GO!
with Microsoft®

Office for Mac 2011
Volume 1

**Shelley Gaskin, Carolyn McLellan,
Robert L. Ferrett, and Alicia Vargas**

PEARSON

Boston   Columbus   Indianapolis   New York   San Francisco   Upper Saddle River
Amsterdam   Cape Town   Dubai   London   Madrid   Milan   Munich   Paris   Montreal   Toronto
Delhi   Mexico City   São Paulo   Sydney   Hong Kong   Seoul   Singapore   Taipei   Tokyo

Editor in Chief: Michael Payne
Executive Editor: Jenifer Niles
Editorial Project Manager: Carly Prakapas
Product Development Manager: Laura Burgess
Development Editor: Ginny Munroe
Editorial Assistant: Andra Skaalrud
Executive Marketing Manager: Nate Anderson
Marketing Coordinator: Susan Osterlitz
Marketing Assistant: Darshika Vyas
Managing Editor: Camille Trentacoste
Senior Production Project Manager: Rhonda Aversa
Senior Operation Manager/Site Lead: Nick Sklitsis

Operations Specialist: Maura Zaldivar-Garcia
Senior Art Director: Jonathan Boylan
Cover Photo: Cheetah: © Ben Durrant/Laptop: © IMG_191 LLC/Shutterstock
Associate Director of Design: Blair Brown
Director of Media Development: Taylor Ragan
Media Project Manager, Production: John Cassar
Full-Service Project Management: PreMediaGlobal
Composition: PreMediaGlobal
Printer/Binder: Webcrafters, Inc.
Cover Printer: Lehigh-Phoenix Color/Hagerstown
Text Font: MinionPro

Credits and acknowledgments borrowed from other sources and reproduced, with permission, in this textbook appear on the appropriate page within text.

Microsoft and/or its respective suppliers make no representations about the suitability of the information contained in the documents and related graphics published as part of the services for any purpose. All such documents and related graphics are provided "as is" without warranty of any kind. Microsoft and/or its respective suppliers hereby disclaim all warranties and conditions with regard to this information, including all warranties and conditions of merchantability, whether express, implied or statutory, fitness for a particular purpose, title and non-infringement. In no event shall Microsoft and/or its respective suppliers be liable for any special, indirect or consequential damages or any damages whatsoever resulting from loss of use, data or profits, whether in an action of contract, negligence or other tortious action, arising out of or in connection with the use or performance of information available from the services.

The documents and related graphics contained herein could include technical inaccuracies or typographical errors. Changes are periodically added to the information herein. Microsoft and/or its respective suppliers may make improvements and/or changes in the product(s) and/or the program(s) described herein at any time. Partial screen shots may be viewed in full within the software version specified.

Microsoft® and Windows® are registered trademarks of the Microsoft Corporation in the U.S.A. and other countries. This book is not sponsored or endorsed by or affiliated with the Microsoft Corporation.

Many of the designations by manufacturers and sellers to distinguish their products are claimed as trademarks. Where those designations appear in this book, and the publisher was aware of a trademark claim, the designations have been printed in initial caps or all caps.

Library of Congress Cataloging in Publication details
Go! with Microsoft Office for Mac 2011 / Shelley Gaskin ... [et al.].
    p. cm.
  Includes index.
  ISBN 978-0-13-310987-0 (alk. paper)
1. Microsoft Office. 2. Macintosh (Computer) 3. Business—Computer programs. I. Gaskin, Shelley.
  HF5548.4.M525G6258 2013
  005.5—dc23

2012030176

10 9 8 7 6 5 4 3 2 1

ISBN 10: 0-13-310987-9
ISBN 13: 978-0-13-310987-0

Brief Contents

Contents

Word

Chapter 1 Creating Documents with Microsoft Word for Mac 2011........57

Chapter 2 Using Tables and Templates to Create Resumes and Cover Letters 115

Excel

Chapter 3   Analyzing Data with Pie Charts, Line Charts, and What-If Analysis Tools 373

PowerPoint

Chapter 1   Getting Started with Microsoft Office PowerPoint 435

About the Authors

Shelley Gaskin, Series Editor, is a professor in the Business and Computer Technology Division at Pasadena City College in Pasadena, California. She holds a bachelor's degree in Business Administration from Robert Morris College (Pennsylvania), a master's degree in Business from Northern Illinois University, and a doctorate in Adult and Community Education from Ball State University. Before joining Pasadena City College, she spent 12 years in the computer industry where she was a systems analyst, sales representative, and Director of Customer Education with Unisys Corporation. She also worked for Ernst & Young on the development of large systems applications for their clients. She has written and developed training materials for custom systems applications in both the public and private sector, and has written and edited numerous computer application textbooks.

This book is dedicated to my students, who inspire me every day.

Robert L. Ferrett recently retired as the Director of the Center for Instructional Computing at Eastern Michigan University, where he provided computer training and support to faculty. He has authored or co-authored more than 70 books on Access, PowerPoint, Excel, Publisher, WordPerfect, Windows, Word, OpenOffice, and Computer Fundamentals. He has been designing, developing, and delivering computer workshops for more than three decades. Before writing for the *GO! Series*, Bob was a series editor for the Learn Series. He has a bachelor's degree in Psychology, a master's degree in Geography, and a master's degree in Interdisciplinary Technology from Eastern Michigan University. His doctoral studies were in Instructional Technology at Wayne State University.

I'd like to dedicate this book to my wife Mary Jane,
whose constant support has been so important all these years.

Alicia Vargas is a faculty member in Business Information Technology at Pasadena City College. She holds a master's and a bachelor's degree in business education from California State University, Los Angeles, and has authored several textbooks and training manuals on Microsoft Word, Microsoft Excel, and Microsoft PowerPoint.

This book is dedicated with all my love to my husband Vic, who makes
everything possible; and to my children Victor, Phil, and Emmy, who are an
unending source of inspiration and who make everything worthwhile.

Carolyn McLellan is the Dean of the Division of Information Technology and Business at Tidewater Community College in Virginia Beach, Virginia. She has a master's degree in Secondary Education from Regent University and a bachelor's degree in Business Education from Old Dominion University. She taught for Norfolk Public Schools for 17 years in Business Education and served as a faculty member at Tidewater Community College for eight years teaching networking, where she developed over 23 new courses and earned the Microsoft Certified Trainer and Microsoft Certified System Engineer industry certifications. In addition to teaching, Carolyn loves to play volleyball, boogie board at the beach, bicycle, crochet, cook, and read.

This book is dedicated to my daughters, Megan and Mandy, who have my
eternal love; to my mother, Jean, who always believes in me and encouraged
me to become a teacher; to my sister Debbie, who was my first student and
who inspires me with her strength in overcoming hardships; to my niece
Jenna, for her bravery, composure, and beauty; to my grandsons, Damon
and Jordan, who bring me happiness and a renewed joie de vie; and to
the students and IT faculty at Tidewater Community College.

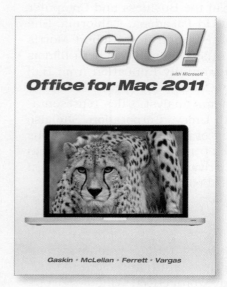

GO! with Office for Mac 2011 is based on the Mac version of Microsoft Office 2011, and therefore it only covers the features that are available in the Mac version of the Office software.

This book is intended for courses using Macintosh computers. MyITLab and all related media are based on Microsoft Office 2010 for PCs. If your course uses MyITLab, you will need to download the MyITLab Mac Compatibility Solution.

The MyITLab Mac Compatibility Solution uses a remote desktop client to run MyITLab in a virtual Windows environment. Two installations are necessary. The first is one time only. The second must be done each time you access MyITLab. Visit http://wps.prenhall.com/bp_myitlab2010_macuser for instructions on how to download the MyITLab Mac Compatibility Solution.

Note the following:

- You must be running Mac OS 10.5 to 10.7.
- Training Simulations are based on the Windows/PC version of Microsoft Office.
- This solution is not intended for MyITLab Grader Project activities. If you need to complete any of the MyITLab Grader Project activities for your course, you will need to complete these on a PC.
- This solution is supported only for customers in the United States and Canada.

A Microsoft® Office textbook designed for student success!

- **Project-Based** – Students learn by creating projects that they will use in the real world.

- **Microsoft Procedural Syntax** – Steps are written to put students in the right place at the right time.

- **Teachable Moment** – Expository text is woven into the steps—at the moment students need to know it—not chunked together in a block of text that will go unread.

- **Sequential Pagination** – Students have actual page numbers instead of confusing letters and abbreviations.

Student Outcomes and Learning Objectives – Objectives are clustered around projects that result in student outcomes.

Project Activities – A project summary stated clearly and quickly.

Project Files – Clearly shows students which files are needed for the project and the names they will use to save their documents.

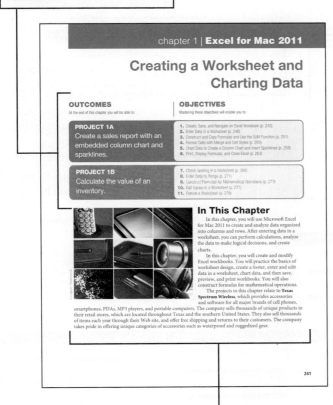

Scenario – Each chapter opens with a story that sets the stage for the projects the student will create.

Project Results – Shows students how their final outcome will appear.

Microsoft Procedural Syntax – Steps are written to put the student in the right place at the right time.

Color Coding – Color variations between the two projects in each chapter make it easy to identify which project students are working on.

Objective 1 | Create, Save, and Navigate an Excel Workbook

On startup, Excel displays the Excel Workbook Gallery, and the Excel Workbook template is selected. A *workbook*—the Excel document that stores your data—contains one or more pages called a *worksheet*. A worksheet—or *spreadsheet*—is stored in a workbook and is formatted as a pattern of uniformly spaced horizontal rows and vertical columns. The intersection of a column and a row forms a box referred to as a *cell*.

Activity 1.01 | Starting Excel and Naming and Saving a Workbook

1 Open **Excel**. In the **Excel Workbook Gallery**, be sure that **Excel Workbook** is selected, and then in the lower right corner, click **Choose**. If necessary, increase the size of the Excel window to fill the screen by clicking the Zoom button or by dragging the lower right corner of the Excel window. On the Standard toolbar, click the **Zoom arrow**, and then click **125%**.

Increases in the Zoom setting are used so that when you compare your screen with the figures used in this textbook, the text in the figures referenced in the project steps can be viewed more easily.

2 On the **File** menu, click **Save As**, and then in the **Save As** dialog box, navigate to the location where you will store your workbooks for this chapter.

3 In your storage location, create a new folder named **Excel Chapter 1** In the **Save As** box, notice that *Workbook1* displays as the default file name.

4 In the **Save As** box, if necessary, double-click *Workbook1* to select it, and then using your own name, type **Lastname_Firstname_1A_Quarterly_Sales** being sure to include the underscore (_) instead of spaces between words. Compare your screen with Figure 1.2.

Another Way

Figure 1.2
File name with your name and underscores between words

Excel Chapter 1 folder created

Save button

Project 1A: Sales Report with Embedded Column Chart and Sparklines | **Excel 243**

Activity 1.02 | Navigating a Worksheet and a Workbook

1 Take a moment to study Figure 1.5 and the table in Figure 1.6 to become familiar with the Excel workbook window.

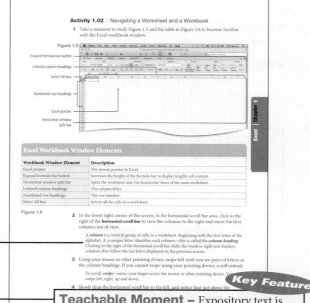

Figure 1.5
Expand formula bar button
Lettered column headings
Select All box
Numbered row headings
Excel pointer
Horizontal window split bar

Excel Workbook Window Elements

Workbook Window Element	Description
Excel pointer	The mouse pointer in Excel.
Expand formula bar button	Increases the height of the formula bar to display lengthy cell content.
Horizontal window split bar	Splits the worksheet into two horizontal views of the same worksheet.
Lettered column headings	The column letter.
Numbered row headings	The row number.
Select All box	Selects all the cells in a worksheet.

Figure 1.6

2 In the lower right corner of the screen, in the horizontal scroll bar area, click to the right of the **horizontal scroll bar** to view the columns to the right and move the first columns out of view.

A **column** is a vertical group of cells in a worksheet. Beginning with the first letter of the alphabet, A, a unique letter identifies each column—this is called the *column heading*. Clicking to the right of the horizontal scroll bar shifts the window right and displays columns that follow the last letter displayed on the previous screen.

3 Using your mouse or other pointing device, swipe left until you see pairs of letters as the column headings. If you cannot swipe using your pointing device, scroll instead.

To scroll, *swipe*—move your finger across the mouse or other pointing device. You swipe left, right, up and down.

4 Slowly drag the horizontal scroll bar to the left, and notice that just above the

Sequential Pagination – Students are given actual page numbers to navigate through the textbook instead of confusing letters and abbreviations.

Teachable Moment – Expository text is woven into the steps—at the moment students need to know it—not chunked together in a block of text that will go unread.

End-of-Chapter

Content-Based Assessments – Assessments with defined solutions.

Objective List - Every project includes a listing of covered objectives from Projects A and B.

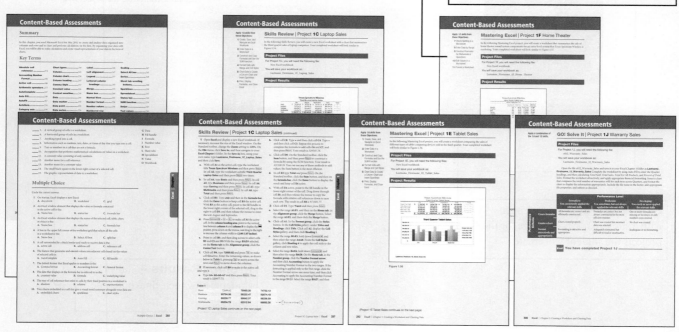

End-of-Chapter

Outcomes-Based Assessments – Assessments with open-ended solutions.

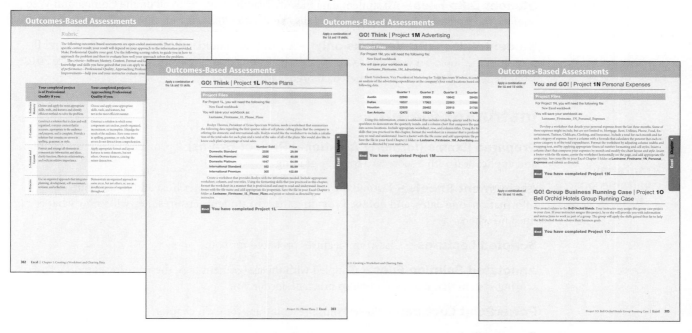

Task-Specific Rubric – A matrix specific to the **GO! Solve It** projects that states the criteria and standards for grading these defined-solution projects.

Outcomes Rubric – A matrix specific to the **GO! Think** projects that states the criteria and standards for grading these open-ended assessments.

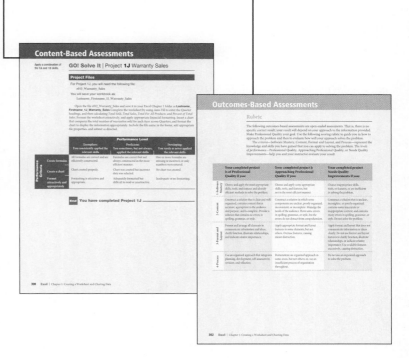

Student Materials

Student Data Files – All student data files are readily available to all on the Companion Web Site: www.pearsonhighered.com/go; then select *GO! with Office for Mac 2011.*

Student Videos (PC Versions only) – A visual and audio walk-through of every A and B project in the book. To view these videos, visit the Companion Web Site for GO! with Office 2010 Volume 1, 2e at www.pearsonhighered.com/go.

Instructor Materials

All
Instructor
materials
available on
the IRC

Prepared Exams (formerly Additional Project Exams) – provided by project, chapter, and application with a scorecard for easy grading.

Assignment Sheets – Lists all the assignments for the chapter. Just add in the course information, due dates, and points. Providing these to students ensures they will know what is due and when.

Scripted Lectures – Classroom lectures prepared for you.

Annotated Solution Files – Coupled with the assignment tags, these create a grading and scoring system that makes grading so much easier for you.

PowerPoint Lectures – PowerPoint presentations for each chapter.

Scoring Rubrics – Can be used either by students to check their work or by you as a quick check-off for the items that need to be corrected.

Syllabus Templates – For 8-week, 12-week, and 16-week courses.

Test Bank – Includes a variety of test questions for each chapter.

Companion Website – Online content such as the Chapter Review (formerly Online Study Guide), Glossary, and Student Data Files are all at www.pearsonhighered.com/go.

Using the Common Features of Microsoft Office for Mac 2011

OUTCOMES
At the end of this chapter you will be able to:

OBJECTIVES
Mastering these objectives will enable you to:

PROJECT 1A
Create, save, and print a Microsoft Office for Mac 2011 file.

1. Use Finder to Locate Files and Folders (p. 3)
2. Locate and Open a Microsoft Office for Mac 2011 Application (p. 7)
3. Enter and Edit Text in an Office for Mac 2011 Application (p. 11)
4. Perform Commands from a Dialog Box (p. 14)
5. Create a Folder, Save a File, and Close an Application (p. 16)
6. Add Document Properties and Print a File (p. 20)

PROJECT 1B
Use the Ribbon and dialog boxes to perform common commands in a Microsoft Office for Mac 2011 file.

7. Open an Existing File and Save It with a New Name (p. 24)
8. Explore Options for an Application (p. 30)
9. Perform Commands from the Menu Bar, Standard Toolbar, and Ribbon (p. 32)
10. Apply Formatting in Office Applications (p. 41)
11. Use the Microsoft Office for Mac 2011 Help System (p. 50)
12. Compress Files (p. 52)

© Christy Thompson / Shutterstock

In This Chapter

In this chapter, you will use Finder to navigate the Mac folder structure, create a folder, and save files in Microsoft Office for Mac 2011 applications. You will also practice using the features of Microsoft Office for Mac 2011 that are common across the major applications that comprise the Microsoft Office for Mac 2011 suite. These common features include creating, saving, and printing files.

You will apply formatting, perform commands, and compress files. You will see that creating professional-quality documents is easy and quick in Microsoft Office for Mac 2011, and that finding your way around is fast and efficient.

The projects in this chapter relate to **Oceana Palm Grill**, which is a chain of 25 casual, full-service restaurants based in Austin, Texas. The Oceana Palm Grill owners plan an aggressive expansion program. To expand by 15 additional restaurants in North Carolina and Florida by 2020, the company must attract new investors, develop new menus, and recruit new employees, all while adhering to the company's quality guidelines and maintaining its reputation for excellent service. To succeed, the company plans to build on its past success and maintain its quality elements.

Project 1A PowerPoint File

Project Activities

In Activities 1.01 through 1.06, you will create a PowerPoint file, save it in a folder that you create by using Finder, and then print the file or submit it electronically as directed by your instructor. Your completed PowerPoint slide will look similar to Figure 1.1.

Project Files

For Project 1A, you will need the following file:

New Presentation

You will save your file as:

Lastname_Firstname_1A_Menu_Plan

Project Results

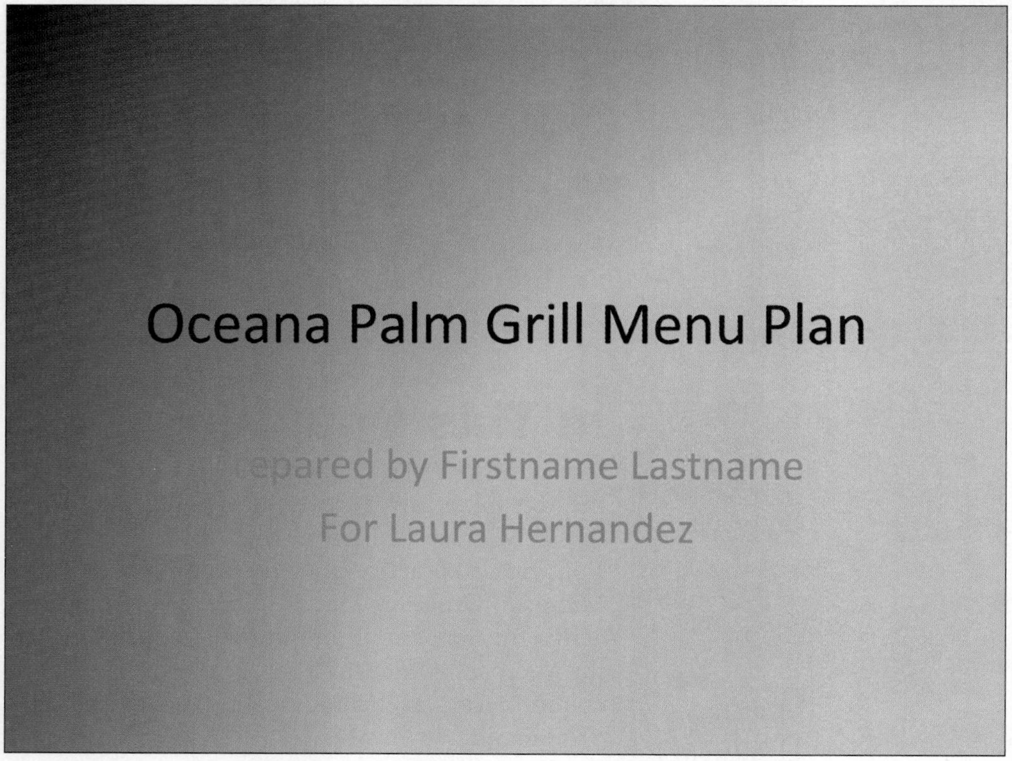

Figure 1.1
Project 1A Menu Plan

Objective 1 | Use Finder to Locate Files and Folders

A *file* is a collection of information stored on a computer under a single name, for example, a Word document or a PowerPoint presentation. Every file is stored in a *folder*—a container in which you store files—or a *subfolder*, which is a folder within a folder. Your Mac operating system stores and organizes your files and folders, which is a primary task of an operating system.

You *navigate*—explore within the organizing structure of the Mac—to create, save, and find your files and folders by using the *Finder* application. When you start up your computer, the Finder application opens and the desktop displays. Finder is used to organize and locate almost everything on the Mac, including documents, pictures, movies, and any other files you may have. Finder displays the files and folders on your computer in a *window*. A window is a rectangular area on a computer screen in which applications and content appear; a window can be moved, resized, maximized, minimized, or closed.

Activity 1.01 | Using Finder to Locate Files and Folders

1 Turn on your computer and display the Mac *desktop*—the opening screen that simulates your work area. Depending upon how your computer is configured, you may have to log in after starting the computer. Compare your screen with Figure 1.2.

> The desktop displays, and the Finder application is open by default. Your desktop may differ, depending on how your applications are installed and how your computer is configured. At the top of the window is the *menu bar*, a horizontal bar that contains the menus of *commands*—instructions to the computer program that causes an action to be performed. Display a menu by *clicking* on its name in the menu bar. To click, tap or press the mouse or pointing device one time.

> The name of the application displays to the right of the *Apple menu* , which enables you to configure your computer, shut down your computer, and log out. The *status menus*, which are displayed as icons, are on the right side of the menu bar. These menus display the status of your computer or give you quick access to features such as volume control or wireless connections.

> At the bottom of the desktop is the *Dock*, which displays *icons* for applications—the icons that display on your Dock may differ. Icons are pictures that represent a program, a file, a folder, or some other object. You can move the dock to the right or left side of the window or customize it to meet your needs. Move your mouse pointer over an icon on the Dock to display the name of the application. The Finder icon is represented by the blue smiling face.

Note | Comparing Your Screen with the Figures in This Textbook

Your screen will match the figures shown in this textbook if you set your screen resolution to 1024 × 768. At other resolutions, your screen will closely resemble, but not match, the figures shown. To view your screen's resolution, on Apple menu, click System Preferences, and then under Hardware, click Displays. After changing the screen resolution, close dialog box. You can also click the System Preferences icon if it displays on the Dock.

Figure 1.2

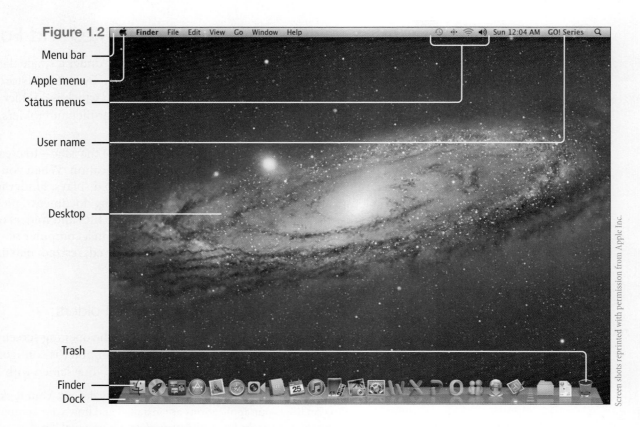

Menu bar

Apple menu

Status menus

User name

Desktop

Trash

Finder

Dock

Screen shots reprinted with permission from Apple Inc.

Another Way

In Finder, press Shift + Command ⌘ + C

2 On the **Finder** menu bar, click **Go**. On the **Go** menu, click **Computer**, and then compare your screen with Figure 1.3. If your screen differs, click the Icons view button ⊞.

On the left side of the Finder window is a *sidebar* that displays icons and names that help you locate files, applications, documents, shared computers, and devices such as CDs, DVDs, or removable storage. Your menu may differ from Figure 1.3 depending upon your computer setup. The Mac operating system organizes items on your computer in folders. The internal hard disk, which is named *Macintosh HD*, contains many important folders with files that are necessary for your computer to function properly. To view the contents of a folder, *double-click* the folder. To double-click, tap or press your mouse or pointing device two times in rapid succession. It is recommended that you store your files in the Documents folder, the Home folder, or on a removable storage device.

Figure 1.3

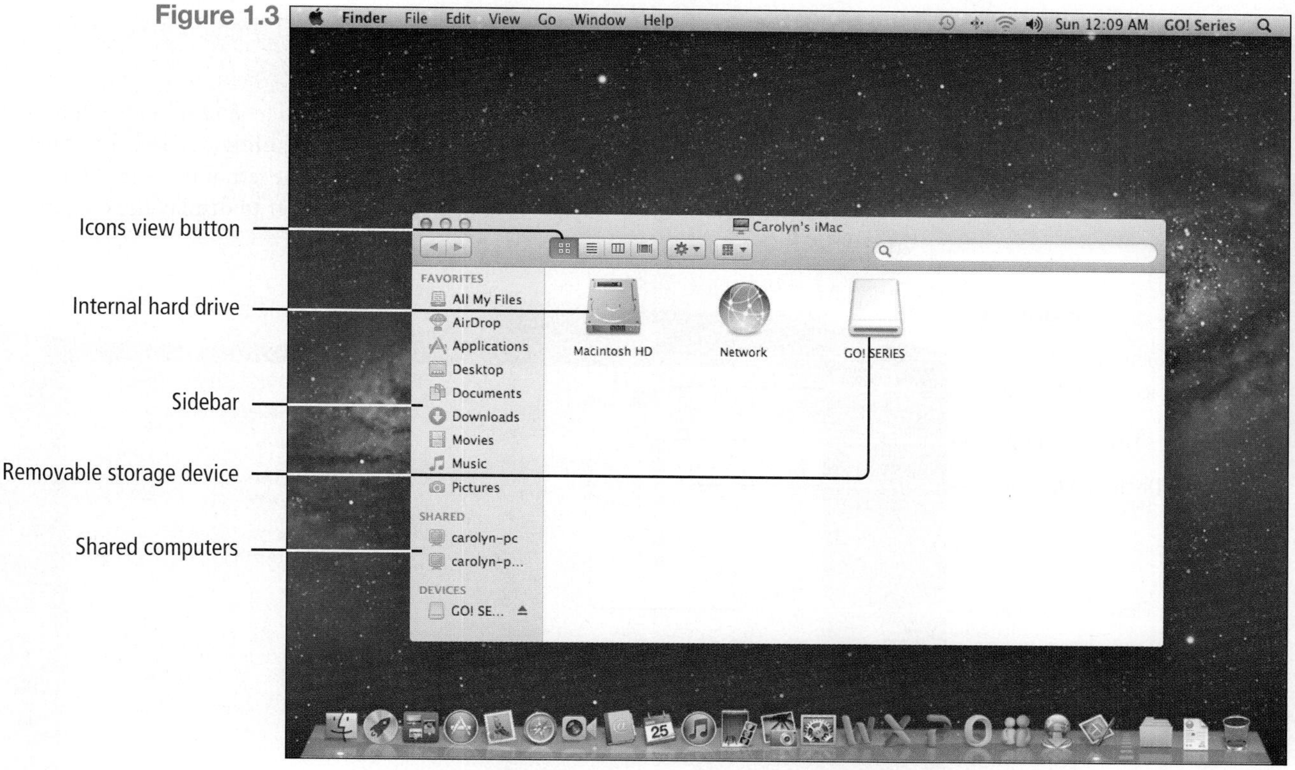

Icons view button

Internal hard drive

Sidebar

Removable storage device

Shared computers

Another Way

In Finder, press Shift +
Command ⌘ + H

3 On the menu bar, click **Go**. On the **Go** menu, click **Home** to open the Home folder, and then compare your screen with Figure 1.4.

The *Home folder*, which has the same name as your user account, makes it easy for you to organize your files. It contains your personal folders and files and cannot be renamed. The *Desktop folder* includes files that you save on your desktop. The *Documents folder* is a convenient place to store most of the files that you create. The folders in the Home folder also display in the Finder sidebar. Store files that you want to share with others in the *Public folder*.

To view the contents of a folder, double-click the folder.

You can display the contents of folders in different views by clicking one of the view buttons. By *default*, the items in Finder display in *Icons view*—a view that displays folders and files as icons or small pictures. Default refers to the current selection or setting that is automatically used by an application unless you specify otherwise. Finder displays folders and files in the view that you selected previously.

Figure 1.4

Contents of Home folder—name of user

View buttons

4 In the Home folder window, click the **List** button ▤ and then compare your screen with Figure 1.5.

> The views in any Finder window enable you to display folders and files in different ways. In *List view*, details about the folders and files display, including the date modified, the size of a file, and the type of a file, such as Word. To the left of the folder name is a *disclosure triangle*, which, when clicked, expands the folder to display the contents of that folder.

Figure 1.5

Columns view button
Icons view button
List view button
Disclosure triangle
Cover Flow view button

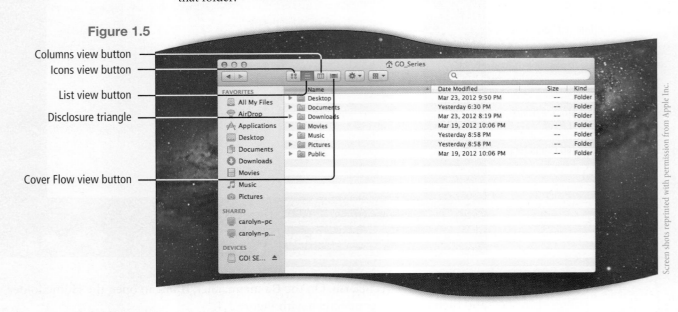

Screen shots reprinted with permission from Apple Inc.

5 In the **Name** column, to the left of **Documents**, click the **disclosure triangle** ▶ to expand the Documents folder.

> The contents of the Documents folder depend on what you have stored on your computer and the applications you have installed. To open a document, double-click on the document name.

6 To the left of the **Documents**, click the **disclosure triangle** ▼ to collapse the Documents folder. In the Home folder window, click the **Columns** view button ▥.

> In *Columns view*, folders and files are displayed in columns. To expand folders, click in the column to the right of a folder. When you click on a file, a *thumbnail*—a miniature version of the file—displays along with information about the file, such as the size of the file and the dates created, modified, and last opened.

7 In the **sidebar**, click **Documents**, then click the **Cover Flow** button ▥, and then compare your screen with Figure 1.6—the contents of your Documents folder will differ from those shown in Figure 1.6.

> *Cover Flow view* is similar to List view, except that it adds a set of previews in the top part of the window that you can flip through. You can navigate through the folders and files by the next folder or file in the preview part of the window or by clicking the folder or file name in the list part of the window. To display the contents of a folder, double-click the folder. In Finder, use the left and right navigation buttons to display folders and files that you have previously viewed.

Figure 1.6

Back navigation button

Forward navigation button

Preview

List of folders and files

8 Practice using the preview part of the Cover Flow view, the list part of the Cover Flow view, and the Finder navigation buttons to navigate the folders and files. When you are finished practicing, in the **sidebar**, click **Documents**; and in the Documents folder window, click the **List** button. In the Documents folder window, click the **Close** button 🔘 to close the Documents folder.

Note | How to Obtain the Student Data Files to Complete Projects in This Book

Projects in this book begin either with a new blank file or from a student data file that has already been started for you. Follow the directions on the inside flap of the back cover of this textbook to download the student data files from the Pearson Web site. Your instructor might direct you to other locations where these files are stored; for example, on a shared network drive or in your learning management system.

More Knowledge | Finding Files on Your Computer

In Finder, on the right side of the menu bar, click the Spotlight button—magnifying glass. In the Spotlight search box, type a few characters that might be in the file name that you are trying to locate; for example, type your last name. The Spotlight will display a list of results. If the file you are trying to locate displays on the list of results, simply click it to open it. If you are not sure that the file listed is the correct one, point to the file to see a preview of the file.

Objective 2 | Locate and Open a Microsoft Office for Mac 2011 Application

Microsoft Office for Mac 2011 includes applications for individuals, small organizations, and large enterprises. An *application*, also referred to as a *program*, is a set of instructions used by a computer to perform a task, such as word processing or accounting.

Activity 1.02 | Locating and Opening a Microsoft Office for Mac 2011 Application

Another Way

Press Shift + Command ⌘ + A. Or, if displayed on the Dock, click the Applications icon.

1 In **Finder**, on the **Go** menu, click **Applications**. Be sure you are displaying the applications in **List** view ≣.

2 In the **Applications** window, locate and double-click **Microsoft Office 2011**. Compare your screen with Figure 1.7, which displays the applications that are included in the Microsoft Office for Mac Home & Business 2011 group of applications—your group of applications may vary.

Microsoft Word is a word processing application, which enables you to create and share documents by using its writing tools.

Microsoft Excel is a spreadsheet application, which enables you to calculate and analyze numbers and create charts.

Microsoft PowerPoint is a presentation application, which enables you to communicate information with high-impact graphics and video.

Additional popular Office applications include *Microsoft Outlook* for managing email and organizational activities, and *Microsoft Document Connection* for sharing and managing files on a Microsoft SharePoint site or on Microsoft's SkyDrive *cloud service*. Cloud service is online storage of data hosted by third parties.

Figure 1.7

Microsoft Office 2011 folder

Applications included with Office (yours may differ)

Screen shots reprinted with permission from Apple Inc.

Another Way

Click the PowerPoint icon on the Dock instead of opening up Applications.

3 Double-click **Microsoft PowerPoint**, and then compare your screen with Figure 1.8.

The PowerPoint Presentation Gallery displays, which enables you to use a theme, template, or guided method to create your presentation. A *gallery* is an Office feature that displays a list of potential results instead of just the command name. The PowerPoint Presentation Gallery windows displays on top of the Microsoft Office 2011 window.

Alert! | **Does a Welcome to PowerPoint Screen Display?**

The first time you open PowerPoint, the Welcome to PowerPoint 2011 screen may display. Click Continue to display the PowerPoint Presentation Gallery.

Alert! | **Does a Blank PowerPoint Presentation Display?**

When installed, the default setting for PowerPoint is to display the PowerPoint Presentation Gallery. Your computer administrator may have changed the default settings for your Office applications. If this is the case, skip to Step 5.

Figure 1.8

PowerPoint Presentation Gallery window

Microsoft Office 2011 window

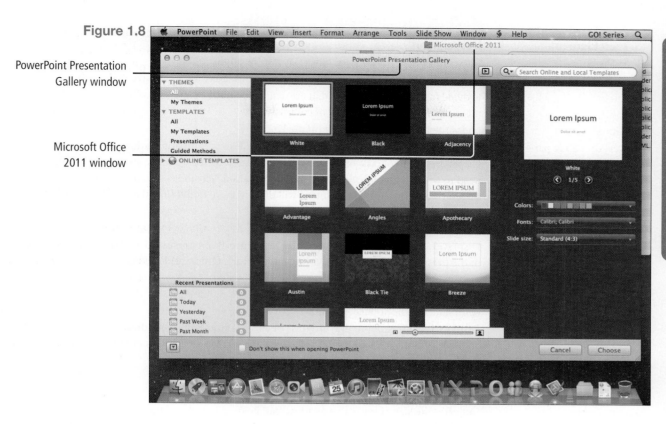

4 In the left pane, under **THEMES**, if All is not selected, click it. In the gallery, double-click the **White** theme to display a new blank presentation in the PowerPoint window. Compare your screen with Figure 1.9, and then take a moment to study the description of the screen elements in the table in Figure 1.10.

Figure 1.9 Menu bar   Zoom button   Title bar

Close button
Standard toolbar
Ribbon tabs
Minimize button
Ribbon

Slides/Outline pane

Group names

Zoom setting

PowerPoint Slide pane

Zoom slider

Status bar

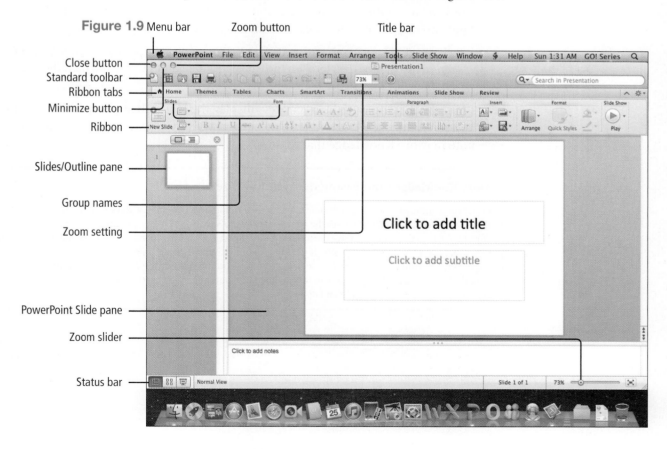

Screen Element	Description
Close button	Closes the active window, but does not exit the application.
Group names	Indicate the name of the groups of related commands on the displayed tab.
Menu bar	Provides access to commands that are available on the Standard toolbar and the Ribbon. Click a menu name to display a menu of commands.
Minimize button	Hides the window by placing it on the Dock.
PowerPoint Slide pane	Displays a large image of the active slide in the PowerPoint application.
Ribbon	Displays a group of task-oriented tabs that contain the commands, styles, and resources you need to work in an Office for Mac 2011 application. The look of your Ribbon depends on your screen resolution. A high resolution will display more individual items and button names on the Ribbon.
Ribbon tabs	Display the names of the task-oriented tabs relevant to the open application.
Slides/Outline pane	Displays either thumbnails of the slides in a PowerPoint presentation (Slides tab) or the outline of the presentation's content (Outline tab). In each Office 2011 application, different panes display in different ways to assist you.
Standard toolbar	Displays a row of buttons that provide a one-click method to perform the most common commands in the application such as Save and Print.
Status bar	Displays file information, the progress of current tasks, and the status of certain commands and keys. On the left side are buttons to change the view of the document. On the right side is a Zoom slider to adjust the size of the displayed document.
Title bar	Displays the name of the file.
Zoom button	Increases or decreases the size of the window.
Zoom setting	Indicates the size of the active window; can be used in place of the Zoom slider.
Zoom slider	Decreases or increases the size of the active slide displayed in the PowerPoint Slide pane.

Figure 1.10

Another Way

Press Option + Command ⌘ + D to hide or unhide the Dock.

5 On the title bar, click the **Zoom** button 🔘 to increase the size of the PowerPoint window, and notice that the Dock still displays at the bottom of the screen. On the **Apple** menu 🍎, point to **Dock**, and then click **Turn Hiding On**.

The Dock is hidden from view. To see the Dock, move the pointer to the bottom of the screen. To unhide the Dock, on the Apple menu, point to Dock, and then click Turn Hiding Off.

6 Point to the bottom of the desktop to display the Dock; then point to the top of the desktop to hide the Dock. If the PowerPoint window does not fill the screen, see the note in More Knowledge that follows.

More Knowledge | Increasing the Window Size

Depending upon your screen resolution, clicking the Zoom button does not always increase the window to fill the entire screen, but instead moves the window to the top left corner of the application window. To manually adjust the size of the window, move the mouse pointer to the right border of the window; the pointer will change to a double-headed horizontal arrow. If the mouse pointer remains as a single-headed arrow, the window is at its maximum width. Drag the right edge of the window to the right until you can drag no further. You can drag the bottom edge of the window in this manner also, but drag it down. Alternatively, drag the bottom right corner of the window to the right and down.

Objective 3 | Enter and Edit Text in an Office for Mac 2011 Application

All of the applications in Office for Mac 2011 require you to type text. Your keyboard is still the primary method of entering information into your computer. Techniques to *edit*—make changes to—text are similar among all of the Office applications.

Activity 1.03 | Entering and Editing Text in an Office for Mac 2011 Application

1 On the standard toolbar, click in the **Zoom** box ⬚100%⬚, and then type **100** to increase the size of the slide in the window. Notice the vertical scroll bar that displays on the right side of the window, an indication that the entire slide is not displayed in the active window. In the middle of the PowerPoint slide pane, *point*—move your mouse pointer—to the text *Click to add title* to display the ⬚I⬚ pointer, and then click one time.

> The *insertion point*—a blinking vertical line that indicates where text or graphics will be inserted—displays.

> In Office for Mac 2011 applications, the mouse *pointer*—any symbol that displays on your screen in response to moving your mouse device—displays in different shapes depending on the task you are performing and the area of the screen to which you are pointing.

Note | Changes to the Zoom Setting

The Zoom setting has no effect on the outcome of this project. Increases in the Zoom setting are used so that when you compare your screen with the figures used in this textbook, you can more easily see the text in the figures referenced in the project steps.

---

2 Type **Oceana Grille Info** and notice how the insertion point moves to the right as you type. Point slightly to the right of the letter *e* in *Grille* and click to place the insertion point there. Compare your screen with Figure 1.11.

Figure 1.11

Zoom changed to 100%

Insertion point

Vertical scroll bar—
indicates that the entire
slide is not displayed

Dock hidden

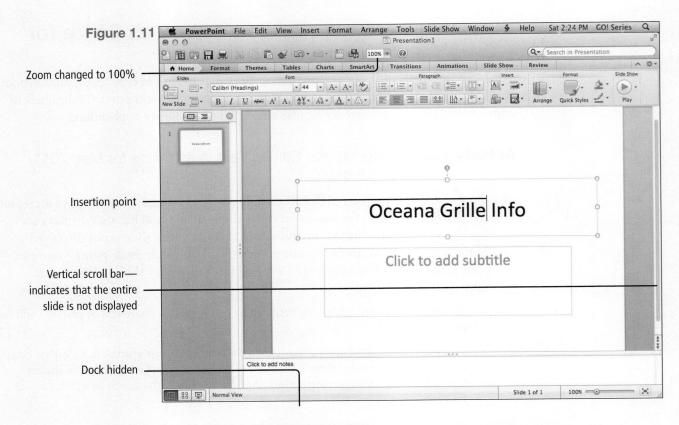

3 On your keyboard, locate and press the ⌦ key to delete the letter *e*.

Pressing ⌦ removes a character to the left of the insertion point.

4 Point slightly to the left of the *I* in *Info* and click one time to place the insertion point there. Type **Menu** and then press ␣ one time. Compare your screen with Figure 1.12.

By default, when you type text in an Office application, existing text moves to the right to make space for new typing.

Figure 1.12

Menu inserted

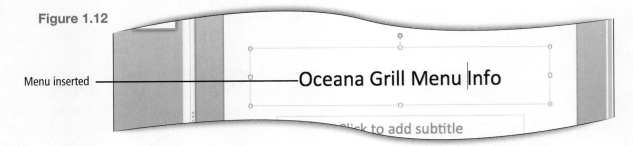

5 Double-click *Info* and then type **Plan**

Select a word by double-clicking it. To *select* refers to highlighting areas of text or data or graphics so that the selection can be edited, formatted, copied, or moved. In any Microsoft Office for Mac 2011 application, selected text is deleted and then replaced when you begin to type new text. You will save time by developing good techniques to select and then edit or replace selected text, which is easier than pressing the ⌦ key numerous times to delete text.

6 With your insertion point blinking after the word *Plan*, on your keyboard, hold down the Option key. While holding down Option, press ← three times.

> This is a **keyboard shortcut**—a key or combination of keys that performs a task that would otherwise require a mouse. This keyboard shortcut moves the insertion point to the beginning of the previous word.
>
> A keyboard shortcut is indicated as a combination of keys such as Option + ← to indicate that you hold down the first key while pressing the second key. A keyboard shortcut can also include three keys, in which case you hold down the first two and then press the third. For example, Option + Shift + ← selects words to the left of the insertion point.

7 With the insertion point blinking at the beginning of the word *Grill*, type **Palm** and press Spacebar.

8 Click anywhere in the text *Click to add subtitle*. With the insertion point blinking, type the following and include the spelling error: **Prepered by Annabel Dunham**

9 With your mouse, point slightly to the left of the *A* in *Annabel*, press down on the mouse, and then **drag**—press down on the mouse while moving your mouse—to the right to select the text *Annabel Dunham*, and then release the mouse button.

> The action of dragging includes releasing the mouse at the end of the area you want to select. Selecting text may require some practice. If you are not satisfied with your result, click anywhere outside of the selection, and then begin again.

10 With the text *Annabel Dunham* selected, type your own firstname and lastname.

11 Notice that the misspelled word *Prepered* displays with a wavy red underline; additionally, all or part of your name might display with a wavy red underline.

> Office for Mac 2011 has a dictionary of words against which all entered text is checked. In Word and PowerPoint, words that are *not* in the dictionary display a wavy red line, indicating a possible misspelled word or a proper name or an unusual word—none of which are in the Office dictionary. In Excel, you can initiate a check of the spelling, but wavy red underlines do not display. You can check spelling in PowerPoint, but you cannot check grammar.

12 Click anywhere in *Prepered*, hold down Control, and then click your mouse one time. Compare your screen with Figure 1.13.

> A **shortcut menu** displays. A shortcut menu displays commands and options relevant to the selected text or object—known as **context-sensitive commands** because they relate to the item for which you pressed Control and clicked.
>
> Here, the shortcut menu displays commands related to the misspelled word. You can click the suggested correct spelling *Prepared*, click Ignore All to ignore the misspelling, add the word to the Office dictionary, or click Spelling to display a **dialog box**. A dialog box is a small window that contains options for completing a task. Whenever you see a command followed by an **ellipsis** (…), which is a set of three dots indicating incompleteness, clicking the command will always display a dialog box.
>
> By default, spelling is checked automatically as you type. To disable this feature, on the PowerPoint menu, click Preferences, click Spelling, and then clear the Check spelling as you type check box. To check spelling all at once, on the Tools menu, click Spelling. The Spelling dialog box will not open if no spelling errors are detected or if the word you are trying to add already exists in the dictionary. All of the Office applications have Preferences that can be changed.

Figure 1.13

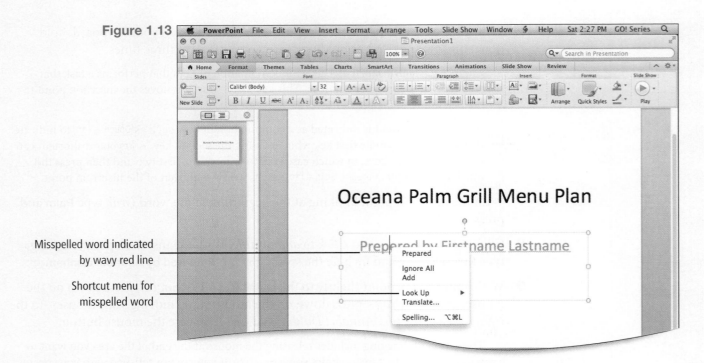

Misspelled word indicated by wavy red line

Shortcut menu for misspelled word

13 On the shortcut menu, click **Prepared** to correct the misspelled word. If necessary, point to any part of your name that displays a wavy red underline, press Control and click, and then on the shortcut menu, click Ignore All so that Office will no longer mark your name with a wavy underline in this file.

> **More Knowledge | Adding to the Office Dictionary**
>
> The main dictionary contains the most common words, but does not include all proper names, technical terms, or acronyms. You can add words, acronyms, and proper names to the Office dictionary by clicking Add when they are flagged, and you might want to do so for your own name and other proper names and terms that you type often.

Objective 4 | Perform Commands from a Dialog Box

In a dialog box, you make decisions about an individual object or topic. A dialog box also offers a way to adjust a number of settings at one time.

Activity 1.04 | Performing Commands from a Dialog Box

1 Point anywhere in the blank area above the title *Oceana Palm Grill Menu Plan* to display the ▶ pointer.

2 Press Control and then click to display a shortcut menu. Notice the command *Format Background* followed by an ellipsis (…). Compare your screen with Figure 1.14.

Recall that a command followed by an ellipsis indicates that a dialog box will display if you click the command.

Figure 1.14

Shortcut menu for
slide background

Ellipsis indicates dialog
box will open

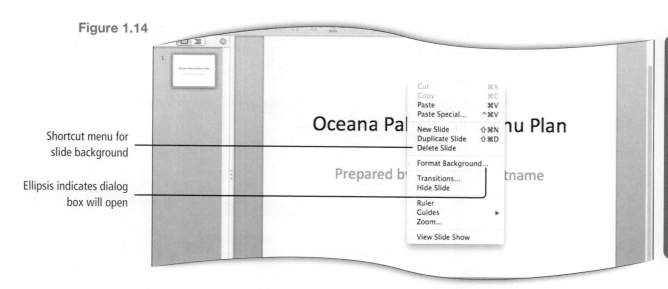

Another Way

On the Format menu,
click Slide Background.

3 Click **Format Background** to display the **Format Background** dialog box, and then
compare your screen with Figure 1.15.

Figure 1.15

Fill selected

Format Background
dialog box

Tabs for background fill
options; Solid tab is active

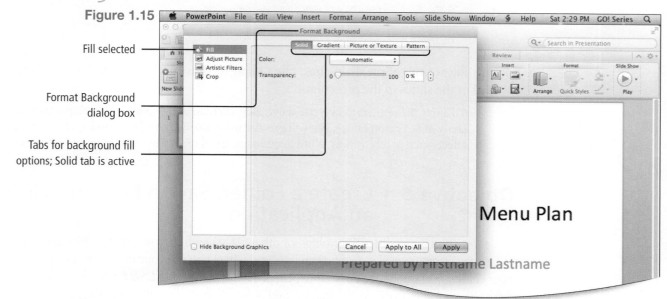

4 On the left, be sure that **Fill** is selected to display the **Fill** options.

Fill is the inside color of an object. Here, the dialog box displays a set of tabs across the
top from which you can display different sets of options.

5 Click the **Gradient tab**.

The dialog box displays additional settings related to the gradient fill option. In a *gradient
fill*, one color fades into another.

6 Under **Styles and direction**, click the **Style arrow**—the arrow in the box to the right of
the text *None*—and then click **Radial** to set the pattern of the fill color.

7 Under **Color and transparency**, click the **Color arrow**, and then in the gallery under
Theme Colors in the fourth row, point to the fifth fill color to display the ScreenTip
Accent 1, Lighter 40%.

A *ScreenTip* displays useful information when you perform various mouse actions, such
as pointing to screen elements or dragging.

8 Click **Accent 1, Lighter 40%**, and then notice that the fill color is applied to your slide. Click the **Add Color** button to add more of the lighter color to the pattern, and then compare your screen with Figure 1.16.

Figure 1.16

Radial style

Add Color button

Apply to All button

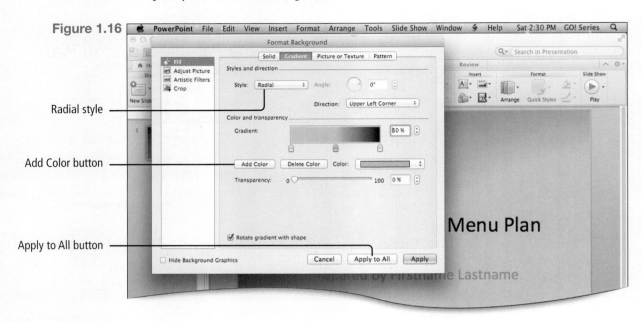

9 At the bottom of the dialog box, click **Apply to All** to apply the gradient fill settings to all of the slides in the presentation.

> To apply the settings to only the active slide, click the Apply button. As you progress in your study of Microsoft Office, you will practice using many dialog boxes and applying dramatic effects such as this to your Word documents, Excel spreadsheets, and PowerPoint slides.

Objective 5 | Create a Folder, Save a File, and Close an Application

A *location* is any disk drive, folder, or other place in which you can store files and folders. Where you store your files depends on how and where you use your data. For example, for your classes, you might decide to store primarily on a removable *USB flash drive* so that you can carry your files to different locations and access your files on different computers. A USB flash drive is a small data storage device that plugs into a computer USB port.

If you do most of your work on a single computer, for example your home desktop system or your laptop computer that you take with you to school or work, store your files in one of the folders—Documents, Movies, Music, or Pictures—provided by your Mac operating system.

Although the Mac operating system helps you to create and maintain a logical folder structure, take the time to name your files and folders in a consistent manner.

Activity 1.05 | Creating a Folder, Saving a File, and Closing an Application

A PowerPoint presentation is an example of a file. Office for Mac 2011 applications use a common dialog box provided by the Mac operating system to assist you in saving files. In this activity, you will create a folder on a USB flash drive in which to store files. If you prefer to store on your hard drive, you can use similar steps to store files in your Documents folder in your Home folder.

1 Insert a USB flash drive into your computer. If you are not using a USB flash drive, go to Step 2.

> As the first step in saving a file, determine where you want to save the file, and if necessary, insert a storage device.

2 At the top of your screen, on the title bar, notice that *Presentation1* displays.

> Most Office for Mac 2011 applications open with a new unsaved file with a default name—*Presentation1*, *Document1*, and so on. As you create your file, your work is temporarily stored in the computer's memory until you initiate a Save command, at which time you must choose a file name and location in which to save your file.

Another Way

Press Command ⌘ + S, or on the File menu, click Save.

3 On the Standard toolbar, click the **Save** button 🖫 to display the **Save As** dialog box. On your keyboard, locate the ⎓ key. To type an underscore character, hold down the Shift key when pressing this key. In the **Save As** box with the text selected, and using your own last name and first name, type **Lastname_Firstname_1A_Menu_Plan** Do not press the Return key.

> You can use spaces in file names; however, some individuals prefer not to use spaces because some applications, especially those that transfer files over the Internet, may not work well with spaces in file names. In general, unless you encounter a problem, it is OK to use spaces. In this textbook, underscores are used instead of spaces in file names.

4 In the **Where** box, notice the ⬍ arrows, which indicate that a pop-up menu will display for this option when you click in the box. Click in the **Where** box to display the menu, and then compare your screen with Figure 1.17 (your screen will differ).

> A ***pop-up menu*** displays—pops up—when you select an option and contains a menu of commands that stay on the screen only until one of the commands is selected. The storage devices for your computer display, including your computer and removable storage devices such as a USB flash drive, CD, or DVD. The default storage location is the Documents folder in your Home folder. This menu also displays the other folders that are located in your Home folder and Recent Places—folders—that you have accessed.

Alert! | Is the Where Box Missing?

If you have previously saved documents and changed the settings in the Save As dialog box, the Where box displays under the Save As box, but does not display with the heading of Where. If this is the case, to the right of the Save As box, click the Less button ▲ so that your dialog box matches the one in Figure 1.17.

Figure 1.17

Name of presentation

Default folder

Storage devices (yours will vary)

Folders in Home folder (yours may vary)

Where menu

Folders recently opened (yours will vary)

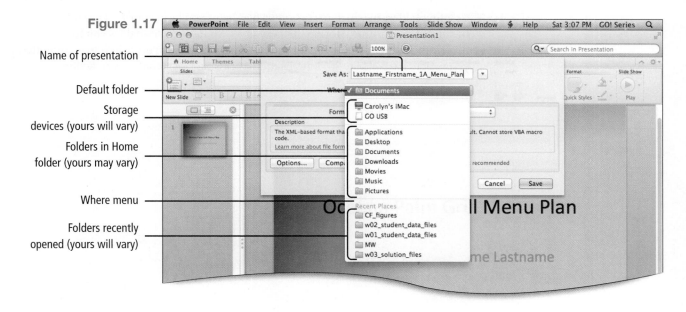

5 Click your USB flash drive, and notice that the menu no longer displays. To the right of the **Save As** box, click the **More arrow** ▼ to display the contents of your USB flash drive. Compare your screen with Figure 1.18.

Clicking a *More arrow* expands the selection and enables you to select more options. For Save As, the window expands and shows the contents of the selected storage device similar to the Finder window in Columns view. This expanded window enables you to create a new folder on the USB flash drive without having to leave the PowerPoint application. To the right of the Save As box, the More arrow changes to a Less arrow, which, when clicked, collapses the Save As options.

Figure 1.18

Click to collapse
Save As options

Storage location—USB
flash drive (yours will vary)

New folder button

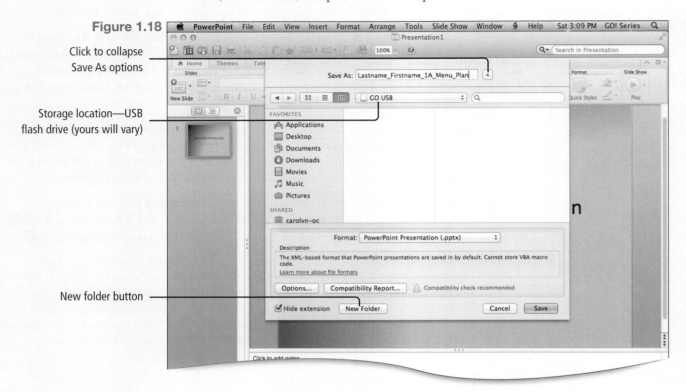

6 At the bottom of the dialog box, click **New Folder**. In the **New Folder** dialog box, type **GO! Office 2011** and then click **Create** or press ⟨Return⟩. **Create** a **New Folder** with the name **Common Features Chapter 1** and then compare your screen with Figure 1.19.

Creating folders in which to store your files helps you keep your files organized and find the files at a later time. Storing the files on a USB flash drive enables you to retrieve the files from another computer when you insert the USB flash drive into that computer. In your Microsoft for Mac 2011 applications, pressing ⟨Return⟩ confirms an action.

Figure 1.19

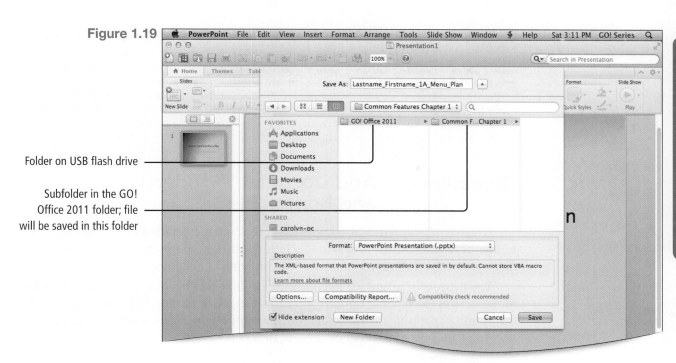

Folder on USB flash drive ————

Subfolder in the GO!
Office 2011 folder; file
will be saved in this folder ————

7 In the lower right corner of the **Save As** dialog box, click **Save** or press Return, and then compare your screen with Figure 1.20.

> Your new file name displays on the title bar, indicating that the file has been saved to the location that you specified. When you are saving something for the first time, for example a new PowerPoint presentation, the Save and Save As commands are identical. That is, the Save As dialog box will display if you click Save or if you click Save As.

Figure 1.20

File name on title bar ————

8 In the text that begins *Prepared by*, click to position the insertion point at the end of your name, and then press Return to move to a new line. Type **For Laura Hernandez**

9 Click anywhere off the slide to remove the box around the subtitle. On the Standard toolbar, click the **Save** button 🖫.

> A brief message displays stating that the file is being saved. The presentation is saved in the same location with the same name and with the change that you just made.

Objective 6 | Add Document Properties and Print a File

Document properties, also known as *metadata*, are details about a file that describe or identify it. Document properties include the title, author name, and *keywords*—words that are searchable and help describe the content of a document.

The process of printing a file is similar in all of the Office applications. There are differences in the types of options you can select. For example, in PowerPoint, you have the option of printing the full slide, with each slide printing on a full sheet of paper, or of printing handouts with small pictures of slides on a page.

Activity 1.06 | Adding Document Properties and Printing a File

1 On the **File** menu, click **Properties**, and then compare your screen with Figure 1.21.

The Properties dialog box for your 1A_Menu_Plan document displays with the Summary tab active. PowerPoint automatically inserted a variation of the slide title in the Title box. Property settings are grouped on tabs.

Figure 1.21

Tabs for file properties

Active tab

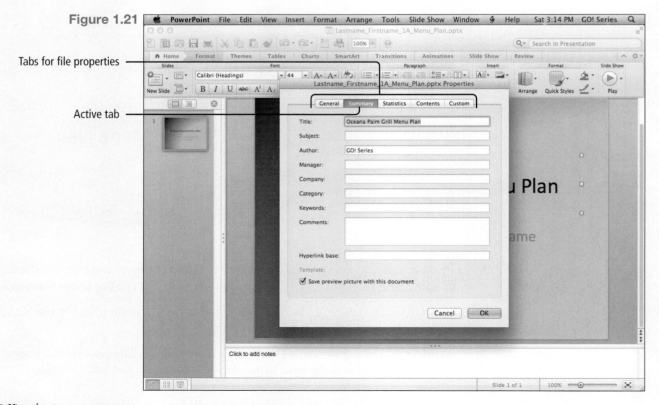

2 If necessary, change the text in the **Title** box to **Oceana Palm Grill Menu Plan** and then press Tab to move to the **Subject** box. Type your course name and section number, press Tab to move to the **Author** box and to select the existing text. If necessary, type your Firstname and Lastname. In the **Keywords** box, type **menu plan** and click the tabs at the top of the dialog box to display the different types of information stored as document properties. In the **Properties** dialog box, click the **Summary tab**, and then click **OK**.

> Adding properties to your documents will make them easier to search for in systems such as Microsoft SharePoint and SkyDrive.

Another Way
Press Command ⌘ + P

3 On the **File** menu, click **Print** to open the **Print** dialog box. Compare your screen with Figure 1.22. (Your settings will differ.)

> Near the top of the dialog box, the name of the printer installed on your system displays. If multiple printers are available, click the printer box to display a menu, and then select a printer. The Copies and Slides area is where you select print options, such as the number of copies, particular slides, and how you want the slides to print.

> On the left, the *Print Preview* displays, which is a view of a document as it will appear on the paper when you print it.

> Under the Print Preview area, on the left, the number of pages and navigation arrows with which you can move among the pages in Print Preview are displayed. By default, all of the slides will print with each slide on a full sheet of paper.

Figure 1.22

Print dialog box (your settings will differ)

Printer box—arrows indicate pop-up menu available

All slides in presentation will print

Each slide prints on a full sheet of paper

Preview of current slide

Navigation buttons to move among multiple slides

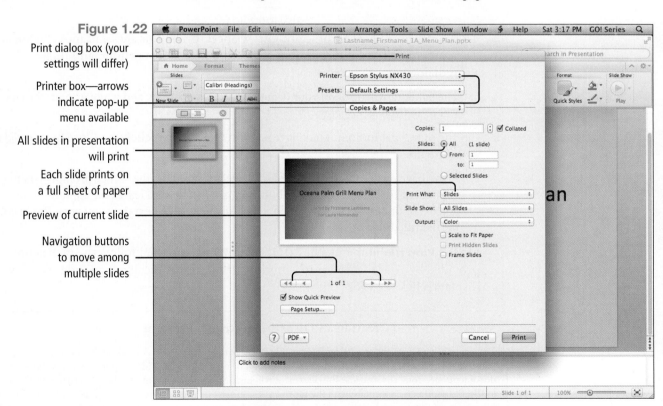

4 Click in the **Print What** box to display a menu. Click **Handouts (2 slides per page)**, and then compare your screen with Figure 1.23.

> The Print Preview changes to show how your slide will print on the paper in this arrangement. If there were multiple slides in this presentation, two slides would print on each piece of paper.

Figure 1.23

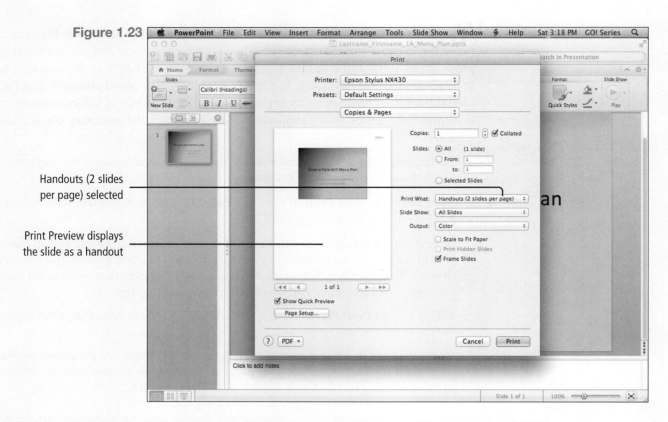

Handouts (2 slides per page) selected

Print Preview displays the slide as a handout

5 To submit your file electronically, click Cancel to skip this step and move to Step 6. To print your slide, be sure your system is connected to a printer, and then in the **Print** dialog box, click **Print**.

> The handout will print on your default printer—on a black and white printer, the colors will print in shades of gray.

Another Way

Press Command ⌘ + W to close a file.

6 On the Standard toolbar, click **Save** 🖫. On the title bar, click the **Close** button 🔘 to close the file.

> If you have made changes to the file or have not saved the file, Office prompts you to save your changes. Clicking the Close button closes the file, and leaves the application open for you to continue working. If you do not close the file, the next time you open PowerPoint, the file will display.

Another Way

Press Command ⌘ + Q to quit or exit any Microsoft for Mac 2011 application.

7 On the **PowerPoint** menu, click **Quit PowerPoint**, and then follow the instructions provided by your instructor to submit your file electronically. If a Finder window displays, click the Close button.

More Knowledge | **Creating a PDF as an Electronic Printout**

You can save an Office file as a *PDF file*. *Portable Document Format* (PDF) is a format that creates an image of your file that preserves the look of your file, but cannot be easily changed. This is a popular format for sending documents electronically, because the document will display on most computers. There are two ways to create a PDF file within an application with the file open. 1) On the File menu, click Save As. If necessary, modify the file name and the storage location. Click in the Format box. In the menu, under Common Formats, click PDF. In the Save As dialog box, click Save. 2) On the File menu, click Print. In the lower left corner of the Print dialog box, click PDF, and then click Save as PDF. In the Save dialog box, if necessary, modify the file name, storage location, and document properties; and then click Save. In the message box, click *Use .pdf* to change the file extension from *.pptx* to *.pdf*.

End **You have completed Project 1A**

Project 1B Word File

Project Activities

In Activities 1.07 through 1.16, you will open, edit, save, and then compress a Word file. Your completed document will look similar to Figure 1.24.

Project Files

For Project 1B, you will need the following file:

cf01B_Cheese_Promotion

You will save your Word document as:

Lastname_Firstname_1B_Cheese_Promotion

Project Results

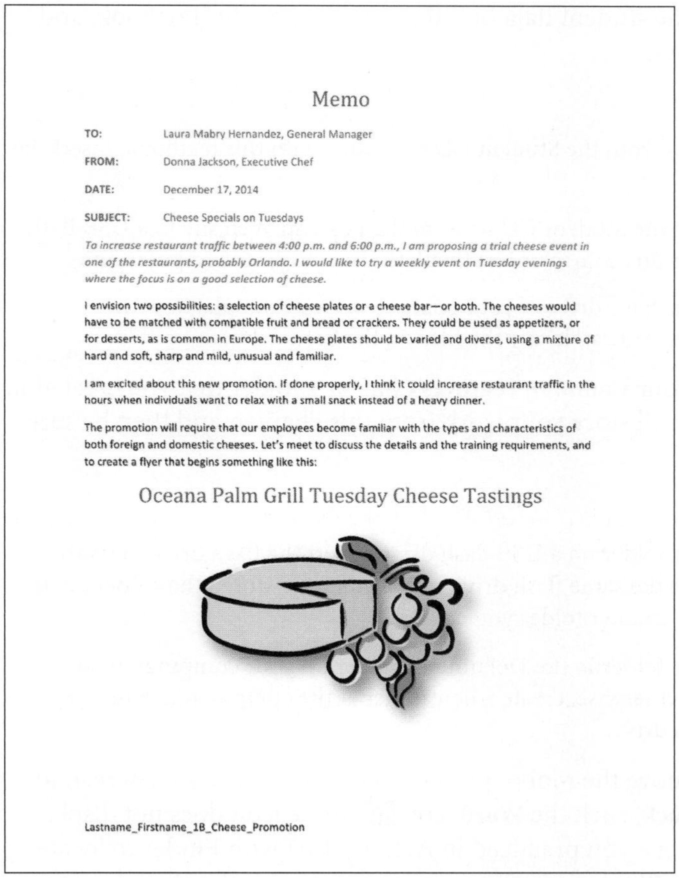

Memo

TO: Laura Mabry Hernandez, General Manager

FROM: Donna Jackson, Executive Chef

DATE: December 17, 2014

SUBJECT: Cheese Specials on Tuesdays

To increase restaurant traffic between 4:00 p.m. and 6:00 p.m., I am proposing a trial cheese event in one of the restaurants, probably Orlando. I would like to try a weekly event on Tuesday evenings where the focus is on a good selection of cheese.

I envision two possibilities: a selection of cheese plates or a cheese bar—or both. The cheeses would have to be matched with compatible fruit and bread or crackers. They could be used as appetizers, or for desserts, as is common in Europe. The cheese plates should be varied and diverse, using a mixture of hard and soft, sharp and mild, unusual and familiar.

I am excited about this new promotion. If done properly, I think it could increase restaurant traffic in the hours when individuals want to relax with a small snack instead of a heavy dinner.

The promotion will require that our employees become familiar with the types and characteristics of both foreign and domestic cheeses. Let's meet to discuss the details and the training requirements, and to create a flyer that begins something like this:

Oceana Palm Grill Tuesday Cheese Tastings

Lastname_Firstname_1B_Cheese_Promotion

Figure 1.24
Project 1B Cheese Promotion

Objective 7 | Open an Existing File and Save It with a New Name

In any Office application, use the Open command to display the *Open dialog box*, from which you can navigate to and then open an existing file that was created in that same application.

The Open dialog box, along with the Save and Save As dialog boxes, are referred to as *common dialog boxes*. These dialog boxes, which are provided by the Mac programming interface, display in all of the Office applications in the same manner. Thus, the Open, Save, and Save As dialog boxes will all look and perform the same in each Office application.

Activity 1.07 | Opening an Existing File and Saving It with a New Name

In this activity, you will display the Open dialog box, open an existing Word document, and then save it in your storage location with a new name.

1 Determine the location of the student data files that accompany this textbook, and be sure you can access these files.

> For example:

> If you are accessing the files from the Student CD that came with this textbook, insert the CD now.

> If you copied the files from the Student CD or from the Pearson Web site to a USB flash drive that you are using for this course, insert the flash drive in your computer now.

> If you copied the files to the hard drive of your computer—for example, in your Documents folder—be sure you can locate the files on the hard drive.

2 Determine the location of your **Common Features Chapter 1** folder that you created in Activity 1.05, in which you will store your work from this chapter, and then be sure you can access that folder.

> For example:

> If you created your chapter folder on a USB flash drive, insert the flash drive in your computer now. This can be the same flash drive where you have stored the student data files; just be sure to use the chapter folder you created.

> If you created your chapter folder in the Documents folder on your computer, be sure you can locate the folder. Otherwise, create a new folder at the computer at which you are working, or on a USB flash drive.

3 If the Dock is still hidden, move the mouse pointer to the bottom of your screen to display the Dock. On the **Dock**, click the **Word** icon ![Word icon]. If the icon does not display on the Dock, use the technique you practiced in Activity 1.02 with Finder to locate and then open the **Microsoft Word** application on your system. If the Dock is not hidden, on the Apple menu ![Apple icon], point to Dock, and then click Turn Hiding On. Compare your screen with Figure 1.25.

> The Word Document Gallery displays, which enables you to use a template or a view to create your document. The default template is a blank Word Document, which is selected. On the right side of the gallery, the selected template displays in Preview. You can search online for templates and locate documents that you have accessed recently.

Figure 1.25

Word Document Gallery ——

Selected template ——

Templates in different views ——

Recent documents ——

Preview of selected template ——

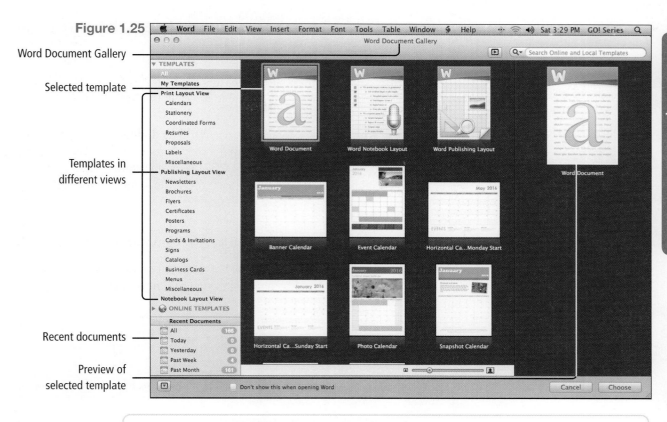

Another Way

Press Command ⌘ + O.

4 On the **File** menu, click **Open**. In the **Open** dialog box, click the **Zoom** button 🔘 to increase the size of the dialog box. In the sidebar under **Favorites**, click **Documents**, and then compare your screen with Figure 1.26.

> The Open dialog box displays the folders and files contained in the Documents folder. The Open dialog box size is increased, which enables you to see more on the screen. You need to determine where your student data files are located. For the purpose of these instructions, the student data files were downloaded from the Pearson Web site and saved in the Documents folder in a subfolder named GO_student_data_files—your storage location will differ.
>
> For example:
>
> If you are accessing the files from a CD/DVD, under Devices, click the CD/DVD.
>
> If you are accessing the files from a USB flash drive, under Devices, click the flash drive name.
>
> If you are accessing the files from the Documents folder of your computer, click the folder name.

Figure 1.26

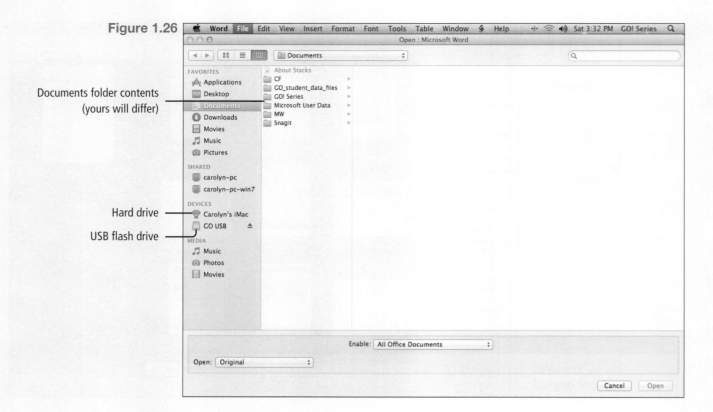

Documents folder contents (yours will differ)

Hard drive

USB flash drive

5 Using the techniques you practiced in Project 1A's Finder, navigate to your student data files for the Common Features chapter. Locate and double-click the Word file **cf01B_Cheese_Promotion** to open and display the file in the Word window. If necessary, click the Zoom button to increase the size of the Word window. If your Word window does not fill the screen, drag the lower right corner of the window down and to the right until the window fills the screen. In the Standard toolbar, click the **Zoom arrow** 100% , click **125%**, and then compare your screen with Figure 1.27.

Like the PowerPoint window, the Word window has a menu bar, Standard toolbar, a Ribbon with tabs to group commands, and a status bar. On the title bar, the file name displays. If you opened the document from a CD or DVD, *(Read Only)* will display. If you opened the document from another source to which the files were copied, *(Read-Only)* might not display. **Read-Only** is a property assigned to a file that prevents the file from being modified or deleted; it indicates that you cannot save any changes to the displayed document unless you first save it with a new name. The Zoom setting is changed to increase the size of the active window, in order to enable you to compare more easily your screen with the figures in this textbook.

Figure 1.27

Zoom button

Standard toolbar

Ribbon

Menu bar

Active window size
increased to 125%

Document displays
in Word window

File name displays on
the title bar (Read-only
will display if opened
from a CD/DVD)

Status bar

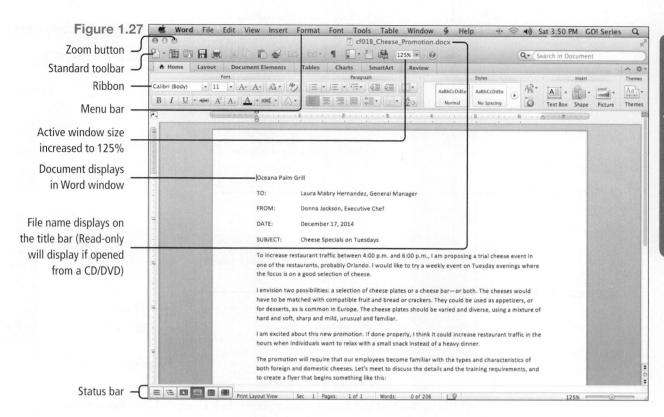

Another Way

Press Shift +
Command ⌘ + S .

6 On the **File** menu, click **Save As** to display the **Save As** dialog box. In the sidebar, click **Documents**, and then compare your screen with Figure 1.28.

The Save As command displays the Save As dialog box where you can name and save a *new* document based on the currently displayed document. After you name and save the new document, the original document closes, and the new document—based on the original one—displays.

At the bottom of the Save As dialog box is the message *Compatibility check recommended*. Office for Mac checks the *compatibility*—the ability to work with other applications—of the file with other Office for Mac versions and with Windows versions of Office, and creates a Compatibility Report. To view the Compatibility Report, click the Compatibility Report button to display any compatibility issues so that you can correct them. You can ignore the Compatibility Report if you do not plan to share the file with others or if you plan to share the file with individuals who are using the same version of Office for Mac. The Compatibility Report checks for compatibility issues with Office 98 for Mac through Microsoft Office for Mac 2011 and with Windows versions from Office 97 through Microsoft Office 2010.

Figure 1.28

Save As dialog box ——

File name box ——

Compatibility message ——

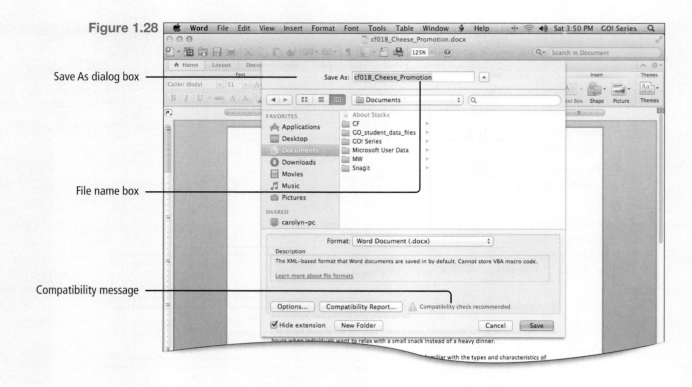

7 At the bottom of the **Save As** dialog box, click **Compatibility Report**, and then compare your screen with Figure 1.29.

> A message displays indicating that the compatibility check was run and no issues were found. If issues were found, they would be displayed in the Compatibility Report task pane.

Figure 1.29

Compatibility Report task pane—no issues found ——

Message box ——

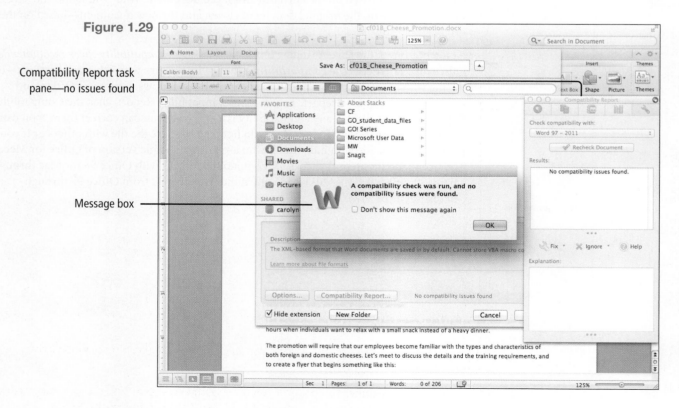

8 In the message box, click **OK**. **Close** 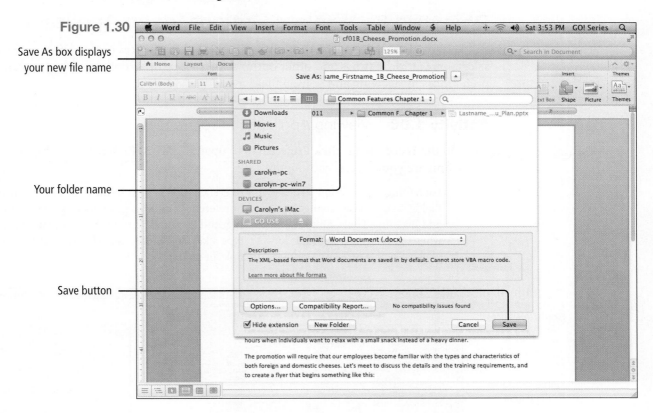 the **Compatibility Report** task pane, and notice that in the **Save As** dialog box, to the right of the **Compatibility Report** button, the text is changed to *No compatibility issues found*.

> A message displays indicating that the compatibility check was run and no issues were found. If issues were found, they would be displayed in the Compatibility Report task pane.

9 In the **Save As** dialog box, navigate to the **Common Features Chapter 1** folder that you created in Project 1A and click the folder. To display more items in the sidebar, move the mouse pointer to the sidebar, and then by using your mouse, *scroll*—slide or swipe your finger on the mouse or other mouse pointer device—until you see the device where you are saving your files.

> When windows are not large enough to display all of the data, you must scroll—slide or swipe your finger on the mouse—to see the data. How you scroll depends on your version of the Mac operating system and the settings for your mouse or other pointing device. If your operating system is Mac OS X, the manner in which you scroll is set to *natural* to match how individuals swipe or move their fingers on other devices, such as phones and iPads. To display the top of a screen, scroll down. To see the bottom of the screen, scroll up. Using the standard mouse, you scroll by sliding your finger on the mouse or other pointing device. You can scroll to the left or right and up or down.

10 Click in the **Save As** box, and then drag to select the existing text. Using your own name, type **Lastname_Firstname_1B_Cheese_Promotion** and then compare your screen with Figure 1.30.

Figure 1.30

Save As box displays your new file name

Your folder name

Save button

11 In the lower right corner of the **Save As** dialog box, click **Save**; or press `Return`. Compare your screen with Figure 1.31.

> The original document closes, and your new document—based on the original—displays with the name in the title bar. The insertion point is blinking at the beginning of the document.

Figure 1.31

New file name on title bar ——

Insertion point at
beginning of document ——

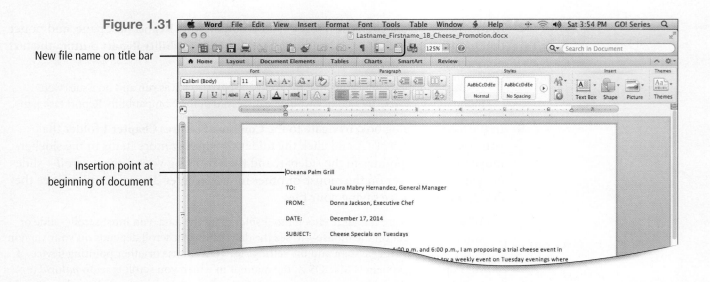

More Knowledge | Changing Mouse Preferences

If you are used to scrolling using a Windows computer or using versions of Mac prior to Mac OS X, you can
change your mouse settings. In any application, click the Apple menu, and then click System Preferences.
Under Hardware, click Mouse. On the Point & Click tab click Scroll direction: natural to deselect this setting. In
this same dialog box, you can set your mouse to right-click.

Objective 8 | Explore Options for an Application

Within each Office application, you can open a *Preferences dialog box* where you can
select application settings and other options and preferences. For example, you can set
preferences for viewing and editing files.

Activity 1.08 | Viewing Application Preferences

Another Way

Press Command ⌘ + [,]

1 On the **Word** menu, click **Preferences** to open the **Word Preferences** dialog box.
Compare your screen with Figure 1.32.

Each Office application has its own Preferences dialog box. In the Word Preferences
dialog box, you can change options or preferences in three general categories: Authoring
and Proofing Tools, Output and Sharing, and Personal Settings. If you are not sure of
where a preference setting is located, type a keyword in the *Search box*—the box in which
you can type a word or a phrase—to look for an item.

Figure 1.32

Word Preferences
dialog box ——

Three categories
of preferences ——

Search box ——

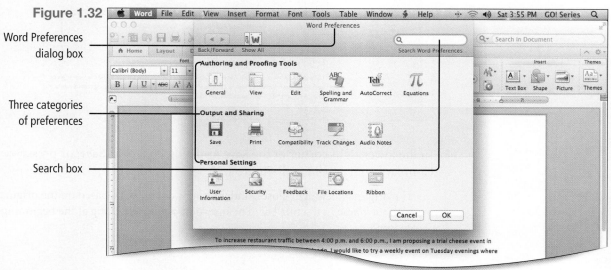

2 In the Search box, type **par** and notice that Word suggests words or phrases based on the characters you enter. Notice that the first suggestion is highlighted, and under **Authoring and Proofing Tools**, Word indicates the location of the preference setting by placing a bright spotlight on **Edit**. **View** has a less bright spotlight because it is the location of a preference setting for one or more of the other suggestions. Compare your screen with Figure 1.33.

> Three suggestions display based on your entering *par* in the Search box. You want to locate preference settings for displaying paragraph marks in the document, but you did not have to enter the entire word *paragraph*. To limit the number of suggestions, type more characters, similar to searching for information by using an Internet search engine.

Figure 1.33

Typed first three letters of *paragraph*—searching for *paragraph* marks

Location of preference setting for one or more other suggestions

Location of preference setting for selected suggestion—*Default Paragraph Style*

Three suggestions

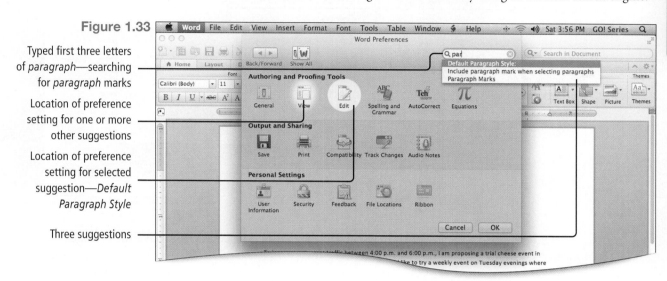

3 Press ↓ two times to select **Paragraph Marks**, and notice that the spotlight indicates the preference setting is located in **View**. In the list of suggestions, click **Paragraph Marks**.

> The View dialog box displays. Clicking a suggestion opens the location of the preference setting. Alternatively, click the setting—in this example, View.

4 Under **Nonprinting characters**, point to **Tab Characters**, and notice that at the bottom of the dialog box a description of the preference displays. Under **Nonprinting characters**, point to each of the preferences and read the description of the preference. Click **All**, and then compare your screen with Figure 1.34.

> This preference setting displays all nonprinting characters listed under nonprinting characters in the Word document; however, they will not display on a printed page. These screen characters do not print and are referred to as *nonprinting characters* or *formatting marks*. The description notes that you can display all nonprinting characters by clicking the Show/Hide button on the Standard toolbar—in other words, you do not need to change the preference setting to display the nonprinting characters. By changing the Preference setting, the default setting will be that nonprinting characters display in a Word document on the screen. When you press Tab, an arrow displays; when you press Spacebar, a dot displays between words; when you press Return, a paragraph mark displays. Displaying these screen characters enables you to edit your document more precisely.

Figure 1.34

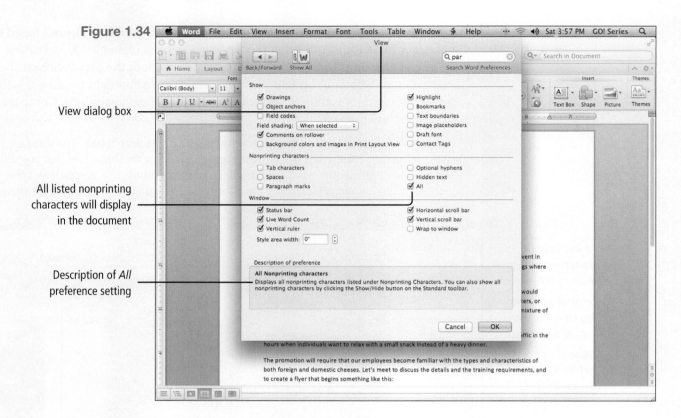

View dialog box

All listed nonprinting characters will display in the document

Description of *All* preference setting

5 In the lower right corner of the dialog box, click **OK** to save the changes to Preferences.

Objective 9 | Perform Commands from the Menu, Standard Toolbar, and Ribbon

Each Office for Mac 2011 application has a menu bar, a Standard toolbar, and a Ribbon from which you can select commands to perform actions within your document. The **Ribbon**, which displays below the Standard toolbar, groups commands and features in a manner that you would most logically use them. Each Office application's Ribbon is slightly different, but all contain the same three elements: *tabs*, *groups*, and commands.

Tabs display across the top of the Ribbon, and each tab relates to a type of activity— for example, laying out a page. Groups are sets of related commands for specific tasks. Commands—instructions to computer applications—are arranged in groups, and might display as a button, a menu, or a box in which you type information.

You can also minimize the Ribbon so only the tab names display. In the minimized Ribbon view, when you click a tab, the Ribbon expands to show the groups and commands; and then when you click a command, the Ribbon returns to its minimized view. Most Office users, however, prefer to leave the complete Ribbon in view at all times.

Activity 1.09 | Performing Commands from the Menu, Standard Toolbar, and Ribbon

1 Take a moment to examine the document on your screen. On the Standard toolbar, notice that the **Show/Hide** button ¶ is selected. Compare your screen with Figure 1.35.

> This document is a memo from the executive chef to the general manager regarding a new restaurant promotion. Because you changed the preference to display all nonprinting characters, symbols display in the document to represent keys pressed on the keyboard. On the Standard toolbar, the Show/Hide button is selected because you changed the preference. By default, the ruler displays, which helps you see how margin settings affect your document and how text aligns. Additionally, if you set a tab or an indent, its location is visible on the ruler.

Figure 1.35

Standard toolbar —
Ribbon —
Home Tab —
Ruler —
Paragraph group on Home tab —
Represents keyboard [Tab] —
Represents keyboard [Return] —
Show/Hide button selected because of preference setting —
Menu bar —

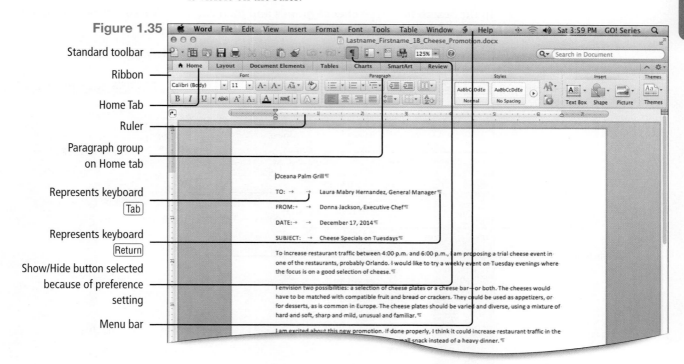

2 On the menu bar, click **View**, and notice that there is a check mark to the left of **Ruler**.

> The View menu enables you to change how your document displays. A check mark to the left of a menu item indicates that the command is active. In this example, the Ruler is visible in the Word window. To hide any item that is active, click the menu item, and the check mark will no longer display.

3 In the **View** menu, click **Ruler** to hide it from the document window and to give you more space to work. To temporarily display the hidden ruler, point to the bottom of the Ribbon.

4 On the Standard toolbar, click the **Show/Hide** button ¶, and notice that the nonprinting characters no longer display in the document. Point to the button to display information about the button, and then click the **Show/Hide** button ¶ to display the nonprinting characters.

> When the Show/Hide button is active, formatting marks display. Because formatting marks guide your eye in a document—like a map and road signs guide you along a highway—these marks will display throughout this instruction. Many expert Word users keep these marks displayed while creating documents. You can display nonprinting characters any time by clicking this button; you do not need to change the Preference setting.

5 In the first line of the document, be sure your insertion point is blinking to the left of the *O* in *Oceana*. Press Return one time to insert a blank paragraph, and then click to the left of the new paragraph mark (¶) in the new line—the line above *Oceana Palm Grill*.

> The *paragraph symbol* is a formatting mark that displays when the Show/Hide command is active each time you press Return.

6 On the Ribbon, be sure that the **Home tab** is active. In the **Insert group**, click the **Picture** button, and then click **Clip Art Gallery**.

> The *Clip Gallery* organizes collections of *clip art*—predefined graphics included with Microsoft Office or downloaded from the Web. The Clip Gallery also organizes collections of photographs, animations, sounds, and videos.

7 In the **Search** box, type **cheese grapes** and then click the **Search** button. Compare your screen with Figure 1.36.

> No clip art of cheese and grapes was found in the Clip Gallery.

Figure 1.36

Clip Gallery

Search button

No clips found

Search words entered

Online button

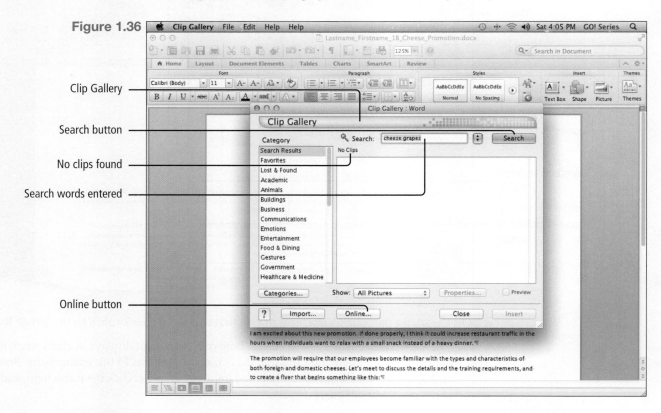

8 At the bottom of the **Clip Gallery** dialog box, click the **Online** button. In the message box, click **Yes** to launch your Internet browser to search for clip art online—you must be able to access the Internet for this command to work. Compare your screen with Figure 1.37—your display may differ if your window is not maximized.

> Your Internet browser opens the Microsoft Office Images Web page where you can search for images or clip art.

Alert! | Does the Web Page Differ From From Figure 1.37?

Web pages are updated frequently. You should still be able to navigate the Office Images page to find the elements you need to find pictures.

Figure 1.37

Safari browser window opened to search for online clip art (your browser application may vary)

Enter search text in this Search box

Microsoft Office search page for images

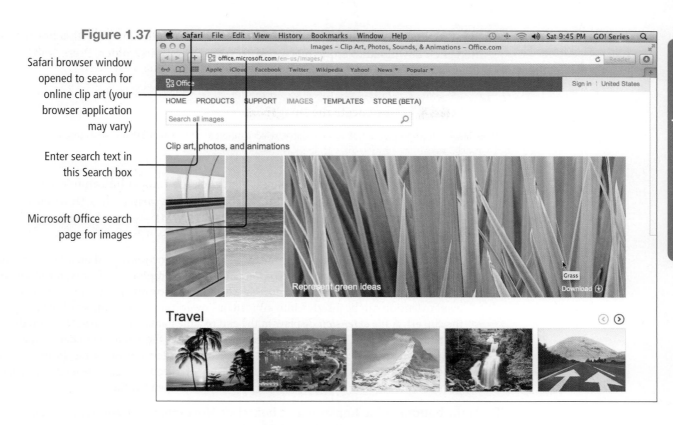

9 Click in the **Search** box, type **cheese grapes** and then press Return. Compare your screen with Figure 1.38.

Figure 1.38

Image to download

Search results for *cheese grapes*—your results may vary

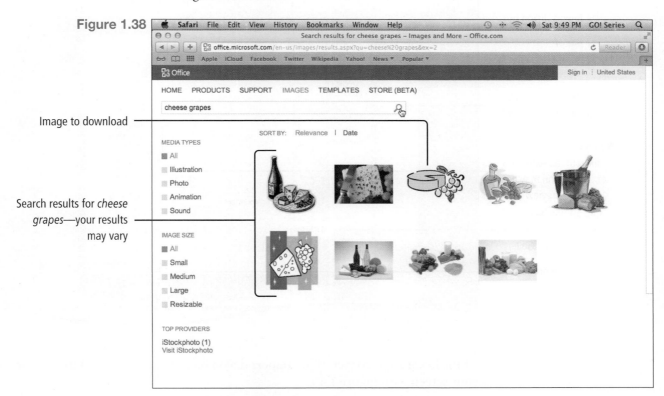

Alert! | Are Your Images Different from Those in Figure 1.38?

Images and clip art are added and removed from the Web, so your images may differ from those shown in Figure 1.38.

10 Point to the image indicated in Figure 1.38 to surround the image with a border, and then click **download** to copy the clip art to your Downloads folder. Press ⌈Command ⌘⌉ + ⌈Q⌉ to exit the browser application.

> **Alert! | Can You Not Locate the Image?**
>
> If the image shown in Figure 1.38 is unavailable, select a different cheese image that is appropriate.

11 At the bottom of the **Clip Gallery** dialog box, click the **Import** button to open the **Import** dialog box. If necessary, in the sidebar under **Favorites**, click **Downloads**, and then click the file you downloaded—**MC900250815.WMF**—your file name may differ if you selected a different clip art image.

By default, files that have a wmf name extension cannot be previewed on a Mac computer. A file with a .wmf extension is a *Windows metafile*—a graphics file format for Microsoft Windows systems. Because Office for Mac 2011 is a Microsoft application, clip art with a .wmf extension can be inserted into a Word or PowerPoint document, which will display the clip art. A file *extension* displays at the end of a file name and is separated from the file name by a period. A computer operating system uses the extension to determine the program that is needed to open the file. For example, a file name of *Cheese_Promotion.docx* has an extension of *.docx*, which is a Word document. If you change a file name's extension, your computer's operating system may not be able to open the file.

12 At the bottom of the **Import** dialog box, click **Move into Clip Gallery**, and then compare your screen with Figure 1.39.

Figure 1.39

Import dialog box

Downloaded clip art (yours may vary)

Folder where clip art was downloaded

No preview available for file with an extension of *.wmf*—you may not have a preview area

Clip art will be moved from Downloads folder to the Clip Gallery

Import button

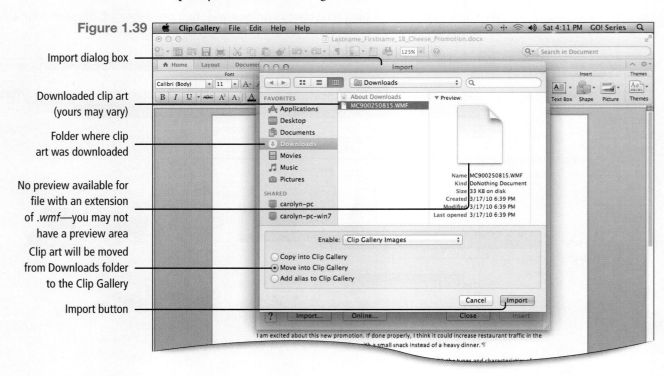

13 At the lower right corner of the **Import** dialog box, click **Import**, and then compare your screen with Figure 1.40.

The Properties dialog box for the clip art displays. In this dialog box, you can enter a description of the clip art, add it to a category in the Clip Gallery, and enter keywords for the clip art so that you can search for the image. The image also displays in Preview.

Figure 1.40

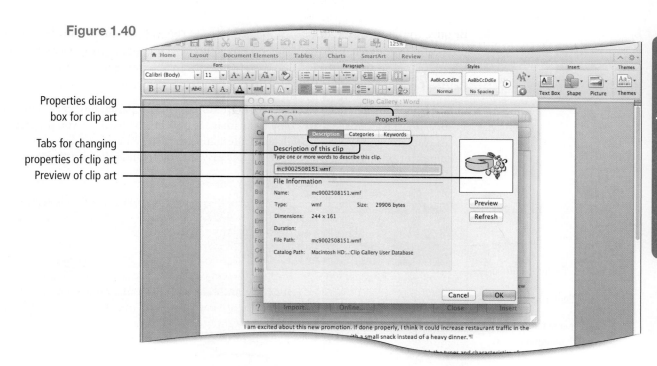

Properties dialog
box for clip art

Tabs for changing
properties of clip art

Preview of clip art

14 In the **Description** box, type **cheese and grapes** and then click the **Keywords tab**. Click **New Keyword**. In the **New Keyword** dialog box, type **cheese** and then click **OK**. Using the same technique, add a **New Keyword** of **grapes** and then compare your screen with Figure 1.41.

You will be able to locate this image in the Clip Gallery by searching for one of the keywords.

Figure 1.41

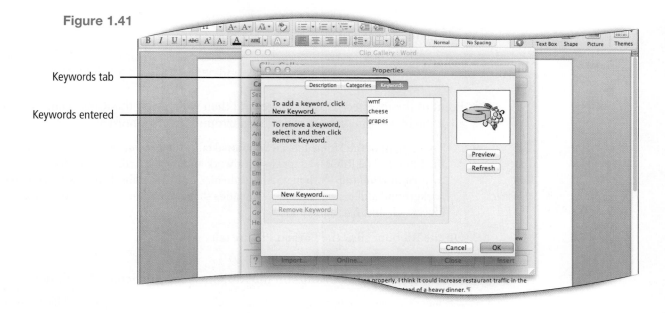

Keywords tab

Keywords entered

15 In the **Properties** dialog box, click **OK**, and then notice in the **Clip Gallery** that the clip art you downloaded from Microsoft displays with the description—*cheese and grapes*—that you entered in the Properties dialog box.

16 In the **Clip Gallery**, click the **cheese and grapes** image, and then click **Insert**.

The clip art is inserted into your Word document at the location of the insertion point.

17 Be sure that your insertion point displays to the right of the clip art and to the left of the paragraph mark and that your image is not selected—surrounded by a border. If necessary, on the Ribbon, click the Home tab. In the **Paragraph group**, click the **Center Text** button ![center], and then compare your screen with Figure 1.42.

Paragraph formats such as Center Text are stored with the paragraph mark. This method of centering an image works only if the image is on a line by itself. As you progress in your study of Word, you will learn alternative ways of centering images. Because nonprinting characters are displayed, it is easy for you to place the insertion point exactly where it is needed to perform a task.

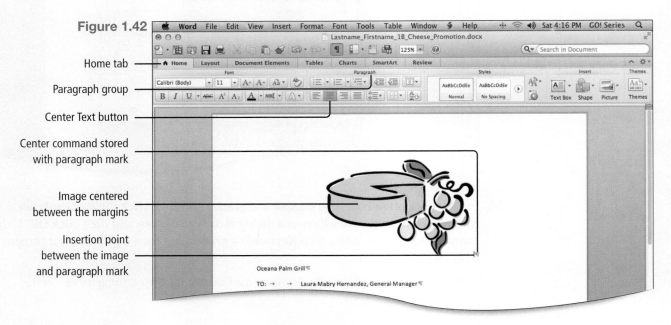

Figure 1.42

Home tab

Paragraph group

Center Text button

Center command stored with paragraph mark

Image centered between the margins

Insertion point between the image and paragraph mark

Alert! | Is the Image Not Centered?

If the image did not center, be sure to click to the left of the paragraph mark located to the right of the image and be sure that the image is not selected. Then on the Home tab, in the Paragraph group, click the Center Text button.

---

18 Point to the inserted clip art image, and then watch how the Ribbon changes as you click the image one time to select it—surround it with a border.

To the right of the Home tab, an additional tab—the *Format Picture* tab—is added to the Ribbon. The Ribbon adapts to your work and displays additional tabs—referred to as ***contextual tabs***—when you need them. Contextual tabs display with a colored background and include special commands that are used to work with the selected object—in this case, a picture.

19 On the Ribbon, click the **Format Picture tab**.

Alert! | Does the Size of Groups on the Ribbon Vary with Screen Resolution?

Your monitor's screen resolution might be set higher than the resolution used to capture the figures in this book. In Figure 1.43 below, the resolution is set to 1024 × 768, which is used for all of the figures in this book. Compare that with Figure 1.44 below, where the screen resolution is set to 1280 × 1024.

At a higher resolution, the Ribbon expands some groups to show more commands than are available with a single click, such as those in the Picture Styles group. Or, the group expands to add descriptive text to some buttons, such as those in the Arrange group. Regardless of your screen resolution, all Office commands are available to you. In higher resolutions, you will have a more robust view of the commands.

In addition to screen resolution, as you resize the window by clicking the Zoom button or by dragging one of the corners of the window, the size of groups may change.

Figure 1.43

Picture Styles group at 1024 x 768 resolution

Arrange group at 1024 x 768 resolution

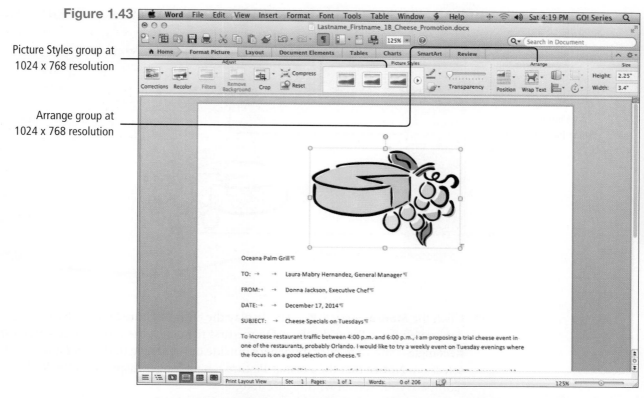

Figure 1.44

Picture Styles group at 1280 x 1024 resolution

More styles display

Arrange group at 1280 x 1024 resolution

Expanded buttons

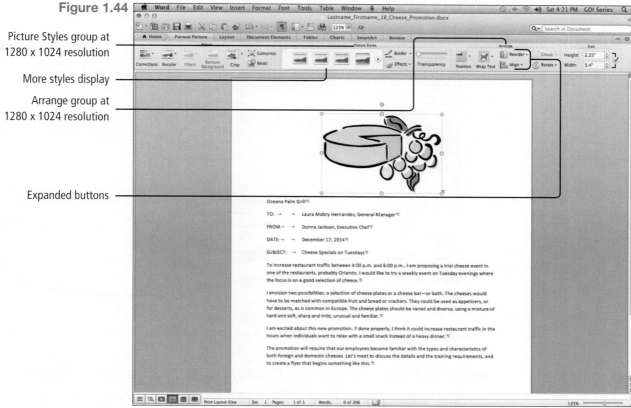

20 On the **Format Picture tab**, in the **Picture Styles group**, point to the third style to display the ScreenTip *Metal Frame*, and then compare your screen with Figure 1.45.

You can apply a picture style or special effect to a picture to make it more visually attractive. Clicking the Picture Style of Metal Frame inserts a metallic-looking frame around the selected image. When you point to a Picture Style, a ScreenTip displays information about the style, and arrows display to the right and at the bottom of the Picture Styles gallery.

Figure 1.45

Scroll right button—click
to display more styles
to the right

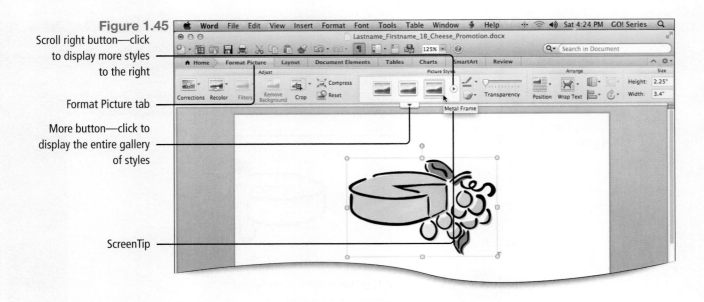

Format Picture tab

More button—click to
display the entire gallery
of styles

ScreenTip

21 Click the **More arrow** [▼] to display the entire Picture Style gallery—do not be concerned if the Ruler displays. On the first row, click the fourth style—**Drop Shadow Rectangle**—and then click anywhere outside of the image to *deselect* it—cancel the selection. Notice that the Format Picture tab no longer displays on the Ribbon. Compare your screen with Figure 1.46.

Contextual tabs display only when you need them.

Figure 1.46

Format Picture tab no
longer displays on
the Ribbon

Drop Shadow Rectangle
picture style applied

22 On the Standard toolbar, click the **Save** button 🖫 to save the changes you have made.

Another Way

On the right side of the
Ribbon, click the 🔺
button; or press Option +
Command ⌘ + R; or on
the View menu, click
Ribbon.

Activity 1.10 | Minimizing, Displaying, and Restoring the Ribbon

Some individuals prefer to minimize the Ribbon in order to maximize available screen space and to display more of the document.

1 Be sure that the Home tab is the active tab. Click the **Home tab**, and notice that only the Ribbon tabs display.

To minimize the Ribbon, you must click the active tab. If you click any other tab, then that tab will become active and will display the groups and buttons associated with the tab.

2 Click anywhere in the document, and notice that the Ribbon remains minimized.

When you need to use a command on the Ribbon, click the tab; and the Ribbon will display.

3 Click the **Home tab**, and notice that the Ribbon is restored.

Most Office users prefer to have the full Ribbon display at all times. You can click any tab to restore the Ribbon.

Objective 10 | Apply Formatting in Office Applications

Formatting is the process of establishing the overall appearance of text, graphics, and pages in an Office file—for example, in a Word document.

Activity 1.11 | Formatting and Viewing Pages

In this activity, you will practice common formatting techniques used in Office applications.

> **Another Way**
>
> On the View menu, click Header and Footer.

1 In the document, scroll to display the bottom of the document. Point to the bottom edge of the document to display the ⬚ pointer, and then double-click to display the **Footer** area. Compare your screen with Figure 1.47.

The Header and Footer tab is added to the Ribbon. A *footer* is a reserved area for text or graphics that displays at the bottom of each page in a document. Likewise, a *header* is a reserved area for text or graphics that displays at the top of each page in a document. When the Footer (or Header) area is active, the document area is inactive (dimmed).

Figure 1.47

Header and Footer contextual tab

Closes the Footer area

Indicates Footer is being created or edited

Footer area

Insertion point left aligned

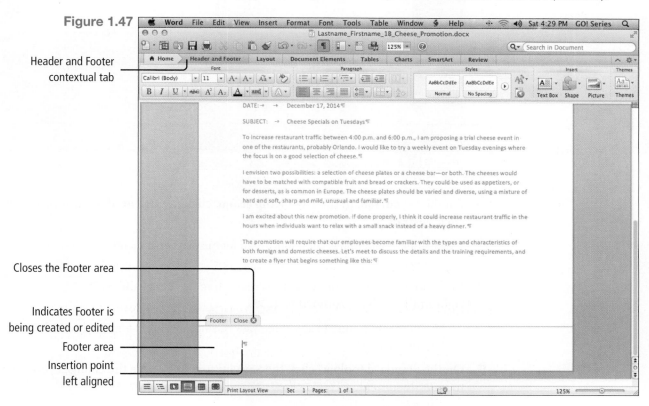

2 In the **Footer** area, using your own name, type the file name of this document **Lastname_Firstname_1B_Cheese_Promotion** and then above the text you typed, click **Close**.

3 On the Ribbon, click the **Layout tab**. In the **Page Setup group**, click the **Orientation** button, and notice that two orientations display—*Portrait and Landscape*. Click **Landscape**.

> In *portrait orientation*, the paper is taller than it is wide. In *landscape orientation*, the paper is wider than it is tall.

4 In the lower right corner of the screen, locate the **Zoom slider** .

> To *zoom* means to increase or decrease the viewing area. You can zoom in to look closely at a section of a document, and then zoom out to see an entire page on the screen. You can also zoom to view multiple pages on the screen.

5 Drag the **Zoom slider** to the left until you have zoomed to approximately **50%**. Compare your screen with Figure 1.48. Your display may differ based on your screen resolution or size of your window.

Figure 1.48

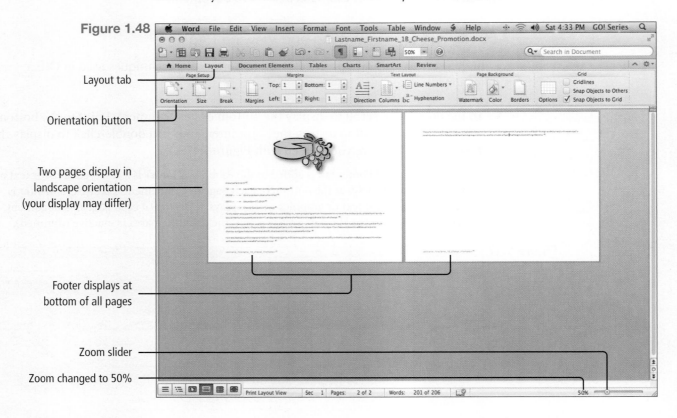

Layout tab

Orientation button

Two pages display in landscape orientation (your display may differ)

Footer displays at bottom of all pages

Zoom slider

Zoom changed to 50%

6 On the **Layout tab**, in the **Page Setup group**, click the **Orientation** button, and then click **Portrait**.

> Portrait orientation is commonly used for business documents, such as letters and memos.

Another Way

On the Standard toolbar, click the Zoom arrow, and then click 125%.

7 In the lower right corner of your screen, drag the **Zoom slider** to the right until you have zoomed to **125%**.

> Use the zoom feature to adjust the view of your document for editing and for your viewing comfort.

8 On the Standard toolbar, click the **Save** button 🖫 to save the changes you have made to your document.

Activity 1.12 | Formatting Text

1 If necessary, scroll to display the top of the document. To the left of *Oceana Palm Grill*, point in the margin area to display the ⬈ pointer and click one time to select the entire line. Compare your screen with Figure 1.49.

> Use this technique to select a line from the margin area. Additionally, with this technique you can drag downward to select multiple-line paragraphs—which is faster and more efficient than dragging through text.

Figure 1.49

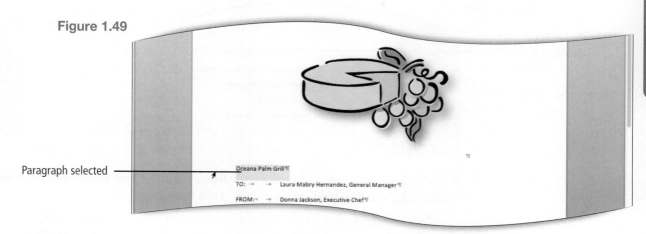

Paragraph selected ————→

> Oceana Palm Grill¶
> TO: → → Laura Mabry Hernandez, General Manager¶
> FROM:→ → Donna Jackson, Executive Chef¶

2 On the Ribbon, click the **Home tab**, and then in the **Paragraph group**, click the **Center Text** button ≡ to center the paragraph.

> *Alignment* refers to the placement of paragraph text relative to the left and right margins. *Center alignment* refers to text that is centered horizontally between the left and right margins. You can also align text at the left margin, which is the default alignment for text in Word, or at the right margin.

3 On the **Home tab**, in the **Font group**, click the **Font arrow** `Calibri (Headings) ▼`. At the top of the list, notice that to the right of **Cambria,** *(Theme Headings)* displays.

> A *font* is a set of characters with the same design and shape. The font in this Word document is Calibri, which is a *sans serif* font—a font design with no lines or extensions on the ends of characters.

> The Cambria font is a *serif* font—a font design that includes small line extensions on the ends of the letters to guide the eye in reading from left to right.

> A *theme* is a predesigned set of colors, fonts, lines, and fill effects that go well together and that can be applied to your entire document or to specific items. A theme combines two sets of fonts—one for text and one for headings. In the default Office theme, Cambria is the suggested font for headings.

> The list of fonts displays as a gallery showing potential results. For example, in the Font gallery, you can see the actual design and format of each font as it would look if applied to text.

4 Scroll in the font list, and then click **Cambria**. With the paragraph *Oceana Palm Grill* still selected, on the **Home tab**, in the **Font group**, click the **Font Size arrow** `11 ▼`, and then click **20**.

> Fonts are measured in *points*, with one point equal to 1/72 of an inch. A higher point size indicates a larger font size. Headings and titles are often formatted by using a larger font size. The word *point* is abbreviated as *pt*.

5 With *Oceana Palm Grill* still selected, on the **Home tab**, in the **Font group**, click the **Font Color arrow** A. Under **Theme Colors**, in the last row, click the seventh color— **Accent 3, Darker 50%**. Click anywhere to deselect the text.

6 To the left of *TO:*, point in the left margin area to display the ⬚ pointer, press down on the mouse, and then drag down to select the four memo headings. Compare your screen with Figure 1.50.

Use this technique to select complete paragraphs from the margin area—dragging downward to select multiple-line paragraphs—which is faster and more efficient than dragging through text.

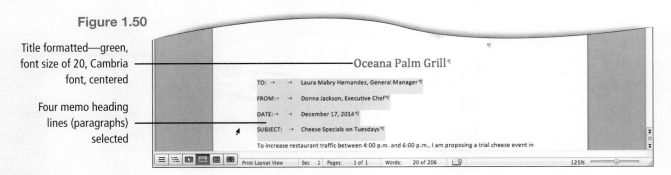

Figure 1.50

Title formatted—green, font size of 20, Cambria font, centered

Four memo heading lines (paragraphs) selected

7 With the four paragraphs selected, on the **Home tab** in the **Font group**, click the **Font Color** button ⬚, which now displays a dark green bar.

The font color button retains its most recently used color—Accent 3, Darker 50%. As you progress in your study of Microsoft Office, you will use other buttons that behave in this manner; that is, they retain their most recently used format.

Another Way
Triple-click anywhere in the paragraph to select the paragraph.

8 To the left the paragraph that begins *To increase,* point in the left margin area to display the ⬚ pointer, and then double-click to select the entire paragraph. If you click too many times, the entire document may be selected—if this occurs, click anywhere and begin again.

9 With the entire paragraph selected, in the **Font group**, click the **Font Color arrow** ⬚, and then under **Theme Colors**, in the first row, click the sixth color—**Accent 2**.

10 In the memo headings area, select the text *TO:* by dragging through the text, and then in the **Font group**, click the **Bold** button ⬚ and the **Italic** button ⬚.

Font styles include bold, italic, and underline. Font styles emphasize text and are a visual cue to draw the reader's eye to important text.

11 With *TO:* still selected, in the **Font group**, click the **Italic** button ⬚ again to turn off the Italic formatting.

A button that behaves in this manner is referred to as a *toggle button*, which means it can be turned on by clicking it once, and then turned off by clicking it again.

12 With *TO:* still selected, on the Standard toolbar, click the **Format Painter** button ⬚. Then, move your mouse under the word *Laura*, and notice the + to the left of the ⬚ mouse pointer.

You can use *Format Painter* to copy the formatting of specific text or of a paragraph and then apply it in other locations in your document. The pointer contains the formatting information from the selected text where the insertion point is positioned. Information about Format Painter and how to turn it off displays in the status bar.

13 With this pointer, drag to select the text *FROM:* and notice that the Bold formatting is applied. *FROM:* still selected, *double-click* the **Format Painter** button ⬚.

14 Select the text *DATE:* to copy the Bold formatting, and notice that the pointer retains the + to the left of its shape.

> When you *double-click* the Format Painter button, the Format Painter feature remains active until you either click the Format Painter button again, or press Esc to cancel it.

15 With Format Painter still active, select the text *SUBJECT:*, and then on the Standard toolbar, notice that the **Format Painter** button is active. Compare your screen with Figure 1.51.

Figure 1.51

Format Painter button
on Standard toolbar active

Memo headings
formatted with Bold

SUBJECT: still selected

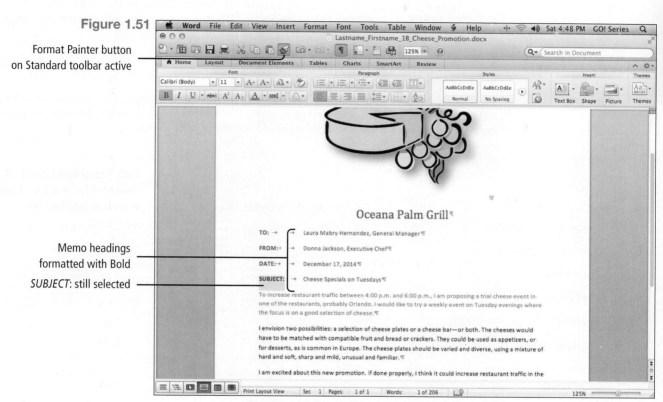

16 On the Standard toolbar, click the **Format Painter** button to turn the command off.

17 In the margin area to the left of the paragraph that begins *To increase*, double-click again to select the entire paragraph. On the **Home tab**, in the **Font group**, click the **Bold** button B and the **Italic** button I. Click anywhere to deselect the paragraph.

18 On the Standard toolbar, click the **Save** button to save the changes you have made to your document.

Activity 1.13 | Using the Clipboard to Cut, Copy, and Paste

The *Clipboard* is a temporary storage area on your computer that holds text or graphics that you select and then copy or cut. When you *copy* text or graphics, a copy is placed on the Clipboard and the original text or graphic remains in place. When you *cut* text or graphics, a copy is placed on the Clipboard, and the original text or graphic is removed—cut—from the document.

After cutting or copying, the contents of the Clipboard are available for you to *paste*—insert—in a new location in the current document, or into another Office file.

1 Hold down Command ⌘, hold down fn, and then press ← to move to the beginning of your document, and then take a moment to study the table in Figure 1.52, which describes similar keyboard shortcuts with which you can navigate quickly in a document.

These keyboard shortcuts used in this textbook are for a Mac OS X operating system using an Apple wireless keyboard that is included with every new iMac. The keyboard shortcuts may also work with a track pad. The keyboard shortcuts for a full-sized keyboard that includes a numeric keypad can be determined by clicking Help on the menu bar, clicking Word Help typing *word keyboard shortcuts* in the search box, and then clicking the *Word keyboard shortcuts* link in the list.

Alert! | **Do Your Keyboard Shortcuts Differ?**

The settings in some versions of the Mac operating system and some utility applications may conflict with the keyboard shortcuts and function key operations in Office. Some keyboard shortcuts also depend on the type of keyboard you are using. Some keyboard shortcuts differ if you are using a laptop.

To Move	Apple Wireless Keyboard	Full-Sized Keyboard (if shortcut keys differ from Wireless Keyboard)
To the beginning of a document	Command ⌘ + fn + ←	Command ⌘ + Home
To the end of a document	Command ⌘ + fn + →	Command ⌘ + End
To the beginning of a line	Command ⌘ + ←	Home or Command ⌘ + ←
To the end of a line	Command ⌘ + →	End or Command ⌘ + →
To the beginning of the previous word	Option + ←	
To the beginning of the next word	Option + →	
To the beginning of the current word (if insertion point is in the middle of a word)	Option + ←	
To the beginning of a paragraph	Command ⌘ + ↑	
To the beginning of the next paragraph	Command ⌘ + ↓	
To the beginning of the current paragraph (if insertion point is in the middle of a paragraph)	Command ⌘ + ↑	
Up one screen	fn + ↑	PageUp
Down one screen	fn + ↓	PageDown

Figure 1.52

Another Way
Press Command ⌘ + C to copy.

2 To the left of *Oceana Palm Grill*, point in the left margin area to display the ⦧ pointer, and then click one time to select the entire line, including the paragraph mark. On the Standard toolbar, click the **Copy** button 🗐.

Anything that you select and then copy—or cut—is placed on the Clipboard. There is no visible indication that your copied selection has been placed on the Clipboard.

3 Press Command ⌘ + fn + → to move to the end of your document. Press Return one time to create a new blank paragraph. On the Standard toolbar, click the **Paste** button 🖻, and then compare your screen with Figure 1.53.

> The Paste command pastes the most recently copied item from the Office Clipboard at the insertion point location. If you click the lower portion of the Paste button, a list of *Paste Options* displays. The paste options enable you to change the format of a pasted item.

Figure 1.53

Copy button

Paste button

Pasted text

Paste Options button

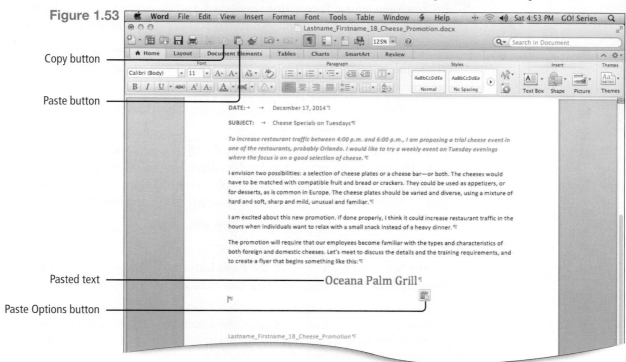

4 Click the **Paste Options** button 🖻 that displays below the pasted text, and then compare your screen with Figure 1.54.

> How Word formats a selection when you paste is determined by whether the selection includes a paragraph mark. Recall that some formatting commands, such as Center Text are stored with the paragraph mark. Because you selected the entire line, which included the paragraph mark, the pasted text retained its formatting—centered. If you do not include the paragraph mark in your selection, character formatting such as font, font color, font size, and bold are always applied to the pasted text.

> When you copy or cut text and then paste it within the same document or another Word document, you can retain the original format and change the formatting to match the surrounding text where it is pasted. To retain the original formatting, you do not need to perform any specific action—you can ignore the Paste Options button.

Figure 1.54

Click to apply formatting of destination paragraph to pasted text

Default setting if you do not change Paste Options

Discards all formatting; most often used for pictures and tables that have been pasted

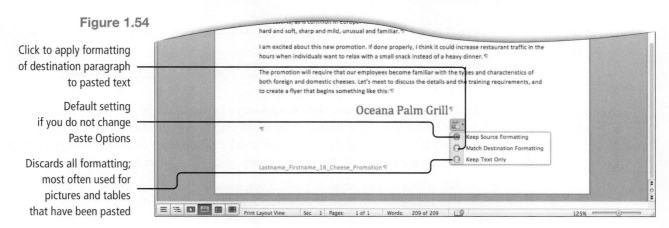

5 Be sure **Keep Source Formatting** is selected, and then press ⎋ to close the Paste Options list; the button displays until you take some other screen action.

Another Way
Press Command ⌘ + X to cut.

6 Press Command ⌘ + fn + ← to move to the top of the document, and then click the **cheese image** one time to select it. Notice that the paragraph mark is not included in the selection. On the Shortcut toolbar, click the **Cut** button ✂.

Recall that the Cut command cuts—removes—the selection from the document and places it on the Clipboard.

7 Point in the left margin area to display the ↗ pointer, and then click one time to select the paragraph mark that displays directly above *Oceana Palm Grill*. Press Delete one time to remove the blank paragraph from the top of the document, and then press Command ⌘ + fn + → to move to the end of the document.

The insertion point is blinking to the left of the last paragraph mark at the end of the document.

8 On the Standard toolbar, click the **Paste** button. Below the pasted image, click the **Paste Options** button, and then compare your screen with Figure 1.55.

Because you selected an image, the Paste Options button displays commands that differ from a selection of text. For images, the default action is to use the Destination Theme— no themes have been applied to this document. Recall that a theme is a predesigned set of colors, fonts, lines, and fill effects that look good together and that can be applied to your entire document or to specific items.

The image displays at the left margin because you did not include the paragraph mark with the image when you selected it—the center command is stored with the paragraph mark.

Figure 1.55

Pasted image at left margin

Oceana Palm Grill¶

Default setting for images if you do not change Paste Options

Keep Source Formatting
Use Destination Theme

Another Way
Press Command ⌘ + E to center.

9 In the **Paste Options** list, click **Keep Source Formatting**. To the left of the pasted image, point in the left margin area to display the ↗ pointer, and then click one time to select the image and the paragraph mark that displays to the right of the image. On the **Home tab**, in the **Paragraph group**, click the **Center Text** button.

When selecting an image to paste, if you wish to retain the formatting in its pasted location, be sure to include the paragraph mark in the selection.

10 Above the cheese picture, click to position the insertion point at the end of the word *Grill*, press Spacebar one time, and then type **Tuesday Cheese Tastings** Compare your screen with Figure 1.56.

Figure 1.56

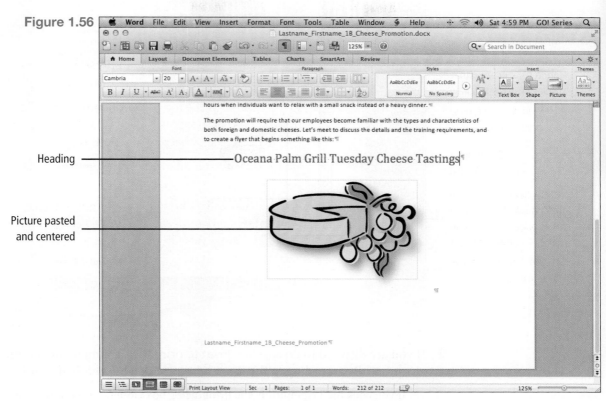

Heading ——————— Oceana Palm Grill Tuesday Cheese Tastings

Picture pasted and centered

More Knowledge | Displaying the Clipboard on a Mac

Display Finder. On the Edit menu, click Show Clipboard to display the current contents of the Clipboard.

Activity 1.14 | Viewing Print Preview and Printing a Word Document

1 Press Command ⌘ + fn + ← to move to the top of your document. Select the text *Oceana Palm Grill*, and then replace the selected text by typing **Memo**.

2 On the **File** menu, click **Properties**. In the **Properties** dialog box, on the **Summary tab**, in the **Title** box, type **Cheese Promotion** and in the **Subject** box, type your course name and section number. In the **Author** box, replace the existing author name with your first and last name. In the **Keywords** box, type **cheese promotion** and then click **OK**.

3 On the Standard toolbar, click the **Save** button 💾 to save the changes you have made to your document.

Another Way

Press Command ⌘ + P to print.

4 On the **File** menu, click **Print**. Compare your screen with Figure 1.57.

For convenience, a Page Setup button displays here, so that you can make last-minute adjustments without closing the Print dialog box. To save the document as a PDF file, click the PDF button. If you need to make corrections to the document, in the Print dialog box, click Cancel.

It is good practice to examine the Print Preview before printing or submitting your work electronically. Then, make any necessary corrections, re-save, and redisplay Print Preview.

Figure 1.57

Printer (yours will vary)

Preview of document (if you have a non-color printer as your default printer, the preview may display in shades of gray)

Navigation buttons to preview other pages

Show Quick Preview selected

Page Setup button—to make quick changes such as page orientation to the document

PDF button—to save document as PDF file

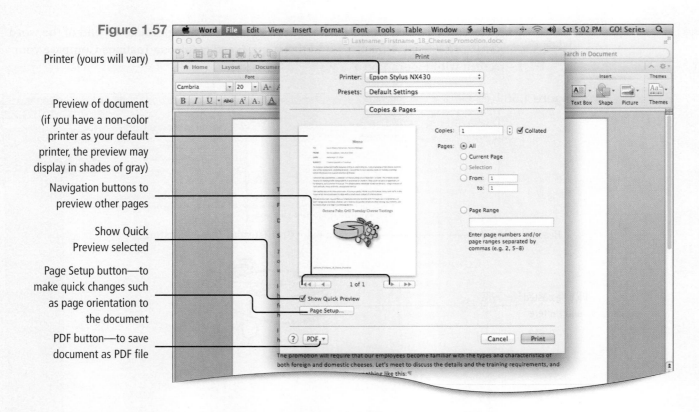

5 If you are directed to do so, click **Print** to print the document; or submit your file electronically according to the directions provided by your instructor.

> If you click the Print button, the Print dialog box closes and the Word window redisplays.

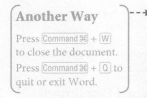

Another Way

Press Command ⌘ + W to close the document. Press Command ⌘ + Q to quit or exit Word.

6 On the left side of the title bar, click the **Close** button 🔘 to close the document. On the **Word** menu, click **Quit Word**.

> When you close a document, the application remains open. You should close your document before exiting Word; otherwise, the next time you open Word, the document will open with the application. If no other applications have been opened, Finder displays.

Objective 11 | Use the Microsoft Office for Mac 2011 Help System

Within each Office application, the Help feature provides information about the application's features and displays step-by-step instructions for performing many tasks.

Activity 1.15 | Using the Microsoft Office for Mac 2011 Help System in Excel

In this activity, you will use the Microsoft Help feature to find the location of a command on the menu and information about adjusting the column size to see everything in Excel.

1 Open the **Microsoft Excel** application. If necessary, click the Zoom button 🔘 or drag the lower right corner of the window down and to the right to increase the size of the Excel window. On the menu bar, click **Help**. In the **Search** box, type **copy** and then compare your screen with Figure 1.58.

> As you type characters, Excel suggests words or phrases based on the characters you enter. In the list of results, Menu Items will display the location on the menu for the command. Help Topics will display information about the selected item.

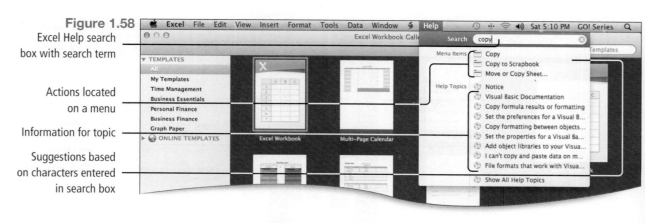

Figure 1.58
Excel Help search
box with search term

Actions located
on a menu

Information for topic

Suggestions based
on characters entered
in search box

2 In the list of results, point to **Copy**, and then compare your screen with Figure 1.59.

Excel points to the Copy command in the Edit menu.

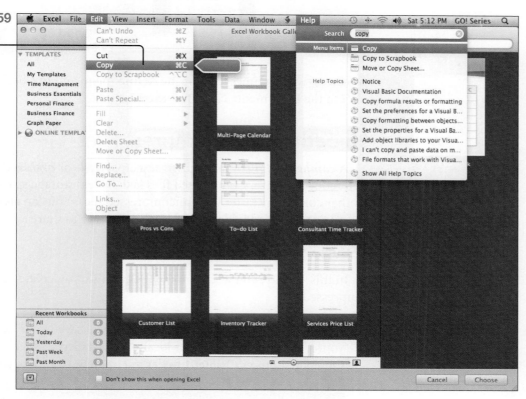

Figure 1.59
Edit menu—location of
Copy command

3 Press ⎋ to remove the search term. On the **Help** menu, click **Excel Help**—located below the Search box—to display the **Help Center** dialog box.

In the Help Center dialog box, you can find help by typing in the Search Help box, by going online to Microsoft's Web site, or by clicking a link such as *Entering and Importing Data*.

4 In the **Search Help** box, type **adjust** and notice the suggestions for terms. In the list of suggestions, click **adjust the column size to see everything**. In the list of results, click **Adjust the column size to see everything**. Scroll to display all of the steps and notice that at the bottom under *See also* are suggestions for other topics.

5 At the top left of the **Help Center** dialog box, click the **Action** button ⚙▾, and then compare your screen with Figure 1.60.

Click the Action button, and then click Print if you want to print a copy of this information for your reference.

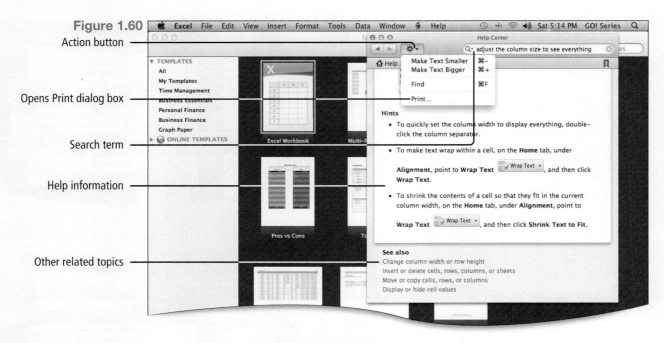

Figure 1.60

Action button

Opens Print dialog box

Search term

Help information

Other related topics

6 Press ⎋ two times to close the Action menu and to close the Help Center window. On the **Excel** menu, click **Quit Excel**.

Objective 12 | Compress Files

A *compressed file*—also known as a *zipped file* or *archived file*—is a file that has been reduced in size. Compressed files take up less storage space and can be transferred to other computers faster than uncompressed files. You can also combine a group of files into one compressed folder, which makes it easier to share a group of files.

Activity 1.16 | Compressing Files

In this activity, you will combine the two files you created in this chapter into one compressed file.

1 In **Finder**, navigate to the location where you saved your two files for this chapter— your USB flash drive or other location—and display the folder window for your **Common Features Chapter 1** folder in **List** view. Compare your screen with Figure 1.61.

Figure 1.61

Finder

List view button

Your chapter files (your name displays)

Common Features Chapter 1 folder contents

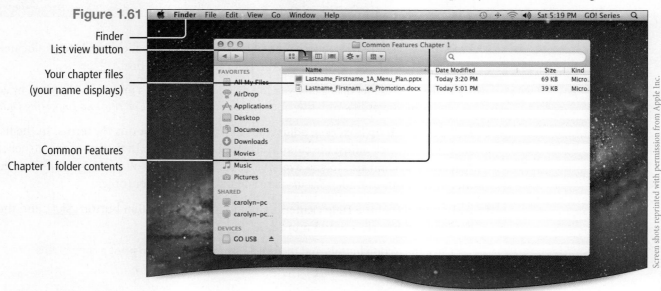

Screen shots reprinted with permission from Apple Inc.

2 In the file list, click your **Lastname_Firstname_1A_Menu_Plan** file one time to select it.

3 Hold down Command ⌘ and then click your **Lastname_Firstname_1B_Cheese_ Promotion** file to select both files. Release Command ⌘.

In any Mac-based application, holding down Command ⌘ while selecting enables you to select multiple items.

4 Point anywhere over the two selected files, hold down Control and click, and then compare your screen with Figure 1.62.

A shortcut menu displays from which you can compress the selected files. Because you have selected two files, the compress command displays as *Compress 2 Items*.

Figure 1.62

Chapter files selected

Shortcut menu

Compress command

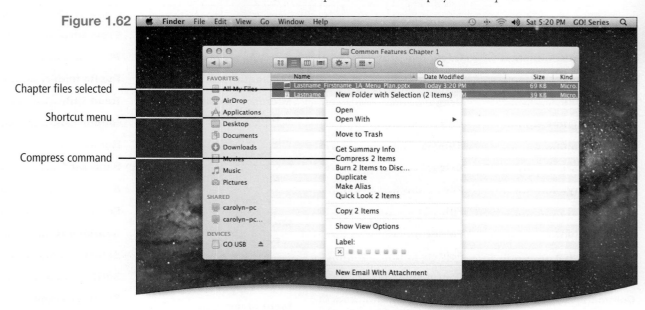

5 On the shortcut menu, click **Compress 2 Items**, and notice that the file *Archive.zip* displays in the Common Features Chapter 1 folder.

Your Mac system creates a compressed file containing a *copy* of each of the selected files. If you compress a single file, the archive file retains the original file name with a .zip extension. If you compress more than one file, the files are compressed into a file named *Archive.zip*. The compressed file should be renamed so that you can more easily identify its contents.

6 Point to **Archive.zip** and click one time to select the file. Click one more time to select the file name—do not double-click or the Archive.zip file will decompress and display the two files within the compressed file. Be sure that only *Archive* is selected—you do not want to change the extension of .zip. Using your own name, type **Lastname_Firstname_Common_Features_Ch01** and press Return.

The compressed folder is now ready to attach to an e-mail or share in some other electronic format.

7 **Close** ⊘ the folder window. If directed to do so by your instructor, submit your compressed folder electronically.

More Knowledge | **Extracting Compressed Files**

Extract means to decompress, or pull out, files from a compressed form. When you extract a file, an uncompressed copy is placed in the folder that you specify. The original file remains in the compressed folder. To extract the files, double-click the compressed file.

End **You have completed Project 1B**

Content-Based Assessments

Summary

In this chapter, you used Finder to navigate the Mac folder structure. You also used features that are common across the Microsoft Office for Mac 2011 applications.

Key Terms

Matching

Match each term in the second column with its correct definition in the first column by writing the letter of the term on the blank line in front of the correct definition.

A Apple menu

B Application

C Command

D Disclosure triangle

E File

F Finder

G Folder

H Home folder

I Icons

J Keyboard shortcut

K Microsoft Excel

L Ribbon

M Sidebar

N Subfolder

O Title bar

_____ 1. A collection of information stored on a computer under a single name.

_____ 2. A container in which you store files.

_____ 3. A folder within a folder.

_____ 4. The application that displays the files and folders on your computer.

_____ 5. A folder with the same name as the user account that contains your personal folders and files and that cannot be renamed.

_____ 6. A menu that enables you to configure your computer, shut down your computer, and log out.

_____ 7. A triangle that displays to the left of a folder name, which, when clicked, expands the folder to display the contents of that folder.

_____ 8. An area on the left side of the Finder window that displays icons that help you locate files, applications, documents, shared computers, and devices such as CDs, DVDs, or removable storage.

_____ 9. An instruction to a computer application that carries out an action.

_____ 10. Small pictures that represent an application, a file, a folder, or an object.

_____ 11. A set of instructions that a computer uses to perform a specific task.

_____ 12. A spreadsheet application used to calculate numbers and create charts.

_____ 13. The user interface that groups commands on tabs at the top of the application window.

_____ 14. A bar at the top of the application window displaying the current file name.

_____ 15. One or more keys pressed to perform a task that would otherwise require a mouse.

Multiple Choice

Circle the correct answer.

1. The area at the bottom of the desktop that displays icons for applications is the:
   A. Dock   **B.** menu bar   **C.** status bar

2. In Finder, a view that displays details about the folders and files, including the date modified, the size of a file, and the type of a file is:
   A. Columns   **B.** Icons   **C.** List

3. The toolbar that displays a row of buttons that provide a one-click method to perform the most common commands in the application such as Save and Print is the:
   A. Dock   **B.** menu bar   **C.** Standard toolbar

4. A button on the left side of the title bar that increases or decreases the size of the window is the:
   A. Close   **B.** Minimize   **C.** Zoom

5. Details about a file, including the title, author name, subject, and keywords are known as:
   A. document properties   **B.** formatting marks   **C.** ScreenTips

6. A button that can be turned on by clicking it once, and then turned off by clicking it again is a:
   A. Close button **B.** gallery **C.** toggle button

7. A type of formatting emphasis applied to text, such as bold, italic, and underline, is called a:
   A. font **B.** font style **C.** keyword

8. An Office feature that copies formatting from one selection of text to another is:
   A. copy **B.** Format Painter **C.** paste

9. A temporary storage area that holds text or graphics that you select and then cut or copy is the:
   A. Clipboard **B.** Clipboard Gallery **C.** Finder

10. A file that has been reduced in size is:
    A. a compressed file **B.** an extracted file **C.** a PDF file

Creating Documents with Microsoft Word for Mac 2011

OUTCOMES
At the end of this chapter you will be able to:

OBJECTIVES
Mastering these objectives will enable you to:

PROJECT 1A
Create a flyer with a picture.

1. Create a New Document and Insert Text (p. 59)
2. Insert and Format Graphics (p. 61)
3. Insert and Modify Text Boxes and Shapes (p. 67)
4. Preview and Print a Document (p. 71)

PROJECT 1B
Format text, paragraphs, and documents.

5. Change Document and Paragraph Layout (p. 75)
6. Create and Modify Lists (p. 82)
7. Set and Modify Tab Stops (p. 86)
8. Insert a SmartArt Graphic (p. 89)

© Pattie Steib/Shutterstock

In This Chapter

In this chapter, you will use Microsoft Word, which is one of the most common programs found on computers and one that almost everyone has a reason to use. You will use many of the new tools found in Word for Mac 2011. When you learn word processing, you are also learning skills and techniques that you need to work efficiently on a computer. You can use Microsoft Word to perform basic word processing tasks such as writing a memo, a report, or a letter. You can also use Word to complete complex word processing tasks, such as creating sophisticated tables, embedding graphics, writing blogs, creating publications, and inserting links into other documents and the Internet. Word is a program that you can learn gradually, and then add more advanced skills one at a time.

The projects in this chapter relate to **Laurel College**. The college offers this diverse geographic area a wide range of academic and career programs, including associate degrees, certificate programs, and non-credit continuing education and personal development courses. The college makes positive contributions to the community through cultural and athletic programs and partnerships with businesses and nonprofit organizations. The college also provides industry-specific training programs for local businesses through its growing Economic Development Center.

Project 1A Flyer

Project Activities

In Activities 1.01 through 1.12, you will create a flyer announcing a new rock climbing class offered by the Physical Education Department at Laurel College. Your completed document will look similar to Figure 1.1.

Project Files

For Project 1A, you will need the following files:

New blank Word document
w01A_Fitness_Flyer
w01A_Rock_Climber

You will save your document as:

Lastname_Firstname_1A_Fitness_Flyer

Project Results

Figure 1.1
Project 1A Fitness Flyer

Objective 1 | Create a New Document and Insert Text

When you create a new document, you can type all of the text, or you can type some of the text and then insert additional text from another source.

Activity 1.01 | Starting a New Word Document and Inserting Text

1 Open **Word**, and in the **Word Document Gallery**, notice that the blank **Word Document** template is selected, and a preview displays on the right side of the gallery. If the Word Document template is not selected, on the left side of the screen, under TEMPLATES, click All, and then click Word Document. In the lower right corner of the **Word Document Gallery**, click **Choose**. If necessary, increase the size of the Word window by clicking the Zoom button ⊙ or by dragging the lower right corner of the window. On the Standard toolbar, if necessary, click the Show/Hide button ¶ so that it is active to display the formatting marks. If the rulers do not display, on the menu bar, click View, and then click Ruler. If necessary, on the Standard toolbar, click the Zoom arrow [100% ▾], and then click 125% to increase the size of the active document.

2 Type **Rock Climbing 101** and then press Return three times. As you type the following text, press the Spacebar only one time at the end of a sentence: **Increase your fitness level by learning basic rock climbing using the new Laurel College Gymnasium rock climbing wall. The Physical Education Department is offering Rock Climbing 101 as part of its Recreational Fitness Program.**

As you type, the insertion point moves to the right. When it approaches the right margin, Word determines whether the next word in the line will fit within the established right margin. If the word does not fit, Word moves the entire word down to the next line. This feature is called *wordwrap* and means that you press Return *only* when you reach the end of a paragraph—it is not necessary to press Return at the end of each line of text.

> **Note | Spacing Between Sentences**
>
> Although you might have learned to add two spaces following end-of-sentence punctuation, the common practice now is to space only one time at the end of a sentence.

3 Press Return two times. Take a moment to study the table in Figure 1.2 to become familiar with the default document settings in Microsoft Word, and then compare your screen with Figure 1.3.

When you press Return, Spacebar, or Tab on your keyboard, characters display in your document to represent these keystrokes. These characters do not print and are referred to as *nonprinting characters marks* or *formatting marks*. These marks will display throughout this instruction.

Default Document Settings in a New Word Document

Setting	Default format
Font and font size	The default font is Cambria (Body) and the default font size is 12.
Line spacing	The default line spacing is single spacing.
Margins	The default top and bottom margins are 1 inch; the default left and right margins are 1.25 inches; margin settings display on the Layout tab.
Paragraph spacing	The default paragraph spacing places 0 pts (points) of blank space after each paragraph.
Style	The default style is Normal; the Normal style stores all of the default settings for a blank Word document.
View	The default view is Print Layout view, which displays the page borders and displays the document as it will appear when printed.

Figure 1.2

Figure 1.3

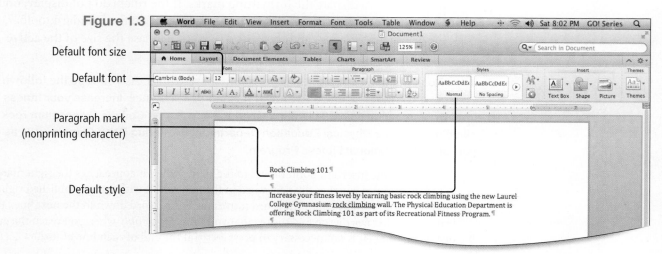

Default font size
Default font
Paragraph mark (nonprinting character)
Default style

Another Way

Open the file, copy the required text, close the file, and then paste the text into the current document.

4 On the menu bar, click **Insert**, and then click **File**. In the **Insert File** dialog box, navigate to the student files that accompany this textbook, locate and click **w01A_Fitness_Flyer**, and then click **Insert**. Compare your screen with Figure 1.4.

A *copy* of the text from the w01A_Fitness_Flyer file displays at the insertion point location; the text is not removed from the original file.

Figure 1.4

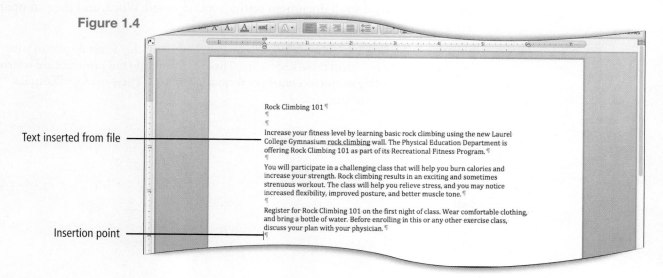

Text inserted from file

Insertion point

5 On the Standard toolbar, click the **Save** button [image]. In the **Save** dialog box, navigate to the location where you are saving your files for this chapter, and then create a new folder named **Word Chapter 1** With this new folder selected, in the **Save As** box, replace the existing text with **Lastname_Firstname_1A_Fitness_Flyer** and then click **Save** or press Return.

Objective 2 | Insert and Format Graphics

To add visual interest to a document, you can insert *graphics*. Graphics include pictures, clip art, charts, and *drawing objects*—shapes, diagrams, lines, and so on. For additional visual interest, you can convert text to an attractive graphic format; add, resize, move, and format pictures; and add an attractive page border.

Activity 1.02 | Formatting Text Using Text Effects

Text effects are decorative formats, such as shadowed or mirrored text, text glow, 3-D effects, and colors that make text stand out.

1 Including the paragraph mark, select the first paragraph of text—*Rock Climbing 101*. On the **Home tab**, in the **Font group**, click the **Text Effects** button [A] to display a gallery.

2 In the **Text Effects** gallery, in the first row, click the first effect. With the text still selected, in the **Font group**, click in the **Font Size** box [11] to select the existing font size. Type **50** and then press Return.

> When you want to change the font size of selected text to a size that does not display in the Font Size list, type the number in the Font Size box and press Return to confirm the new font size.

3 With the text still selected, in the **Paragraph group**, click the **Center Text** button [image] to center the text. Compare your screen with Figure 1.5.

Figure 1.5

Font Size changed to 50

Text Effects button

Center button darker, indicating centering applied

Text Effects applied to title (title selected)

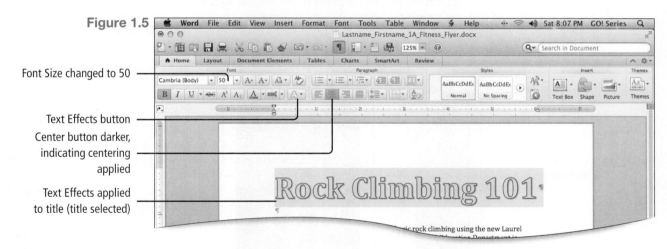

4 With the text still selected, in the **Font group**, click the **Text Effects** button [A]. Point to **Shadow**, and then under **Outer**, in the second row, click the third style—**Outside Left**.

5 With the text still selected, in the **Font group**, click the **Font Color arrow** [A]. Under **Theme Colors**, in the first row, click the fourth color—**Text 2**.

6 Click anywhere in the document to deselect the text, and then compare your screen with Figure 1.6.

Figure 1.6

Title color changed and shadow added ————— **Rock Climbing 101**

...is rock climbing using the new Laurel

7 **Save** 🖫 your document.

Activity 1.03 | Inserting and Resizing Pictures

1 In the paragraph that begins *Increase your fitness*, click to position the insertion point at the beginning of the paragraph.

2 On the **Home tab**, in the **Insert group**, click the **Picture** button, and then click **Picture from File**. In the **Choose a Picture** dialog box, navigate to your student data files, locate and click **w01A_Rock_Climber.jpg**, and then click **Insert**.

Word inserts the picture as an ***inline object***; that is, the picture is positioned directly in the text at the insertion point, just like a character in a sentence. Sizing handles surround the picture, indicating that it is selected.

3 If necessary, scroll to view the entire picture. Notice the round and square sizing handles around the border of the selected picture, as shown in Figure 1.7.

The round corner sizing handles resize the graphic proportionally. The square sizing handles resize a graphic vertically or horizontally only; however, sizing with these will distort the graphic. A green rotate handle, with which you can rotate the graphic to any angle, displays above the top center sizing handle.

Figure 1.7

Center sizing handle
Rotate handle

Corner sizing handles

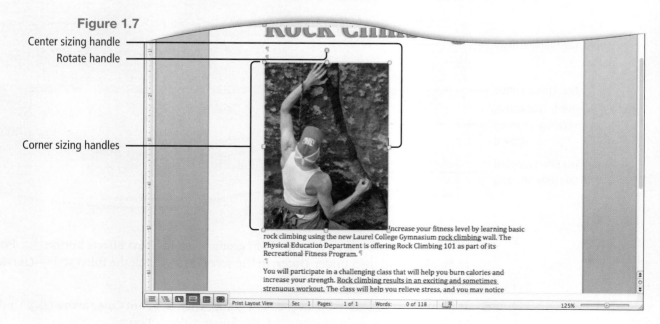

Increase your fitness level by learning basic rock climbing using the new Laurel College Gymnasium rock climbing wall. The Physical Education Department is offering Rock Climbing 101 as part of its Recreational Fitness Program.

You will participate in a challenging class that will help you burn calories and increase your strength. Rock climbing results in an exciting and sometimes strenuous workout. The class will help you relieve stress, and you may notice

Print Layout View   Sec 1   Pages: 1 of 1   Words: 0 of 118   125%

4 At the lower right corner of the picture, point to the round sizing handle until the ⬉ pointer displays. Drag upward and to the left until the **ScreenTip** displays that the **Width** is **2.04″** and the **Height** is **2.72″** as shown in Figure 1.8, and then release the mouse button. Notice that the graphic is proportionally resized.

Figure 1.8

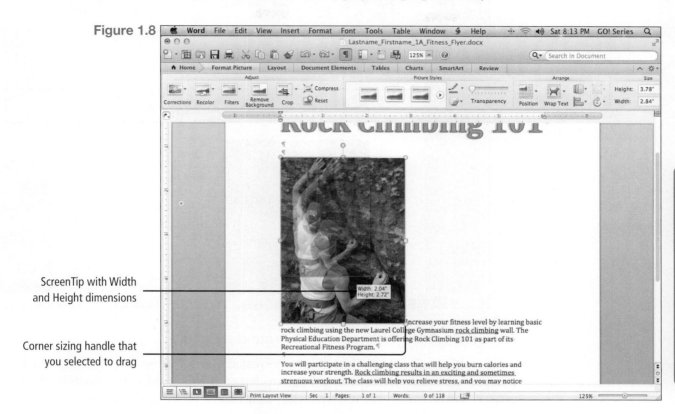

ScreenTip with Width and Height dimensions

Corner sizing handle that you selected to drag

5 On the Standard toolbar, click the **Undo** button 🔙 to undo the resizing of the picture.

This action discards all formatting changes that you made to the picture.

6 Be sure the picture is selected—you know it is selected if the sizing handles display. On the Ribbon, click the **Format Picture tab**. In the **Size group**, double-click in the **Height** box to select the existing text. Type **4.5** and then press Return. In the document, scroll to view the entire picture on your screen, compare your screen with Figure 1.9, and then **Save** 💾 your document.

When you use the Height and Width boxes to change the size of a graphic, the graphic will always resize proportionally; that is, the width adjusts as you change the height and vice versa.

Figure 1.9

Format Picture tab

Undo button

Picture Height changed
to 4.5″

Width changes to keep
picture in proportion

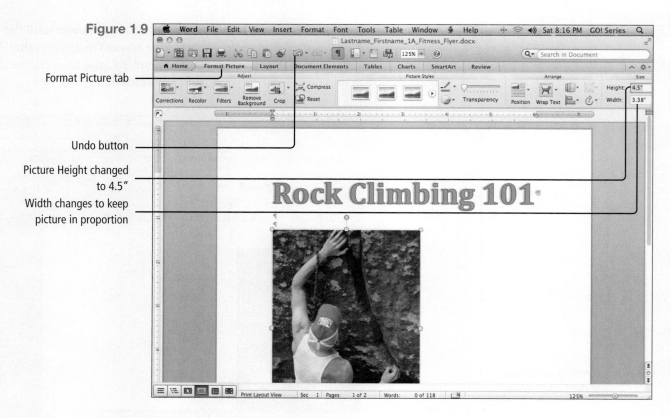

Activity 1.04 | Wrapping Text Around a Picture

Graphics inserted as inline objects are treated like characters in a sentence, which can result in unattractive spacing. You can change an inline object to a *floating object*—a graphic that can be moved independently of the surrounding text characters.

1 Be sure the picture is selected. On the **Format Picture tab**, in the **Arrange group**, click the **Wrap Text** button to display a list of text wrapping arrangements.

> *Text wrapping* refers to the manner in which text displays around an object.

2 On the list, click **Square** to wrap the text around the graphic, and then notice the *anchor* symbol to the left of the first line of the paragraph. Compare your screen with Figure 1.10.

> Select square text wrapping when you want to wrap the text to the left or right of the image. When you apply text wrapping, the object is always associated with—anchored to—a specific paragraph.

Figure 1.10

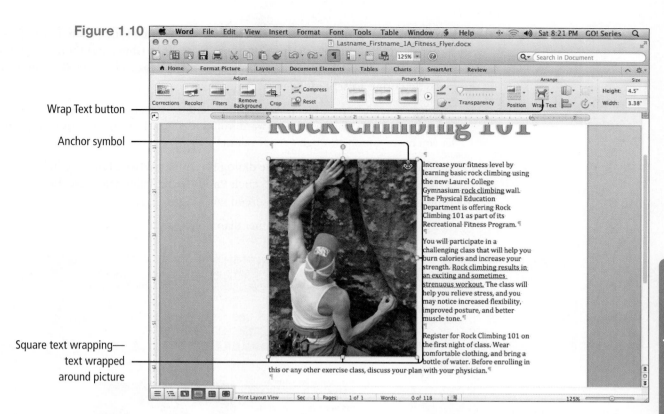

Wrap Text button

Anchor symbol

Square text wrapping—
text wrapped
around picture

3 **Save** 📄 your document.

Activity 1.05 | Moving a Picture

1 Point to the selected rock climber picture to display the ⬥ pointer.

2 Drag the picture to the right until the right edge of the picture aligns at approximately **6 inches on the horizontal ruler**, and then release the mouse button. Compare your screen with Figure 1.11.

Figure 1.11

Right edge aligned
with right margin

Top edge aligned with
top of paragraph

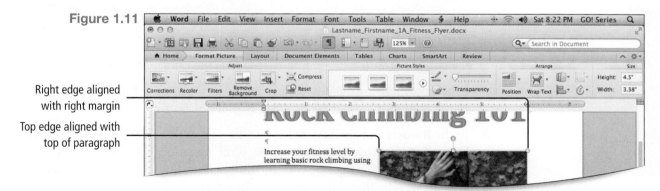

3 If necessary, press any of the arrow keys on your keyboard to *nudge*—move in small increments—the picture in any direction so that the text wraps to match Figure 1.11. **Save** 📄 your document.

Activity 1.06 | Applying Picture Styles and Artistic Effects

Picture styles include shapes, shadows, frames, borders, and other special effects with which you can stylize an image. *Artistic effects* are formats that make pictures look more like sketches or paintings.

Another Way

On the Format menu, click Picture, and then in the Format Picture dialog box click Glow & Soft Edges.

1 Be sure the rock climber picture is selected. On the **Format Picture tab**, in the **Picture Styles group**, click the **Picture Effects** button ▢. Point to **Glow**, and then click **Glow Options**. In the **Format Picture** dialog box, under **Soft Edges**, click the **Size spin box up arrow** ▢ five times to set **Soft Edges** at **5 pt**.

> The Soft Edges feature fades the edges of the picture. The number of points you choose determines how far the fade goes inward from the edges of the picture. *Spin box* arrows let you move rapidly through a set of values by clicking.

2 On the left side of the **Format Picture** dialog box, click **Artistic Filters**. Click in the **Artistic filter** box, and on the list, click **Paint Brush**. Click **OK**, **Save** ▢ your document, and then compare your screen with Figure 1.12.

> The picture looks like a painting, rather than a photograph.

Figure 1.12

Soft Edges and Paint Brush artistic effects applied to picture

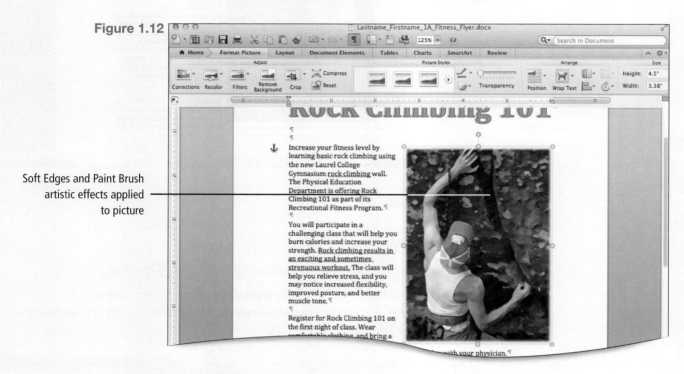

Activity 1.07 │ Adding a Page Border

Page borders frame a page and help to focus the information on the page.

1 Click anywhere outside the picture to deselect it. On the Ribbon, click the **Layout tab**. In the **Page Background group**, click the **Borders** button.

2 In the **Borders and Shading** dialog box, be sure that the **Page Border tab** is selected. Under **Setting**, click **Box**. Under **Style**, scroll down the list about a third of the way and click the heavy top line with the thin bottom line—check the **Preview** area to be sure the heavier line is the nearest to the edges of the page.

3 Click the **Color arrow**, and then in the first row, click the fourth color—**Text 2**.

4 Under **Apply to**, be sure *Whole document* is selected, and then compare your screen with Figure 1.13.

Figure 1.13

Borders button

Borders and Shading dialog box

Border style

Box setting

Border color

Page border preview

Border width

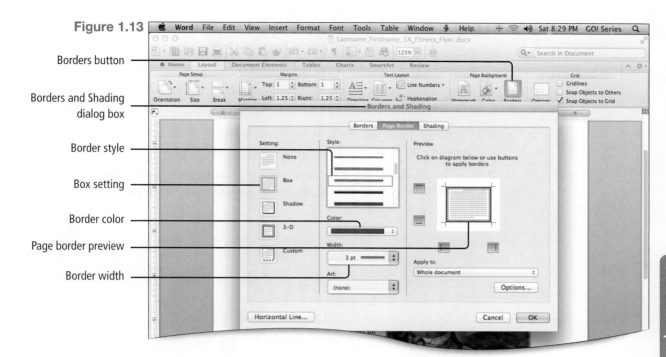

5 At the bottom of the **Borders and Shading** dialog box, click **OK**.

6 Press Command ⌘ + fn + ← to move to the top of the document, and then compare your page border with Figure 1.14. **Save** 🖫 your document.

Figure 1.14

Page border added to document

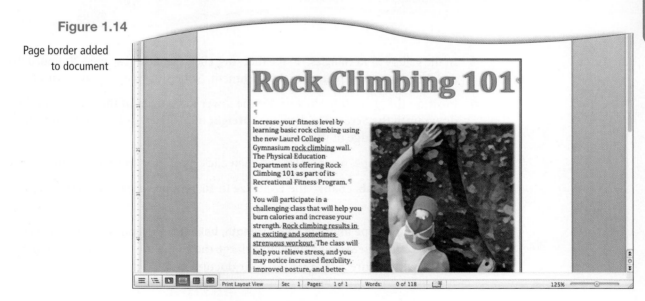

Objective 3 | Insert and Modify Text Boxes and Shapes

Word provides predefined *shapes* and *text boxes* that you can add to your documents. A shape is an object such as a line, arrow, box, callout, or banner. A text box is a movable, resizable container for text or graphics. Use these objects to add visual interest to your document.

Activity 1.08 | Inserting a Shape

1   Press ⬇ one time to move to the blank paragraph—or blank line—below the title. Press Return eight times to make space for a text box—there will be ten paragraph marks between the title and the first paragraph of text. Notice that the picture anchored to the paragraph moves with the text.

2   Press Command ⌘ + fn + ➡ to move to the end of the document, and notice that your insertion point is positioned in the empty paragraph at the end of the document.

3   On the Ribbon, click the **Home tab**, and then in the **Insert group**, click the **Shape** button to display a list of shape categories. Point to **Rectangles**, and then compare your screen with Figure 1.15.

Figure 1.15

Shape button

Rounded Rectangle shape

List of Shape categories

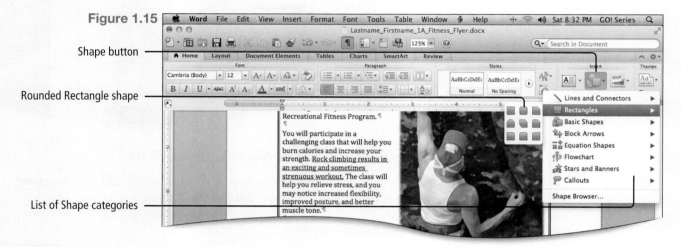

4   In the gallery of **Rectangles**, on the first row, click the second shape—**Rounded Rectangle**—and then move your pointer in the document. Notice that the ⊞ pointer displays.

5   Position the ⊞ pointer just under the lower left corner of the picture, and then drag down until the **ScreenTip** displays a **Height** of **1″**. Then drag to the right until aligned with the right edge of the picture.

6   Point to the shape, press Control and then click. From the shortcut menu, click **Add Text**.

7   On the **Home tab**, change the **Font Size** to **16**, and be sure **Center Text** 🖺 alignment is selected.

8   In the shape, type **Improve your strength, balance, and coordination** If necessary, use the lower middle sizing handle to enlarge the shape to view your text. Compare your screen with Figure 1.16. **Save** 🖫 your document.

Figure 1.16

Rounded Rectangle shape inserted and formatted, text added

Activity 1.09 | Inserting a Text Box

A text box is useful to differentiate portions of text from other text on the page. You can move a text box anywhere on the page.

1 Press Command ⌘ + fn + ← to move to the top of the document.

2 On the **Home tab**, in the **Insert group**, click the **Text Box** button. Position the 🔲 pointer below the letter *c* in *Rock*, on the first blank line—where the first paragraph mark displays. Drag down and to the right to create a text box with a **Height** of **1.5″** and a **Width** of **4″**. If the text box displays above the title of the report, use the keyboard arrows to nudge it down.

3 With the insertion point blinking in the text box, type the following, pressing Return two times after each of the first two lines to create a new paragraph and a blank line:

> **Meets Tuesdays and Thursdays, 7-9 p.m.**
>
> **Begins September 13, ends December 16**
>
> **College Gymnasium, Room 104**

4 Compare your screen with Figure 1.17.

Figure 1.17

Text box inserted with text ——————

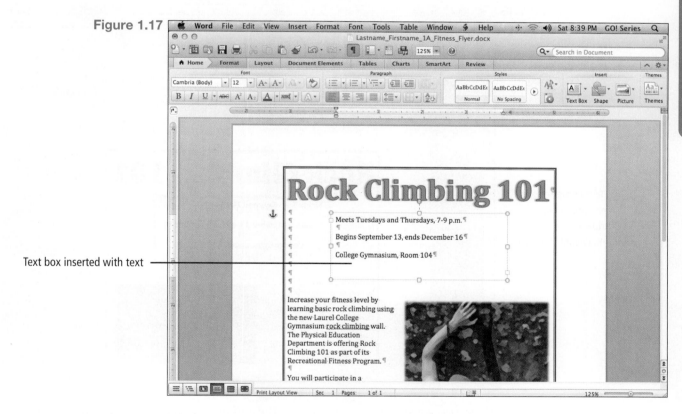

5 **Save** 💾 your document.

Activity 1.10 | Moving, Resizing, and Formatting Shapes and Text Boxes

1 In the text box you just created in the upper portion of the flyer, select all of the text. On the **Home tab**, change the **Font Size** to **14**, apply **Bold** **B** and then **Center** ☰ the text.

2 On the Ribbon, click the **Format tab**, and in the **Size group**, notice the **Height** setting of *1.5″* and **Width** setting of *4″* for the selected text box.

> To adjust the size of a text box, drag the sizing handles; or change the Height and Width settings on the Format tab.

3 In the **Shape Styles group**, click the **Effects** button. Point to **Shadow**, and then under **Outer**, in the first row, click the first style—**Outside Bottom Right**.

4 In the **Shape Styles group**, click the **Shape Outline arrow** . In the first row, click the fourth color—**Text 2**—to change the color of the text box border.

5 Click the **Shape Outline arrow** again, point to **Weights**, and then click **3 pt**.

6 Click anywhere in the document to deselect the text box. Notice that with the text box deselected, you can see all the measurements on the horizontal ruler.

7 Click anywhere in the text box and point to the text box border to display the pointer. By dragging, visually center the text box vertically and horizontally in the space below the *Rock Climbing 101* title. Then, if necessary, press any of the arrow keys on your keyboard to nudge the text box in precise increments to match Figure 1.18.

Figure 1.18

Text formatted and centered in text box, shadow added, border color and weight changed

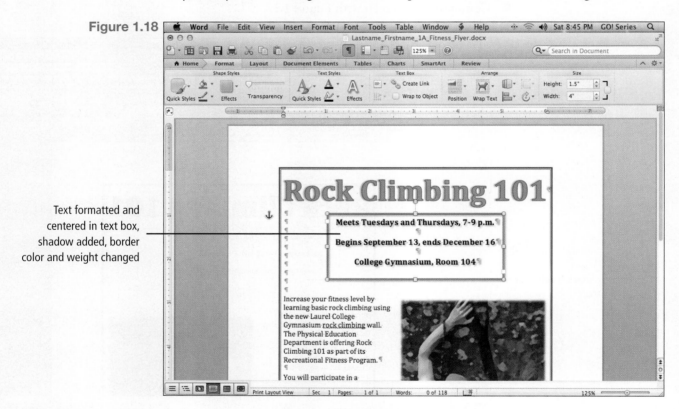

8 Press Command ⌘ + fn + → to move to the end of the document. Click on the border of the rounded rectangular shape to select it.

9 On the **Format tab**, in the **Size group**, click the **Height spin arrows** as necessary to change the height of the shape to **0.8″**.

10 In the **Shape Styles group**, click the **Shape Fill arrow** , and then at the bottom of the gallery, click **Fill Effects**. In the **Format Shape** dialog box, click the **Gradient tab**. Click in the **Style** box, click **Path** to change the gradient style from the default of Linear, and then click **OK**.

11 In the **Shape Styles group**, click the **Shape Outline arrow** . In the first row, click the sixth color—**Accent 2**.

12 Click the **Shape Outline arrow** 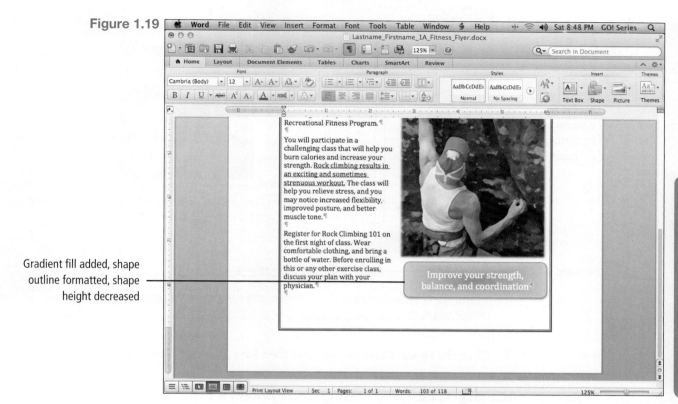 again, point to **Weights**, and then click **1 1/2 pt**. Click anywhere in the document to deselect the shape. Compare your screen with Figure 1.19, and then **Save** your document.

Figure 1.19

Gradient fill added, shape outline formatted, shape height decreased

Objective 4 | Preview and Print a Document

While you are creating your document, it is useful to preview it periodically to be sure that you are getting the result you want. Then, before printing, make a final preview to be sure the document layout is what you intended.

Activity 1.11 | Adding a File Name to the Footer

Information in headers and footers helps to identify a document when it is printed or displayed electronically. Recall that a header is information that prints at the top of every page, and a footer is information that prints at the bottom of every page. In this textbook, you will insert the file name in the footer of every Word document.

Another Way

On the View menu, click Header and Footer.

1 If necessary, scroll to display the bottom of the document. Point to the bottom edge of the document to display the pointer, and then double-click to display the **Footer** area.

The footer area displays with the insertion point blinking at the left edge; and on the Ribbon, the Header and Footer tab displays.

2 On the **Insert** menu, point to **AutoText**, click **Filename**, and then compare your screen with Figure 1.20.

Your filename displays in the Footer area. *AutoText* is a feature that quickly enables you to insert stored information into a document; for example, a file name, or the author of the document. When the Footer or Header area is active, the body of the document is dimmed—it is inactive. Conversely, when the body of the document is active, the footer or header text is dimmed.

Figure 1.20

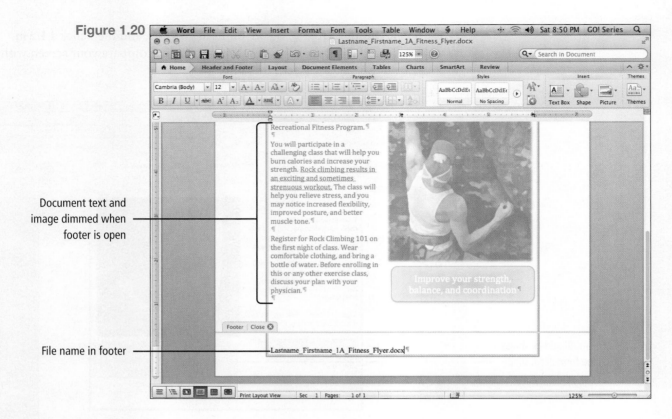

Document text and image dimmed when footer is open

File name in footer

Another Way

Double-click anywhere in the document to close the Footer area.

- - - ▶ **3**   Click the **Footer Close** button, and then **Save** 🖫 your document.

Activity 1.12 │ Previewing and Printing a Document

To ensure that you are getting the result you want, it is useful to periodically preview your document. Then, before printing, make a final preview to be sure the document layout is what you intended.

1   Press Command ⌘ + fn + ← to move the insertion point to the top of the document. On the **File** menu, click **Properties**. In the **Subject** box, type your course name and section number. In the **Author** box, delete any text, and then type your firstname and lastname. In the **Keywords** box, type **fitness, rock climbing** and then click **OK**. **Save** 🖫 your document.

Another Way

Press Command ⌘ + P to display the Print dialog box.

- - - ▶ **2**   On the **File** menu, click **Print** to display the **Print** dialog box. Compare your screen with Figure 1.21.

The Print dialog box displays a preview of the document. If a preview does not display, be sure *Show Quick Preview* is selected. If you do not wish to preview the document or make changes to the number of copies or pages, you can click the Print button on the Standard toolbar to print quickly.

Figure 1.21

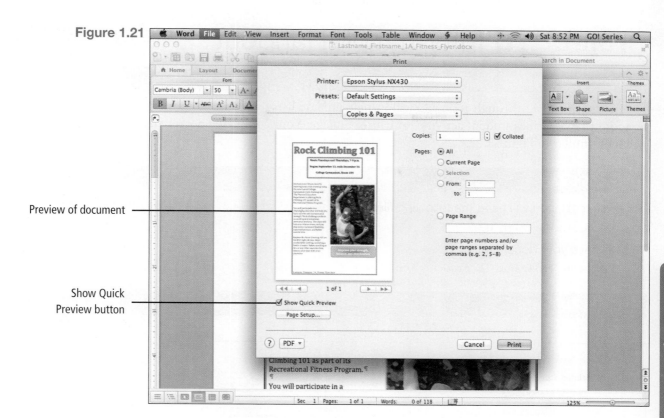

Preview of document

Show Quick
Preview button

3 In the **Print** dialog box, click **Print**. Or, submit your document electronically as directed by your instructor.

4 **Close** your document. On the **Word** menu, click **Quit Word** to exit Word.

End You have completed Project 1A ————————————

Project 1B Information Handout

Project Activities

In Activities 1.13 through 1.23, you will format and add lists to an information handout that describes student activities at Laurel College. Your completed document will look similar to Figure 1.22.

Project Files

For Project 1B, you will need the following file:

w01B_Student_Activities

You will save your document as:

Lastname_Firstname_1B_Student_Activities

Project Results

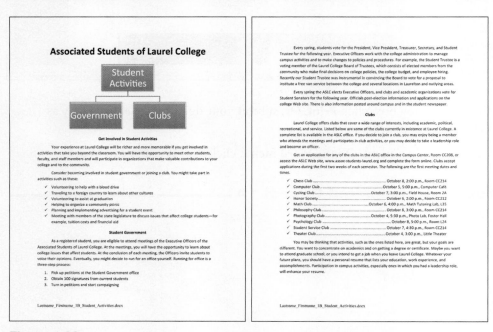

Figure 1.22
Project 1B Student Activities

Objective 5 | Change Document and Paragraph Layout

Document layout includes *margins*—the space between the text and the top, bottom, left, and right edges of the paper. Paragraph layout includes line spacing, indents, and tabs. In Word, the information about paragraph formats is stored in the paragraph mark at the end of a paragraph. When you press the Return, the new paragraph mark contains the formatting of the previous paragraph, unless you take steps to change it.

Activity 1.13 | Setting Margins

Another Way

Press Command ⌘ + O to display the Open dialog box.

1 Open **Word**. On the **File** menu, click **Open** to display the **Open** dialog box. From your student files, locate and double-click the document **w01B_Student_Activities**. On the Standard toolbar, be sure the **Show/Hide** button ¶ is active so that you can view the nonprinting characters. If necessary, increase the size of the window so that it fills the entire screen. On the Standard toolbar, click the **Zoom arrow** [100% ▼], and then click **125%** to increase the size of the active document.

2 On the **File** menu, click **Save As** to display the **Save As** dialog box. Navigate to your **Word Chapter 1** folder, and then **Save** the document as **Lastname_Firstname_1B_Student_Activities**

3 On the Ribbon, click the **Layout tab**. In the **Margins group**, click the **Left spin box down arrow** ◌ five times to change the left margin setting to **1**. Double-click in the **Right** box, type **1** and then press Return. Compare your screen with Figure 1.23.

Use the spin box or type directly in the margin box to change a setting. These actions change the left and right margins to 1 inch on all pages of the document.

Figure 1.23

Margins group

Layout tab

Left and Right margins changed

Zoom set at 125%

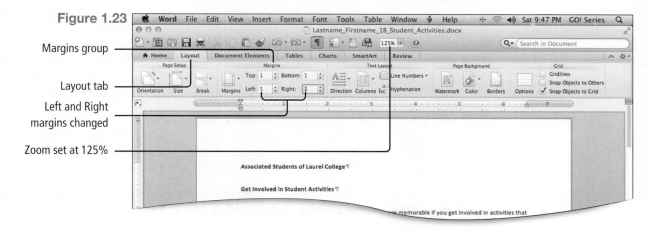

4 If the ruler below the Ribbon is not displayed, on the menu bar, click View, and then click Ruler. Scroll to view the bottom of **Page 1** and the top of **Page 2**. Notice that the page edges display, and the page number and total number of pages display in the middle of the status bar.

5 Point to the bottom edge of **Page 1** to display the ▣ pointer, and then double-click to display the **Footer** area.

6 On the **Insert** menu, point to **AutoText**, and then click **Filename** to insert your file name in the **Footer** area. **Close** the **Footer** area, and then **Save** 🖫 your document.

Activity 1.14 | Aligning Text

Alignment refers to the placement of paragraph text relative to the left and right margins. Most paragraph text uses *left alignment*—aligned at the left margin, leaving the right margin uneven. Three other types of paragraph alignment are: *center alignment*—centered between the left and right margins; *right alignment*—aligned at the right margin with an uneven left margin; and *justified alignment*—text aligned evenly at both the left and right margins. See the table in Figure 1.24.

Paragraph Alignment Options

Alignment	Button	Description and Example
Align Text Left		Align Text Left is the default paragraph alignment in Word. Text in the paragraph aligns at the left margin, and the right margin is uneven.
Center Text		Center alignment aligns text in the paragraph so that it is centered between the left and right margins.
Align Text Right		Align Text Right aligns text at the right margin. Using Align Text Right, the left margin, which is normally even, is uneven.
Justify Text		The Justify alignment option adds additional space between words so that both the left and right margins are even. Justify is often used when formatting newspaper-style columns.

Figure 1.24

1 Scroll to position the middle of **Page 2** on your screen, look at the left and right margins, and notice that the text is justified—both the right and left margins of multiple-line paragraphs are aligned evenly at the margins. On the Ribbon, click the **Home tab**, and in the **Paragraph group**, notice that the **Justify Text** button is active.

2 In the paragraph that begins *Every spring, students vote*, in the first line, look at the space following the word *Every*, and then compare it with the space following the word *Trustee* in the second line. Notice how some of the spaces between words are larger than others.

To achieve a justified right margin, Word adjusts the size of spaces between words in this manner, which can result in unattractive spacing in a document that spans the width of a page. Many individuals find such spacing difficult to read.

> **Another Way**
>
> On the Edit menu, click Select All.

3 Press [Command ⌘] + [A] to select all of the text in the document, and then on the **Home tab**, in the **Paragraph group**, click the **Align Text Left** button.

4 Press [Command ⌘] + [fn] + [←] to move to the top of the document. At the top of the document, in the left margin area, point to the left of the first paragraph—*Associated Students of Laurel College*—until the pointer displays, and then click one time to select the paragraph. On the **Home tab**, in the **Font group**, change the **Font Size** to **26**.

Use this technique to select entire lines of text.

5 Point to the left of the first paragraph—*Associated Students of Laurel College*—to display the pointer again, and then drag down to select the first two paragraphs, which form the title and subtitle of the document.

6 On the **Home tab**, in the **Paragraph group**, click the **Center Text** button ☰ to center the title and subtitle between the left and right margins, and then compare your screen with Figure 1.25.

Figure 1.25

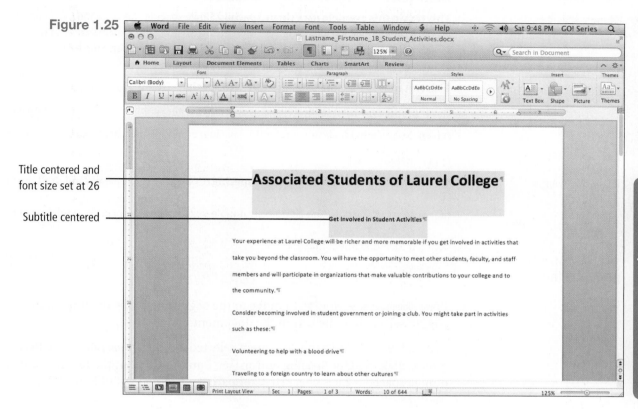

Title centered and font size set at 26

Subtitle centered

7 Scroll to view the bottom of **Page 1**, and then locate the first bold subheading— *Student Government*. Point to the left of the paragraph to display the ⤢ pointer, and then click one time.

8 With *Student Government* selected, use your mouse or the vertical scroll bar to bring the lower portion of **Page 2** into view—do not click while scrolling. Locate the subheading *Clubs*. Move the pointer to the left of the paragraph to display the ⤢ pointer, hold down [Command ⌘], and then click one time.

> Two subheadings are selected; in Mac OS X, you can hold down [Command ⌘] to select multiple items.

9 On the **Home tab**, in the **Paragraph group**, click the **Center Text** button ☰ to center both subheadings, and then click **Save** 🖫.

Activity 1.15 | Changing Line Spacing

Line spacing is the distance between lines of text in a paragraph. Three of the most commonly used line spacing options are shown in the table in Figure 1.26.

Line Spacing Options

Alignment	Description, Example, and Information
Single spacing	**This text in this example uses single spacing**. Single spacing was once the most commonly used spacing in business documents. Now, because so many documents are read on a computer screen rather than on paper, single spacing is becoming less popular. Single spacing is the default spacing in Microsoft Word for Mac 2011.
Multiple 1.15 spacing	**This text in this example uses multiple 1.15 spacing**. This line spacing is equivalent to single spacing with an extra 1/6 line added between lines to make the text easier to read on a computer screen. Many individuals now prefer this spacing, even on paper, because the lines of text appear less crowded.
Double spacing	**This text in this example uses double spacing**. College research papers and draft documents that need space for notes are commonly double-spaced; there is space for a full line of text between each document line.

Figure 1.26

1 Press ⌘Command ⌘ + fn + ← to move to the beginning of the document. Press ⌘Command ⌘ + A to select all of the text in the document.

2 With all of the text in the document selected, on the **Home tab**, in the **Paragraph group**, click the **Line Spacing** button, and notice that the text in the document is double spaced—**2.0** is checked. Compare your screen with Figure 1.27.

Figure 1.27

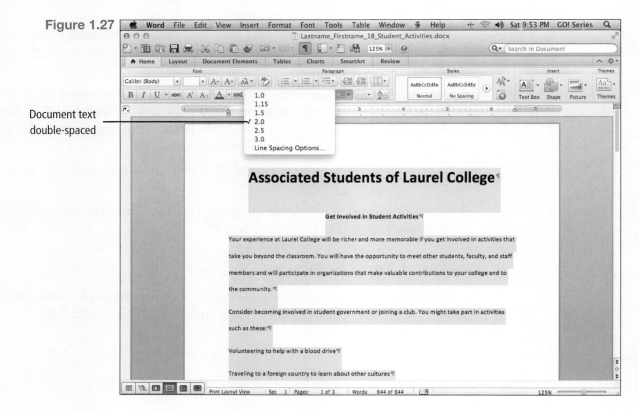

Document text double-spaced

3 On the **Line Spacing** list, click the second setting—**1.15**—and then click anywhere in the document to deselect the text. Compare your screen with Figure 1.28, and then **Save** 🖫 your document.

> Double spacing is most commonly used in research papers and rough draft documents. Recall that on a computer screen, spacing of 1.15 is easier to read than single spacing. Because a large percentage of Word documents are read on a computer screen, 1.15 is the preferred spacing for a Word document.

Figure 1.28

Line spacing changed to 1.15

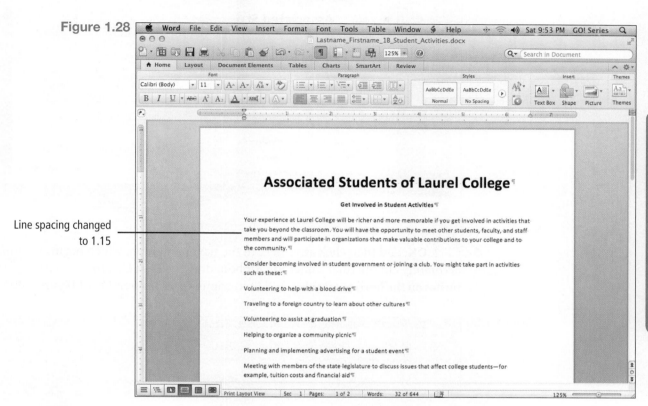

Activity 1.16 | Indenting Text and Adding Space After Paragraphs

Common techniques to distinguish paragraphs include adding space after each paragraph, indenting the first line of each paragraph, or both.

1 Below the title and subtitle of the document, click anywhere in the paragraph that begins *Your experience.*

Another Way

On the Format menu, click Paragraph; or press Option + Command ⌘ + M.

2 On the **Home tab**, in the **Paragraph group**, click the **Line Spacing** button ⊞▾, and then click **Line Spacing Options** to open the **Paragraph** dialog box.

3 In the **Paragraph** dialog box, on the **Indents and Spacing tab**, under **Indentation**, click the **Special arrow**, and then click **First line** to indent the first line by 0.5″, which is the default indent setting. Compare your screen with Figure 1.29.

Figure 1.29

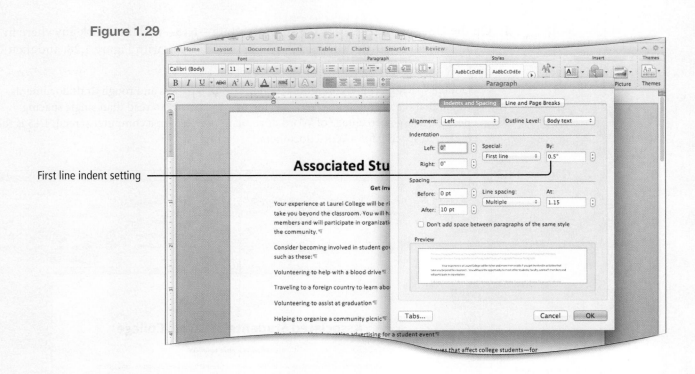

First line indent setting

4 Click **OK**, and then click anywhere in the next paragraph, which begins *Consider becoming*. On the ruler under the Ribbon, drag the **First Line Indent** button to **0.5 inches on the horizontal ruler**, and then compare your screen with Figure 1.30.

Figure 1.30

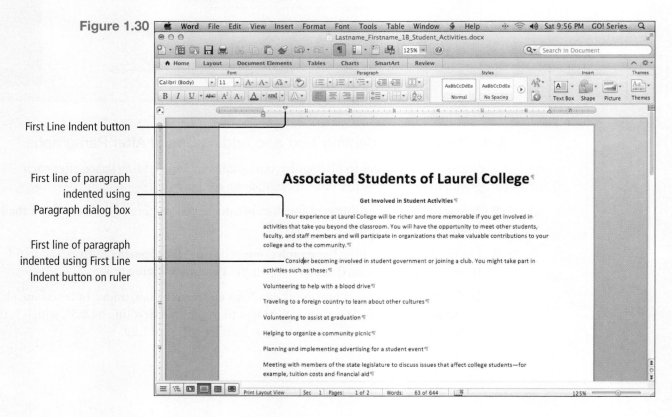

First Line Indent button

First line of paragraph indented using Paragraph dialog box

First line of paragraph indented using First Line Indent button on ruler

5 By using either of the techniques you just practiced, or by using Format Painter, apply a first line indent of **0.5"** in the paragraph that begins *As a registered* to match the indent of the remaining paragraphs in the document.

6 Press Command ⌘ + A to select all of the text in the document. On the **Home tab**, in the **Paragraph group**, click the **Line Spacing** button, and then click **Line Spacing Options**. In the **Paragraph** dialog box, under **Spacing**, click the **After spin box down arrow** one time to change the value to **6 pt**, and then compare your screen with Figure 1.31.

> The Preview displays the effect of changes to the spacing. To change the value in the box, you can also select the existing number, type a new number, and then press Return. This document will use 6 pt spacing after paragraphs.

Figure 1.31

Paragraph dialog box —————

Spacing After set at 6 pt —————

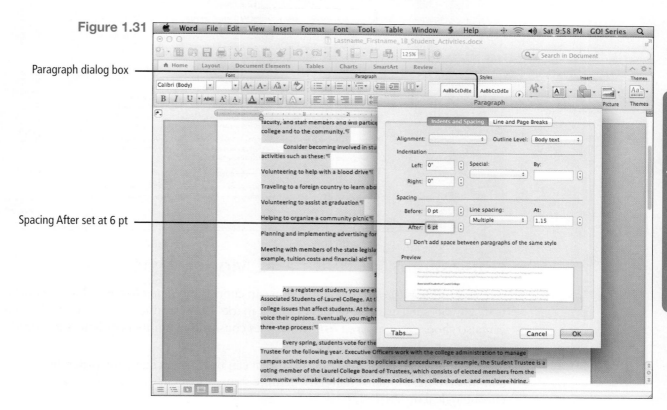

7 In the **Paragraph** dialog box, click **OK**. Press Command ⌘ + fn + ← to move to the top of your document, and notice that there is less space after each paragraph mark.

8 Scroll to view the middle and lower portions of **Page 1**. Select the subheading *Student Government*, including the paragraph mark following it, hold down Command ⌘, and then select the subheading *Clubs*.

9 With both subheadings selected, on the **Format** menu, click **Paragraph**. In the **Paragraph** dialog box, under **Spacing**, click the **Before up spin box arrow** two times to set the **Spacing Before** to **12 pt**, and then click **OK**. Compare your screen with Figure 1.32, and then **Save** your document.

> This action increases the amount of space above each of the two subheadings, which will make them easy to distinguish in the document. The formatting is applied only to the two selected paragraphs.

Figure 1.32

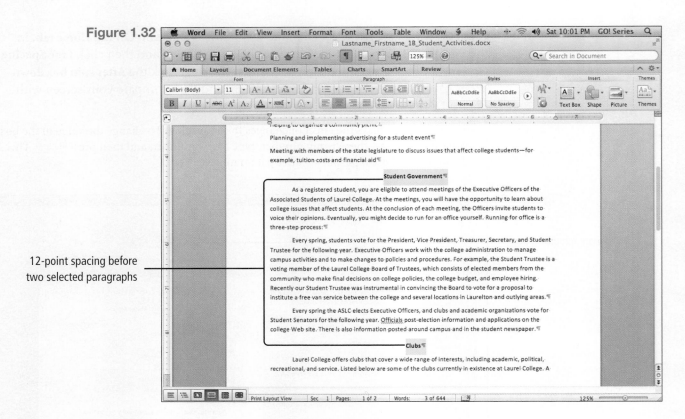

12-point spacing before two selected paragraphs

Objective 6 | Create and Modify Lists

To display a list of information, you can choose a **bulleted list**, which uses **bullets**—text symbols such as small circles or check marks—to introduce each item in a list. You can also choose a **numbered list**, which uses consecutive numbers or letters to introduce each item in a list.

Use a bulleted list if the items in the list can be introduced in any order; use a numbered list for items that have definite steps, a sequence of actions, or are in chronological order.

Activity 1.17 | Creating a Bulleted List

1 In the upper portion of **Page 1**, locate the paragraph that begins *Volunteering to help*, and then point to this paragraph from the left margin area to display the ⬛ pointer. Drag down to select this paragraph and the next five paragraphs.

2 On the **Home tab**, in the **Paragraph group**, click the **Bulleted List** button ⬛ ▾ to change the selected text to a bulleted list.

The spacing between each of the bulleted points changes to the spacing between lines in a paragraph—in this instance, 1.15 line spacing. The spacing after the last item in the list is the same as the spacing after each paragraph—in this instance, 6 pt. Each bulleted item is automatically indented.

3 On the ruler, point to the **First Line Indent** button ⬛, read the ScreenTip, and then point to the **Hanging Indent** button ⬛. Compare your screen with Figure 1.33.

By default, Word formats bulleted items with a first line indent of 0.25″ and adds a Hanging Indent at 0.5″. The hanging indent maintains the alignment of text when a bulleted item is more than one line, for example, the last bulleted item in this list.

Figure 1.33

Hanging Indent
button on ruler

Bulleted list

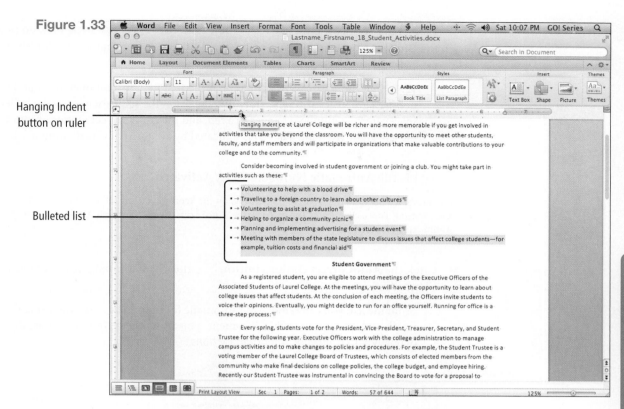

4 Scroll down to view **Page 2**. By using the ⬆ pointer in the left margin area, select all of the paragraphs that indicate the club names and meeting dates, beginning with *Chess Club* and ending with *Theater Club*.

5 In the **Paragraph group**, click the **Bulleted List** button ☰▾, and then **Save** ◨ your document.

Activity 1.18 | Creating a Numbered List

1 Scroll to view **Page 1**, and then under the subheading *Student Government*, in the paragraph that begins *As a registered student*, click to position the insertion point at the *end* of the paragraph following the colon. Press Return to create a blank paragraph.

2 Notice that the paragraph is indented, because the First Line Indent from the previous paragraph carried over to the new paragraph.

3 To change the indent formatting for this paragraph, on the ruler, drag the **First Line Indent** button ▽ to the left so that it is positioned directly above the lower button. Compare your screen with Figure 1.34.

Figure 1.34

First Line Indent button

Paragraph with no
first line indent

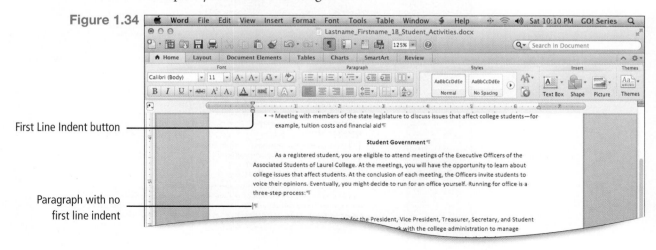

4 Being sure to include the period, type **1.** and press ⌴Spacebar⌴. Type **Pick up petitions at the Student Government office.** and press ⏎Return⏎. Notice that the second number and a tab are added to the next line.

Word determines that this paragraph is the first item in a numbered list and formats the new paragraph accordingly, indenting the list in the same manner as the bulleted list. The space after the number changes to a tab, and the AutoCorrect Options button displays to the left of the list item. The tab is indicated by a right arrow formatting mark.

Alert! | Is the Automatic Numbered List Activated?

If a numbered list does not begin automatically, on the Word menu, click the Preferences. Under Authoring and Proofing Tools, click AutoCorrect. Click the AutoFormat as You Type tab. Under Apply as you type, click Automatic numbered lists, and then click OK.

---

5 Click the **AutoCorrect Options** button 🗍, and then compare your screen with Figure 1.35.

From the list, you can remove the automatic formatting here, or stop using the automatic numbered lists option in this document. You also have the option to open the AutoCorrect dialog box to *Control AutoFormat Options*.

Figure 1.35

AutoCorrect Options button for numbered list

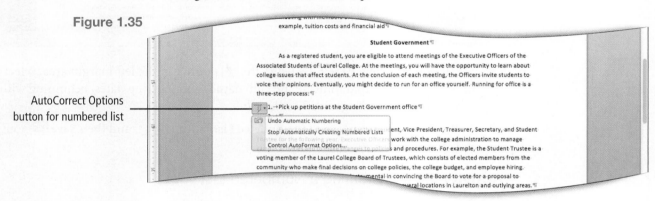

6 Click the **AutoCorrect Options** button again to close the menu without selecting any of the commands.

7 Type **Obtain 100 signatures from current students.** and press ⏎Return⏎. Type **Turn in petitions and start campaigning.** and press ⏎Return⏎. Compare your screen with Figure 1.36.

Figure 1.36

Numbered list

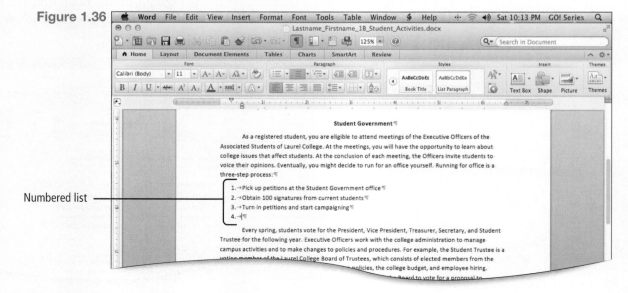

8 Press Delete to turn off the list numbering. Then, press Delete three more times to remove the blank paragraph. Compare your screen with Figure 1.37.

Figure 1.37

Three items in the list; item 4 and extra lines deleted

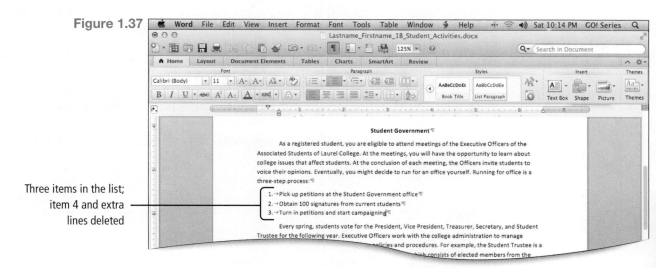

9 Save your document.

> **More Knowledge** │ **To End a List**
>
> To turn a list off, you can press Delete, click the Numbered List or Bulleted List button, or press Return a second time. Both list buttons—Numbered and Bullets—act as *toggle buttons*; that is, clicking the button one time turns the feature on, and clicking the button again turns the feature off.

Activity 1.19 │ Customizing Bullets

1 Press Command ⌘ + fn + → to move to the end of the document, and then scroll as necessary to display the bulleted list containing the list of clubs.

2 Point to the left of the first list item to display the pointer, and then drag down to select all the clubs in the list—the bullet symbols are not highlighted.

3 On the **Home tab**, in the **Paragraph group**, click the **Bulleted List arrow**, and then compare your screen with Figure 1.38.

Figure 1.38

Check mark bullet

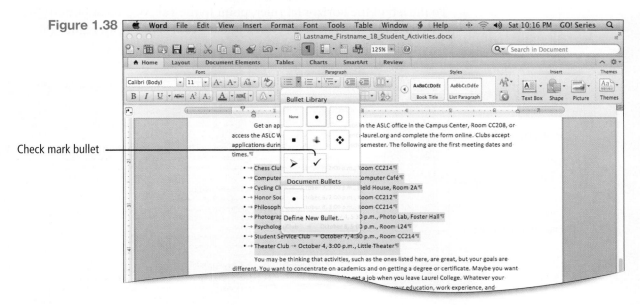

4 Under **Bullet Library**, click the **check mark** symbol. If the check mark is not available, choose another bullet symbol.

5 With the bulleted list still selected, on the Standard toolbar, click the **Format Painter** button ◇.

6 Use the vertical scroll bar or your mouse to scroll to view **Page 1**. Move the pointer to the left of the first item in the bulleted list to display the ◤ pointer, and then drag down to select all of the items in the list and to apply the format of the second bulleted list to this list. Compare your screen with Figure 1.39, and then **Save** 💾 your document.

Figure 1.39

Bullet symbol changed using Format Painter

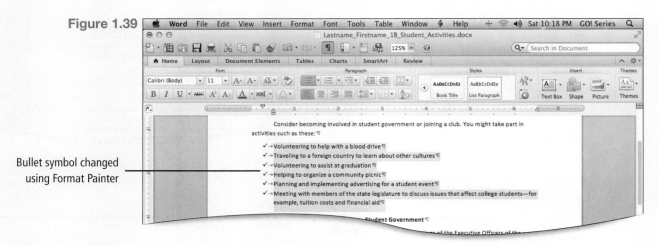

Objective 7 | Set and Modify Tab Stops

Tab stops mark specific locations on a line of text. Use tab stops to indent and align text, and use the [Tab] key to move to tab stops. By default, left tab stops are set every 0.5 inch.

Activity 1.20 | Setting Tab Stops

1 Scroll to view the middle of **Page 2** to view the bulleted list, and then by using the ◤ pointer at the left of the first item, select all of the items in the bulleted list. Notice that there is a tab between the name of the club and the date.

The arrow that indicates a tab is a nonprinting character or formatting mark.

2 To the left of the horizontal ruler, point to the **Tab Alignment** button 🗗 to display the *Left Tab* ScreenTip, and then compare your screen with Figure 1.40.

Figure 1.40

Tab alignment button

Left Tab ScreenTip

Nonprinting tab mark

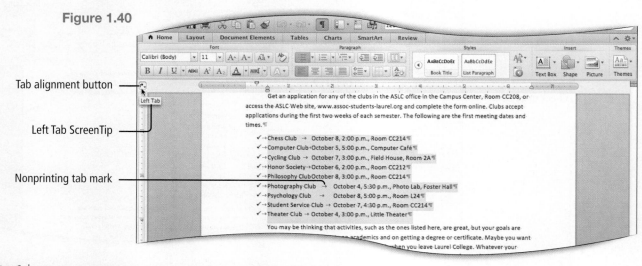

3 Click the **Tab Alignment** button 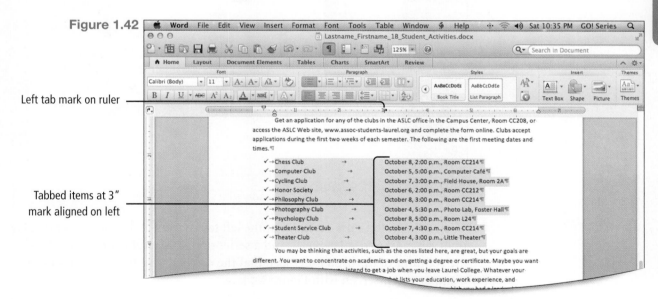 to view the tab alignment options shown in the table in Figure 1.41.

Tab Alignment Options

Type	Tab Alignment Button Displays This Marker	Description
Left		Text is left aligned at the tab stop and extends to the right.
Center		Text is centered around the tab stop.
Right		Text is right aligned at the tab stop and extends to the left.
Decimal		The decimal point aligns at the tab stop.
Bar		A vertical bar displays at the tab stop.

Figure 1.41

4 Be sure that **Left** is selected, and then press Esc to close the list of tabs. With the bulleted list still selected, along the lower edge of the horizontal ruler, point to and then click at **3 inches on the horizontal ruler**. Notice that all of the dates left align at the new tab stop location, and the right edge of the column is uneven.

5 Compare your screen with Figure 1.42, and then **Save** your document.

Figure 1.42

Left tab mark on ruler

Tabbed items at 3″ mark aligned on left

Activity 1.21 | Modifying Tab Stops

Tab stops are a form of paragraph formatting, and thus, the information about tab stops is stored in the paragraph mark in the paragraphs to which they were applied.

1 With the bulleted list still selected, on the ruler, point to the new tab marker, and then when the *Left Tab* ScreenTip displays, drag the tab marker to **3.5 inches on the horizontal ruler**.

In all of the selected lines, the text at the tab stop left aligns at 3.5 inches.

Another Way
On the Format menu,
click Tabs.

2 On the ruler, point to the tab marker to display the ScreenTip, and then double-click to display the **Tabs** dialog box.

3 In the **Tabs** dialog box, under **Tab stop position**, be sure that **3.5″** is selected, and then type **6**

4 Under **Alignment**, click the **Right** option button. Under **Leader**, click the **2** option button. At the lower left corner of the **Tabs** dialog box, click **Set**.

> Because the Right tab will be used to align the items in the list, the tab stop at 3.5″ is no longer necessary.

5 In the **Tabs** dialog box, in the **Tab stop position** box, click **3.5″** to select this tab stop, and then in the lower portion of the **Tabs** dialog box, click the **Clear** button to delete this tab stop, which is no longer necessary. Compare your screen with Figure 1.43.

Figure 1.43

Tab stop position

Right tab selected

Leader 2 selected

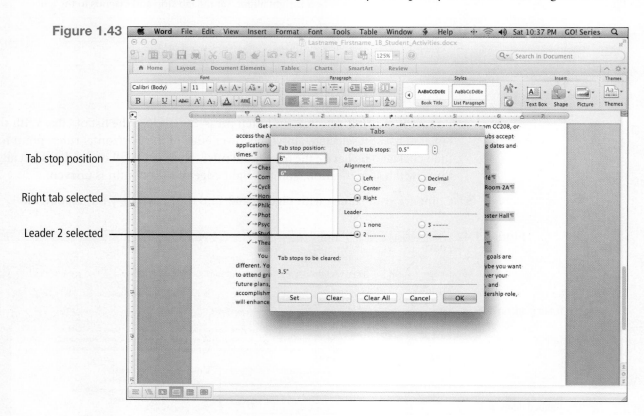

6 Click **OK**. On the ruler, notice that the left tab marker at *3.5″* no longer displays, a right tab marker displays at *6″*, and a series of dots—a ***dot leader***—displays between the columns of the list. Notice also that the right edge of the column is even. Compare your screen with Figure 1.44.

> A ***leader character*** creates a solid, dotted, or dashed line that fills the space to the left of a tab character and draws the reader's eyes across the page from one item to the next. When the character used for the leader is a dot, it is commonly referred to as a dot leader.

Figure 1.44

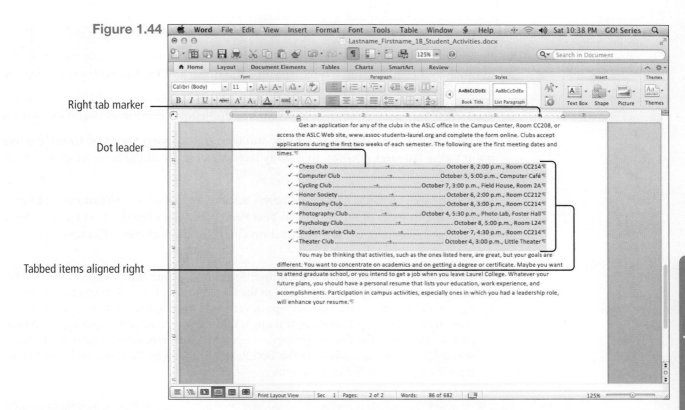

Right tab marker

Dot leader

Tabbed items aligned right

7 In the bulleted list that uses dot leaders, locate the *Honor Society* item, and then click to position the insertion point at the end of that line. Press Return to create a new blank bulleted item.

8 Type **Math Club** and press Tab. Notice that a dot leader fills the space to the right tab marker location.

9 Type **October 6, 4:00 p.m., Math Tutoring Lab, L35** and notice that the text moves to the left to maintain the right alignment of the tab stop.

10 **Save** 🖫 your document.

Objective 8 | Insert a SmartArt Graphic

SmartArt graphics are designer-quality visual representations of information, and Word provides many different layouts from which you can choose. A SmartArt graphic can communicate your messages or ideas more effectively than plain text and adds visual interest to a document or Web page.

Activity 1.22 | Inserting a SmartArt Graphic

1 Press ⌘Command ⌘ + fn + ← to move to the top of the document. Press ⌘Command ⌘ + → to move to the end of the first paragraph—the title—and then press Return to create a blank paragraph.

> Because the paragraph above is 26 pt font size, the new paragraph mark displays in that size.

2 On the Ribbon, click the **SmartArt tab**, and then in the **Insert SmartArt Graphic group**, point to the **Hierarchy** button to display its ScreenTip. Read the ScreenTip, and then click the button.

3 In the **Hierarchy** gallery, in the first row, click the first graphic—**Organization Chart**. Point to the title bar of the displayed **Text Pane**, and then drag the **Text Pane** to the left so that you can view the Organization Chart in the document. Compare your screen with Figure 1.45.

> The SmartArt graphic displays at the insertion point location and consists of two parts— the graphic itself, and the Text Pane. On the Ribbon, the Format tab is inserted to the right of the SmartArt tab. You can type directly into the graphics, or type in the Text Pane. By typing in the Text Pane, you might find it easier to organize your layout. As you click a Text box in the Text Pane, the corresponding Text box in the Organization chart is selected. If you accidentally close the Text Pane, click the Text Pane button located at the top left corner of the SmartArt graphic.

Figure 1.45

Format tab for SmartArt

Hierarchy button

Text Pane to enter text into the Organization Chart

Top Text box in Text Pane and Organization Chart

SmartArt—Organization Chart—inserted in document at insertion point

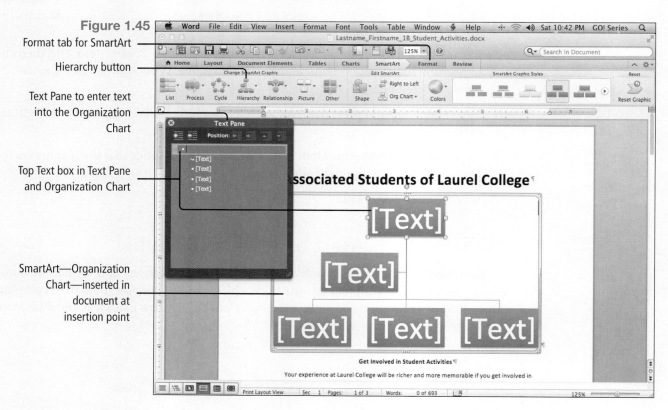

4 **Save** 💾 your document.

Activity 1.23 | Modifying a SmartArt Graphic

Another Way

In the Text Pane, select the bulleted point, and then click the Delete button 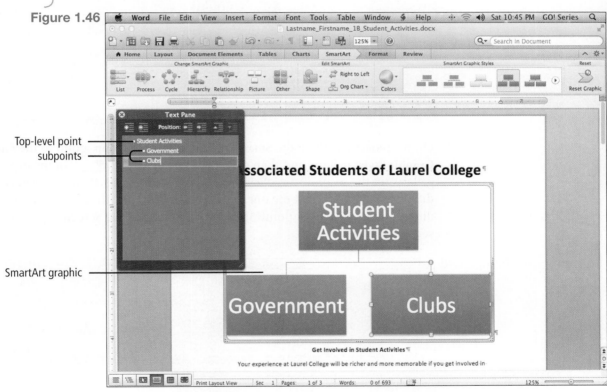 to delete the text box.

1 In the SmartArt graphic, in the second level, click the border of the *[Text]* box to display a *solid* border and sizing handles, and in the Text Pane, notice that the second *[Text]* box is selected. Press Command ⌘ + X to cut—delete—the box. Repeat this procedure in the bottom row to delete the middle *[Text]* box. **Save** 🖫 your document.

2 In the **Text Pane**, click in the top bulleted point, and then type **Student Activities** Notice that the first bulleted point aligns further to the left than the other points.

> The *top-level points* are the main points in a SmartArt graphic. *Subpoints* are indented second-level bullet points.

Another Way

Type the text directly in the SmartArt boxes.

3 Press ⬇. Type **Government** and then press ⬇ again. Type **Clubs** and then compare your screen with Figure 1.46.

Figure 1.46

4 In the upper left corner of the **Text Pane**, click the **Close** button ⊗.

5 Click the border of the SmartArt graphic to deselect any of the text boxes. On the Ribbon, click the **Format tab**, and then in the **Size group**, set the **Height** to **2.5** and the **Width** to **4.2**, and then compare your screen with Figure 1.47.

6 With the SmartArt graphic still selected, click the **SmartArt tab**, and then in the **SmartArt Graphic Styles group**, click the **Colors** button. Under **Colorful**, on the first row, click the second style—**Colorful Range - Accent Colors 2 to 3**.

Figure 1.47

Size group

Format tab for SmartArt

Height and Width set

Text Pane button

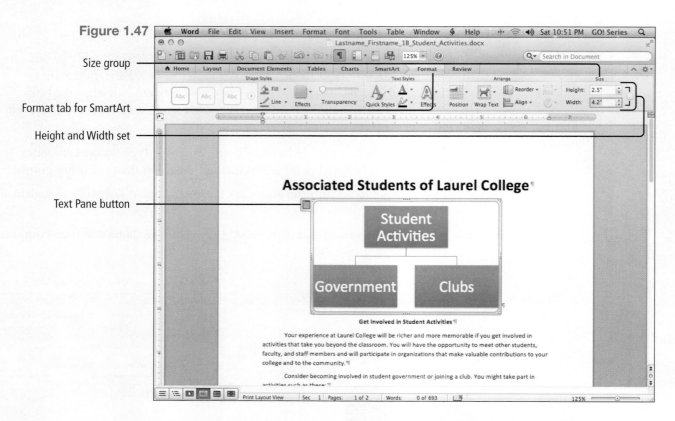

7 On the **SmartArt tab**, in the **SmartArt Graphics Styles group**, point to the **SmartArt Graphic Styles** gallery, and then click the **More** arrow [▼]. In the expanded gallery, on the second row, click the first style—**Polished**. If your screen is set at a different resolution that the one used for this textbook, the location of the style may differ—find the style by pointing to a style to display the ScreenTip. Compare your screen with Figure 1.48.

Figure 1.48

Polished style selected

SmartArt color and style changed

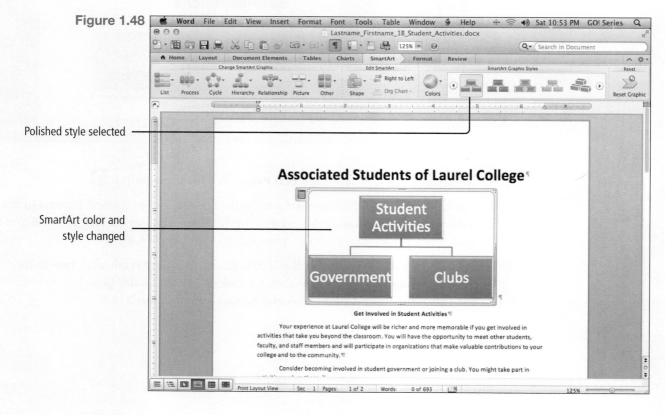

8   Click outside of the graphic to deselect it. On the **File** menu, click **Properties**. In the **Subject** box, type your course name and section number, and in the **Author** box, delete any text and then type your firstname and lastname. In the **Keywords** box, type **Student Activities, Associated Students** and then click **OK**. **Save** 🖫 your document.

9   On the **File** menu, click **Print** to display **Print Preview**. At the bottom of the preview, click the **Next Page** ▶ and **Previous Page** ◀ buttons to move between pages. If necessary, return to the document and make any necessary changes and Save the document.

10 As directed by your instructor, **Print** your document or submit it electronically. **Close** ⊖ the Word document. On the **Word** menu, click **Quit Word**.

More Knowledge | **Changing the Bullet Level in a SmartArt Graphic**

To increase or decrease the level of an item select the text box, and then in Text Pane, click one of the Position buttons.

End **You have completed Project 1B**

Content-Based Assessments

Summary

In this chapter, you created and formatted documents using Microsoft Word for Mac 2011. You inserted and formatted graphics, created and formatted bulleted and numbered lists, and created and formatted text boxes. You also created lists using tab stops with dot leaders, and created and modified a SmartArt graphic.

Key Terms

Matching

Match each term in the second column with its correct definition in the first column by writing the letter of the term on the blank line in front of the correct definition.

_____ 1.	Formats that make pictures look more like sketches or paintings.	**A** Artistic effects
_____ 2.	A small box with an upward- and downward-pointing arrow that enables you to move rapidly through a set of values by clicking.	**B** Bullets
		C Floating object
_____ 3.	Small circles in the corners of a selected graphic with which you can resize the graphic proportionally.	**D** Inline object
		E Justified alignment
_____ 4.	The manner in which text displays around an object.	**F** Left alignment
_____ 5.	An object or graphic that can be moved independently of the surrounding text.	**G** Line spacing
		H Nudge
_____ 6.	The process of using the arrow keys to move an object in small precise increments.	**I** Picture styles
_____ 7.	An object or graphic inserted in a document that acts like a character in a sentence.	**J** Shapes
		K Sizing handles
_____ 8.	Frames, shapes, shadows, borders, and other special effects that can be added to an image to create an overall visual style for the image.	**L** SmartArt
		M Spin box
_____ 9.	Predefined drawing objects, such as stars, banners, arrows, and callouts, included with Microsoft Office, and that can be inserted into documents.	**N** Tab stop
		O Text wrapping
_____10.	A commonly used alignment of text in which text is aligned at the left margin, leaving the right margin uneven.	
_____11.	An alignment of text in which the text is evenly aligned on both the left and right margins.	
_____12.	The distance between lines of text in a paragraph.	

_____13. Text symbols such as small circles or check marks that introduce items in a list.

_____14. A mark on the ruler that indicates the location where the insertion point will be placed when you press the Tab key.

_____15. A designer-quality graphic used to create a visual representation of information.

Multiple Choice

Circle the correct answer.

1. Characters that display on the screen to show the location of paragraphs, tabs, and spaces, but that do not print, are called:

   A. text effects   **B.** bullets   **C.** formatting marks

2. The placement of paragraph text relative to the left and right margins is referred to as:

   A. alignment   **B.** spacing   **C.** indents

3. The symbol that indicates to which paragraph an image is attached is:

   A. a small arrow   **B.** an anchor   **C.** a paragraph mark

4. A movable, resizable container for text or graphics is a:

   A. text box   **B.** dialog box   **C.** SmartArt graphic

5. A rectangle is an example of a predefined:

   A. paragraph   **B.** format   **C.** shape

6. A feature that enables you to quickly insert stored information such as a file name, page number, or author into a document is:

   A. graphics   **B.** AutoText   **C.** SmartArt

7. The space between the text and the top, bottom, left, and right edges of the paper are referred to as:

   A. alignment   **B.** margins   **C.** spacing

8. A group of items in which items are displayed in order to indicate definite steps, a sequence of actions, or chronological order is a:

   A. numbered list   **B.** bulleted list   **C.** outline list

9. A series of dots following a tab that serve to guide the reader's eye is a:

   A. leader   **B.** field   **C.** shape

10. Tab stops are a form of:

    A. line formatting   **B.** document formatting   **C.** paragraph formatting

Content-Based Assessments

Apply 1A skills from these Objectives:

1. Create a New Document and Insert Text
2. Insert and Format Graphics
3. Insert and Modify Text Boxes and Shapes
4. Preview and Print a Document

Skills Review | Project **1C** Recycling

In the following Skills Review, you will create and edit a flyer for the Laurel College recycling program. Your completed document will look similar to Figure 1.49.

Project Files

For Project 1C, you will need the following files:

New blank Word document
w01C_Recycling_Text
w01C_Recycling_Picture

You will save your document as:

Lastname_Firstname_1C_Recycling

Project Results

Figure 1.49

(Project 1C Recycling continues on the next page)

Content-Based Assessments

1 Open **Word** and display a new blank document. On the Standard toolbar, be sure that the **Show/Hide** button is active so that you can view nonprinting characters. If necessary, display rulers and increase the size of the Word window. On the Standard toolbar, click the **Zoom arrow**, and then click **125%**. On the Standard toolbar, click the **Save** button, navigate to your **Word Chapter 1** folder, and then **Save** the document as **Lastname_Firstname_1C_Recycling**

   a. Type **Campus Recycling** and then press Return four times.

   b. Type **The Laurel College Student Government Association encourages students to look for ways to recycle in their classrooms and labs. In April, there will be a special focus on campus recycling, and you can participate by signing up to be a volunteer. Information is available at the kiosk on the south end of the quad.**

   c. Press Return two times. On the **Insert** menu, click **File**. Navigate to your student files, click the file **w01C_Recycling_Text**, and then at the bottom of the **Insert File** dialog box, click **Insert**. **Save** your document.

2 At the top of the document, in the left margin area, point to the left of the first paragraph—*Campus Recycling*—until the pointer displays, and then click one time to select the paragraph. On the **Home tab**, in the **Font group**, click the **Text Effects** button. In the displayed **Text Effects** gallery, in the fourth row, click the second effect—Orange, filled in.

   a. With the text still selected, in the **Font group**, click the **Font Size arrow**, and then click **48**. In the **Paragraph group**, click the **Center Text** button.

   b. With the text still selected, in the **Font group**, click the **Text Effects** button. Point to **Shadow**, and then under **Outer**, in the first row click the third style—**Outside Bottom Left**. In the **Font group**, click the **Font Color arrow**. Under **Standard Colors**, click the sixth color—**Green**.

   c. In the paragraph that begins *The Laurel College*, click to position the insertion point at the beginning of the paragraph. On the **Home tab**, in the **Insert group**, click the **Picture** button, and then click **Picture from File**. From your student data files, **Insert** the file **w01C_Recycling_Picture.jpg**. On the **Format Picture tab**, in the **Size group**, change the **Height** of the picture to **2.5**

   d. With the picture still selected, on the **Format Picture tab**, in the **Arrange group**, click the **Wrap Text** button, and then click **Square**.

   e. Point anywhere in the picture to display the [icon] pointer. Drag the picture down to align the top of the picture with the top of the paragraph that begins *During the week*. Nudge as necessary to match the picture position shown in Figure 1.49.

   f. On the **Format Picture tab**, in the **Picture Styles group**, click the **Picture Effects** button. Point to **Shadow**, and then under **Outer**, in the first row, click the third style—**Outside Bottom Left**.

   g. Click anywhere to deselect the picture. Click the **Layout tab**, and then in the **Page Background group**, click the **Borders** button. In the **Borders and Shading** dialog box, under **Setting**, click **Box**. Under **Style**, scroll about one-third down the list, click the first style with a thick top and thinner bottom line.

   h. Click the **Color arrow**, and then under **Standard Colors**, click the sixth color—**Green**. Click **OK**, and then **Save** your document.

3 Move to the bottom of the document. On the **Home tab**, in the **Insert group**, click the **Text Box** button.

   a. At the bottom of the document, position the [icon] pointer in an open area near the left margin, and then drag down and to the right to create a text box **2.5″** high and **5.5″** wide; you need not be precise.

   b. With the insertion point positioned in the text box, type the following, pressing Return two times after the first four lines:

   Recycling Locations

   Classrooms and Labs: Cans, bottles, paper, and plastics

   Technology Building: All types of batteries

   Campus Printers: Office paper

   To Be Announced: Computer and other electronic equipment

   c. In the text box, select all of the text. On the **Home tab**, in the **Font group**, click in the **Font Size** box, and then type **13** Click the **Bold** button, and then click the **Center Text** button.

   d. On the **Format tab**, in the **Size group**, if necessary click the **Height spin arrows** to change the height of the text box to **2.5″**. If necessary, click the **Width spin arrow** to change the width of the text box to **5.5″**.

(Project 1C Recycling continues on the next page)

e. In the **Shape Styles group**, click the **Effects** button. Point to **Shadow**, and then under **Outer**, in the first row, click the third style—**Outside Bottom Left**. In the **Shape Styles group**, click the **Shape Outline arrow**. Under **Standard Colors**, click the sixth color—**Green**.

f. If necessary, click anywhere inside the text box. Point to the text box border to display the ⊕ pointer. Drag or nudge the text box to the approximate position as shown in Figure 1.49, and then click anywhere outside the text box to deselect it.

g. On the **Home tab**, in the **Insert group**, click the **Shape** button. Point to **Basic Shapes**, and in the first row, click the first shape—**Oval**.

h. Position the ⊞ pointer slightly under the text box and at approximately **2 inches on the horizontal ruler**. Drag down and right to create a small oval shape. With the oval shape selected, on the **Format tab**, in the **Size group**, change the **Height** to **0.9″** and the **Width** to **2″**.

i. With the shape selected, point to the shape. Press Control and click, and then click **Add Text**. Type **Recycle!** and then select the text you typed. On the **Home tab**, in the **Font group**, click the **Font Size arrow**, and then click **22**. Click the **Bold** button, and then if necessary, click the **Center Text** button.

j. On the **Format tab**, in the **Shape Styles group**, click the **Shape Fill arrow**, and then under **Standard Colors**, click the sixth color—**Green**. In the **Shape**

Styles group, click the **Shape Outline arrow**, and then under **Standard Colors**, click the sixth color— **Green**.

k. Point to the shape border until the ⊕ pointer displays, and then position the shape with its widest points aligned with the lower edge of the text box and approximately centered. As necessary, move the shape in small increments by pressing the arrow keys on your keyboard. Refer to Figure 1.49 for approximate placement. **Save** your document.

4 Move your mouse to the bottom of the page to display the ▭ pointer, and then double-click to display the **Footer** area.

a. On the **Insert** menu, point to **AutoText**, and then click **Filename**. **Close** the **Footer** area.

b. Press Command ⌘ + fn + ← to move the insertion point to the beginning of the document. On the **File** menu, click **Properties**. In the **Subject** box, type your course name and section number, and in the **Author** box, delete any text and then type your firstname and lastname. In the **Keywords** box, type **Campus Recycling** and then click **OK**.

c. On the **File** menu, click **Print** to display the **Print Preview**. If necessary, return to the document to make any corrections or adjustments, and then Save your document.

d. **Print** or submit electronically as directed by your instructor, and then **Close** the document, and **Quit Word**.

End **You have completed Project 1C** ————————————————————

Content-Based Assessments

Apply **1B** skills from these Objectives:

5 Change Document and Paragraph Layout

6 Create and Modify Lists

7 Set and Modify Tab Stops

8 Insert a SmartArt Graphic

Skills Review | Project **1D** Athletics

In the following Skills Review, you will edit a document describing the athletics offered at Laurel College. Your completed document will look similar to Figure 1.50.

Project Files

For Project 1D, you will need the following file:

w01D_Athletics

You will save your document as:

Lastname_Firstname_1D_Athletics

Project Results

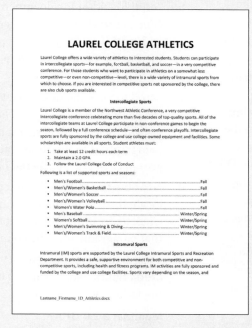

Figure 1.50

(Project 1D Athletics continues on the next page)

Content-Based Assessments

Skills Review | Project 1D Athletics (continued)

1 Open **Word**. From your student files, locate and **Open** the document **w01D_Athletics**. On the **File** menu, click **Save As**. Navigate to your **Word Chapter 1** folder. **Save** the document as **Lastname_Firstname_1D_Athletics**.

a. On the Standard toolbar, be sure that the **Show/Hide** button is active so that you can view nonprinting characters. If necessary, display rulers. On the Ribbon, click the **Layout tab**. In the **Margins group**, change the **Top**, **Bottom**, **Left**, and **Right** margins to **1**, and then click in the document. On the Standard toolbar, click the **Zoom arrow**, and then click **125%**. **Save** the document.

b. Press ⌘Command⌘ + A to select all of the text in the document. On the **Home tab**, in the **Paragraph group**, click the **Align Text Left** button to change the alignment from justified to left aligned.

c. With all of the text still selected, on the **Home tab**, in the **Paragraph group**, click the **Line Spacing** button, and then click **1.15**. Click the **Line Spacing** button, and then click **Line Spacing Options**. In the **Paragraph** dialog box, under **Spacing**, set **After** to **6 pt** spacing after each paragraph, and then click **OK**.

d. At the top of the document, click anywhere in the title. On the **Home tab**, in the **Paragraph group**, click the **Center Text** button. Near the top of **Page 1**, locate and select the subheading paragraph *Intercollegiate Sports*. Hold down ⌘Command⌘. Use your mouse or the vertical scroll bar to locate and then select the subheadings *Intramural Sports* and *Club Sports*. In the **Paragraph group**, click the **Center Text** button.

e. With the three paragraphs still selected, on the **Format** menu, click **Paragraph**. In the **Paragraph** dialog box, under **Spacing**, set **Before** to **12 pt**, and then click **OK**.

f. Scroll to view the bottom of **Page 1**, point anywhere in the bottom margin area to display the ▤ pointer, and then double-click to open the **Footer** area. On the **Insert** menu, point to **AutoText**, and then click **Filename**. Double-click anywhere in the document to close the **Footer** area, and then **Save** the document.

2 Near the middle of **Page 1**, above the *Intramural Sports* subheading, locate the paragraph that begins *Men's Football*, and then move the pointer into the left margin area to display the ⬀ pointer. Drag down to select this paragraph and the next eight paragraphs—ending with the paragraph that begins *Men's/Women's Track & Field*. On the **Home tab**, in the **Paragraph group**, click the **Bulleted List** button. Be sure that the round bullet is selected.

a. Scroll to view the bottom of **Page 1** and the top of **Page 2**. Locate the list of sports that begins with *Tennis*. Move the pointer into the left margin area of that paragraph to display the ⬀ pointer. Drag down to select this paragraph and the next eight paragraphs, ending with the last item on the list—*Wrestling*. On the **Home tab**, in the **Paragraph group**, click the **Bulleted List** button.

b. Scroll to end of the document. Locate the list of *Club Sports* that begins with *Adaptive Sports* and ends with *Ice Hockey*. Select all five paragraphs, and then in the **Paragraph group**, click the **Bulleted List** button.

c. Scroll to view the middle of **Page 2**, and then locate the paragraph that begins *The student athlete must provide*. Select that paragraph and the next two paragraphs. On the **Home tab**, in the **Paragraph group**, click the **Numbered List** button.

d. Near the top of **Page 1**, under *Intercollegiate Sports*, locate the paragraph that ends *Student athletes must:* Click to position the insertion point at the *end* of that paragraph after the colon, and then press Return.

e. Type **1.** and press Spacebar. Type **Take at least 12 credit hours each term** and then press Return. Type the following text for items 2 and 3 in the list:

Maintain a 2.0 GPA

Follow the Laurel College Code of Conduct

f. Near the middle of **Page 1**, select the items in the bulleted list. On the **Home tab**, in the **Paragraph group**, click the **Bulleted List arrow**. Under **Bullet Library**, click the **black square** symbol. If the black square is not available, choose another bullet symbol. Repeat this procedure on the other two bulleted lists. **Save** your document.

3 In the middle of **Page 1**, select the bulleted list. Point to the left tab marker at **3″ on the horizontal ruler**. When the *Left Tab* ScreenTip displays, double-click to open the **Tabs** dialog box.

a. Under **Tab stop position**, select **3″**, and at the bottom of the dialog box, click **Clear** to delete this tab stop. Then, type **6** in the **Tab stop position** box.

(Project 1D Athletics continues on the next page)

Content-Based Assessments

Skills Review | Project **1D** Athletics (continued)

b. Under **Alignment**, click the **Right** option button. Under **Leader**, click the **2** option button. At the bottom of the **Tabs** dialog box, click the **Set** button, and then click **OK**.

4 Press ⌘ Command ⌘ + fn + → to move to the end of the document, and then press Return. On the **Home tab**, in the **Paragraph group**, click the **Bulleted List** button to turn off the bullet point.

a. Click the **SmartArt tab**, and then in the **Insert SmartArt Graphic group**, click the **Process** button. In the fourth row, click the fourth style—**Closed Chevron Process**.

b. In the **Text Pane**, in the top-level points box, type **Intercollegiate** and then press ↓. In the two remaining bullets, type **Intramural** and **Club** If your Text Pane does not display, at the top left side of the SmartArt Graphic, click the Text Pane button.

c. In the upper left corner of the **Text Pane**, click the **Close** button. Click the graphic border to deselect any text boxes. Click the **Format tab**, and then in the **Size group**, by clicking the **spin box arrows**, change the **Height** to **1.5"** and the **Width** to **6.5"**.

d. With the SmartArt graphic still selected, on the **SmartArt tab**, in the **SmartArt Graphic Styles group**, click the **Colors** button. Under **Colorful**, click the first style—**Colorful - Accent Colors**.

e. On the **SmartArt tab**, point to the **SmartArt Graphic Styles group**, and then click the **More** button. On the second row, click the first style—**Polished**. Click anywhere in the document to deselect the graphic. Press ⌘ Command ⌘ + fn + ← to move the insertion point to the beginning of the document. **Save** your document.

f. On the **File** menu, click **Properties.** In the **Subject** box, type your course name and section number, and in the **Author** box, type your firstname and lastname. In the **Keywords** box, type **student athletics** and then click **OK**.

g. **Save** your document. On the **File** menu, click the **Print**. Examine the **Print Preview**. **Print** or submit electronically as directed. **Close** the document, and then **Quit Word**.

End **You have completed Project 1D** ─────────────────

Apply **1A** skills from these Objectives:

1 Create a New Document and Insert Text

2 Insert and Format Graphics

3 Insert and Modify Text Boxes and Shapes

4 Preview and Print a Document

Mastering Word | Project **1E** Geology

In the following Mastering Word project, you will create a flyer announcing a field trip sponsored by the Laurel College Geology Department. Your completed document will look similar to Figure 1.51.

Project Files

For Project 1E, you will need the following files:

New blank Word document
w01E_Geology_Text
w01E_Geology_Picture

You will save your document as:

Lastname_Firstname_1E_Geology

Project Results

Geology Field Trip

The Laurel College Geology Department field trip will explore the Ridge-and-Valley Appalachians physiographic province on September 28. This field trip is a requirement for students in Geology 259.

We can accommodate an additional 25 students who would like to explore this area and gain an introduction to physical and historical geology. If you would like to join the field trip, you can register at www.laurelcollege.edu/geology. These outings are extremely popular, and spaces go very quickly. If you are interested, please register as soon as possible. The $25 fee includes lunch, dinner, and transportation.

The bus will leave from the College Circle at 6 a.m. and will return about 8 p.m. Bring a backpack with snacks, water, sunscreen, and anything else you might need during a 14-hour day. Students in the Geology 259 class should bring a notebook and either a digital camera or a smartphone with a fairly high-resolution camera.

The purpose of this trip is to explore the Ridge-and-Valley Appalachians physiographic province. This province extends from southeastern New York, through parts of New Jersey, into Pennsylvania, and extends south as far as Alabama and Georgia. The geology of this region created a severe obstacle to land travel from east to west in the colonial days, and continues to create travel problems in the region. We will explore the geological history of the region at several points. We will spend about half the day exploring Rickets Glen State Park.

Date: September 28

Place: Science and Technology Lobby

Time: 6 a.m.

Lastname_Firstname_1E_Geology.docx

Figure 1.51

(Project 1E Geology continues on the next page)

Content-Based Assessments

Mastering Word | Project **1E** Geology (continued)

1 Open **Word** and display a new blank document. **Save** the document in your **Word Chapter 1** folder as **Lastname_Firstname_1E_Geology** and then add the file name to the footer. Be sure the nonprinting characters and rulers display. In the Standard toolbar, change the **Zoom** to 125%.

2 At the top of the document, type **Geology Field Trip** and press ⌇Return⌇ three times. Type **The Laurel College Geology Department field trip will explore the Ridge-and-Valley Appalachians physiographic province on September 28. This field trip is a requirement for students in Geology 259**. Press ⌇Return⌇ two times. **Insert** the file **w01E_Geology_Text**.

3 Select the title *Geology Field Trip*. On the **Home tab**, in the **Font group**, display the **Text Effects** gallery, and then in the third row, apply the third effect. Change the **Font Size** to **50 pt**. Apply a **Shadow** text effect using the third effect under **Outer—Outside Bottom Left**. Change the **Font Color** to **Accent 1**—in the first row, the fifth color. **Center** the title.

4 Click to position the insertion point at the beginning of the paragraph that begins *The Laurel College Geology*, and then from your student files, **Insert** the picture **w01E_Geology_Picture**. Change the **Height** of the picture to **3.25** and then set the **Wrap Text** to **Square**. Move the picture so that the top edge aligns with the top of the paragraph that begins *We can accommodate*. Using the **Format Picture** dialog box, apply a **Watercolor Sponge Artistic Effect**—in the third row, the second effect. From **Picture Effects**, add a **2pt Soft Edge**.

5 Scroll to view the lower portion of the page. **Insert** a **Text Box** beginning at the left margin with a **Width** of **5″** and a **Height** of **1.75″**. Type the following text in the text box pressing ⌇Return⌇ two times after the first two lines:

> **Date: September 28**
>
> **Place: Science and Technology Lobby**
>
> **Time: 6 a.m.**

6 Select the text in the text box. Change the **Font Size** to **18** pt, apply **Bold**, and **Center** the text. Change the **Font Color** to **Text 2**—first row, fourth color. Add a **Shape Fill** to the text box using the theme color, **Text 2, Lighter 60%**—third row, fourth color. Then apply a **Gradient Fill** using the **Rectangular Style**. Change the **Shape Outline** color to **Background 1**—first row, first color. Cancel the selection of text, and then click the border of the text box. Drag or nudge the text box as necessary to center it horizontally between the left and right margins, and vertically between the last line of text and the footer.

7 On the **Layout tab**, add a **Box Page Border**. Change the border color to **Text 2**—first row, fourth color, and change the border **Width** to **3 pt**.

8 Display the **File Properties**. In the **Subject** box, type your course name and section number, and in the **Author** box, type your firstname and lastname. In the **Keywords** box, type **geology, field trip** and then click **OK**.

9 **Save** and preview your document, make any necessary adjustments, and then **Print** your document or submit it electronically as directed. **Close** the document and then **Quit Word**.

End **You have completed Project 1E**

Mastering Word | Project **1F** Grades

In the following Mastering Word project, you will create a flyer about grade improvement strategies sponsored by the Laurel College Student Counseling Services. Your completed document will look similar to Figure 1.52.

Project Files

For Project 1F, you will need the following file:

> w01F_Grades

You will save your document as:

> Lastname_Firstname_1F_Grades

Project Results

Improve Your Grades!

Are you having problems figuring out what to study? Do you find that after class your notes don't seem to have captured the important points of a lecture? Do you find yourself running out of time to finish your homework and other projects? When you find time to study, do you have trouble concentrating?

There are simple, time-proven techniques to solve these and other barriers to better grades. Laurel College Student Counseling Services will be offering several sessions to any interested students that will cover the following topics:

✓ Keys for taking effective notes
✓ Tips about how to study
✓ Strategies for taking tests
✓ Techniques to improve time management
✓ Tips on how to retain information

These sessions will be held on the following days and times. The sessions on Wednesday, Thursday, and Friday will last three hours. The Saturday session is more intensive, and will last from 10 a.m. until 4 p.m. with a lunch break at noon. You are welcome to sign up for more than one session:

Wednesday, September 8 .... Noon .... Student Union, Room 225
Thursday, September 9 .... 8 a.m. .... Student Union, Room 117
Friday, September 10 .... 7 p.m. .... Student Union, Room 225
Saturday, September 11 .... 10 a.m. .... Science and Technology Building Auditorium

Lastname_Firstname_1F_Grades.docx

Figure 1.52

(Project 1F Grades continues on the next page)

Mastering Word | Project **1F** Grades (continued)

1 Open **Word**. From your student files **Open** the document **w01F_Grades**. **Save** the document in your **Word Chapter 1** folder as **Lastname_Firstname_1F_ Grades** Add the file name to the footer. Display nonprinting characters and rulers. On the Standard toolbar, change the **Zoom** setting to **125%**.

2 Set the **Top** margin to **1.25** and the other three margins to **1**. Select all of the text in the document, including the title. Add **12 pt** spacing after all paragraphs. Change the **Line Spacing** to **1.15**. Change the alignment to **Align Text Left. Center** the title—*Improve Your Grades!*— and then change the **Font Size** to **32**.

3 Locate the paragraph that begins *Keys for taking*. Select that paragraph and the four paragraphs that follow it. Create a bulleted list from the selected text, using the **check mark** symbol.

4 Position the insertion point in the blank paragraph at the end of the document. On the **Format** menu, display the **Tabs** dialog box. Add a **Center** tab stop at **3″**. In the **Tabs** dialog box, add a dot leader. **Set** the tab stop, and then **Set** a **Right** tab stop with a dot leader at **6.5″**.

5 Type the text shown in **Table 1**, pressing $\boxed{\text{Tab}}$ between columns and $\boxed{\text{Return}}$ at the end of the first three lines. Refer to Figure 1.52.

6 Select the first three lines in the tabbed list and change the **Spacing After** to **0 pt**. Press $\boxed{\text{Command} \, \mathcal{H}} + \boxed{\text{fn}} + \boxed{\rightarrow}$

to move to the end of the document, and press $\boxed{\text{Return}}$. Insert a **SmartArt Graphic**, select the **Process** category, scroll down to display more of the gallery, and then in the near the bottom of the list, select **Equation**—as shown in Figure 1.52.

7 If necessary, display the Text Pane. In the upper left corner of the **Text Pane**, click the **Add Shape** button— round green button—three times to display five circles to the left of the equal sign. Add the following text in this order: **Time Tips** and **Study Tips** and **Test Tips** and **Note Tips** and **Memory Tips** and **Better Grades**

8 **Close** the **Text Pane**. Click the SmartArt border. On the **Format tab**, set the **Height** of the SmartArt graphic to **2.5″** and the **Width** to **6.5″**. On the **SmartArt tab**, from the **SmartArt Graphics Styles** gallery, apply the **Brick Scene** style, and change the **Color** to the fourth color under **Colorful—Colorful Range – Accent Colors 4 to 5**. On the **Home tab**, click the **Bold** button.

9 Display the **File Properties**. In the **Subject box**, type your course name and section, and in the **Author** box, type your firstname and lastname. In the **Keywords** box, type **improve grades**

10 **Save** your document. Preview your document, check for and make any adjustments, and then **Print** your document or submit it electronically as directed. **Close** your document, and then **Quit Word**.

Table 1

Wednesday, September 8	Noon	Student Union, Room 225
Thursday, September 9	8 a.m.	Student Union, Room 117
Friday, September 10	7 p.m.	Student Union, Room 225
Saturday, September 11	10 a.m.	Science and Technology Building Auditorium

----→ (Return to Step 6)

End **You have completed Project 1F** ————————————————————

Content-Based Assessments

Apply a combination of 1A and 1B skills:

1 Create a New Document and Insert Text

2 Insert and Format Graphics

3 Insert and Modify Text Boxes and Shapes

4 Preview and Print a Document

5 Change Document and Paragraph Layout

6 Create and Modify Lists

7 Set and Modify Tab Stops

8 Insert a SmartArt Graphic

Mastering Word | Project 1G Web Sites

In the following Mastering Word project, you will edit guidelines for club Web sites at Laurel College. Your completed document will look similar to Figure 1.53.

Project Files

For Project 1G, you will need the following files:

> New blank Word document
> w01G_Chess_Club_Picture
> w01G_Web_Sites_Text

You will save your document as

> Lastname_Firstname_1G_Web_Sites

Project Results

Figure 1.53

(Project 1G Web Sites continues on the next page)

Mastering Word | Project **1G** Web Sites (continued)

1 Open **Word** and display a new blank document. Display nonprinting characters and rulers. On the Standard toolbar, change the **Zoom** to **125%**. **Save** the document in your **Word Chapter 1** folder as **Lastname_Firstname_1G_Web_Sites** Add the file name to the footer.

Change the **Left** and **Right Margins** to **1″**. At the top of the document, type **Club Web Sites** and then press Return two times. Select the title you just typed. From the **Text Effects** gallery, in the fourth row, apply the second effect, change the **Font Size** to **60 pt**, and **Center** the title.

2 Click in the last blank line in the document. Locate and insert the file **w01G_Web_Sites_Text**. *Except* for the document title and the blank line below it, select all of the document text. **Align Text Left**, change the **Line Spacing** to **1.15**, and change the **Spacing After** to **6 pt**. Locate and **Center** the document subtitle that begins *Published by*.

3 In the middle of **Page 1**, under the subheading *Be sure that*, select the six paragraphs down to, but not including, the *General information* subheading. Format the selected text as a bulleted list, selecting the check mark as the bullet symbol. Near the bottom of **Page 1** and the top of **Page 2**, under the *Web Site Design Guidelines* subheading, select all of the paragraphs to the end of the document—not including the blank paragraph mark—and create another bulleted list, selecting the black round bullet symbol.

4 Under the subheading that begins *General information about the club*, select the six paragraphs and format as a numbered list.

Near the top of the document, position the insertion point to the left of the paragraph that begins *The Web site*. **Insert** the picture **w01G_Chess_Club_Picture**. Set **Wrap Text** to **Square**. Decrease the picture **Width** to **2.7″**. If necessary, drag or nudge the picture down so that the subtitle displays centered between the margins and above the picture and so that you do not have a single line of text wrapping below the picture. Apply the **Picture Style** of **Soft Edge Rectangle**. Using the **Format Picture** dialog box, apply **Soft Edges** of **5 pt**.

5 Press Command ⌘ + fn + → to move to the blank line at the end of the document. Type **For assistance, Student Computing Services hours are:** and then press Return. Set a **Left** tab stop at **1.5″**. Display the **Tabs** dialog box. At **5** add a **Right** tab stop with a **dot leader** and click **Set**. Click **OK** to close the dialog box, press Tab to begin, and then

type the following information. Be sure to press Tab to begin each line and press Tab between the days and the times and press Return at the end of each line.

Monday–Thursday	8 a.m. to 10 p.m.
Friday	8 a.m. to 5 p.m.
Saturday	8 a.m. to 12 noon

6 At the top of **Page 2**, position the insertion point to the left of the subheading *Web Site Design Guidelines*. Press Return one time, and then click in the blank paragraph you just created. **Insert** a **SmartArt** graphic, and then from the **Process** gallery, select the **Basic Chevron Process**—in the fourth row, the third graphic. Click the border of the graphic, and then on the **Format tab**, set the **Height** of the graphic to **1″** and the **Width** of the graphic to **6.5″**. In the upper left corner outside of the graphic, click the **Text Pane** button to display the **Text Pane**. In the **Text Pane**, type **Club** and **Web Site** and **New Members** in the order specified. **Close** the **Text Pane**. Click the border of the SmartArt graphic. Change the **SmartArt Graphic Style** to **Inset** and scroll to display the bottom of the **Colors** gallery. Under **Accent 6**, click the first color—**Colored Fill – Accent 6**.

7 At the bottom of **Page 2**, **Insert** a **Text Box** and set the height to **0.7″** and the width to **6″**. In the text box, type: **The Student Computing Services office is located in the Cedar Building, Room 114, call (215) 555-0932.**

Select the text in the text box. Change the **Font Size** to **16 pt**, apply **Bold**, and **Center** the text. Change the **Shape Fill** to **Accent 6, Darker 25%**—fifth row, last color. From the **Shape Effects** gallery, apply the **Bevel Circle** effect. Cancel the section of the text, and then click the Text box border. Drag or nudge the text box to visually center it horizontally between the left and right margins and vertically between the tabbed list and the footer.

8 In **File Properties**, in the **Subject** box, type your course name and section number, and in the **Author** box, type your firstname and lastname. In the **Keywords** box, type **Web sites, guidelines, Student Computing Services Save** your document, examine the Print Preview, check for and make any adjustments, and then **Print** your document or submit it electronically as directed. **Close** the document, and **Quit Word**.

End **You have completed Project 1G**

Content-Based Assessments

GO! Fix It | Project **1H** Guidelines

Project Files

For Project 1H, you will need the following file:

  w01H_Guidelines

You will save your document as:

  Lastname_Firstname_1H_Guidelines

From the student files that accompany this textbook, locate and open the file **w01H_Guidelines**, and then save the file in your Word Chapter 1 folder as **Lastname_Firstname_1H_Guidelines**

This document contains errors that you must find and correct. Read and examine the document, and then edit to correct any errors that you find and to improve the overall document format. Types of errors could include, but are not restricted to:

- Wasted space due to text not wrapping around pictures
- Inconsistent line spacing in paragraphs
- Inconsistent spacing between paragraphs
- Inconsistent paragraph indents
- Inconsistent indenting of lists
- Titles that do not extend across the page
- Text boxes that are too small
- Tabbed lists with wide spaces that do not contain leaders
- Spaces between paragraphs created using empty paragraphs rather than space after paragraphs

Things you should know to complete this project:

- Displaying nonprinting characters will assist in locating spacing errors.
- There are no errors in the fonts, although the title font size is too small.
- The final flyer should fit on one page.

Save your document and add the file name to the footer. In File Properties, type your course name and section number in the Subject box, type your firstname and lastname in the Author box, and in the Keywords box, type **Web site guidelines** and then save your document and submit as directed.

End **You have completed Project 1H** ——————————————————

Content-Based Assessments

Apply a combination of the **1A** and **1B** skills.

GO! Make It | Project 1I Flyer

Project Files

For Project 1I, you will need the following files:

> w01I_Team_Building
> w01I_Park_Picture

You will save your document as:

> Lastname_Firstname_1I_Team_Building

From the student files that accompany this textbook, locate and open the file w01I_Team_Building, and then save the file in your Word Chapter 1 folder as **Lastname_Firstname_1I_Team_Building**

Using the skills you have practiced, create the document shown in Figure 1.54. The title uses a Text Effect and is 48 pt. The SmartArt graphic uses the Radial Cycle with an Intense Effect style, is 3″ high and 6″ wide, and has the Colorful Range – Accent Colors 2 to 3 applied. The following are typed in the shapes: **Effective Leadership**, **Executive Officers**, **Student Senators**, **Club Presidents**, **Judicial Review Board** The w01I_Park_Picture picture has a 2 pt Soft Edge, and is 2.5″ wide. The page border uses 3 pt dark blue color—Text 2.

Add the file name to the footer. In File Properties, add your course name and section number, your name, and the keywords **team building** Save your document, and then submit as directed.

Project Results

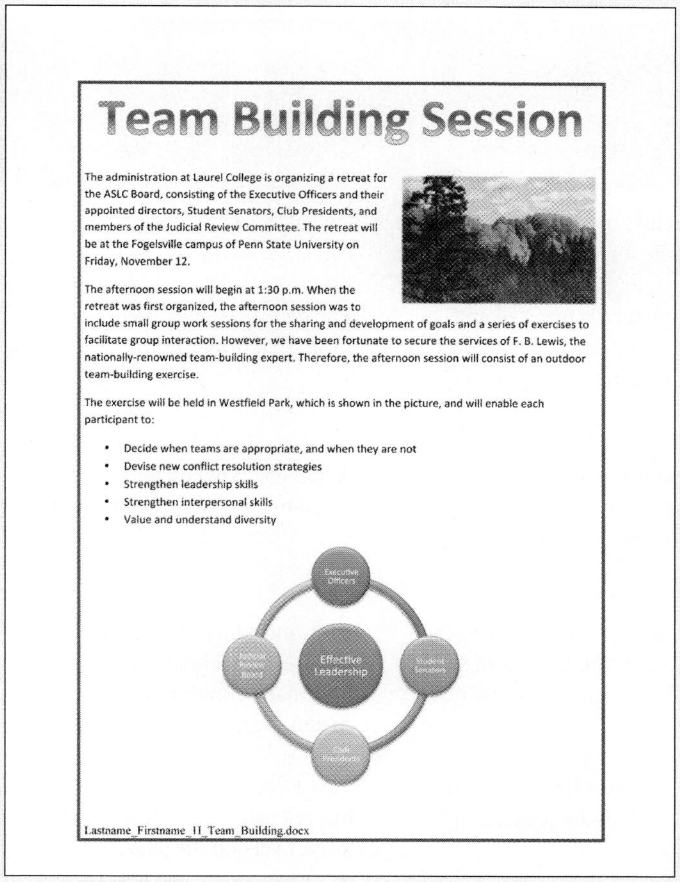

Figure 1.54

Content-Based Assessments

Apply a combination of the 1A and 1B skills.

GO! Solve It | Project 1J Food Drive

Project Files

For Project 1J, you will need the following files:

New blank Word document
w01J_Food_Drive

You will save your document as:

Lastname_Firstname_1J_Food_Drive

Create a new document and save it in your Word Chapter 1 folder as **Lastname_Firstname_1J_Food_Drive** Use the following information to create a flyer that includes a title that uses Text Effects, introductory text, two lists of an appropriate type, one text box, and a picture with appropriate formatting and text wrapping. Use your own picture or w01J_Food_Drive. Set the left and right margins at 1″, line spacing at 1.15, and spacing after the paragraphs at 6 pt.

This Thanksgiving, the Associated Students of Laurel College (ASLC) is sponsoring a food drive for the local community. All college clubs are invited to participate. Results will be adjusted for club membership by measuring the results in pounds of food per member. Three kinds of food are acceptable: canned goods, nonperishable dry goods, and boxed or canned dry drink mixes, such as coffee, tea, or lemonade.

To participate, a club must follow this procedure: fill out a competition form, collect the goods, and then turn in the food on November 13. The address and telephone number for the ASLC is the Cedar Building, Room 222, Laurelton, PA 19100, (215) 555-0902.

Add the file name to the footer. To File Properties, add your course name and section number, your name, and the keywords **food drive, clubs**

	Performance Level		
	Exemplary: You consistently applied the relevant skills	**Proficient: You sometimes, but not always, applied the relevant skills**	**Developing: You rarely or never applied the relevant skills**
Create and format lists	Both lists use the proper list type and are formatted correctly.	One of the lists is formatted correctly.	Neither of the lists are formatted correctly.
Insert and format a picture	The picture is inserted and positioned correctly, and text is wrapped around the picture.	The picture is inserted but not formatted properly.	No picture is inserted.
A text box with appropriate information is inserted and formatted	A text box with appropriate information is inserted and formatted.	A text box is adequately formatted but is difficult to read or unattractive.	No text box is inserted.
Insert introductory text	Introductory text explains the reason for the flyer, with no spelling or grammar errors.	Some introductory text is included, but does not contain sufficient information and/or includes spelling or grammar errors.	No introductory text, or insufficient introductory text.
Insert title using Text Effects	Text Effects title inserted and centered on the page.	Text Effects title is inserted, but not centered or formatted attractively on the page.	No Text Effects title is included.

Performance Criteria

End You have completed Project 1J

Content-Based Assessments

Apply a combination of the **1A** and **1B** skills.

GO! Solve It | Project **1K** Fitness Services

Project Files

For Project 1K, you will need the following files:

> New blank Word document
> w01K_Volleyball

You will save your document as:

> Lastname_Firstname_1K_Fitness_Services

Create a new file and save it in your Word Chapter 1 folder as **Lastname_Firstname_1K_ Fitness Services** Use the following information to create a flyer that includes introductory text, a SmartArt graphic, a title that uses Text Effects, and a picture that has an artistic effect applied and uses text wrapping. Use your own picture or w01K_Volleyball. Set the left and right margins at 1", line spacing at 1.15, and spacing after the paragraphs at 10 pt.

The Associated Students of Laurel College sponsors fitness activities. These take place both on campus and off campus. The activities fall into two categories: Fitness Services and Intramural Sports. Fitness Services are noncompetitive activities, with the most popular being Kickboxing, Jogging, and Aerobics. The most popular Intramural Sports activities—which include competitive team and club sports—are Field Hockey, Volleyball, and Basketball.

Add the file name to the footer, and to File Properties, add your course name and section number, your name, and the keywords **fitness, sports**

Performance Criteria		Performance Level		
		Exemplary: You consistently applied the relevant skills	**Proficient: You sometimes, but not always, applied the relevant skills**	**Developing: You rarely or never applied the relevant skills**
	Insert title using Text Effects	Text Effects title inserted and centered on the page.	Text Effects title is inserted, but not centered on the page.	No Text Effects title is included.
	Insert introductory text	Introductory text explains the reason for the flyer, with no spelling or grammar errors.	Some introductory text is included, but does not sufficiently explain the topic and/or includes spelling or grammar errors.	No or insufficient introductory text is included.
	Insert and format a picture	The picture is inserted and positioned correctly, an artistic effect is applied, and text is wrapped around the picture.	The picture is inserted but not formatted properly.	No picture is inserted in the document.
	Insert and format SmartArt	The SmartArt graphic displays both categories of fitness activities and examples of each type.	The SmartArt graphic does not display fitness activities by category.	No SmartArt graphic inserted.

End **You have completed Project 1K**

Outcomes-Based Assessments

Rubric

The following outcomes-based assessments are open-ended assessments. That is, there is no specific correct result; your result will depend on your approach to the information provided. Make Professional Quality your goal. Use the following scoring rubric to guide you in how to approach the problem and then to evaluate how well your approach solves the problem.

The *criteria*—Software Mastery, Content, Format and Layout, and Process—represent the knowledge and skills you have gained that you can apply to solving the problem. The *levels of performance*—Professional Quality, Approaching Professional Quality, or Needs Quality Improvements—help you and your instructor evaluate your result.

	Your completed project is of Professional Quality if you:	Your completed project is Approaching Professional Quality if you:	Your completed project Needs Quality Improvements if you:
1-Software Mastery	Choose and apply the most appropriate skills, tools, and features and identify efficient methods to solve the problem.	Choose and apply some appropriate skills, tools, and features, but not in the most efficient manner.	Choose inappropriate skills, tools, or features, or are inefficient in solving the problem.
2-Content	Construct a solution that is clear and well organized, contains content that is accurate, appropriate to the audience and purpose, and is complete. Provide a solution that contains no errors in spelling, grammar, or style.	Construct a solution in which some components are unclear, poorly organized, inconsistent, or incomplete. Misjudge the needs of the audience. Have some errors in spelling, grammar, or style, but the errors do not detract from comprehension.	Construct a solution that is unclear, incomplete, or poorly organized; contains some inaccurate or inappropriate content; and contains many errors in spelling, grammar, or style. Do not solve the problem.
3-Format and Layout	Format and arrange all elements to communicate information and ideas, clarify function, illustrate relationships, and indicate relative importance.	Apply appropriate format and layout features to some elements, but not others. Overuse features, causing minor distraction.	Apply format and layout that does not communicate information or ideas clearly. Do not use format and layout features to clarify function, illustrate relationships, or indicate relative importance. Use available features excessively, causing distraction.
4-Process	Use an organized approach that integrates planning, development, self-assessment, revision, and reflection.	Demonstrate an organized approach in some areas, but not others; or, use an insufficient process of organization throughout.	Do not use an organized approach to solve the problem.

Outcomes-Based Assessments

Apply a combination of
the **1A** and **1B** skills.

GO! Think | Project **1L** Academic Services

Project Files

For Project 1L, you will need the following file:

New blank Word document

You will save your document as:

Lastname_Firstname_1L_Academic_Services

The Services Coordinator of the Associated Students of Laurel College (ASLC) needs to create a flyer to inform students of academic services available at the ASLC office. Referrals are available for medical, legal, and counseling services, as well as tutoring and volunteer organizations. Among the services offered at the ASLC office are free printing (up to 250 pages per semester), help with minor legal issues, housing information, bicycle repair, minor computer repair, and help placing students with volunteer organizations.

Create a flyer with basic information about the services provided. Be sure the flyer is easy to read and understand and has an attractive design. If you need more information about student services available at other colleges, search the Web for **student government** and add whatever services you think might be (or should be) available at your college. Add appropriate information to File Properties. Save the document in your Word Chapter 1 folder as **Lastname_ Firstname_1L_Academic_Services** and submit it as directed.

End **You have completed Project 1L** ————————————————

Apply a combination of
the **1A** and **1B** skills.

GO! Think | Project **1M** Campus Bookstore

Project Files

For Project 1M, you will need the following files:

New blank Word document
w01M_Campus_Bookstore

You will save your document as:

Lastname_Firstname_1M_Campus_Bookstore

The Manager of the Laurel College Bookstore needs to create a flyer that can be handed out by the ASLC to students during Welcome Week. The bookstore gives students attending Welcome Week a discount of 20% on special items such as sweatshirts and other college-related clothing, coffee mugs, calendars, and similar items. Door prizes will also be awarded. The bookstore is open Monday and Thursday from 8 a.m. to 10 p.m., Tuesday and Wednesday from 8 a.m. to 8 p.m., and Friday from 8 a.m. to 5 p.m.

Using your own campus bookstore as a model, create a flyer that gives general information about the bookstore, provides one or more lists of items that are on sale, displays the picture w01M_Campus_Bookstore, and has a highlighted area that gives the store hours.

Add appropriate information to File Properties. Save the document in your Word Chapter 1 folder as **Lastname_Firstname_1M_Campus_Bookstore** and submit it as directed.

End **You have completed Project 1M** ————————————————

Outcomes-Based Assessments

You and GO! | Project **1N** Family Flyer

Project Files

For Project 1N, you will need the following file:

New blank Word document

You will save your document as:

Lastname_Firstname_1N_Family_Flyer

In this project, you will create a one-page flyer that you can send to your family. Include any information that may interest your family members, such as work-related news, school events, vacation plans, and the activities and accomplishments of you, your spouse, your friends, or other family members. Choose any writing style that suits you—chatty, newsy, entertaining, or humorous.

To complete the assignment, be sure to include a title, at least one list, a picture, and either a SmartArt graphic or a text box or shape. Before you submit the flyer, be sure to check it for grammar and spelling errors, and also be sure to format the document in an attractive manner, using the skills you practiced in this chapter.

Save the file in your Word Chapter 1 folder as **Lastname_Firstname_1N_Family_Flyer** Add the file name to the footer, and add, your course name and section number, your name, and the keywords **flyer** and **family** to File Properties. Submit your file as directed.

 End You have completed Project 1N ————————————————

GO! Group Business Running Case | Project **1O**
Bell Orchid Hotels Group Running Case

This project relates to the **Bell Orchid Hotels**. Your instructor may assign this group case project to your class. If your instructor assigns this project, he or she will provide you with information and instructions to work as part of a group. The group will apply the skills gained thus far to help the Bell Orchid Hotels achieve their business goals.

 End You have completed Project 1O ————————————————

Using Tables and Templates to Create Resumes and Cover Letters

OUTCOMES
At the end of this chapter you will be able to:

OBJECTIVES
Mastering these objectives will enable you to:

PROJECT 2A
Create a resume by using a Word table.

1. Create a Table (p. 117)
2. Add Text to a Table (p. 118)
3. Format a Table (p. 122)

PROJECT 2B
Create a cover letter and resume by using a template.

4. Create a New Document from an Existing Document (p. 132)
5. Change and Reorganize Text (p. 135)
6. Use the Proofing Options (p. 144)
7. Create a Document Using a Template (p. 148)

© Michael D. Brown/Shutterstock

In This Chapter

Tables are useful for organizing and presenting data. Because a table is so easy to use, many individuals prefer to arrange tabular information in a Word table rather than setting a series of tabs. Use a table when you want to present rows and columns of information or to create a structure for a document such as a resume.

When using Word to write business or personal letters, use a commonly approved letter format. You will make a good impression on prospective employers if you use a standard business letter style when you are writing a cover letter for a resume. You can create a resume using one of the Microsoft resume templates included with Microsoft Office or available online.

The projects in this chapter relate to **Madison Staffing Services**. Many companies prefer to hire employees through a staffing service, so that both the employer and the employee can determine if the match is a good fit. Madison Staffing Services takes care of the details of recruiting, testing, hiring, and paying the employee. At the end of the employment assignment, neither the employer nor the employee is required to make a permanent commitment. Many individuals find full-time jobs with an employer for whom they initially worked through a staffing agency.

Project 2A Resume

Project Activities

In Activities 2.01 through 2.09, you will create a table to use as the structure for a resume for one of Madison Staffing Services' clients. Your completed document will look similar to Figure 2.1.

Project Files

For Project 2A, you will need the following file:

w02A_Experience

You will save your document as:

Lastname_Firstname_2A_Resume

Project Results

Daniela Johnstone   (608) 555-0588
1343 Siena Lane, Deerfield, WI 53531   djohnstone@alcona.net

OBJECTIVE   Retail sales manager position in the mobile phone industry, using good
                       communication and negotiating skills.

SUMMARY OF   • Five years' experience in retail sales
QUALIFICATIONS   • Excellent interpersonal and communication skills
                       • Proficiency using Microsoft Office
                       • Fluency in spoken and written Spanish

EXPERIENCE   **Retail Sales Representative**, Universe Retail Stores, Deerfield, WI October
                       2015 to October 2016
                       • Exceeded monthly sales goals for 8 months out of 12
                       • Provided technical training on products and services to new sales reps

                       Sales Associate, Computer Products Warehouse, Deerfield, WI July 2013 to
                       September 2015
                       • Demonstrated, recommended, and sold a variety of computer products to
                         customers
                       • Led computer training for other sales associates
                       • Received commendation for sales accomplishments

                       Salesperson (part-time), Home and Garden Design Center, Madison, WI July
                       2011 to June 2013
                       • Helped customers in flooring department with selection and measurement
                         of a variety of flooring products
                       • Assisted department manager with product inventory

EDUCATION   **University of Wisconsin, Madison, WI**
                       Bachelor's in Business Administration, June 2016

                       Madison Area Technical College, Madison, WI
                       Associate's in Information Systems, June 2014

HONORS AND   • Elected to Beta Gamma Sigma, international honor society for business
ACTIVITIES   students
                       • Qualified for Dean's List, six academic periods

Lastname_Firstname_2A_Resume.docx

Figure 2.1
Project 2A Resume

Objective 1 | Create a Table

A ***table*** is an arrangement of information organized into rows and columns. The intersection of a row and a column in a table creates a box called a ***cell*** into which you can type. Tables are useful for presenting information in a logical and orderly manner.

Activity 2.01 | Creating a Table

1 Open **Word**, and in a new blank document, display nonprinting characters and rulers. On the **Home tab**, in the **Paragraph group**, click the **Line Spacing** button [icon], and then click **1.15**. In the **Font group**, click the **Font Size arrow** [11], and then click **11**. On the Ribbon, click the **Layout tab**, and in the **Margins group**, change the **Left** and **Right** margins to **1**. If necessary, on the Standard toolbar, change the Zoom setting to 125%.

> Recall that on a computer screen, spacing of 1.15 is easier to read than single spacing. Because a large percentage of Word documents are read on a computer screen, 1.15 is the preferred spacing for a Word document. Changing left and right margins to 1" and the font size enables you to enter more text per line. Changing the Zoom setting enables you to compare more easily your screen to the figures in this textbook.

2 On the **File** menu, click **Save As**. In the **Save As** dialog box, navigate to the location where you are storing your projects for this chapter. Create a new folder named **Word Chapter 2**

3 **Save** the file in the **Word Chapter 2** folder as **Lastname_Firstname_2A_Resume**

4 Scroll to the bottom of the document to display the [icon] pointer, and then double click to open the **Footer** area. On the **Insert** menu, point to **AutoText**, and then click **Filename** to insert the name of your file in the **Footer** area. **Close** the **Footer** area.

Another Way

On the Table menu, point to Insert, and then click Table to begin the creation of a table.

5 On the Ribbon, click the **Tables tab**, in the **Table Options group**, click the **New** button. In the **Table** grid, in the fourth row, point to the second square, and notice that the cells display in blue and *2 × 4 Table* displays at the top of the grid. Compare your screen with Figure 2.2.

Figure 2.2

Tables tab

New button

Table size

Pointer indicates table size

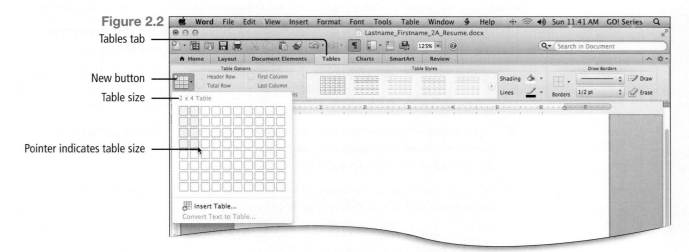

6 Click one time to create the table. Notice that nonprinting characters in each cell indicate the end of the contents of each cell and the character to the right of each row indicates the row end. **Save** 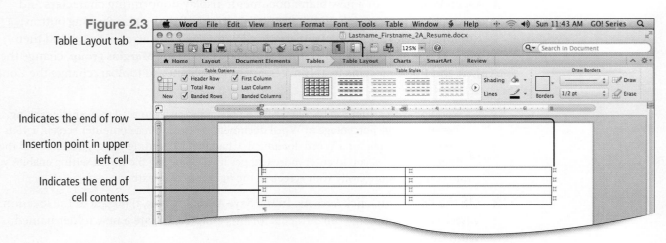 your document, and then compare your screen with Figure 2.3.

> A table with four rows and two columns displays at the insertion point location, and the insertion point displays in the upper left cell. The table fills the width of the page, from the left margin to the right margin. On the Ribbon, the Table Layout tab displays. Borders display around each cell in the table.

Figure 2.3
Table Layout tab

Indicates the end of row

Insertion point in upper left cell

Indicates the end of cell contents

Objective 2 | Add Text to a Table

In a Word table, each cell behaves similarly to a document. For example, as you type in a cell, when you reach the right border of the cell, wordwrap moves the text to the next line. When you press Return, the insertion point moves down to a new paragraph in the same cell. You can also insert text from another document into a table cell.

Activity 2.02 | Adding Text to a Table

There are numerous acceptable formats for resumes, many of which can be found in business communications textbooks. The layout used in this project is suitable for a recent college graduate and places topics in the left column and details in the right column.

1 If necessary, scroll to view the top of the document. With the insertion point blinking in the first cell in the first row, type **OBJECTIVE** and then press Tab.

> Pressing Tab moves the insertion point to the next cell in the row, or, if the insertion point is already in the last cell in the row, pressing Tab moves the insertion point to the first cell in the following row. Pressing Tab in the last cell of the table creates a new row.

2 Type **Retail sales manager position in the mobile phone industry, using good communication and negotiating skills**. Notice that the text wraps in the cell and the height of the row adjusts to fit the text.

3 Press Tab to move to the first cell in the second row. Type **SUMMARY OF QUALIFICATIONS** and then press Tab. Type the following, pressing Return at the end of each line *except* the last line:

> **Five years' experience in retail sales**
>
> **Excellent interpersonal and communication skills**
>
> **Proficiency using Microsoft Office**
>
> **Fluency in spoken and written Spanish**

4 **Save** your document, and then compare your screen with Figure 2.4.

Figure 2.4

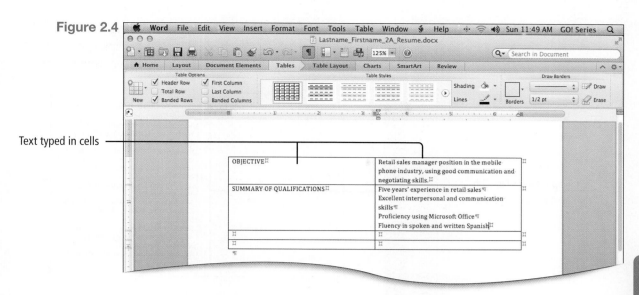

Text typed in cells

Activity 2.03 | Inserting Existing Text into a Table Cell

1 Press [Tab] to move to the first cell in the third row. Type **EXPERIENCE** and then press [Tab].

2 Type the following, pressing [Return] after each line, including the last line:

> **Retail Sales Representative, Universe Retail Stores, Deerfield, WI October 2015 to October 2016**
>
> **Exceeded monthly sales goals for 8 months out of 12**
>
> **Provided technical training on products and services to new sales reps**

3 Be sure your insertion point is positioned in the second column to the left of the cell marker below the last entry—on a blank line. Compare your screen with Figure 2.5.

Figure 2.5

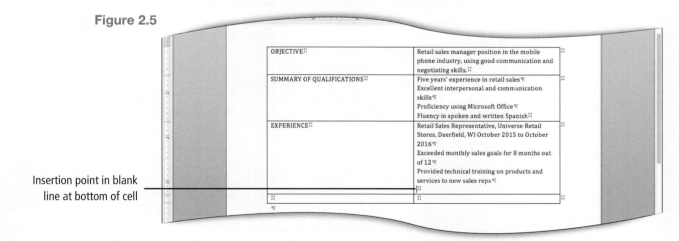

Insertion point in blank line at bottom of cell

Another Way

Open the second document and select the text you want. Copy the text, and then paste at the desired location in the first document.

4 On the **Insert** menu, click **File**. Navigate to your student files, click **w02A_Experience**, and then click **Insert**.

5 Press [Delete] one time to remove the blank line at the end of the inserted text, and then compare your screen with Figure 2.6.

> By default a table has the same defaults as a new blank document—single-spaced, Cambria font, font size of 12. The inserted text has the default document settings.

Figure 2.6

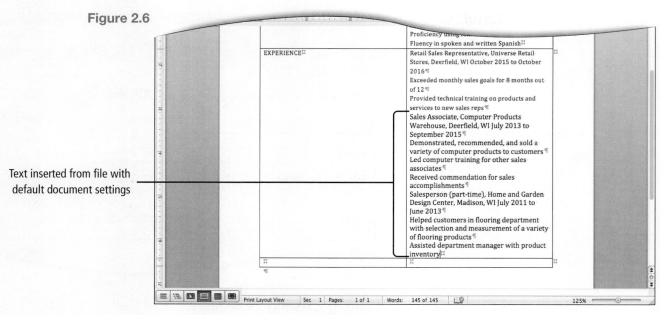

Text inserted from file with default document settings

6 In the cell to the right of *EXPERIENCE*, click anywhere in the paragraph beginning with *Retail Sales*. On the Standard toolbar, click the **Format Painter** button ✎. Select the paragraphs of the inserted text, beginning with *Sales Associate* and ending with the last line in the cell. **Save** 🖫 your document.

> Format Painter copied the paragraph settings—Font, Font Size, and line spacing—to the selected text.

7 Press Tab to move to the first cell in the fourth row. Type **EDUCATION** and then press Tab.

8 Type the following, pressing Return at the end of each item *except* the last one:

> **University of Wisconsin, Madison, WI**
>
> **Bachelor's in Business Administration, June 2016**
>
> **Madison Area Technical College, Madison, WI**
>
> **Associate's in Information Systems, June 2014**

9 Compare your screen with Figure 2.7.

Figure 2.7

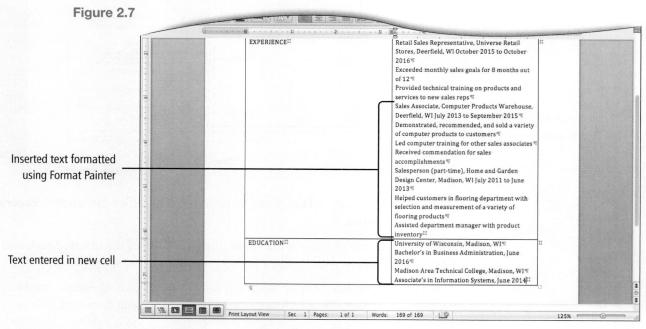

Inserted text formatted using Format Painter

Text entered in new cell

10 Save 🖫 your document.

Activity 2.04 | Creating Bulleted Lists in a Table

1 Scroll to view the top of your document, and then in the cell to the right of *SUMMARY OF QUALIFICATIONS*, select all of the text.

2 On the **Home tab**, in the **Paragraph group**, click the **Bulleted List** button ▤ ▾.

> The selected text displays as a bulleted list. Using a bulleted list in this manner makes each qualification more distinctive.

3 Be sure that the text is still selected, and then in the **Paragraph group**, click the **Decrease Indent** button ▤ one time to align the bullets at the left edge of the cell.

4 On the Standard toolbar, double-click the **Format Painter** button ▨. In the cell to the right of *EXPERIENCE*, select the second and third paragraphs—beginning with *Exceeded* and *Provided*—to create the same style of bulleted list as you did in the previous step.

> When you double-click the Format Painter button, it remains active until you turn it off.

5 In the same cell, under *Sales Associate*, select the three paragraphs that begin with *Demonstrated* and *Led* and *Received* to create another bulleted list aligned at the left edge of the cell.

6 With the Format Painter pointer still active, in the same cell, under *Salesperson (part-time)*, select the paragraphs that begin with *Helped* and *Assisted* to create the same type of bulleted list.

Another Way

Click the Format Painter button again.

- - ▶ **7** Press Esc to turn off the **Format Painter**. Click anywhere in the table to deselect the text, and then compare your screen with Figure 2.8.

Figure 2.8

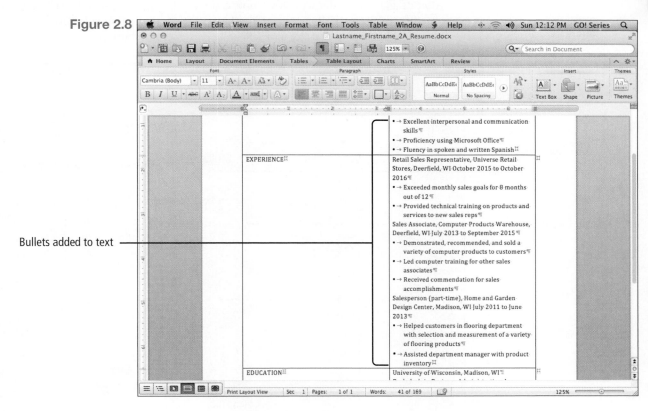

Bullets added to text

8 **Save** ▤ your document.

Objective 3 | Format a Table

Use Word's formatting tools to make your tables attractive and easy to read. Types of formatting you can add to a table include changing the row height and the column width, removing or adding borders, increasing or decreasing the paragraph or line spacing, or enhancing the text.

Activity 2.05 | Changing the Width of Table Columns

When you create a table, all of the columns are of equal width. In this activity, you will change the width of the columns.

1 In any row, point to the vertical border between the two columns to display the ⟺ pointer.

2 Drag the column border to the left to approximately **1.25 inches on the horizontal ruler** or as far left as you can drag the column border.

3 Scroll to the top of the document. Notice that in the second row, the text *SUMMARY OF QUALIFICATIONS* wraps to two lines to accommodate the new column width.

4 If necessary, in the left column, click in any cell. On the Ribbon, click the **Table Layout tab**.

5 In the **Settings group**, click the **Properties** button. In the **Table Properties** dialog box, click the **Column tab**. Under **Column 1**, click the **Preferred width spin arrows** as necessary to change the width of the first column to **1.4"**. Compare your screen with Figure 2.9.

After dragging a border with your mouse, use the Table Properties dialog box to set a precise measurement, if necessary. To change the width of other columns, at the bottom of the Table Properties dialog box, click the Next Column button.

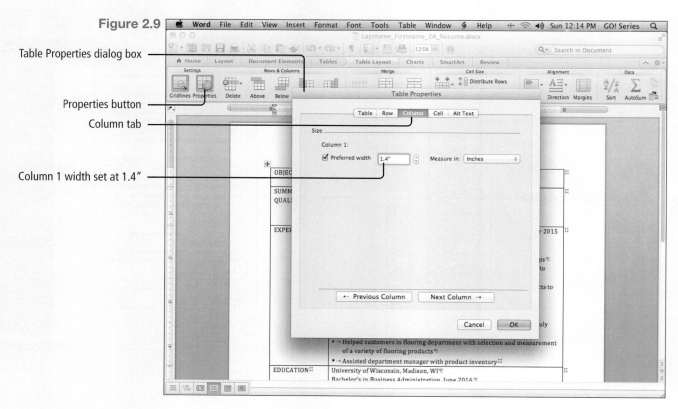

Figure 2.9

Table Properties dialog box

Properties button

Column tab

Column 1 width set at 1.4"

6 In the **Table Properties** dialog box, click **OK**, and then **Save** 🖫 your document.

More Knowledge | Changing Column Widths

You will typically get the best results if you change the column widths starting at the left side of the table, especially in tables with three or more columns. Word can also calculate the best column widths for you. To do this, select the table. Then, on the Table Layout tab, in the Cell Size group, click the AutoFit button and click AutoFit to Contents.

Activity 2.06 | Adding Rows to a Table

You can add rows or columns anywhere in a table.

1 Scroll to view the lower portion of the table. In the last row of the table, click anywhere in the *second* cell that contains the educational information, and then press Tab.

> A new row displays at the bottom of the table. When the insertion point is in the last cell in the bottom row of a table, you can add a row by pressing the Tab key; the insertion point will display in the first cell of the new row.

2 Type **HONORS AND ACTIVITIES** and then press Tab.

3 Type the following, pressing Return after the first item but not the second item:

> **Elected to Beta Gamma Sigma, international honor society for business students**
>
> **Qualified for Dean's List, six academic periods**

4 Select the text you typed in the last cell of the last row—select only the text, not the entire cell. On the **Home tab**, in the **Paragraph group**, click the **Bulleted List** button ▤▾, and then click the **Decrease Indent** button ◁를 one time to align the bullets at the left edge of the cell.

5 Click anywhere in the table to deselect the text, and then compare your screen with Figure 2.10.

Figure 2.10

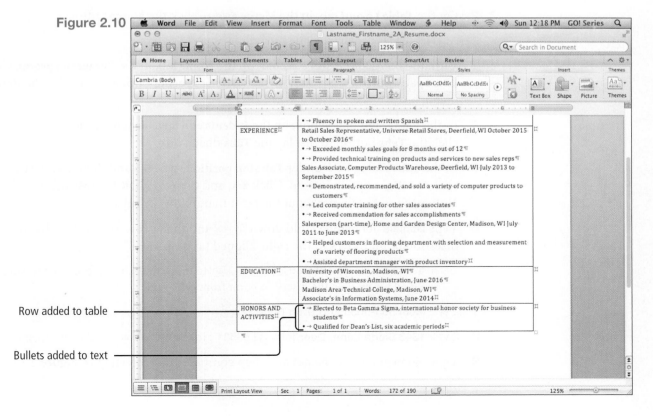

Row added to table

Bullets added to text

6 Click anywhere in the top row of the table.

Another Way

On the Table menu, point to Insert, and then click Rows Above.

7 On the **Table Layout tab**, in the **Rows & Columns group**, click the **Above** button. Compare your screen with Figure 2.11.

A new row displays above the row that contained the insertion point, and the new row is selected.

Figure 2.11

Above button

Row inserted at top of table

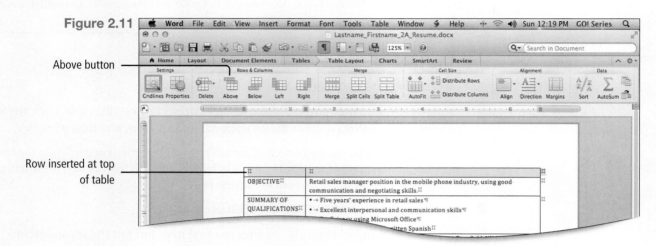

8 **Save** your document.

Activity 2.07 | Merging Cells

The title of a table typically spans all of the columns. In this activity, you will merge cells so that you can position the personal information across both columns.

1 Be sure the two cells in the top row are selected; if necessary, drag across both cells to select them.

Another Way

On the Table menu, click Merge Cells.

2 On the **Table Layout tab**, in the **Merge group**, click the **Merge** button.

The cell border between the two cells no longer displays.

3 With the merged cell still selected, on the **Home tab**, in the **Paragraph group**, click the **Line Spacing arrow** , and then click **Line Spacing Options** to display the **Paragraph** dialog box.

4 In the **Paragraph** dialog box, on the **Indents and Spacing tab**, in the lower left corner, click the **Tabs** button to display the **Tabs** dialog box.

5 In the **Tabs** dialog box, under **Tab stop position**, type **6.5** and then under **Alignment**, click the **Right** option button. Click **Set**, and then click **OK** to close the dialog box. Notice the right tab marker at the right margin on the ruler.

6 Type **Daniela Johnstone** Hold down Control and then press Tab. Notice that the insertion point moves to the right-aligned tab stop at 6.5".

In a Word table, you must use Control + Tab to move to a tab stop because pressing Tab is reserved for moving the insertion point from cell to cell.

7 Type **(608) 555-0588** and then press Return.

8 Type **1343 Siena Lane, Deerfield, WI 53531** Hold down Control and then press Tab.

9 Type **djohnstone@alcona.net** and then compare your screen with Figure 2.12.

Figure 2.12

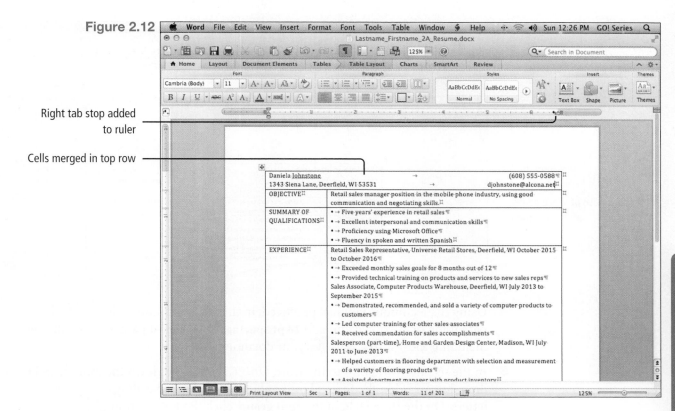

Right tab stop added to ruler

Cells merged in top row

10 Save ⊞ your document.

Activity 2.08 | Formatting Text in Cells

1 In the first row of the table, select the name *Daniela Johnstone*. On the **Home tab**, in the **Font group**, click the **Bold** button B, and then change the **Font Size** 11 ▾ to **16**.

2 Under *Daniela Johnstone*, click anywhere in the second line of text, which contains the address and email address.

3 On the **Home tab**, in the **Paragraph group**, click the **Line Spacing arrow**, and then click **Line Spacing Options** to display the **Paragraph** dialog box. In the **Paragraph** dialog box, on the **Indents and Spacing tab**, under **Spacing**, click the **After up spin arrow** three times to add **18 pt** spacing between the first row of the table and the second row. Click **OK**, and then compare your screen with Figure 2.13.

These actions separate the personal information from the body of the resume and add focus to the applicant's name.

Figure 2.13

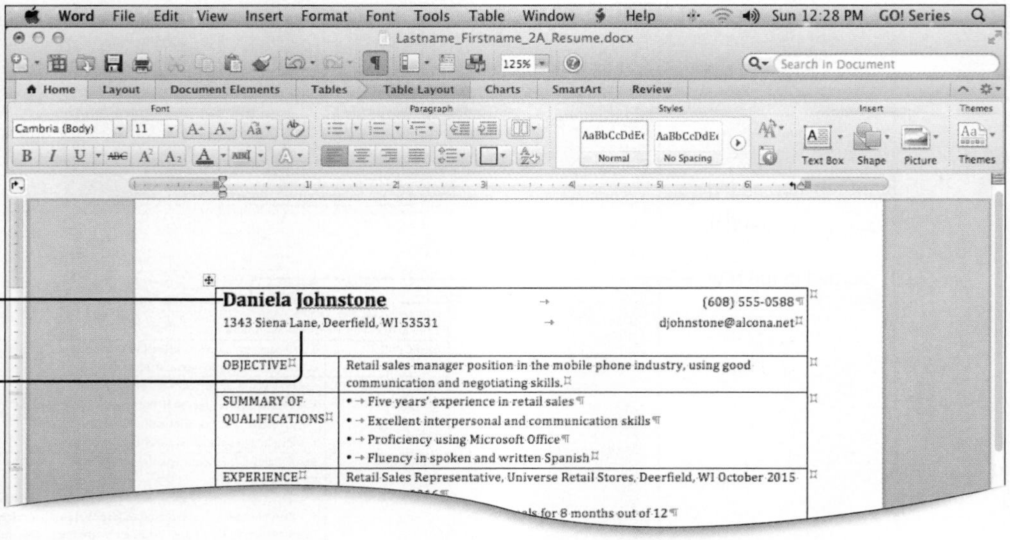

Text formatted

18 pt space added
after paragraph

4 Using the technique you just practiced, in the second column, click in the last paragraph of every cell and add **18 pt Spacing After** the last paragraph of all rows including the last row. **Save** 🖫 your document.

5 In the second row, point to the word *OBJECTIVE*, hold down the mouse, and then drag downward in the first column only to select all the headings in uppercase letters. On the **Home tab**, in the **Font group**, click the **Bold** button B .

> **Note | Selecting Only One Column**
>
> When you drag downward to select the first column, a fast mouse might also begin to select the second column when you reach the bottom. If this happens, drag to the left slightly to deselect the second column and select only the first column.

6 In the cell to the right of *EXPERIENCE*, without selecting the comma that follows, select *Retail Sales Representative* and then apply **Bold** B to the selected text.

7 In the same cell, apply **Bold** B to the other job titles—*Sales Associate* and *Salesperson*—but do not bold *(part time)* or the commas following the job titles.

8 In the cell to the right of *EDUCATION*, apply **Bold** B to *University of Wisconsin, Madison, WI* and *Madison Area Technical College, Madison, WI*.

9 In the same cell, click anywhere in the line beginning with *Bachelor's*. On the **Home tab**, in the **Paragraph group**, click the **Line Spacing arrow** , and then click **Line Spacing Options** to display the **Paragraph** dialog box. In the **Paragraph** dialog box, on the **Indents and Spacing tab**, under **Spacing**, click the **After up spin arrow** two times to add **12 pt** spacing after the paragraph. Click **OK**.

10 In the cell to the right of *EXPERIENCE*, under *Retail Sales Representative*, click anywhere in the second bulleted item, and then add **12 pt Spacing After** the item.

11 In the same cell, repeat this process for the last bulleted item under *Sales Associate*.

12 Scroll to the top of the document, and then compare your screen with Figure 2.14.

Figure 2.14

Space added after
paragraphs in second
column

Bold emphasis applied
to first column

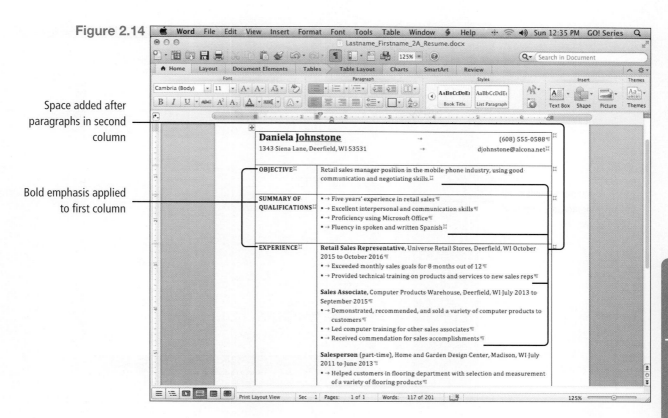

13 Save 🖫 your document.

Activity 2.09 | Changing the Table Borders

When you create a table, all of the cells have black borders. Most resumes do not display any cell borders. A border at the top and bottom of the resume, however, is attractive and adds a professional look to the document.

1 Press Command ⌘ + fn + ← to move the insertion point to the top of the table, and then point slightly outside of the upper left corner of the table to display the **table move handle** ⊞. Point to the table move handle ⊞ to display the 🔾 pointer.

2 Click one time to select the entire table, and notice that the nonprinting row markers at the end of each row are also selected.

Shaded row markers indicate that the entire row is selected.

3 Click the **Tables tab**. In the **Draw Borders group**, click the **Borders arrow**, and then click **None**.

The black borders no longer display; instead, depending on your setup, either nonprinting dimmed borders—the default setting—or no borders display.

4 On the **File** menu, click **Print** to preview the table. Notice that no borders display in the preview, as shown in Figure 2.15.

Figure 2.15

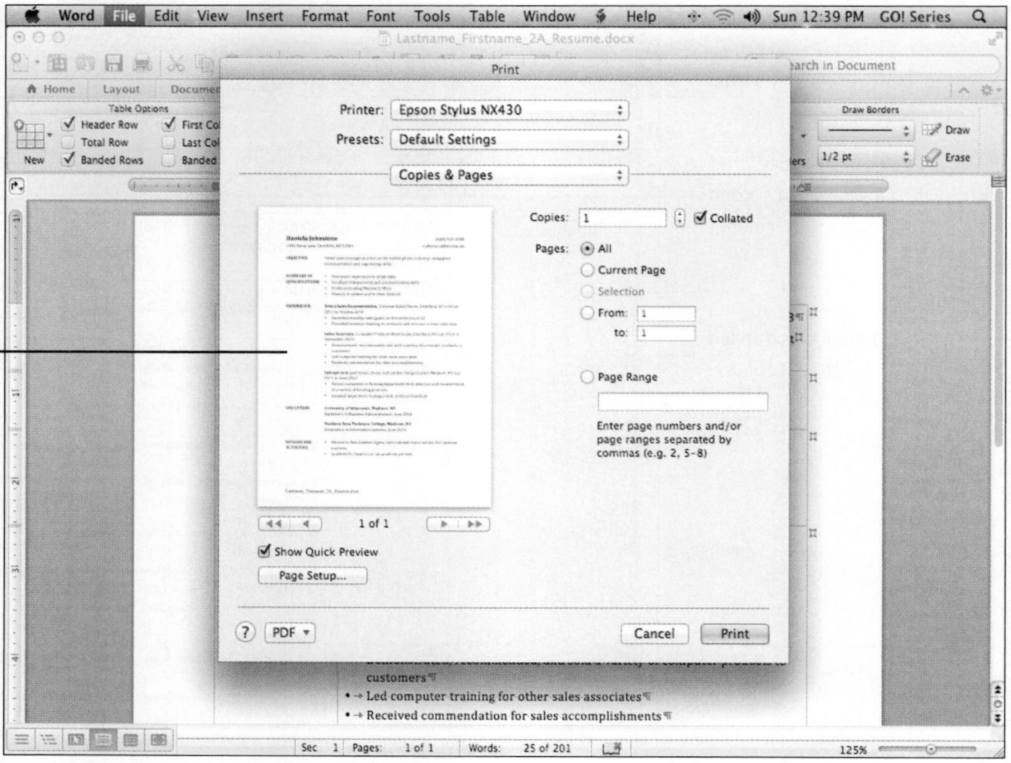

Document preview, all
table borders removed

Another Way

On the Format menu,
click Borders and Shad-
ing, and then select
the Style and edge for
border.

5 In the **Print** dialog box, click **Cancel**. Be sure the table is still selected. In the **Draw Borders group**, click the **Line Style** button ⌐━━━━ ⬦⌐. In the list, click the style with the thick upper line and the thin lower line—the ninth line style under No Border.

6 In the **Draw Borders group**, click the **Borders arrow**, and then click **Top**.

A border is added to the top of the table.

7 In the **Draw Borders group**, click the **Line Style** button ⌐━━━━ ⬦⌐. In the list, click the style with the thin upper line and the thick lower line—the style directly below the selected style. In the **Draw Borders group**, click the **Borders arrow**, and then click **Bottom**.

8 Without canceling the selection, scroll to display the bottom of your document, and then compare your screen with Figure 2.16.

Figure 2.16

Bottom border style selected

Borders button indicates a top and bottom border

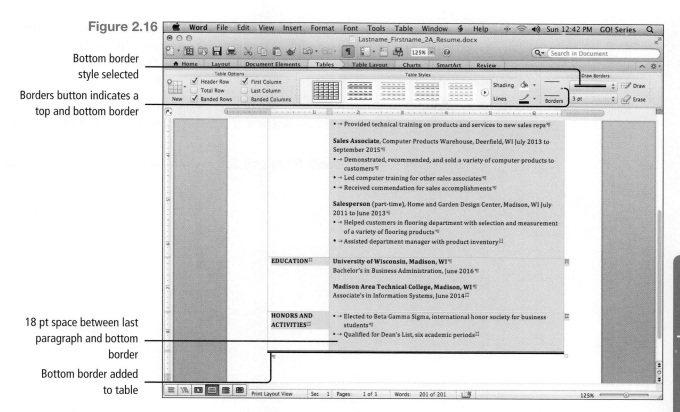

18 pt space between last paragraph and bottom border

Bottom border added to table

9 Click anywhere to cancel the selection, scroll to the top of the document, and then notice that there is only a small amount of space between the top border and the first line of text.

10 Click anywhere in the text *Daniela Johnstone*. On the **Home tab**, in the **Paragraph group**, click the **Line Spacing arrow**, and then click **Line Spacing Options**. In the **Paragraph** dialog box, under **Spacing**, click the **Before up spin arrow** three times to add **18 pt** spacing before the first paragraph, and then click **OK**. **Save** your document, and then compare your screen with Figure 2.17.

Figure 2.17

Top border

18 pt spacing added above first paragraph

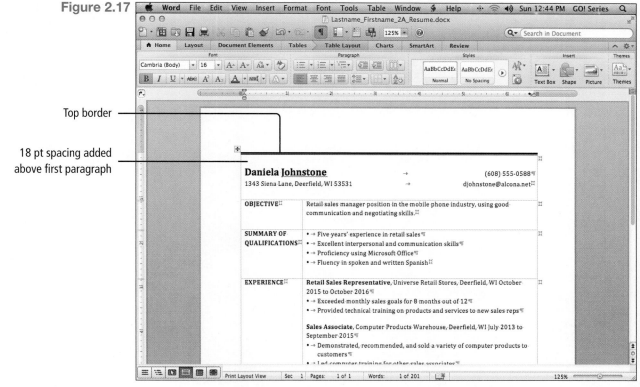

11 On the **File** menu, click **Properties**. In the **Properties** dialog box, on the **Summary tab**, click in the **Subject** box, and then type your course name and section number. In the **Author** box, delete any text and then type your firstname and lastname. In the **Keywords** box, type **resume, Word table** and then click **OK**.

12 **Save** 🖫 and then **Print** your document, or submit it electronically, as directed by your instructor. **Close** 🔘 your document. On the **Word** menu, click **Quit Word**.

End **You have completed Project 2A** ————————————————————

Project 2B Cover Letter and Resume

Project Activities

In Activities 2.10 through 2.22, you will create a letterhead, and then use the letterhead to create a cover letter. You will also create a short resume using a Microsoft template and save it as a Web page. Your completed documents will look similar to Figure 2.18.

Project Files

For Project 2B, you will need the following files:

w02B_Cover_Letter_Text
Blocks Resume Template from Word's installed templates

You will save your documents as:

Lastname_Firstname_2B_Letterhead
Lastname_Firstname_2B_Cover_Letter
Lastname_Firstname_2B_Brief_Resume
Lastname_Firstname_2B_HTML_Resume

Project Results

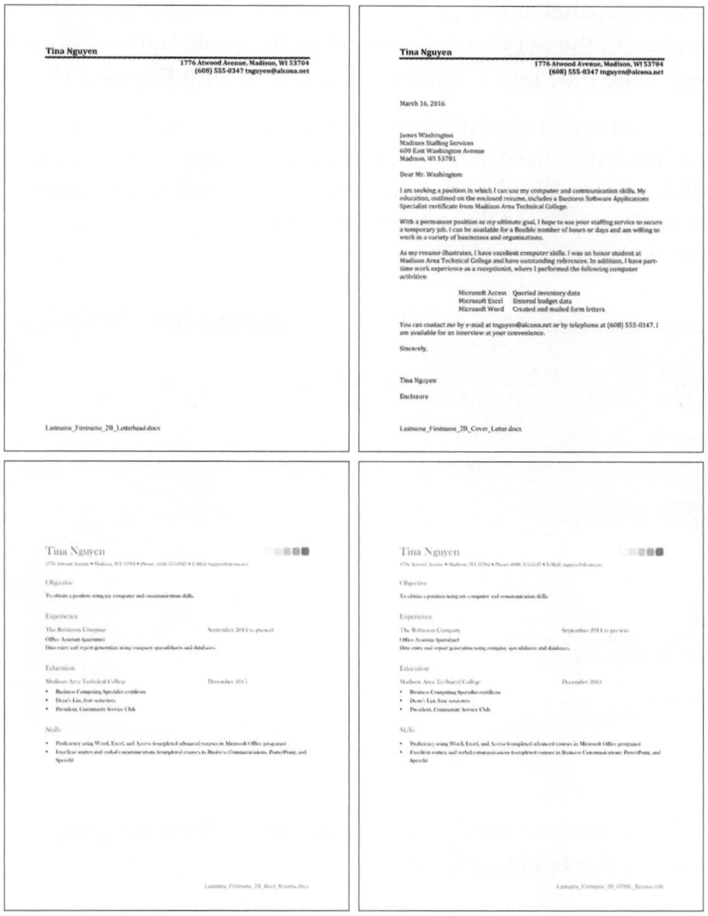

Figure 2.18

Project 2B Cover Letter and Resume

Objective 4 | Create a New Document from an Existing Document

A **template** is an *existing* document that you use as a starting point for a *new* document. The template document opens a copy of itself, unnamed, and then you use the structure—and possibly some content, such as headings—as the starting point for a new document.

All documents are based on a template. When you create a new blank document, it is based on Word's **Normal template**, which serves as the starting point for all new Word documents.

Activity 2.10 | Creating a Letterhead

A **letterhead** is the personal or company information that displays at the top of a letter, and which commonly includes a name, address, and contact information. The term also refers to a piece of paper imprinted with such information at the top.

1 Open **Word**, and in the new blank document, be sure that nonprinting characters and rulers display. On the **Layout tab**, in the **Margins group**, change the **Left** and **Right** margins to **1**. If necessary, on the Standard toolbar, change the Zoom setting to 125%.

2 Type **Tina Nguyen** and then press ⏎ Return.

3 Type **1776 Atwood Avenue, Madison, WI 53704** and then press ⏎ Return.

4 Type **(608) 555-0347 tnguyen@alcona.net** and then press ⏎ Return. Notice that the email address is blue and underlined. On the Standard toolbar, click the **Undo** button 🔄 one time to remove the hyperlink—the blue line. Compare your screen with Figure 2.19.

> Pressing Undo causes the last action—automatic formatting of the email address as a hyperlink—to be canceled. To change the default automatic formatting of Internet and email addresses as hyperlinks, on the Word menu, click Preferences, click AutoCorrect, click the AutoFormat as You Type tab, and then under Replace as you type, clear the Internet and network paths with hyperlinks check box.

Figure 2.19

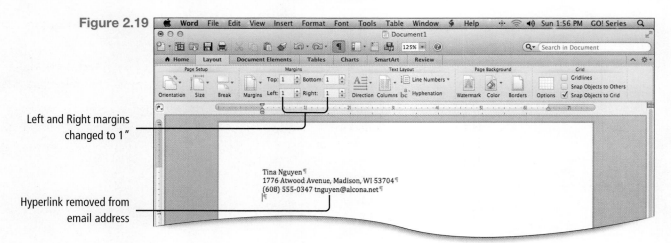

Left and Right margins changed to 1″

Hyperlink removed from email address

5 Select the first paragraph—*Tina Nguyen*—and on the **Home tab**, in the **Font group**, apply **Bold** B, and then change the **Font Size** to **16**.

6 Select the second and third paragraphs—do not select the blank line—and then apply **Bold** B.

7 With the two paragraphs still selected, on the **Home tab**, in the **Paragraph group**, click the **Align Text Right** button.

8 Click anywhere in the first paragraph—*Tina Nguyen*. On the **Format** menu, click **Borders and Shading**. In the **Borders and Shading** dialog box, under **Style**, be sure the first style—a single solid line—is selected.

> Here you can set the style, color, width, and location of the line, all in one dialog box.

9 Click the **Width arrow**, and then click **3 pt**. To the right, under **Preview**, click the bottom border of the diagram. Under **Apply to**, be sure *Paragraph* displays. Compare your screen with Figure 2.20.

Figure 2.20

Borders and Shading dialog box

Line style

Line width changed to 3 pt

Line applied to bottom border of paragraph

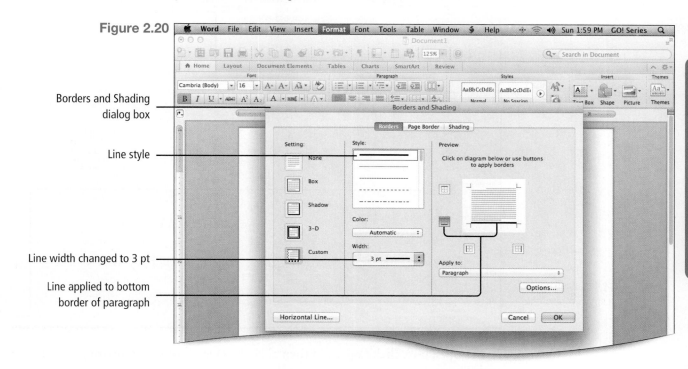

10 Click **OK** to display a 3 pt line that extends from the left margin to the right margin below *Tina Nguyen*,

11 On the **File** menu, click **Save As**. **Save** the document in your **Word Chapter 2** folder as **Lastname_Firstname_2B_Letterhead** and then in the **Footer** area, insert the **Filename**.

12 On the **File** menu, click **Properties**. In the **Properties** dialog box, on the **Summary tab**, click in the **Subject** box, and then type your course name and section number. In the **Author** box, delete any text and then type your firstname and lastname. In the **Keywords** box type **personal letterhead** and then click **OK**.

13 **Save** your document, and then **Print** it or submit electronically as directed. **Close** the document, but leave Word open.

Activity 2.11 | Creating a Document from an Existing Document

To use an existing document as the starting point for a new document, Word provides the Copy command in the Open dialog box.

1 On the **File** menu, click **Open** to display the **Open** dialog box. If necessary, navigate to your **Word Chapter 2** folder, and click your **2B_Letterhead** document to select it. In the lower left corner of the **Open** dialog box, click the **Open** box, and then compare your screen with Figure 2.21.

> By default a document is opened as an Original document. In the Open box, you can open a document as a Copy or as a Read-Only document.

Figure 2.21

Word Chapter 2 folder

Selected 2B_Letterhead document

Open button

Open box

Copy command opens document as copy of the original

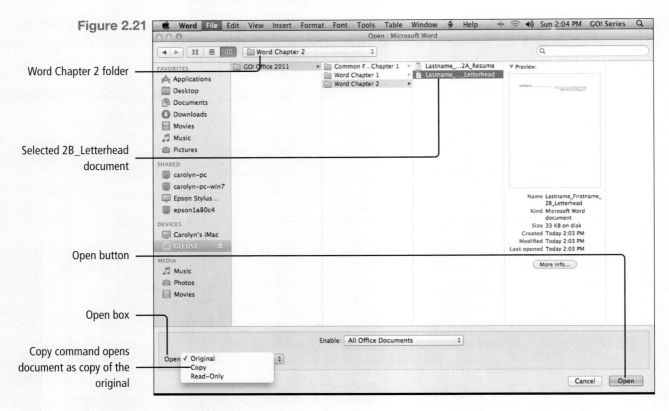

2 In the **Open** box, click **Copy**, and then click the **Open** button. Compare your screen with Figure 2.22.

> Word opens a copy of your 2B_Letterhead document in the form of a new Word document—the title bar indicates *Document* followed by a number. You are not opening the original document, and changes that you make to this new document will not affect the contents of your 2B_Letterhead document.

Figure 2.22

Document opens unnamed (your name may differ)

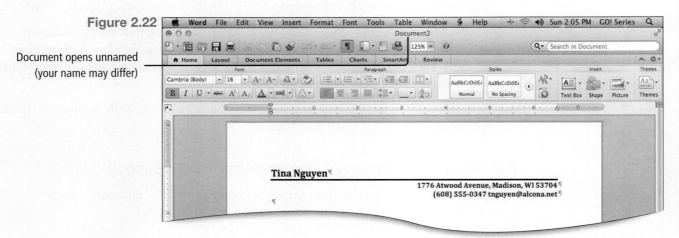

3 On the **File** menu, click **Save As**. Navigate to your **Word Chapter 2** folder. **Save** the file as **Lastname_Firstname_2B_Cover_Letter**

> The personal information that you typed in the 2B_Letterhead File Properties dialog box remains in the new document.

4 Scroll down to view the **Footer** area, and notice that the original footer displays.

> The footer displays because it was included in the document that you opened as a copy. The *Filename* does not automatically update to the new Filename.

┌─ **Another Way**

Press Option + Shift + Command ⌘ + U to update the file name in the Footer area.

5 Point to the **Footer** area and double-click to open the **Footer** area. Point to the footer text—the file name. Press Control and click. On the shortcut menu, click **Update Field**. **Close** the **Footer** area.

6 **Save** 💾 your document.

More Knowledge | Creating a Template File

You can also identify an original document so that Office always knows that you want to create a new unnamed copy. To do so, save your document as a template file instead of a document. Word will then attach the dotx extension to the file, instead of the docx extension that is applied for a document, and will store the template file in a special location with other templates. Then, you can open the template from the Word Document Gallery by clicking *My Templates*.

Objective 5 | Change and Reorganize Text

Business letters follow a standard format and contain the following parts: the current date, referred to as the *date line*; the name and address of the person receiving the letter, referred to as the *inside address*; a greeting, referred to as the *salutation*; the text of the letter, usually referred to as the *body* of the letter; a closing line, referred to as the *complimentary closing*; and the *writer's identification*, which includes the name or job title (or both) of the writer, and which is also referred to as the *writer's signature block*.

Some letters also include the initials of the person who prepared the letter, an optional *subject line* that describes the purpose of the letter, or a list of *enclosures*—documents included with the letter.

Activity 2.12 | Recording AutoCorrect Entries

You can correct commonly misspelled words automatically by using Word's *AutoCorrect* feature. Commonly misspelled words—such as *teh* instead of *the*—are corrected using a built-in list that is installed with Office. If you have words that you frequently misspell, you can add them to the list for automatic correction.

1 On the **Word** menu, click **Preferences**. In the **Word Preferences** dialog box, under **Authoring and Proofing Tools**, click **AutoCorrect**.

2 In the **AutoCorrect** dialog box, be sure that the **AutoCorrect tab** is active. Under **Replace**, type **resumee** and under **With**, type **resume**

> If another student has already added this AutoCorrect entry, a Replace button will display instead of the Add button.

3 Click **Add**. If the entry already exists, click Replace instead, and then click **Yes**.

4 In the **AutoCorrect** dialog box, under **Replace**, type **computr** and under **With**, type **computer** and then compare your screen with Figure 2.23.

Figure 2.23

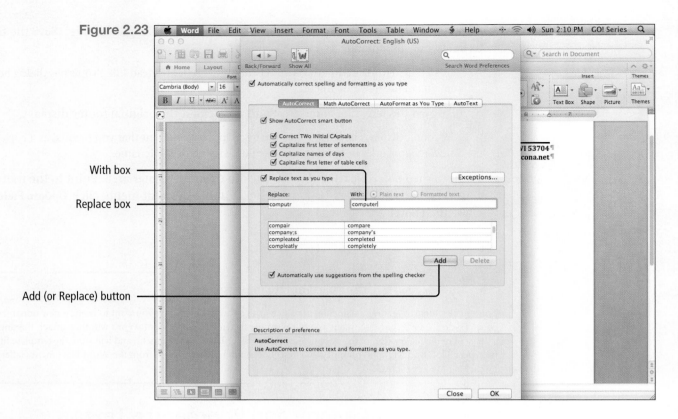

With box

Replace box

Add (or Replace) button

5 Click **Add** (or Replace) and then click **OK** to close the dialog box.

Activity 2.13 | Creating a Cover Letter

There are a variety of accepted letter formats that you will see in reference manuals and business communication texts. The one used in this chapter is a block style cover letter taken from *Business Communication Today*.

1 Press Command ⌘ + fn + → to position the insertion point at the end of the document—on the blank line below the phone number and email address. Press Return three times, and then type **March 16, 2016** to create the dateline.

Most business communication texts recommend that the dateline be positioned at least 0.5 inch (3 blank lines) below the letterhead; or, position the dateline approximately 2 inches from the top edge of the paper.

2 Press Return four times, which leaves three blank lines. Type the following inside address on four lines, but do not press Return following the last line:

James Washington

Madison Staffing Services

600 East Washington Avenue

Madison, WI 53701

The recommended space between the dateline and inside address varies slightly among business communication texts and office reference manuals. However, all indicate that the space can be from one to 10 blank lines depending on the length of your letter.

3 Press Return two times to leave one blank line. Compare your screen with Figure 2.24.

Figure 2.24

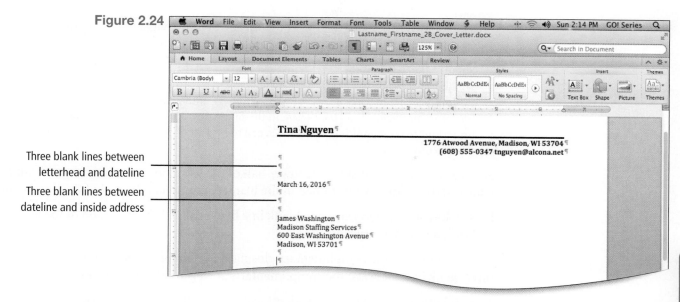

Three blank lines between
letterhead and dateline

Three blank lines between
dateline and inside address

4 Type the salutation **Dear Mr. Washington:** and then press Return two times.

Always leave one blank line above and below the salutation.

5 Type, exactly as shown, the following opening paragraph that includes an intentional word usage error: **I am seeking a position in witch I can use my** and press Spacebar. Type, exactly as shown, **computr** and then watch *computr* as you press Spacebar.

The AutoCorrect feature recognizes the misspelled word, and then changes *computr* to *computer* when you press Spacebar, Return, or a punctuation mark.

6 Type the following, including the misspelled last word: **and communication skills. My education, outlined on the enclosed resumee** and then type **,** (a comma). Notice that when you type the comma, AutoCorrect replaces *resumee* with *resume*.

7 Press Spacebar. Complete the paragraph by typing **includes a Business Software Applications Specialist certificate from MATC.** Compare your screen with Figure 2.25.

Figure 2.25

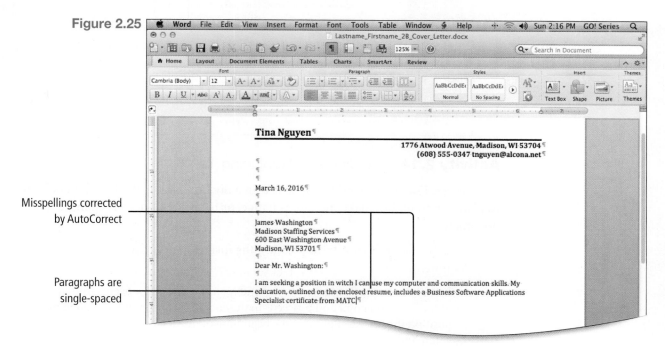

Misspellings corrected
by AutoCorrect

Paragraphs are
single-spaced

8 Press Return two times. On the **Insert** menu, click **File**. Navigate to your student files, locate and **Insert** the file **w02B_Cover_Letter_Text**.

> Some of the words in the cover letter text display red wavy underlines. These indicate possible spelling or word usage errors, and you will correct them before the end of this project. Green wavy lines indicate possible grammatical errors. Some word usage errors are not flagged, such as *witch*, in the first paragraph of the body of the letter. It is important that you not rely solely on Word to find all of errors in a document; you still need to proofread.

9 Scroll as necessary to display the lower half of the letter on your screen, and be sure your insertion point is positioned in the blank paragraph at the end of the document.

10 Press Return one time to leave one blank line between the last paragraph of the letter and the complimentary closing.

11 Type **Sincerely,** as the complimentary closing, and then press Return four times to leave three blank lines between the complimentary closing and the writer's identification.

12 Type **Tina Nguyen** as the writer's identification, and then press Return two times.

13 Type **Enclosure** to indicate that a document is included with the letter. **Save** 🖫 your document, and then compare your screen with Figure 2.26.

Figure 2.26

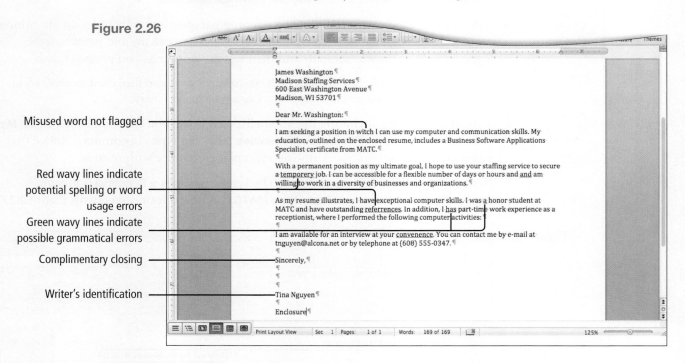

Misused word not flagged

Red wavy lines indicate potential spelling or word usage errors

Green wavy lines indicate possible grammatical errors

Complimentary closing

Writer's identification

Activity 2.14 | Finding and Replacing Text

Use the Find command to locate text in a document quickly. Use the Find and Replace command to make the same change, or to make numerous changes in a document.

1 Press Command ⌘ + fn + ← to position the insertion point at the beginning of the document.

> Because a find operation—or a find and replace operation—begins from the location of the insertion point and proceeds to the end of the document, it is good practice to position the insertion point at the beginning of the document before initiating the command.

Another Way

Press Command ⌘ + F
to place the insertion
point in the Search box.

2 On the right side of the Standard toolbar, click in the **Search in Document** box, and then type **ac** If necessary, scroll down slightly in your document to view the entire body text of the letter, and then compare your screen with Figure 2.27.

> In the document, the search letters *ac* are selected and highlighted in yellow for all three words that contain the letters *ac* together. The first occurrence of *ac* is selected—it has a slight gray background color in the highlighted letters. On the right side of the Search box are navigation arrows that enable you to quickly move to and select the next or previous occurrence of the search term in the document. On the left side of the Search box is the Find button—magnifying glass—which gives you more options when searching or finding text.

Figure 2.27

Find button

Search in Document box
with search text entered

Navigation arrows

Matches found in the
document; first match
selected

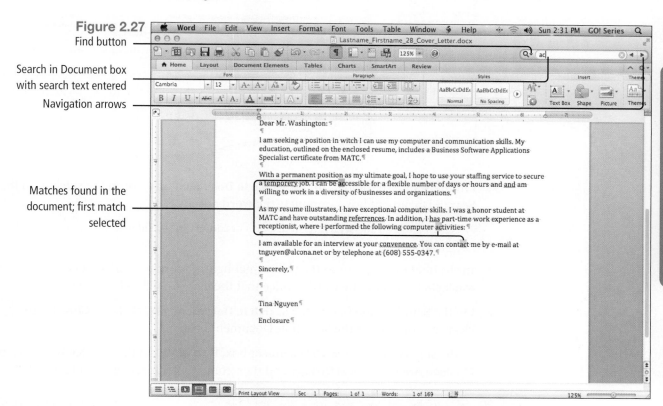

3 Click the **Find** button 🔍, click **List Matches in Sidebar**, and then compare your screen with Figure 2.28.

> The sidebar displays three different areas to accomplish tasks. Matches for the *ac* search text also display highlighted in yellow. To display the match for the second occurrence, in the sidebar, point to the second grouping to fully display the match and surrounding text.

Figure 2.28

Close button for sidebar ——

Sidebar ——

Search text ——

Replace With box ——

3 matches for *ac* ——

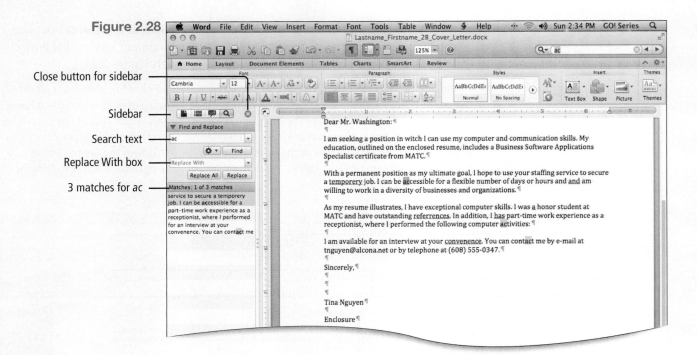

4 On the Standard toolbar, in the **Search in Document** box—or in the sidebar, in the Search Document box—complete the word **accessible**

One match for the search term displays in context in the sidebar and is highlighted in the document.

5 In the document, point to the yellow highlighted word *accessible*, click, and then type **available** to replace the word. Notice that the list of matches is now empty.

6 On the Standard toolbar, in the **Search in Document** box, click the **Close** button to clear the contents of the Search in Document box.

7 In the sidebar, in the **Search Document** box, type **MATC** In the **Replace With** box, type **Madison Area Technical College** and then compare your screen with Figure 2.29.

Figure 2.29

Two matches found for MATC ——

Replacement text ——

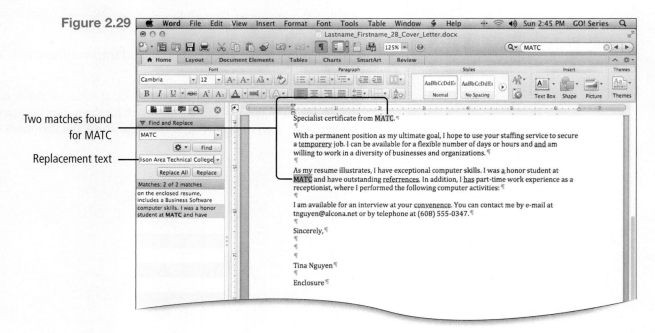

8 In the sidebar, above the *Replace With* box, click the **Actions** button ⚙▾, and then click **Advanced Find & Replace**. In the **Find and Replace** dialog box, click the **Replace tab**. In the bottom left corner, click the **More** arrow ▼ to expand the dialog box, and then under **Search**, click to select the **Match case** check box.

> The acronym *MATC* appears in the document two times. In a formal letter, the reader may not know what the acronym means, so you should include the full text instead of an acronym. In this instance, you must select the *Match case* check box so that the replaced text will match the case you typed in the Replace With box, and *not* display in all uppercase letters in the manner of *MATC*.

9 In the **Find and Replace** dialog box—not the sidebar—click the **Replace All** button to replace both instances of *MATC*. A message box displays that states *2 replacements were made*. Click **Yes** to continue searching at the beginning of the document, and then click **OK** to close the message boxes.

10 In the **Find and Replace** dialog box, clear the **Match case** check box, click the **Less** arrow ▲, and then **Close** 🔵 the **Find and Replace** dialog box. **Close** ⊗ the sidebar. On the Standard toolbar, in the **Search in Document** box, click the **Close** ⊗ button to clear the box.

> The Find and Replace dialog box opens with the settings used the last time it was open. Thus, it is good practice to reset this dialog box to its default settings each time you use it.

11 **Save** 💾 your document.

Activity 2.15 | Selecting and Moving Text to a New Location

By using Word's ***drag-and-drop*** feature, you can use the mouse to drag selected text from one location to another. Drag-and-drop is most effective when the text to be moved and the destination are on the same screen.

1 Take a moment to study the table in Figure 2.30 to become familiar with the techniques you can use to select text in a document quickly.

Selecting Text in a Document

To Select	Do This
A portion of text	Click to position the insertion point at the beginning of the text you want to select, hold down Shift, and then click at the end of the text you want to select. Alternatively, press down on the mouse and drag from the beginning to the end of the text you want to select.
A word	Double-click the word.
A sentence	Hold down Command ⌘ and click anywhere in the sentence.
A paragraph	Triple-click anywhere in the paragraph; or, move the pointer to the left of the paragraph, into the margin area. When the ⬈ pointer displays, double-click.
A line	Move the pointer to the left of the line. When the ⬈ pointer displays, click one time.
One character at a time	Position the insertion point to the left of the first character, hold down Shift, and press ← or → as many times as desired.
A string of words	Position the insertion point to the left of the first word, hold down Option and Shift, and then press ← or → as many times as desired.
Consecutive lines	Position the insertion point to the left of the first line or word, hold down Shift and press ↑ or ↓.
Consecutive paragraphs	Position the insertion point to the left of the first line orword, hold down Shift and Command ⌘ and press ↑ or ↓.
The entire document	Hold down Command ⌘ and press A. Alternatively, move the pointer to the left of any line in the document. When the ⬈ pointer displays, triple-click.

Figure 2.30

2 Be sure you can view the entire body of the letter on your screen. In the paragraph that begins *With a permanent position*, in the second line, locate and double-click *days*.

3 Point to the selected word to display the ⬈ pointer.

4 Drag to the right until the insertion point and dimmed words are positioned to the right of the word *hours* in the same line. Release the mouse button to move the text. Notice that the **Paste Options** button 📋 displays.

5 On the same line, select the word *hours* and drag it to the left of the word *or*—the previous location of the word *days*. Click anywhere in the document to deselect the text.

6 Examine the text that you moved, and add or remove spaces, if necessary.

7 Hold down Command ⌘, and then in the paragraph that begins *I am available*, click anywhere in the first sentence to select the entire sentence.

8 Drag the selected sentence to the end of the paragraph by positioning the insertion point to the right of the period following the phone number. Compare your screen with Figure 2.31.

Figure 2.31

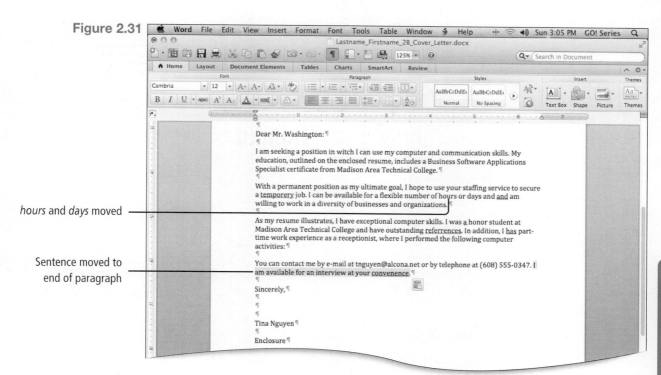

hours and *days* moved

Sentence moved to
end of paragraph

9 **Save** 💾 your document.

Activity 2.16 │ Indenting Text and Adding Space After Paragraphs

1 Locate the paragraph that begins *As my resume*, and then click to position the
insertion point in the blank line below that paragraph. Press Return one time.

2 On the Ribbon, click the **Tables tab**. In the **Table Options group**, click the **New** button.
In the **Table** grid, in the third row, click the second square to insert a 2 x 3 Table.

3 In the first cell of the table, type **Microsoft Access** and then press Tab. Type
Queried inventory data and then press Tab. Complete the table using the following
information:

Microsoft Excel	**Entered budget data**
Microsoft Word	**Created and mailed form letters**

4 Point slightly outside of the upper left corner of the table to display the **table move
handle** button ⊞. Point to the **table move handle** button ⊞ to display the ✛ pointer,
and then click one time to select the entire table.

5 On the **Table Layout tab**, in the **Cell Size group**, click the **AutoFit** button, and then
click **AutoFit to Contents** to have Word adjust the column widths for the two columns
based on the text you entered.

6 On the **Home tab**, in the **Paragraph group**, click the **Center Text** button 🗒 to center
the table between the left and right margins.

7 On the **Tables tab**, in the **Draw Borders group**, click the **Borders arrow**, and then click
None. Click anywhere to cancel the selection of the table, and then compare your
screen with Figure 2.32.

A light gray or dimmed line displays in place of the original table borders.

Figure 2.32

Table inserted in letter, no borders—dimmed

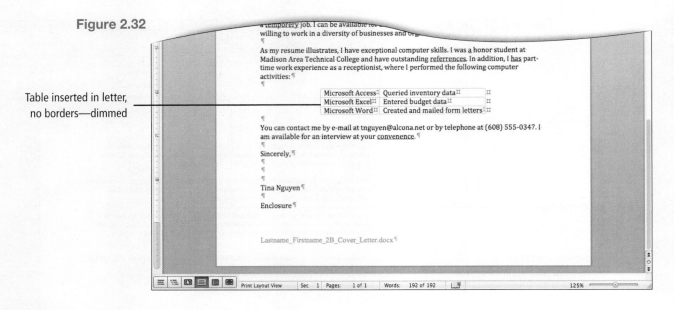

willing to work in a diversity of businesses and org

As my resume illustrates, I have exceptional computer skills. I was a honor student at Madison Area Technical College and have outstanding references. In addition, I has part-time work experience as a receptionist, where I performed the following computer activities: ¶

¶

Microsoft Access	Queried inventory data
Microsoft Excel	Entered budget data
Microsoft Word	Created and mailed form letters

¶

You can contact me by e-mail at tnguyen@alcona.net or by telephone at (608) 555-0347. I am available for an interview at your convenence. ¶

¶

Sincerely, ¶

¶

¶

¶

Tina Nguyen ¶

¶

Enclosure ¶

Lastname_Firstname_2B_Cover_Letter.docx ¶

Print Layout View   Sec   1   Pages: 1 of 1   Words: 192 of 192   125%

8   **Save** 💾 your document.

Objective 6 | Use the Proofing Options

Word compares your typing to words in the Office dictionary and compares your phrases and punctuation to a list of grammar rules. This automatic proofing is set by default. Words that are not in the dictionary are marked with a wavy red underline. Phrases and punctuation that differ from the grammar rules are marked with a wavy green underline.

However, Word will not flag the word *sign* as misspelled even though you intended to type *sing a song* rather than *sign a song*, because both are words contained within Word's dictionary. Your own knowledge and proofreading skills are still required, even when using a sophisticated Word processing program like Word.

Activity 2.17 | Checking Spelling and Grammar Errors

There are three ways to respond to spelling and grammar errors flagged by Word. You can point to the word, press Control and click a flagged word or phrase, and then from the shortcut menu choose a correction or action. You can click the 🖹 icon on the status bar, and then from the shortcut menu choose a correction or action. Or, you can initiate the Spelling and Grammar command to display the Spelling and Grammar dialog box, which provides more options than the shortcut menus.

Alert! | **Is Your Spelling and Grammar Checking Activated?**

If you do not see any wavy red or green lines under words, the automatic spelling and/or grammar checking has been turned off on your system. To activate the spelling and grammar checking, on the Word menu, click Preferences. Under Authoring and Proofing Tools, click Spelling and Grammar. Under Spelling, be sure *Check spelling as you type* and *Always suggest corrections* are selected. Be sure that *Hide spelling errors in this document* is **not** selected. Under Grammar, be sure that *Check grammar as you type* and *Check grammar with spelling* are selected. Be sure that *Hide grammatical errors in this document* is **not** selected. If you make changes in the Spelling and Grammar dialog box, to display the flagged spelling and grammar errors, click the Recheck Document button, and then click OK to close the dialog box.

---

1 Press `Command ⌘` + `fn` + `←` to position the insertion point at the beginning of the document. Scroll to display the body of the letter on your screen, and then examine the text to locate the red and green wavy underlines. Compare your screen with Figure 2.33.

> A list of grammar rules applied by a computer program like Word can never be exact, and a computer dictionary cannot contain all known words and proper names. Thus, you will need to check any words flagged by Word with wavy underlines, and you will also need to proofread for content errors.

Figure 2.33

Word usage problem not flagged

Red wavy underline indicates possible spelling problem

Green wavy underline indicates possible grammatical problem

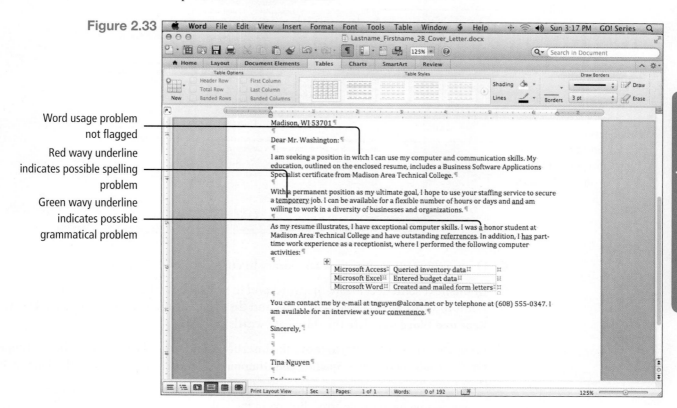

2 In the status bar, locate and point to the [icon] icon to display the ScreenTip *Spelling and Grammar Status*.

> If this button displays with a red X, you know there are possible errors identified in the document.

3 Click the [icon] icon, and then compare your screen with Figure 2.34.

> A shortcut menu displays for the first possible error—*temporery*—that is located to the right of the insertion point. The shortcut menu suggests a correction for the misspelled word. If another word is selected, you did not have the insertion point at the top of the document before completing this step.

Figure 2.34

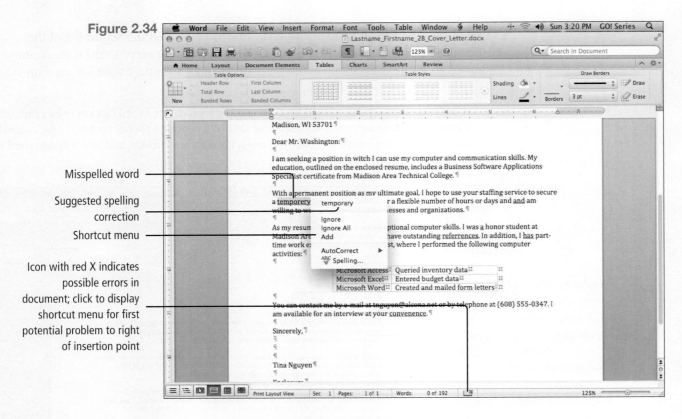

Misspelled word

Suggested spelling correction

Shortcut menu

Icon with red X indicates possible errors in document; click to display shortcut menu for first potential problem to right of insertion point

4 On the shortcut menu, click **temporary** to correct the spelling error.

5 In the next sentence, locate the word *and* that displays with a wavy red underline. Point to word, press Control and click, and then from the shortcut menu, click **Delete Repeated Word** to delete the duplicate word.

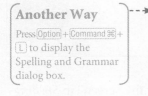

Another Way

Press Option + Command ⌘ + L to display the Spelling and Grammar dialog box.

6 Press Command ⌘ + fn + ← to move the insertion point to the beginning of the document. On the **Tools** menu, click **Spelling and Grammar**. Compare your screen with Figure 2.35.

The word *referrences* is highlighted—a *possible spelling error*—and the sentence containing the possible error displays in the dialog box. A suggested change also displays. Similar to the Find command, position the insertion point at the beginning of the document before you initiate the Spelling and Grammar check command.

Figure 2.35

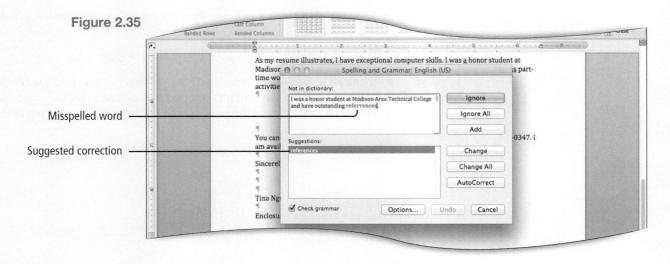

Misspelled word

Suggested correction

7 In the **Spelling and Grammar** dialog box, click the **Change** button to change the spelling to *references*.

The next marked word—a possible grammatical error—displays.

8 Click the **Change** button to change *a* to *an*. Continue the spelling and grammar check and change *has* to *have* and correct the spelling of *convenence* to *convenience*.

9 In the message box that indicates *The spelling and grammar check is complete*, click **OK**.

10 In the first sentence of the body of the letter, locate and double-click *witch* to select the word. Type **which** to correct the spelling of the word that was not found by Word.

11 **Save** 💾 your document.

Activity 2.18 │ Using the Thesaurus

A *thesaurus* is a research tool that lists *synonyms*—words that have the same or similar meaning to the word you selected.

1 Scroll so that you can view the body of the letter. In the paragraph that begins *With a permanent*, point to the word *diversity*, and then press Control and click to display a shortcut menu.

2 On the shortcut menu, point to **Synonyms**, and then compare your screen with Figure 2.36.

A list of synonyms displays; the list will vary in length depending on the selected word.

Figure 2.36

List of synonyms for *diversity*

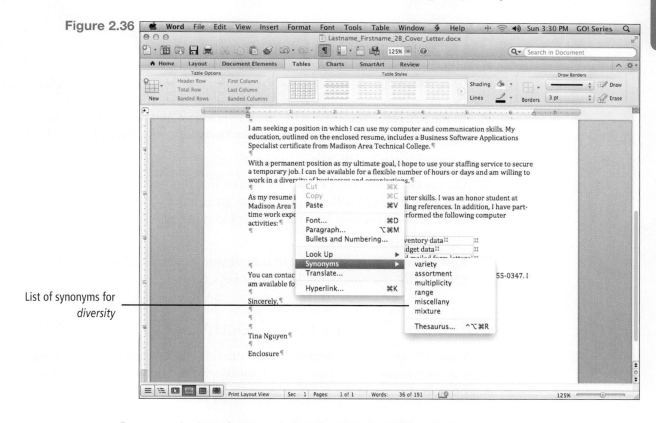

3 From the list of synonyms, click **variety** to replace *diversity* with *variety*.

Another Way

Click in the word, and
on the Tools menu,
click Thesaurus. Or
press Control + Option +
Command ⌘ + R.

4 In the paragraph that begins *As my resume illustrates*, point to the word *exceptional*, press Control and click. In the shortcut menu, point to **Synonyms**, and then click **Thesaurus** to display the **Reference Tools** task pane. Compare your screen with Figure 2.37.

The Reference Tools task pane gives you more options than the shortcut menu.

Figure 2.37

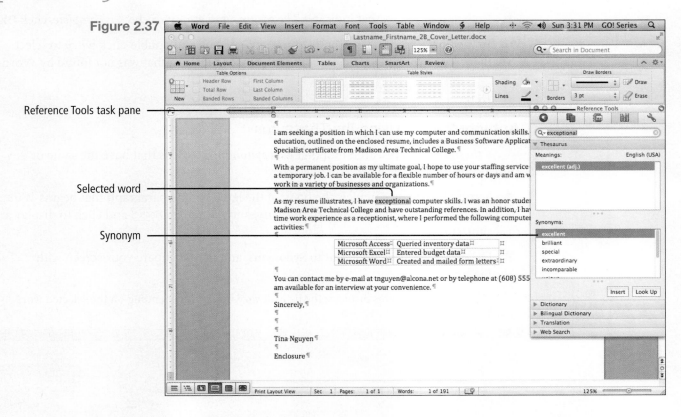

Reference Tools task pane

Selected word

Synonym

5 In the **Reference Tools** task pane, under **Synonyms**, be sure *excellent* is selected, and then click **Insert**. **Close** the **Reference Tools** task pane. **Save** your document.

excellent replaces the word *exceptional*.

6 On the **File** menu, click **Properties**. Notice that this document retained the properties that were included with the original document that was used to create this cover letter. In the **Keywords** box, replace any existing text with **cover letter** and then click **OK**.

7 **Save** your document. **Print** or submit your document electronically as directed. **Close** the document, but leave Word open.

Objective 7 | Create a Document Using a Template

Microsoft provides predesigned templates for letters, resumes, invoices, and other types of documents. When you open a template, it opens unnamed so that you can reuse it as often as you need to.

Activity 2.19 | Locating and Opening a Template

If you need to create a short resume quickly, or if you need ideas about how to format your resume, Microsoft Word provides predesigned resume templates. Some templates are available because they are saved on your computer when you install the Office software; many more are available online. After opening a template, you can add text as indicated, modify the layout and design, and add or remove resume elements.

Another Way

Press Shift +
Command ⌘ + P.

1   In the Word application, on the **File** menu, click **New from Template** to display the **Word Document Gallery**.

2   In the sidebar under **Print Layout View**, click **Resumes**.

3   In the Word Document Gallery, if necessary, click the Blocks Resume. Notice that a preview of the *Blocks Resume* template displays on the right. Compare your screen with Figure 2.38.

Figure 2.38

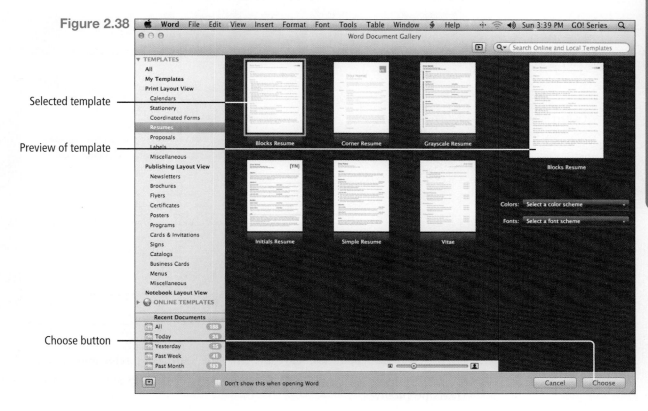

Selected template

Preview of template

Choose button

4   In the lower right corner, click the **Choose** button. If necessary, increase the size of the window by clicking the Zoom button or by dragging the lower right corner of the window. On the Standard toolbar, change the **Zoom** setting to **125%** to enlarge the display of the active document.

The template opens a copy of itself in the form of a new Word document—the title bar indicates *Document* followed by a number. Recall that you are not opening the template itself, and that changes you make to this new document will not affect the contents of the template file.

5   Display the **Save As** dialog box. **Save** the document in your **Word Chapter 2** folder as **Lastname_Firstname_2B_Brief_Resume** and then in the **Footer** area—called the *First Page Footer* in this template—**Insert** the **Filename**. **Close** the **First Page Footer** area. Notice that the file name displays aligned with the right margin.

6   **Save** 🖫 your document.

Activity 2.20 | Replacing Template Placeholder Text

After you save the template file as a Word document, you can begin to substitute your own information in the indicated locations. You can also remove unneeded resume elements that are included with the template.

1 Press [Command ⌘] + [fn] + [←] to move the insertion point to the top of the document, and then compare your screen with Figure 2.39.

> At the top of the document, the name and contact information are located in the Header area—called the First Page Header in this template. The first line typically displays the name of the computer user or computer as indicated on the right side of the menu bar.

Figure 2.39

Zoom changed to 125%

Computer or user name (yours will differ) in header area

Contact information in header area

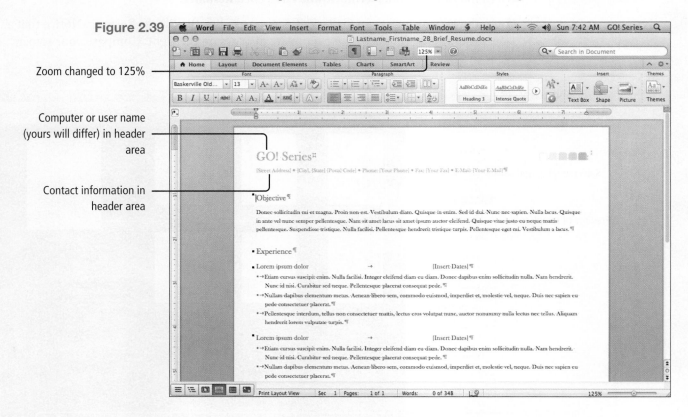

2 In the **Header** area, double-click the first line. Notice the **table move handle** ⊞—the first line and the boxes at the right side are inserted into table cells to better align the text and pictures.

3 Select the displayed user or computer name—GO! Series for this example—and replace the text by typing **Tina Nguyen**

4 In the **First Page Header** area, under *Tina Nguyen*, click anywhere in the Street Address control *[Street Address]*. Type **1776 Atwood Avenue** and then compare your screen with Figure 2.40.

> Text surrounded by brackets is called a ***content control***. There are several different types of content controls, including date, picture, and ***text controls***. Most of the controls in this template are text controls. For the contact information at the top of the document, all of the text controls are grouped together. Each control has ***placeholder text***, text that indicates the type of information to be entered.

Figure 2.40

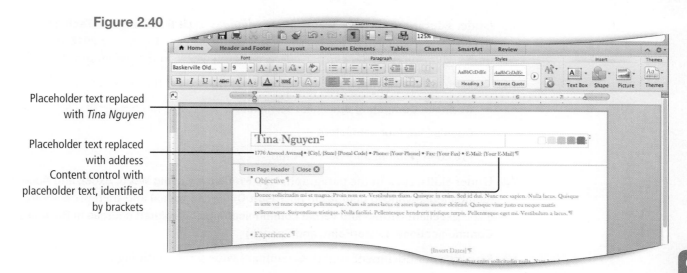

Placeholder text replaced with *Tina Nguyen*

Placeholder text replaced with address

Content control with placeholder text, identified by brackets

5 Click anywhere in the content control *[City]*. Type **Madison** and notice that the comma following *Madison* is included in the template.

6 Complete the contact information by using the following information:

[State]	**WI**
[Postal Code]	**53704**
[Your Phone]	**(608) 555-0347**
[Your Fax]	(skip this control)
[Your E-Mail]	**tnguyen@alcona.net**

7 **Close** the **First Page Header** area. Under *Objective*, click anywhere in the paragraph, and then type **To obtain a position using my computer and communications skills.**

8 Under **Experience**, click the text *Lorem ipsum dolor*, type **The Robinson Company** and then click in the *[Insert Dates]* control. Type **September 2014 to present** and then under *The Robinson Company*, click anywhere in the first bulleted paragraph.

9 Type **Office Assistant (part-time)** and then press Return. Type **Data entry and report generation using company spreadsheets and databases.** Compare your screen with Figure 2.41.

Figure 2.41

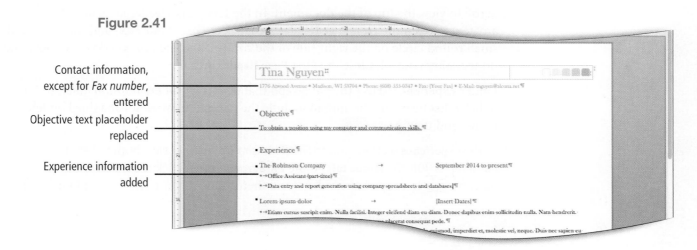

Contact information, except for *Fax number*, entered

Objective text placeholder replaced

Experience information added

Word | Chapter 2

10 Under **Education**, click the text *Aliquam dapibus*, type **Madison Area Technical College** and then click in the *[Insert Dates]* control. Type **December 2015** and then under *Madison Area Technical College*, click anywhere in the paragraph.

11 Type the following, pressing ⟨Return⟩ after every line *except* the last line:

Business Computing Specialist certificate

Dean's List, four semesters

President, Community Service Club

12 Under **Skills**, click in the paragraph, type **Proficiency using Word, Excel, and Access (completed advanced courses in Microsoft Office programs)** and then press ⟨Return⟩. Type **Excellent written and verbal communications (completed courses in Business Communications, PowerPoint, and Speech)**

13 **Save** 🖫 your document, and then compare your screen with Figure 2.42.

Figure 2.42

Placeholder text replaced under *Education* and *Skills*

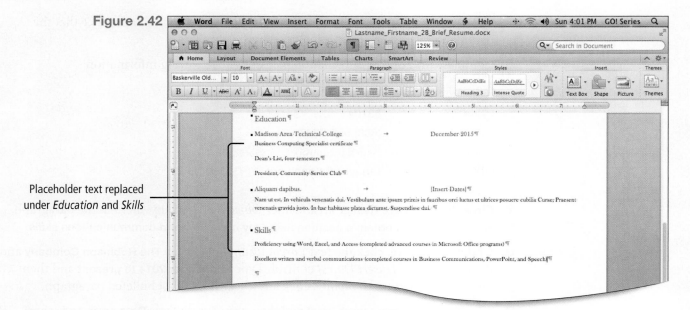

Activity 2.21 | Removing Template Controls and Formatting the Resume

1 Scroll to view the top of the document. In the **First Page Header** area, double-click any text to open the **First Page Header** area. Select *Fax: [Your Fax]* and the space and small round circle on the right side of the control, and then press ⟨Delete⟩ to remove the unnecessary control. **Close** the **First Page Header** area.

2 Under **Experience**, select the paragraph that begins with *Lorem ipsum dolor* and the bulleted list below it—be sure to include the paragraph mark for the third bulleted item—and then press ⟨Delete⟩.

3 In the **Experience** section, under *The Robinson Company*, select both bulleted paragraphs. On the **Home tab**, in the **Paragraph group**, click the **Bulleted List** button 📋▾ to remove the bullets, and then compare your screen with Figure 2.43.

Figure 2.43

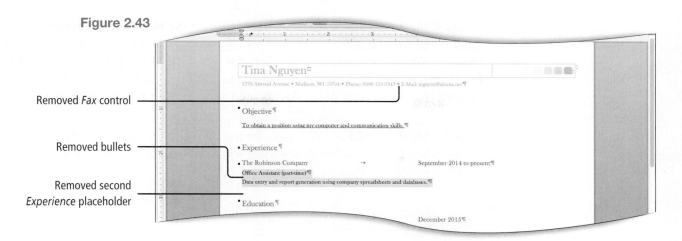

Removed *Fax* control

Removed bullets

Removed second
Experience placeholder

4   Under **Education**, select the paragraph that begins with *Aliquam dapibus* and the paragraph below it—be sure to include the paragraph marks—and then press Delete.

5   In the **Education** section, under *Madison Area Technical College*, select the three paragraphs that begin with *Business*, *Dean's*, and *President*. On the **Home tab**, in the **Paragraph group**, click the **Bulleted List** button ▣ ▾, and then click the **Decrease Indent** button ▣. Click the **Line Spacing** button ▣▾, and then click **Line Spacing Options**. In the **Paragraph** dialog box, under **Spacing**, change **After** to **0**, and then click **OK**.

6   With the three bulleted items still selected, on the Standard toolbar, click the **Format Painter** button ▣. Under **Skills**, point to the left of the first paragraph to display the ▣ pointer, and then drag down to select the two paragraphs under *Skills*. **Save** ▣ your document, and then compare your screen with Figure 2.44.

This action copies the formatting of the bulleted items—bulleted list with decreased indent and spacing after set at 0—under *Education* to the two paragraphs under *Skills*.

Figure 2.44

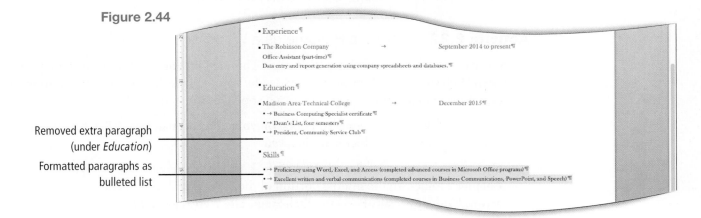

Removed extra paragraph
(under *Education*)

Formatted paragraphs as
bulleted list

7   Click anywhere to cancel the selection. On the **Layout tab**, in the **Margins group**, change the **Top** margin to **2**, the **Bottom** margin to **1**, the **Left** margin to **1**, and the **Right** margin to **1** to make this short resume better fill the page.

8 Double-click in the **First Page Header** area to open the **First Page Header** area. Select all of the text in the header, and then press Command ⌘ + X to cut—remove—the text. **Close** the **First Page Header** area. Click to the left of the *O* in *Objective* to place the insertion point there. Press Command ⌘ + V to paste the text that was in the First Page Header area to the body of the document. Compare your screen with Figure 2.45.

> The header information displays when you print the document; however, in preparation for saving the resume as a Web page, the text must be moved into the body of the document because the header and footer text will not display in a document that is saved as a Web page.

Figure 2.45

Text moved from Header area to body of document

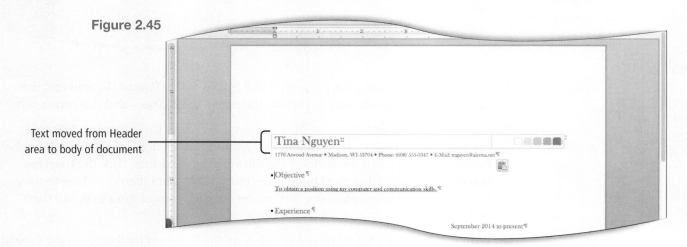

9 On the **File** menu, click **Properties**. In the **Subject** box, type your course name and section number. In the **Author** box, delete any text and then type your firstname and lastname. In the **Keywords** box, type **short resume, template** and then click **OK**.

10 **Save** 🖫 your document, and then **Print** or submit the document electronically as directed. Leave the resume displayed on your screen.

Activity 2.22 | Saving a Resume as a Web Page

You can save your resume as a Web page. This enables you to post the Web page on your own Web site or on Web space provided by your college. It also enables you to send the resume as an email attachment that can be opened using any Web browser.

1 With your **2B_Brief_Resume** still open on your screen, click **Save** 🖫 to be sure the current version of the document is saved.

2 On the **File** menu, click **Save As Web Page**. If necessary, navigate to the **Word Chapter 2** folder. In the middle portion of the **Save As** dialog box, click the **Format arrow**. Under **Specialty Formats**, click **Single File Web Page (.mht)**.

> A *Single File Web Page* is a document saved using the *Hypertext Markup Language (HTML)*. HTML is the language used to format documents that can be opened using a Web browser such as Safari, Firefox, or Internet Explorer. If you save the document with an .htm extension, pictures and other page elements are stored in a separate folder along with the .htm file.

3 At the top of the dialog box, in the **Save As** box, type **Lastname_Firstname_2B_ HTML_Resume** Click **Save**, and then notice that the Web page displays in the Word application. Also notice, that the footer with the filename does not display; however, it will print if printed using the Word application.

4 On the **File** menu, click **Properties**. In the **Subject** box, be sure your course name and section number display. In the **Author** box, be sure your first and last names display. In the **Keywords** box, replace the existing text with **HTML** and then click **OK. Save** 🖫 the document, and then **Print** or submit the document electronically as directed.

5 On the **File** menu, click **Web Page Preview**. Compare your screen with Figure 2.46.

Your Web browser opens and displays the resume. Your display may differ depending upon the Web browser that is installed on your computer. The footer with the Filename does not display, nor will it print.

Figure 2.46

Resume displayed in a Web browser (yours may differ)

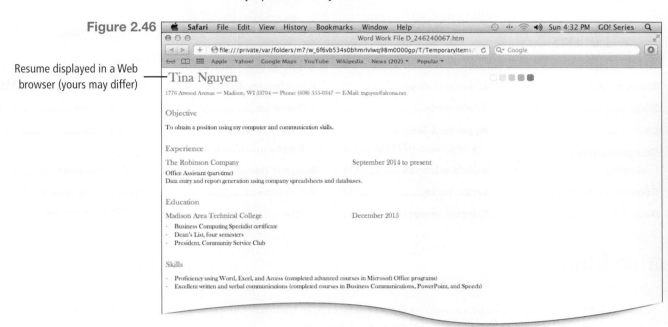

6 **Close** ⊙ the Web page, and then **Quit** your browser. **Close** ⊙ the document, and then **Quit Word**.

End **You have completed Project 2B**

Word | Chapter 2

Content-Based Assessments

Summary

In this chapter, you created a table, and then used the table to create a resume. You created a letterhead template, and then created a document using a copy of the letterhead template. You created a cover letter for the resume, moved text, corrected spelling and grammar, and used the built-in thesaurus. Finally, you created a short resume using a template, and you also saved the resume as a Web page.

Key Terms

AutoCorrect..............135
Body....................135
Cell 117
Complimentary
    closing 135
Content control 150
Date line................135

Drag-and-drop 141
Enclosures 135
Hypertext Markup
    Language (HTML) ...154
Inside address...........135
Letterhead...............132
Normal template........132

Placeholder text 150
Salutation..................135
Single File Web
    Page.......................154
Subject line 135
Synonyms..................147
Table 117

Template 132
Text control..............150
Thesaurus 147
Writer's
    identification..........135
Writer's signature
    block 135

Matching

Match each term in the second column with its correct definition in the first column by writing the letter of the term on the blank line in front of the correct definition.

_____ 1. An arrangement of information organized into rows and columns.

_____ 2. The box at the intersection of a row and column in a table.

_____ 3. A document structure that opens a copy of itself, opens unnamed, and is used as the starting point for another document.

_____ 4. The template that serves as a basis for all new Word documents.

_____ 5. The personal or company information that displays at the top of a letter.

_____ 6. Text in a content control that indicates the type of information to be entered in a specific location.

_____ 7. The first line in a business letter that contains the current date and that is positioned just below the letterhead if a letterhead is used.

_____ 8. The name and address of the person receiving a letter and positioned below the date line.

_____ 9. The greeting line of a letter.

_____ 10. A parting farewell in a letter.

_____ 11. The name and title of the author of a letter, placed near the bottom of the letter under the complimentary closing.

_____ 12. The optional line following the inside address in a business letter that states the purpose of the letter.

_____ 13. Additional documents included with a business letter.

_____ 14. A Word feature that corrects common spelling errors as you type, for example changing *teh* to *the*.

_____ 15. A technique by which you can move, by dragging, selected text from one location in a document to another.

A AutoCorrect

B Cell

C Complimentary
    closing

D Date line

E Drag and drop

F Enclosures

G Inside address

H Letterhead

I Normal template

J Placeholder text

K Salutation

L Subject line

M Table

N Template

O Writer's
    identification

Content-Based Assessments

Multiple Choice

Circle the correct answer.

1. When you create a table, the width of all of cells in the table is:
   A. equal   B. proportional   C. 1 inch

2. To indicate words that might be misspelled because they are not in Word's dictionary, Word flags text with:
   A. blue wavy underlines   B. green wavy underlines   C. red wavy underlines

3. To indicate possible grammar errors, Word flags text with:
   A. blue wavy underlines   B. green wavy underlines   C. red wavy underlines

4. To use an existing document without affecting the original document, open it as a:
   A. copy   B. original   C. read-only

5. A research tool that provides a list of words with similar meanings is:
   A. a thesaurus   B. a dictionary   C. an encyclopedia

6. A word with the same or similar meaning as another word is:
   A. an acronym   B. a search term   C. a synonym

7. In a template, an area indicated by placeholder text into which you can add text, pictures, dates, or lists is a:
   A. text control   B. content control   C. quick control

8. A document saved in HTML, which can be opened using a Web browser, is a:
   A. Web page   B. template   C. resume

9. Using drag-and-drop to move text is most useful when both the text and the destination are on the same:
   A. document   B. section   C. screen

10. To locate specific text in a document quickly, use the:
    A. Find command   B. Replace command   C. Locate command

Apply **2A** skills from
these Objectives:

1 Create a Table
2 Add Text to a Table
3 Format a Table

Skills Review | Project **2C** Student Resume

In the following Skills Review, you will use a table to create a resume for Marissa Johnston. Your completed resume will look similar to Figure 2.47.

Project Files

For Project 2C, you will need the following files:

> **New blank Word document**
> w02C_Skills
> w02C_Experience

You will save your document as:

> Lastname_Firstname_2C_Student_Resume

Project Results

Marissa Johnston

2274 West Pond Street
Sun Prairie, WI 53590
(608) 555-1947
johnstonm@alcona.net

OBJECTIVE	A technical writing position with a technology manufacturing firm that requires good communication and design skills.
SKILLS	**Technical Writing**
	• Technical Writer, Madison Area Technical College IT Department
	• Technical Writer, MATC Faculty and Staff Development Center
	• Reporter, MATC, college newspaper
	• Science and Technology Writer, Sun Prairie High School paper
	Leadership
	• Secretary, MATC Writer's Club
	• Treasurer, Amateur Radio Club, Sun Prairie High School
	Computer Proficiencies
	• Microsoft Office
	• Adobe InDesign
	• Adobe Acrobat Pro
EXPERIENCE	**Technical Writer** (part-time), Madison Area Public Library main computer lab, Madison, WI September 2015 to present
	Summer Assistant, Sun Prairie Library, Madison, WI June 2013to August 2015
EDUCATION	**Madison Area Technical College**, English major, Technical Writing August 2015 to present
	Graduate of Sun Prairie High School June 2015

Lastname_Firstname_2C_Student_Resume.docx

Figure 2.47

(Project 2C Student Resume continues on the next page)

Skills Review | Project **2C** Student Resume (continued)

1 Open **Word**. In a new blank document, be sure that nonprinting characters and rulers display. If necessary, on the Standard toolbar, change the Zoom setting to 125%. On the **Home tab**, in the **Paragraph group**, click the **Line Spacing** button and then click **1.15**. In the **Font group**, click the **Font Size arrow**, and then click **11**. On the Ribbon, click the **Layout tab**, and in the **Margins group**, change the **Left** and **Right** margins to **1**. **Save** the document in your **Word Chapter 2** folder as **Lastname_Firstname_2C_Student_Resume**

a. In the **Footer** area, **Insert** the **Filename**, and then **Close** the **Footer** area. Click the **Tables tab**, and then in the **Table Options group**, click the **New** button. In the **Table** grid, in the fourth row, click the second square to insert a 2 × 4 Table.

b. In the first cell of the table, type **Marissa Johnston** and then press Return. Type the following text, pressing Return after each line *except* the last line:

2274 West Pond Street

Sun Prairie, WI 53590

(608) 555-1947

johnstonm@alcona.net

c. Press ↓ to move to the first cell in the second row. On the Standard toolbar, click the **Undo** button to remove the hyperlink from the email address. Type **SKILLS** and then press ↓ to move to the first cell in the third row.

d. Type **EXPERIENCE** and then press ↓. Type **EDUCATION**

e. **Save** your document.

2 Click in the cell to the right of the cell that displays *SKILLS*, and then type the following, pressing Return after each item, including the last item:

> Technical Writing
>
> Technical Writer, Madison Area Technical College
> > IT Department
>
> Technical Writer, MATC Faculty and Staff
> > Development Center
>
> Reporter, MATC, college newspaper
>
> Science and Technology Writer, Sun Prairie High
> > School paper

a. With the insertion point in the blank line at the bottom of the cell, on the **Insert** menu, click **File**. Navigate to your student files, select **w02C_Skills**, and then click **Insert**. Press Delete one time to remove the blank line.

(Project 2C Student Resume continues on the next page)

b. In the same cell, click in the first line that begins with *Technical Writing*. On the Standard toolbar, click the **Format Painter** button. Select the paragraphs of the inserted text, beginning with *Leadership* and ending with the last line in the cell.

c. Click in the cell to the right of the cell that displays *EXPERIENCE*, and then **Insert** the **File w02C_Experience**. Press Delete one time to remove the blank line. In the cell to the right of the cell that displays *SKILLS*, click in any paragraph, and then click the **Format Painter** button. In the cell to the right of the cell that displays *EXPERIENCE*, select all of the paragraphs to change the formatting to match the rest of the document.

d. Click in the cell to the right of the cell that displays *EDUCATION*, and then type the following, pressing Return after all items *except* the last item:

Madison Area Technical College, English major,
**   Technical Writing**

August 2015 to present

Graduate of Sun Prairie High School

June 2015

3 Click anywhere in the top row of the table. On the **Table Layout tab**, in the **Rows & Columns group**, click the **Below** button. Type **OBJECTIVE** and then press Tab.

a. Type **A technical writing position with a technology manufacturing firm that requires good communication and design skills.**

b. In any row, point to the vertical border between the two columns to display the ╫ pointer. Drag the column border to the left to approximately **1.75 inches on the horizontal ruler**.

c. Click anywhere in the left column. On the **Table Layout tab**, in the **Settings group**, click the **Properties** button. In the **Table Properties** dialog box, click the **Column tab**. In the **Preferred Width** box, if necessary, type **1.75** and then click **OK**.

d. In the first row of the document, drag across both cells to select them. On the **Table Layout tab**, in the **Merge group**, click the **Merge** button. On the **Home tab**, in the **Paragraph group**, click the **Center Text** button.

e. In the first row, select the first paragraph of text— *Marissa Johnston*. In the **Font group**, change the **Font Size** to **22** and apply **Bold**.

Word | Chapter 2

Skills Review | Project **2C** Student Resume (continued)

f. In the second row, point to the word *OBJECTIVE*, hold down the mouse, and then drag down to select all of the row headings that display in uppercase letters. In the **Font group**, click the **Bold** button. **Save** your document.

4 Click in the cell to the right of the cell that displays *OBJECTIVE*. On the **Home tab**, in the **Paragraph group**, click the **Line Spacing** button, and then click **Line Spacing Options**. In the **Paragraph** dialog box, on the **Indents and Spacing tab**, under **Spacing**, click the **After up spin arrow** three times to change the spacing after the paragraph to **18 pt**. Click **OK**.

a. In the cell to the right of *SKILLS*, apply **Bold** to the words *Technical Writing, Leadership*, and *Computer Proficiencies*. Then, under each bold heading in the cell, select the lines of text, and create a bulleted list.

b. In the first two bulleted lists, click in the last bullet item, and then, set the **Spacing After** to **12 pt**.

c. In the last bulleted list, click in the last bullet item, and then set the **Spacing After** to **18 pt**.

d. In the cell to the right of *EXPERIENCE*, apply **Bold** to *Technical Writer* and *Summer Assistant*. Click in the line *September 2015 to present* and apply **Spacing After** of **12 pt**. Click in the line *June 2013 to August 2015* and apply **Spacing After** of **18 pt**.

e. In the cell to the right of *EDUCATION*, apply **Bold** to *Madison Area Technical College* and *Graduate of Sun Prairie High School*.

f. In the same cell, click in the line *August 2015 to present* and apply **Spacing After** of **12 pt**. Click in the line *June 2015* and apply **Spacing After** of **24 pt**.

g. In the first row, click in the last line—*johnstonm@ alcona.net*—and then change the **Spacing After** to **18 pt**. Click in the first line—*Marissa Johnston*—and set the **Spacing Before** to **24 pt** and the **Spacing After** to **6 pt**.

5 Point to the upper left corner of the table, and then click the **table move handle** button to select the entire table. On the **Tables tab**, in the **Draw Borders group**, click the **Borders arrow**, and then click **None**.

a. On the **Tables tab**, in the **Draw Borders group**, click the **Line Weight** button, and then click **1 1/2 pt**. Click the **Borders arrow** again, and then click **Top**. Click the **Borders arrow** again, and then click **Bottom**. **Save** your document.

b. Click anywhere to cancel the selection. On the **File** menu, click **Properties**. In the **Subject** box, type your course name and section number. In the **Author** box, delete any text and then type your firstname and lastname, and in the **Keywords** box type **resume, table** and then click **OK**.

c. **Save**, and then, as directed by your instructor, **Print** your document or submit it electronically. **Close** the document, and then **Quit Word**.

End **You have completed Project 2C** —————————————————————

Content-Based Assessments

Apply **2B** skills from these Objectives:

4 Create a New Document from an Existing Document

5 Change and Reorganize Text

6 Use the Proofing Options

7 Create a Document Using a Template

Skills Review | Project **2D** Cabrera Letter

In the following Skills Review, you will create a letterhead, and then create a new document from the letterhead to create a resume cover letter. You will also create a short resume using a Microsoft template and save it as a Web page. Your completed documents will look similar to Figure 2.48.

Project Files

For Project 2D, you will need the following files:

> New blank Word document
> w02D_Letter_Text
> Corner Resume Template from Word's installed templates

You will save your documents as:

> Lastname_Firstname_2D_Cabrera_Letterhead
> Lastname_Firstname_2D_Cabrera_Letter
> Lastname_Firstname_2D_Resume
> Lastname_Firstname_2D_Web_Resume

Project Results

Figure 2.48

(Project 2D Cabrera Letter continues on the next page)

Skills Review | Project **2D** Cabrera Letter (continued)

1 Open **Word**. In a new blank document, be sure that nonprinting characters and rulers display. If necessary, on the Standard toolbar, change the Zoom setting to 125%. Change the **Left** and **Right** margins to **1**.

a. Type **Carlos Cabrera** and then press ⟨Return⟩. Type **7719 Reese Drive** and press ⟨Return⟩. Type **Monona, WI 53716** and then press ⟨Return⟩.

b. Type **(608) 555-1447** and then press ⟨Return⟩. Type **ccabrera@alcona.net** and then press ⟨Return⟩ one time. On the Standard toolbar, click **Undo** one time to remove the hyperlink. Press ⟨Return⟩ two more times.

c. Select all five lines of the personal information, but do not select the blank paragraphs. Change the **Font** to **Arial Rounded MT Bold**. On the **Home tab**, in the **Paragraph group**, click the **Align Text Right** button. Select the first paragraph—*Carlos Cabrera*—and then apply **Bold** and change the **Font Size** to **20**.

d. Select the five lines of text you just formatted. On the **Format** menu, click **Borders and Shading**. In the **Borders and Shading** dialog box, under **Style**, be sure that the first style—a single solid line—is selected. Click the **Width arrow**, and then click **3 pt**. In the **Preview** area, click the right border, and then click **OK**.

e. On the **File** menu, click **Save As**. **Save** the document in your **Word Chapter 2** folder as **Lastname_ Firstname_2D_Cabrera_Letterhead**

f. In the **Footer** area, **Insert** the **Filename**, and then **Close** the **Footer** area. On the **File** menu, click **Properties**. In the **Subject** box, type your course name and section number. In the **Author** box, delete any text and then type your firstname and lastname. In the **Keywords** box, type **personal letterhead** and then click **OK**.

g. **Save** your document. **Print** the document, or submit it electronically as directed. **Close** the document, but leave Word open.

2 On the **File** menu, click **Open**. If necessary, navigate to your **Word Chapter 2** folder, and click your **2D_Cabrera_ Letterhead** document to select it. In the lower left corner of the **Open** dialog box, click the **Open** box, click **Copy**, and then click the **Open** button. On the **File** menu, click **Save As**. Navigate to your **Word Chapter 2** folder, and **Save** the file as **Lastname_Firstname_2D_Cabrera_Letter** In the **Footer** area, double-click, and then point to the file

name. Press ⟨Control⟩ and click. On the shortcut menu, click **Update Field**. **Close** the **Footer** area, and then **Save** your document.

a. On the **Word** menu, click **Preferences**. In the **Word Preferences** dialog box, under **Authoring and Proofing Tools**, click **AutoCorrect**.

b. In the **AutoCorrect** dialog box, be sure that the **AutoCorrect tab** is active. Under **Replace**, type **Madisin** and under **With**, type **Madison** Click **Add**. If the entry already exists, click *Replace* instead, and then click Yes. Click **OK** to close the dialog box.

c. Press ⟨Command ⌘⟩ + ⟨fn⟩ + ⟨→⟩ to move to the end of the document, type **May 25, 2016** and then press ⟨Return⟩ four times. Type the following inside address, pressing ⟨Return⟩ after every line, *except* the last line:

Ms. Marilyn Kelly

Madison Staffing Services

600 East Washington Avenue

Madison, WI 53701

d. Press ⟨Return⟩ two times, type **Dear Ms. Kelly:** and then press ⟨Return⟩ two times. On the **Insert** menu, click **File**. Navigate to your student files, locate and insert the file **w02D_Letter_Text**.

e. Scroll to view the lower portion of the page, and be sure your insertion point is in the empty paragraph mark at the end. Press ⟨Return⟩, type **Sincerely,** and then press ⟨Return⟩ four times. Type **Carlos Cabrera** and press ⟨Return⟩ two times. Type **Enclosure** and then **Save** your document.

f. Near the top of the document, locate the paragraph that begins *I am interested in* and click to position the insertion point at the beginning of the paragraph. Type **I recently moved to the** Press ⟨Spacebar⟩, and then type the misspelled word **Madisin** Press ⟨Spacebar⟩ and notice that AutoCorrect corrects the misspelling. Type **area from Minneapolis, and** Press ⟨Spacebar⟩.

g. Press ⟨Command ⌘⟩ + ⟨fn⟩ + ⟨←⟩ to move to the top of the document. On the right side of the Standard toolbar, on the left side of the **Search in Document** box, click the **Find** button. 🔍, and then click **Replace**. In the sidebar, in the **Search Document** box, type **think** In the **Replace with** box, type **believe** and then click **Replace All**. **Close** the **Find and Replace** sidebar.

(Project 2D Cabrera Letter continues on the next page)

Content-Based Assessments

h. In the paragraph that begins *I recently moved*, double-click *job*. Point to the selected word, and then drag the word to the left of *working*. Adjust spacing if necessary.

i. Below the paragraph that begins *I have worked*, click to position the insertion point in the second blank line. On the **Tables tab**, in the **Table Options group**, click the **New** button. In the **Table** grid, in the third row, click the second square to insert a 2 × 3 Table. Type the following information in the table:

Non-profit experience:	Fundraising, financial management
Computer proficiency:	Word, Excel, Access
Education focus:	Business Administration

j. Point outside of the upper left corner and click the **table move handle** button to select the entire table. On the **Table Layout tab**, in the **Cell Size group**, click the **AutoFit** button, and then click **AutoFit to Contents**. On the **Home tab**, in the **Paragraph group**, click the **Center Text** button. On the **Tables tab**, in the **Draw Borders group**, click the **Borders arrow**, and then click **None**. **Save** your document.

3 If you do not see any wavy red and green lines under words, refer to the Alert in Activity 2.17 to enable the default settings for automatic proofing.

a. In the paragraph that begins *I recently moved*, locate and point to *Businesss*, and then press [Control] and click. From the shortcut menu, click **Business**. In the following paragraph, locate and display the shortcut menu for *Comunity*. From the shortcut menu, click **Community**.

b. Press [Command ⌘] + [fn] + [←] to move to the top of the document. On the status bar, click the [⌨️✗] icon. From the shortcut menu, click **have** to change *has* to *have*.

c. Press [Command ⌘] + [fn] + [←] to move to the top of the document. On the **Tools** menu, click **Spelling and Grammar**. In the **Spelling and Grammar** dialog box, click **Change** to change the spelling of *permnent* to *permanent*, and then click **OK** to close the message box.

d. In the paragraph that begins *I recently moved*, point to *job* and then press [Control] and click. In the shortcut menu, point to **Synonyms**, and then click **career**.

In the first line of the paragraph that begins *I am available*, point to *additional*, press [Control] and click, and replace it with the synonym **further**.

e. On the **File** menu, click **Properties**. Be sure that your course and section number are in the **Subject** box, and your firstname and lastname are in the **Author** box. In the **Keywords** box, replace any existing text with **cover letter** and then click **OK**. **Save** your document, and then **Print** or submit the document electronically as directed. **Close** the document, but leave Word open.

4 On the **File** menu, click **New from Template**. In the sidebar, under **Print Layout View**, click **Resumes**. In the **Word Document Gallery**, click **Corner Resume**, and then click **Choose**. If necessary, increase the width of the window by clicking the Zoom button or dragging the lower right corner of the window. On the Standard toolbar, change the **Zoom** setting to **125%** to increase the display of the document.

a. **Save** the document in your **Word Chapter 2** folder as **Lastname_Firstname_2D_Resume** and then in the **First Page Footer** area, **Insert** the **Filename**. **Close** the **First Page Footer** area. At the top of the resume, double-click the square that displays *yn* to open the **First Page Header** area. In the top left corner of the header area, click the **table move handle**, and then press [Command ⌘] + [X] to cut the table from the header. Press [Delete] to delete a blank line from the header area. **Close** the **First Page Header** area.

b. At the top of the document click the first control, which displays the user or computer name. Replace this text by typing **Carlos Cabrera** Click the *[Street Address]* control, and then type **7719 Reese Drive** Click the *[City]* control, and then type **Monona** Click the *[State]* control, and then type **WI** Click the *[Postal Code]* control, and then type **53716** Click the *[Your Phone]* control, and then type **(608) 555-1447** Click the *[Your E-Mail]* control, and then type **ccabrera@alcona.net** and then click in the line above the email address.

c. On the same line as the email address, select *F: [Your Fax]*, and then press [Delete].

d. To the right of *Objective*, click the paragraph, and then type **A temporary or permanent position in a non-profit organization in the Madison area, where my fundraising, computer, and organizational skills will be of benefit to the organization.**

(Project 2D Cabrera Letter continues on the next page)

e. To the right of *Experience*, click *Lorem ipsum dolor*, and type **Fundraising Assistant** Click the *[Insert Dates]* control, and then type **May 2014 to May 2016** Under *Fundraising Assistant*, click the paragraph, and then type the following, pressing Return after the first item:

International Falls Community Fund, 217 Hennepin St., International Falls, MN 56649

Participated in fundraising in Northern Minnesota counties, organized fundraising events, performed financial analyses, and tracked donations.

f. To the right of *Education*, click *Aliquam dapibus*, and then type **Bachelor of Business Administration, University of Minnesota** Click the *[Insert Dates]* control, and then type **May 2016** Under the degree, click the paragraph, and then type the following list, pressing Return after the first three items:

Dean's List, final two terms

H. W. Walker Business Administration partial scholarship

Student Assistant, Financial Aid

3.2 GPA

g. To the right of *Skills*, click the paragraph, and then type the following list, pressing Return after the first two items:

Organizing fundraising events

Computer proficiency in Word, Excel, and Access

Written and oral communications

h. To the right of *Experience*, select the paragraphs that are placeholders for information—do not include the paragraphs where you typed information. Press Delete to delete the placeholders. Press Delete to remove the extra blank line. At the bottom of the document point to the left of the last row to display the ⬆ pointer and drag up to include the blank row above it—select two rows. Press Delete to delete the two rows.

i. In the *Education* section, select the four paragraphs under *Bachelor of Business Administration*—the lines beginning with *Dean's*, *H. W.*, *Student*, and *3.2*. On the **Home tab**, in the **Paragraph group**, click the **Bulleted List** button. On the Standard toolbar, click the **Format Painter** button, and then select the three items in the *Skills* section to apply the Bulleted List style.

j. On the **Layout tab**, in the **Margins group**, change the **Top** margin to **2**, the **Bottom** margin to **1**, the **Left** margin to **1**, and the **Right** margin to **1**.On the **File** menu, click **Properties**. In the **Subject** box, type your course and section number. Type your firstname and lastname as the **Author**. In the **Keywords** box, type **resume, template** and then click **OK**. **Save** your document. **Print** or submit the document electronically as directed. Leave the document open.

k. On the **File** menu, click **Save As Web Page**. If necessary, navigate to the **Word Chapter 2** folder. In the middle of the **Save As** dialog box, click the **Format arrow**, and under **Specialty Formats**, click **Single File Web Page (.mht)**. At the top of the dialog box, in the **Save As** box, type **Lastname_ Firstname_2D_Web_Resume** and then click **Save**.

l. Display the **File Properties**, and then in the **Keywords** box, add **HTML** to the list of keywords. Click **OK** and **Save** your document. **Print** or submit the document electronically as directed.

m. On the **File** menu, click **Web Page Preview** to view the resume in your Web browser. **Close** the Web browser window, and then **Quit** your browser. **Close** the document, and then **Quit Word**.

End **You have completed Project 2D**

Content-Based Assessments

Apply **2A** skills from these Objectives:

1 Create a Table
2 Add Text to a Table
3 Format a Table

Mastering Word | Project **2E** Job Listings

In the following Mastering Word project, you will create an announcement for new job postings at Madison Staffing Services. Your completed document will look similar to Figure 2.49.

Project Files

For Project 2E, you will need the following files:

New blank Word document
w02E_Legal_Jobs

You will save your document as:

Lastname_Firstname_2E_Job_Listings

Project Results

Madison Staffing Services
Job Alert! Several New Positions in the Legal Profession!
March 15

Madison Staffing Services has several new openings for both full- and part-time positions in the legal profession. Some of these jobs are temporary, some are for a specific project with a defined beginning and ending date, and some are open-ended with the potential for permanent employment. The following jobs were posted in the past week. These listings are just in, so apply now to be one of the first candidates considered!

Position	Type	Location
Paralegal	Part-time	Oconomowoc
Records Clerk	Part-time	Madison
Legal Receptionist	Full-time, two months	Baraboo
Legal Word Processor	Full-time, open ended	Milwaukee

For further information about any of these new jobs, or a complete listing of jobs that are available through Madison Staffing Services, please call Marilyn Kelly at (608) 555-0386 or visit our Web site at www.madisonstaffing.com.

To help prepare yourself before applying for these jobs, we recommend that you review the following articles on our Web site at www.madisonstaffing.com.

Topic	Article Title
Legal skills and knowledge	*Maintaining Your Legal Skills*
Legal etiquette	*Legal Protocol and Social Networking*
General information	*Working in a Legal Office*

Lastname_Firstname_2E_Job_Listings.docx

Figure 2.49

(Project 2E Job Listings continues on the next page)

Content-Based Assessments

Mastering Word | Project 2E Job Listings (continued)

1 Open **Word** and in a new blank document be sure that nonprinting characters and rulers display. If necessary, increase the size of the window, and on the Standard toolbar, change the Zoom setting to 125%. Change the **Left** and **Right** margins to **1**. **Save** the document in your **Word Chapter 2** folder as **Lastname_Firstname_2E_Job_Listings** and then in the **Footer** area, **Insert** the **Filename**.

2 At the top of the document, type **Madison Staffing Services** and press ⏎Return. Type **Job Alert! Several New Positions in the Legal Profession!** and press ⏎Return. Type **March 15** and press ⏎Return two times. Insert the file **w02E_Legal_Jobs**. Press Command ⌘ + A to select the entire document. Change the **Font Size** to **11**, and the **Line Spacing** to **1.15**.

3 At the top of the document, select and **Center** the three title lines. Select the title *Madison Staffing Services* and change the **Font Size** to **24 pt** and apply **Bold**. Apply **Bold** to the second and third title lines and change the **Font Size** to **12**. Locate the paragraph that begins *For further information*, and then click to the left of *For* and press ⏎Return to insert a blank line. Press ⬆ one time to position the insertion point in the blank line. Insert a **3 × 4 Table**. Enter the following:

Position	Type	Location
Paralegal	Part-time	Oconomowoc
Legal Receptionist	Full-time, two months	Baraboo
Legal Word Processor	Full-time, open ended	Milwaukee

4 In the table, click anywhere in the second row, and then insert a row below. Add the following information:

Records Clerk	Part-time	Madison

5 Select the entire table. On the **Tables tab**, in the **Table Styles group**, click the second table style—**Light Shading**.

6 With the table still selected, on the **Table Layout tab**, in the **Cell Size group**, click the **AutoFit** button, click **AutoFit to Contents**, and then **Center** the table. With the table still selected, add **6 pt Spacing Before**.

7 At the bottom of the document, click to position the insertion point on the blank line. Insert a **2 × 4 Table**. Enter the following:

Topic	Article Title
Legal skills and knowledge	Maintaining Your Legal Skills
Legal etiquette	Legal Protocol and Social Networking
General information	Working in a Legal Office

8 Select the entire table. On the **Table Layout tab**, in the **Cell Size group**, click the **AutoFit** button, and then click **AutoFit to Contents**. **Center** the table, and then apply **6 pt Spacing Before** and **6 pt Spacing After**.

9 With the table still selected, remove all table borders, and then add a **1 pt** solid line **Top** border and **Bottom** border. Select the cells in the first row, apply **Bold**, and then **Center** the text. Apply **Italic** to the three article titles.

10 Click in the paragraph that begins with *Madison Staffing Services has several*, and then change the **Spacing After** to **12 pt**. Change the **Spacing After** to **12 pt** for the paragraphs that begin with *For further information* and *To help prepare*.

11 In the **File Properties**, add course information, your name, and the **Keywords new listings, legal Save** and then **Print** or submit the document electronically as directed. **Close** the document, and then **Quit Word**.

 You have completed Project 2E ——————

Content-Based Assessments

Apply **2B** skills from these Objectives:

4 Create a New Document from an Existing Document

5 Change and Reorganize Text

6 Use the Proofing Options

7 Create a Document Using a Template

Mastering Word | Project **2F** Job Tips

In the following Mastering Word project, you will create a fax and a memo that includes job tips for Madison Staffing Services employees. Your completed documents will look similar to Figure 2.50.

Project Files

For Project 2F, you will need the following files:

> w02F_Heading
> w02F_Tips_Text
> Capital Fax template from Word's installed templates

You will save your documents as:

> Lastname_Firstname_2F_Resume_Tips
> Lastname_Firstname_2F_Fax

Project Results

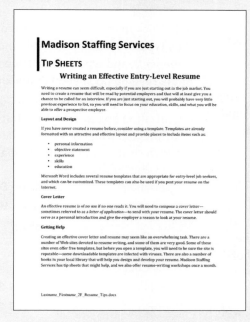

Figure 2.50

(Project 2F Job Tips continues on the next page)

Content-Based Assessments

1 Open **Word**. On the **File** menu, click **Open**, and then navigate to your student files. Locate and click **w02F_Heading**. **Open** the document as a **Copy**. If necessary, display nonprinting characters and rulers, and increase the size of the window.

2 Display the **File Properties**, add your course information, name, and the **Keywords memo, associates**

3 **Save** the document in your **Word Chapter 2** folder as **Lastname_Firstname_2F_Resume_Tips** In the **Footer** area, **Insert** the **Filename**.

4 At the top of the document, click to position the insertion point in the blank paragraph below the heading. **Insert** the file **w02F_Tips_Text** and press Delete to remove the blank line at the end of the inserted text.

5 Select and **Center** the title that begins *Writing an Effective*, and then change the **Font Size** to **20**. By using either the **Spelling and Grammar** dialog box, or by displaying the shortcut menu for selected words, correct all spelling and grammatical errors—ignore the five paragraphs that begin with lowercase letters.

6 In the second line of the paragraph that begins *Writing a resume*, locate and point to *prospective*. Press Control and click, and from the shortcut menu, click the synonym **potential**.

7 At the bottom of the document, select both the heading *Cover Letter* and the paragraph below that title. Drag the selected text above the heading *Getting Help*. Remove the blank paragraph at the end of the document. In the paragraph that begins *The cover letter*, select the first sentence of the paragraph and drag it to the end of the same paragraph. Adjust spacing if necessary.

8 Near the top of the document, select the five paragraphs that begin with lowercase letters, starting with *personal information* and ending with *education*. Create a bulleted list.

9 **Save** the document, and then **Print** or submit the document electronically as directed. **Close** the document but leave Word open.

10 From **Coordinated Forms templates**, create a document based on the **Capital Fax** template. If necessary, increase the size of the window. On the Standard toolbar, change the **Zoom** setting to **125%**. **Save** the document in your **Word Chapter 2** folder as **Lastname_Firstname_2F_Fax** and then in the **First Page Footer** area, **Insert** the **Filename**.

11 Click *Date:* and then press Tab so that the insertion point is in the second cell. After typing the information for the control, press ↓. Type the following for the template controls, skipping those that are not listed:

Date:	May 12, 2016
Send To:	James Washington
From:	Kevin Rau
Phone Number:	(608) 555-1348
Total Pages Including Cover:	2

12 Click in the box to the right of *Please Review*, and then type an **X** Click in the cell under the cell that displays *Comments*, and type **James: Here is a copy of the draft of the resume tip sheet. Let me know what you think**.

13 At the top of the document, double-click in the organization box to open the **First Page Header** section. Type the following for the template controls, and delete the **Web** control and the blank space:

organization	Madison Staffing Services
[Street Address]	600 East Washington Avenue
[City]	Madison
[State]	WI
[Postal Code]	53701
[Your Phone]	(608) 555-2344
[Your Fax]	(608) 555-2388
[Your E-Mail]	krau@madisonstaffing.com

14 In the **File Properties**, add your course information, your name, and the **Keywords resume tips, fax Save** the document, and then **Print** or submit the document electronically as directed.

15 **Close** the document, and then **Quit Word**.

End **You have completed Project 2F** —————

Content-Based Assessments

Apply a combination of
2A and **2B** skills:

1 Create a Table

2 Add Text to a Table

3 Format a Table

4 Create a New
Document from an
Existing Document

5 Change and
Reorganize Text

6 Use the Proofing
Options

7 Create a Document
Using a Template

Mastering Word | Project **2G** Job Letter

In the following Mastering Word project, you will create a new document from an existing document, format a table, and then create a fax cover using a template. Your completed documents will look similar to Figure 2.51.

Project Files

For Project 2G, you will need the following files:

> w02G_Letter_Text
> w02G_Letterhead
> w02G_Resume
> **Revolution Fax template from Word's installed templates**

You will save your documents as:

> Lastname_Firstname_2G_Job_Letter
> Lastname_Firstname_2G_Resume
> Lastname_Firstname_2G_Fax

Project Results

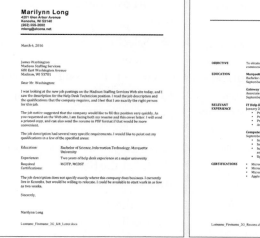

Figure 2.51

(Project 2G Job Letter continues on the next page)

Mastering Word | Project **2G** Job Letter (continued)

1 Open **Word** and display nonprinting characters and rulers and increase the size of the window. If necessary, on the Standard toolbar, change the Zoom setting to 125%. By using the **Open** dialog box and the **Copy** feature, create a document from the file **w02G_Letterhead**. **Save** the document in your **Word Chapter 2** folder as **Lastname_Firstname_2G_Job_Letter** In the **Footer** area, **Insert** the **Filename**. Move to the end of the document, and then type **March 6, 2016** and then press Return four times. Type the following, pressing Return after the first three lines:

> **James Washington**
> **Madison Staffing Services**
> **600 East Washington Avenue**
> **Madison, WI 53701**

2 Press Return two times, type **Dear Mr. Washington:** and press Return two times. **Insert** the text from the file **w02G_Letter_Text** and remove the blank line at the bottom of the inserted text.

3 Move to the top of the document, and then by using either the **Spelling and Grammar** dialog box, or by displaying the shortcut menu for selected words, correct spelling and grammatical errors. In the paragraph that begins *I was looking*, in the third line, point to *corporation* and then press Control and click. Use the shortcut menu to change the word to the synonym **company**. In the same sentence, change *correct* to the synonym **right**.

4 In the paragraph that begins *I currently*, select the first sentence of the paragraph and drag it to the end of the second sentence in the same paragraph. In the second blank line below the paragraph that begins *The job description had several*, insert a **2 × 3 Table**, and then type the text shown in **Table 1** below.

5 Select the entire table. **AutoFit to Contents**, **Center** the table, remove the table borders, and then add **3 pt Spacing Before** and **3 pt Spacing After**. Click anywhere in the document to deselect the table. Change the **Top**

margin to **0.5** and the **Bottom** margin to **0.75** so that the entire letter fits on one page.

6 In the **File Properties**, add your course information, name, and the **Keywords job letter Save** the document, and then **Print** or submit the document electronically as directed. **Close** the document, but leave Word open.

7 From your student files, **Open w02G_Resume**. **Save** the document in your **Word Chapter 2** folder as **Lastname_Firstname_2G_Resume** In the **Footer** area, **Insert** the **Filename**. If necessary, display nonprinting characters and rulers and increase the size of the window. If necessary, on the Standard toolbar, change the **Zoom** setting to **125%**.

8 Insert a new second row in the table. In the first cell of the new row, type **OBJECTIVE** and then press Tab. Type **To obtain a Help Desk Technician position that will use my technical and communication skills and computer support experience.** In the same cell, add **12 pt Spacing After**.

9 Select the entire table. **AutoFit to Contents**, and remove the table borders, and then with the table selected, create a single solid line **1 1/2 pt** top border.

10 In the first row of the table, select both cells and then **Merge Cells**. **Center** the five lines and apply **Bold**. In the first row, select *Marilynn Long* and change the **Font Size** to **20 pt** and add **36 pt Spacing Before**. In the email address at the bottom of the first row, add **24 pt Spacing After**.

11 In the first column, apply **Bold** to the four headings. In the cell to the right of *EDUCATION*, **Bold** the names of the two schools. Add **12 pt Spacing After** to the two lines that begin *September*.

12 In the cell to the right of *RELEVANT EXPERIENCE*, **Bold** the names of the two jobs—*IT Help Desk Specialist* and *Computer Technician*. In the same cell, below the line that begins *January 2014*, apply bullets to the four lines that comprise the job duties. Create a similar bulleted

Table 1

Education:	Bachelor of Science, Information Technology, Marquette University
Experience:	Two years of help desk experience at a major university
Required Certifications:	MCITP, MCDST

(Return to Step 5)

(Project 2G Job Letter continues on the next page)

Content-Based Assessments

Mastering Word | Project 2G Job Letter (continued)

list for the duties as a Computer Technician. Add **12 pt Spacing After** to the last line of each of the bulleted lists.

13 In the cell to the right of *CERTIFICATIONS*, select all four lines and create a bulleted list. **Decrease** the **Indent** for this bulleted list. In the **File Properties**, add your course information, name, and the **Keywords help desk resume Save** the document, and then **Print** or submit the document electronically as directed. **Close** the document, but leave Word open

14 From **Coordinated Forms templates**, create a document based on the **Revolution Fax** template. If necessary, display nonprinting characters and rulers and increase the size of the window. On the Standard toolbar,

change the **Zoom** setting to **125%**. **Save** the document in your **Word Chapter 2** folder as **Lastname_Firstname_2G_Fax** and then in the **First Page Header** area, **Insert** the **Filename**.

15 Type the text shown in **Table 2** for the content controls, skipping controls that are not listed in Table 2.

16 Delete the *[Web Address]* control and any extra spaces that result after the deletion. In the **File Properties**, add your course information, your name, and the **Keywords fax cover page Save** the document, and then **Print** or submit the document electronically as directed. **Close** the document, and then **Quit Word**.

Word | Chapter 2

Table 2

organization	**Marilynn Long**
[Street Address]	**4201 Glen Arbor Avenue**
[City] [State] [Postal Code]	**Kenosha WI 53140**
[Your Phone]	**(262) 555-2002**
[Your Fax]	**(262) 555-2002**
[Your E-Mail]	**mlong@alcona.net**
Date:	**3/6/2016**
Send To:	**James Washington, Recruiter**
From:	**Marilynn Long**
Phone Number:	**(608) 555-1348**
Total Pages Including Cover:	**3**
Please Review	**X**
Comments:	**Two pages to follow that include my resume and a cover letter for the position of Help Desk Technician.**

(Return to Step 16)

End **You have completed Project 2G** ————————————————————

Content-Based Assessments

GO! Fix It | Project 2H New Jobs

Project Files

For Project 2H, you will need the following file:

> w02H_New_Jobs

You will save your document as:

> Lastname_Firstname_2H_New_Jobs

From the student files that accompany this textbook, locate and open the file w02H_New_Jobs, and then save the file in your Word Chapter 2 folder as **Lastname_Firstname_2H_New_Jobs**

This document contains errors that you must find and correct. Read and examine the document, and then edit to correct the errors that you find and to improve the overall document format. Types of errors could include, but are not restricted to:

- Spelling errors
- Grammar errors
- Duplicate words
- Unattractive table column widths
- Title not merged across the top row of the table
- Inconsistent spacing before and after paragraphs in the table

Things you should know to complete this project:

- Viewing the document in Print Preview will help identify some of the problems
- The Spelling and Grammar checker will be useful
- Adjust the column widths *before* merging the title

Save your document and add the file name to the footer area. In File Properties, type your course name and section number in the Subject box and your firstname and lastname in the Author box. In the Keywords box, type **job listings** and then save your document and print or submit electronically as directed.

End You have completed Project 2H ————————————————

Content-Based Assessments

Apply a combination of the **2A** and **2B** skills.

GO! Make It | Project 2I Training

Project Files

For Project 2I, you will need the following file:

New blank Word document

You will save your document as:

Lastname_Firstname_2I_Training

Open Word, and then save the new blank document in your Word Chapter 2 folder as **Lastname_Firstname_2I_Training**

Use the skills you practiced in this chapter to create the table shown in Figure 2.52. The first row font is Cambria 16 pt, the remainder is Cambria 14 pt. The spacing after the first row is 36 pt, the spacing after the bottom of the remaining rows is 12 pt. All margins are 1".

Add the file name to the footer. In the File Properties, add your course information, your name, and the keywords **online training** Save your document, and then submit as directed.

Project Results

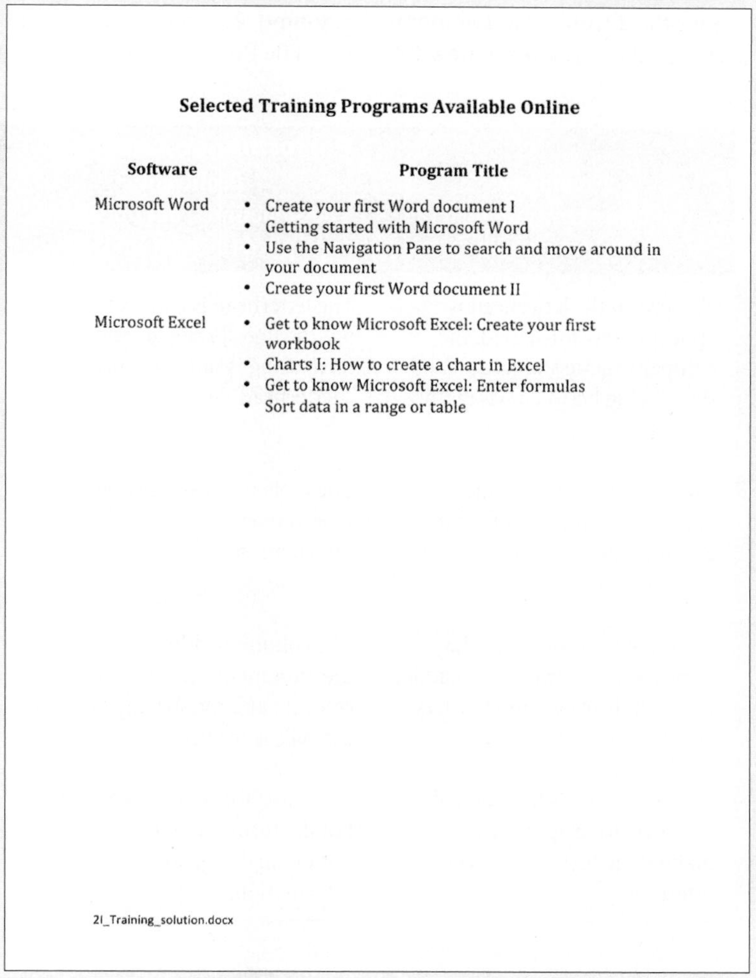

Selected Training Programs Available Online

Software	Program Title
Microsoft Word	• Create your first Word document I • Getting started with Microsoft Word • Use the Navigation Pane to search and move around in your document • Create your first Word document II
Microsoft Excel	• Get to know Microsoft Excel: Create your first workbook • Charts I: How to create a chart in Excel • Get to know Microsoft Excel: Enter formulas • Sort data in a range or table

2I_Training_solution.docx

Figure 2.52

End You have completed Project 2I

Content-Based Assessments

GO! Solve It | Project 2J Job Posting

Project Files

For Project 2J, you will need the following files:

New blank Word document
w02J_Job_Postings

You will save your documents as:

Lastname_Firstname_2J_Letterhead
Lastname_Firstname_2J_Job_Postings

Print the w02J_Job_Postings document, and use the information to complete this project. Create a new company letterhead and save it in your Word Chapter 2 folder as **Lastname_Firstname_2J_Letterhead** Add the file name to the footer. Add your course information, your name, and the keyword **letterhead** in the File Properties.

Create a new document using a copy of the file you just created. The new document will be a list of new jobs posted by Madison Staffing Services. The job posting should include the letterhead, introductory text, and a table that includes the information about the new jobs that are currently available. The job list should be in table format. Use either two or three columns, and label the columns appropriately. Format the table, the table borders, and the text in an attractive, readable manner.

Save the document as **Lastname_Firstname_2J_Job_Postings** Add the file name to the footer, and change the keywords to **new jobs** in the File Properties. Submit your two files as directed.

		Performance Level	
	Exemplary: You consistently applied the relevant skills	**Proficient:** You sometimes, but not always, applied the relevant skills	**Developing:** You rarely or never applied the relevant skills
Create and format a letterhead template	The text in the letterhead is appropriately formatted, the company name stands out, and the spacing between paragraphs is attractive.	The letterhead is complete, but the line spacing or text formatting is not appropriate for a letterhead.	The spacing and formatting is not appropriate for a letterhead.
Insert a table	The inserted table has the appropriate number of columns and rows to display the information.	The table is not structured to effectively display the information.	No table is inserted in the document.
Format the table structure	Table column widths fit the information, extra space is added between the rows, and borders are attractively formatted.	The column widths do not reflect the amount of information in the column, and the spacing between the cells is insufficient.	Table displays only default column widths and spacing.
Format the text in the table	Important text is highlighted and formatted appropriately, making the text easy to read and interpret.	Some text formatting is added, but the formatting does not highlight the important information.	No text formatting is included.

(Performance Criteria — left vertical label)

End You have completed Project 2J

Content-Based Assessments

Apply a combination of the **2A** and **2B** skills.

GO! Solve It | Project **2K** Agenda

Project Files

For Project 2K, you will need the following file:

> **Agenda template from Coordinated Forms templates**

You will save your document as:

> **Lastname_Firstname_2K_Agenda**

Create a new document based on an agenda template—such as the *Capital Agenda* template—from the Coordinated Forms templates on your computer. Save the agenda as **Lastname_Firstname_2K_Agenda** Use the following information to prepare an agenda for a Madison Staffing Services meeting. Madison Staffing Services is located at 600 East Washington Avenue, Madison, WI 53701. The phone number is (608) 555-0386. Change headings in the template as necessary to describe the text that you enter next to the item; for example change *Meeting Called By:* to *Date:*

The meeting will be facilitated by Marilyn Kelly. It will be the monthly meeting of the company administrators—Kevin Rau, Marilyn Kelly, Andre Randolph, Susan Nguyen, and Charles James. The meeting will be held on March 15, 2016, at 3:00 p.m. Topic A discussion is old business (open issues) that includes 1) expanding services into the printing and food service industries; 2) recruitment at the UW-Madison and MATC campuses; and 3) the addition of a part-time trainer. Topic B discussion is new business that includes 1) recruitment at the University of Wisconsin, Milwaukee; 2) rental of office space in or around Milwaukee; 3) purchase of new computers for the training room; and 4) renewal of snow removal service contract.

In the header area, delete any unused controls. If necessary, in the body of the agenda, delete any unused rows so that the agenda prints on one page. Add the file name to the footer, and add your course name and section number, your name, and the keywords **agenda, monthly administrative meeting** in the File Properties. Submit as directed.

Performance Criteria	Performance Level		
	Exemplary: You consistently applied the relevant skills	**Proficient:** You sometimes, but not always, applied the relevant skills	**Developing:** You rarely or never applied the relevant skills
Select an agenda template	Agenda template is appropriate for the information provided for the meeting.	Agenda template is used, but does not fit the information provided.	No template is used for the agenda.
Add appropriate information to the template	All information is inserted in the appropriate places. All unused controls are removed.	All information is included, but not in the appropriate places, and not all of the unused controls are removed.	Information is missing and unused placeholders are not removed.
Format template information	All text in the template is properly aligned and formatted.	All text is included, but alignment or formatting is inconsistent.	No additional formatting has been added.

End **You have completed Project 2K**

Rubric

The following outcomes-based assessments are open-ended assessments. That is, there is no specific correct result; your result will depend on your approach to the information provided. Make Professional Quality your goal. Use the following scoring rubric to guide you in how to approach the problem and then to evaluate how well your approach solves the problem.

The *criteria*—Software Mastery, Content, Format and Layout, and Process—represent the knowledge and skills you have gained that you can apply to solving the problem. The *levels of performance*—Professional Quality, Approaching Professional Quality, or Needs Quality Improvements—help you and your instructor evaluate your result.

	Your completed project is of Professional Quality if you:	Your completed project is Approaching Professional Quality if you:	Your completed project Needs Quality Improvements if you:
1-Software Mastery	Choose and apply the most appropriate skills, tools, and features and identify efficient methods to solve the problem.	Choose and apply some appropriate skills, tools, and features, but not in the most efficient manner.	Choose inappropriate skills, tools, or features, or are inefficient in solving the problem.
2-Content	Construct a solution that is clear and well organized, contains content that is accurate, appropriate to the audience and purpose, and is complete. Provide a solution that contains no errors in spelling, grammar, or style.	Construct a solution in which some components are unclear, poorly organized, inconsistent, or incomplete. Misjudge the needs of the audience. Have some errors in spelling, grammar, or style, but the errors do not detract from comprehension.	Construct a solution that is unclear, incomplete, or poorly organized; contains some inaccurate or inappropriate content; and contains many errors in spelling, grammar, or style. Do not solve the problem.
3-Format and Layout	Format and arrange all elements to communicate information and ideas, clarify function, illustrate relationships, and indicate relative importance.	Apply appropriate format and layout features to some elements, but not others. Overuse features, causing minor distraction.	Apply format and layout that does not communicate information or ideas clearly. Do not use format and layout features to clarify function, illustrate relationships, or indicate relative importance. Use available features excessively, causing distraction.
4-Process	Use an organized approach that integrates planning, development, self-assessment, revision, and reflection.	Demonstrate an organized approach in some areas, but not others; or, use an insufficient process of organization throughout.	Do not use an organized approach to solve the problem.

Outcomes-Based Assessments

GO! Think | Project **2L** Workshops

Project Files

For Project 2L, you will need the following files:

> New blank Word document
> w02L_Workshop_Information

You will save your document as:

> Lastname_Firstname_2L_Workshops

Madison Staffing Services offers a series of workshops for its employee-clients. Any temporary employee who is available during the workshop hours can attend the workshops and there is no fee. Currently, the company offers three-session workshops covering Excel and Word, a two-session workshop covering Business Communication, and a one-session workshop covering *Creating a Resume*.

Print the w02L_Workshop_Information file and use the information to complete this project. Create an announcement with a title, an introductory paragraph, and a table listing the workshops and the topics covered in each workshop. Use the file w02L_Workshop_Information for help with the topics covered in each workshop. Format the table cells appropriately. Add an appropriate footer and information to the File Properties. Save the document in your Word Chapter 2 folder as **Lastname_Firstname_2L_Workshops** and submit it as directed.

End You have completed Project 2L ⎯⎯⎯⎯⎯⎯⎯⎯⎯⎯

GO! Think | Project **2M** Calendar

Project Files

For Project 2M, you will need the following files:

> Calendar template
> w02M_Workshop_Information

You will save your document as:

> Lastname_Firstname_2M_Calendar

To keep track of workshops provided to employees, the trainer fills out a monthly calendar. Each workshop lasts two hours. Print the w02M_Workshop_Information file and use part or all of the information to complete this project.

Create a new document using a template, for example the *Banner Calendar* template found in the Calendars category under Print Layout View. Create a template for a month in 2016, and decide on the dates and times to hold the training sessions. The computer skills workshops are held in the Lab, the others are held in Room 104. The trainer always schedules the hour before each workshop for preparation. Fill out the calendar and use your choice of formatting to indicate that the workshops cover a two-hour period. Include your name somewhere in the template. Add appropriate information to the File Properties. Save the document in your Word Chapter 2 folder as **Lastname_Firstname_2M_Calendar** and submit it as directed.

End You have completed Project 2M ⎯⎯⎯⎯⎯⎯⎯⎯⎯⎯

Word | Chapter 2

Outcomes-Based Assessments

Apply a combination of the **2A** and **2B** skills.

You and GO! | Project **2N** Personal Resume

Project Files

For Project 2N, you will need the following file:

New blank Word document

You will save your documents as:

Lastname_Firstname_2N_Personal_Resume
Lastname_Firstname_2N_Cover_Letter

Locate and print the information for a job for which you would like to apply, and then create your own personal resume using a table and a cover letter. Include any information that is appropriate, including your objective for a specific job, your experience, skills, education, honors, or awards. Create your own letterhead and cover letter, using the cover letter you created in Project 2B as a guide.

To complete the assignment, be sure to format the text appropriately, resize the table columns in the resume to best display the information, and check both documents for spelling and grammar errors.

Save the resume as **Lastname_Firstname_2N_Personal_Resume** and the cover letter as **Lastname_Firstname_2N_Cover_Letter** in your Word Chapter 2 folder. Add the file name to the footer, and add your course name and section number, your name, and the keywords **my resume** and **cover letter** to the File Properties. Submit your file as directed.

 You have completed Project 2N ——————————————

Apply a combination of the **2A** and **2B** skills.

GO! Group Business Running Case | Project **2O**
Bell Orchid Hotels Group Running Case

This project relates to the **Bell Orchid Hotels**. Your instructor may assign this group case project to your class. If your instructor assigns this project, he or she will provide you with information and instructions to work as part of a group. The group will apply the skills gained thus far to help the Bell Orchid Hotels achieve their business goals.

 You have completed Project 2O ——————————————

Creating Research Papers, Newsletters, and Merged Mailing Labels

OUTCOMES
At the end of this chapter you will be able to:

OBJECTIVES
Mastering these objectives will enable you to:

PROJECT 3A
Create a research paper that includes citations and a bibliography.

1. Create a Research Paper (p. 181)
2. Insert Footnotes in a Research Paper (p. 184)
3. Create Citations and a Bibliography in a Research Paper (p. 188)

PROJECT 3B
Create a multiple-column newsletter and merged mailing labels.

4. Format a Multiple-Column Newsletter (p. 198)
5. Use Special Character and Paragraph Formatting (p. 204)
6. Create Mailing Labels Using Mail Merge (p. 208)

© wawritto / Shutterstock

In This Chapter

Microsoft Word provides many tools for creating complex documents. For example, Word has tools that enable you to create a research paper that includes citations, footnotes, and a bibliography. You can also create multiple-column newsletters, format the nameplate at the top of the newsletter, use special character formatting to create distinctive title text, and add borders and shading to paragraphs to highlight important information.

In this chapter, you will edit and format a research paper, create a two-column newsletter, and then create a set of mailing labels to mail the newsletter to multiple recipients.

The projects in this chapter relate to **Memphis Primary Materials**, located in the Memphis area. In addition to collecting common recyclable materials, the company collects and recycles computers, monitors, copiers and fax machines, cell phones, wood pallets, and compostable materials. The company's name comes from the process of capturing the "primary materials" of used items for reuse. Memphis Primary Materials ensures that its clients comply with all state and local regulations. They also provide training to clients on the process and benefits of recycling.

Project 3A Research Paper

Project Activities

In Activities 3.01 through 3.07, you will edit and format a research paper that contains an overview of recycling activities in which businesses can engage. This paper was created by Elizabeth Freeman, a student intern working for Memphis Primary Metals, and will be included in a customer information packet. Your completed document will look similar to Figure 3.1.

Project Files

For Project 3A, you will need the following file:

w03A_Green_Business

You will save your document as:

Lastname_Firstname_3A_Green_Business

Project Results

Figure 3.1
Project 3A Green Business

Objective 1 | Create a Research Paper

When you write a research paper or a report for college or business, follow a format prescribed by one of the standard *style guides*—a manual that contains standards for the design and writing of documents. The two most commonly used styles for research papers are those created by the *Modern Language Association (MLA)* and the *American Psychological Association (APA)*; there are several others.

Activity 3.01 | Formatting Text and Page Numbers in a Research Paper

When formatting the text for your research paper, refer to the standards for the style guide that you have chosen. In this activity, you will create a research paper using MLA style. MLA style uses 1-inch margins, a 0.5" first line indent, and double spacing throughout the body of the document, with no extra space above or below paragraphs.

1   Open **Word**. From your student files, locate and open the document **w03A_Green_Business**. If necessary, display the formatting marks and rulers and increase the size of the window to fill the entire screen. On the Standard toolbar, click the **Zoom arrow** `100%`, and then click **125%**. In the location where you are storing your projects for this chapter, create a new folder named **Word Chapter 3** and then **Save** the file in the folder as **Lastname_Firstname_3A_Green_Business**

> Changing the Zoom setting enables you to compare more easily your screen to the figures in this textbook.

2   Press Command ⌘ + A to select the entire document. On the **Home tab**, in the **Paragraph group**, click the **Line Spacing** button, and then change the line spacing to **2.0**. On the **Layout tab**, in the **Margins group**, change the **Left** margin to **1**, and then change the **Right** margin to **1**. In the document, click anywhere in the document to cancel the selection of the Right margin setting.

3   Press Command ⌘ + fn + ← to cancel the selection of the document and to move to the beginning of the document. Press Return one time to create a blank line at the top of the document, and then click to position the insertion point in the blank line. Type **Elizabeth Freeman** and press Return.

4   Type **Henry Miller** and press Return. Type **Marketing** and press Return. Type **April 15, 2016** and press Return. Type **Going Green Benefits Business** With your insertion point in the last line you typed, on the **Home tab**, in the **Paragraph group**, click the **Center Text** button. Compare your screen with Figure 3.2.

Figure 3.2

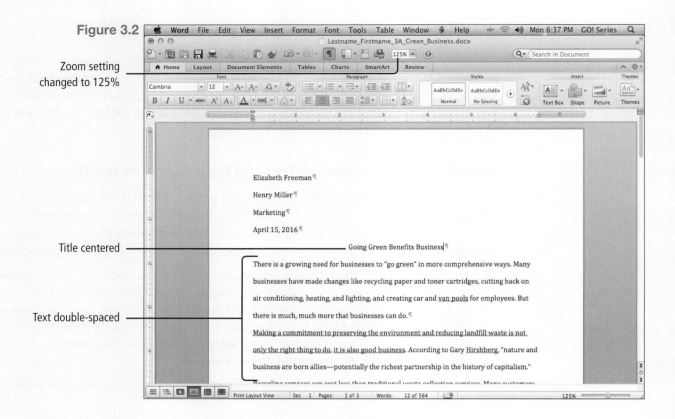

Zoom setting changed to 125%

Title centered

Text double-spaced

> **More Knowledge | Creating a Document Heading for a Research Paper**
>
> On the first page of an MLA-style research paper, on the first line, type the report author. On the second line, type the person for whom the report is prepared—for example, your professor or supervisor. On the third line, type the name of the class or department or organization. On the fourth line, type the date. On the fifth line, type the report title and center it.

5 At the top of **Page 1**, point anywhere in the white top margin area to display the ▣ pointer, and then double-click to display the **Header** area. In the **Header** area, type **Freeman** and then press Spacebar.

> Recall that the text you insert into a header or footer displays on every page of a document. Within a header or footer, you can insert many different types of information; for example, automatic page numbers, the date, the time, the file name, or images.

6 On the **Header and Footer tab**, in the **Insert group**, click the **Page #** button. Select the text and page number. On the **Home tab**, in the **Font group**, change the **Font Size** to **12**. Click anywhere in the **Header** area to cancel the selection, and then compare your screen with Figure 3.3.

> The page number is inserted in the header at the position of the insertion point, and the font size matches the rest of the document. The default font size for the header and footer areas is 11 pt.

Figure 3.3

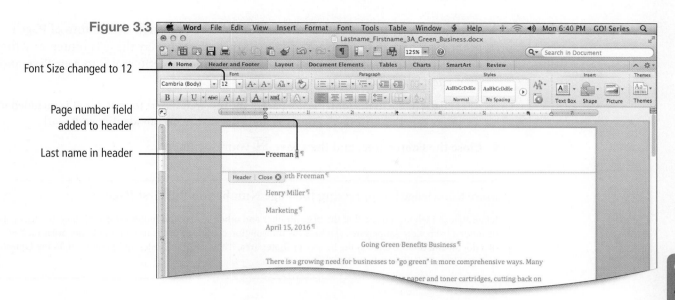

Font Size changed to 12

Page number field added to header

Last name in header

7 On the **Home tab**, in the **Paragraph group**, click the **Align Text Right** button ⬚. **Close** the **Header** area.

8 Near the top of **Page 1**, in the body of the document, locate the first paragraph beginning *There is a growing*, and then click to position the insertion point at the beginning of the paragraph. Without clicking anywhere else in the document, scroll to the end of the document, hold down Shift, and then click to right of the last paragraph mark to select all of the text from the insertion point to the end of the document. Release Shift.

Another Way

With the text selected, on the Format menu, click Paragraph. On the Indents and Spacing tab, under Indentation, click the Special arrow, and then click First line. Under Indentation, in the By box, be sure 0.5" displays.

9 With the text selected, on the ruler, point to the **First Line Indent** button ▽, and then drag the button to **0.5" on the horizontal ruler**. Compare your screen with Figure 3.4.

The MLA style uses 0.5-inch indents at the beginning of the first line of every paragraph. Indenting—moving the beginning of the first line of a paragraph to the right or left of the rest of the paragraph—provides visual cues to help the reader find the beginning of a paragraph and makes the document easier to read.

Figure 3.4

First Line Indent button moved to 0.5" on the ruler

First line indented 0.5 inch

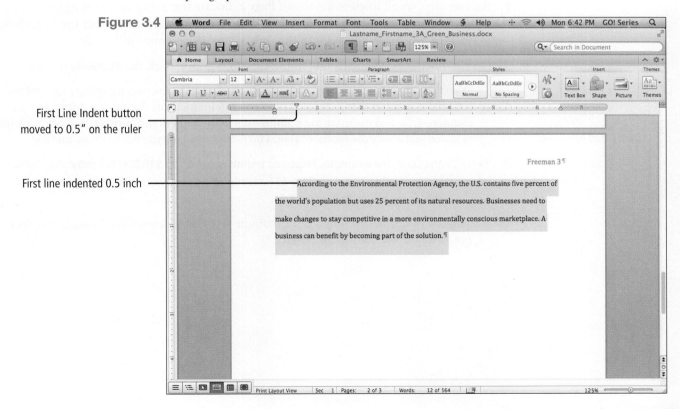

10 Click anywhere to cancel the selection of text. Scroll to view the bottom of **Page 1**, point anywhere in the bottom white margin area to display the ▣ pointer, and then double-click to display the **Footer** area. On the **Insert** menu, point to **AutoText**, and then click **Filename**.

> The file name in the footer is *not* part of the research report format, but it is included in projects in this textbook so that you and your instructor can identify your work.

11 **Close** the **Footer** area, and then **Save** 🔲 your document.

> **More Knowledge** | **Suppressing the Page Number on the First Page**
>
> Some style guidelines require that the page number and other header and footer information on the first page be hidden from view—*suppressed*. To hide the information contained in the header and footer areas on Page 1 of a document, double-click in the header or footer area. Then, on the Header and Footer tab, in the Options group, select the Different First Page check box.

Objective 2 | Insert Footnotes in a Research Paper

Reports and research papers typically include information that you find in other sources, and these must be credited. Within report text, numbers mark the location of *notes*—information that expands on the topic being discussed but that does not fit well in the document text. The numbers refer to *footnotes*—notes placed at the bottom of the page containing the note, or to *endnotes*—notes placed at the end of a document or chapter.

Activity 3.02 | Inserting Footnotes

Footnotes can be added as you type the document or after the document is complete. Word renumbers the footnotes automatically, so footnotes do not need to be entered in order, and if one footnote is removed, the remaining footnotes renumber automatically.

1 If necessary, scroll to view the top of **Page 2**. Locate the paragraph that begins *Consumers and businesses*. In the eighth line of text, toward the end of the line, click to position the insertion point to the right of the period after *followed*.

Another Way

On the Insert menu, click Footnote, which opens the Footnote and Endnote dialog box.

2 On the **Document Elements tab**, in the **Citations group**, click the **Footnote** button.

> Word creates space for a footnote in the footnote area at the bottom of the page and adds a footnote number to the text at the insertion point location. Footnote *1* displays in the footnote area, and the insertion point moves to the right of the number. A short black line is added just above the footnote area. You do not need to type the footnote number.

3 Type **Tennessee, for example, imposes penalties of up to $10,000 for providing false information regarding the recycling of hazardous waste.** Notice that the footnote is single-spaced as shown in Figure 3.5.

> This is an explanatory footnote; the footnote provides additional information that does not fit well in the body of the report.

Figure 3.5

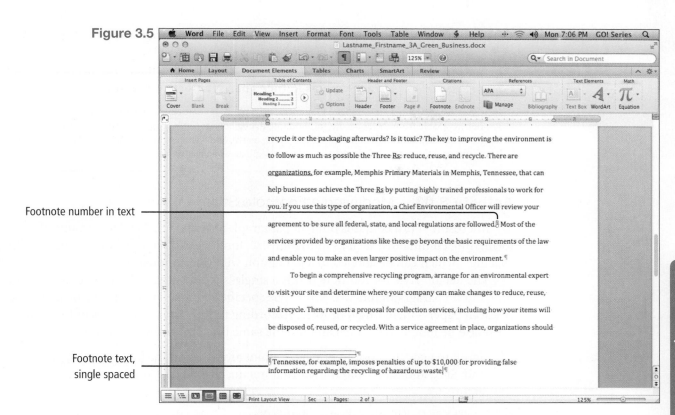

Footnote number in text

Footnote text, single spaced

4 Scroll to view the top of **Page 2**, and then locate the paragraph that begins *There are many common*. In the third line of text, click to position the insertion point to the right of the period following *environment*.

5 On the **Document Elements tab**, in the **Citations group**, click the **Footnote** button. Type **Exposure to lead can harm the human nervous system and cause learning problems.** Notice that the footnote you just added becomes the new footnote 1, as shown in Figure 3.6.

The first footnote is renumbered as footnote *2*.

Figure 3.6

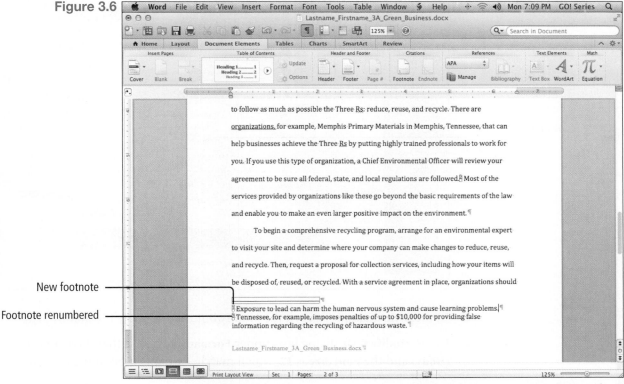

New footnote

Footnote renumbered

6 **Save** ⊞ your document.

Activity 3.03 | Modifying a Footnote Style

Microsoft Word contains built-in paragraph formats called *styles*—groups of formatting commands, such as font, font size, font color, paragraph alignment, and line spacing—which can be applied to a paragraph with one command.

The default style for footnote text is a single-spaced paragraph that uses a 12-point font and no paragraph indents. MLA style specifies double-spaced text in all areas of a research paper—including footnotes. According to MLA style, first lines of footnotes must also be indented 0.5 inch and use the same font size as the report text.

Another Way

On the Format menu, click Style.

1 Scroll to view the bottom of **Page 2**. Point anywhere in the footnote text, press Control and click, and then from the shortcut menu, click **Style**. Compare your screen with Figure 3.7.

The Style dialog box displays, listing the styles currently in use in the document, in addition to some of the word processing elements that come with special built-in styles. Because you pressed Control and clicked on the footnote text, under Styles, the selected style is Footnote Text.

Figure 3.7

Style dialog box

Footnote Text Style Description

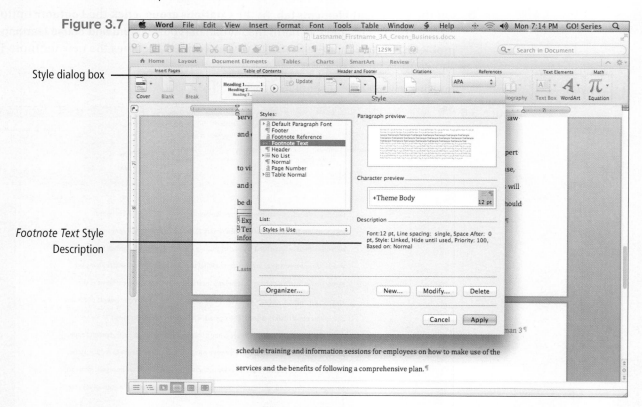

2 In the **Style** dialog box, click the **Modify** button to display the **Modify Style** dialog box.

3 In the **Modify Style** dialog box, under **Formatting**, notice that the **Font** is **Cambria (Body)** and the **Font Size** is **12**, which matches what is used in the document.

4 In the lower left corner of the dialog box, click the **Format** button, and then click **Paragraph**. In the **Paragraph** dialog box, under **Indentation**, click in the **Special** box, and then click **First line**.

5 Under **Spacing**, click in the **Line spacing** box, and then click **Double**. Compare your screen with Figure 3.8.

Figure 3.8

First line indent selected ——

Line spacing set to *Double* ——

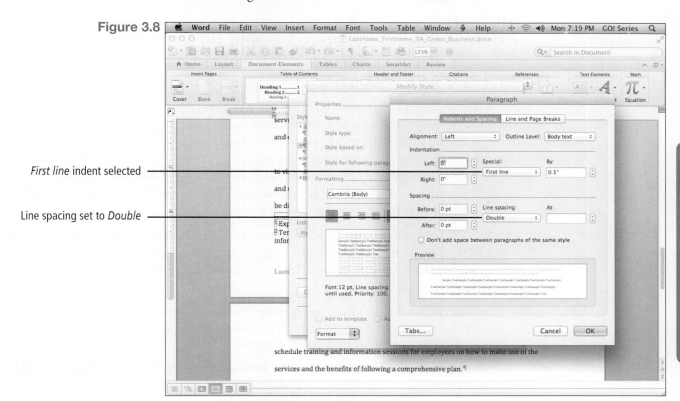

6 Click **OK** to close the **Paragraph** dialog box, click **OK** to close the **Modify Style** dialog box, and then click **Apply** to apply the new style and to close the Style dialog box. **Save** 💾 your document, and then compare your screen with Figure 3.9.

Your inserted footnotes are formatted with the new Footnote Text paragraph style; any new footnotes that you insert will also use this format.

Figure 3.9

First line indented ——

Footnote text
double-spaced ——

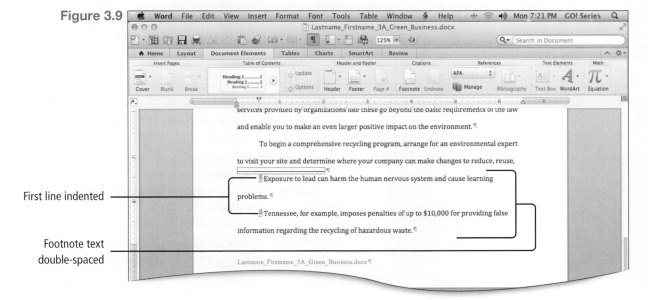

Objective 3 | Create Citations and a Bibliography in a Research Paper

When you use quotations from, or detailed summaries of, other people's work, you must specify the source of the information. A *citation* is a note inserted into the text of a report or research paper that refers the reader to a source in the bibliography. Create a *bibliography* at the end of a document to list the sources referred to in the document. Such a list is typically titled *Works Cited* (in MLA style), *Bibliography*, *Sources*, or *References*.

Activity 3.04 | Adding Citations

When writing a long research paper, you will likely reference numerous books, articles, and Web sites. Some of your research sources may be referenced many times, others only one time. References to sources within the text of your research paper are indicated in an *abbreviated* manner. However, as you enter a citation for the first time, you can also enter the *complete* information about the source. Then, when you have finished your paper, you will be able to automatically generate the list of sources that must be included at the end of your research paper.

1 Press Command ⌘ + fn + ← to position the insertion point at the top of the document, and then locate the paragraph that begins *Making a commitment*. In the fourth line, following the word *capitalism*, click to position the insertion point to the right of the quotation mark.

> The citation in a document points to the full source information in the bibliography, which typically includes the name of the author, the full title of the work, the year of publication, and other publication information.

2 On the **Document Elements tab**, in the **References group**, click the **Bibliography Style** button APA , and then click **MLA** to insert a reference using MLA style.

3 In the **References group**, click the **Manage** button, and then compare your screen with Figure 3.10.

> The Citations tool displays where you can manage the citations that you add to your document.

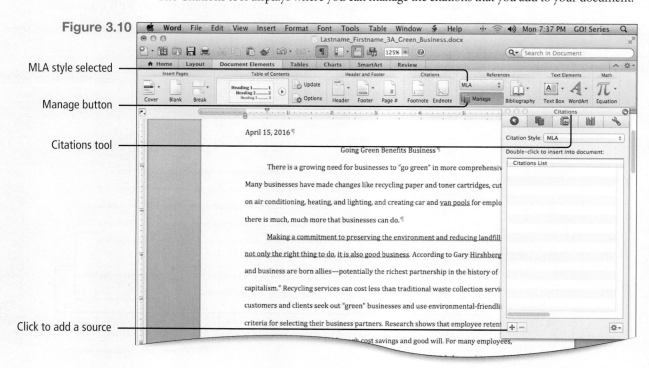

Figure 3.10

MLA style selected

Manage button

Citations tool

Click to add a source

4 At the bottom left corner of the **Citations** tool, click ⊞ to display the **Create New Source** dialog box. Be sure *Book* is selected as the **Type of Source**. Add the following information, and then compare your screen with Figure 3.11:

Author:	**Hirshberg, Gary**
Title:	**Stirring it Up: How to Make Money and Save the World**
City:	**New York**
Publisher:	**Hyperion**
Year:	**2012**

In the MLA style, citations that refer to items on the *Works Cited* page are placed in parentheses and are referred to as ***parenthetical references***—references that include the last name of the author or authors and the page number in the referenced source, which you add to the reference. No year is indicated, and there is no comma between the name and the page number.

Figure 3.11

Create New Source dialog box

Source type

MLA style selected

Citation information

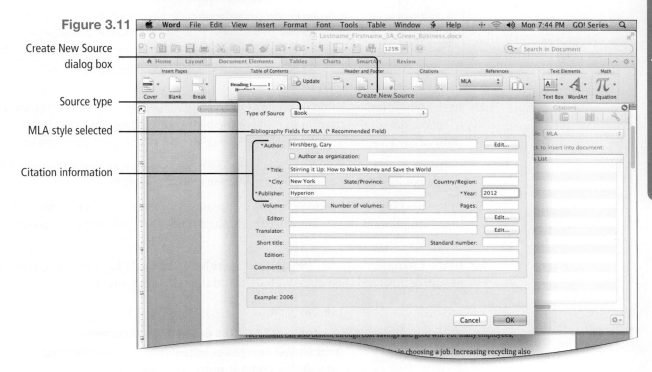

Note | Citing Corporate Authors

If the author of a document is identified as the name of an organization only, select the Author as organization check box and type the name of the organization in the Author as organization box.

---

5 Click **OK** to close the **Create New Source** dialog box and to insert the citation in the document and in the **Citations** tool in the **Citations List**. In the paragraph, point to *(Hirshberg)* and click one time to select the citation.

A blue frame displays around the citation.

6 On the right side of the blue frame that surrounds the citation, click the **arrow**, and then click **Edit This Citation**.

7 In the **Edit Citation** dialog box, under **Add**, in the **Pages** box, type **1** to indicate that you are citing from Page 1 of this source. Compare your screen with Figure 3.12.

Figure 3.12

Citation added to
Citations tool

Page number

Parenthetical reference
with blue frame
surrounding it

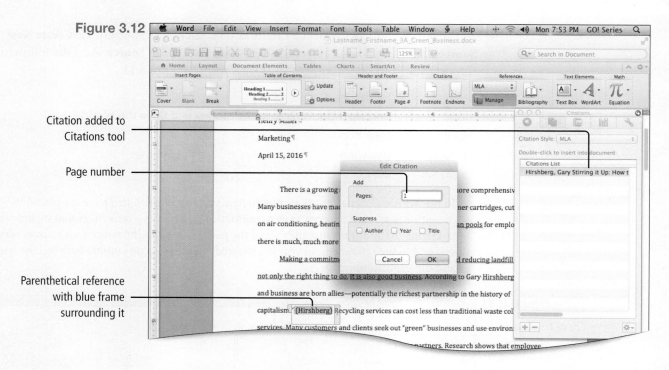

8 In the **Edit Citation** dialog box, click **OK** to display the page number of the citation. Click outside of the citation to remove the blue frame. Then type a period to the right of the citation, and delete the period to the left of the quotation mark.

In MLA style, if the reference occurs at the end of a sentence, the parenthetical reference always displays to the left of the punctuation mark that ends the sentence.

9 In the next paragraph, which begins *Government contractors*, click to position the insertion point at the end of the paragraph, but to the left of the period that ends the sentence.

10 In the **Citations** tool, click ➕. In the **Create New Source** dialog box, click in the **Type of Source** box, and then click **Web site**. Add the following information:

Author:	**Aitoro, Jill R.**
Name of Web page:	**Nextgov - GSA Drives Green IT Procurements**
URL:	**http://www.nextgov.com/technology-news/2008/02/ gsa-drives-green-it-procurements/41870**
Year:	**2008**
Month:	**February**
Day:	**21**
Year accessed:	**2016**
Month accessed:	**January**
Day accessed:	**17**

11 Compare your screen with Figure 3.13, and then click **OK** to close the **Create New Source** dialog box and add the citation.

A parenthetical reference is added. Because the cited Web page has no page numbers, only the author name is used in the parenthetical reference. The Web site citation is added to the Citations tool.

Figure 3.13

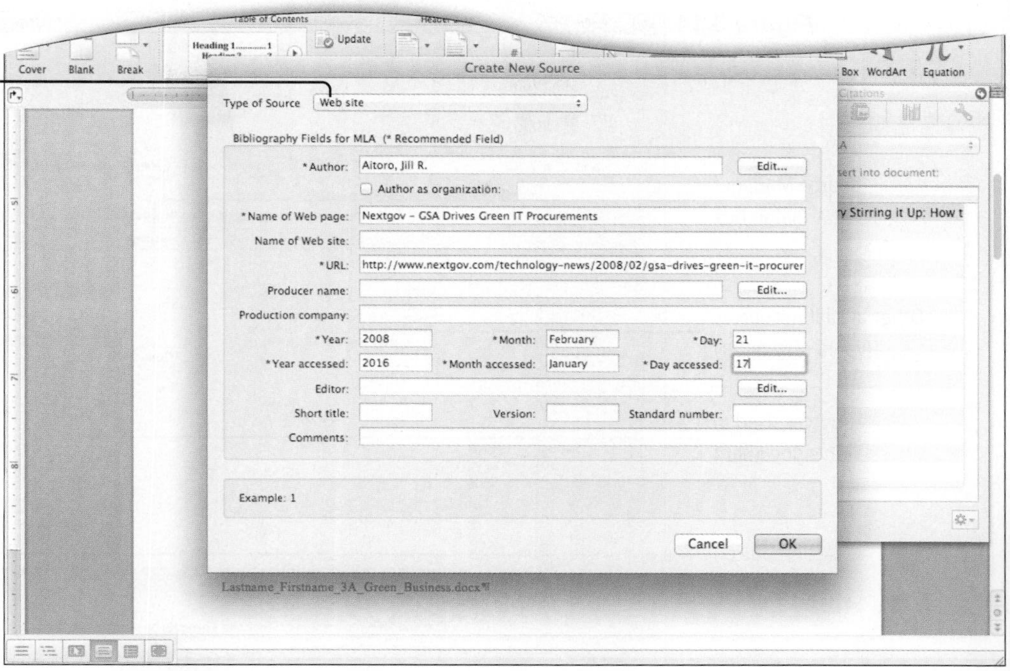

Web site citation

12 Double-click the title bar of the **Citations** tool to collapse it so that you can see more of the document. Near the top of **Page 2**, in the paragraph that begins *Consumers and businesses*, in the third line, click to position the insertion point following the word *toxic* to the left of the question mark.

13 Double-click the title bar of the **Citations** tool to expand it. In the **Citations** tool, click ✚. In the **Create New Source** dialog box, click in the **Type of Source** box, click **Book**, and then add the following information:

Author:	**Scott, Nicky**
Title:	**Reduce, Reuse, Recycle: An Easy Household Guide**
City:	**White River Junction**
State/Province:	**Vermont**
Publisher:	**Chelsea Green Publishing**
Year:	**2011**

14 Click **OK**. Click the inserted citation—*(Scott)*—to select it. On the blue frame that surrounds the citation, click the **arrow**, and then click **Edit This Citation**.

15 In the **Edit Citation** dialog box, in the **Pages** box, type **7** to indicate that you are citing from Page 7 of this source. Click **OK**. Click in the document to remove the frame from the citation.

16 In the lower right corner of the **Citations** tool, click the **Action** button ⚙▾, and then click **Citation Source Manager**. In the **Source Manager** dialog box, under **Current list**, click the third source, which displays the author name of *Scott*, and then compare your screen with Figure 3.14.

> The Source Manager dialog box displays. Other citations on your computer display in the *Master list* box. The citations for the current document display in the *Current list* box. Word maintains the Master list so that if you use the same sources regularly, you can copy sources from your Master list to the current document.

Figure 3.14

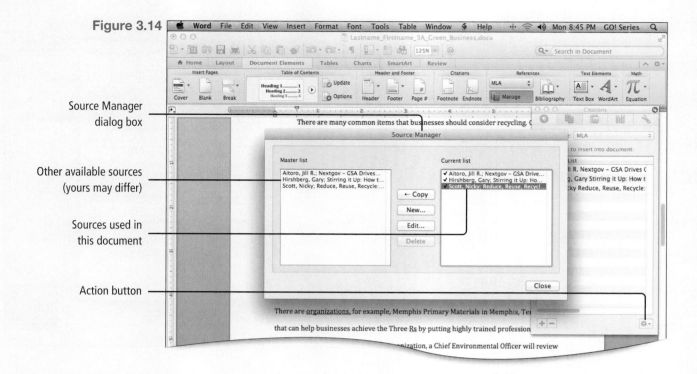

Source Manager
dialog box

Other available sources
(yours may differ)

Sources used in
this document

Action button

17 At the bottom of the **Source Manager** dialog box, click **Close**. **Close** the **Citations** tool, and then **Save** your document.

Activity 3.05 | Inserting Page Breaks

In this activity you will insert a manual page break so that you can begin your bibliography on a new page.

1 Press Command ⌘ + fn + → to move the insertion point to the end of the document.

┌ **Another Way**
On the Layout tab, in the Page Setup group, click the Break button, and then click Page.

--→ **2** On **Insert** menu, point to **Break**, and then click **Page Break**.

A ***manual page break*** forces a page to end at the insertion point location, and then places any subsequent text at the top of the next page. Recall that the new paragraph retains the formatting of the previous paragraph, so the first line is indented.

3 On the ruler, point to the **First Line Indent** button, and then drag the **First Line Indent** button to the left to **0 inches on the horizontal ruler**. **Save** your document.

4 Scroll as necessary to view the last paragraph for **Page 3**, and then compare your screen with Figure 3.15.

A ***page break indicator***, which shows where a manual page break was inserted, displays after the last paragraph on Page 3. The page-break indicator displays because you are showing formatting marks or nonprinting characters. If there were a footnote on this page, it would display at the bottom of the page below the page break indicator.

Figure 3.15

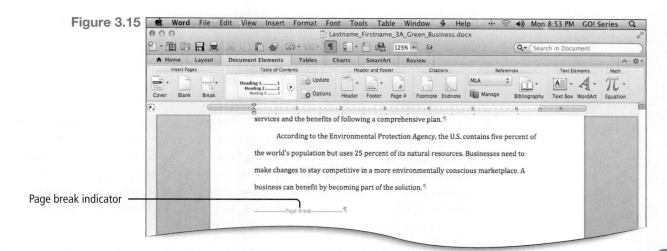

Page break indicator

Activity 3.06 | Creating a Reference Page

At the end of a report or research paper, include a list of each source referenced. *Works Cited* is the reference page heading used in the MLA style guidelines. Other styles may refer to this page as a *Bibliography* (Business Style) or *References* (APA Style). This information is always displayed on a separate page.

1 Scroll to view the top of **Page 4**. With the insertion point blinking in the blank line of **Page 4**, on the **Document Elements tab**, in the **References group**, in the **Bibliography Style** box, be sure *MLA* displays.

2 In the **References group**, click the **Bibliography** button, and then click the **Works Cited** box.

> An alphabetical list of the sources displays under the title *Works Cited*.

3 Click anywhere in the inserted text, and then compare your screen with Figure 3.16.

> The bibliography entries that you created display as a field, which is indicated by the gray shading when you click in the text. A blue frame surrounds the title and references. The field links to the Source Manager for the citations.

Figure 3.16

Click to display Bibliography options menu

Formatted *Works Cited* title automatically included

Entries display as a field, indicated by gray shading when selected

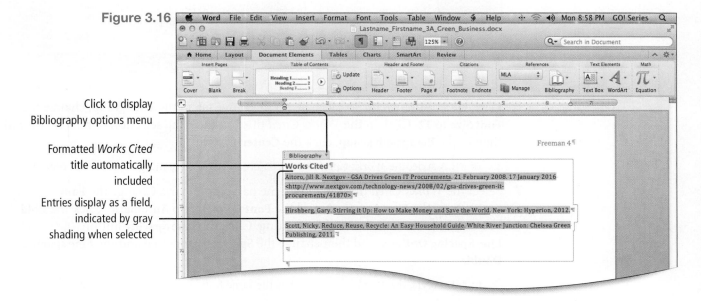

4 In the blue frame above *Works Cited*, click the **Bibliography arrow**, and then click **Convert Bibliography to Static Text**.

> The bibliography entries no longer display with gray shading because they are no longer contained in a field. Once you are certain that your sources are typed correctly, convert the bibliography entries to text so that you can format them in the latest MLA style.

5 In the bibliography, point to the left of the first entry—beginning *Aitoro, Jill*—to display the ![pointer] pointer. Drag down to select all three references. On the **Home tab**, in the **Paragraph group**, click the **Line Spacing** button ![button], and then click **Line Spacing Options**. In the **Paragraph** dialog box, on the **Indents and Spacing tab**, under **Indentation**, click in the **Special** box, and then click **Hanging**. Under **Spacing**, change **After** to **0**. Click in the **Line spacing** box, and then click **Double**. Compare your screen with Figure 3.17.

> The entries will be formatted according to MLA guidelines; the text is double-spaced, the extra space between paragraphs is removed, and each entry uses a *hanging indent*—the first line of each entry extends 0.5 inch to the left of the remaining lines of the entry.

Figure 3.17

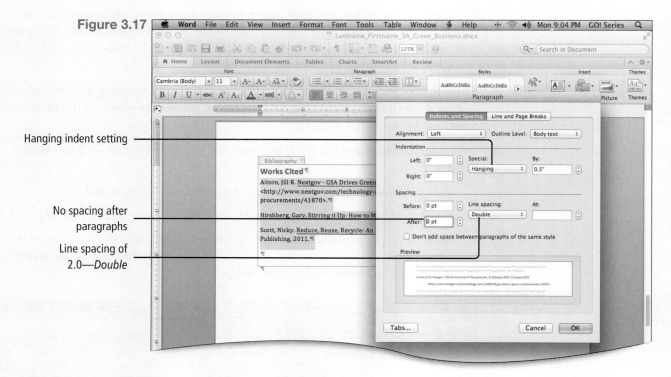

Hanging indent setting

No spacing after paragraphs

Line spacing of 2.0—*Double*

6 Click **OK**. With the entries selected, on the **Home tab** in the **Font group**, change the **Font Size** to **12**. Click in the *Works Cited* title to cancel the selection of references, and then in the **Paragraph group**, click the **Center Text** button ![button].

> In MLA style, the *Works Cited* title is centered between the margins of the document.

7 Select the *Works Cited* title, including the paragraph mark. Change the **Font** to **Cambria**, the **Font Size** to **12**, and the **Font Color** ![A] to **Automatic**. Click the **Bold** button ![B] to remove the bold formatting. Click the **Line Spacing** button ![button], click **Line Spacing Options**, and then change the **Spacing Before** to **0** and the **Line spacing** to **Double**.

> In MLA style, the *Works Cited* title has the same font and spacing as the text.

8 In the **Paragraph** dialog box, click **OK**. In the framed **Bibliography**, click in the blank line below the last source, and then press ⌦ to remove the extra blank line. Click below the framed **Bibliography** to remove the frame, **Save** 🖫 your document, and then compare your screen with Figure 3.18.

> MLA styles change. Be sure to consult with your instructor or an MLA style guide to format your bibliography in the correct manner. Although it takes some extra work to format the bibliography, time is saved because the entries are automatically generated from the Source Manager.

Figure 3.18

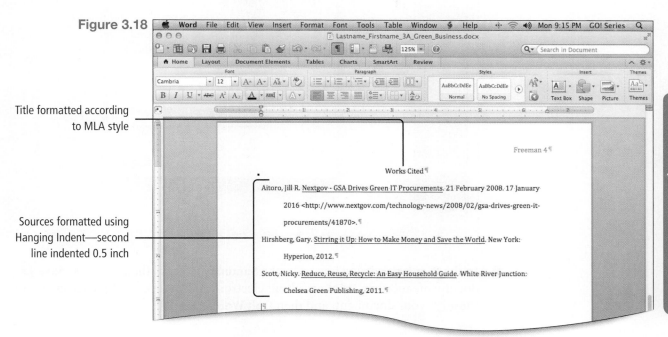

Title formatted according to MLA style

Sources formatted using Hanging Indent—second line indented 0.5 inch

Activity 3.07 | Managing File Properties

Recall that document property information is stored in the File Properties. An additional group of property categories is also available.

1 On the **File** menu, click **Properties**. On the **Summary tab**, in the **Title** box, type, **Going Green Benefits Business** and then in the **Subject** box, type your course information. In the **Author** box, select the existing text, and then type your firstname and lastname.

2 In the **Manager** box, type **Henry Miller** and in the **Company** box, type **Memphis Primary Materials**

3 In the **Category** box, type **Marketing Documents** and in the **Keywords** box, type **green business, research paper**

4 In the **Comments** box, type **Draft copy of a research report that will be included in the marketing materials packet**

5 In the **Properties** dialog box, click the **Statistics tab**, and then compare your screen with Figure 3.19.

> The document statistics show the number of revisions made to the document, the last time the document was edited, and the number of paragraphs, lines, words, and characters in the document.

Figure 3.19

Statistics tab

Document statistics
(yours may vary slightly)

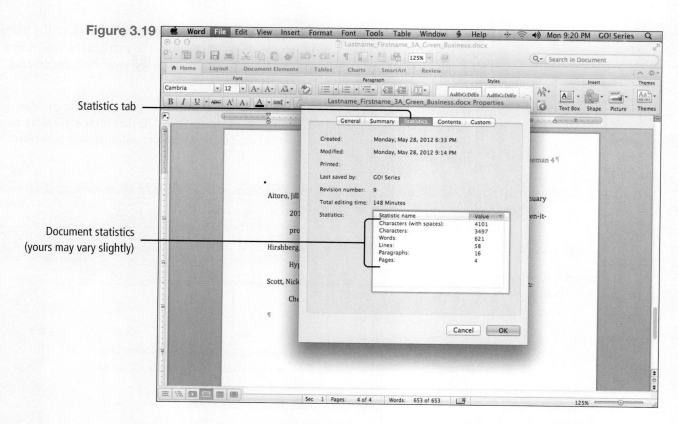

6 In the **Properties** dialog box, click the **Summary tab**, and then click **OK**. **Save** [H] your document, and then **Print** or submit electronically as directed by your instructor. **Close** [⊗] your document, and then **Quit Word**.

End **You have completed Project 3A** ——————————

Project 3B Newsletter with Mailing Labels

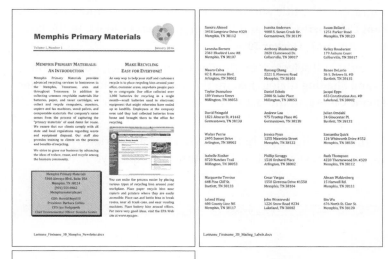

Figure 3.20
Project 3B Memphis Newsletter

Objective 4 | Format a Multiple-Column Newsletter

All newspapers and most magazines and newsletters use multiple columns for articles because text in narrower columns is easier to read than text that stretches across a page. Word has a tool with which you can change a single column of text into two or more columns, and then format the columns. If a column does not end where you want it to, you can end the column at a location of your choice by inserting a *manual column break*.

Activity 3.08 | Changing One Column of Text to Two Columns

Newsletters are usually two or three columns wide. When using 8.5 × 11-inch paper in portrait orientation, avoid creating four or more columns because they are so narrow that word spacing looks awkward, often resulting in one long word on a line by itself.

1 Open **Word**. From your student files, locate and open the document **w03B_Memphis_Newsletter**. If necessary, display the formatting marks and rulers and increase the size of the window to fill the entire screen. On the Standard toolbar, click the **Zoom arrow** , and then click **125%**. **Save** the file in your **Word Chapter 3** folder as **Lastname_Firstname_3B_Memphis_Newsletter** and then insert the file name in the **Footer** area.

> The document is formatted using 1" margins, 1.15 line spacing, 10-pt spacing after paragraphs, and 11-pt font size to make it easier to read online.

2 Select the first paragraph of text—*Memphis Primary Materials*. On the **Home tab**, in the **Font group**, change the **Font** to **Arial Black** and the **Font Size** to **24**.

3 Select the first two paragraphs—the title and the volume information and date. In the **Font group**, click the **Font Color arrow** $\boxed{A}$, and then under **Theme Colors**, in the last row, click the fifth color—**Accent 1, Darker 50%**.

4 With the first two paragraphs still selected, on the **Format** menu, click **Borders and Shading**. In the **Borders and Shading** dialog box, on the **Borders tab**, click in the **Color** box, and then under **Theme Colors**, in the last row, click the fifth color—**Accent 1, Darker 50%**.

Another Way

In the Preview area, click the Bottom Border button.

5 Click in the **Width** box, and then click **3 pt**. In the **Preview** box at the right, point to the *bottom* border of the small preview and click one time. Compare your screen with Figure 3.21.

Figure 3.21

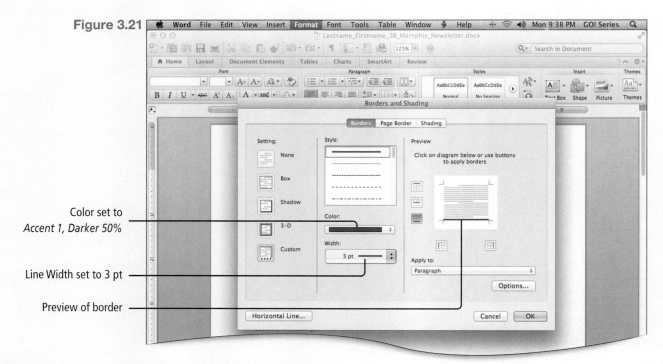

Color set to *Accent 1, Darker 50%*

Line Width set to 3 pt

Preview of border

6   In the **Borders and Shading** dialog box, click **OK**.

> The line visually defines the newsletter *nameplate*—the banner on the front page of a newsletter that identifies the publication.

7   Below the nameplate, beginning with the paragraph *Memphis Primary Materials: An Introduction*, select all of the text to the end of the document, which extends to two pages.

8   On the **Home tab**, in the **Paragraph group**, click the **Columns** button ⊞▾, and then click **Two**.

9   Without clicking in the document, scroll to view the top of **Page 1**, **Save** 🖫 your document, and then compare your screen with Figure 3.22.

> Word divides the text into two columns, and inserts a *section break* below the nameplate, dividing the one-column section of the document from the two-column section of the document. A *section* is a portion of a document that can be formatted differently from the rest of the document. A section break marks the end of one section and the beginning of another section. Do not be concerned if your columns do not break at the same line as shown in the figure.

Figure 3.22

Columns button

Section Break inserted

Text displays in two columns

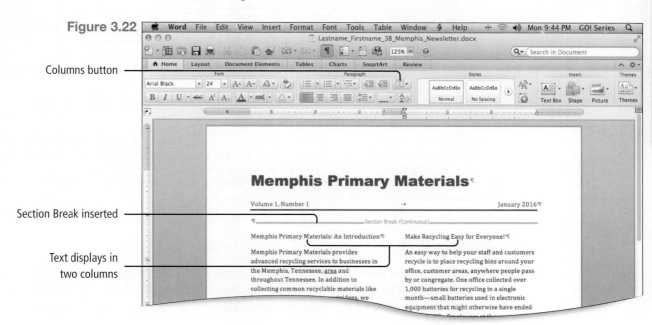

Activity 3.09 | Formatting Multiple Columns

The uneven right margin of a single page-width column is easy to read. When you create narrow columns, justified text is sometimes preferable. Depending on the design and layout of your newsletter, you might decide to reduce extra space between paragraphs and between columns to improve the readability of the document.

1   With the two columns of text still selected, on the **Home tab**, in the **Paragraph group**, click the **Line Spacing** button 🔲▾, and then click **Line Spacing Options**. Under **Spacing**, click the **After down spin arrow** one time to change the spacing after to **6 pt**, and then click **OK**.

2   On the **Home tab**, in the **Paragraph group**, click the **Justify Text** button 🔲.

3   Click anywhere in the document to deselect the text, **Save** 🖫 your document, and then compare your screen with Figure 3.23.

Figure 3.23

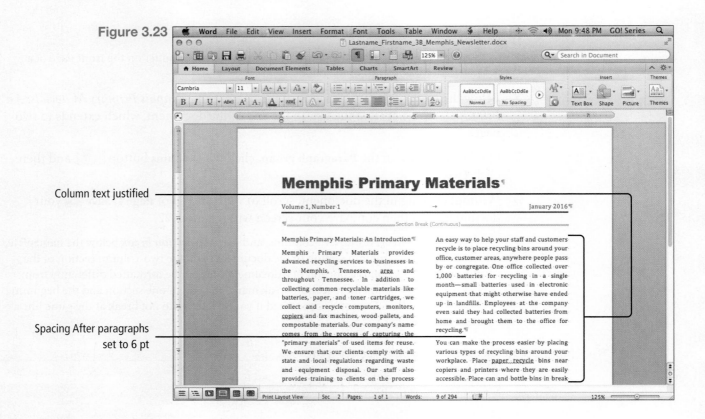

Column text justified

Spacing After paragraphs
set to 6 pt

More Knowledge | Justifying Column Text

Although many magazines and newspapers still justify text in columns, there are a variety of opinions about whether to justify the columns, or to use left alignment and leave the right edge uneven. Justified text tends to look more formal and cleaner, but in a word processing document, it also results in uneven spacing between words. It is the opinion of some authorities that justified text is more difficult to read, especially in a page-width document. Let the overall look and feel of your newsletter be your guide.

Activity 3.10 | Inserting a Column Break

1 Scroll to view the lower portion of the page. In the first column, locate the company address that begins with the paragraph *Memphis Primary Materials*, and then select that paragraph and the three following paragraphs, ending with the telephone number.

2 On the **Home tab**, in the **Paragraph group**, click the **Line Spacing** button [icon], and then click **Line Spacing Options**. Under **Spacing**, click the **After down spin arrow** one time to change the spacing after to **0 pt**, and then click **OK**.

3 Select the three paragraphs that begin with *CEO* and end with *CFO*, and then change the **Spacing After** to **0 pt**.

4 Near the bottom of the first column, click to position the insertion point at the beginning of the line that begins *Make Recycling*.

5 On the **Layout tab**, in the **Page Setup group**, click the **Break** button to display the gallery of Page Breaks and Section Breaks. Compare your screen with Figure 3.24.

Figure 3.24

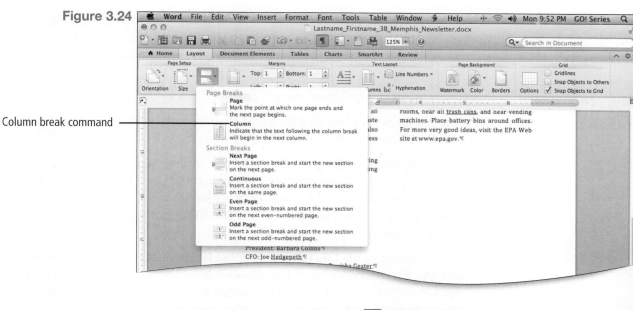

Column break command

6 Under **Page Breaks**, click **Column**. **Save** your document. If necessary, scroll to view the bottom of the first column, and then compare your screen with Figure 3.25.

A *column break indicator*—a dotted line containing the words *Column Break*—displays at the bottom of the column. The text to the right of the column break moved to the top of the next column. The column break indicator displays because you are showing formatting marks or nonprinting characters in this document.

Figure 3.25

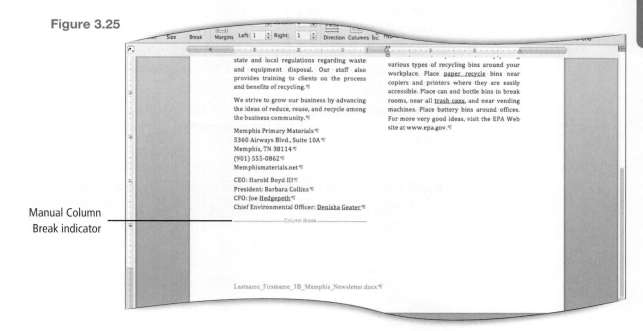

Manual Column Break indicator

Activity 3.11 | Inserting a ClipArt Image

Clip art images—predefined graphics included with Microsoft Office or downloaded from the Web—can make your document visually appealing and more interesting.

1 Press Command ⌘ + fn + ← to move the insertion point to the beginning of the document. On the **Home tab**, in the **Insert group**, click the **Picture** button, and then click **Clip Art Gallery**.

2 At the bottom of the **Clip Gallery**, click the **Online** button. In the message box, click **Yes** to launch your browser—a message box may not display if you previously launched the browser and clicked the *Don't ask me again* check box in the message box.

> Your browser application opens the Microsoft Office Images Web page.

3 Click in the **Search** box, and then type **environmental awareness recycling arrows** so that Word can search for images that contain these keywords. Press Return.

4 Locate the image of the green heart with three blue, bent arrows in it. Point to the image, and then click **view details**. Be sure that the name of the image is *Recycling symbol in green heart*—if it is not, click the back button in your browser and then select the correct image. Click the **Download** button. **Close** ⊖ the Web page, and then **Quit** your browser.

5 At the bottom of the **Clip Gallery**, click the **Import** button to display the **Import** dialog box and the contents of your **Downloads** folder. Select the file you downloaded—*MC900441848.WMF*. At the bottom of the **Import** dialog box, click the **Move into Clip Gallery** option button, and then click **Import**.

> The image is moved from your Downloads folder to the Clip Gallery.

6 In the **Properties** dialog box, in the **Description of this clip** box, type **Recycle** In the **Properties** dialog box, click the **Keywords tab**, and then click **New Keyword**. In the **New Keyword** box, type **environmental awareness** and then click **OK**. In the **Properties** dialog box, click **OK**. In the **Clip Gallery**, click in the **Search** box, type **environmental awareness** and then click the **Search** button to locate the image that you downloaded and moved to the Clip Gallery.

7 If necessary, click the **Recycle** image, and then click **Insert** to insert the clip art in your document. In the document, click the image to select it, and then compare your screen with Figure 3.26.

> Recall that when you insert a graphic, it is inserted as an inline object; that is, it is treated as a character in a line of text. Here, the inserted clip art becomes the first character in the nameplate.

Figure 3.26

Image inserted in
document and selected

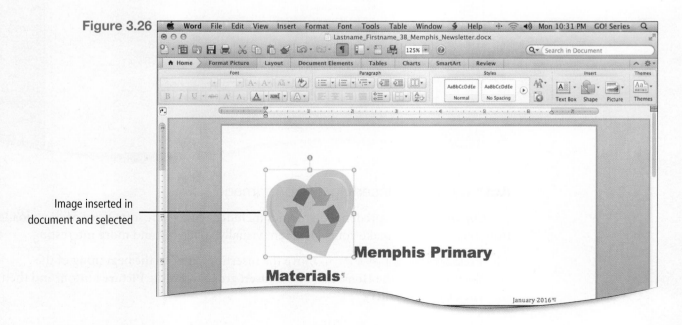

8 With the image still selected, on the **Format Picture tab**, in the **Size group**, triple-click in the **Height** box, type **1** and then press ⏎Return. In the **Arrange group**, click the **Wrap Text** button, and then click **Square**.

9 Point to the image to display the ✥ pointer, and then drag the image to the right so that the bottom edge aligns slightly above *January 2016*, and the right side aligns with the right margin. Recall that you can press the arrow keys as necessary to nudge the image in small, precise increments.

10 **Save** 💾 the document, and then compare your screen with Figure 3.27.

Figure 3.27

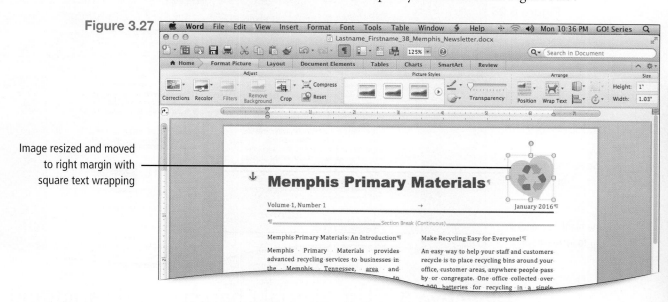

Image resized and moved to right margin with square text wrapping

Activity 3.12 │ Inserting a Screenshot

A *screenshot* is an image of an active window on your computer that you can paste into a document. Screenshots are especially useful when you want to insert an image of a Web site into a document you are creating in Word. You can insert a screenshot of any open window on your computer.

1 Without closing Word, from the **Dock**, open your Internet browser. If necessary, click the Zoom button 🔘 or drag the lower right corner of the window down and to the right to increase the size of the browser window so that it fills the entire screen. In your browser window, in the address bar, type **www.epa.gov/wastes/conserve/rrr** and press ⏎Return.

> **Alert!** │ **If Web Page is Not Found**
>
> Web page locations or addresses often change. If the Web page *www.epa.gov/wastes/conserve/rrr* is not found, in the address bar, type *www.epa.gov* and then search the site for the keyword recycle and find a Web page to use for the activity.

2 Press ⌘Command ⌘ + Control + Shift + 3. **Close** 🔘 your Web page, and then **Quit** your browser.

> If the sound on your computer is on, you will hear what sounds like a camera click. A copy of the screen is saved to the Clipboard.

3 If the Word application does not display, from the Dock, click the 📱 icon to redisplay your *3B_Memphis_Newletter* document. In the second column, click to position the insertion point at the beginning of the paragraph that begins *You can make*.

Another Way

On Standard toolbar,
click the Paste button.

4 Press Command ⌘ + V to paste the screenshot from the Clipboard into the document. Press Return one time to add space between the screenshot and the paragraph that begins with *You can make*. **Save** 🖬 the document, and then compare your screen with Figure 3.28.

The screenshot is inserted at the insertion point, and the image resizes to fit between the column margins.

Figure 3.28

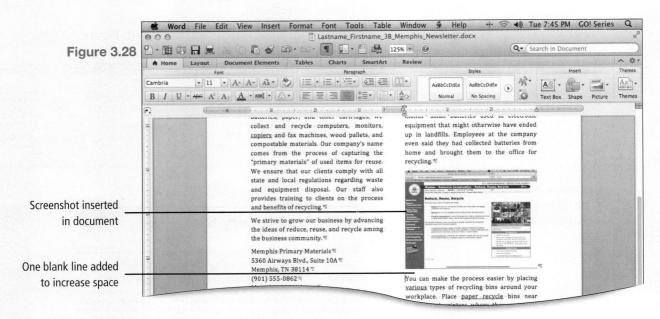

Screenshot inserted
in document

One blank line added
to increase space

Objective 5 | Use Special Character and Paragraph Formatting

Special text and paragraph formatting are useful to emphasize text, and they make your newsletter look more professional. For example, you can place a border around one or more paragraphs or add shading to a paragraph. When adding shading, use light colors; dark shading can make the text difficult to read.

Activity 3.13 | Applying the Small Caps Font Effect

For headlines and titles, *small caps* is an attractive font effect. The effect changes lowercase letters to uppercase letters, but with the same height of the lowercase letters.

1 At the top of the first column, select the paragraph *Memphis Primary Materials: An Introduction* including the paragraph mark.

Another Way

Press Command ⌘ + D
to display the Font
dialog box.

2 On the **Format** menu, click **Font** to display the **Font** dialog box. Click in the **Font color** box, and then under **Theme Colors**, in the last row, click the fifth color—**Accent 1, Darker 50%**.

3 Under **Font style**, click **Bold**. Under **Size**, click **16**. Under **Effects**, select the **Small caps** check box. Compare your screen with Figure 3.29.

The Font dialog box provides more options than are available on the Ribbon and enables you to make several changes at the same time. In the Preview box, the text displays with the selected formatting options applied.

Figure 3.29

Bold selected

Font color selected

Small caps effect selected

16-pt font size selected

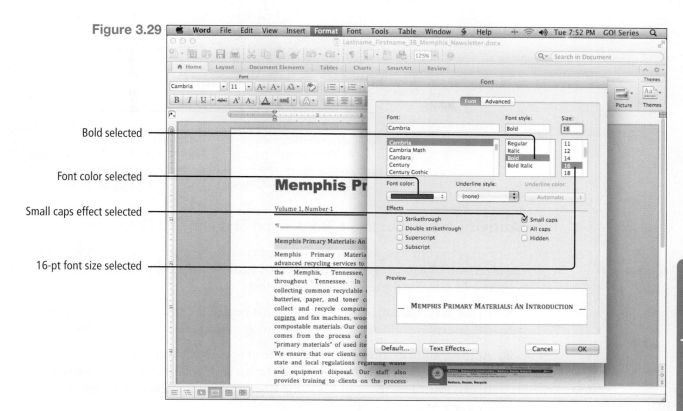

4 In the **Font** dialog box, click **OK**. On the **Home tab**, in the **Paragraph group**, click the **Center Text** button.

5 With the text still selected, on the Standard toolbar, click the **Format Painter** button. Then, at the top of the second column, select the paragraph *Make Recycling Easy for Everyone!* to apply the same formats. Notice that the column title wraps, which places a single word on the second line.

6 Position the insertion point to the left of the word *Easy*, and then press Delete to remove the space between *Recycling* and *Easy*. Hold down Shift and then press Return.

Holding down Shift while pressing Return inserts a ***manual line break***, which moves the text to the right of the insertion point to a new line while keeping the text in the same paragraph. If you simply press Return, the second line of the heading will be in its own paragraph and will not have the same line spacing applied to it as the first line of the heading. A ***line break indicator***, in the shape of a bent arrow, indicates that a manual line break is inserted. Similar to the Section Break and Column Break indicators, the line break indicator displays because you are showing formatting marks or nonprinting characters.

7 **Save** the document, and then compare your screen with Figure 3.30.

Figure 3.30

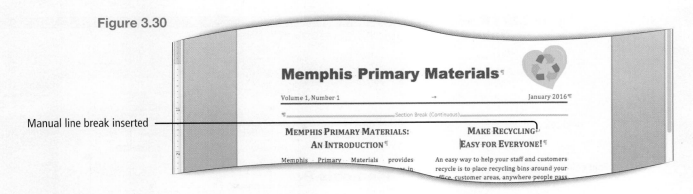

Manual line break inserted

Activity 3.14 | Adding a Border and Shading to a Paragraph

Paragraph borders provide strong visual cues to the reader. Paragraph shading can be used with or without borders. When used with a border, light shading can be very effective in drawing the reader's eye to the text.

1 In the first column, in the paragraph that begins *We strive to grow*, click to position the insertion point at the end of the paragraph, and then press Return one time.

2 At the bottom of the column, select the nine lines of company information, beginning with *Memphis Primary Materials* and ending with the paragraph that begins *Chief Environmental*. On the **Home tab**, in the **Paragraph group**, click the **Center Text** button.

3 With the text still selected, on the **Format** menu, click **Borders and Shading**. In the **Borders and Shading** dialog box, with the **Borders tab** active, under **Setting**, click **Shadow**. Compare your screen with Figure 3.31.

In the lower right portion of the Borders and Shading dialog box, the *Apply to* box displays *Paragraph*. The *Apply to* box directs where the border will be applied—in this instance, the border will be applied only to the selected paragraphs. Word saves the last line color and width settings that you used in the document, so the Color is set at Accent 1, Darker 50%, and the Width is set at 3 pt.

Figure 3.31

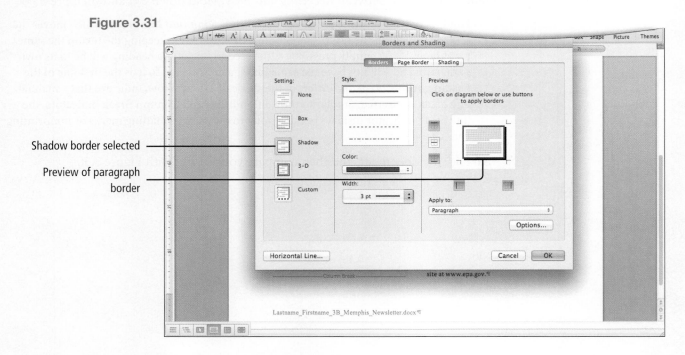

Shadow border selected

Preview of paragraph border

4 At the top of the **Borders and Shading** dialog box, click the **Shading tab**.

5 Under **Fill** in the gallery of colors, in the last row, click the sixth color—**Pale Blue**. Notice that the shading change is reflected in the Preview area on the right side of the dialog box, and that *Pale Blue* displays in the box above the *More Colors* button.

6 At the bottom of the **Borders and Shading** dialog box, click **OK**. Click anywhere in the document to deselect the text, **Save** 🖫 the document, and then compare your screen with Figure 3.32.

Figure 3.32

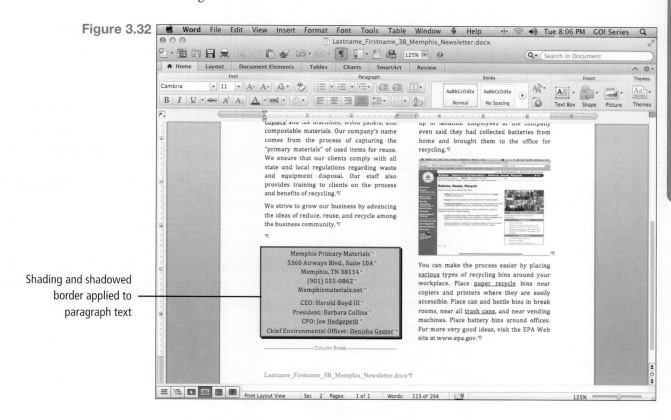

Shading and shadowed border applied to paragraph text

7 On the **File** menu, click **Properties**, and then be sure that the **Summary tab** is active. In the **Subject** box, type your course name and section number, and in the **Author** box, delete any text and then type your firstname and lastname. In the **Keywords** box, type **newsletter, January** and then click **OK**. **Save** 🖫 your document.

8 On the **File** menu, click **Print**, and then view the Preview of the document. **Print** or submit your document electronically as directed by your instructor. **Close** ⊗ the document, leaving Word open for the next activity.

Objective 6 | Create Mailing Labels Using Mail Merge

Word's ***mail merge*** feature joins a ***main document*** and a ***data source*** to create customized letters or labels. The main document contains the text or formatting that remains constant. For labels, the main document contains the formatting for a specific label size. The data source contains information including the names and addresses of the individuals for whom the labels are being created. Names and addresses in a data source might come from a Word table, an Excel spreadsheet, or an address book.

The easiest way to perform a mail merge is to use the Mail Merge Manager, which lists the steps and guides you through the mail merge process.

Activity 3.15 | Opening and Using the Mail Merge Manager

In this activity, you will open the data source for the mail merge, which is a Word table containing names and addresses.

Another Way
Press Command ⌘ + N

1 If necessary, open Word. On the **File** menu, click **New Blank Document**. If necessary, display the formatting marks and rulers and increase the size of the window to fill the entire screen. If necessary, on the Standard toolbar, click the Zoom arrow 100% ▾, and then click 125%.

> The blank document is where the mailing labels will display once the merge is completed.

2 With your new document open on the screen, from your student files, **Open** the file **w03B_Addresses**. If necessary, increase the size of the window to fill the entire screen. If necessary, on the Standard toolbar, click the Zoom arrow 100% ▾, and then click 125%. **Save** the address file in your **Word Chapter 3** folder as **Lastname_Firstname_3B_ Addresses** and then **Insert** the **Filename** in the **Footer** area.

> This document contains a table of addresses. The first row contains the column names. The remaining rows contain the names and addresses.

3 Click to position the insertion point in the last cell in the table, and then press ⟨Tab⟩ to create a new row. Enter the following information, pressing ⟨Tab⟩ to move between the cells, and then compare your screen with Figure 3.33:

First Name	**John**
Last Name	**Wisniewski**
Address 1	**1226 Snow Road**
Unit	**#234**
City	**Lakeland**
State	**TN**
ZIP Code	**38002**

Figure 3.33

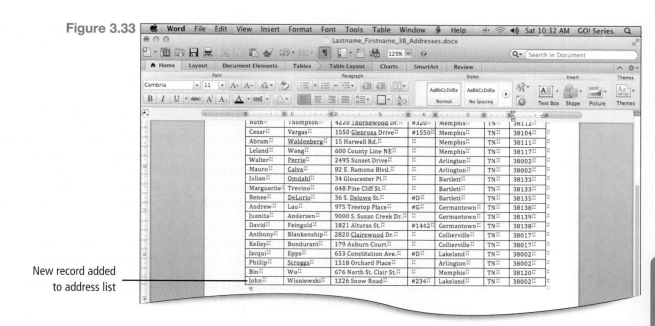

New record added to address list

4 **Save** 🖫 your document, and then **Close** 🔘 the table of addresses. Your blank document is the active document.

5 On the **Tools** menu, click **Mail Merge Manager** to display the **Mail Merge Manager**. If necessary, point to the title bar of the **Mail Merge Manager** to display the 🔍 pointer, and then drag the tool to the left side of your screen to view more of the document.

6 In the **Mail Merge Manager**, under **1. Select Document Type**, click the **Create New** button, and then click **Labels**. In the **Label Options** dialog box, in the **Label products** box, be sure that **Avery standard** displays. Under **Product number**, be sure that **5160 – Address** displays. Under **Label** information, notice the details about the selected address label. Compare your screen with Figure 3.34.

> The Avery 5160 address label is a commonly used label, and is automatically selected when you are creating labels. The pre-cut sheets contain three columns of 10 labels each—for a total of 30 labels per sheet. Each label is 1" high and 2.63" wide.

Figure 3.34

Mail Merge Manager—lists steps to merge documents

Label Options dialog box

Default Label product

Default Product number for Avery standard label

Label information

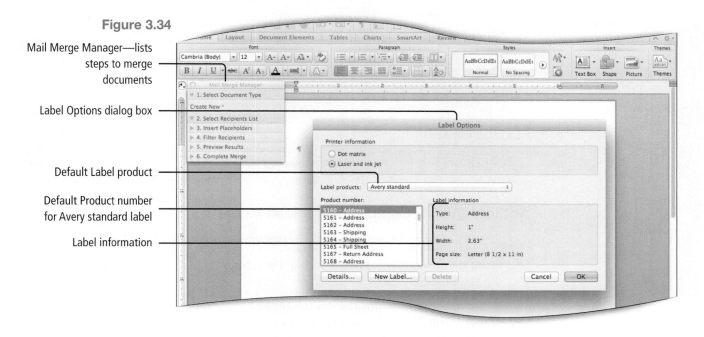

7 At the bottom of the **Label Options** dialog box, click **OK**. In the **Mail Merge Manager**, notice that Step **1**, where you clicked *Create New*, displays information about the merge—the name of the main document and the fact that you are creating mailing labels.

> The label page is set up with three columns and ten rows. Each label is identified by <<Next Record>>, and the labels display in cells in a table. The label borders may or may not display on your screen, depending on your settings. In Step 2 of the Mail Merge Manager, you must identify the recipients—the data source. For your recipient data source, you can choose to use an existing list—for example, a list of names and addresses that you have in a FileMaker Pro database, an Excel worksheet, a Word table, or your Outlook or Apple contacts list. If you do not have an existing data source, you can type a new list at this step.

8 If label borders do not display, on the Ribbon, click the Table Layout tab. In the Settings group, click the Gridlines button, and then notice that each label is outlined.

9 In the **Mail Merge Manager**, under **2. Select Recipients List**, click the **Get List** button, and then click **Open Data Source**.

10 In the **Choose a File** dialog box, navigate to your **Word Chapter 3** folder, select your **Lastname_Firstname_3B_Addresses** file, and then click **Open**. In the **Edit Labels** dialog box, click in the **Insert Merge Field** box, and then compare your screen with Figure 3.35.

> In the Edit Labels dialog box, the column headings from the text in the first row of your Word table of addresses display. Each row of information that contains data for one person is referred to as a *record*. The column headings—for example, *First_Name* and *Last_Name*—are referred to as *fields*. An underscore replaces the spaces between words in the field name headings.

Figure 3.35

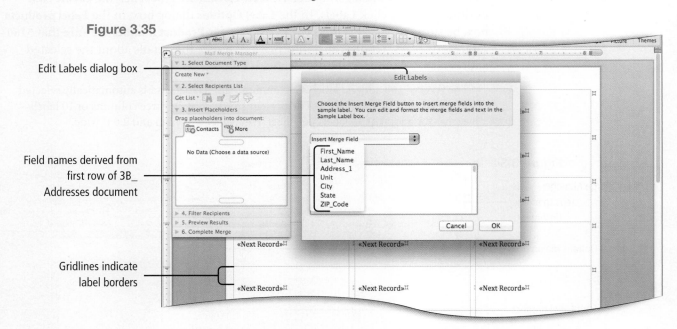

Edit Labels dialog box

Field names derived from first row of 3B_ Addresses document

Gridlines indicate label borders

Activity 3.16 | Completing the Mail Merge

You can add or edit names and addresses while completing the Mail Merge.

1 From the **Insert Merge Field** list, click **First_Name**, and notice the text that displays in the **Sample label** box.

> <<*First_Name*>> displays, which is the field name for the column in your 3B_Addresses document. This field name serves as a placeholder for the first name of a record. The insertion point is positioned to the right of the field name.

2 Press Spacebar. Click in the **Insert Merge Field** box, and then click **Last_Name**. Press Return to move the insertion point to the next line of the label.

3 Click in the **Insert Merge Field** box, and then click **Address_1**, which is the field name for the street address. Press Spacebar, and then insert the **Unit** field name, which is the apartment or unit number. Press Return, insert the **City** field name, and then type **,** (a comma). Press the Spacebar, insert the **State** field name, press Spacebar, and then insert the **ZIP_Code** field name. Compare your screen with Figure 3.36.

> If you make a mistake entering a space or comma, use the same techniques you use in any document to insert or delete characters.

Figure 3.36

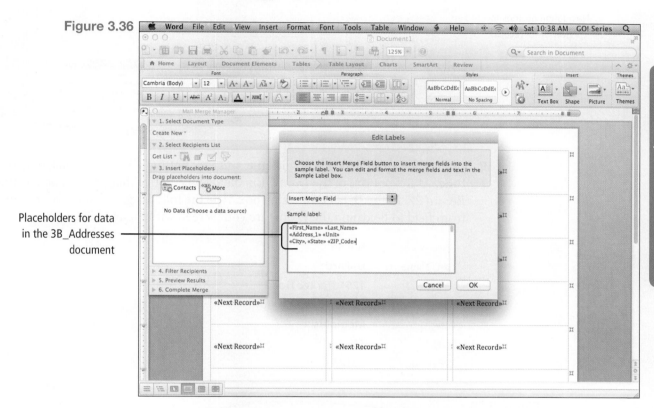

Placeholders for data in the 3B_Addresses document

4 In the **Edit Labels** dialog box, click **OK**. In the **Mail Merge Manager**, notice that in Step **3**, the placeholders are inserted under Contacts. Also notice that the labels within the document are populated with the field names.

5 In the **Mail Merge Manager**, under Step **2**, to the right of *Get List*, point to the icons to display the ScreenTip for each icon, and then click the **Edit Data Source** button. Compare your screen with Figure 3.37.

> Click the Edit Data Source button to edit existing records in the data source—3B_Addresses—or to add records to the data source. The navigation buttons at the bottom of the dialog box enable you to view other records in the data source. The first record for *Taylor Dunnahoo* displays in the Data Form dialog box.

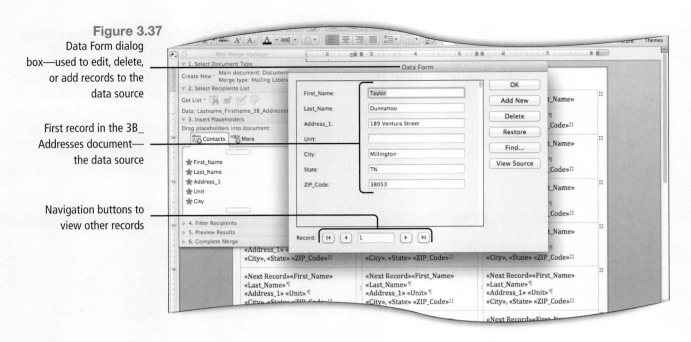

Figure 3.37
Data Form dialog
box—used to edit, delete,
or add records to the
data source

First record in the 3B_
Addresses document—
the data source

Navigation buttons to
view other records

6 In the **Data Form** dialog box, click the **Add New** button—be sure to click only one time. At the bottom of the *Data Form* dialog box, notice that you will be creating *Record 27*. In the **Data Form** dialog box, type the following, pressing Tab to move from field to field, and then compare your screen with Figure 3.38.

First_Name	**Susan**
Last_Name	**Ballard**
Address_1	**1251 Parker Road**
Unit:	
City	**Memphis**
State	**TN**
ZIP_Code	**38123**

Figure 3.38

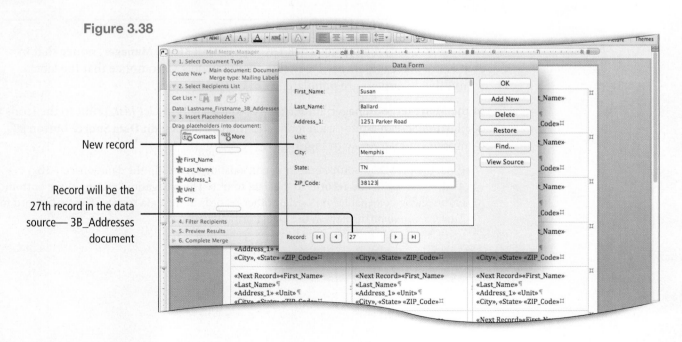

New record

Record will be the
27th record in the data
source— 3B_Addresses
document

7 In the **Data Form** dialog box, click **OK**. In the **Mail Merge Manager**, click **5. Preview Results** to expand the section. Without clicking, point to each icon to display its ScreenTip, and then click the **View Merged Data** button ![icon]. Scroll to view the bottom of the document, notice the new record you just entered, and then compare your screen with Figure 3.39.

Preview the labels before completing the merge so that you can correct any formatting errors. In the Mail Merge Manager window, click Step 4 to select records to include in the merge that match specified criteria, such as records for individuals living in Memphis.

Figure 3.39

Preview displays labels as they will print when merge is completed

View Merged Data button

New record in data source

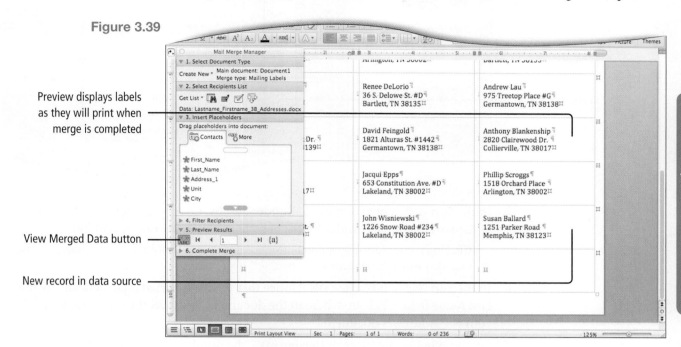

8 **Close** ![icon] the **Mail Merge Manager** so that you can see the entire document of labels.

Activity 3.17 | Previewing, Sorting, and Printing the Mail Merge Document

If you discover that you need to make further changes to your labels, you can still make them even though the Mail Merge Manager is closed.

1 Scroll to view the top of the document, and notice that the labels do not display in alphabetical order.

2 On **Tools** menu, click **Mail Merge Manager**. In the **Mail Merge Manager**, under Step **2**, click the **Edit Data Source** button ![icon]. In the **Data Form** dialog box, click the **View Source** button to display the list of names and addresses in the **3B_Addresses** document. Scroll to the bottom of the document, and notice that the record for *Susan Ballard* was added to this file.

3 Scroll to the top of the **3B_Addresses** document, move the mouse pointer above the **Last Name** field heading to display the ![icon] pointer, and then click to select the column.

4 On the **Home tab**, in the **Paragraph** group, click the **Sort** button ![icon], and then compare your screen with Figure 3.40.

Mailing labels are often sorted by either last name or by ZIP Code.

Figure 3.40

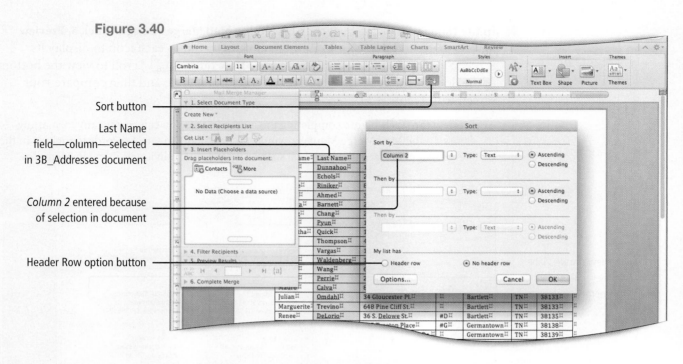

Sort button

Last Name field—column—selected in 3B_Addresses document

Column 2 entered because of selection in document

Header Row option button

5 In the **Sort** dialog box, be sure that under **Sort by**, *Column 2* displays. At the bottom of the **Sort** dialog box, under **My list has**, click the **Header row** option button.

Clicking the *Header row* option button informs Word that the first row should not be included when the records are sorted.

6 In the **Sort** dialog box, click **OK**. Notice that the list is sorted alphabetically by the **Last Name** field. Click anywhere in the document to cancel the selection. **Save** 🖫 your *3B_Addresses* document.

7 On the **Window** menu, click **Document1**—the number following *Document* may differ depending on how many blank documents you have opened.

Use the Window menu to move between open documents.

8 Notice that the labels are not sorted. In the **Mail Merge Manager**, under Step **5**, click the **View Merged Data** button ⟨⟨⟩⟩ABC to display the field names, and then click the **View Merged Data** button ⟨⟨⟩⟩ABC three more times to redisplay the all of the labels sorted by the last name.

When you edit the source file, click the View Merged Data button four times to be sure that the labels display correctly. Clicking it one time displays the field names. Clicking the button a second time displays labels, but some may have data displayed incorrectly, and some labels may not display. Clicking the button a third time displays the field names. Clicking the button a fourth time displays the labels correctly.

9 In the **Mail Merge Manager**, click **6. Complete Merge**, and then click the **Merge to New Document** button 🖫. Notice that a new document—*Labels1*—displays.

Merge the labels to a new document if you need to save the labels to print at a later time.

More Knowledge | Why You Should Merge to a New Document

When you merge the labels to a new document, Word removes the link to the source document, which enables you to open and view the file no matter where the document is saved or if the document has been renamed. If you save the original document—in this activity, Document1—on another computer or in another location or with a new name, and then open the document, Word attempts to locate the source document because the label file is linked to it. An error message will display, stating that Word cannot locate the source document, and you will have to take further action in the message boxes to remove the Data/Header Source information from the document to open it.

---

10 **Close** 🔘 the **Mail Merge Manager**. With the *Labels1* document active, on the **File** menu, click **Save As**, navigate to your **Word Chapter 3** folder, and save as **Lastname_Firstname_3B_Mailing_Labels**

11 Press Command ⌘ + fn + → to position the insertion point at the end of the document—on the blank line under the last label in the first column. Move the pointer to the **Footer** area, and notice that the 🖳 pointer does not display because the last row of the labels extends into the **Footer** area.

12 On the **View** menu, click **Header and Footer**. The insertion point displays in the **Header -Section 1-** area of the document. Scroll to view the bottom of the first page, and then click in the **Footer -Section 1-** area. On the **Insert** menu, point to **AutoText**, and then click **Filename**. **Close** the **Footer** area, which also closes the Header area.

13 At the top of **Page 2**, click anywhere in the empty table row, and then click the **Table Layout tab**. In the **Rows & Columns group**, click the **Delete** button, and then click **Delete Rows**. **Save** 💾 your document.

> Adding footer text to a label sheet moves the last row of labels to the top of the next page. In this instance, a blank second page is created, which you can delete by deleting the blank row.

14 On the **File** menu, click **Properties**. In the **Subject** box, type your course name and section number, and in the **Author** box, delete any text and then type your firstname and lastname. In the **Keywords** box, type **newsletter mailing labels** and then click **OK**. **Save** 💾 your document.

15 **Print** your document or submit electronically as directed by your instructor.

> If you print, the labels will print on whatever paper is in the printer; unless you have preformatted labels available, the labels will print on a sheet of paper. Printing the labels on plain paper enables you to proofread the labels before you print them on more expensive label sheets.

16 **Close** 🔘 your **3B_Mailing_Labels** document. **Close** 🔘 the **Document1** file, and in the message box, click **Don't Save**—you merged the file to a new document. **Print** or submit electronically your **3B_Addresses** document. **Close** 🔘 your **3B_Addresses** document; and if prompted, save changes to the document.

17 In addition to your labels and address document, submit your **3B_Memphis_ Newsletter** document as directed. **Quit Word**.

End **You have completed Project 3B** ——————————————

Content-Based Assessments

Summary

In this chapter, you created a research paper using the MLA style. You added a header, footnotes, citations, and a bibliography, and changed the footnote style. You created a newsletter that used multiple columns. You added a column break, a page break, and a manual line break. You added special font effects, and added a border and shading to a paragraph. Finally, you used the Mail Merge Manager tool to create a set of mailing labels for the newsletter.

Key Terms

Matching

Match each term in the second column with its correct definition in the first column by writing the letter of the term on the blank line in front of the correct definition.

_____ 1. A manual that contains standards for the design and writing of documents.

_____ 2. One of two commonly used style guides for formatting research papers.

_____ 3. An image of an active window on your computer that you can paste into a document.

_____ 4. In a research paper, information that expands on the topic, but that does not fit well in the document text.

_____ 5. In a research paper, a note placed at the bottom of the page.

_____ 6. In a research paper, a note placed at the end of a document or chapter.

_____ 7. A list of cited works in a report or research paper, also referred to as Works Cited, Sources, or References, depending upon the report style.

_____ 8. In the MLA style, a list of cited works placed at the end of a research paper or report.

_____ 9. A group of formatting commands, such as font, font size, font color, paragraph alignment, and line spacing that can be applied to a paragraph with one command.

_____10. A note, inserted into the text of a research paper that refers the reader to a source in the bibliography.

_____11. In the MLA style, a citation that refers to items on the Works Cited page, and which is placed in parentheses; the citation includes the last name of the author or authors, and the page number in the referenced source.

_____12. The action of forcing a page to end and placing subsequent text at the top of the next page.

A American Psychological Association (APA)

B Bibliography

C Citation

D Endnote

E Footnote

F Hanging indent

G Manual column break

H Manual page break

I Note

J Page break indicator

K Parenthetical reference

L Screenshot

M Style

N Style guide

O Works Cited

_____13. A dotted line with the text Page Break that indicates where a manual page break was inserted.

_____14. An indent style in which the first line of a paragraph extends to the left of the remaining lines, and that is commonly used for bibliographic entries.

_____15. An artificial end to a column to balance columns or to provide space for the insertion of other objects.

Multiple Choice

Circle the correct answer.

1. Column text that is aligned to both the left and right margins is referred to as:
   A. centered   B. justified   C. indented

2. The banner on the front page of a newsletter that identifies the publication is the:
   A. heading   B. nameplate   C. title

3. A portion of a document that can be formatted differently from the rest of the document is a:
   A. tabbed list   B. paragraph   C. section

4. A font effect, commonly used in titles, that changes lowercase text into uppercase letters using a reduced font size is:
   A. Small Caps   B. Level 2 Head   C. Bevel

5. To end a line before the normal end of the line, without creating a new paragraph, hold down the Shift key while pressing the:
   A. Return key   B. Ctrl key   C. Option key

6. The nonprinting symbol that displays where a manual line break is inserted is the:
   A. short arrow   B. bent arrow   C. anchor

7. In mail merge, the document that contains the text or formatting that remains constant is the:
   A. data source   B. mailing list   C. main document

8. In mail merge, the list of variable information, such as names and addresses, that is merged with a main document to create customized form letters or labels is the:
   A. data source   B. mailing list   C. main document

9. In mail merge, a row of information that contains data for one person is a:
   A. record   B. field   C. label

10. To perform a mail merge using Word's step-by-step guided process, use the:
    A. Mail Merge Template   B. Mail Merge tool   C. Mail Merge Manager

Word | Chapter 3

Content-Based Assessments

Apply **3A** skills from these Objectives:

1 Create a Research Paper

2 Insert Footnotes in a Research Paper

3 Create Citations and a Bibliography in a Research Paper

Skills Review | Project **3C** Batteries

In the following Skills Review, you will format and edit a research paper for Memphis Primary Materials. The research topic is recycling batteries. Your completed document will look similar to Figure 3.41.

Project Files

For Project 3C, you will need the following file:

w03C_Batteries

You will save your document as:

Lastname_Firstname_3C_Batteries

Project Results

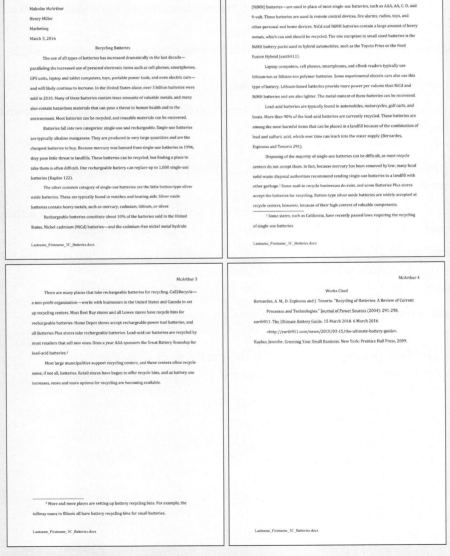

Figure 3.41

(Project 3C Batteries continues on the next page)

Skills Review | Project **3C** Batteries (continued)

1 Open **Word**. From your student files, locate and open the document **w03C_Batteries**. If necessary, display the formatting marks and rulers and increase the size of the window to fill the entire screen. If necessary, on the Standard toolbar, click the Zoom arrow, and then click 125%. **Save** the file in your **Word Chapter 3** folder as **Lastname_Firstname_3C_Batteries**

a. Press Command ⌘ + A to select the entire document. On the **Home tab**, in the **Paragraph group**, click the **Line Spacing** button, and then change the line spacing to **2.0**. On the **Layout tab**, in the **Margins group**, change the **Left** margin to **1** and then change the **Right** margin to **1**. Click in the document to cancel the selection of the Right margin setting.

b. Press Command ⌘ + fn + ← to cancel the selection of the document and to move to the beginning of the document. Press Return to create a blank line at the top of the document, and then click to position the insertion point in the blank line. Type **Malcolm McArthur** and then press Return. Type **Henry Miller** and then press Return. Type **Marketing** and then press Return. Type **March 3, 2016** and then press Return.

c. Type **Recycling Batteries** and then on the **Home tab**, in the **Paragraph group**, click the **Center Text** button to center the title.

d. At the top of **Page 1**, point anywhere in the white top margin area to display the ▣ pointer, and then double-click to display the **Header** area. Type **McArthur** and then press Spacebar. On the **Header and Footer tab**, in **the Insert group**, click the **Page #** button. Select the text and page number. On the **Home tab**, in the **Font group**, change the **Font** to **Cambria**, and then change the **Font Size** to **12**. On the **Home tab**, in the **Paragraph group**, click the **Align Text Right** button. **Close** the **Header** area.

e. Near the top of **Page 1**, locate the paragraph beginning *The use of,* and then click to position the insertion point at the beginning of the paragraph. Without clicking in the document, scroll to the end of the document, hold down Shift, and then click to the right of the last paragraph mark to select all of the text from the insertion point to the end of the document. On the horizontal ruler, drag the **First Line Indent** button to **0.5"**.

f. Click anywhere to cancel the selection of the text. Scroll to view the bottom of **Page 1**, point in the bottom white margin area to display the ▣ pointer, and then double-click to display the **Footer** area. On the **Insert** menu, point to **AutoText**, and then click **Filename**.

g. **Close** the **Footer** area, and then **Save** your document.

2 Scroll to view the middle of **Page 2**, locate the paragraph that begins *Disposing of the majority,* and then at the beginning of the fourth line, click to position the insertion point to the right of the period following *garbage.* On the **Document Elements tab**, in the **Citations group**, click the **Footnote** button.

a. Type **Some states, such as California, have recently passed laws requiring the recycling of single-use batteries.** **Save** your document.

b. At the top of **Page 3**, locate the paragraph that ends with *lead-acid batteries.* Click to position the insertion point at the end of the paragraph to the right of the period and insert a footnote.

c. As the footnote text, type **More and more places are setting up battery recycling bins. For example, the tollway oases in Illinois all have battery recycling bins for small batteries.** **Save** your document.

d. At the bottom of **Page 3**, point anywhere in the footnote text, press Control and click. From the shortcut menu, click **Style**. In the **Style** dialog box, click the **Modify** button. In the **Modify Style** dialog box, under **Formatting**, click the **Font arrow**, scroll down the list, and then click **Cambria**.

e. In the lower left corner of the dialog box, click the **Format** button, and then click **Paragraph**. In the **Paragraph** dialog box, under **Indentation**, click in the **Special** box, and then click **First line**. Under **Spacing**, click in the **Line spacing** box, and then click **Double**.

f. In the **Paragraph** dialog box, click **OK**. In the **Modify Style** dialog box, click **OK**. In the **Style** dialog box, click **Apply** to apply the new style. Scroll to view the bottom of **Page 2**, and notice that the first footnote also reflects the changes you made to the footnote on **Page 3**. **Save** your document.

3 Scroll to view the middle of **Page 1**, and then locate the paragraph that begins *Batteries fall.* Click to position the insertion point to the left of the period at the end of the paragraph.

(Project 3C Batteries continues on the next page)

Skills Review | Project **3C** Batteries (continued)

a. On the **Document Elements tab**, in the **References group**, be sure that the **Bibliography Style** is **MLA**. In the **References group**, click the **Manage** button to open the **Citations** tool. At the bottom left corner of the **Citations** tool, click ⊞. In the **Create New Source** dialog box, be sure that **Type of Source** is **Book**. In the **Create New Source** dialog box, add the following information:

Author:	**Kaplan, Jennifer**
Title:	**Greening Your Small Business**
City:	**New York**
Publisher:	**Prentice Hall Press**
Year:	**2009**

b. In the **Create New Source** dialog box, click **OK** to close the dialog box and to insert the citation. In the text, click to select the citation—*(Kaplan)*. On the right side of the blue frame that surrounds the citation, click the **arrow**, and then click **Edit This Citation**. In the **Edit Citation** dialog box, under **Add**, in the **Pages** box, type **122** and then click **OK**. Click outside of the blue frame of the citation to cancel the selection. At the top of **Page 2**, at the end of the first paragraph, click to position the insertion point to the left of the period following *Fusion Hybrid*. In the **Citations** tool, click ⊞. In the **Create New Source** dialog box, click in the **Type of Source** box, click **Web site**, and then add the following information (before typing Author information, select Author as organization check box; type the URL on one line):

Author as organization:	**earth911**
Name of Web page:	**The Ultimate Battery Guide**
URL:	**http://earth911.com/news/2010/ 03-15/the-ultimate-battery-guide**
Year:	**2010**
Month:	**March**
Day:	**15**
Year accessed:	**2016**
Month accessed:	**March**
Day accessed:	**6**

c. In the **Create New Source** dialog box, click **OK**. Near the bottom of **Page 2**, in the paragraph that begins

Lead acid batteries, position the insertion point at the end of the paragraph to the left of the period. In the **Citations** tool, click ⊞. In the **Create New Source** dialog box, click in the **Type of Source** box, click **Article in a journal**, and then add the following information (type the Author and Title information on one line):

Author:	**Bernardes, A. M.; Espinosa, D.; Tenorio, J.**
Title:	**Recycling of Batteries: A Review of Current Processes and Technologies**
Journal name:	**Journal of Power Sources**
Year:	**2004**
Pages:	**291–298**

d. In the **Create New Source** dialog box, click **OK**. Double-click the **Citations** tool title bar to collapse it. In the document, click to select the citation— begins with *Bernardes*—and on the right side of the blue frame that surrounds the citation, click the **arrow**, and then click **Edit This Citation**. In the **Edit Citation** dialog box, under **Add**, in the **Pages** box, type **291** and then click **OK**. Click in the document to cancel the selection of the citation. **Close** the **Citations** tool, and then **Save** your document.

e. Press Command ⌘ + fn → to move the insertion point to the end of the document. On the **Insert** menu, point to **Break**, and then click **Page Break** to insert a manual page break. On the ruler, drag the **First Line Indent** button to the left to **0 inches on the horizontal ruler**.

f. On the **Document Elements tab**, in the **References group**, in the **Bibliography Style** box, be sure **MLA** displays. In the **References group**, click the **Bibliography** button, and then click the **Works Cited** box. Click anywhere in the inserted references. In the blue frame above *Works Cited*, click the **Bibliography arrow**, and then click **Convert Bibliography to Static Text**.

g. In the bibliography, point to the left of the first entry—beginning *Bernardes*—to display the ⬈ pointer. Drag down to select all three references. On the **Home tab**, in the **Paragraph group**, click the **Line Spacing** button, and then click **Line Spacing Options**. In the **Paragraph** dialog box, on the

(Project 3C Batteries continues on the next page)

Indents and Spacing tab, under **Indentation**, click in the **Special** box, and then click **Hanging**. Under **Spacing**, change **After** to **0**. Click in the **Line spacing** box, and then click **Double**. In the **Paragraph** dialog box, click **OK**.

h. With the entries still selected, on the **Home tab** in the **Font group**, change the **Font** to **Cambria** and the **Font Size** to **12**. Click in the *Works Cited* title to cancel the selection, and then in the **Paragraph group**, click the **Center Text** button. Select the *Works Cited* title, including the paragraph mark. Change the **Font Size** to **12** and the **Font Color** to **Automatic**. Click the **Bold** button to remove the bold formatting. Click the **Line Spacing** button, click **Line Spacing Options**, and then change the **Spacing Before** to **0** and the **Line spacing** to **Double**. In the **Paragraph** dialog box, click **OK**. In the framed **Bibliography**, click in the last paragraph—the blank line below the last source—and then press Delete to remove the extra blank line. Click outside of the framed Bibliography to remove the frame, and then **Save** your document.

4 On the **File** menu, click **Properties**.

a. In the **Properties** dialog box, on the **Summary tab**, fill in the following information:

Title:	**Recycling Batteries**
Subject:	Your course information
Author:	Your firstname and lastname
Company:	**Memphis Primary Materials**
Keywords:	**recycling, nature, research paper**
Comments:	**Draft of a new white paper research report on recycling batteries**

b. At the bottom of the **Properties** dialog box, click **OK**. **Save** your document, and then **Print** or submit electronically as directed by your instructor. **Close** the document, and then **Quit Word**.

End **You have completed Project 3C** ————————————

Content-Based Assessments

Apply **3B** skills from these Objectives:

4 Format a Multiple-Column Newsletter

5 Use Special Character and Paragraph Formatting

6 Create Mailing Labels Using Mail Merge

Skills Review | Project **3D** February Newsletter

In the following Skills Review, you will format a newsletter for Memphis Primary Materials, and then create a set of mailing labels for the newsletter. Your completed documents will look similar to Figure 3.42.

Project Files

For Project 3D, you will need the following files:

New blank Word document
w03D_February_Newsletter
w03D_Addresses

You will save your documents as:

Lastname_Firstname_3D_February_Newsletter
Lastname_Firstname_3D_Addresses
Lastname_Firstname_3D_Labels

Project Results

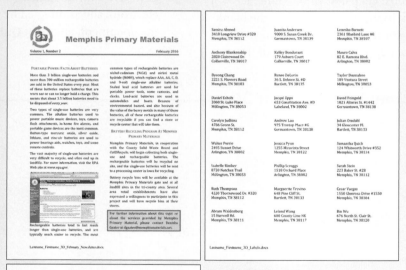

Figure 3.42

(Project 3D February Newsletter continues on the next page)

Skills Review | Project **3D** February Newsletter (continued)

1 Open **Word**. From your student files, **Open** the document **w03D_February_Newsletter**. If necessary, display the formatting marks and rulers and increase the size of the window to fill the entire screen. If necessary, on the Standard toolbar, click the Zoom arrow, and then click 125%. **Save** the file in your **Word Chapter 3 folder** as Lastname_Firstname_3D_February_Newsletter and then **Insert** the **Filename** in the **Footer** area.

a. Select the first paragraph of text—*Memphis Primary Materials*. On the **Home tab**, in the **Font group**, change the **Font** to **Arial Black** and the **Font Size** to **24**. Click the **Font Color arrow**, and then under **Theme Colors**, in the first row, click the sixth color—**Accent 2**. On the **Home tab**, in the **Paragraph group**, click the **Align Text Right** button.

b. Select the second paragraph—beginning with *Volume 1* and ending with *February 2016*. On the **Format** menu, click **Borders and Shading**. In the **Borders and Shading** dialog box, with the **Borders tab** active, click in the **Color** box, and then under **Theme Colors**, in the fifth row, click the sixth color—**Accent 2, Darker 25%**. Click in the **Width** box, and then click **3 pt**. In the **Preview** area, click the *bottom* border of the small preview and then click **OK**.

c. Below the nameplate, locate the paragraph that begins *Portable Power*, and then select all of the text from that point to the end of the document, including the last paragraph mark. On the **Home tab**, in the **Paragraph group**, click the **Columns** button, and then click **Two**.

d. With the text still selected, in the **Paragraph group**, click the **Line Spacing** button, and then click **Line Spacing Options**. Set **Spacing After** to **6 pt**, and then in the **Paragraph** dialog box, click **OK**. In the **Paragraph group**, click the **Justify Text** button, and then **Save** the newsletter.

e. Press Command ⌘ + fn + ← to cancel the selection and to move the insertion point to the beginning of the document. On the **Home tab**, in the **Insert group**, click the **Picture** button, and then click **Clip Art Gallery**.

f. At the bottom of the **Clip Gallery**, click the **Online** button, and, if necessary, in the message box, click Yes to launch your browser. On the Office Images Web page, in the **Search** box, type **recycle**

batteries and then press Return. Locate the image of two batteries, as shown in Figure 3.42. Point to the image, and then click **Download**. **Close** the Web page, and then **Quit** your browser.

g. At the bottom of the **Clip Gallery**, click the **Import** button. In the **Import** dialog box, select the file you downloaded—*MC900014527.WMF*. At the bottom of the **Import** dialog box, click the **Move into Clip Gallery** option button, and then click **Import**. In the **Properties** dialog box, in the **Description of this clip** box, type **Batteries** In the **Properties** dialog box, click the **Keywords tab**, and then click **New Keyword**. In the **New Keywords** box, type **batteries** and then click **OK**. Add **recycle** as a **Keyword** and then click **OK**. In the **Properties** dialog box, click **OK**.

h. In the **Clip Gallery Search** box, type **batteries** and then click the **Search** button. If necessary, click the **Batteries** picture, and then click **Insert** to insert the image into your document. In the document, click the image to select it. On the **Format Picture tab**, in the **Size group**, triple-click in the **Height** box, type **1** and then press Return. In the **Arrange group**, click the **Wrap Text** button, and then click **Square**. Drag or nudge the image to the location shown in Figure 3.42.

i. From the **Dock**, open your Web browser. In the address bar, type **www.epa.gov/wastes/conserve/materials/battery.htm** and then press Return. Maximize the browser window. Press Command ⌘ + Control + Shift + 3 to copy the screen. **Close** the Web page, and then **Quit** your browser to return to your document. Near the bottom of the first column, click to position the insertion point at the beginning of the paragraph that begins *Rechargeable batteries*. Press Command ⌘ + V to paste the screenshot from the Clipboard into your document. **Save** your document.

2 At the top of the first column, select the paragraph that begins *Portable Power*. Be sure to include the paragraph mark. On the **Format** menu, click **Font**. In the **Font** dialog box, click in the **Font** box, and then under **Theme Colors**, in the fifth row, click the sixth color—**Accent 2, Darker 25%**. Under **Font style**, click **Bold**. Under **Size**, click **12**. Under **Effects**, select the **Small caps** check box.

(Project 3D February Newsletter continues on the next page)

a. In the **Font** dialog box, click **OK**. On the **Home tab**, in the **Paragraph group**, click the **Center Text** button.

b. With the text still selected, on the Standard toolbar, click the **Format Painter** button. Near the middle of the second column, select the paragraph, including the paragraph mark, that begins *Battery Recycling Program* to apply the same formatting.

c. At the bottom of the second column, in the paragraph that begins *For further*, select the entire paragraph, including the paragraph mark. On the **Home tab**, in the **Font group**, click the **Bold** button.

d. With the paragraph still selected, on the **Format** menu, click **Borders and Shading**. In the **Borders and Shading** dialog box, with the **Borders tab** active, under **Setting**, click **Box**. Be sure that the **Color** is **Accent 2, Darker 25%**, the **Width** is **3 pt**, and **Apply to** is **Paragraph**—Word retains the settings from your last command.

e. At the top of the **Borders and Shading** dialog box, click the **Shading tab**. Under **Fill**, in the gallery of colors, in the last row, click the second color—**Tan**. At the bottom of the **Borders and Shading** dialog box, click **OK**. Click anywhere in the document to cancel the selection, and then **Save** your document.

f. On the **File** menu, click **Properties**. In the **Properties** dialog box, in the **Subject** box, type your course information, and in the **Author** box, replace existing text with your name. Add the **Keywords** of **newsletter, energy** and then click **OK**. **Save** your document, and then **Print** or submit electronically as directed. **Close** the document, but leave Word open.

3 In Word, on the **File** menu, click **New Blank Document**. If necessary, display the formatting marks and rulers and increase the size of the window to fill the entire screen. If necessary, on the Standard toolbar, click the Zoom arrow, and then click 125%. With your new document still displayed, **Open** the file **w03D_Addresses**. If necessary, increase the size of the window to fill the entire screen and change the Zoom setting to 125%. **Save** the address file in your **Word Chapter 3** folder as **Lastname_Firstname_3D_Addresses** and then **Insert** the **Filename** in the **Footer** area.

a. Click to position the insertion point in the last cell in the table, and then press Tab to create a new row. Enter the following new record, pressing Tab to move to the next field—do not press Tab after entering data for the ZIP Code:

First Name	Sarah
Last Name	Stein
Address 1	223 Baker St.
Unit	#2B
City	Memphis
State	TN
ZIP Code	38112

b. **Save**, and then **Close** the table of addresses. Your blank document is the active document. On the **Tools** menu, click **Mail Merge Manager**. If necessary, drag the Mail Merge Manager to the left or right to view more of the document. In the **Mail Merge Manager**, under **1. Select Document Type**, click **Create New**, and then click **Labels**.

c. In the **Label Options** dialog box, in the **Label products** box, be sure that **Avery standard** displays. Under **Product number**, be sure that **5160 – Address** displays. At the bottom of the **Label Options** dialog box, click **OK**. If borders do not display around the labels in the document, on the Table Layout tab, in the Settings group, click the Gridlines button.

d. In the **Mail Merge Manager**, under **2. Select Recipients List**, click the **Get List** button, and then click **Open Data Source**. In the **Choose a File** dialog box, navigate to your **Word Chapter 3** folder, select your **Lastname_Firstname_3D_Addresses** file, and then click **Open**.

e. In the **Edit Labels** dialog box, click in the **Insert Merge Field** box, click **First_Name**, and then press Spacebar. Click in the **Insert Merge Field** box, click **Last_Name**, and then press Return. Insert the **Address_1** field name, press Spacebar, insert the **Unit** field name, and then press Return. Insert the **City** field name, and then type **,** (a comma). Press Spacebar, insert the **State** field name, press Spacebar, and then insert the **ZIP_Code** field name. In the **Edit Labels** dialog box, click **OK**.

f. In the **Mail Merge Manager**, under **2. Select Recipients List**, click the **Edit Data Source** button. In

(Project 3D February Newsletter continues on the next page)

Skills Review | Project **3D** February Newsletter (continued)

the **Data Form** dialog box, click the **Add New** button to create Record 27. In the **Data Form** dialog box, type the following, pressing ⟮Tab⟯ to move from field to field.

First_Name:	**Carolyn**
Last_Name:	**Judkins**
Address_1:	**4786 Green St.**
Unit:	
City:	**Memphis**
State:	**TN**
ZIP_Code:	**38112**

g. In the **Data Form** dialog box, click **OK**. In the **Mail Merge Manager**, click **5. Preview Results**, and then click the **View Merged Data** button. **Close** the **Mail Merge Manager**. Scroll to view the bottom of the document, and notice the new record you just entered.

4 Scroll to view the top of the document, and notice that the labels are not in alphabetical order by the last name. On the **Tools** menu, click **Mail Merge Manager**. In the **Mail Merge Manager**, under Step **2**, click the **Edit Data Source** button. In the **Data Form** dialog box, click the **View Source** button.

a. In your **3D_Addresses** document, move the mouse pointer above the **Last Name** field heading to display the ⬇ pointer, and then click to select the column. On the **Home tab**, in the **Paragraph group**, click the **Sort** button. In the **Sort** dialog box, be sure that under **Sort by**, *Column 2*, displays. Under **My list has**, click the **Header row** option button, and then click **OK**. Click anywhere in the document to

cancel the selection, and then **Save** your addresses document.

b. On the **Window** menu, click **Document1**—the number following *Document* may differ. In the **Mail Merge Manager**, under Step **5**, click the **View Merged Data** button four times to display all of the labels sorted by last name.

c. In the **Mail Merge Manager**, click **6. Complete Merge**, and then click the **Merge to New Document** button. **Close** the **Mail Merge Manager**. With the *Labels1* document active, on the **File** menu, click **Save As**, navigate to your **Word Chapter 3** folder, and then save the document as **Lastname_Firstname_3D_Labels**

d. On the **View** menu, click **Header and Footer**. Scroll to view the bottom of the first page, and then click in the **Footer -Section 1-** area. On the **Insert** menu, point to **AutoText**, and then click **Filename**. **Close** the **Footer** area. At the top of **Page 2**, click anywhere in the empty table row. On the **Table Layout tab**, in the **Rows & Columns group**, click the **Delete** button, and then click **Delete Rows**. **Save** your document.

e. On the **File** menu, click **Properties**. Type your course information, your name, and the **Keywords** of **newsletter mailing labels** and then click **OK**. **Save** the labels, and then **Print** or submit electronically as directed. **Close** your **3D_Labels** document, and then **Close** the **Document1** file without saving changes. **Print** your **3D_Addresses** document or submit electronically as directed by your instructor. **Close** your **3D_Addresses** document, saving changes if prompted, and then **Quit Word**.

End **You have completed Project 3D**

Word | Chapter 3

Content-Based Assessments

Apply 3A skills from these Objectives:

1. Create a Research Paper
2. Insert Footnotes in a Research Paper
3. Create Citations and a Bibliography in a Research Paper

Mastering Word | Project 3E Refrigerant

In the following Mastering Word project, you will edit and format a research paper for Memphis Primary Materials, the topic of which is removing refrigerant from appliances. Your completed document will look similar to Figure 3.43.

Project Files

For Project 3E, you will need the following file:

w03E_Refrigerant

You will save your document as:

Lastname_Firstname_3E_Refrigerant

Project Results

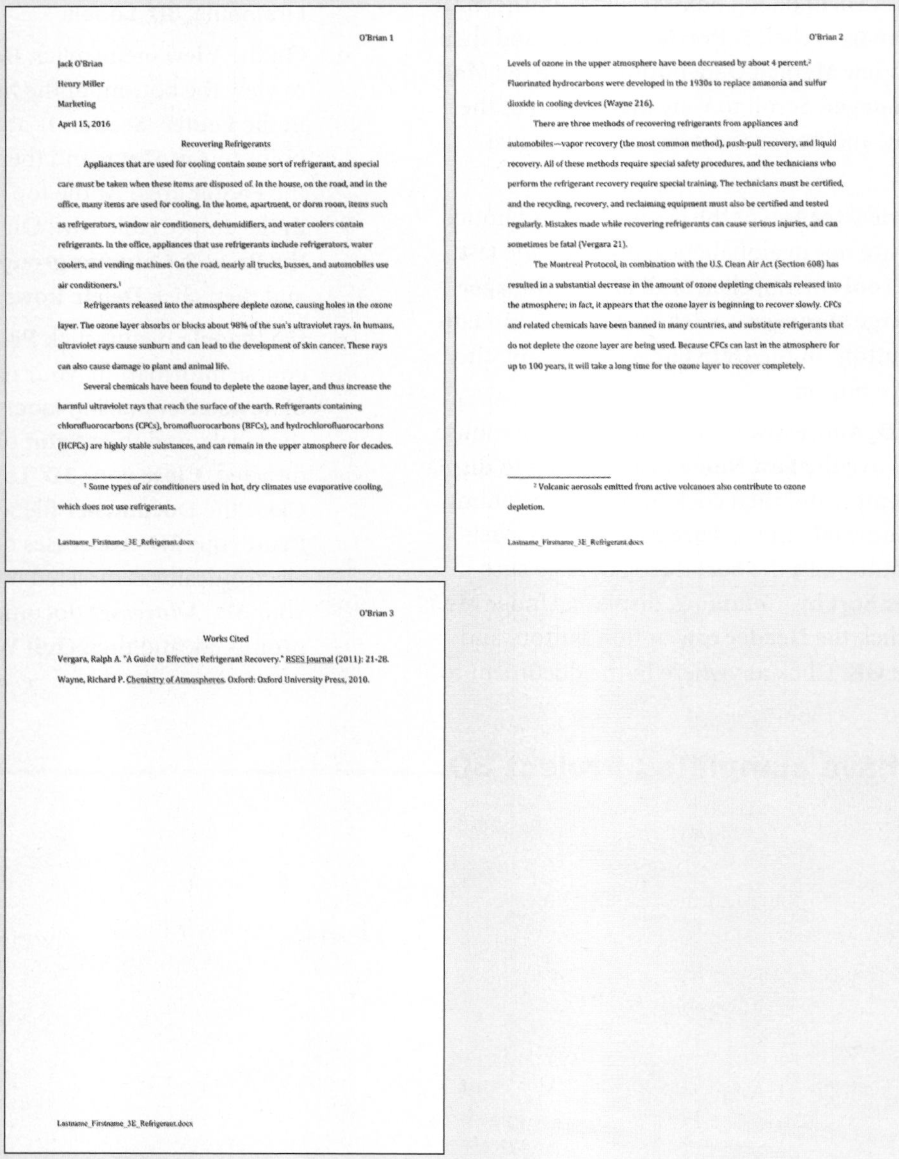

O'Brian 1

Jack O'Brian

Henry Miller

Marketing

April 15, 2016

Recovering Refrigerants

Appliances that are used for cooling contain some sort of refrigerant, and special care must be taken when these items are disposed of. In the house, on the road, and in the office, many items are used for cooling. In the home, apartment, or dorm room, items such as refrigerators, window air conditioners, dehumidifiers, and water coolers contain refrigerants. In the office, appliances that use refrigerants include refrigerators, water coolers, and vending machines. On the road, nearly all trucks, busses, and automobiles use air conditioners.[1]

Refrigerants released into the atmosphere deplete ozone, causing holes in the ozone layer. The ozone layer absorbs or blocks about 98% of the sun's ultraviolet rays. In humans, ultraviolet rays cause sunburn and can lead to the development of skin cancer. These rays can also cause damage to plant and animal life.

Several chemicals have been found to deplete the ozone layer, and thus increase the harmful ultraviolet rays that reach the surface of the earth. Refrigerants containing chlorofluorocarbons (CFCs), bromofluorocarbons (BFCs), and hydrochlorofluorocarbons (HCFCs) are highly stable substances, and can remain in the upper atmosphere for decades.

[1] Some types of air conditioners used in hot, dry climates use evaporative cooling, which does not use refrigerants.

Lastname_Firstname_3E_Refrigerant.docx

O'Brian 2

Levels of ozone in the upper atmosphere have been decreased by about 4 percent.[2] Fluorinated hydrocarbons were developed in the 1930s to replace ammonia and sulfur dioxide in cooling devices (Wayne 216).

There are three methods of recovering refrigerants from appliances and automobiles—vapor recovery (the most common method), push-pull recovery, and liquid recovery. All of these methods require special safety procedures, and the technicians who perform the refrigerant recovery require special training. The technicians must be certified, and the recycling, recovery, and reclaiming equipment must also be certified and tested regularly. Mistakes made while recovering refrigerants can cause serious injuries, and can sometimes be fatal (Vergara 21).

The Montreal Protocol, in combination with the U.S. Clean Air Act (Section 608) has resulted in a substantial decrease in the amount of ozone depleting chemicals released into the atmosphere; in fact, it appears that the ozone layer is beginning to recover slowly. CFCs and related chemicals have been banned in many countries, and substitute refrigerants that do not deplete the ozone layer are being used. Because CFCs can last in the atmosphere for up to 100 years, it will take a long time for the ozone layer to recover completely.

[2] Volcanic aerosols emitted from active volcanoes also contribute to ozone depletion.

Lastname_Firstname_3E_Refrigerant.docx

O'Brian 3

Works Cited

Vergara, Ralph A. "A Guide to Effective Refrigerant Recovery." RSES Journal (2011): 21-28.

Wayne, Richard P. Chemistry of Atmospheres. Oxford: Oxford University Press, 2010.

Lastname_Firstname_3E_Refrigerant.docx

Figure 3.43

(Project 3E Refrigerant continues on the next page)

Content-Based Assessments

Mastering Word | Project **3E** Refrigerant (continued)

1 Open **Word**. From your student files, **Open** the document **w03E_Refrigerant**. If necessary, display the formatting marks and rulers and increase the size of the window to fill the entire screen. If necessary, on the Standard toolbar, click the Zoom arrow, and then click 125%. **Save** the document in your **Word Chapter 3** folder as **Lastname_Firstname_3E_Refrigerant** Select all of the text in the document. Change the **Line Spacing** to **2.0**, and then change the **Left** and **Right** margins to **1**.

2 Click in the document to cancel the selection of the margin setting, and then press Command ⌘ + fn + ← to position the insertion point at the beginning of the document. Press Return to insert a blank line, click in the blank line, type **Jack O'Brian** and then press Return. Type **Henry Miller** and press Return. Type **Marketing** and press Return. Type **April 15, 2016** Click anywhere in the title *Recovering Refrigerants*, and then apply **Center Text** to the title.

3 Display the **Header** area, type **O'Brian** and then press Spacebar. Insert a page number. Select the text in the **Header** area, change the **Font** to **Cambria** and the **Font Size** to **12**. Apply **Align Text Right** formatting to the header. **Insert** the **Filename** in the **Footer** area.

Near the top of **Page 1**, starting with the paragraph that begins *Appliances that*, select the text from that point to the end of the document including the last paragraph mark, and then set the **First Line Indent** to **0.5"** on the horizontal ruler.

4 Near the top of **Page 1**, in the paragraph that begins *Appliances that are used*, click to position the insertion point to the right of the period at the end of the paragraph following *air conditioners*, and then add the following footnote:

> **Some types of air conditioners used in hot, dry climates use evaporative cooling, which does not use refrigerants.**

At the bottom of **Page 1**, in the paragraph that begins *Several chemicals have* click to position the insertion point to the right of the period following *4 percent*, and then add the following footnote:

> **Volcanic aerosols emitted from active volcanoes also contribute to ozone depletion.**

5 Press Control and click anywhere in the footnote, modify the **Style** to set the **Font** to **Cambria**, the **Font Size** to **12**, and then change the **Format** of **Paragraph** to

add a **Special First line** indent and use **Line spacing** of **Double**.

Scroll to view the top of **Page 2**. In the same paragraph, click to position the insertion point to the left of the period following *cooling devices* at the end of the paragraph. In the **MLA** format, add the following **Book** citation:

Author:	**Wayne, Richard P.**
Title:	**Chemistry of Atmospheres**
City:	**Oxford**
Country/Region	**England**
Publisher:	**Oxford University Press**
Year:	**2010**

6 In the middle of **Page 2**, locate the paragraph that begins *There are three*, and then click to position the insertion point to the left of the period following *sometimes be fatal* at the end of the paragraph. Add the following **Article in a journal** citation:

Author:	**Vergara, Ralph A.**
Title:	**A Guide to Effective Refrigerant Recovery**
Journal name:	**RSES Journal**
Year:	**2011**
Pages:	**21-28**

Select the *Vergara* citation and add the page number **21** and then select the *Wayne* citation and add the page number **216**

7 Move to the end of the document, and then **Insert** a manual **Page Break** to create a new page. Add the **Bibliography** in the form of **Works Cited**. Click anywhere in the *Works Cited* text, and then **Convert** the **Bibliography to Static Text**. Select the two references, set a **Hanging** indent, change the **Spacing After** to **0**, set **Line spacing** to **Double**, change the **Font** to **Cambria**, and change the **Font Size** to **12**. Select the *Works Cited* title, including the paragraph mark. Change the **Font** to **Cambria**, the **Font Size** to **12**, and the **Font Color** to **Automatic**. Remove the **Bold** formatting, and then apply **Center Text**. Change the **Line Spacing Before** to **0** and the **Line spacing** to **Double**. In the framed **Bibliography**, delete the extra blank line.

8 Display **File Properties** and add your course information, your name, and the **Keywords** of **recycling refrigerants Save** your document, and then **Print** or submit electronically as directed. **Close** the document, and then **Quit Word**.

End **You have completed Project 3E**

Apply **3B** skills from these Objectives:

4 Format a Multiple-Column Newsletter

5 Use Special Character and Paragraph Formatting

6 Create Mailing Labels Using Mail Merge

Mastering Word | Project **3F** Spring Newsletter

In the following Mastering Word project, you will format a newsletter for Memphis Primary Materials, and then create a set of mailing labels for the newsletter. Your completed documents will look similar to Figure 3.44.

Project Files

For Project 3F, you will need the following files:

New blank Word document
w03F_March_Newsletter
w03F_Addresses

You will save your documents as:

Lastname_Firstname_3F_March_Newsletter
Lastname_Firstname_3F_Labels
Lastname_Firstname_3F_Addresses

Project Results

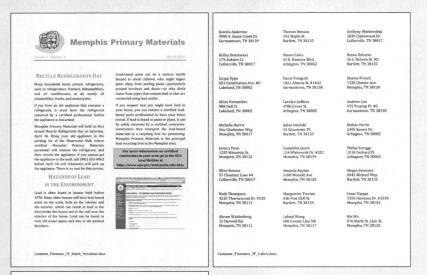

Figure 3.44

(Project 3F Spring Newsletter continues on the next page)

Mastering Word | Project **3F** Spring Newsletter (continued)

1 Open **Word**, and then from your student files, **Open w03F_March_Newsletter**. If necessary, display the formatting marks and rulers and increase the size of the window to fill the entire screen. If necessary, on the Standard toolbar, click the Zoom arrow, and then click 125%. **Save** the document in your **Word Chapter 3** folder as **Lastname_Firstname_3F_March_Newsletter** and then **Insert** the **Filename** in the **Footer** area.

Select the first line of text—*Memphis Primary Materials*. Change the **Font** to **Arial Black**, the **Font Size** to **24**, the **Font Color** to **Text 2, Lighter 40%** (fourth row, fourth color), and **Align Text Right**.

Select the second line of text—the volume and date. Change the **Font Color** to **Text 2, Lighter 40%**. Display the **Borders and Shading** dialog box, and then add a **Text 2, Lighter 40%, 3 pt** line below the paragraph.

2 Move to the beginning of the document. Display the **Clip Art Gallery**, search **Online** for an image of a **kitchen refrigerator** and then **Download** the image of the blue refrigerator as shown in Figure 3.44. **Import** the downloaded file, and **Move** it **into** the **Clip Gallery** from the *Downloads* folder. Add an appropriate description for the image, and then **Insert** the image into your document. Change the **Height** of the image to **1** and then apply **Square** text wrapping. Drag or nudge the image to the location shown in Figure 3.44.

Starting with the paragraph that begins *Recycle Refrigerants*, select all of the text from that point to the end of the document, including the last paragraph mark. Change the **Spacing After** to **6 pt**, format the text in two columns, and apply **Justify Text** alignment.

3 At the top of the first column, select the paragraph *Recycle Refrigerants Day*. From the **Font** dialog box, change the **Font Size** to **18**, apply **Bold**, add the **Small caps** effect, and change the **Font color** to **Text 2, Lighter 40%**. Apply **Center Text** to the paragraph. Near the bottom of the same column, apply the same formatting to the paragraph that begins *Hazards of Lead*. Add a manual line break between *Lead* and *in*, being sure to delete any extra spaces.

From the **Dock**, open your Web browser, and then navigate to the **www.epa.gov/lead/pubs/nlic.htm** Web site. If necessary, increase the size of the browser window so that it fills the entire screen, and then press Command ⌘ + Control + Shift + 3 to copy the screen to the Clipboard. **Close** the Web page, and then **Quit** your Web browser

to return to the Word document. In the second column, click to position the insertion point in the second blank paragraph. Press Command ⌘ + V to paste a copy of the screenshot of the EPA Web page into the document.

4 Above the screenshot, select the paragraph that begins with *For more information*. Apply **Center Text** alignment and **Bold** formatting. Add a **Shadow** border to the paragraph, and be sure that the **Color** is **Text 2, Lighter 40%**. Change the **Width** to **1 1/2 pt**, and then on the **Shading tab** of the dialog box, apply a **Fill** of **Pale Blue**—in the last row, the sixth color.

At the bottom of the first column, locate the paragraph that begins with *Lead-based paint*, and then click to the left of *Lead*. Insert a column break.

Display **File Properties** and add your course information, your name, and the **Keywords** of **March newsletter Save** the document, and then **Print** or submit electronically as directed. **Close** the document but leave Word open.

5 Display a **New Blank Document**. If necessary, display the formatting marks and rulers and increase the size of the window to fill the entire screen. If necessary, on the Standard toolbar, click the Zoom arrow, and then click 125%.

With the new document open, **Open** the file **w03F_Addresses**, **Save** the address file in your **Word Chapter 3** folder as **Lastname_Firstname_3F_Addresses** and then **Insert** the **Filename** in the **Footer** area. **Save** and then **Close** the address file.

With the new document open, display the **Mail Merge Manager**. Under Step **1**, click **Create New**, and then click **Labels**. In the **Label Options** dialog box, be sure **Avery standard 5160 – Address** displays.

Under Step **3**, click **Get List**, click **Open Data Source**, and then navigate to your **Word Chapter 3** folder and **Open** your **3F_Addresses** document. In the **Edit Labels** dialog box, insert the appropriate field names for a mailing address and be sure to include proper spacing, punctuation, and returns.

Under Step **5**, click the **View Merged Data** button, and then notice the labels are not in alphabetical order. Under Step **2**, click the **Edit Data Source** button, and in the **Data Form** dialog box, click the **View Source** button. **Sort** the list of addresses by **Last Name**, being sure not to include the column headings in the sort. **Save** your **3F_Addresses** document, and then from the **Window** menu, display **Document1**. Click the **View Merged Data** button two

(Project 3F Spring Newsletter continues on the next page)

times. In the message box that displays stating that *Record 2 does not have the same number of fields as the first row*, click **OK**. In the second message box, click **OK**. In the **Mail Merge Manager**, click the **View Merged Data** button two more times to display all of the sorted labels.

In the **Mail Merge Manager**, under Step **6**, click the **Merge to New Document** button. **Close** the **Mail Merge Manager**. **Save** the *Labels1* document in your **Word Chapter 3** folder as **Lastname_Firstname_3F_Labels** Add the file name to the **Footer** area, and then delete the empty row at the bottom of the table.

6 Display **File Properties**, and then add your course information, your name, and the **Keywords** of **mailing labels Save** the document, and then **Print** or submit electronically as directed. **Close** your **3F_Labels** document and save changes, if prompted. **Close** the **Document1** file without saving changes. With your **3F_Addresses** document displayed, **Print** or submit electronically as directed. **Close** your **3F_Addresses** file, saving changes if prompted, and then **Quit Word**.

End **You have completed Project 3F** ————————————

Content-Based Assessments

Apply a combination of
3A and 3B skills:

1 Create a Research Paper

2 Insert Footnotes in a Research Paper

3 Create Citations and a Bibliography in a Research Paper

4 Format a Multiple-Column Newsletter

5 Use Special Character and Paragraph Formatting

6 Create Mailing Labels Using Mail Merge

Mastering Word | Project 3G Economics

In the following Mastering Word project, you will edit and format a newsletter and a research paper for Memphis Primary Materials on the topic of environmental economics. Your completed documents will look similar to Figure 3.45.

Project Files

For Project 3G, you will need the following files:

New blank Word document
w03G_Economics
w03G_Addresses
w03G_April_Newsletter

You will save your documents as:

Lastname_Firstname_3G_Economics
Lastname_Firstname_3G_April_Newsletter
Lastname_Firstname_3G_Labels
Lastname_Firstname_3G_Addresses

Project Results

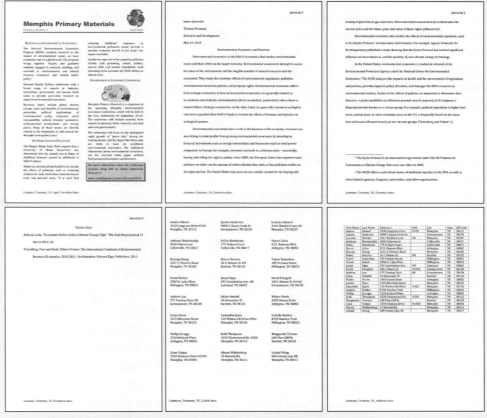

Figure 3.45

(Project 3G Economics continues on the next page)

Mastering Word | Project **3G** Economics (continued)

1 Open **Word**, and then from your student files, **Open** the document **w03G_April_Newsletter**. If necessary, display the formatting marks and rulers and increase the size of the window to fill the entire screen. If necessary, on the Standard toolbar, click the Zoom arrow, and then click 125%. **Save** the document in your **Word Chapter 3** folder as **Lastname_Firstname_3G_April_Newsletter Insert** the **Filename** in the **Footer** area, and then **Save** your document.

Starting with the paragraph that begins *Research on Environmental Economics*, select all of the text from that point to the end of the document—the document text extends to two pages. Set the **Spacing After** to **6 pt**, format the selected text as two columns, and set the alignment to **Justify Text**.

2 At the bottom of the first column, in the paragraph that begins *Maine has already*, click to position the insertion point to the left of the fifth line, which begins *reducing childhood*. Insert a column break.

At the top of the first column, select the paragraph *Research on Environmental Economics*. Display the **Font** dialog box, set the Font **Size** to **12**, set the **Font style** to **Bold**, set the **Font color** to **Text 2**—first row, fourth color—and then add the **Small caps** effect. Apply **Center Text** to the paragraph. Use the **Format Painter** to apply the same formatting to the paragraphs *The Hard Costs of Pollution* located near the bottom of the first column and to *Environmental Economics Conference* in the second column.

3 At the bottom of the second column, select the last two paragraphs of text beginning with *For more information* and ending with the paragraph mark following *MEEC*. From the **Borders and Shading** dialog box, apply a **1 1/2 pt**, **Shadow** border using the **Text 2** color, and then on the **Shading tab**, apply a **Fill** of **Pale Blue**—last row, sixth color.

In the second column, click to position the insertion point at the beginning of the paragraph that begins *Memphis Primary Materials is a cosponsor*. Display the **Clip Art Gallery**. Search **Online** for an image of a **business conference**. **Download** the image shown in Figure 3.45, **Close** the Web page, and then **Quit** your Web browser. **Import** the image from your Downloads folder by moving it into the Clip Gallery. Add an appropriate description of the image, locate the image in the Clip Gallery, and then **Insert** the image into the newsletter. Change the **Height** of the image to **1** Apply **Top and Bottom** text wrapping, and then position the image as shown in Figure 3.45 by either dragging or nudging.

In **File Properties**, type your course information, your name, and the **Keywords** of **April newsletter Save** your document, and then **Print** or submit electronically as directed. **Close** the document, but leave Word open.

4 From your student files, **Open** the document **w03G_Economics**. If necessary, display the formatting marks and rulers and increase the size of the window to fill the entire screen. If necessary, on the Standard toolbar, click the Zoom arrow, and then click 125%. **Save** the document in your **Word Chapter 3** folder as **Lastname_Firstname_3G_Economics** Select the entire document. Change the **Line Spacing** to **2.0** and the **Left** and **Right** margins to **1**. Display the **Header** area, type **Jaworski** and then press ⌈Spacebar⌋. Insert a page number. Select the text, change the **Font** to **Cambria** and the **Font Size** to **12**, and then apply **Align Text Right**. In the **Footer** area, **Insert** the **Filename**, and then **Save** your document.

Near the top of the document, apply **Center Text** to the title *Environmental Economics and Business*. Beginning with the text below the centered title that begins with *Environmental economics is the field*, select the text from that point to the end of the document, including the last paragraph mark, and then set a **First Line Indent** at **0.5"**.

5 At the top of **Page 2**, in the paragraph that begins *Environmental economics also studies*, in the second line, click to position the insertion point to the right of the comma following *Protocol*, and then insert the following footnote:

> **The Kyoto Protocol is an international agreement under the UN Framework Convention on Climate Change that went into effect in 2005.**

In the next paragraph, which begins *In the United States*, in the second line, position the insertion point to the right of the period following *Economics*, and then insert the following footnote:

> **The NCEE offers a centralized source of technical expertise to the EPA, as well as other federal agencies, Congress, universities, and other organizations.**

Display the shortcut menu for the footnote, and then for the **Style**, **Modify** to set the **Font** to **Cambria** and the **Format** of the **Paragraph** to include a **First line** indent and **Line spacing** of **Double**. **Save** your document.

6 Near the bottom of **Page 1**, in the paragraph that begins *Environmental economists have a role*, position the insertion point to the left of the period following *rights* at the end of the paragraph, which displays on **Page 2**. Using

(Project 3G Economics continues on the next page)

Mastering Word | Project **3G** Economics (continued)

MLA format, add the following **Article in periodical** citation (type the Title on one line):

Author:	**Abboud, Leila**
Title:	**Economist Strikes Gold in Climate-Change Fight**
Periodical Title:	**The Wall Street Journal**
Year:	**2012**
Month:	**March**
Day:	**13**
Pages	**A1**

In the document, select the *Abboud* citation, and then edit the citation to include the page number **A1** In the middle of **Page 2**, in the paragraph that begins *In the United States*, click to position the insertion point to the left of the period following *groups* at the end of the paragraph. Add the following **Book** citation in **MLA** format (type the Author and Title on one line):

Author:	**Tietenberg, Tom; Folmer, Henk, Editors**
Title:	**The International Yearbook of Environmental Resource Economics, 2010/2011**
City:	**Northampton**
State/Province	**MA**
Publisher:	**Edward Elgar Publishers**
Year:	**2011**

7 Select the *Tietenberg* citation, and then edit the citation to include the page number **1** At the end of the document, **Insert** a manual **Page Break**. At the top of **Page 3**, insert the **Bibliography** as **Works Cited**. **Convert** the **Bibliography to Static Text**. Select the inserted references, change the **Font** to **Cambria** and the **Font Size** to **12**. Set the **Indentation** to **Hanging**, the **Spacing After** to **0 pt**, and the **Line spacing** to **Double**. Select the *Works Cited* title, including the paragraph mark. Change the **Font** to **Cambria**, the **Font Size** to **12**, the **Font Color** to **Automatic**, **Spacing Before** to **0 pt**, and **Line spacing** to **Double**. Apply **Center Text** to the title, and remove the **Bold** formatting. Delete the extra blank line after the second reference in the framed Bibliography.

Display **File Properties** and add your course information, your name, and the **Keywords** of **environmental economics Save** your document, and then **Print** or

submit electronically as directed. **Close** the document, but leave Word open.

8 Display a **New Blank Document**. If necessary, display the formatting marks and rulers and increase the size of the window to fill the entire screen. If necessary, on the Standard toolbar, click the Zoom arrow, and then click 125%. With the new document open, from your student files, **Open** the file w03G_Addresses, and then **Save** the addresses document in your **Word Chapter 3** folder as **Lastname_Firstname_3G_Addresses Insert** the **Filename** in the **Footer** area, **Save** the document, and then **Close** the addresses document.

With the new document open, display the **Mail Merge Manager**. Under Step **1**, **Create New Labels**. Be sure that in the **Label Options** dialog box, the **Avery standard 5160 – Address** label is selected. Under Step **2**, click **Get List**, and then click **Open Data Source**. Navigate to your **Word Chapter 3** folder and **Open** your **3G_Addresses** file. In the **Edit Labels** dialog box, insert the appropriate field names for a mailing address and be sure to include proper spacing, punctuation, and returns.

Under Step **5**, click the **View Merged Data** button, and notice that the labels are not in alphabetical order. Under Step **2**, click the **Edit Data Source** button, and in the **Data Form** dialog box, click the **View Source** button. **Sort** the list of addresses by **Last Name**, being sure not to include the column headings in the sort. **Save** your **3G_Addresses** document, and then from the **Window** menu, display your **Document1** file. Click the **View Merged Data** button four times to display all of the sorted labels.

In the **Mail Merge Manager**, under Step **6**, click the **Merge to New Document** button. **Close** the **Mail Merge Manager**. **Save** the *Labels1* document in your **Word Chapter 3** folder as **Lastname_Firstname_3G_Labels** Add the file name to the **Footer** area, and then select and delete the last two empty rows of the table.

9 Display **File Properties**, and then add your course information, your name, and the **Keywords** of **mailing labels Save** your **3G_Labels** document, and then **Print** or submit electronically as directed. **Close** your **3G_Labels** document and save changes, if prompted. **Close** the **Document1** file without saving changes. With your **3G_Addresses** file displayed, **Print** or submit electronically as directed. **Close** your **3G_Addresses** file, saving changes if prompted, and then **Quit Word**.

End **You have completed Project 3G**

Content-Based Assessments

GO! Fix It | Project **3H** Metals Report

Project Files

For Project 3H, you will need the following file:

> w03H_Metals_Report

You will save your document as:

> Lastname_Firstname_3H_Metals_Report

From the student files, open the file w03H_Metals_Report. If necessary, display the formatting marks and rulers and increase the size of the window to fill the entire screen. Save the file in your Word Chapter 3 folder as **Lastname_Firstname_3H_Metals_Report**

This document contains errors that you must find and correct. Read and examine the document, and then edit to correct any errors that you find and to improve the overall document format. Types of errors could include, but are not restricted to:

- Formatting does not match MLA style guidelines that you practiced in the chapter
- Incorrect header format
- Incorrect spacing between paragraphs
- Incorrect paragraph indents
- Incorrect line spacing
- Incorrect footnote format
- Incorrectly formatted reference page

Things you should know to complete this project:

- Displaying formatting marks will assist in locating spacing errors.
- There are no errors in the parenthetical references in the document.
- There are no errors in the information in the footnotes or bibliographical references.

Save your document and add the file name to the footer area. In File Properties, add your course information, your name, and the keywords **valuable metals, recycling** Save your document and print or submit electronically as directed.

End **You have completed Project 3H** ———————————

Content-Based Assessments

Apply a combination of the **3A** and **3B** skills.

GO! Make It | Project **3I** Green Newsletter

Project Files

For Project 3I, you will need the following files:

New blank Word document
w03I_Competition
w03I_Kids

You will save your document as:

Lastname_Firstname_3I_Green_Newsletter

Start with a new blank Word document, and then save the file in your Word Chapter 3 folder as **Lastname_Firstname_3I_Green_Newsletter** Create the document shown in Figure 3.46, using 1-inch left and right margins, a 0.5-inch top margin, and a Font Size of 11 pt. Create a nameplate, and then insert the files **w03I_Competition** and **w03I_Kids**. The title is Arial Black, 24 pt, Text 2—first row, fourth color. Other titles and borders are Text 2. The two headings in the columns are Cambria, 14 pt. The clip art image can be found online by using the search term **recycle computer** and the screenshot can be found at the Web address in the last line of the newsletter.

Add the file name to the footer area. In File Properties, add your course information, your name, and the keywords **green, campuses, kids** Save your document and print or submit electronically as directed.

Project Results

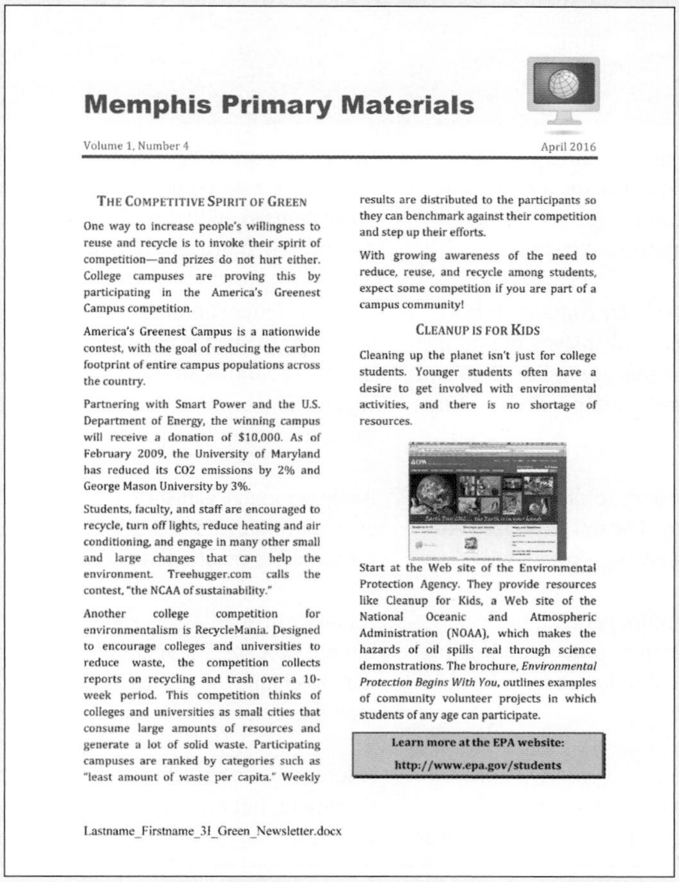

Figure 3.46

Memphis Primary Materials

Volume 1, Number 4   April 2016

THE COMPETITIVE SPIRIT OF GREEN

One way to increase people's willingness to reuse and recycle is to invoke their spirit of competition—and prizes do not hurt either. College campuses are proving this by participating in the America's Greenest Campus competition.

America's Greenest Campus is a nationwide contest, with the goal of reducing the carbon footprint of entire campus populations across the country.

Partnering with Smart Power and the U.S. Department of Energy, the winning campus will receive a donation of $10,000. As of February 2009, the University of Maryland has reduced its CO2 emissions by 2% and George Mason University by 3%.

Students, faculty, and staff are encouraged to recycle, turn off lights, reduce heating and air conditioning, and engage in many other small and large changes that can help the environment. Treehugger.com calls the contest, "the NCAA of sustainability."

Another college competition for environmentalism is RecycleMania. Designed to encourage colleges and universities to reduce waste, the competition collects reports on recycling and trash over a 10-week period. This competition thinks of colleges and universities as small cities that consume large amounts of resources and generate a lot of solid waste. Participating campuses are ranked by categories such as "least amount of waste per capita." Weekly

results are distributed to the participants so they can benchmark against their competition and step up their efforts.

With growing awareness of the need to reduce, reuse, and recycle among students, expect some competition if you are part of a campus community!

CLEANUP IS FOR KIDS

Cleaning up the planet isn't just for college students. Younger students often have a desire to get involved with environmental activities, and there is no shortage of resources.

Start at the Web site of the Environmental Protection Agency. They provide resources like Cleanup for Kids, a Web site of the National Oceanic and Atmospheric Administration (NOAA), which makes the hazards of oil spills real through science demonstrations. The brochure, *Environmental Protection Begins With You*, outlines examples of community volunteer projects in which students of any age can participate.

**Learn more at the EPA website:
http://www.epa.gov/students**

Lastname_Firstname_3I_Green_Newsletter.docx

End You have completed Project 3I

Content-Based Assessments

GO! Solve It | Project 3J Municipal Newsletter

Project Files

For Project 3J, you will need the following file:

New blank Word document

You will save your documents as:

Lastname_Firstname_3J_Municipal_Newsletter

Memphis Primary Materials writes an informational newsletter for customers. Create a new document and save it in your Word Chapter 3 folder as **Lastname_Firstname_3J_Municipal_Newsletter** Use the following information to create a newsletter that includes a nameplate, multiple columns, at least two articles with article titles formatted so that they stand out, at least one clip art image, one screenshot, and one paragraph that includes a border and shading.

This issue (Volume 1, Number 6—June 2016) will focus on municipal solid waste—the waste generated by households and small businesses. This category of waste does not include hazardous, industrial, or construction waste. The articles you write can be on any topic regarding municipal waste, and might include an introduction to the topic and a discussion of recycling in the United States or in the Memphis community. You will need to research this topic on the Web. A good place to start is www.epa.gov, which has many articles on solid municipal waste, and also provides links to further articles on the topic. You might also consider doing a Web search for the term **municipal solid waste recycling**

Add the file name to the footer area. To File Properties, add your course information, your name, and the keywords **municipal solid waste recycling** Save your document and print or submit electronically as directed.

Performance Criteria		Performance Level		
		Exemplary: You consistently applied the relevant skills	**Proficient:** You sometimes, but not always, applied the relevant skills	**Developing:** You rarely or never applied the relevant skills
	Create and format nameplate	The nameplate includes both the company name and the date and volume information, and is formatted attractively.	One or more of the nameplate elements are done correctly, but other items are either omitted or not formatted properly.	The newsletter does not include a nameplate.
	Insert at least two articles in multiple-column format	The newsletter contains at least two articles, displayed in multiple columns that are well written and are free of grammar and spelling errors.	The newsletter contains only one article, or the text is not divided into two columns, or there are spelling and grammar errors in the text.	The newsletter contains only one article, the article is not divided into multiple columns, and there are spelling and grammar errors.
	Insert and format at least one clip art image	An appropriate clip art image is included. The image is sized and positioned appropriately.	A clip art image is inserted, but is either inappropriate, or is formatted or positioned poorly.	No clip art image is included.
	Border and shading added to a paragraph	One or more paragraphs display an attractive border with shading that enables the reader to read the text.	A border or shading is displayed, but not both; or, the shading is too dark to enable the reader to easily read the text.	No border or shading is added to a paragraph.
	Insert a screenshot	A screenshot is inserted in one of the columns; the screenshot is related to the content of the article.	A screenshot is inserted in the document, but does not relate to the content of the article.	No screenshot is inserted.

End You have completed Project 3J

Content-Based Assessments

Apply a combination of the **3A** and **3B** skills.

GO! Solve It | Project **3K** Paper Report

Project Files

For Project 3K, you will need the following file:

New blank Word document

You will save your document as:

Lastname_Firstname_3K_Paper_Report

Create a new file and save it in your Word Chapter 3 folder as **Lastname_Firstname_3K_Paper_Report** Use the following information to create a report written in the MLA format. The report should include at least two footnotes, at least two citations, and should include a *Works Cited* page.

Memphis Primary Materials writes and distributes informational reports on topics of interest to the people of Memphis. This report will be written by Sarah Stanger for the head of marketing, Henry Miller. Information reports are provided as a public service of the company, and are distributed free of charge.

The topic of the report is recycling and reuse of paper and paper products. The report should contain an introduction, and then details about how much paper is used, what it is used for, the increase of paper recycling over time, and how paper products can be recycled or reused. A good place to start is www.epa.gov, which has many articles on paper use and recycling, and also provides links to further articles on the topic. You might also consider doing a Web search for the terms **paper recycling**

Add the file name to the footer area; and to File Properties, add your course information, your name, and the keywords **paper products, recycling** Save your document and print or submit electronically as directed.

Performance Criteria	Performance Level		
	Exemplary: You consistently applied the relevant skills	**Proficient:** You sometimes, but not always, applied the relevant skills	**Developing:** You rarely or never applied the relevant skills
Format the header and heading	The last name and page number are right-aligned in the header, and the report has a four-line heading and a centered title.	The header and heading are included, but are not formatted according to MLA style guidelines.	The header or heading is missing or incomplete.
Format the body of the report	The report is double-spaced, with no space after paragraphs. The first lines of paragraphs are indented 0.5".	Some, but not all, of the report formatting is correct.	The majority of the formatting does not follow MLA guidelines.
Footnotes are included and formatted correctly	Two or more footnotes are included, and the footnote text is 11 pt, double-spaced, and the first line of each footnote is indented.	The correct number of footnotes is included, but the footnotes are not formatted properly.	No footnotes are included.
Citations and bibliography are included and formatted according to MLA guidelines	At least two citations are included in parenthetical references, with page numbers where appropriate, and the sources are included in a properly formatted Works Cited page.	Only one citation is included, or the citations and sources are not formatted correctly.	No citations or Works Cited page are included.

End You have completed Project 3K

Outcomes-Based Assessments

Rubric

The following outcomes-based assessments are open-ended assessments. That is, there is no specific correct result; your result will depend on your approach to the information provided. Make Professional Quality your goal. Use the following scoring rubric to guide you in how to approach the problem and then to evaluate how well your approach solves the problem.

The *criteria*—Software Mastery, Content, Format and Layout, and Process—represent the knowledge and skills you have gained that you can apply to solving the problem. The *levels of performance*—Professional Quality, Approaching Professional Quality, or Needs Quality Improvements—help you and your instructor evaluate your result.

	Your completed project is of Professional Quality if you:	Your completed project is Approaching Professional Quality if you:	Your completed project Needs Quality Improvements if you:
1-Software Mastery	Choose and apply the most appropriate skills, tools, and features and identify efficient methods to solve the problem.	Choose and apply some appropriate skills, tools, and features, but not in the most efficient manner.	Choose inappropriate skills, tools, or features, or are inefficient in solving the problem.
2-Content	Construct a solution that is clear and well organized, contains content that is accurate, appropriate to the audience and purpose, and is complete. Provide a solution that contains no errors in spelling, grammar, or style.	Construct a solution in which some components are unclear, poorly organized, inconsistent, or incomplete. Misjudge the needs of the audience. Have some errors in spelling, grammar, or style, but the errors do not detract from comprehension.	Construct a solution that is unclear, incomplete, or poorly organized; contains some inaccurate or inappropriate content; and contains many errors in spelling, grammar, or style. Do not solve the problem.
3-Format and Layout	Format and arrange all elements to communicate information and ideas, clarify function, illustrate relationships, and indicate relative importance.	Apply appropriate format and layout features to some elements, but not others. Overuse features, causing minor distraction.	Apply format and layout that does not communicate information or ideas clearly. Do not use format and layout features to clarify function, illustrate relationships, or indicate relative importance. Use available features excessively, causing distraction.
4-Process	Use an organized approach that integrates planning, development, self-assessment, revision, and reflection.	Demonstrate an organized approach in some areas, but not others; or, use an insufficient process of organization throughout.	Do not use an organized approach to solve the problem.

Outcomes-Based Assessments

Apply a combination of the **3A** and **3B** skills.

GO! Think | Project **3L** Jobs Newsletter

Project Files

For Project 3L, you will need the following file:

New blank Word document

You will save your document as:

Lastname_Firstname_3L_Jobs_Newsletter

The marketing manager of Memphis Primary Materials needs to create the next issue of the company's monthly newsletter (Volume 1, Number 7—July 2016), which will focus on "green jobs." Green jobs are jobs associated with environmentally friendly companies or are positions with firms that manufacture, sell, or install energy-saving or resource-saving products.

Use the following information to create a newsletter that includes a nameplate, multiple columns, at least two articles with article titles formatted so that they stand out, at least one clip art image, one screenshot, and one paragraph that includes a border and shading.

The articles you write can be on any topic regarding green jobs, and might include an introduction to the topic, information about a recent (or future) green job conference, and a discussion of green jobs in the United States. You will need to research this topic on the Web. A good place to start is www.epa.gov. You might also consider doing a Web search for the terms **green jobs** or **green jobs conference**

Add the file name to the footer area. Add appropriate information to File Properties. Save the document in your Word Chapter 3 folder as **Lastname_Firstname_3L_Jobs_Newsletter** and print or submit electronically as directed.

End **You have completed Project 3L** —————————————

Apply a combination of the **3A** and **3B** skills.

GO! Think | Project **3M** Construction Report

Project Files

For Project 3M, you will need the following file:

New blank Word document

You will save your document as:

Lastname_Firstname_3M_Construction_Report

As part of the ongoing research provided on environment topics by the staff of Memphis Primary Materials, the Marketing Director, Henry Miller, has asked a summer intern, James Bodine, to create a report on recycling and reuse in the construction and demolition of buildings.

Create a new file and save it in your Word Chapter 3 folder as **Lastname_Firstname_3M_Construction_Report** Use the following information to create a report written in the MLA format. The report should include at least two footnotes, at least two citations, and should include a *Works Cited* page.

The report should contain an introduction, and then details about, for example, how much construction material can be salvaged from existing buildings, how these materials can be reused in future buildings, and how materials can be saved and recycled on new building projects. A good place to start is www.epa.gov, which has a number of articles on recycling and reuse of materials during construction and demolition. You might also consider doing a Web search for the terms **construction recycling** or **demolition recycling** or **construction and demolition**

Add the file name to the footer area. Add appropriate information to File Properties, save your document, and then print or submit electronically as directed.

End **You have completed Project 3M** —————————————

Word | Chapter 3

Apply a combination of the 3A and 3B skills.

You and GO! | Project **3N** College Newsletter

Project Files

For Project 3N, you will need the following file:

New blank Word document

You will save your document as:

Lastname_Firstname_3N_College_Newsletter

In this project, you will create a one-page newsletter. The newsletter should include at least one article describing your college and one article about an academic or athletic program at your college.

Be sure to include a nameplate, at least two articles, at least one clip art or screenshot image, and a bordered paragraph or paragraphs. Before you submit the newsletter, be sure to check it for grammar and spelling errors, and also be sure to format the newsletter in an attractive manner by using the skills you practiced in this chapter.

Save the file in your Word Chapter 3 folder as **Lastname_Firstname_3N_College_Newsletter** Add the file name to the footer area, and add your course information, your name, and the keywords **newsletter** and **college** to File Properties. Save and print or submit electronically as directed.

 You have completed Project 3N _____

Apply a combination of the 3A and 3B skills.

GO! Group Business Running Case | Project **3O**
Bell Orchid Hotels Group Running Case

This project relates to the **Bell Orchid Hotels**. Your instructor may assign this group case project to your class. If your instructor assigns this project, he or she will provide you with information and instructions to work as part of a group. The group will apply the skills gained thus far to help the Bell Orchid Hotels achieve their business goals.

 You have completed Project 3O _____

Creating a Worksheet and Charting Data

OUTCOMES

At the end of this chapter you will be able to:

OBJECTIVES

Mastering these objectives will enable you to:

PROJECT 1A

Create a sales report with an embedded column chart and sparklines.

1. Create, Save, and Navigate an Excel Workbook (p. 243)
2. Enter Data in a Worksheet (p. 246)
3. Construct and Copy Formulas and Use the SUM Function (p. 251)
4. Format Cells with Merge and Cell Styles (p. 255)
5. Chart Data to Create a Column Chart and Insert Sparklines (p. 258)
6. Print, Display Formulas, and Close Excel (p. 263)

PROJECT 1B

Calculate the value of an inventory.

7. Check Spelling in a Worksheet (p. 269)
8. Enter Data by Range (p. 271)
9. Construct Formulas for Mathematical Operations (p. 273)
10. Edit Values in a Worksheet (p. 277)
11. Format a Worksheet (p. 279)

© rangizzz / Shutterstock

In This Chapter

In this chapter, you will use Microsoft Excel for Mac 2011 to create and analyze data organized into columns and rows. After entering data in a worksheet, you can perform calculations, analyze the data to make logical decisions, and create charts.

In this chapter, you will create and modify Excel workbooks. You will practice the basics of worksheet design, create a footer, enter and edit data in a worksheet, chart data, and then save, preview, and print workbooks. You will also construct formulas for mathematical operations.

The projects in this chapter relate to **Texas Spectrum Wireless**, which provides accessories and software for all major brands of cell phones, smartphones, PDAs, MP3 players, and portable computers. The company sells thousands of unique products in their retail stores, which are located throughout Texas and the southern United States. They also sell thousands of items each year through their Web site, and offer free shipping and returns to their customers. The company takes pride in offering unique categories of accessories such as waterproof and ruggedized gear.

Project 1A Sales Report with Embedded Column Chart and Sparklines

In Activities 1.01 through 1.15, you will create an Excel worksheet for Roslyn Thomas, the President of Texas Spectrum Wireless. The worksheet displays the first quarter sales of wireless accessories for the current year and includes a chart to visually represent the data. Your completed worksheet will look similar to Figure 1.1.

Project Files

For Project 1A, you will need the following file:

New Excel workbook

You will save your workbook as:

Lastname_Firstname_1A_Quarterly_Sales

Project Results

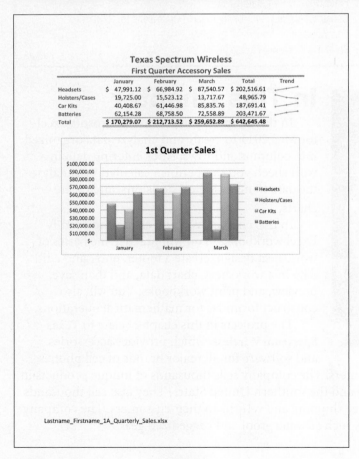

Figure 1.1
Project 1A Quarterly Sales

Objective 1 | Create, Save, and Navigate an Excel Workbook

On startup, Excel displays the Excel Workbook Gallery, and the Excel Workbook template is selected. A **workbook**—the Excel document that stores your data—contains one or more pages called a **worksheet**. A worksheet—or **spreadsheet**—is stored in a workbook and is formatted as a pattern of uniformly spaced horizontal rows and vertical columns. The intersection of a column and a row forms a box referred to as a **cell**.

Activity 1.01 | Starting Excel and Naming and Saving a Workbook

1 Open **Excel**. In the **Excel Workbook Gallery**, be sure that **Excel Workbook** is selected, and then in the lower right corner, click **Choose**. If necessary, increase the size of the Excel window to fill the screen by clicking the Zoom button 🔘 or by dragging the lower right corner of the Excel window. On the Standard toolbar, click the **Zoom arrow** 100% ▾, and then click **125%**.

> Increases in the Zoom setting are used so that when you compare your screen with the figures used in this textbook, the text in the figures referenced in the project steps can be viewed more easily.

> **Another Way**
>
> Use the keyboard shortcut Shift + Command ⌘ + S to display the Save As dialog box.

2 On the **File** menu, click **Save As**, and then in the **Save As** dialog box, navigate to the location where you will store your workbooks for this chapter.

3 In your storage location, create a new folder named **Excel Chapter 1** In the **Save As** box, notice that *Workbook1* displays as the default file name.

4 In the **Save As** box, if necessary, double-click *Workbook1* to select it, and then using your own name, type **Lastname_Firstname_1A_Quarterly_Sales** being sure to include the underscore (_) instead of spaces between words. Compare your screen with Figure 1.2.

Figure 1.2

File name with your name and underscores between words

Excel Chapter 1 folder created

Save button

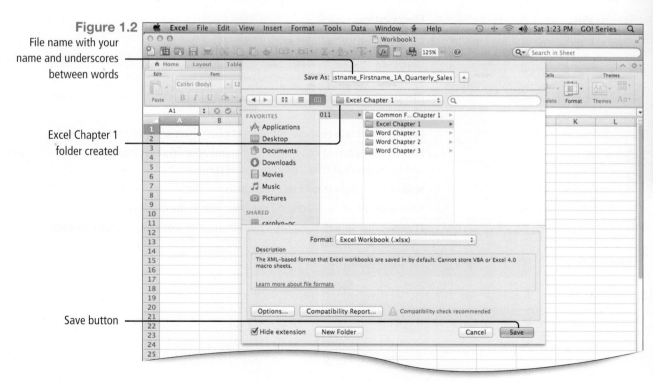

5 Click **Save**. Compare your screen with Figure 1.3, and then take a moment to study the Excel window parts in the table in Figure 1.4.

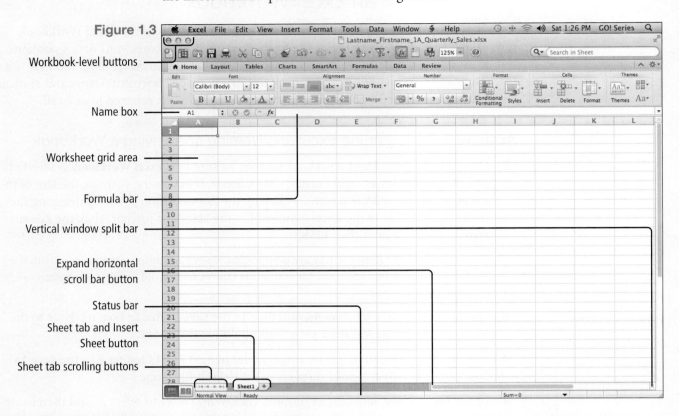

Figure 1.3

Workbook-level buttons

Name box

Worksheet grid area

Formula bar

Vertical window split bar

Expand horizontal scroll bar button

Status bar

Sheet tab and Insert Sheet button

Sheet tab scrolling buttons

Parts of the Excel Window

Screen Part	Description
Expand horizontal scroll bar button	Increases the width of the horizontal scroll bar.
Formula bar	Displays the value or formula contained in the active cell; also permits entry or editing.
Name box	Displays the name of the selected cell, table, chart, or object.
Sheet tab and Insert Sheet button	Identify the worksheet in a workbook and inserts an additional worksheet.
Sheet tab scrolling buttons	Display sheet tabs that are not in view when there are numerous sheet tabs.
Status bar	Displays the current cell mode, page number, worksheet information, view buttons, and for numerical data, common calculations such as Sum and Average.
Vertical window split bar	Splits the worksheet into two vertical views of the same worksheet.
Workbook-level buttons	Minimize, close, or restore the previous size of the displayed workbook.
Worksheet grid area	Displays the columns and rows that intersect to form the worksheet's cells.

Figure 1.4

Activity 1.02 | Navigating a Worksheet and a Workbook

1 Take a moment to study Figure 1.5 and the table in Figure 1.6 to become familiar with the Excel workbook window.

Figure 1.5

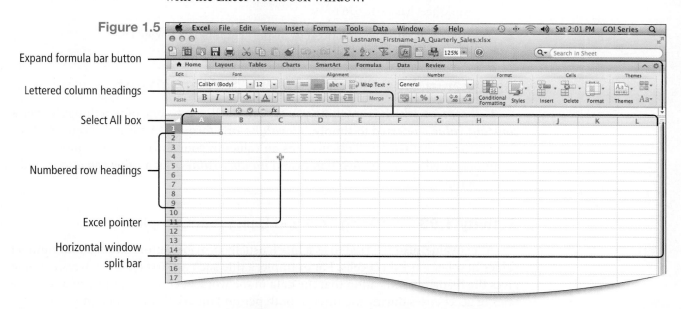

Expand formula bar button

Lettered column headings

Select All box

Numbered row headings

Excel pointer

Horizontal window split bar

Excel Workbook Window Elements

Workbook Window Element	Description
Excel pointer	The mouse pointer in Excel.
Expand formula bar button	Increases the height of the formula bar to display lengthy cell content.
Horizontal window split bar	Splits the worksheet into two horizontal views of the same worksheet.
Lettered column headings	The column letter.
Numbered row headings	The row number.
Select All box	Selects all the cells in a worksheet.

Figure 1.6

2 In the lower right corner of the screen, in the horizontal scroll bar area, click to the right of the **horizontal scroll bar** to view the columns to the right and move the first columns out of view.

> A *column* is a vertical group of cells in a worksheet. Beginning with the first letter of the alphabet, *A*, a unique letter identifies each column—this is called the *column heading*. Clicking to the right of the horizontal scroll bar shifts the window right and displays columns that follow the last letter displayed on the previous screen.

3 Using your mouse or other pointing device, swipe left until you see pairs of letters as the column headings. If you cannot swipe using your pointing device, scroll instead.

> To scroll, *swipe*—move your finger across the mouse or other pointing device. You can swipe left, right, up and down.

4 Slowly drag the horizontal scroll bar to the left, and notice that just above the scroll box, ScreenTips with the column letters display as you drag. By dragging the horizontal scroll bar or by swiping, position **column Z** near the center of your screen.

> Column headings after column Z use two letters starting with AA, AB, and so on, through ZZ. After that, columns begin with three letters beginning with AAA. This pattern provides 16,384 columns. The last column is XFD. You do not have to point to the horizontal scroll bar to scroll left and right; you can scroll by swiping anywhere in the worksheet.

5 Swipe up or scroll to move **row 1** out of view.

A *row* is a horizontal group of cells. Beginning with number 1, a unique number identifies each row—this is the *row heading*, located at the left side of the worksheet. A single worksheet has 1,048,576 rows.

6 Use the skills you just practiced to display **column A** and **row 1**.

Objective 2 | Enter Data in a Worksheet

Cell content, which is anything you type in a cell, can be one of two things: either a *constant value*—referred to simply as a *value*—or a *formula*. A formula is an equation that performs mathematical calculations on values in your worksheet. The most commonly used values are *text values* and *number values*, but a value can also include a date or a time of day.

Activity 1.03 | Entering Text and Using AutoComplete

A text value, also referred to as a *label*, usually provides information about number values in other worksheet cells. For example, a title such as *First Quarter Accessory Sales* gives the reader an indication that the data in the worksheet relates to information about sales of accessories during the three-month period January through March.

1 If necessary, point to and then click the cell at the intersection of **column A** and **row 1** to make it the *active cell*—the cell is outlined in a color such as blue or red and is ready to accept data.

The intersecting column letter and row number form the *cell reference*—also called the *cell address*. When a cell is active, its column letter and row number are highlighted. The cell reference of the selected cell, *A1*, displays in the Name box.

2 With cell **A1** as the active cell, type the worksheet title **Texas Spectrum Wireless** and then press Return. Compare your screen with Figure 1.7.

Text or numbers in a cell are referred to as *data*. You must confirm the data you type in a cell by pressing Return or by some other keyboard movement, such as pressing Tab or an arrow key. Pressing Return moves the selection to the cell below—in this case, cell A2.

Figure 1.7

Name box displays active cell—A2

Column heading and row heading of the active cell highlighted

Worksheet title entered

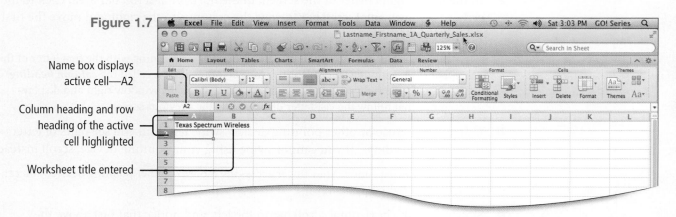

3 In cell **A1**, notice that the text does not fit; the text spills over and displays in cell **B1** to the right.

If text is too long for a cell and cells to the right are empty, the text will display. If the cells to the right contain other data, only the text that will fit in the cell displays.

4 In cell **A2**, type the worksheet subtitle **First Quarter Accessory Sales** and then press Return. Compare your screen with Figure 1.8.

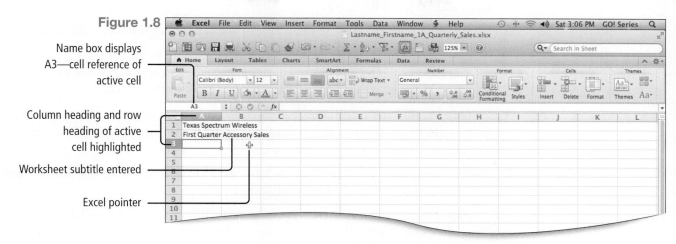

Figure 1.8

Name box displays A3—cell reference of active cell

Column heading and row heading of active cell highlighted

Worksheet subtitle entered

Excel pointer

5 Press Return again to make cell **A4** the active cell. In cell **A4**, type **Headsets** which will form the first row title, and then press Return.

The text characters that you typed align at the left edge of the cell—referred to as *left alignment*—and cell A5 becomes the active cell. Left alignment is the default for text values.

6 In cell **A5**, type **H** and notice the text from the previous cell displays.

If the first characters you type in a cell match an existing entry in the column, Excel fills in the remaining characters for you. This feature, called *AutoComplete*, assists only with alphabetic values.

7 Continue typing the remainder of the row title **olsters/Cases** and press Return.

The AutoComplete suggestion is removed when the entry you are typing differs from the previous value.

> **Another Way**
>
> Use the keyboard shortcut Command ⌘ + S to Save changes to your workbook.

8 In cell **A6**, type **Car Kits** and press Return. In cell **A7**, type **Batteries** and press Return. In cell **A8**, type **Total** and press Return. On the Standard toolbar, click **Save** 🔲.

Activity 1.04 | Using Auto Fill and Keyboard Shortcuts

1 Click cell **B3**. Type **J** and notice that when you begin to type in a cell, on the **formula bar**, the **Cancel** ⊗ and **Enter** ⊘ buttons become active, as shown in Figure 1.9.

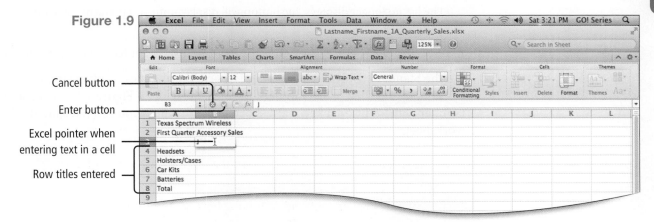

Figure 1.9

Cancel button

Enter button

Excel pointer when entering text in a cell

Row titles entered

2 Continue to type **anuary** On the **formula bar**, notice that values you type in a cell also display there. Then, on the **formula bar**, click the **Enter** button ⊘ to confirm the entry and keep cell **B3** active.

3 With cell **B3** active, locate the small blue or red square in the lower right corner of the selected cell.

> You can drag this *fill handle*—the small square in the lower right corner of a selected cell—to adjacent cells to fill the cells with values based on the first cell.

4 Point to the **fill handle** until the ✛ pointer displays, press down on the mouse, drag to the right to cell **D3**, and as you drag, notice the ScreenTips *February* and *March*. Release the mouse.

5 Under the text that you just filled, click the **Auto Fill Options** button ▦ that displays, and then compare your screen with Figure 1.10.

> *Auto Fill* generates and extends a *series* of values into adjacent cells based on the value of other cells. A series is a group of things that come one after another in succession; for example, *January, February, March*.
>
> The Auto Fill Options button displays options to fill the data; options vary depending on the content and program from which you are filling, and the format of the data you are filling. *Fill Series* is selected, indicating the action that was taken. Because the options are related to the current task, the button is referred to as being *context sensitive*.

Figure 1.10

Auto Fill Options button

Fill handle

January, February, March
display in cells
B3, C3, and D3

Auto Fill Options list

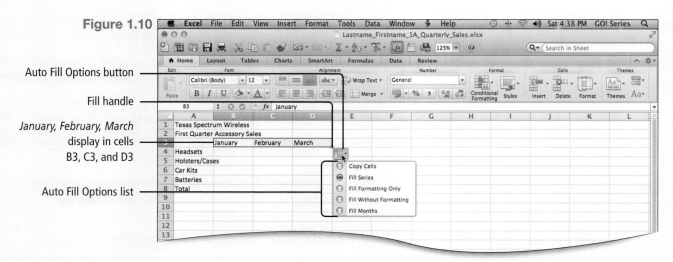

6 Click in any cell to cancel the display of the Auto Fill Options list.

> The list no longer displays; the button will display until you perform some other screen action.

7 Press Command ⌘ + fn + ←, which is the keyboard shortcut to make cell **A1** active.

8 On the Standard toolbar, click **Save** 🖫 to save the changes you have made to your workbook, and then take a moment to study the table in Figure 1.11 to become familiar with additional keyboard shortcuts with which you can navigate the Excel worksheet.

Keyboard Shortcuts to Navigate the Excel Window

To Move the Location of the Active Cell:	Press:
Up, down, right, or left one cell	⬆, ⬇, ➡, ⬅
Down one cell	Return
Up one cell	Shift + Return
Up one full screen	fn + ⬆
Down one full screen	fn + ⬇
To column A of the current row	fn + ⬅
To the last cell in the last column of the active area (the rectangle formed by all the rows and columns in a worksheet that contain entries)	Command ⌘ + fn + ➡
To cell A1	Command ⌘ + fn + ⬅
Right one cell	Tab or ➡

Figure 1.11

Activity 1.05 | Aligning Text and Adjusting the Size of Columns

1 In the **column heading area**, point to the vertical line between **column A** and **column B** to display the ⬌ pointer, press down on the mouse, and then compare your screen with Figure 1.12.

A ScreenTip displays information about the width of the column. The default width of a column is 10 characters or 0.90 inches using the default Excel font of Calibri and the default font size of 12. An average of 10 characters in 12-point Calibri font will fit in a cell.

Figure 1.12

ScreenTip

Column heading area

Mouse pointer
Auto Fill Options button

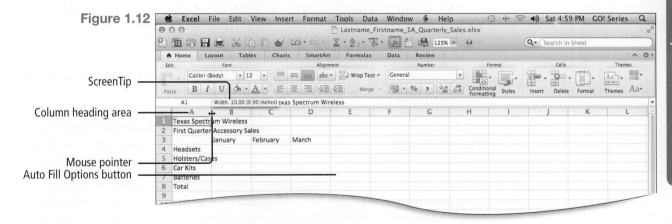

2 Drag to the right, and when the number of characters indicated in the ScreenTip reaches **13.00 (1.16 inches)**, release the mouse. If you are not satisfied with your result, on the Standard toolbar, click Undo ↺ and begin again.

This width accommodates the longest row title in cells A4 through A8—*Holsters/Cases*. The worksheet title and subtitle in cells A1 and A2 span more than one column and still do not fit in column A.

Excel | Chapter 1

3 Click cell **B3** and then drag across to select cells **B3**, **C3**, and **D3**. Compare your screen with Figure 1.13; if you are not satisfied with your result, click anywhere and begin again.

> The three cells, B3 through D3, are selected and form a ***range***—two or more cells on a worksheet that are adjacent (next to each other) or nonadjacent (not next to each other). This range of cells is referred to as *B3:D3*. When you see a colon (:) between two cell references, the range includes all the cells between the two cell references.
>
> A range of cells that is selected in this manner is indicated by a colored border, and Excel treats the range as a single unit so you can make the same changes to more than one cell at a time. The selected cells in the range are highlighted except for the first cell in the range, which displays in the Name box.

Figure 1.13

First cell in selected range—B3—displays in Name box

Column A widened to 13 (1.16 inches)

Range B3:D3 selected

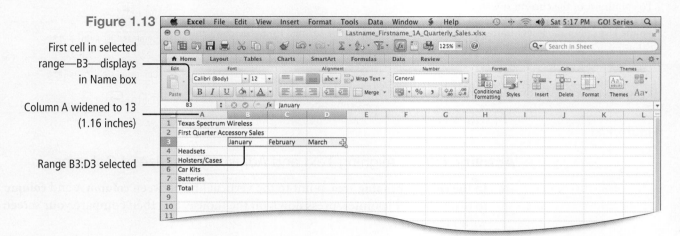

4 With the range **B3:D3** selected, on the **Home tab**, in the **Alignment group**, click the **Center Text** button ⬚. On the Standard toolbar, click the **Save** 🖫 button.

> The column titles *January*, *February*, and *March* align in the center of each cell.

Activity 1.06 | Entering Numbers

To type number values, use either the number keys across the top of your keyboard or the numeric keypad if you have one.

1 Under *January*, click cell **B4**, type **47991.12** and then on the **formula bar**, click the **Enter** button ⬚ to maintain cell **B4** as the active cell. Compare your screen with Figure 1.14.

> By default, *number* values align at the right edge of the cell. The default ***number format***—a specific way in which Excel displays numbers—is the ***general format***. In the default general format, whatever you type in the cell will display, with the exception of trailing zeros to the right of a decimal point. For example, in the number 237.50 the *0* following the *5* is a trailing zero.
>
> Data that displays in a cell is the ***displayed value***. Data that displays in the formula bar is the ***underlying value***. The number of digits or characters that display in a cell—the displayed value—depends on the width of the column. Calculations on numbers are always based on the underlying value, not the displayed value.

Figure 1.14

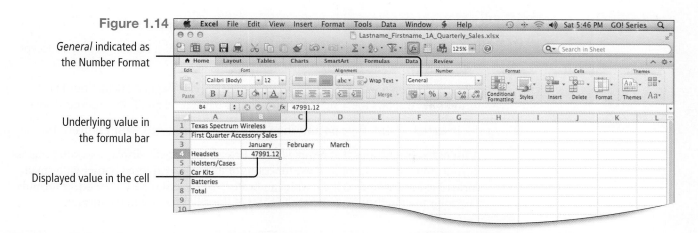

General indicated as
the Number Format

Underlying value in
the formula bar

Displayed value in the cell

2 Press Tab to make cell **C4** active. Then, enter the remaining sales numbers as shown by using the following technique: Press Tab to confirm your entry and move across the row, and then press Return at the end of a row to move to the next row.

	January	February	March
Headsets	47991.12	66984.92	87540.57
Holsters/Cases	19725	15523.12	13717.67
Car Kits	40408.67	61446.98	85835.76
Batteries	62154.28	68758.50	72558.89

3 Compare the numbers you entered with Figure 1.15 and then **Save** 🔲 your workbook.

> In the default general format, trailing zeros to the right of a decimal point will not display. For example, when you type *68758.50*, the cell displays *68758.5* instead.

Figure 1.15

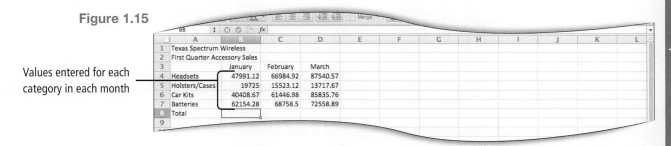

Values entered for each
category in each month

Objective 3 | Construct and Copy Formulas and Use the SUM Function

A cell contains either a constant value (text or numbers) or a formula. A formula is an equation that performs mathematical calculations on values in other cells, and then places the result in the cell containing the formula. You can create formulas or use a *function*—a prewritten formula that looks at one or more values, performs an operation, and then returns a value.

Activity 1.07 | Constructing a Formula and Using the SUM Function

In this activity, you will practice three different ways to sum a group of numbers in Excel.

1 If necessary, click cell **B8** to make it the active cell and type **=**

The equal sign (=) displays in the cell with the insertion point blinking, ready to accept more data.

All formulas begin with the = sign, which signals Excel to begin a calculation. The formula bar displays the = sign, and the formula bar Cancel and Enter buttons display.

2 At the insertion point, type **b4** and then compare your screen with Figure 1.16.

A list of Excel functions that begin with the letter *B* may briefly display—as you progress in your study of Excel, you will use functions of this type. A colored border with small corner boxes surrounds cell B4, which indicates that the cell is part of an active formula. The color used in the box matches the color of the cell reference in the formula.

Figure 1.16

Cell B4 outlined in blue—or another color—to show it is part of an active formula

Cell B8 displays the beginning of the formula, with *b4* in blue—or another color—to match outlined cell

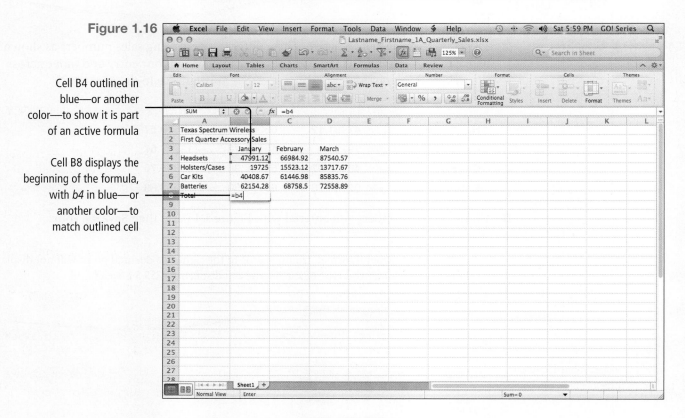

3 At the insertion point, type **+** and then type **b5**

A border of another color surrounds cell B5, and the color matches the color of the cell reference in the active formula. When typing cell references, it is not necessary to use uppercase letters.

4 At the insertion point, type **+b6+b7** and then press Return.

The result of the formula calculation—*170279.07*—displays in the cell. Recall that in the default General format, trailing zeros do not display.

5 Click cell **B8** again, look at the **formula bar**, and then compare your screen with Figure 1.17.

The formula adds the values in cells B4 through B7, and the result displays in cell B8. In this manner, you can construct a formula by typing. Although cell B8 displays the *result* of the formula, the formula itself displays in the formula bar. This is referred to as the *underlying formula*.

Always view the formula bar to be sure of the exact content of a cell—a displayed number may actually be a formula.

Figure 1.17

Formula displays
in formula bar

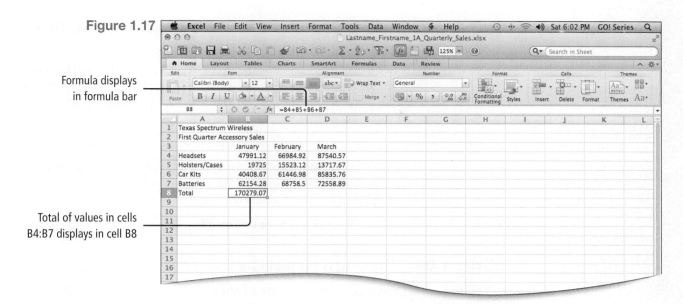

Total of values in cells
B4:B7 displays in cell B8

6 Click cell **C8** and type **=** to signal the beginning of a formula. Then, point to cell **C4** and click one time.

> The reference to the cell C4 is added to the active formula. A moving border surrounds the referenced cell, and the border color and the color of the cell reference in the formula are color coded to match.

7 At the insertion point, type **+** and then click cell **C5**. Repeat this process to complete the formula to add cells **C6** and **C7**, and then press Return.

> The result of the formula calculation—*212713.52*—displays in the cell. This method of constructing a formula is the ***point and click method***.

Another Way

Use the keyboard shortcut Command ⌘ + Shift + T; or, on the Formulas tab, in the Function group, click the AutoSum button.

8 Click cell **D8**. On the Standard toolbar, click the **Sum** button Σ, and then compare your screen with Figure 1.18.

> *SUM* is an Excel function—a prewritten formula. A moving border surrounds the range D4:D7 and *=SUM(D4:D7)* displays in cell D8.
>
> The = sign signals the beginning of a formula, *SUM* indicates the type of calculation that will take place (addition), and *(D4:D7)* indicates the range of cells on which the sum calculation will be performed.

Figure 1.18

Sum button

SUM function displays
in formula bar

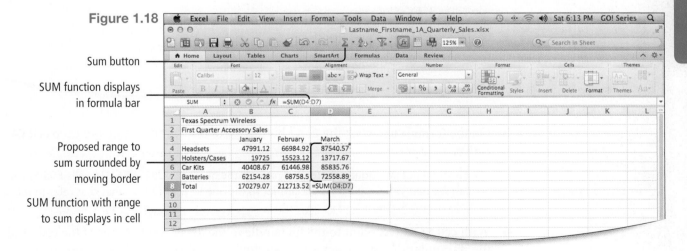

Proposed range to
sum surrounded by
moving border

SUM function with range
to sum displays in cell

Excel | Chapter 1

9 Look at the **formula bar**, and notice that the formula also displays there. Then, look again at the cells surrounded by the moving border.

> When you activate the ***Sum function***, Excel first looks *above* the active cell for a range of cells to sum. If no range is above the active cell, Excel will look to the *left* for a range of cells to sum. If the proposed range is not what you want to calculate, you can select a different group of cells.

10 Press Return to construct a formula by using the prewritten SUM function.

> Your total is *259652.89*. Because the Sum function is frequently used, it has its own button on the Standard toolbar. A larger version of the button also displays on the Formulas tab in the Function group. This button is also referred to as ***AutoSum***.

11 On the Standard toolbar, click the **Save** button 🖫.

Activity 1.08 | Copying a Formula by Using the Fill Handle

You have practiced three ways to create a formula—by typing, by using the point-and-click technique, and by using a function button from the Ribbon. You can also copy formulas. When you copy a formula from one cell to another, Excel adjusts the cell references to fit the new location of the formula.

1 Click cell **E3**, type **Total** and then press Return.

> The text in cell E3 is centered because the centered format continues from the adjacent cell—D3.

2 With cell **E4** as the active cell, on the Standard toolbar, click the **Sum** button Σ. Compare your screen with Figure 1.19.

> Recall that Excel first looks above the selected cell for a proposed range of cells to sum, and if no data is detected, Excel looks to the left and proposes a range of cells to sum.

Figure 1.19

SUM function displays in formula bar

SUM function displays in cell

Proposed range to sum outlined with moving border

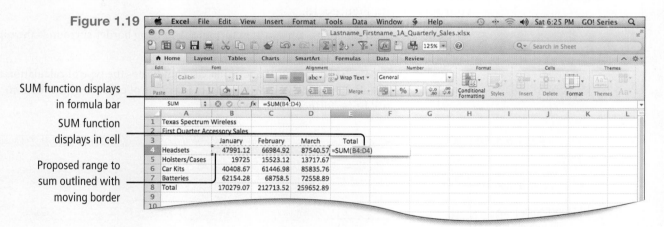

3 On the **formula bar**, click the **Enter** button ✓ to display the result and keep cell **E4** active.

> The total dollar amount of *Headsets* sold in the quarter is *202516.61*. In cells E5:E8, you can see that you need a formula similar to the one in E4, but formulas that refer to the cells in row 5, row 6, and so on.

4 With cell **E4** active, point to the fill handle in the lower right corner of the cell until the ➕ pointer displays. Click and then drag down through cell **E8**; if you are not satisfied with your result, on the Standard toolbar, click the Undo button ↩, and begin again. Compare your screen with Figure 1.20.

Figure 1.20

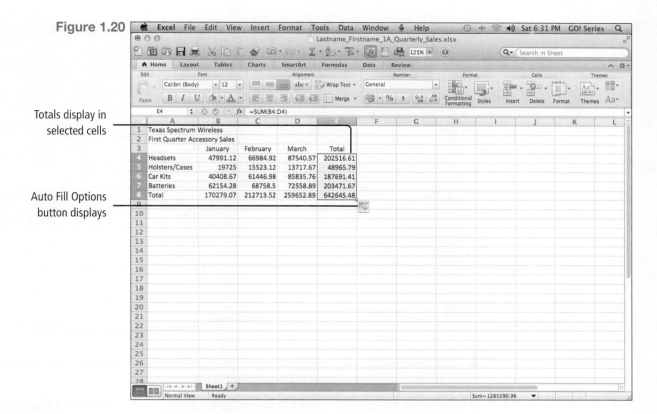

Totals display in selected cells

Auto Fill Options button displays

5 Click cell **E5**, look at the **formula bar**, and notice the formula *=SUM(B5:D5)*. Click cell **E6**, look at the **formula bar**, and then notice the formula *=SUM(B6:D6)*.

In each row, Excel copied the formula but adjusted the cell references *relative* to the row number. This is called a ***relative cell reference***—a cell reference based on the relative position of the cell that contains the formula and the cells referred to.

The calculation is the same, but it is performed on the cells in that particular row. Use this method to insert numerous formulas into spreadsheets quickly.

6 Click cell **F3,** type **Trend** and then press Return. **Save** 🖫 your workbook.

Objective 4 | Format Cells with Merge and Cell Styles

Format—change the appearance of—cells to make your worksheet attractive and easy to read.

Activity 1.09 | Using Merge and Applying Cell Styles

1 By dragging, select the range **A1:F1**, and then on the **Home tab**, in the **Alignment group**, click the **Merge** button. Select the range **A2:F2**, and then click the **Merge** button.

The *Merge* command joins selected cells into one larger cell and centers the contents in the new cell; individual cells in the range B1:F1 and B2:F2 can no longer be selected—they are merged into cells A1 and A2 respectively.

2 Click cell **A1**. On the **Home tab**, in the **Format group**, click the **Styles** button to display the **Cell Styles** gallery, and then compare your screen with Figure 1.21.

A ***cell style*** is a defined set of formatting characteristics, such as font, font size, font color, cell borders, and cell shading.

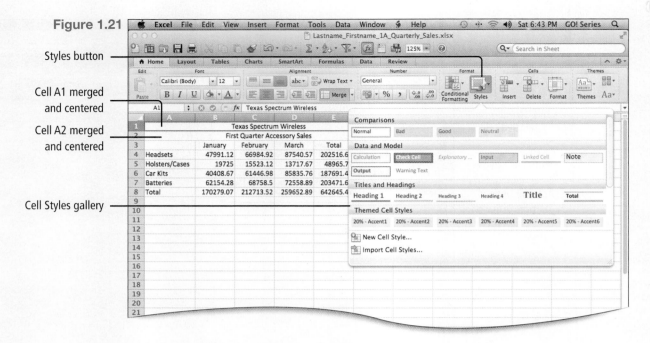

Figure 1.21

Styles button

Cell A1 merged and centered

Cell A2 merged and centered

Cell Styles gallery

3 In the gallery, under **Titles and Headings**, click **Title**, and notice that the row height adjusts to accommodate this larger font size.

4 Click cell **A2**, display the **Cell Styles** gallery, and then under **Titles and Headings**, click **Heading 1**.

Use cell styles to maintain a consistent look in a worksheet and across worksheets in a workbook.

5 Select the range **B3:F3**, hold down Command ⌘, and then select the range **A4:A8** to select the column titles and the row titles.

Use this technique to select two or more ranges that are nonadjacent—not next to each other.

6 Display the **Cell Styles** gallery, click **Heading 4** to apply this cell style to the column titles and row titles, and then **Save** 🖫 your workbook.

Activity 1.10 | Formatting Financial Numbers

Another Way

In the Name box type b4:e4,b8:e8 and then press Return.

1 Select the range **B4:E4**, hold down Command ⌘, and then select the range **B8:E8**.

This range is referred to as *b4:e4,b8:e8* with a comma separating the references to the two nonadjacent ranges.

Another Way

Display the Cell Styles gallery, scroll, and under Number Format, click Currency.

2 On the **Home tab**, in the **Number group**, click the **Number Format arrow** `General`, and then click **Accounting**. Notice that the formatting is applied to both ranges. If the format is applied only to the first range, once again, click the Number Format arrow `General`, and click Accounting. Compare your screen with Figure 1.22.

The *Accounting Number Format* applies a thousand comma separator where appropriate, inserts a fixed U.S. dollar sign aligned at the left edge of the cell, applies two decimal places, and leaves a small amount of space at the right edge of the cell to accommodate a parenthesis when negative numbers are present. Excel widens the columns to accommodate the formatted numbers.

Figure 1.22

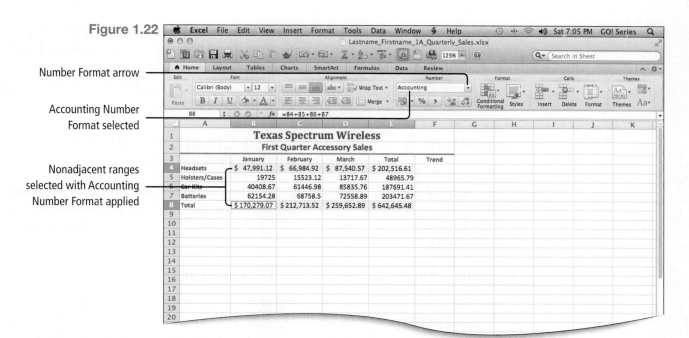

Number Format arrow

Accounting Number
Format selected

Nonadjacent ranges
selected with Accounting
Number Format applied

Another Way

Display the Cell Styles
gallery, scroll, and
under Number Format,
click Comma.

3 Select the range **B5:E7**, and then in the **Number group**, click the **Comma Style** button .

The **Comma Style** inserts thousand comma separators where appropriate and applies two decimal places. Comma Style also leaves space at the right to accommodate a parenthesis when negative numbers are present.

When preparing worksheets with financial information, the first row of dollar amounts and the total row of dollar amounts are formatted in the Accounting Number Format; that is, with thousand comma separators, dollar signs, two decimal places, and space at the right to accommodate a parenthesis for negative numbers, if any. Rows that are *not* the first row or the total row should be formatted with the Comma Style.

4 Select the range **B8:E8**. In the **Format group**, click the **Styles** button to display the **Cell Styles** gallery, and then under **Titles and Headings**, click **Total**. Click any blank cell to cancel the selection, and then compare your screen with Figure 1.23.

This is a common way to apply borders to financial information. The single border indicates that calculations were performed on the numbers above, and the double border indicates that the information is complete. Sometimes financial documents do not display values with cents; rather, the values are rounded up. You can do this by selecting the cells, and then clicking the Decrease Decimal button two times.

Figure 1.23

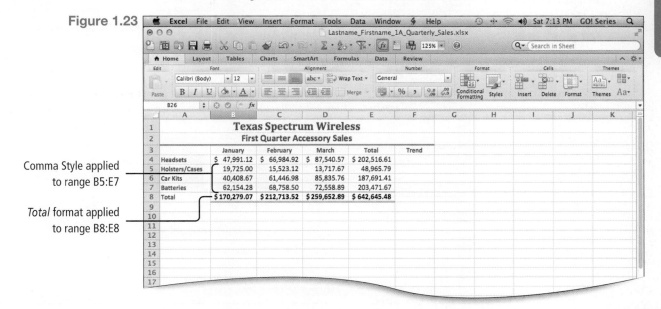

Comma Style applied
to range B5:E7

Total format applied
to range B8:E8

Excel | Chapter 1

5 On the **Home tab**, in the **Themes group**, click the **Themes** button. Click the **Black** theme, and notice that the cell styles change to match the new theme. **Save** 🔲 your workbook.

> Recall that a theme is a predefined set of colors, fonts, lines, and fill effects that look good together.

Objective 5 | Chart Data to Create a Column Chart and Insert Sparklines

A *chart* is a graphic representation of data in a worksheet. Data presented as a chart is easier to understand than a table of numbers. *Sparklines* are tiny charts embedded in a cell and give a visual trend summary alongside your data. A sparkline makes a pattern more obvious to the eye.

Activity 1.11 | Charting Data in a Column Chart

In this activity, you will create a *column chart* showing the monthly sales of accessories by category during the first quarter. A column chart is useful for illustrating comparisons among related numbers. The chart will enable the company president, Rosalyn Thomas, to see a pattern of overall monthly sales.

1 Select the range **A3:D7**. Click the **Charts tab**, and then in the **Insert Chart group**, click the **Column** button to display a gallery of column chart types.

> When charting data, typically you should *not* include totals—include only the data you want to compare. By using different *chart types*, you can display data in a way that is meaningful to the reader—common examples are column charts, pie charts, and line charts.

2 In the gallery of column chart types, under **2-D Column**, click **Clustered Column**. Compare your screen with Figure 1.24.

> A column chart displays in the worksheet, and the charted data is bordered by colored lines. Because the chart object is selected—surrounded by a border and displaying sizing handles—contextual tabs named *Chart Layout* and *Format* display to the right of the Charts tab on the Ribbon.

Figure 1.24

Two additional contextual tabs display for Charts— *Chart Layout* and *Format*

Charted data range bordered by colored lines (green = legend, blue = columns, purple = category labels)

Border and sizing handles indicate chart is selected

Clustered column chart displays in worksheet

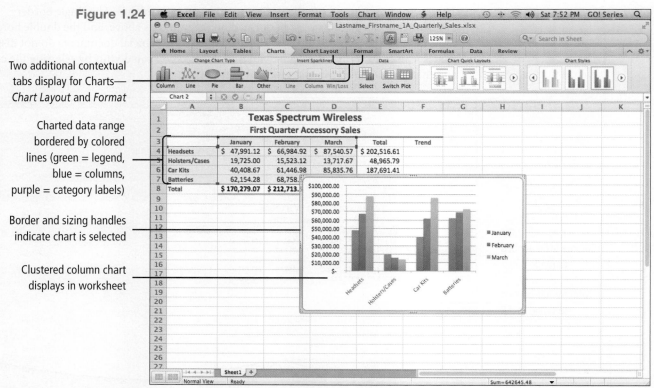

3 Point to the top border of the chart to display the 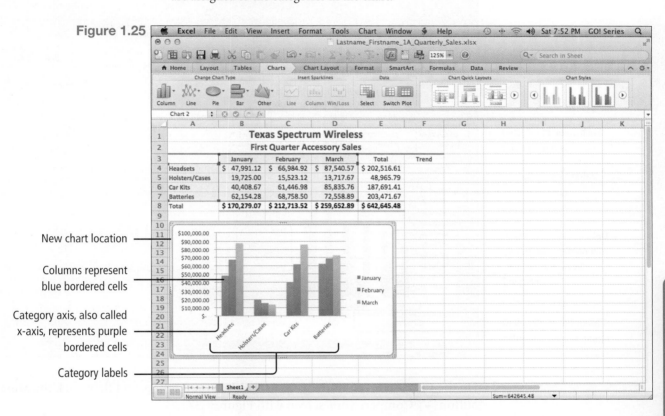 pointer, and then drag the upper left corner of the chart just inside the upper left corner of cell **A10**, approximately as shown in Figure 1.25.

> Based on the data you selected in your worksheet, Excel constructs a column chart and adds *category labels*—the labels that display along the bottom of the chart to identify the category of data. This area is referred to as the *category axis* or the *x-axis*. Excel uses the row titles as the category names.
>
> On the left, Excel includes a numerical scale on which the charted data is based; this is the *value axis* or the *y-axis*. On the right is a *legend* that identifies the patterns or colors that are assigned to the categories in the chart.

Figure 1.25

New chart location

Columns represent
blue bordered cells

Category axis, also called
x-axis, represents purple
bordered cells

Category labels

4 On the Ribbon, locate the contextual tabs to the right of **Charts** and click the **Chart Layout tab** and then the **Format tab** to display the tools that are available for working with charts.

> When a chart is selected, two tabs provide commands for working with the chart.

5 Locate the group of cells bordered in a color—your color may be red, blue, or another.

> Each of the bordered twelve cells is referred to as a *data point*—a value that originates in a worksheet cell. Each data point is represented in the chart by a *data marker*—a column, bar, area, dot, pie slice, or other symbol in a chart that represents a single data point.
>
> Related data points form a *data series*; for example, there is a data series for *January*, for *February*, and for *March*. Each data series has a unique color or pattern represented in the chart legend.

Excel | Chapter 1

6 On the **Charts tab**, in the **Data group**, click the **Switch** button, and then compare your screen with Figure 1.26. If the Switch button does not work as expected, in the Data group, click the Select button, and in the Select Data Source dialog box, click Switch Row/Column, and then click OK.

> In this manner, you can easily change the categories of data from the row titles, which is the default, to the column titles. Whether you use row or column titles as your category names depends on how you want to view your charted data. Here, the president wants to see monthly sales and the breakdown of product categories within each month.

Figure 1.26

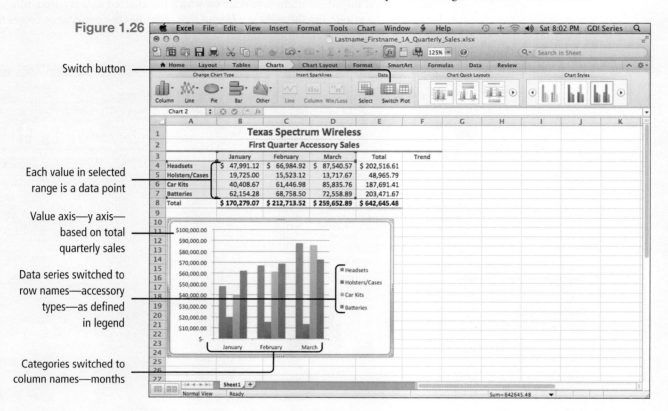

Switch button

Each value in selected range is a data point

Value axis—y axis—based on total quarterly sales

Data series switched to row names—accessory types—as defined in legend

Categories switched to column names—months

7 On the **Charts tab**, point to the **Chart Quick Layouts group**, and then click the **More** button. Compare your screen with Figure 1.27.

> In the *Chart Quick Layouts gallery*, you can select a predesigned *chart layout*—a combination of chart elements, which can include a title, legend, labels for the columns, and the table of charted cells.

Figure 1.27

More button

Chart Quick
Layouts gallery

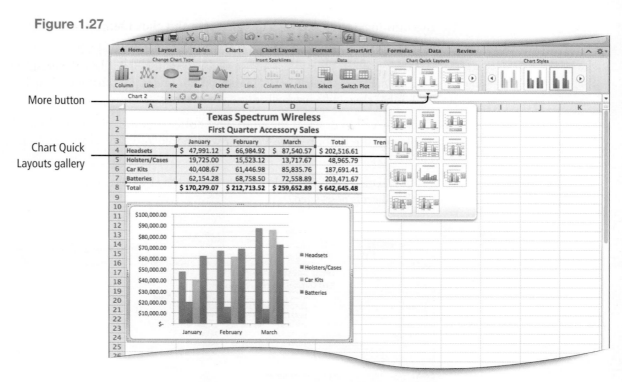

8 Using the ScreenTips as your guide, locate and click **Layout 1**.

9 In the chart, click anywhere in the text *Chart Title* to select the title box, type **1st Quarter Sales** and then click anywhere inside the chart border to cancel the selection of the title.

10 On the **Charts tab**, point to the **Chart Styles group**, click the **More** button , and then compare your screen with Figure 1.28.

The ***Chart Styles gallery*** displays an array of pre-defined ***chart styles***—the overall visual look of the chart in terms of its colors, backgrounds, and graphic effects such as flat or beveled columns.

Figure 1.28

Chart Styles gallery

Title added to chart

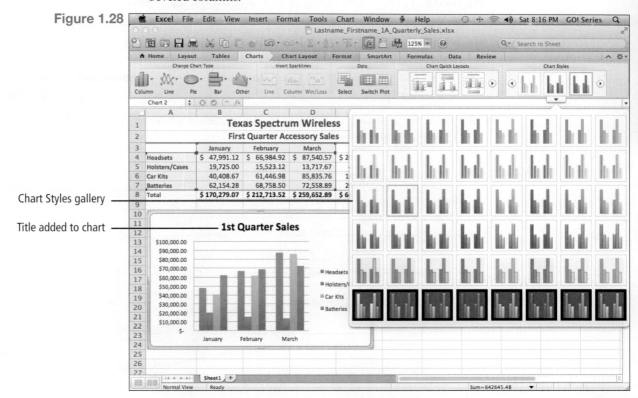

11 By counting across and then down, locate and click the 26th style.

This style uses a white background, formats the columns with theme colors, and applies a beveled effect. With this clear visual representation of the data, the president can see the sales of all product categories in each month, and can see that the sale of headsets and car kits has risen quite markedly during the quarter.

12 Click any cell to deselect the chart, and notice that the two contextual tabs no longer display on the Ribbon. **Save** 🖫 your workbook, and then compare your screen with Figure 1.29.

Contextual tabs display when an object is selected, and then are removed from view when the object is deselected.

Figure 1.29

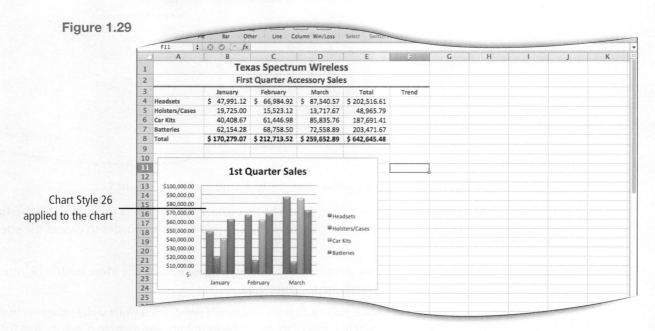

Chart Style 26 applied to the chart

Activity 1.12 | Creating and Formatting Sparklines

By creating sparklines, you provide a context for your numbers. Your readers will be able to see the relationship between a sparkline and its underlying data quickly.

Another Way

In the worksheet, select the range F4:F7 to insert it into the *Select where to place sparklines* box.

1 Select the range **B4:D7**. On the **Charts tab**, in the **Insert Sparklines group**, click **Line**. In the **Insert Sparklines** dialog box, notice that the selected data range *B4:D7* displays.

2 With the insertion point blinking in the **Select where to place sparklines** box, type **f4:f7** Compare your screen with Figure 1.30.

Figure 1.30

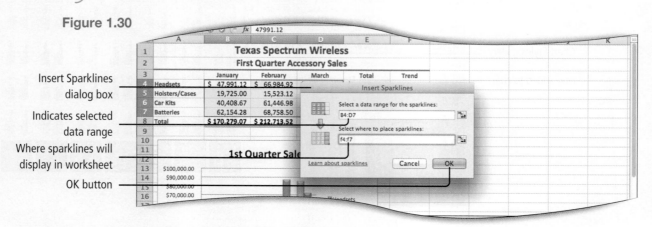

Insert Sparklines dialog box

Indicates selected data range

Where sparklines will display in worksheet

OK button

3 Click **OK** to insert the trend lines in the range F4:F7, and then on the **Sparklines tab**, in the **Markers group**, click to select the **All** check box.

Alongside each row of data, the sparkline provides a quick visual trend summary for sales of each accessory item over the three-month period. For example, you can see instantly that of the four items, only Holsters/Cases had declining sales for the period.

4 In the **Format group**, point to the **Sparkline Styles**—sparklines with marker points— and then click the **More** button ☑. By using the ScreenTips as your guide, click **Sparkline Style Accent 4, Darker 25%**. Click cell **A1** to deselect the range. **Save** ☐ your workbook, and then compare your screen with Figure 1.31.

Use markers, colors, and styles in this manner to further enhance your sparklines.

Figure 1.31

Sparklines inserted and formatted

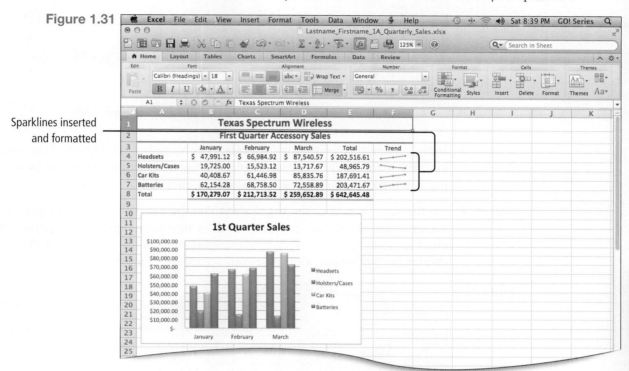

Objective 6 | Print, Display Formulas, and Close Excel

Use *Page Layout View* and the commands on the Page Layout tab to prepare for printing.

Activity 1.13 | Creating a Footer, Changing Views, and Using Print Preview

For each Excel project in this textbook, you will create a footer containing your name and the project name.

1 Be sure the chart is *not* selected. On the **View** menu, click **Header and Footer** to display the **Page Setup** dialog box with the **Header/Footer tab** active.

2 In the **Page Setup** dialog box, click **Customize Footer**. In the **Footer** dialog box, notice that the insertion point is blinking in the **Left section** box. Compare your screen with Figure 1.32.

Text or document elements such as the file name or page number can be inserted at the left margin, centered between the margins, or aligned with the right margin. Above the section boxes are buttons you can click to insert document elements or to format text or pictures.

Figure 1.32

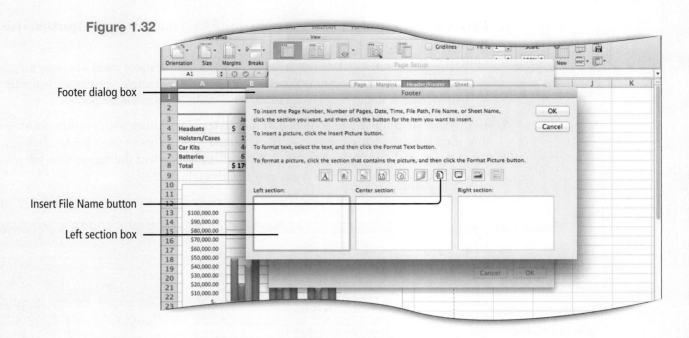

Footer dialog box

Insert File Name button

Left section box

3 In the **Footer** dialog box, click the **Insert File Name** button 🔲 to add the name of your file to the footer—&*[File]* displays in the **Left** section box. In the **Footer** dialog box, click **OK**. In the **Page Setup** dialog box, click **OK**.

> **Another Way**
>
> On the Layout tab, in the View group, click the Page Layout button; or, on the View menu, click Page Layout.

4 On the status bar, click the **Page Layout View** button 🔲🔲. Scroll to display the footer—your file name—and then scroll to view your chart. Click a corner of the chart to select it, and then point to the small dots on the right edge of the chart to display the 🔲 pointer. Compare your screen with Figure 1.33.

Figure 1.33

Border indicates chart is selected

Horizontal resize pointer

	January	February	March	Total	Trend
Headsets	$ 47,991.12	$ 66,984.92	$ 87,540.57	$ 202,516.61	
Holsters/Cases	19,725.00	15,523.12	13,717.67	48,965.79	
Car Kits	40,408.67	61,446.98	85,835.76	187,691.41	
Batteries	62,154.28	68,758.50	72,558.89	203,471.67	
Total	$ 170,279.07	$ 212,713.52	$ 259,652.89	$ 642,645.48	

1st Quarter Sales

5 Drag the 🔲 pointer to the right so that the right border of the chart is just inside the right border of **column F**. Be sure the left and right borders of the chart are just slightly **inside** the left border of **column A** and the right border of **column F**—adjust as necessary.

6 Click any cell to deselect the chart. On the **Layout tab**, in the **Page Setup group**, click the **Margins** button, and then click **Custom Margins**. In the **Page Setup** dialog box, under **Center on page**, select the **Horizontally** check box.

> This action will center the data and chart horizontally on the page, as shown in the Preview area.

7 In the **Page Setup** dialog box, click **OK**, and then **Save** 🖫 your workbook.

8 On the **File** menu, click **Properties**. In the **Subject** box, type your course name and section number. In the **Author** box, replace the existing text with your firstname and lastname. In the **Keywords** box, type **accessory sales** and then click **OK**.

9 On the **Layout tab**, in the **Print group**, click the **Preview** button, and then compare your screen with Figure 1.34.

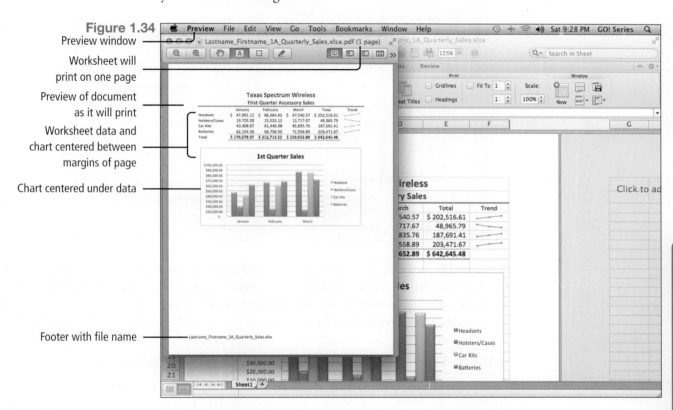

Figure 1.34
Preview window
Worksheet will print on one page
Preview of document as it will print
Worksheet data and chart centered between margins of page
Chart centered under data
Footer with file name

10 Note any adjustments that need to be made, and then **Close** 🔘 the **Print Preview**. On the **Preview** menu, click **Quit Preview** to return to the Excel application and worksheet. On the **Layout tab**, in the **View group**, click the **Normal** button to return to the Normal view, and then press Command ⌘ + fn + ← to return to cell **A1**.

> *Normal View* maximizes the number of cells visible on your screen and keeps the column letters and row numbers closer. The vertical dotted line between columns indicates that as currently arranged, only the columns to the left of the dotted line will print on the first page. The exact position of the vertical line may vary depending on your default printer setting.

11 If necessary, make adjustments, and then **Save** 🖫 your workbook.

Activity 1.14 | Printing a Worksheet

1 On the **File** menu, click **Print**. Be sure **Copies** indicates *1*, and be sure **Print What** indicates *Active Sheets*. Compare your screen with Figure 1.35.

Figure 1.35

Copies indicates 1

Print Preview

Prints *Active Sheets*

PDF button

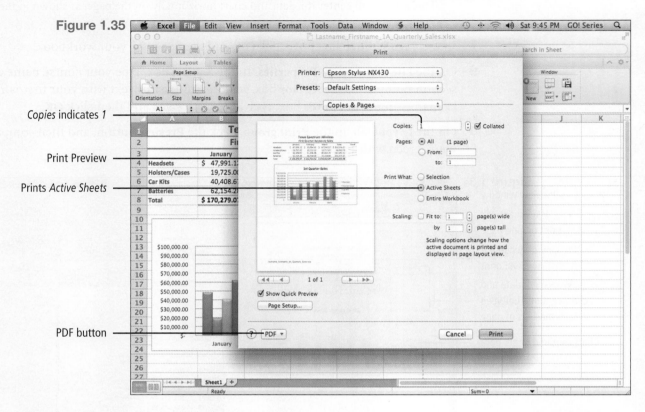

2 To print on paper, be sure that a printer is available, and then click the **Print** button. To create an electronic printout, in the **Print** dialog box, click the **PDF** button, and then click **Save as PDF**. In the **Save** dialog box, navigate to your storage location, and then click the **Save** button. In the message box, click **Use .pdf** to create the PDF file.

Activity 1.15 | Displaying, Printing, and Hiding Formulas

When you type a formula in a cell, the cell displays the *results* of the formula calculation. Recall that this value is called the displayed value. You can view and print the underlying formulas in the cells. When you do so, a formula often takes more horizontal space to display than the result of the calculation.

1 If necessary, redisplay your worksheet. Because you will make some temporary changes to your workbook, on the Standard toolbar, click the **Save** button ⊞ to be sure your work is saved up to this point.

Another Way

Hold down Control, and then press ` (usually located below Esc).

2 On the **Formulas tab**, in the **Function group**, click the **Show arrow**, and then click **Show Formulas**. Then, in the **column heading area**, point to the **column A** heading to display the ⬇ pointer, press down on the mouse, and then drag to the right to select columns **A:F**. Being careful not to click in the worksheet, scroll to display columns **B:F** on the screen, and then compare your screen with Figure 1.36.

Figure 1.36

Dotted line indicates page break

Underlying formulas displayed in cells

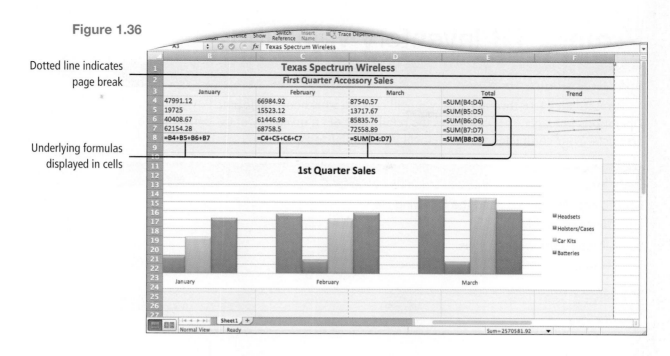

> **Note** | Turning the Display of Formulas On and Off
>
> To turn the display of formulas off, on the Formulas tab, in the Function group, click the Show arrow, and then click Show Formulas; or use the keyboard shortcut of [Control] + [~].

3 Point to the column heading boundary between any two of the selected columns to display the ⬌ pointer, and then double-click to AutoFit the selected columns. If necessary, scroll to display columns **A:F**.

> *AutoFit* adjusts the width of a column to fit the cell content of the *widest* cell in the column.

Another Way

In the Print dialog box, to the right of Scaling, select the *Fit to* check box.

4 On the **Layout tab**, in the **Page Setup group**, click the **Orientation** button, and then click **Landscape**. In the **Print** group, select the **Fit To** check box to scale the data to fit onto one page.

> *Scaling* shrinks the width (or height) of the printed worksheet to fit a maximum number of pages, and is convenient for printing formulas. Although it is not always the case, formulas frequently take up more space than the actual data.

5 Check to be sure your chart is centered below the data and the left and right edges are slightly inside column A and column F—drag a chart edge and then deselect the chart if necessary. Display the **Print Preview**, and then submit your worksheet with formulas displayed, either printed or electronically, as directed by your instructor.

6 **Close** 🖿 the workbook, and in the message box, click **Don't Save** so that you do *not* save the changes you made—displaying formulas, changing column widths and orientation, and scaling—to print your formulas.

Another Way

To quit Excel, press [Command ⌘] + [Q].

7 On the **Excel** menu, click **Quit Excel**.

End **You have completed Project 1A**

Excel | Chapter 1

Project 1B Inventory Valuation

Project Activities

In Activities 1.16 through 1.23, you will create a workbook for Josette Lovrick, Operations Manager, that calculates the retail value of an inventory of car convenience products. Your completed worksheet will look similar to Figure 1.37.

Project Files

For Project 1B, you will need the following file:

New Excel workbook

You will save your workbook as:

Lastname_Firstname_1B_Car_Products

Project Results

Texas Spectrum Wireless
Car Products Inventory Valuation

	Warehouse Location	Quantity In Stock	Retail Price	Total Retail Value	Percent of Total Retail Value
As of December 31					
Antenna Signal Booster	Dallas	1,126	$ 19.99	$ 22,508.74	8.27%
Car Power Port Adapter	Dallas	3,546	19.49	69,111.54	25.39%
Repeater Antenna	Houston	1,035	39.99	41,389.65	15.21%
SIM Card Reader and Writer	Houston	2,875	16.90	48,587.50	17.85%
Sticky Dash Pad	Houston	3,254	11.99	39,015.46	14.33%
Window Mount GPS Holder	Dallas	2,458	20.99	51,593.42	18.95%
Total Retail Value for All Products				$ 272,206.31	

Lastname_Firstname_1B_Car_Products.xlsx

Figure 1.37
Project 1B Car Products

Objective 7 | Check Spelling in a Worksheet

In Excel, the spelling checker performs similarly to the other Microsoft Office programs.

Activity 1.16 | Checking Spelling in a Worksheet

1 Open **Excel** and display a new Excel workbook. If necessary, increase the size of the window to fill the screen. On the Standard toolbar, change the **Zoom** setting 100% ▾ to **125%.** In cell **A1**, type **Texas Spectrum Wireless** and press Return. In cell **A2**, type **Car Products Inventory** and press Return.

2 On the **File** menu, click **Save As**, and then in the **Save As** dialog box, navigate to your **Excel Chapter 1** folder. In the **Save As** box, type **Lastname_Firstname_1B_Car_Products** and then click **Save**.

3 Press Tab to move to cell **B3**, type **Quantity** and press Tab. In cell **C3**, type **Average Cost** and press Tab. In cell **D3**, type **Retail Price** and press Tab.

4 In cell **E3**, type **Total Retail Value** and press Tab. In cell **F3**, type **Percent of Total Retail Value** and press Return.

5 Click cell **E3** and then look at the **formula bar**. Notice that in the cell, the displayed value is cut off; however, in the **formula bar**, the entire text value—the underlying value—displays. Compare your screen with Figure 1.38.

> Text that is too long to fit in a cell spills over to cells on the right only if they are empty. If the cell to the right contains data, the text in the cell to the left is truncated. The entire value continues to exist but is not completely visible.

Figure 1.38

Entire contents of cell E3 display in formula bar

Cell E3 active, text cut off

Text in F3 displays because there is nothing entered in cell G3

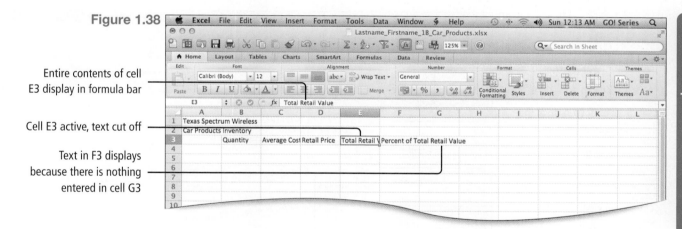

6 Click cell **A4**. *Without* correcting the spelling error, type **Antena Signal Booster** and then press Return. In the range **A5:A10**, type the remaining row titles shown below. Then compare your screen with Figure 1.39.

     Car Power Port Adapter

     Repeater Antenna

     SIM Card Reader and Writer

     Sticky Dash Pad

     Window Mount GPS Holder

     Total Retail Value for All Products

Figure 1.39

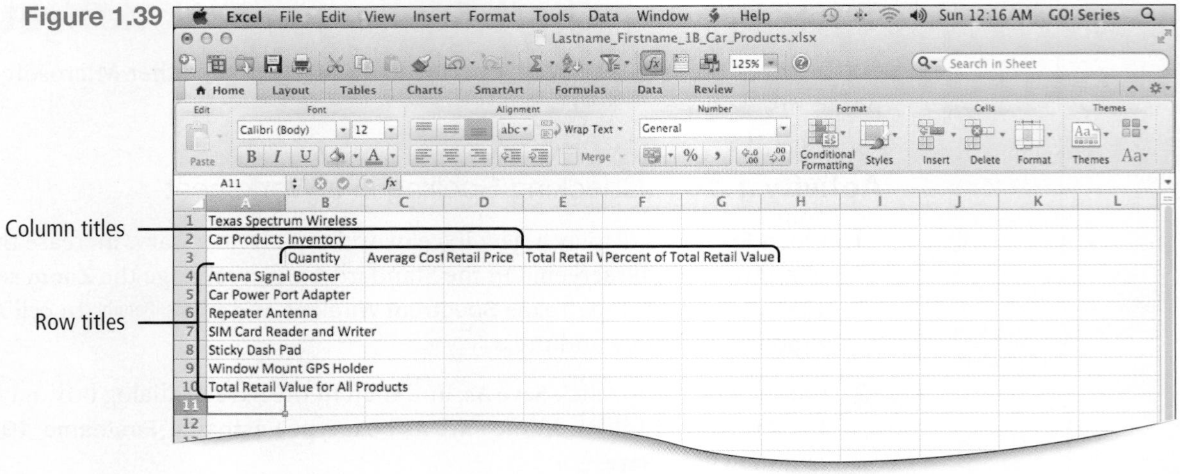

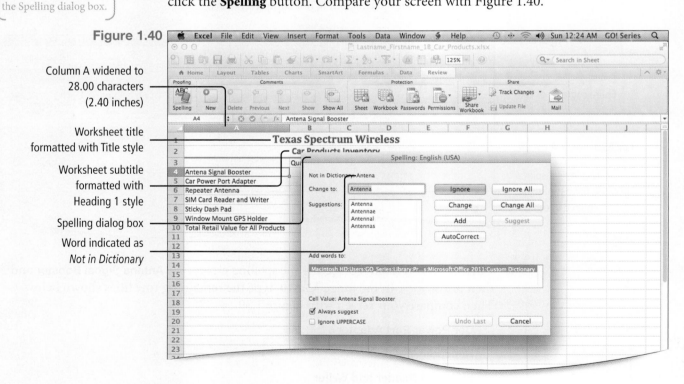

Column titles

Row titles

7 In the **column heading area**, point to the right boundary of **column A** to display the ⟺ pointer, and then drag to the right to widen **column A** to **28.00 (2.40 inches)**.

8 Select the range **A1:F1**. On the **Home tab**, in the **Alignment group**, click the **Merge** button to merge and center the text. In the **Format group**, click the **Styles** button. From the **Cell Styles** gallery, apply the **Title** style.

9 Select the range **A2:F2**, **Merge** the text, and then from the **Cell Styles** gallery, apply the **Heading 1** style. Click cell **A1**.

> **Another Way**
>
> From the Tools menu, click Spelling to display the Spelling dialog box.

10 With cell **A1** as the active cell, click the **Review tab**, and then in the **Proofing group**, click the **Spelling** button. Compare your screen with Figure 1.40.

Figure 1.40

Column A widened to 28.00 characters (2.40 inches)

Worksheet title formatted with Title style

Worksheet subtitle formatted with Heading 1 style

Spelling dialog box

Word indicated as *Not in Dictionary*

11 In the **Spelling** dialog box, to the right of **Not in Dictionary**, notice the word *Antena*.

The spelling tool does not have this word in its dictionary. In the Change to box, Excel suggests a spelling. In the Suggestions box, Excel provides a list of suggested spellings.

12 Click the **Change** button.

Antena, a typing error, is changed to *Antenna,* and the spelling tool indicates that *SIM* is not in the dictionary.

13 Click **Ignore,** and then correct any other errors you may have made. When the message displays, *The spell check is complete for the entire sheet,* click **OK. Save** 🖫 your workbook.

Because the spelling check begins its checking process starting with the currently selected cell, it is good practice to return to cell A1 before starting the Spelling command.

> **Alert** | **Does a Message Display Asking if You Want to Continue Checking at the Beginning of the Sheet?**
>
> If a message displays asking if you want to continue checking at the beginning of the sheet, click Yes. The Spelling command begins its checking process with the currently selected cell and moves to the right and down. Thus, if your active cell was a cell after A1, this message may display.

Objective 8 | Enter Data by Range

You can enter data by first selecting a range of cells. This is a time-saving technique, especially if you use a numeric keypad to enter the numbers.

Activity 1.17 | Entering Data by Range

1 Select the range **B4:D9,** type **1126** and then press Return.

The value displays in cell B4, and cell B5 becomes the active cell.

2 With cell **B5** active in the range, and pressing Return after each entry, type the following, and then compare your screen with Figure 1.41:

> **4226**
>
> **1035**
>
> **2875**
>
> **3254**
>
> **2458**

After you enter the last value and press Return, the active cell moves to the top of the next column within the selected range. Although it is not required to enter data in this manner, you can see that selecting the range before you enter data saves time because it confines the movement of the active cell to the selected range.

Figure 1.41

Cell C4 active

Range B4:D9 selected

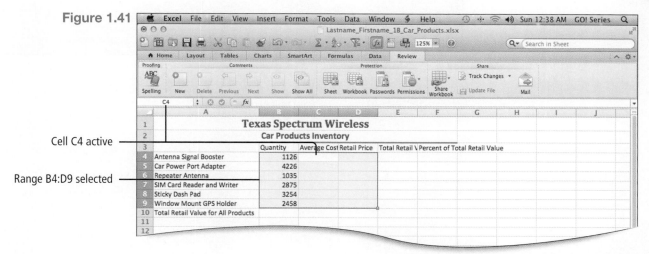

3 With the selected range still active, from the following table, beginning in cell **C4** and pressing Return after each entry, enter the data for the **Average Cost** column and then the **Retail Price** column. If you prefer, deselect the range to enter the values—typing in a selected range is optional.

Average Cost	Retail Price
9.75	19.99
9.25	19.49
16.90	39.99
9.55	16.90
4.20	12.99
10.45	20.99

Recall that the default number format for cells is the *General* number format, in which numbers display exactly as you type them and trailing zeros do not display, even if you type them.

4 Click any blank cell, and then compare your screen with Figure 1.42. Correct any errors you may have made while entering data, and then **Save** 💾 your workbook.

Figure 1.42

Data entered

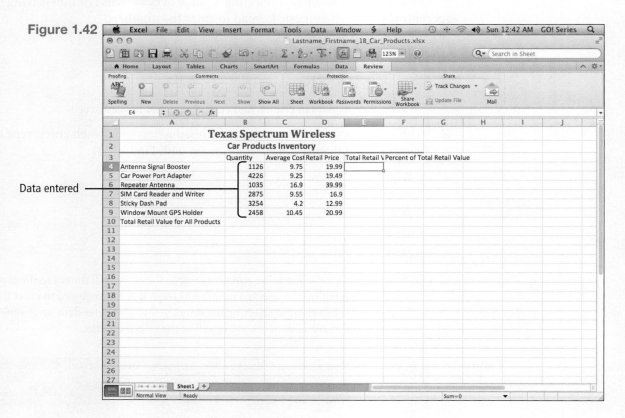

Objective 9 | Construct Formulas for Mathematical Operations

Operators are symbols with which you can specify the type of calculation you want to perform in a formula.

Activity 1.18 | Using Arithmetic Operators

1 Click cell **E4**, type **=b4*d4** and notice that the two cells are outlined as part of an active formula. Then press Return.

> The *Total Retail Value* of all *Antenna Signal Booster* items in inventory—*22508.74*—equals the *Quantity* (1126) times the *Retail Price* (selling price) of 19.99. In Excel, the asterisk (*) indicates multiplication.

2 Take a moment to study the symbols you will use to perform basic mathematical operations in Excel, as shown in the table in Figure 1.43, which are referred to as *arithmetic operators*.

Symbols Used in Excel for Arithmetic Operators	
Operator Symbol	**Operation**
+	Addition
-	Subtraction (also negation)
*	Multiplication
/	Division
%	Percent
^	Exponentiation

Figure 1.43

3 Click cell **E4**.

> You can see that in cells E5:E9, you need a formula similar to the one in E4, but one that refers to the cells in row 5, row 6, and so on. Recall that you can copy formulas and the cell references will change *relative to* the row number.

4 With cell **E4** selected, position your pointer over the fill handle in the lower right corner of the cell until the ⊞ pointer displays. Then, drag down through cell **E9** to copy the formula.

Another Way

Select the range, display the Cell Styles gallery, and then under Number Format, click Comma [0].

5 Select the range **B4:B9**, and then on the **Home tab**, in the **Number group**, click the **Comma Style** button. Then, in the **Number group**, click the **Decrease Decimal** button two times to remove the decimal places from these values.

> Comma Style formats a number with two decimal places. Because these are whole numbers referring to quantities, no decimal places are necessary.

6 Select the range **E4:E9**, and then at the bottom of your screen, in the status bar, notice the displayed value for **Sum**—*288713.51*.

> When you select numerical data, the Sum calculation displays in the status bar by default. Here, Excel indicates that if you summed the selected values, the result would be 288713.51.

7 Click cell **E10**, and on the Standard toolbar, click the **Sum** button ∑. Notice that Excel selects the range above cell E10 to sum. Press Return to display the total *288713.51.*

8 Select the range **C5:E9** and apply the **Comma Style** ﹐.

9 Select the range **C4:E4**, hold down Command ⌘, and then click cell **E10**. Release Command ⌘ and then on the **Home tab**, in the **Number group**, click the **Number Format arrow** General ▾, and then click **Accounting** to apply the Accounting Number Format to the range **C4:E4**. If the formatting is applied only to the first range, click the Number Format arrow General ▾, and then click Accounting to apply the same formatting to cell E10. Notice that Excel widened **column E**.

10 Click cell **E10**, and then in the **Format group**, click the **Styles** button. From the **Cell Styles** gallery, apply the **Total** style. Click any blank cell, **Save** 💾 your workbook, and then compare your screen with Figure 1.44.

Figure 1.44

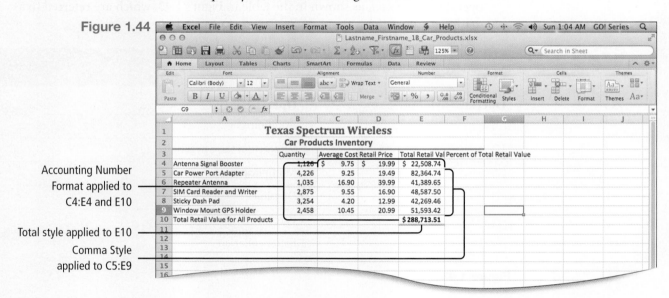

Accounting Number Format applied to C4:E4 and E10

Total style applied to E10

Comma Style applied to C5:E9

More Knowledge | Status Bar Calculations

You can display six calculations on the status bar. To change from the default calculation of Sum, on the status bar, to the right of the Sum total, click the More arrow, and then click Average, Count, Count Nums (the number of selected cells that contain a number value), Max, or Min. If you do not wish to display a calculation in the status bar, click None.

Activity 1.19 | Copying Formulas Containing Absolute Cell References

In a formula, a relative cell reference refers to a cell by its position *in relation to* the cell that contains the formula. An ***absolute cell reference***, on the other hand, refers to a cell by its *fixed* position in the worksheet, for example, the total in cell E10.

A relative cell reference automatically adjusts when a formula is copied. In some calculations, you do *not* want the cell reference to adjust; rather, you want the cell reference to remain the same when the formula is copied.

1 Click cell **F4**, type **=** and then click cell **E4**. Type **/** and then click cell **E10**.

> The formula =*E4/E10* indicates that the value in cell E4 will be *divided* by the value in cell E10. Why? Because Ms. Lovrick wants to know the percentage by which each product's Total Retail Value makes up the Total Retail Value for All Products.
>
> Arithmetically, the percentage is computed by dividing the *Total Retail Value* for each product by the *Total Retail Value for All Products*. The result will be a percentage expressed as a decimal.

2 Press [Return]. Click cell **F4** and notice that the formula displays in the **formula bar**. Then, point to cell **F4** and double-click.

> The formula, with the two referenced cells displayed in different colors and bordered with the same colors, displays in the cell. This feature, called the **range finder**, is useful for verifying formulas because it visually indicates which workbook cells are included in a formula calculation.

3 Press [Return] to redisplay the result of the calculation in the cell, and notice that approximately 8% of the total retail value of the inventory is made up of Antenna Signal Boosters.

4 Click cell **F4** again, and then drag the fill handle down through cell **F9**. Compare your screen with Figure 1.45.

> Each cell displays an error message—*#DIV/0!* and a green triangle in the upper left corner of each cell indicates that Excel detects an error.
>
> Like a grammar checker, Excel uses rules to check for formula errors and flags errors in this manner. Additionally, the Auto Fill Options button displays, from which you can select formatting options for the copied cells.

Figure 1.45

Cells F5:F9 display error messages and green triangles

Auto Fill Options button

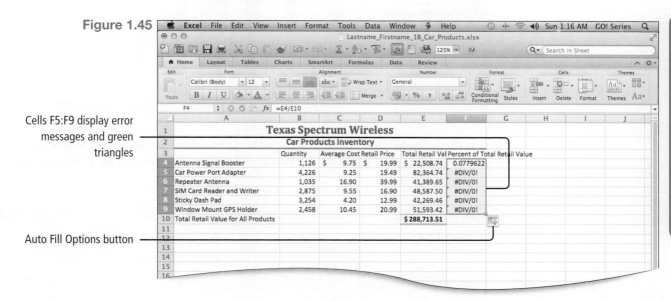

5 Click cell **F5**, and to the left of the cell, point to the **Error Checking** button ⊕▾ to display its ScreenTip—*The formula or function used is dividing by zero or empty cells*.

> In this manner, Excel suggests the cause of an error.

6 Look at the **formula bar** and examine the formula.

> The formula is =*E5/E11*. The cell reference to E5 is correct, but the cell reference following the division operator (/) is *E11*, and E11 is an *empty* cell.

7 Click cell **F6**, point to the **Error Checking** button ⬦▾, and in the **formula bar** examine the formula.

> Because the cell references are relative, Excel builds the formulas by increasing the row number for each equation. But in this calculation, the divisor must always be the value in cell E10—the *Total Retail Value for All Products.*

8 Point to cell **F4**, and then double-click to place the insertion point within the cell.

Another Way

On the Formulas tab, in the Function group, click the Switch Reference button; or edit the formula so that it indicates =E4/E10.

9 Within the cell, use the arrow keys as necessary to position the insertion point to the left of *E10*, and then press Command ⌘ + T. Compare your screen with Figure 1.46.

> Dollar signs ($) display, which changes the reference to cell E10 to an absolute cell reference. The use of the dollar sign to denote an absolute reference is not related in any way to whether or not the values you are working with are currency values. It is simply the symbol that Excel uses to denote an absolute cell reference. You can position the insertion point anywhere in the E10 cell reference; it does not need to be placed to the left of the cell reference.

Figure 1.46

Edited formula with dollar signs denoting an absolute cell reference

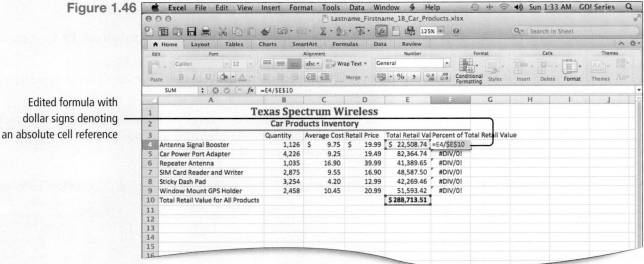

10 On the **formula bar**, click the **Enter** button ✓ so that **F4** remains the active cell. Then, drag the fill handle to copy the new formula down through cell **F9**. Compare your screen with Figure 1.47.

Figure 1.47

Formula containing absolute cell reference for the first cell in selected range

Percentage of total (E10) calculated for each product (your results may vary slightly)

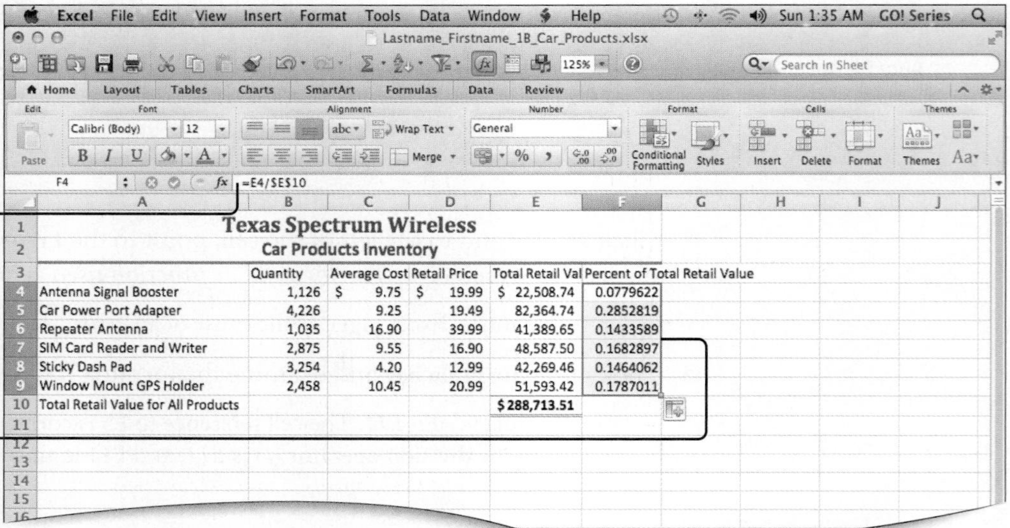

11 Click cell **F5**, examine the formula in the **formula bar**, and then examine the formulas for cells **F6**, **F7**, **F8**, and **F9**.

> For each formula, the cell reference for the *Total Retail Value* of each product changed relative to its row; however, the value used as the divisor—*Total Retail Value for All Products* in cell E10—remained absolute. Thus, using either relative or absolute cell references, it is easy to duplicate formulas without typing them.

12 Save 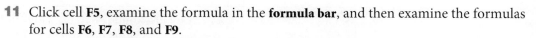 your workbook.

> **More Knowledge** | **Calculate a Percentage if You Know the Amount and the Total**
>
> Using the equation *amount/total = percentage*, you can calculate the percentage by which a part makes up a total—with the percentage formatted as a decimal. For example, if on a test you score 42 points correctly out of 50, your percentage of correct answers is 42/50 = 0.84 or 84%.

Objective 10 | Edit Values in a Worksheet

Excel performs calculations on numbers; that is why you use Excel. If you make changes to the numbers, Excel automatically *recalculates*. This is one of the most powerful and valuable features of Excel.

Activity 1.20 | Editing Values in a Worksheet

You can edit text and number values directly within a cell or on the formula bar.

1 In cell **E10**, notice the column total *$288,713.51*. Then, click cell **B5**, and to change its value, type **3546** Watch cell **E5** as you press Return.

> Excel formulas *recalculate* if you change the value in a cell that is referenced in a formula. It is not necessary to delete the old value in a cell; selecting the cell and typing a new value replaces the old value with your new typing.
>
> The *Total Retail Value* of all *Car Power Port Adapters* items recalculates to *69,111.54* and the total in cell E10 recalculates to *$275,460.31*. Additionally, all of the percentages in column F recalculate.

2 Point to cell **D8**, and then double-click to place the insertion point within the cell. Use the arrow keys to move the insertion point to right of *2*, press Delete to delete *2*, and then type **1** so that the new Retail Price is *11.99*.

3 Watch cells **E8** and **E10** as you press Return, and then notice the recalculation of the formulas in those two cells.

> Excel recalculates the value in cell E8 to *39,015.46* and the value in cell E10 to *$272,206.31*. Additionally, all of the percentages in column F recalculate because the *Total Retail Value for All Products* recalculated.

4 Point to cell **A2** so that the ⊞ pointer is positioned slightly to the right of the word *Inventory*, and then double-click to place the insertion point in the cell. Press Spacebar, type **Valuation** and then press Return to add *Valuation* after *Inventory*.

5 Click cell **B3**, and then in the **formula bar**, click to place the insertion point after the letter *y*. Press Spacebar one time, type **In Stock** and then on the **formula bar**, click the **Enter** button ⊘. Save 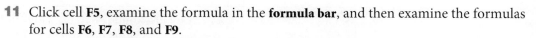 your workbook, and then compare your screen with Figure 1.48.

> Recall that if text is too long to fit in the cell and the cell to the right contains data, the text is truncated—cut off—but the entire value still exists as the underlying value.

Figure 1.48

In Stock added to column title

Valuation added to subtitle

New value in cell B5

New value in cell D8

Recalculated total

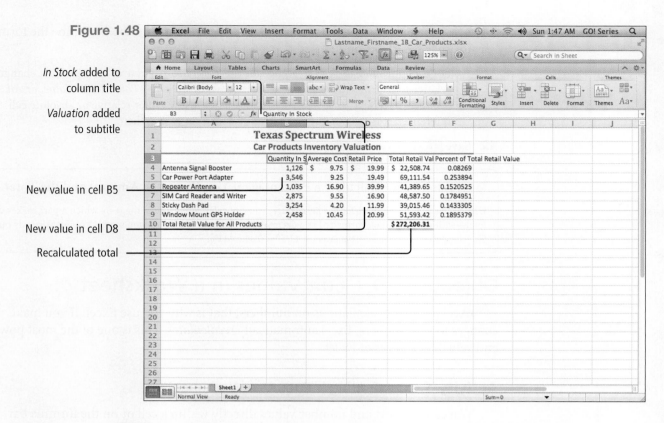

Activity 1.21 | Formatting Cells with the Percent Style

A percentage is part of a whole expressed in hundredths. For example, 75 cents is the same as 75 percent of one dollar. The **Percent Style** button formats the selected cell as a percentage rounded to the nearest hundredth by multiplying the underlying value by 100 and displaying a percent symbol (%) on the right side of the displayed value.

1 Click cell **F4**, and then on the **Home tab**, in the **Number group**, click the **Percent Style** button.

Your result is 8%, which is *0.08269* rounded to the nearest hundredth and expressed as a percentage. Percent Style displays the value of a cell as a percentage.

2 Select the range **F4:F9**, click the **Percent Style** button, click the **Increase Decimal** button two times, and then click the **Center Text** button.

Percent Style may not offer a percentage precise enough to analyze important financial information—adding additional decimal places to a percentage makes data more precise.

3 Click any cell to cancel the selection, **Save** your workbook, and then compare your screen with Figure 1.49.

Figure 1.49

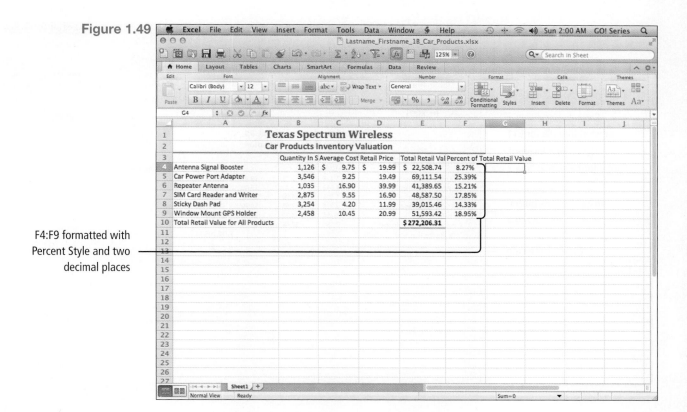

F4:F9 formatted with
Percent Style and two
decimal places

Objective 11 | Format a Worksheet

Formatting refers to the process of specifying the appearance of cells and the overall layout of your worksheet. Formatting is accomplished through various commands on the Ribbon, for example, applying Cell Styles, and also from shortcut menus, keyboard shortcuts, and the Format Cells dialog box.

Activity 1.22 | Inserting and Deleting Rows and Columns

1 In the **row heading area** on the left side of your screen, point to the row heading for **row 3** to display the ➡ pointer, and then press Control and click to simultaneously select the row and display a shortcut menu.

> **Another Way**
>
> With the row selected, on the Home tab, in the Cells group, click the Insert button arrow, and then click Insert Rows. Or, with the row selected, click the Insert button—the default setting of the button inserts a new sheet row above the selected row.

‑‑➤ **2** On the shortcut menu, click **Insert** to insert a new **row 3**.

The rows below the new row 3 move down one row, and the Insert Options button displays. By default, the new row uses the formatting of the row *above*.

3 Click cell **E11**. On the **formula bar**, notice that the range changed to sum the new range **E5:E10**. Compare your screen with Figure 1.50.

If you move formulas by inserting additional rows or columns in your worksheet, Excel automatically adjusts the formulas. Excel adjusted all of the formulas in the worksheet that were affected by inserting this new row.

Excel | Chapter 1

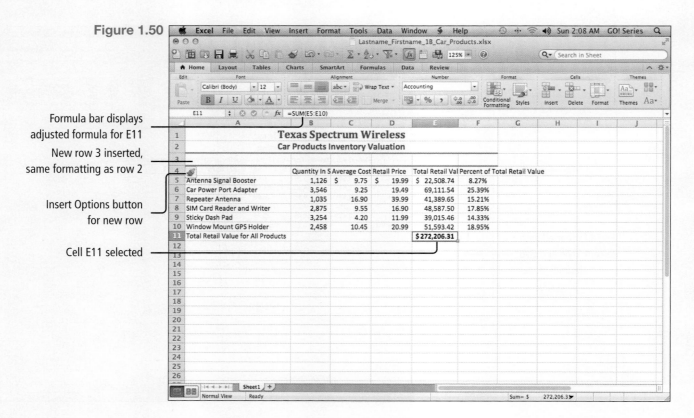

Figure 1.50

Formula bar displays adjusted formula for E11

New row 3 inserted, same formatting as row 2

Insert Options button for new row

Cell E11 selected

4 Click cell **A3**, type **As of December 31** and then on the **formula bar**, click the **Enter** button to maintain **A3** as the active cell. Select the range **A3:F3**, and then on the **Home tab**, in the **Alignment group**, click the **Merge** button to merge the cells and to center the text. In the **Format group**, click the **Styles** button to display the **Cell Styles** gallery, and then click **Heading 2**.

5 In the **column heading area**, point to **column B** to display the ⬇ pointer, press [Control] and click, and then click **Insert**.

By default, the new column uses the formatting of the column to the *left*.

6 Click cell **B4**, type **Warehouse Location** and then press [Return].

7 In cell **B5**, type **Dallas** and then type **Dallas** again in cells **B6** and **B10**. Use AutoComplete to speed your typing by clicking the AutoComplete suggestion. In cells **B7**, **B8**, and **B9**, type **Houston**

8 In the **column heading area**, point to **column D**, press [Control] and click, and then click **Delete**.

The remaining columns shift to the left, and Excel adjusts all the formulas in the worksheet accordingly. You can use a similar technique to delete a row in a worksheet.

9 **Save** 💾 your workbook, and then compare your screen with Figure 1.51.

Figure 1.51

Average Cost
column deleted

New column B with
warehouse locations
added

Text entered and
formatted in cell A3

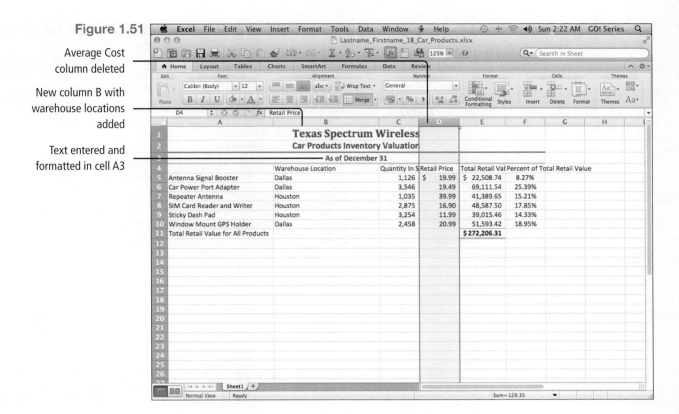

Activity 1.23 | Adjusting Column Widths and Wrapping Text

Use the Wrap Text command to display the contents of a cell on multiple lines.

1 In the **column heading area**, point to the **column B** heading to display the ⬇ pointer, click, and then drag to the right to select **columns B:F**.

2 With the columns selected, in the **column heading area**, point to the right boundary of any of the selected columns to display the ⬌ pointer, and then drag to set the **Width** to **12.00 (1.07 inches)**.

Use this technique to format multiple columns or rows simultaneously.

3 Select the range **B4:F4** that comprises the column headings, and then on the **Home tab**, in the **Alignment group**, click the **Wrap Text** button, and then click **Wrap Text**. Notice that the row height adjusts.

4 With the range **B4:F4** still selected, in the **Alignment group**, click the **Center Text** button 🔳 and the **Align Text Middle** button 🔳. With the range **B4:F4** still selected, apply the **Heading 4** cell style.

The Align Text Middle command aligns text so that it is centered between the top and bottom margins of the cell.

5 Select the range **B5:B10**, and then click the **Center Text** button 🔳. Click cell **A11**, and then from the **Cell Styles** gallery, scroll, and then under **Themed Cell Styles**, click **40% - Accent1**. Click any blank cell, and then compare your screen with Figure 1.52.

Excel | Chapter 1

Figure 1.52

Width of columns B:F set to 12.00 (1.07 inches)

Column heading text wrapped and formatted

Warehouse locations centered

Cell style applied to cell A11

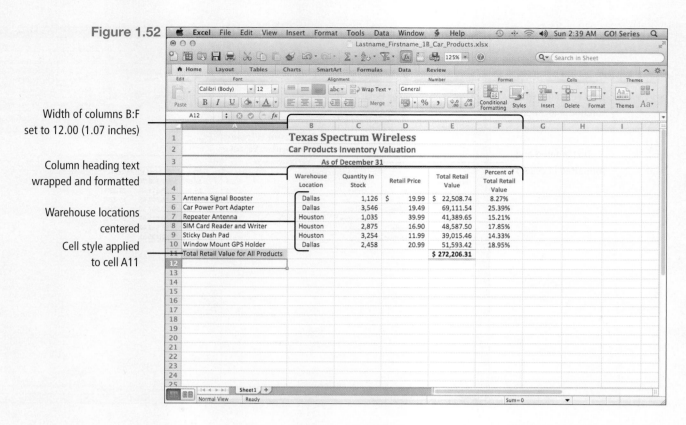

6 On the **View** menu, click **Header and Footer**, and then click **Customize Footer**. With the insertion point in the **Left section** box, click the **Insert File Name** button 📄 to add the name of your file to the footer—*&[File]* displays. In the **Footer** dialog box, click **OK**. In the **Page Setup** dialog box, click **OK**. On the **Layout tab**, in the **View group**, click the **Page Layout** button, and notice that the worksheet will print on two pages.

7 On the **Layout tab**, in the **Page Setup group**, click the **Orientation** button, and then click **Landscape**. Click the **Margins** button, and then click **Custom Margins**. In the **Page Setup** dialog box, under **Center on page**, select the **Horizontally** check box; and then click **OK**.

8 On the **File** menu, click **Properties**. In the **Subject** box, type your course name and section number. In the **Author** box, replace the existing text with your firstname and lastname. In the **Keywords** box, type **car products, inventory** and then click **OK**.

9 On the **Layout tab**, in the **View group**, click the **Preview** button, and notice that the worksheet will print on one page. Compare your screen with Figure 1.53.

Figure 1.53

Worksheet displays in Preview application

Worksheet will print on one page

Worksheet displays in landscape orientation

Footer with your file name

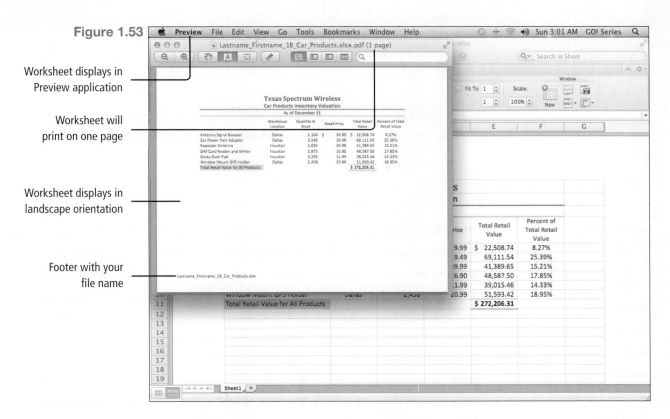

10 Note any additional adjustments or corrections that need to be made, and then **Close** the **Preview** of the worksheet. On the **Preview** menu, click **Quit Preview** to display the Excel application and your worksheet. On the left side of the status bar, click the **Normal View** button to return to the Normal View, and then press Command ⌘ + fn + ← to return to cell **A1**.

11 Make any necessary corrections, and then **Save** your workbook.

12 **Print** or submit your worksheet electronically as directed by your instructor. If required by your instructor, print or create an electronic version of your worksheet with formulas displayed using the instructions in Activity 1.15 in Project 1A.

13 **Close** your workbook, and then on the **File** menu, click **Quit Excel**.

End You have completed Project 1B _____

Excel | Chapter 1

Summary

In this chapter, you used Microsoft Excel for Mac 2011 to create and analyze data organized into columns and rows and to chart and perform calculations on the data. By organizing your data with Excel, you will be able to make calculations and create visual representations of your data in the form of charts.

Key Terms

Absolute cell reference 274

Accounting Number Format 256

Active cell 246

Arithmetic operators .273

AutoComplete 247

Auto Fill....................248

AutoFit 267

AutoSum....................254

Category axis 259

Category labels 259

Cell 243

Cell address 246

Cell content...............246

Cell reference 246

Cell style 255

Chart.........................258

Chart layout 260

Chart Quick Layouts gallery....................260

Chart styles...............261

Chart Styles gallery ...261

Chart types...............258

Column......................245

Column chart.............258

Column heading 245

Comma Style 257

Constant value 246

Context sensitive.......248

Data 246

Data marker 259

Data point 259

Data series................259

Displayed value 250

Expand formula bar button 245

Expand horizontal scroll bar button 244

Fill handle 248

Format.......................255

Formula.....................246

Formula bar...............244

Function 251

General format 250

Horizontal window split bar.................245

Label 246

Left alignment............247

Legend 257

Lettered column headings 245

Merge.......................255

Name box 244

Normal View 265

Number format 250

Number values 246

Numbered row headings 245

Operators 273

Page Layout View 263

Percent Style.............278

Point and click method..................253

Range.......................250

Range finder..............275

Relative cell reference 255

Row..........................246

Row heading 246

Scaling 267

Select All box 245

Series........................248

Sheet tab scrolling buttons...................244

Sparklines 258

Spreadsheet..............243

Status bar..................244

SUM function.............254

Swipe 245

Text values................246

Underlying formula....232

Underlying value........250

Value 246

Value axis..................259

Vertical window split bar..................244

Workbook 243

Workbook-level buttons...................244

Worksheet.................243

X-axis 259

Y-axis 259

Matching

Match each term in the second column with its correct definition in the first column by writing the letter of the term on the blank line in front of the correct definition.

_____ 1. An Excel file that contains one or more worksheets.

_____ 2. Another name for a worksheet.

_____ 3. The intersection of a column and a row.

_____ 4. The labels along the lower border of the Excel window that identify each worksheet.

A Cell

B Cell address

C Cell content

D Chart

E Column

F Constant value

_____ 5. A vertical group of cells in a worksheet.

_____ 6. A horizontal group of cells in a worksheet.

_____ 7. Anything typed into a cell.

_____ 8. Information such as numbers, text, dates, or times of day that you type into a cell.

_____ 9. Text or numbers in a cell that are not a formula.

_____ 10. An equation that performs mathematical calculations on values in a worksheet.

_____ 11. A constant value consisting of only numbers.

_____ 12. Another name for a cell reference.

_____ 13. Another name for a constant value.

_____ 14. The small black square in the lower right corner of a selected cell.

_____ 15. The graphic representation of data in a worksheet.

G Data

H Fill handle

I Formula

J Number value

K Row

L Sheet tabs

M Spreadsheet

N Value

O Workbook

Multiple Choice

Circle the correct answer.

1. On startup, Excel displays a new Excel:
   A. document   **B.** worksheet   **C.** grid

2. An Excel window element that displays the value or formula contained in the active cell is the:
   A. Name box   **B.** status bar   **C.** formula bar

3. An Excel window element that displays the name of the selected cell, table, chart, or object is the:
   A. Name box   **B.** status bar   **C.** formula bar

4. A box in the upper left corner of the worksheet grid that selects all the cells in a worksheet is the:
   A. Name box   **B.** Select All box   **C.** split bar

5. A cell surrounded by a black border and ready to receive data is the:
   A. active cell   **B.** address cell   **C.** reference cell

6. The feature that generates and extends values into adjacent cells based on the values of selected cells is:
   A. AutoComplete   **B.** Auto Fill   **C.** fill handle

7. The default format that Excel applies to numbers is the:
   A. Comma format   **B.** Accounting format   **C.** General format

8. The data that displays in the formula bar is referred to as the:
   A. constant value   **B.** formula   **C.** underlying value

9. The type of cell reference that refers to cells by their fixed position in a worksheet is:
   A. absolute   **B.** relative   **C.** exponentiation

10. Tiny charts embedded in a cell that give a visual trend summary alongside your data are:
    A. embedded charts   **B.** sparklines   **C.** chart styles

Content-Based Assessments

Apply 1A skills from these Objectives:

1 Create, Save, and Navigate an Excel Workbook

2 Enter Data in a Worksheet

3 Construct and Copy Formulas and Use the SUM Function

4 Format Cells with Merge and Cell Styles

5 Chart Data to Create a Column Chart and Insert Sparklines

6 Print, Display Formulas, and Close Excel

Skills Review | Project **1C** Laptop Sales

In the following Skills Review, you will create a new Excel worksheet with a chart that summarizes the third quarter sales of laptop computers. Your completed worksheet will look similar to Figure 1.54.

Project Files

For Project 1C, you will need the following file:

New Excel workbook

You will save your workbook as:

Lastname_Firstname_1C_Laptop_Sales

Project Results

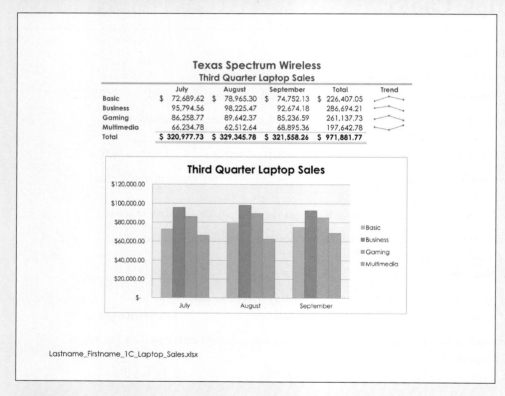

Figure 1.54

(Project 1C Laptop Sales continues on the next page)

Content-Based Assessments

Skills Review | Project **1C** Laptop Sales (continued)

1 Open **Excel** and display a new Excel workbook. If necessary, increase the size of the Excel window. On the Standard toolbar, change the **Zoom** setting to **125%**. On the **File** menu, click **Save As**, and then navigate to your **Excel Chapter 1** folder. In the **Save As** box, using your own name, type **Lastname_Firstname_1C_Laptop_Sales** and then click **Save**.

a. With cell **A1** as the active cell, type the worksheet title **Texas Spectrum Wireless** and then press Return. In cell **A2**, type the worksheet subtitle **Third Quarter Laptop Sales** and then press Return two times.

b. In cell **A4**, type **Basic** and then press Return. In cell **A5**, type **Business** and then press Return. In cell **A6**, type **Gaming** and then press Return. In cell **A7**, type **Multimedia** and then press Return. In cell **A8**, type **Total** and then press Return.

c. Click cell **B3**. Type **July** and then in the **formula bar**, click the **Enter** button to keep cell **B3** the active cell. With **B3** as the active cell, point to the fill handle in the lower right corner of the selected cell, drag to the right to cell **D3**, and then release the mouse to enter the text *August* and *September*.

d. Press Command ⌘ + fn + ←, to make cell **A1** the active cell. In the **column heading area**, point to the vertical line between **column A** and **column B** to display the ✛ pointer, press down on the mouse, and drag to the right to increase the column width to **12.00 (1.07 inches)**.

e. Point to cell **B3**, and then drag across to select cells **B3** and **C3** and **D3**.With the range **B3:D3** selected, on the **Home tab** in the **Alignment group**, click the **Center Text** button.

f. Click cell **B4**, type **72689.62** and press Tab to make cell **C4** active. Enter the remaining values, as shown below in **Table 1**, pressing Tab to move across the rows and Return to move down the columns.

2 If necessary, click cell **B8** to make it the active cell and type =

a. Type **b4+ b5+b6+b7** and then press Return. Your result is *320977.73*.

b. Click cell **C8**. Type = and then click cell **C4**. Type + and then click cell **C5**. Repeat this process to complete the formula to add cells **C6** and **C7**, and then press Return. Your result is *329345.78*.

c. Click cell **D8**. On the Standard toolbar, click the **Sum** button, and then press Return to construct a formula by using the SUM function. Your result is *321558.26*. You can use any of these methods to add values; the Sum button is the most efficient.

d. In cell **E3** type **Total** and press Return. On the Standard toolbar, click the **Sum** button, and then on the **formula bar**, click the **Enter** button to display the result and keep cell **E4** active.

e. With cell **E4** active, point to the fill handle in the lower right corner of the cell. Drag down through cell **E8**, and then release the mouse to copy the formula with relative cell references down to sum each row. The result in cell **E8** is *971881.77*.

3 Click cell **F3**. Type **Trend** and then press Return.

a. Select the range **A1:F1**, and then on the **Home tab**, in the **Alignment group**, click the **Merge** button. Select the range **A2:F2**, and then click the **Merge** button.

b. Click cell **A1**. In the **Format group**, click the **Styles** button. In the **Cell Styles** gallery, under **Titles and Headings**, click **Title**. Click cell **A2**, display the **Cell Styles** gallery, and then click **Heading 1**.

c. Select the range **B3:F3**, hold down Command ⌘, and then select the range **A4:A8**. From the **Cell Styles** gallery, click **Heading 4** to apply this cell style to the column and row titles.

d. Select the range **B4:E4**, hold down Command ⌘, and then select the range **B8:E8**. On the **Home tab**, in the **Number group**, click the **Number Format arrow**, and then click **Accounting** button to apply the Accounting Number Format to the two ranges. If the formatting is applied only to the first range, click the Number Format arrow one more time, and then click Accounting to apply the Accounting Number Format to the range B8:E8. Select the range **B5:E7**, and then

Table 1

Basic	72689.62	78965.30	74752.13
Business	95794.56	98225.47	92674.18
Gaming	86258.77	89642.37	85236.59
Multimedia	66234.78	62512.64	68895.36

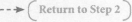 --→ (Return to Step 2)

(Project 1C Laptop Sales continues on the next page)

Skills Review | Project **1C** Laptop Sales (continued)

in the **Number group**, click the **Comma Style** button. Select the range **B8:E8**. In the **Format group**, click the **Styles** button to display the **Cell Styles** gallery, and then under **Titles and Headings**, click **Total**.

e. On the **Home tab**, in the **Themes group**, click the **Themes** button to display the **Themes** gallery. Click the **Austin** theme.

4 Select the range **A3:D7**. On the **Charts tab**, in the **Insert Chart group**, click **Column**. From the gallery of column chart types, under **2-D Column**, click the first chart—**Clustered Column**.

a. On the Standard toolbar, click the **Save** button to be sure that you have saved your work up to this point. Point to the top border of the chart to display the ⊕ pointer, and then drag to position the chart inside the upper left corner of cell **A10**.

b. On the **Charts tab**, in the **Data group**, click the **Switch** button so that the months display on the Horizontal (Category) axis and the types of laptops display in the legend. If the Switch button does not work as expected, in the Data group, click the Select button, and in the Select Data Source dialog box, click Switch Row/Column, and then click OK.

c. On the **Charts tab**, in the **Chart Quick Layouts group**, click the first layout—**Layout 1**.

d. In the chart, click anywhere in the text *Chart Title* to select the text box. Type **Third Quarter Laptop Sales** and then click anywhere in a blank area within the borders of the chart to cancel the selection of the chart title.

e. On the **Charts tab**, point to the **Chart Styles group**, and then click the **More** button. By counting across and then down, locate and click the **34th** style.

f. Point to the lower right corner of the chart to display the ⬊ pointer, and then drag down and to the right so that the lower right border of the chart is positioned just inside the lower right corner of cell **F26**.

5 Select the range **B4:D7**. On the **Charts tab**, in the **Insert Sparklines group**, click **Line**. In the **Insert Sparklines** dialog box, in the **Select where to place sparklines** box, type **f4:f7** and then click **OK** to insert the sparklines.

a. On the **Sparklines tab**, in the **Markers group**, select the **All** check box to display markers in the sparklines.

b. On the **Sparklines tab**, in the **Format group**, point to the styles, click the **More** button to display a gallery, and then using the ScreenTips as your guide, click the **Sparkline Style Accent 4, Darker 25%** style.

6 On the **View** menu, click **Header and Footer**, and then in the **Page Setup** dialog box, click **Customize Footer**. With the insertion point positioned in the **Left section** box, click the **Insert File Name** button; and then click **OK**. In the **Page Setup** dialog box, click **OK**.

a. On the **Layout tab**, in the **View group**, click the **Page Layout** button, and notice that your worksheet will print on two pages. On the **Layout tab**, in the **Page Setup group**, click the **Orientation** button, and then click **Landscape**.

b. Scroll to display the page footer with your file name. In the **View group**, click the **Normal** button to return to Normal View, and then **Save** your workbook.

7 Press ⌘ Command + fn + ← to make cell **A1** active.

a. On the **File** menu, click **Properties**. In the **Subject** box, type your course name and section number. In the **Author** box, delete any text and type your firstname and lastname. In the **Keywords** box, type **laptop sales** and then click **OK**.

b. On the **Layout tab**, in the **Page Setup group**, click the **Margins** button, and then click **Custom Margins**. In the **Page Setup** dialog box, under **Center on page**, select the **Horizontally** check box, and then click **OK**.

c. On the **Layout tab**, in the **Print group**, click the **Preview** button, and notice that the worksheet will print in Landscape orientation on one page. **Close** the **Preview** window, and then **Quit Preview**. If necessary, make any corrections and resize and move your chart so that it is centered under the worksheet.

d. On the Standard toolbar, click the **Save** button to be sure that you have saved your work up to this point.

e. **Print** or submit your workbook electronically as directed by your instructor. If required by your instructor, print or create an electronic version of your worksheet with formulas displayed by using the instructions in Activity 1.15. **Close** the workbook without saving so that you do not save the changes you made to print formulas, and then **Quit Excel**.

End **You have completed Project 1C** ——————

Content-Based Assessments

Apply 1B skills from these Objectives:

7 Check Spelling in a Worksheet

8 Enter Data by Range

9 Construct Formulas for Mathematical Operations

10 Edit Values in a Worksheet

11 Format a Worksheet

Skills Review | Project 1D Laptop Bags

In the following Skills Review, you will create a worksheet that summarizes the inventory of laptop messenger-style bags. Your completed worksheet will look similar to Figure 1.55.

Project Files

For Project 1D, you will need the following file:

New Excel workbook

You will save your workbook as:

Lastname_Firstname_1D_Laptop_Bags

Project Results

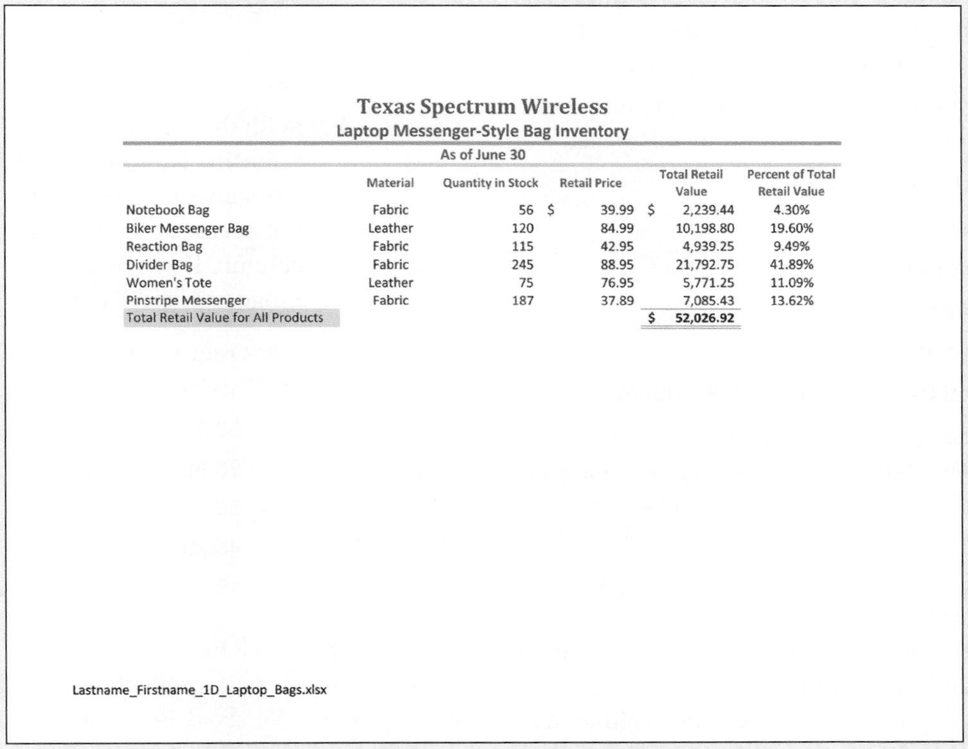

Texas Spectrum Wireless
Laptop Messenger-Style Bag Inventory

		As of June 30			
	Material	Quantity in Stock	Retail Price	Total Retail Value	Percent of Total Retail Value
Notebook Bag	Fabric	56	$ 39.99	$ 2,239.44	4.30%
Biker Messenger Bag	Leather	120	84.99	10,198.80	19.60%
Reaction Bag	Fabric	115	42.95	4,939.25	9.49%
Divider Bag	Fabric	245	88.95	21,792.75	41.89%
Women's Tote	Leather	75	76.95	5,771.25	11.09%
Pinstripe Messenger	Fabric	187	37.89	7,085.43	13.62%
Total Retail Value for All Products				$ 52,026.92	

Lastname_Firstname_1D_Laptop_Bags.xlsx

Figure 1.55

(Project 1D Laptop Bags continues on the next page)

Skills Review | Project **1D** Laptop Bags (continued)

1 Open **Excel** and display a new Excel workbook. If necessary, increase the size of the Excel window. On the Standard toolbar, change the **Zoom** setting to **125%**. On the **File** menu, click **Save As**, and then navigate to your **Excel Chapter 1** folder. In the **Save As** box, using your own name, type **Lastname_Firstname_1D_Laptop_Bags** and then click **Save**.

a. In cell **A1** type **Texas Spectrum Wireless** and in cell **A2** type **Laptop Messenger-Style Bag Inventory** Click cell **B3**, type **Quantity in Stock** and press (Tab). In cell **C3** type **Average Cost** and press (Tab). In cell **D3**, type **Retail Price** and press (Tab). In cell **E3**, type **Total Retail Value** and press (Tab). In cell **F3** type **Percent of Total Retail Value** and press (Return).

b. Click cell **A4**, type **Notebook Bag** and press (Return). In the range **A5:A10**, type the remaining row titles as shown below, including any misspelled words.

Biker Messenger Bag

Reaction Bag

Divider Bag

Women's Tote

Pinstrip Messenger

Total Retail Value for All Products

c. Press (Command ⌘) + (fn) + (←) to move to cell **A1**. On the **Review tab**, in the **Proofing group**, click the **Spelling** button. Correct *Pinstrip* to **Pinstripe** and any other spelling errors you may have made, and then when the message displays, *The spell check is complete for the entire sheet*, click **OK**.

d. In the **column heading area**, point to the right boundary of **column A** to display the ⬌ pointer, and then drag to the right to widen **column A** to **29.00 (2.49 inches)**.

e. In the **column heading area**, point to the **column B** heading to display the ⬇ pointer, click, and then drag to the right to select **columns B:F**. With the columns selected, in the **column heading area**, point to the right boundary of any of the selected columns, and then drag to the right to set the width to **13.00 (1.16 inches)**.

f. Select the range **A1:F1**. On the **Home tab**, in the **Alignment group**, click the **Merge** button. In the **Format group**, click the **Styles** button, and then from the **Cell Styles** gallery, apply the **Title** style. Select the range **A2:F2**. **Merge** the text across the selection, and

then from the **Cell Styles** gallery, apply the **Heading 1** style.

2 In the **Themes group**, click the **Themes** button, and from the **Themes** gallery, click **Adjacency**. Select the empty range **B4:D9**. With cell **B4** active in the range, type **56** and then press (Return).

a. With cell **B5** active in the range, and pressing (Return) after each entry, type the following data in the **Quantity in Stock** column:

120

125

245

75

187

b. With the selected range still active, from the following table, beginning in cell **C4** and pressing (Return) after each entry, enter the following data for the **Average Cost** column and then the **Retail Price** column. If you prefer, type without selecting the range first; recall that this is optional.

Average Cost	Retail Price
19.75	39.99
52.25	84.99
26.90	42.95
58.55	88.95
45.20	76.95
18.45	37.89

3 In cell **E4**, type **=b4*d4** and then press (Return) to construct a formula that calculates the *Total Retail Value* of the *Notebook Bags* (Quantity in Stock X Retail Price).

a. Click cell **E4**, position your pointer over the fill handle, and then drag down through cell **E9** to copy the formula with relative cell references.

b. Select the range **B4:B9**, and then on the **Home tab**, in the **Number group**, click the **Comma Style** button. Then, in the **Number group**, click the **Decrease Decimal** button two times to remove the decimal places from these non-currency values.

c. Click cell **E10**. On the Standard toolbar, click the **Sum** button, and then press (Return) to calculate the *Total Retail Value for All Products*. Your result is *52456.42*.

(Project 1D Laptop Bags continues on the next page)

Skills Review | Project **1D** Laptop Bags (continued)

d. Select the range **C5:E9** and apply the **Comma Style**. Select the range **C4:E4**, hold down Command ⌘, and then click cell **E10**. With the nonadjacent cells selected, apply the **Accounting Number Format**. You may have to repeat the steps to be sure that the Accounting Number format is applied to the second range. Click cell **E10**, and then from the **Cell Styles** gallery, apply the **Total** style.

e. Click cell **F4**, type **=** and then click cell **E4**. Type **/** and then click cell **E10**. Press Command ⌘ + T to make the reference to cell *E10* absolute, and then on the **formula bar**, click the **Enter** button so that cell **F4** remains the active cell. Drag the fill handle to copy the formula down through cell **F9**.

f. Point to cell **B6**, and then double-click to place the insertion point within the cell. Use the arrow keys to move the insertion point to the right of *2*, and press Delete to delete *2*, type **1** and then press Return so that the new *Quantity in Stock* is *115*. Notice the recalculations in the worksheet.

4 Select the range **F4:F9**, and then on the **Home tab**, in the **Number group**, click the **Percent Style** button. Click the **Increase Decimal** button two times, and then apply **Center Text** to the selection.

a. In the **row heading area** on the left side of your screen, point to **row 3** to display the ➡ pointer, and then press Control and click to simultaneously select the row and display a shortcut menu. On the shortcut menu, click **Insert** to insert a new **row 3**.

b. Click cell **A3**, type **As of June 30** and then on the **formula bar**, click the **Enter** button to keep cell **A3** as the active cell. **Merge** the text across the range **A3:F3**, and then apply the **Heading 2** cell style.

5 In the **column heading area**, point to **column B**. When the ⬇ pointer displays, press Control and click, and then click **Insert** to insert a new column.

a. Click cell **B4**, type **Material** and then press Return. In cell **B5**, type **Fabric** and then press Return. In cell **B6,** type **Leather** and then press Return.

b. Using AutoComplete to speed your typing by clicking the AutoComplete suggestion, in cells **B7**, **B8**, and **B10** type **Fabric** and in cell **B9** type **Leather**

c. In the **column heading area**, point to the right boundary of **column B**, and then drag to the left to set the width to **13.00 (1.16 inches)**. In the **column heading area**, point to **column D**, press Control and click, and then click **Delete** to delete the *Average Cost* column.

d. Select the column titles in the range **B4:F4**, and then on the **Home tab**, in the **Alignment group**, click the **Wrap Text** button and then click **Wrap Text**. With the range still selected, click the **Center Text** button, and then click **Align Text Middle** button. With the range still selected, apply the **Heading 4** cell style.

e. Select the range **B5:B10**, and then in the **Alignment group**, click the **Center Text** button. Click cell **A11**, and then from the **Cell Styles** gallery, under **Themed Cell Styles**, click **40% - Accent1**.

6 On the **View** menu, click **Header and Footer**, and then in the **Page Setup** dialog box, click **Customize Footer**. With the insertion point in the **Left section** box, click the **Insert File Name** button, and then click **OK**. In the **Page Setup** dialog box, click **OK**.

a. Press Command ⌘ + fn + ← to move the insertion point to cell **A1**. On the **Layout tab**, in the **Page Setup group**, click the **Orientation** button, and then click **Landscape**.

b. In the **Page Setup group**, click the **Margins** button, and then click **Custom Margins**. In the **Page Setup** dialog box, under **Center on page**, select the **Horizontally** check box, and then click **OK**.

c. On the **File** menu, click **Properties**. In the **Subject** box type your course name and section number. In the **Author** box, delete any text and type your firstname and lastname. In the **Keywords** box, type **laptop messenger-style bags** and then click **OK**.

d. **Save** your file and then **Print** or submit your workbook electronically as directed by your instructor. If required by your instructor, print or create an electronic version of your worksheet with formulas displayed by using the instructions in Activity 1.15. **Close** the workbook without saving so that you do not save the changes you made to print formulas, and then **Quit Excel**.

End **You have completed Project 1D**

Content-Based Assessments

Apply 1A skills from these Objectives:

1 Create, Save, and Navigate an Excel Workbook

2 Enter Data in a Worksheet

3 Construct and Copy Formulas and Use the SUM Function

4 Format Cells with Merge and Cell Styles

5 Chart Data to Create a Column Chart and Insert Sparklines

6 Print, Display Formulas, and Close Excel

Mastering Excel | Project **1E** Tablet Sales

In the following Mastering Excel project, you will create a worksheet comparing the sales of different types of tablet computing devices sold in the third quarter. Your completed worksheet will look similar to Figure 1.56.

Project Files

For Project 1E, you will need the following files:

  New Excel workbook

You will save your workbook as:

  Lastname_Firstname_1E_Tablet_Sales

Project Results

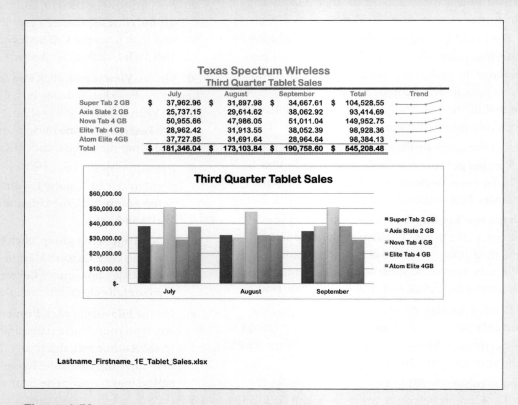

Figure 1.56

(Project 1E Tablet Sales continues on the next page)

Content-Based Assessments

1 Open **Excel** and display a new Excel workbook. If necessary, increase the size of the Excel window. On the Standard toolbar, change the **Zoom** setting to **125%.** On the **File** menu, click **Save As**, and then navigate to your **Excel Chapter 1** folder. In the **Save As** box, using your own name, type **Lastname_Firstname_1E_Tablet_Sales** and then click **Save**.

2 In cell **A1**, type **Texas Spectrum Wireless** and in cell **A2**, type **Third Quarter Tablet Sales** Change the **Theme** to **Sky.** In cell **B3**, type **July** and then use the fill handle to enter the months *August* and *September* in the range **C3:D3**. In cell **E3**, type **Total** and in cell **F3**, type **Trend**

3 **Center** the column titles in the range **B3:F3**. **Merge** the title across the range **A1:F1**, and apply the **Title** cell style. **Merge** the subtitle across the range **A2:F2**, and then apply the **Heading 1** cell style.

4 Widen **column A** to **13:00 (1.51 inches)**, and then in the range **A4:A9**, type the following row titles:

    Super Tab 2GB

    Axis Slate 2GB

    Nova Tab 4GB

    Elite Tab 4GB

    Atom Elite 4GB

    Total

5 Widen columns **B:F** to **12:00 (1.40 inches)**, and then in the range **B4:D8**, enter the monthly sales figures for each type of tablet device, as shown in the table below:

	July	August	September
Super Tab 2GB	37962.96	31897.98	34667.61
Axis Slate 2GB	25737.15	29614.62	38062.92
Nova Tab 4GB	50955.66	47986.05	51011.04
Elite Tab 4GB	28962.42	31913.55	38052.39
Atom Elite 4GB	37727.85	31691.64	28964.64

6 In cell **B9**, **Sum** the *July* sales, and then copy the formula across to cells **C9:D9**. In cell **E4**, **Sum** the *Super Tab 2GB* sales, and then copy the formula down to cells **E5:E9**.

7 Apply the **Heading 4** cell style to the row titles and the column titles. Apply the **Total** cell style to the totals in the range **B9:E9**. Apply the **Number Format** of **Accounting** to the first row of sales figures and to the total row. Apply the **Comma Style** to the remaining sales figures.

8 To compare the monthly sales of each product visually, select the range that represents the sales figures for the three months, including the month names and the product names—do not include any totals in the range. With this data selected, insert a **Clustered Column** chart. **Switch** the Row/Column data so that the months display on the category axis and the types of tablet devices display in the legend. If the Switch button does not work as expected, in the Data group, click the Select button, and in the Select Data Source dialog box, click Switch Row/Column, and then click OK.

9 Position the upper left corner of the chart slightly inside the lower right portion of cell **A11** so that the chart is visually centered below the worksheet, as shown in Figure 1.56. Apply the **26th Chart Style**, and then modify the **Chart Quick Layout** by applying **Layout 1**. Change the **Chart Title** to **Third Quarter Tablet Sales**

10 In the range **F4:F8**, insert **Line** sparklines that compare the monthly data. Do not include the totals. Show **All** of the sparkline **Markers** and apply **Sparkline Style Accent 2, Darker 50%.**

11 Insert a **Footer** with the **File Name** in the **Left section**. Display the **File Properties**, add your course name and section, your name, and the keywords **tablet, sales** Change the **Orientation** to **Landscape**, and then center the worksheet **Horizontally** on the page. Check your worksheet by previewing it in **Preview**, and then make any necessary corrections to be sure that the worksheet prints on one page.

12 **Save** your workbook, and then **Print** or submit electronically as directed. If required by your instructor, print or create an electronic version of your worksheet with formulas displayed by using the instructions in Activity 1.15. **Close** the workbook without saving so that you do not save the changes you made to print formulas, and then **Quit Excel**.

End **You have completed Project 1E**

Apply **1B** skills from
these Objectives:

7 Check Spelling in a
Worksheet

8 Enter Data by Range

9 Construct Formulas
for Mathematical
Operations

10 Edit Values in a
Worksheet

11 Format a Worksheet

Mastering Excel | Project **1F** Home Theater

In the following Mastering Excel project, you will create a worksheet that summarizes the sale of home theater sound system components for an entry-level system that Texas Spectrum Wireless is marketing. Your completed worksheet will look similar to Figure 1.57.

Project Files

For Project 1F, you will need the following file:

New Excel workbook

You will save your workbook as:

Lastname_Firstname_1F_Home_Theater

Project Results

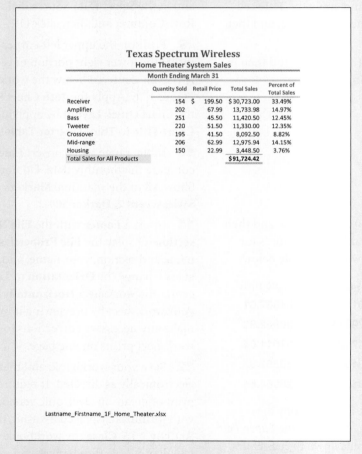

Texas Spectrum Wireless
Home Theater System Sales

	Quantity Sold	Retail Price	Total Sales	Percent of Total Sales
	Month Ending March 31			
Receiver	154	$ 199.50	$ 30,723.00	33.49%
Amplifier	202	67.99	13,733.98	14.97%
Bass	251	45.50	11,420.50	12.45%
Tweeter	220	51.50	11,330.00	12.35%
Crossover	195	41.50	8,092.50	8.82%
Mid-range	206	62.99	12,975.94	14.15%
Housing	150	22.99	3,448.50	3.76%
Total Sales for All Products			$91,724.42	

Lastname_Firstname_1F_Home_Theater.xlsx

Figure 1.57

(Project 1F Home Theater continues on the next page)

Content-Based Assessments

Mastering Excel | Project **1F** Home Theater (continued)

1 Open **Excel** and display a new Excel workbook. If necessary, increase the size of the Excel window. On the Standard toolbar, change the **Zoom** setting to **125%.** In your **Excel Chapter 1** folder, save your workbook as **Lastname_Firstname_1F_Home_Theater**

2 In cell **A1**, type **Texas Spectrum Wireless** In cell **A2**, type **Home Theater System Sales** and then **Merge** the title and the subtitle across **columns A:F**—be sure to merge each row separately. Apply the **Title** and **Heading 1** cell styles respectively. Beginning in cell **B3**, type the following column titles:

    Product Number

    Quantity Sold

    Retail Price

    Total Sales

    Percent of Total Sales

3 Beginning in cell **A4**, type the following row titles, including misspelled words:

    Receiver

    Amplifyer

    Bass

    Tweeter

    Crossover

    Mid-range

    Housing

    Total Sales for All Products

4 Make cell **A1** the active cell, and then check spelling in your worksheet. Correct *Amplifyer* to **Amplifier**, and make any other necessary corrections. Widen **column A** to **25.00 (2.16 inches)** and **columns B:F** to **10.50 (0.94 inches)**.

5 In the range **B4:D10**, type the following data:

	Product Number	Quantity Sold	Retail Price
Receiver	**RS-3**	154	199.50
Amplifier	**AS-8**	202	67.99
Bass	**WS-2**	251	45.50
Tweeter	**TS-4**	220	51.50
Crossover	**CS-5**	195	51.50
Mid-range	**MS-6**	206	62.99
Housing	**HS-8**	165	22.99

6 In cell **E4**, construct a formula to calculate the *Total Sales* of the *Receiver* by multiplying the *Quantity Sold* times the *Retail Price*. Copy the formula down for the remaining products. In cell **E11**, use the **SUM** function to calculate the *Total Sales for All Products*, and then apply the **Total** cell style to the cell.

7 Using absolute cell references as necessary so that you can copy the formula, in cell **F4**, construct a formula to calculate the *Percent of Total Sales* for the first product by dividing the *Total Sales* of the *Receiver* by the *Total Sales for All Products*. Copy the formula down for the remaining products. To the computed percentages, apply **Percent Style** with two decimal places, and then **Center** the percentages.

8 Apply the **Comma Style** with no decimal places to the *Quantity Sold* figures. To cells **D4**, **E4**, and **E11**, apply the **Number Format** of **Accounting**. To the range **D5:E10**, apply the **Comma Style**.

9 Change the *Retail Price* of the *Crossover* to **41.50** and the *Quantity Sold* of the *Housing* to **150** Delete **column B**, and then **Insert** a new **row 3**. In cell **A3**, type **Month Ending March 31** and then **Merge** the text across the range **A3:E3**. Apply the **Heading 2** cell style. To cell **A12**, apply the **20% - Accent1** cell style. Select the four column titles, apply **Wrap Text**, **Align Text Middle**, and **Center Text** formatting, and then apply the **Heading 3** cell style.

10 Insert a **Footer** with the **File Name** in the **Left section**. Display the **File Properties**, add your course name and section, your name, and the keywords **home theater, sales**

11 Center the worksheet **Horizontally** on the page. Preview the worksheet in **Preview**, and then make any necessary corrections to print the worksheet on one page.

12 **Save** your workbook, and then **Print** or submit electronically as directed. If required by your instructor, print or create an electronic version of your worksheet with formulas displayed by using the instructions in Activity 1.15. **Close** the worksheet without saving so that you do not save the changes you made to print formulas, and then **Quit Excel**.

End **You have completed Project 1F**

Mastering Excel | Project **1G** Sales Comparison

In the following Mastering Excel project, you will create a new worksheet that compares annual laptop sales by store location. Your completed worksheet will look similar to Figure 1.58.

Project Files

For Project 1G, you will need the following file:

New Excel workbook

You will save your workbook as

Lastname_Firstname_1G_Sales_Comparison

Project Results

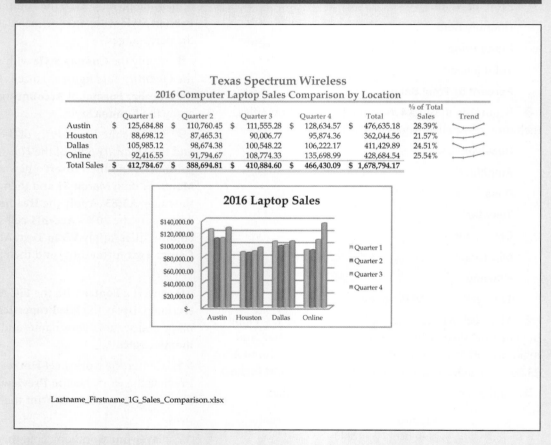

Figure 1.58

(Project 1G Sales Comparison continues on the next page)

Content-Based Assessments

Mastering Excel | Project **1G** Sales Comparison (continued)

1 Open **Excel** and display a new Excel workbook. If necessary, increase the size of the Excel window. On the Standard toolbar, change the **Zoom** setting to **125%.** In your **Excel Chapter 1** folder, save your workbook as **Lastname_Firstname_1G_Sales_Comparison**

2 In cell **A1**, type **Texas Spectrum Wireless** As the worksheet subtitle, in cell **A2**, type **2016 Computer Laptop Sales Comparison by Location** In cell **B3**, type **Quarter 1** and then use the fill handle to enter *Quarter 2, Quarter 3,* and *Quarter 4* in the range **C3:E3**. In cell **F3**, type **Total** In cell **G3**, type **% of Total Sales** In cell **H3**, type **Trend**

3 In the range **A4:A7**, type the following row titles: **Austin** and **Houston** and **Online** and **Total Sales**

4 Widen columns **B:F** to **14.00 (1.23 inches)**. **Merge** the title across the range **A1:H1**, and then apply the **Title** cell style. **Merge** the subtitle across the range **A2:H2**, and then apply the **Heading 1** cell style. Select the seven column titles, apply **Center Text** formatting, **Wrap Text**, and then apply the **Heading 4** cell style.

5 In the range **B4:E6**, enter the sales values for each Quarter as shown in **Table 1** at the bottom of the page.

6 **Sum** the *Quarter 1* sales, and then copy the formula across for the remaining Quarters. **Sum** the sales for the *Austin* location, and then copy the formula down through cell **F7**. Apply the **Number Format** of **Accounting** to the first row of sales figures and to the total row, and the **Comma Style** to the remaining sales figures. Format the totals in **row 7** with the **Total** cell style.

7 **Insert** a new **row 6** with the row title **Dallas** and the following sales figures for each quarter: **105985.12** and **98674.38** and **100548.22** and **106222.17** Copy the formula in cell **F5** down to cell **F6** to sum the new row.

8 Using absolute cell references as necessary so that you can copy the formula, in cell **G4** construct a formula to calculate the *Percent of Total Sales* for the first location by dividing the *Total* for the *Austin* location by the *Total Sales* for all Quarters. Copy the formula down for the remaining locations. To the computed percentages, apply

Percent Style with two decimal places, and then **Center** the percentages.

9 Insert **Line** sparklines in the range **H4:H7** that compare the quarterly data. Do not include the totals. Show **All** of the sparkline **Markers** and apply the **Sparkline Style Accent 2, Darker 25%** style.

10 **Save** your workbook. To compare the quarterly sales of each location visually, select the range that represents the sales figures for the four quarters, including the quarter names and each location—do not include any totals in the range. With this data selected, insert a **Column, Clustered Cylinder** chart.

11 **Switch** the row/column data so that the locations display on the category axis—if the Switch button does not perform as expected, on the Charts tab in the Data group, click the Select button; and then in the Edit Data Source dialog box, click Switch Row/Column and then click OK. Position the top edge of the chart in **row 10** and visually center it below the worksheet data. Apply the **26th Chart Style**, and then modify the **Chart Quick Layout** by applying **Layout 1**. Change the **Chart Title** to **2016 Laptop Sales**

12 Deselect the chart. Change the **Orientation** to **Landscape**, center the worksheet **Horizontally** on the page, and then change the **Theme** to **Saddle**. **Scale** the worksheet so that the **Width** fits to **1 page**. Insert a **Footer** with the **File Name** in the **Left section**. Make **A1** the active cell so that you can view the top of your worksheet.

13 Display the **File Properties**, add your course name and section, your name, and the keywords **laptops, sales** View your worksheet in **Preview**, and then make any necessary corrections to be sure that the worksheet prints on one page.

14 **Save** your workbook, and then **Print** or submit electronically as directed. If required by your instructor, print or create an electronic version of your worksheet with formulas displayed by using the instructions in Activity 1.15. **Close** your workbook without saving so that you do not save the changes you made to print formulas, and then **Quit Excel**.

Table 1

	Quarter 1	Quarter 2	Quarter 3	Quarter 4
Austin	125684.88	110760.45	111555.28	128634.57
Houston	88698.12	87465.31	90006.77	95874.36
Online	92416.55	91794.67	108774.33	135698.99

- - ► (Return to Step 6)

 End **You have completed Project 1G**

GO! Fix It | Project **1H** Team Sales

Project Files

For Project 1H, you will need the following file:

> e01H_Team_Sales

You will save your workbook as:

> Lastname_Firstname_1H_Team_Sales

In this project, you will edit a worksheet that summarizes sales by each sales team member at the Texas Spectrum Wireless San Antonio location for the month of February. From the student files that accompany this textbook, open the file e01H_Team_Sales, and then save the file in your Excel Chapter 1 folder as **Lastname_Firstname_1H_Team_Sales**

To complete the project, you must find and correct errors in formulas and formatting. View each formula in the formula bar and edit as necessary. In addition to errors that you find, you should know:

- There are two spelling errors.

- Worksheet titles should be merged and centered and appropriate cell styles should be applied.

- Appropriate number and accounting format with zero decimals should be applied to the data, and text should be wrapped where necessary. Percent style formatting should be applied appropriately where necessary.

- Column headings should be formatted with the Heading 4 style.

- In the chart, the team member names should display on the Horizontal (Category) axis and the week names should display in the legend. Note: If the Switch button does not work as expected, in the Data group, click the Select button, and in the Select Data Source dialog box, click Switch Row/Column, and then click OK.

- The chart should include the title **February Team Member Sales**

- The worksheet should be centered horizontally on one page in Landscape orientation.

- A footer should be inserted that includes the file name, and file properties should include the keywords **team sales, San Antonio**

Save your workbook, and then print or submit electronically as directed. If required by your instructor, print or create an electronic version of your worksheet with formulas displayed by using the instructions in Activity 1.15. Close the workbook without saving so that you do not save the changes you made to print formulas, and then Quit Excel.

End **You have completed Project 1H** ─────────────────────

Content-Based Assessments

GO! Make It | Project 1I Printer Sales

Project Files

For Project 1I, you will need the following file:

New Excel workbook

You will save your workbook as:

Lastname_Firstname_1I_Printer_Sales

Create the worksheet shown in Figure 1.59. Use the Pushpin theme and change the Orientation to Landscape. Construct formulas in the Total Sold, Total Sales, and Percent of Total Sales columns, and in the Total row. Apply cell styles and number formatting as shown. Use the 26th style for the chart. Insert sparklines for the monthly data using the Sparkline Style Accent 1, Darker 25% style. Add your course name and section, your name, and the keywords **inkjet, printer, sales** to the file properties. Save the file in your Excel Chapter 1 folder as **Lastname_Firstname_1I_Printer_Sales**

Project Results

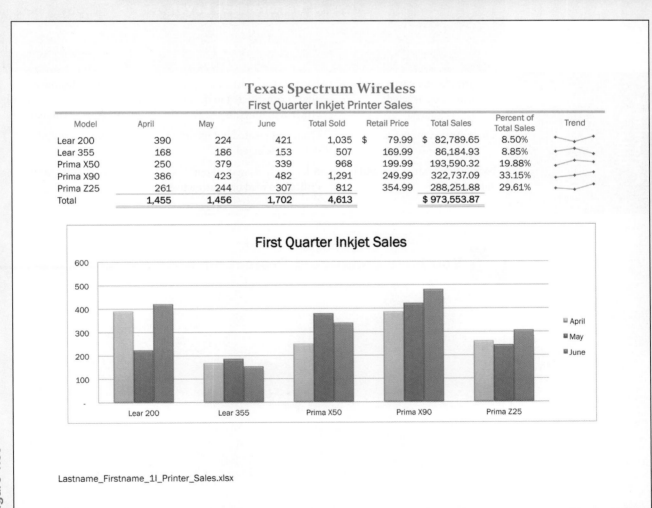

Figure 1.59

Lastname_Firstname_1I_Printer_Sales.xlsx

Excel | Chapter 1

End You have completed Project 1I

Content-Based Assessments

GO! Solve It | Project **1J** Warranty Sales

Project Files

For Project 1J, you will need the following file:

e01J_Warranty_Sales

You will save your workbook as:

Lastname_Firstname_1J_Warranty_Sales

Open the file e01J_Warranty_Sales and save it in your Excel Chapter 1 folder as **Lastname_Firstname_1J_Warranty_Sales** Complete the worksheet by using Auto Fill to enter the Quarter headings, and then calculating *Total Sold*, *Total Sales*, *Total For All Products*, and *Percent of Total Sales*. Format the worksheet attractively, and apply appropriate financial formatting. Insert a chart that compares the total number of warranties sold for each item across Quarters, and format the chart to display the information appropriately. Include the file name in the footer, add appropriate file properties, and submit as directed.

		Performance Level	
	Exemplary: You consistently applied the relevant skills	**Proficient:** You sometimes, but not always, applied the relevant skills	**Developing:** You rarely or never applied the relevant skills
Create formulas	All formulas are correct and are efficiently constructed.	Formulas are correct but not always constructed in the most efficient manner.	One or more formulas are missing or incorrect; or only numbers were entered.
Create a chart	Chart created properly.	Chart was created but incorrect data was selected.	No chart was created.
Format attractively and appropriately	Formatting is attractive and appropriate.	Adequately formatted but difficult to read or unattractive.	Inadequate or no formatting.

(left sidebar label: **Performance Criteria**)

End **You have completed Project 1J** ———————————

Content-Based Assessments

GO! Solve It | Project **1K** Service Receipts

Project Files

For Project 1K, you will need the following file:

e01K_Service_Receipts

You will save your workbook as:

Lastname_Firstname_1K_Service_Receipts

Open the file e01K_Service_Receipts and save it in your Excel Chapter 1 folder as **Lastname_Firstname_1K_Service_ Receipts** Complete the worksheet by using Auto Fill to complete the month headings, and then calculating the Total Receipts for each month and for each product. Insert and format appropriate sparklines in the Trend column. Format the worksheet attractively with a title and subtitle, check spelling, adjust column width, and apply appropriate financial formatting. Insert a chart that compares the total sales receipts for each product with the months displaying as the categories, and format the chart attractively. Include the file name in the footer, add appropriate file properties, and submit as directed.

Performance Criteria		Performance Level		
		Exemplary: You consistently applied the relevant skills	**Proficient:** You sometimes, but not always, applied the relevant skills	**Developing:** You rarely or never applied the relevant skills
	Create formulas	All formulas are correct and are efficiently constructed.	Formulas are correct but not always constructed in the most efficient manner.	One or more formulas are missing or incorrect; or only numbers were entered.
	Create a chart	Chart created properly.	Chart was created but incorrect data was selected.	No chart was created.
	Insert and format sparklines	Sparklines inserted and formatted properly.	Sparklines were inserted but incorrect data was selected or sparklines were not formatted.	No sparklines were inserted.
	Format attractively and appropriately	Formatting is attractive and appropriate.	Adequately formatted but difficult to read or unattractive.	Inadequate or no formatting.

End **You have completed Project 1K**

Outcomes-Based Assessments

Rubric

The following outcomes-based assessments are open-ended assessments. That is, there is no specific correct result; your result will depend on your approach to the information provided. Make Professional Quality your goal. Use the following scoring rubric to guide you in how to approach the problem and then to evaluate how well your approach solves the problem.

The *criteria*—Software Mastery, Content, Format and Layout, and Process—represent the knowledge and skills you have gained that you can apply to solving the problem. The *levels of performance*—Professional Quality, Approaching Professional Quality, or Needs Quality Improvements—help you and your instructor evaluate your result.

	Your completed project is of Professional Quality if you:	Your completed project is Approaching Professional Quality if you:	Your completed project Needs Quality Improvements if you:
1-Software Mastery	Choose and apply the most appropriate skills, tools, and features and identify efficient methods to solve the problem.	Choose and apply some appropriate skills, tools, and features, but not in the most efficient manner.	Choose inappropriate skills, tools, or features, or are inefficient in solving the problem.
2-Content	Construct a solution that is clear and well organized, contains content that is accurate, appropriate to the audience and purpose, and is complete. Provide a solution that contains no errors in spelling, grammar, or style.	Construct a solution in which some components are unclear, poorly organized, inconsistent, or incomplete. Misjudge the needs of the audience. Have some errors in spelling, grammar, or style, but the errors do not detract from comprehension.	Construct a solution that is unclear, incomplete, or poorly organized; contains some inaccurate or inappropriate content; and contains many errors in spelling, grammar, or style. Do not solve the problem.
3-Format and Layout	Format and arrange all elements to communicate information and ideas, clarify function, illustrate relationships, and indicate relative importance.	Apply appropriate format and layout features to some elements, but not others. Overuse features, causing minor distraction.	Apply format and layout that does not communicate information or ideas clearly. Do not use format and layout features to clarify function, illustrate relationships, or indicate relative importance. Use available features excessively, causing distraction.
4-Process	Use an organized approach that integrates planning, development, self-assessment, revision, and reflection.	Demonstrate an organized approach in some areas, but not others; or, use an insufficient process of organization throughout.	Do not use an organized approach to solve the problem.

Outcomes-Based Assessments

GO! Think | Project **1L** Phone Plans

Project Files

For Project 1L, you will need the following file:

New Excel workbook

You will save your workbook as:

Lastname_Firstname_1L_Phone_Plans

Roslyn Thomas, President of Texas Spectrum Wireless, needs a worksheet that summarizes the following data regarding the first quarter sales of cell phone calling plans that the company is offering for domestic and international calls. Roslyn would like the worksheet to include a calculation of the total sales for each plan and a total of the sales of all of the plans. She would also like to know each plan's percentage of total sales.

	Number Sold	Price
Domestic Standard	2556	29.99
Domestic Premium	3982	49.99
Domestic Platinum	1647	64.99
International Standard	582	85.99
International Premium	365	102.99

Create a worksheet that provides Roslyn with the information needed. Include appropriate worksheet, column, and row titles. Using the formatting skills that you practiced in this chapter, format the worksheet in a manner that is professional and easy to read and understand. Insert a footer with the file name and add appropriate file properties. Save the file in your Excel Chapter 1 folder as **Lastname_Firstname_1L_Phone_Plans** and print or submit as directed by your instructor.

End **You have completed Project 1L** ————————————

Outcomes-Based Assessments

GO! Think | Project **1M** Advertising

Project Files

For Project 1M, you will need the following file:

New Excel workbook

You will save your workbook as:

Lastname_Firstname_1M_Advertising

Eliott Verschoren, Vice President of Marketing for Texas Spectrum Wireless, is conducting an analysis of the advertising expenditures at the company's four retail locations based on the following data:

	Quarter 1	Quarter 2	Quarter 3	Quarter 4
Austin	22860	25905	18642	28405
Dallas	18557	17963	22883	25998
Houston	32609	28462	25915	31755
San Antonio	12475	15624	13371	17429

Using this information, create a workbook that includes totals by quarter and by location, sparklines to demonstrate the quarterly trends, and a column chart that compares the quarterly data across locations. Include appropriate worksheet, row, and column titles. Using the formatting skills that you practiced in this chapter, format the worksheet in a manner that is professional and easy to read and understand. Insert a footer with the file name and add appropriate file properties. Save the file in your Excel Chapter 1 folder as **Lastname_Firstname_1M_Advertising** and print or submit as directed by your instructor.

End **You have completed Project 1M** ——————————————

Apply a combination of the **1A** and **1B** skills.

You and GO! | Project **1N** Personal Expenses

Project Files

For Project 1N, you will need the following file:

New Excel workbook

You will save your workbook as:

Lastname_Firstname_1N_Personal_Expenses

Develop a worksheet that details your personal expenses from the last three months. Some of these expenses might include, but are not limited to, Mortgage, Rent, Utilities, Phone, Food, Entertainment, Tuition, Childcare, Clothing, and Insurance. Include a total for each month and for each category of expense. Insert a column with a formula that calculates the percent that each expense category is of the total expenditures. Format the worksheet by adjusting column widths and wrapping text, and by applying appropriate financial number formatting and cell styles. Insert a column chart that compares your expenses by month and modify the chart layout and style. Insert a footer with the file name, center the worksheet horizontally on the page, and add appropriate file properties. Save your file in your Excel Chapter 1 folder as **Lastname_Firstname_1N_Personal_Expenses** and submit as directed.

 You have completed Project 1N ——————————————

Apply a combination of the **1A** and **1B** skills.

GO! Group Business Running Case | Project **1O**
Bell Orchid Hotels Group Running Case

This project relates to the **Bell Orchid Hotels**. Your instructor may assign this group case project to your class. If your instructor assigns this project, he or she will provide you with information and instructions to work as part of a group. The group will apply the skills gained thus far to help the Bell Orchid Hotels achieve their business goals.

 You have completed Project 1O ——————————————

Excel | Chapter 1

Using Functions, Creating Tables, and Managing Large Workbooks

OUTCOMES

At the end of this chapter you will be able to:

OBJECTIVES

Mastering these objectives will enable you to:

PROJECT 2A

Analyze inventory by applying statistical and logical calculations to data and by sorting and filtering data.

1. Use the SUM, AVERAGE, MEDIAN, MIN, and MAX Functions (p. 309)
2. Move Data, Resolve Error Messages, and Rotate Text (p. 314)
3. Use COUNTIF and IF Functions and Apply Conditional Formatting (p. 316)
4. Use Date and Time Functions and Freeze Panes (p. 321)
5. Create, Sort, and Filter an Excel Table (p. 323)
6. Format and Print a Large Worksheet (p. 327)

PROJECT 2B

Summarize the data on multiple worksheets.

7. Navigate a Workbook and Rename Worksheets (p. 331)
8. Enter Dates, Clear Contents, and Clear Formats (p. 332)
9. Copy and Paste Cells (p. 336)
10. Edit and Format Multiple Worksheets at the Same Time (p. 337)
11. Create a Summary Sheet with Column Sparklines (p. 343)
12. Format and Print Multiple Worksheets in a Workbook (p. 347)

© Ronald Sumners / Shutterstock

In This Chapter

In this chapter, you will use statistical functions to calculate the average of a group of numbers and use other logical and date and time functions. You will use the counting functions and apply conditional formatting to make data easy to visualize. In this chapter, you will also create a table and analyze the table's data by sorting and filtering the data. You will summarize a workbook that contains multiple worksheets.

The projects in this chapter relate to **Laurales Herbs and Spices**. After ten years as an executive chef, Laura Morales started her own business, which offers quality products for cooking, eating, and entertaining in retail stores and online. In addition to herbs and spices, the business offers a wide variety of condiments, confections, jams, sauces, oils, and vinegars. Later this year, Laura will add a line of tools, cookbooks, and gift baskets. The company name is a combination of Laura's first and last names, and also the name of an order of plants related to cinnamon.

Project 2A Inventory Status Report

Project Activities

In Activities 2.01 through 2.15, you will edit a worksheet for Laura Morales, President, detailing the current inventory of flavor products at the Oakland production facility. Your completed worksheet will look similar to Figure 2.1.

Project Files

For Project 2A, you will need the following file:

e02A_Flavor_Inventory

You will save your workbook as:

Lastname_Firstname_2A_Flavor_Inventory

Project Results

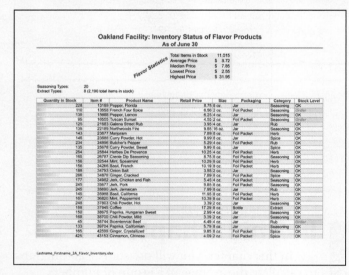

Figure 2.1
Project 2A Flavor Inventory

Objective 1 | Use the SUM, AVERAGE, MEDIAN, MIN, and MAX Functions

A *function* is a predefined formula—a formula that Excel has already built for you—that performs calculations by using specific values in a particular order or structure. *Statistical functions*, which include the AVERAGE, MEDIAN, MIN, and MAX functions, are useful to analyze a group of measurements.

Activity 2.01 | Using the SUM and AVERAGE Functions

Laura has a worksheet with information about the inventory of types of flavor products currently in stock at the Oakland facility. In this activity, you will use the SUM and AVERAGE functions to gather information about the product inventory.

1 Open **Excel**. On the **File** menu, click **Open**, and then from the student files that accompany this textbook, locate and **Open e02A_Flavor_Inventory**. If necessary, increase the size of the Excel window to fill the screen by clicking the Zoom button or by dragging the corner of the Excel window. If necessary, on the Standard toolbar, click the Zoom arrow 100%, and then click 125%.

2 On the **File** menu, click **Save As**. In the **Save As** dialog box, navigate to the location where you are storing your projects for this chapter. **Create** a new folder named **Excel Chapter 2** and then in the **Save As** box, type **Lastname_Firstname_2A_Flavor_Inventory** Click **Save** or press Return.

3 Notice that the worksheet contains data related to types of flavor products in the inventory, including information about the *Quantity in Stock, Item #, Product Name, Retail Price, Size, Packaging,* and *Category.*

4 In cell **A4**, type **Total Items in Stock** In cell **A5**, type **Average Price** In cell **A6**, type **Median Price**

5 Click cell **B4**. On the **Formulas tab**, in the **Function group**, click the **AutoSum** button. Compare your screen with Figure 2.2.

> The *SUM function* is a predefined formula that adds all the numbers in a selected range of cells. Because it is frequently used, there are several ways to insert the function.
>
> For example, you can insert the SUM function from the Standard toolbar, by using the keyboard shortcut Command ⌘ + Shift + T, or from the Math and Trigonometry list displayed after clicking the Insert button in the Function group on the Formulas tab.

Figure 2.2

AutoSum button on Standard toolbar

AutoSum button on Formulas tab in Function group

Row 3 blank

Row titles entered

Sum function in cell B4

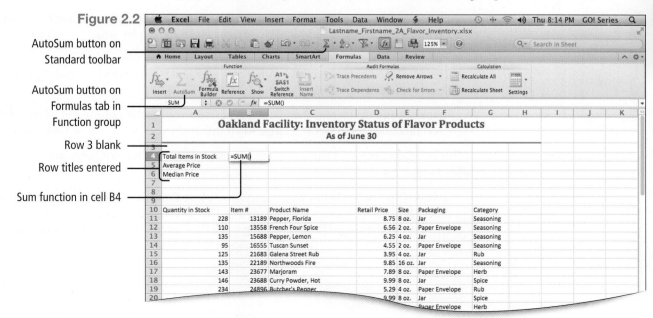

6 With the insertion point blinking in the function, select the range **A11:A65**, dragging down as necessary—a ScreenTip of *55R x 1C* displays—and then press Return. Scroll to view the top of your worksheet, and notice the result in cell **B4**, *11015*.

> The ScreenTip of *55R x 1C* indicates that you have selected 55 rows in 1 column.

7 Click cell **B4** and look at the formula bar. Compare your screen with Figure 2.3.

> *SUM* is the name of the function. The values in parentheses are the ***arguments***—the values that an Excel function uses to perform calculations or operations. In this instance, the argument consists of the values in the range A11:A65.

Figure 2.3

Function and arguments display in formula bar

Result of SUM function displays in cell B4

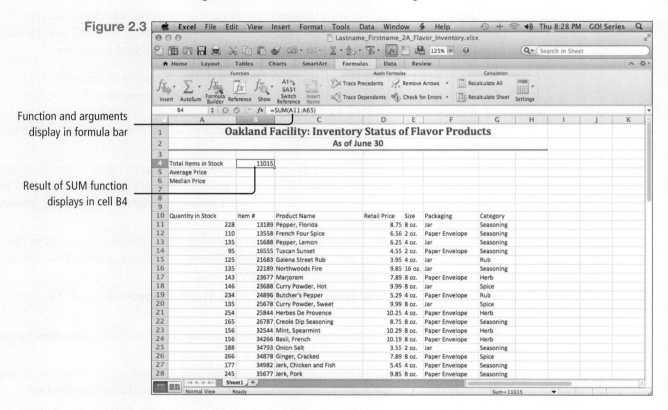

8 Click cell **B5**. In the **Function group**, click the **AutoSum arrow**, click **Average**, and then notice that *B4* displays as the argument.

> By clicking the AutoSum arrow, you can select common functions, such as Sum, Average, Count Numbers, Max, and Min. These same functions display when you click the Sum arrow on the Standard toolbar.

> The ***AVERAGE function*** adds a group of values, and then divides the result by the number of values in the group.

> In the cell and the formula bar, Excel proposes to average the value in cell B4. Recall that Excel functions will propose a range when data is above or to the left of a selected cell.

Another Way
Select the range
D11:D65 and press
Return.

9 With *B4* still selected in the function, type **d11:d65** and then compare your screen with Figure 2.4.

> A ScreenTip displays below B5 that gives you a hint about the arguments that are needed for the AVERAGE function, and the range D11:D65 is selected. Because you want to average the values in the range D11:D65—and not cell B4—you must edit the proposed range.

Figure 2.4

Formula bar displays function name and arguments

Range of cells to be averaged typed in argument of function

ScreenTip for AVERAGE function

Range of cells to be averaged selected

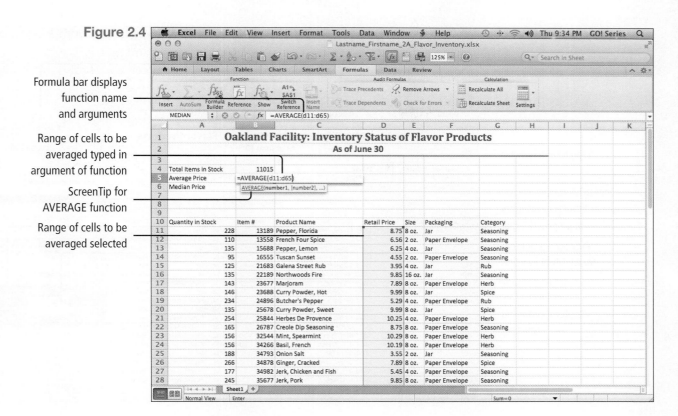

10 Press Return, and then **Save** 🖫 your workbook.

> In cell B5, the result indicates that the average Retail Price of all products is *8.72*. You have used two methods for entering the argument—dragging through the cells and typing the range of cells.

Activity 2.02 | Using the MEDIAN Function

> The **MEDIAN function** is a statistical function that describes a group of data—you may have seen it used to describe the price of houses in a particular geographical area. The MEDIAN function finds the middle value that has as many values above it in the group as are below it. It differs from AVERAGE in that the result is not affected as much by a single value that is greatly different from the others.

> **Another Way**
>
> In the Function group, click the Formula Builder button.

1 If necessary, click cell **B6**. On the Standard toolbar, click the **Sum arrow** Σ, and then click **More Functions**. In the **Formula Builder** window, in the **Search for a function box**, type **med** and notice that *MEDIAN* displays under *Statistical*. Double-click **MEDIAN**, and then compare your screen with Figure 2.5.

> The Formula Builder window displays a Description of the function, has a link to More help on this function, and at the bottom of the dialog box has an area for you to enter the argument for the function. Excel proposes a range of B4:B5—the values above the selected cell—for the MEDIAN function.

Figure 2.5

Formula Builder window

Search term entered

MEDIAN function listed under Statistical category

Values in proposed range

Proposed argument for MEDIAN function

Arguments box

Result for proposed argument

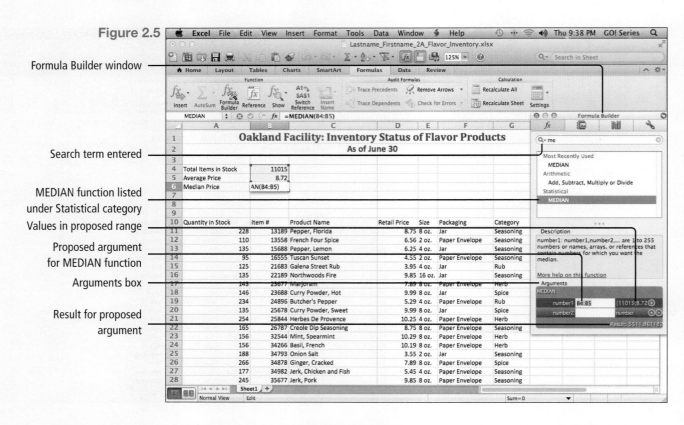

2 At the bottom of the **Formula Builder** window, in the **Arguments** box, with the range *B4:B5* selected in the **number1** box, in the worksheet, click cell **D11**, and then drag down through cell **D65** to select the range **D11:D65**. Notice in the **Formula Builder** window how the range in the **number1** box and the result change as you drag to select the range. Compare your screen with Figure 2.6.

> When indicating which cells you want to use in the function's calculation—known as *defining the arguments*—you can either select the values with your mouse or type the range of values, whichever you prefer.

Figure 2.6

Formula bar displays function and argument

Selected range surrounded by moving border

Range of cells used in argument

Result using the selected range

3 Press Return, and then **Close** 🔘 the **Formula Builder** window. Notice that the **Median Price** in cell **B6** is *7.85*.

> In the range of prices, 7.85 is the middle value. Half of all flavor products are priced *above* 7.85 and half are priced *below* 7.85.

4 If necessary, scroll to view row 1. Select the range **B5:B6**. On the **Home tab**, in the **Number group**, click the **Number Format arrow** [General ▾], and then click **Accounting**.

5 Click cell **B4**. In the **Number group**, click the **Comma Style** button [,], and then click the **Decrease Decimal** button [.00] two times. **Save** 🔘 your workbook, and then compare your screen with Figure 2.7.

Figure 2.7

Comma Style applied
with no decimal places

Accounting Number
Format applied

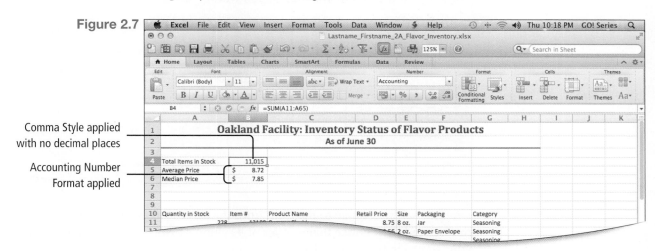

Activity 2.03 | Using the MIN and MAX Functions

The statistical *MIN function* determines the smallest value in a selected range of values. The statistical *MAX function* determines the largest value in a selected range of values.

1 In cell **A7**, type **Lowest Price** and then in cell **A8**, type **Highest Price**

2 Click cell **B7**. On the Standard toolbar, click the **AutoSum arrow** [Σ], and then click **Min**. In the worksheet, select the range **D11:D65**, and then press Return. Scroll to display cell **B7**.

> The lowest Retail Price is *2.55*.

3 Click cell **B8**, and then by using a similar technique, insert the **Max** function to determine the highest **Retail Price**—*31.95*.

4 Select the range **B7:B8** and apply the **Number Format** [General ▾] of **Accounting**. **Save** 🔘 your workbook, and then compare your screen with Figure 2.8.

Figure 2.8

MIN function calculates
lowest price

MAX function calculates
highest price

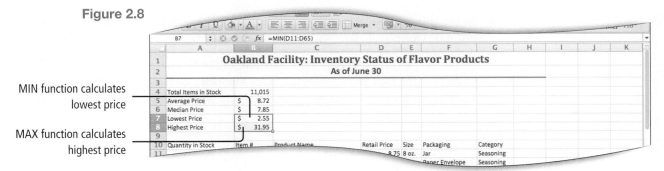

Excel | Chapter 2

Objective 2 | Move Data, Resolve Error Messages, and Rotate Text

When you move a formula, the cell references within the formula do not change, no matter what type of cell reference you use. If you move cells into a column that is not wide enough to display number values, Excel displays a message so that you can adjust as necessary. You can reposition data within a cell at an angle by rotating the text.

Activity 2.04 | Moving Data and Resolving a ##### Error Message

1 Select the range **A4:B8**. Point to the right edge of the selected range to display the ✋ pointer, and then compare your screen with Figure 2.9.

Figure 2.9

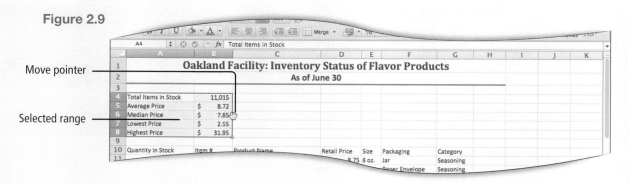

Move pointer

Selected range

2 Drag the selected range to the right until the **ScreenTip** displays **D4:E8**, release the mouse, and then notice that a series of # symbols displays in **column E**. Compare your screen with Figure 2.10.

Using this technique, cell contents can be moved from one location to another; this is referred to as *drag and drop*.

If a cell width is too narrow to display the entire number, Excel displays the ##### error because displaying only a portion of a number would be misleading. The actual values remain in the cells but cannot be displayed because the cell widths are not wide enough.

Figure 2.10

symbols display because cell width is too narrow to display underlying value

Range moved to D4:E8

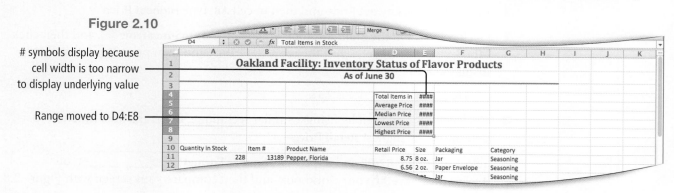

3 In the **column heading area**, point to the right boundary of **column E** to display the ↔ pointer. Double-click to AutoFit the column to accommodate the widest entry.

4 Select the range **D4:E8**. On the **Home tab**, in the **Format group**, click the **Styles** button to display the **Cell Styles** gallery. Under **Themed Cell Styles**, click **20%- Accent1**, and then AutoFit **column D** to accommodate the widest entry. **Save** 💾 your workbook.

Activity 2.05 | Rotating Text

Another Way

To display the Format Cells dialog box, press Command ⌘ + 1 ; or, press Control and click, and then from the shortcut menu, click Format Cells.

1 In cell **C6**, type **Flavor Statistics** and then press Return. Select the range **C4:C8**, and then on the **Home tab**, in the **Alignment group**, click the **Merge** button. On the **Format** menu, click **Cells** to display the **Format Cells** dialog box. In the **Format Cells** dialog box, click the **Alignment tab**. Under **Text control**, notice that the **Merge cells** check box is selected because you clicked the Merge button.

2 In the upper right portion of the dialog box, under **Orientation**, point to the **red diamond**, and then drag the diamond upward until the **Degrees** box indicates **30**. Alternatively, in the degrees box, type *30*. Compare your screen with Figure 2.11.

Figure 2.11

Format Cells dialog box

Text orientation set to 30 degrees

Merge cells selected—you clicked Merge button in Alignment group

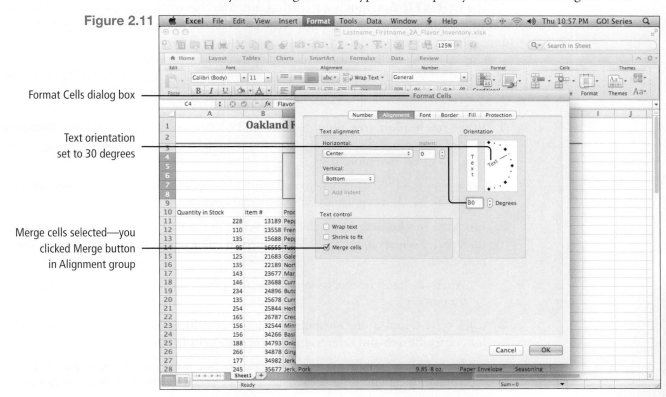

3 In the lower right corner of the **Format Cells** dialog box, click **OK**.

4 With the merged cell still selected, on the **Home tab**, in the **Font group**, change the **Font Size** to **14**, and then apply **Bold** B and **Italic** I. Click the **Font Color arrow** A ▾, and then in the first row, click the fourth color—**Text 2**.

5 In the **Alignment group**, click the **Align Text Right** button. Click cell **A1**, **Save** 💾 your workbook, and then compare your screen with Figure 2.12.

Figure 2.12

Text rotated and formatted

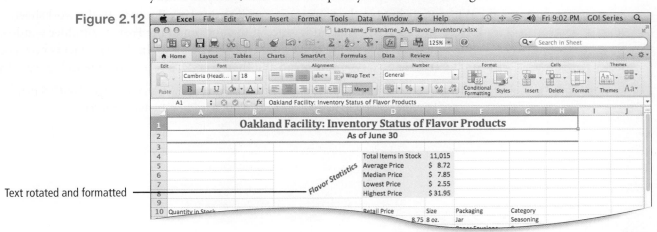

Excel | Chapter 2

Objective 3 | Use COUNTIF and IF Functions and Apply Conditional Formatting

Recall that statistical functions analyze a group of measurements. Another group of Excel functions, referred to as *logical functions*, test for specific conditions. Logical functions typically use conditional tests to determine whether specified conditions—called *criteria*—are true or false.

Activity 2.06 | Using the COUNTIF Function

The *COUNTIF function* is a statistical function that counts the number of cells within a range that meet the given condition—the criteria that you provide. The COUNTIF function has two arguments—the range of cells to check and the criteria.

The seasonings of Laurales Herbs and Spices will be featured on an upcoming segment of a TV shopping channel. In this activity, you will use the COUNTIF function to determine the number of *seasoning* products currently available in inventory.

1 In the **row heading area**, point to **row 9** and click to select the row. On the **Home tab**, in the **Cells group**, click the **Insert** button to insert a row. Press Command ⌘ + Y two times to insert two more rows.

> Command ⌘ + Y is a useful keyboard shortcut to repeat commands in Microsoft Office programs. Most commands can be repeated in this manner.

2 From the **row heading area**, select **rows 9:11**. On the **Edit** menu, point to **Clear**, and then click **Formats** to remove the blue accent color in columns D and E from the new rows.

> When you insert rows or columns, formatting from adjacent rows or columns repeats in the new cells.

3 Click cell **E4**, look at the **Formula Bar**, and then notice that the arguments of the **SUM** function adjusted and refer to the appropriate cells in rows 14:68.

> The referenced range updates to *A14:A68* after you insert the three new rows. In this manner, Excel adjusts the cell references in a formula relative to their new locations.

4 In cell **A10**, type **Seasoning Types:** and then press Tab.

5 With cell **B10** as the active cell, on the **Formulas tab**, in the **Function group**, click the **Formula Builder** button. In the **Formula Builder** window, in the **Search for a function** box, type **countif** and then under **Statistical**, double-click **COUNTIF**.

> Recall that the COUNTIF function counts the number of cells within a range that meet the given condition.

6 Without clicking in the worksheet, scroll to display **column G**. In the worksheet, select the range **G14:G68**, and notice at the bottom of the **Formula Builder** window in the **Arguments** box, in the **range** box, *G14:G68* displays. In the **Arguments** box, click in the **criteria** box, type **seasoning** and then compare your screen with Figure 2.13.

> The COUNTIF function counts the number of cells within the range G14:G68 that contain the criteria of *seasoning*. You do not need to capitalize criteria.

Figure 2.13

Function with two
arguments displays in
formula bar

ScreenTip for
COUNTIF function

Function arguments

Range of *G14:G68*

Criteria of *seasoning*

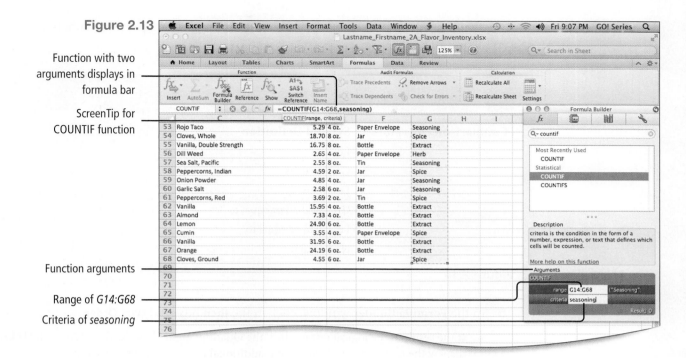

7 Press Return, and then **Close** the **Formula Builder** window. If necessary, scroll to display cell **B10**.

> There are *20* different *Seasoning* products available to feature on the TV show.

8 With cell **B10** selected, on the **Home tab**, in the **Alignment group**, click the **Align Text Left** button to place the result closer to the row title. **Save** your workbook.

Activity 2.07 | Using the IF Function

A *logical test* is any value or expression that you can evaluate as being true or false. The *IF function* uses a logical test to check whether a condition is met, and then returns one value if true, and another value if false. For example, *C14 = 228* is an expression that can be evaluated as true or false. If the value in cell C14 is equal to 228, the expression is true. If the value in cell C14 is not 228, the expression is false.

In this activity, you will use the IF function to determine the inventory levels and determine whether more products should be ordered.

1 Click cell **H13**, type **Stock Level** and then press Return.

2 In cell **H14**, on the **Formulas tab**, in the **Function group**, click the **Formula Builder** button. In the **Formula Builder** window, in the **Search for a function** box, type **if** and then scroll to display the **Logical** category. Under **Logical**, double-click **IF**. Without clicking in the worksheet, if necessary, scroll to display cell *A14*.

3 In the **Formula Builder** window, in the **Arguments** box, click in the **value1** box. With the insertion point in the **value1** box, in the worksheet, click cell **A14**. Without clicking in the worksheet, scroll to display cell *H14*. In the **Formula Builder** window, under the **value1** box to the right of **is True**, click the arrows. From the list, click **< (Less Than)**. In the **value2** box, type **125** and then look at the function and its argument in the Formula Bar.

> This logical test will look at the value in cell A14, which is *228*, and then determine if the number is less than 125. The expression *<125* includes the < *comparison operator*, which means *less than*. Comparison operators compare values.

4 Examine the table in Figure 2.14 for a list of comparison operator symbols and their definitions.

Comparison Operators

Comparison Operators	Symbol Definition
=	Equal to
>	Greater than
<	Less than
>=	Greater than or equal to
<=	Less than or equal to
<>	Not equal to

Figure 2.14

5 In the **Formula Builder** window, click in the **then** box, and type **Order**

If the result of the logical test is true—the Quantity in Stock is less than 125—cell H14 will display the text *Order*, indicating that additional product must be ordered.

6 Click in the **else** box, type **OK** and then compare your screen with Figure 2.15.

If the result of the logical test is false—the Quantity in Stock is *not* less than 125—then Excel will display *OK* in the cell.

Figure 2.15

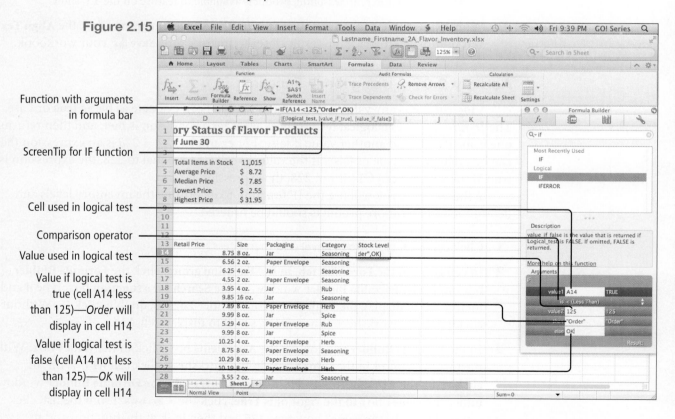

Function with arguments in formula bar

ScreenTip for IF function

Cell used in logical test

Comparison operator

Value used in logical test

Value if logical test is true (cell A14 less than 125)—*Order* will display in cell H14

Value if logical test is false (cell A14 not less than 125)—*OK* will display in cell H14

7 Press Return to display the result *OK* in cell **H14**. **Close** the **Formula Builder** window.

In the argument, if the value to be inserted into a cell is text, Excel inserts quotation marks around the text—"*Order*" and "*OK*".

8 Using the fill handle, copy the function in cell **H14** down through cell **H68**. Then scroll as necessary to view cell **A18**, which displays *125*. Look at cell **H18** and notice that the **Stock Level** displays *OK*. Notice that cell **A15** displays *110* and notice that cell **H15** displays *Order* because 110 is less than 125. **Save** 🖫 your workbook, and then compare your screen with Figure 2.16.

The comparison operator is <125 (less than 125), and thus a value of *exactly* 125 is indicated as OK.

Figure 2.16

Function in column H copied using fill handle

Cell H15 displays *Order*—cell A15 contains *110*, which is less than 125

Cell H18 displays *OK*—cell A18 contains *125*

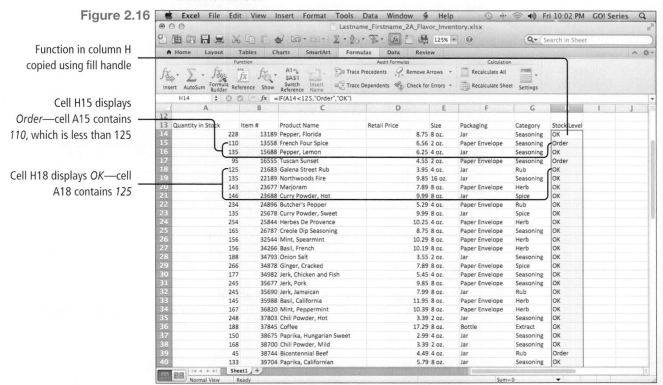

Activity 2.08 | Applying Conditional Formatting by Using Highlight Cells Rules and Data Bars

A **conditional format** changes the appearance of a cell based on a condition—a criteria. If the condition is true, the cell is formatted based on that condition; if the condition is false, the cell is *not* formatted. In this activity, you will use conditional formatting as another way to draw attention to the Stock Level of products.

1 Be sure the range **H14:H68** is selected. On the **Home tab**, in the **Format group**, click the **Conditional Formatting** button. In the list, point to **Highlight Cells Rules**, and then click **Text that Contains**.

2 In the **New Formatting Rule** dialog box, with the insertion point blinking in the empty box, type **Order** and notice that in the **Format with** box, the default setting is to highlight the cell with **light red fill with dark red text.**

3 In the **Format with** box, click the ⬍ **arrows**, and then in the list, click **custom format**.

Here, in the Format Cells dialog box, you can select any combination of formats to apply to the cell if the condition is true. The custom format you specify will be applied to any cell in the selected range if it contains the text *Order*.

4 In the **Format Cells** dialog box, on the **Font tab**, under **Font style**, click **Bold Italic**. Click in the **Color** box, and then under **Theme Colors**, in the first row, click the sixth color—**Accent 2**. Click **OK**, and then compare your screen with Figure 2.17.

In the range, if the cell meets the condition of containing *Order*, the font color will change to Bold Italic, Accent 2.

Figure 2.17

Conditional Formatting button

New Formatting Rule dialog box

Only cells with the text *Order* will be formatted

Custom format used

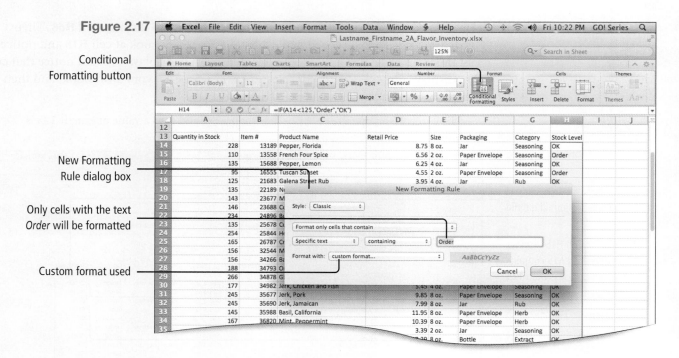

5 In the **New Formatting Rule** dialog box, click **OK**, click anywhere to cancel the selection, and then notice how the formatting is applied to the cells that display *Order*.

6 Select the range **A14:A68**. In the **Format group**, click the **Conditional Formatting** button. Point to **Data Bars**, and then under **Gradient Fill**, click **Orange Data Bar**. Click anywhere to cancel the selection. **Save** your workbook, and then compare your screen with Figure 2.18.

> A **data bar** provides a visual cue to the reader about the value of a cell relative to other cells. The length of the data bar represents the value in the cell. A longer bar represents a higher value and a shorter bar represents a lower value. Data bars are useful for identifying higher and lower numbers quickly within a large group of data, such as very high or very low levels of inventory.

Figure 2.18

Orange Data Bars applied to stock quantities

Conditional font formatting applied to *Order*

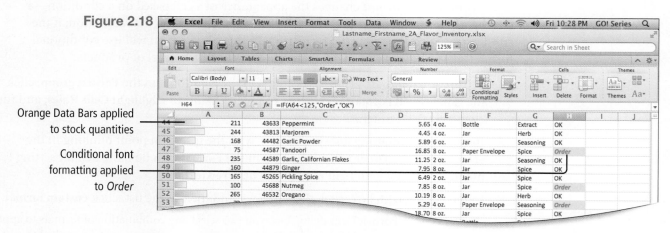

Activity 2.09 | Using Find and Replace

The **Find and Replace** feature searches the cells in a worksheet—or in a selected range—for matches, and then replaces each match with a replacement value of your choice.

Comments from customers on the company's blog indicate that, for dried herbs and seasonings, customers prefer a sealable foil packet rather than a paper envelope.

Thus, all products of this type have been repackaged. In this activity, you will replace all occurrences of *Paper Envelope* with *Foil Packet*.

1 Select the range **F14:F68**.

> Restrict the find and replace operation to a specific range in this manner, especially if there is a possibility that the name occurs elsewhere.

2 On the **Edit** menu, click **Replace**. In the **Replace** dialog box, in the **Find what** box, type **Paper Envelope** and then in the **Replace with** box, type **Foil Packet** Compare your screen with Figure 2.19.

Figure 2.19

Replace dialog box ⎯⎯⎯⎯⎯⎯

Find *Paper Envelope* ⎯⎯⎯⎯

Replace with *Foil Packet* ⎯

Replace All button ⎯⎯⎯⎯

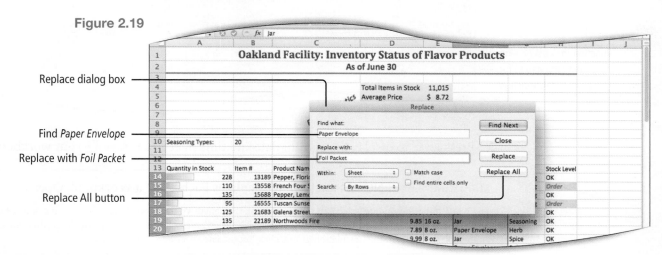

3 Click the **Replace All** button. In the message box, notice that 19 replacements were made, and then click **OK**. In the **Replace** dialog box, click **Close**, and then **Save** 🖫 your workbook.

Objective 4 | Use Date and Time Functions and Freeze Panes

Excel can obtain the date and time from your computer's calendar and clock and display this information on your worksheet.

By freezing or splitting panes, you can view two areas of a worksheet and lock rows and columns in one area. When you freeze panes, you select the specific rows or columns that you want to remain visible when scrolling in your worksheet.

Activity 2.10 | Using the NOW Function to Display a System Date

The *NOW function* retrieves the date and time from your computer's calendar and clock and inserts the information into the selected cell. The result is formatted as a date and time.

1 Scroll as necessary, and then click cell **A70**. Type **Edited by Frank Barnes** and then press Return.

2 With cell **A71** as the active cell, on the **Formulas tab**, in the **Function group**, click the **Insert** button, point to **Date and Time**, and then click **NOW**. Compare your screen with Figure 2.20.

> If you were to use the Formula Builder window to insert this function, you would notice that this function does not require an argument. This function is *volatile*, meaning the date and time will not remain as entered, but rather the date and time will automatically update each time you open this workbook.

Figure 2.20

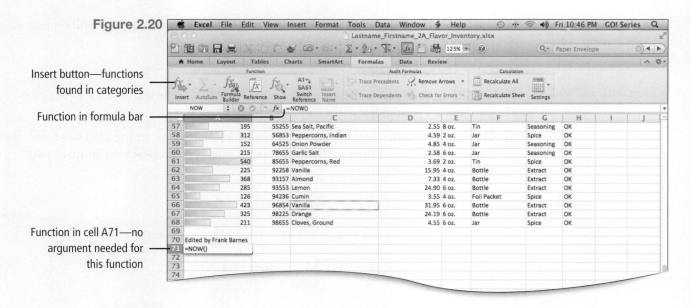

Insert button—functions found in categories

Function in formula bar

Function in cell A71—no argument needed for this function

3 Press Return to display the current date and time in cell **A71**. **Save** 🖫 your workbook.

> **More Knowledge | NOW Function Recalculates Each Time a Workbook Opens**
>
> The NOW function updates each time the workbook is opened. With the workbook open, you can force the NOW function to update by pressing Command ⌘ + Shift + =, for example, to update the time. Alternatively, on the Formulas tab, in the Calculation group, click Recalculate Sheet for the active sheet.

Activity 2.11 | Freezing and Unfreezing Panes

In a large worksheet, if you scroll to display the bottom of the worksheet or scroll beyond the right column, you will no longer see the top rows or first column of your worksheet where identifying information about the data is usually placed. You will find it easier to work with your data if you can always view the identifying row or column titles.

The *Freeze Panes* command enables you to select one or more rows or columns and then freeze (lock) them into place. The locked rows and columns become separate panes. A *pane* is a portion of a worksheet window bounded by and separated from other portions by vertical or horizontal bars.

1 Press Command ⌘ + fn + ← to make cell **A1** the active cell. Scroll until **row 40** displays at the top of your Excel window, and notice that all of the identifying information in the column titles is out of view.

> **Another Way**
>
> To freeze panes, on the Window menu, click Freeze Panes.

2 Press Command ⌘ + fn + ← again, and then from the **row heading area**, select **row 14**. On the **Layout tab**, in the **Window group**, click the **Freeze Panes** button 🔲, and then click **Freeze Panes**. Click any cell to deselect the row, and then notice that a line displays along the upper border of **row 14**.

> By selecting row 14, the rows above—rows 1–13—are frozen in place and will not move as you scroll down.

3 Watch the row numbers below **row 13**, and then scroll to bring **row 40** into view again. Notice that **rows 1:13** are frozen in place. Compare your screen with Figure 2.21.

> The remaining rows of data continue to scroll. Use this feature when you have long or wide worksheets.

Figure 2.21

Freeze Panes button in Windows group

Freeze Panes command freezes rows 1–13

Row 40 in view

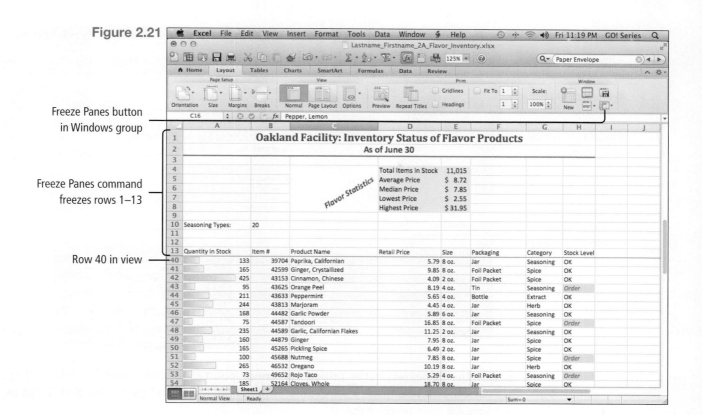

Quantity in Stock	Item #		Product Name	Retail Price	Size	Packaging	Category	Stock Level
40	133	39704	Paprika, Californian	5.79	8 oz.	Jar	Seasoning	OK
41	165	42599	Ginger, Crystallized	9.85	8 oz.	Foil Packet	Spice	OK
42	425	43153	Cinnamon, Chinese	4.09	2 oz.	Foil Packet	Spice	OK
43	95	43625	Orange Peel	8.19	4 oz.	Tin	Seasoning	Order
44	211	43633	Peppermint	5.65	8 oz.	Bottle	Extract	OK
45	244	43813	Marjoram	4.45	4 oz.	Jar	Herb	OK
46	168	44482	Garlic Powder	5.89	6 oz.	Jar	Seasoning	OK
47	75	44587	Tandoori	16.85	8 oz.	Foil Packet	Spice	Order
48	235	44589	Garlic, Californian Flakes	11.25	2 oz.	Jar	Seasoning	OK
49	160	44879	Ginger	7.95	8 oz.	Jar	Spice	OK
50	165	45265	Pickling Spice	6.49	2 oz.	Jar	Spice	OK
51	100	45688	Nutmeg	7.85	8 oz.	Jar	Spice	Order
52	265	46532	Oregano	10.19	8 oz.	Jar	Herb	OK
53	73	49652	Rojo Taco	5.29	4 oz.	Foil Packet	Seasoning	Order
54	185	52164	Cloves, Whole	18.70	8 oz.	Jar	Spice	OK

Another Way

To unfreeze panes, on the Window menu, click Unfreeze Panes.

4 In the **Window group**, click the **Freeze Panes** button, and then click **Unfreeze** to unlock all rows and columns. **Save** your workbook.

> **More Knowledge | Freeze Columns or Freeze Both Rows and Columns**
>
> You can freeze columns that you want to remain in view on the left. Select the column to the right of the column(s) that you want to remain in view while scrolling to the right, and then click the Freeze Panes command. You can also use the command to freeze both rows and columns; click a *cell* to freeze the rows *above* the cell and the columns to the *left* of the cell.

Objective 5 | Create, Sort, and Filter an Excel Table

To analyze a group of related data, you can convert a range of cells to an *Excel table*. An Excel table is a series of rows and columns that contains related data that is managed independently from the data in other rows and columns in the worksheet.

Activity 2.12 | Creating an Excel Table

1 Be sure that you have applied the Unfreeze command—no rows on your worksheet are locked. Then, click any cell in the data below row 13.

Another Way

Select the range of cells that make up the table, including the header row, and then click the New button.

2 On the **Tables tab**, in the **Table Options group**, click the **New arrow**, and then click **Insert Table with Headers**. Compare your screen with Figure 2.22.

The column titles in row 13 form the table headers. Excel selects all of the row and columns for the table, and formats the Excel table with alternating colors—banded rows. Sorting and filtering arrows display in the table's header row.

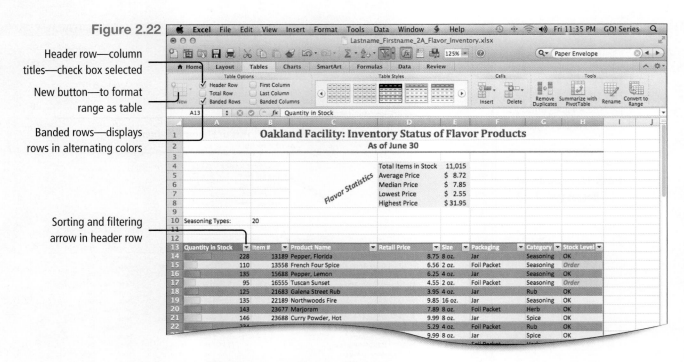

Figure 2.22

Header row—column titles—check box selected

New button—to format range as table

Banded rows—displays rows in alternating colors

Sorting and filtering arrow in header row

3 On the **Tables tab**, in the **Table Styles group**, point to the bottom of the styles gallery, click the **More** button ▾, and then under **Light**, locate and click **Table Style Light 16**. **Save** 🖫 your workbook.

Activity 2.13 | Sorting and Filtering an Excel Table

You can *sort* tables—arrange all the data in a specific order—in ascending or descending order. You can *filter* tables—display only a portion of the data based on matching a specific value—to show only the data that meets the criteria that you specify.

1 In the header row of the table, click the **Retail Price arrow**, and then in the **Sort and Filter** task pane, under **Sort**, click **Ascending**. If necessary, point to the title bar of the task pane, and drag the task pane up slightly so that the top of the table header row displays. In the header row, next to the **Retail Price arrow**, notice the small **up arrow** indicating an ascending (smallest to largest) sort. Compare your screen with Figure 2.23.

The rows in the table are sorted from the lowest retail price to highest retail price.

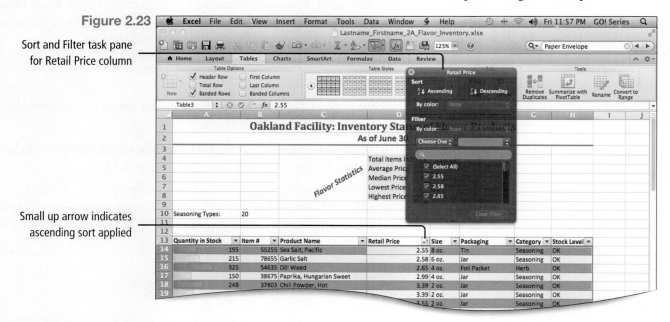

Figure 2.23

Sort and Filter task pane for Retail Price column

Small up arrow indicates ascending sort applied

2 In the table header row, click the **Category arrow**. In the **Sort and Filter** task pane, under **Sort**, click **Ascending**. In the table header row, next to the **Category arrow**, notice the small **up arrow** indicating an ascending (A to Z) sort.

> The rows in the table are sorted alphabetically by Category. The sort is removed from the Retail Price column.

3 In the **Sort and Filter** task pane, click **Descending**.

> The rows in the table are sorted in reverse alphabetic order by Category name, and the small arrow points downward, indicating a descending (Z to A) sort.

4 In the **Sort and Filter** task pane, under **Filter**, click the **(Select All)** check box to clear all of the check boxes. Click to select only the **Extract** check box, drag the task pane up slightly so that the top of the table header row displays, and then compare your screen with Figure 2.24.

> Only the rows containing *Extract* in the Category column display—the remaining rows are hidden from view. A small funnel—the filter icon—indicates that a filter is applied to the data in the table. Additionally, the row numbers display in blue to indicate that some rows are hidden from view. A filter hides entire rows in the worksheet.

Figure 2.24

Sort and Filter task pane
for Category column

(*Select All*) check box
cleared

Extract check box
selected

Funnel indicates
filter applied

Small down arrow
indicates descending sort

Blue row numbers indicate
that some rows are hidden

Only products in *Extract*
category display

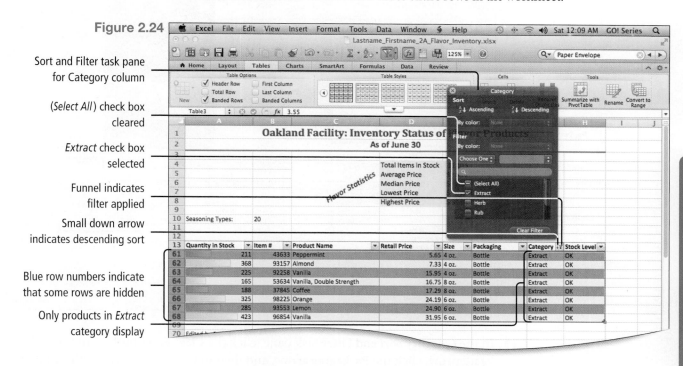

Excel | Chapter 2

5 Click any cell in the table so that the task pane closes and the table is selected. On the **Tables tab**, in the **Table Options group**, select the **Total Row** check box.

> *Total* displays in cell A69. In cell H69, the number *8* indicates that eight rows currently display.

6 Click cell **A69**, click the **arrows** that display to the right of cell **A69**, and then in the list, click **Sum**.

> Excel sums only the visible rows in Column A, and indicates that *2190* products in the Extract category are in stock. In this manner, you can use an Excel table to quickly find information about a group of data.

7 Click cell **A11**, type **Extract Types:** and press ⌧Tab. In cell **B11**, type **8 (2,190 total items in stock)** and then press ⌧Return.

8   In the table header row, click the **Category arrow**—displays small down arrow and filter—and then in the task pane, click the **Clear Filter** button.

All the rows in the table redisplay. The descending sort on Category remains in effect.

9   Click the **Packaging arrow**, click the **(Select All)** check box to clear all the check boxes, and then click to select the **Foil Packet** check box.

10 Click the **Category arrow**, click the **(Select All)** check box to clear all the check boxes, and then click the **Herb** check box. If necessary, drag the task pane up slightly so that the top of the table header row displays, and then compare your screen with Figure 2.25.

By applying multiple filters, Laura can quickly determine that seven items in the Herb category are packaged in foil packets with a total of 1,346 such items in stock.

Figure 2.25

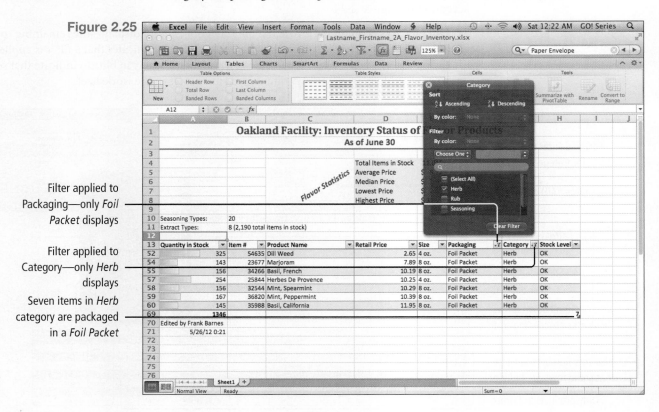

Filter applied to Packaging—only *Foil Packet* displays

Filter applied to Category—only *Herb* displays

Seven items in *Herb* category are packaged in a *Foil Packet*

11 In the **Category Sort and Filter** task pane, click the **Clear Filter** button. In the table header row, click the **Packaging arrow**, and then in the task pane, click **Clear Filter**.

12 In the table header row, click the **Item # arrow**, and then in the **Sort and Filter** task pane, click **Ascending**, which will apply an ascending sort to the data using the *Item#* column. Click anywhere in the table to close the task pane, and then **Save** 🖫 your workbook.

Activity 2.14 │ Converting a Table to a Range of Data

When you are finished answering questions about the data in a table by sorting, filtering, and totaling, you can convert the table into a normal range. Doing so is useful if you want to use the feature only to apply an attractive Table Style to a range of cells. For example, you can insert a table, apply a Table Style, and then convert the table to a normal range of data but keep the formatting.

Another Way

With any table cell
selected, press [Control]
and click, and from the
shortcut menu click
Convert to Range.

1 With the table active—you clicked in a cell in the table—on the **Tables tab**, in the **Table Options group**, click the **Total Row** check box to clear the check mark and remove the Total row from the table.

2 On the **Tables tab**, in the **Tools group**, click the **Convert to Range** button. In the message box, click **Yes**. **Save** 🔲 your workbook, and then compare your screen with Figure 2.26.

Figure 2.26

Convert to Range button ——

Table converted to normal range, table style formatting remains

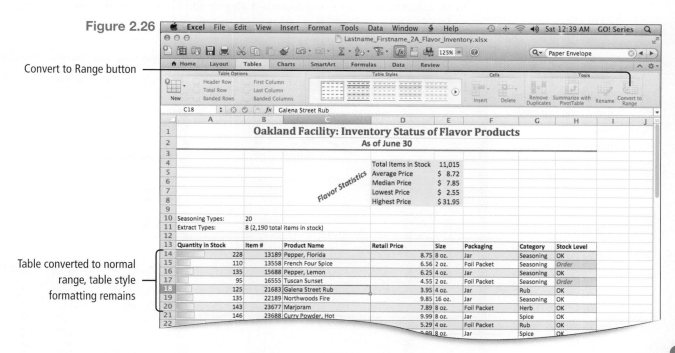

Objective 6 | Format and Print a Large Worksheet

A worksheet might be too wide, too long—or both—to print on a single page. Use Excel's *Print Titles* and *Scale to Fit* commands to create pages that are attractive and easy to read.

The Print Titles command enables you to specify rows and columns to repeat on each printed page. Scale to Fit commands enable you to stretch or shrink the width, height, or both, of printed output to fit a maximum number of pages.

Activity 2.15 | Printing Titles and Scaling to Fit

1 Press [Command ⌘] + [fn] + [←] to display the top of your worksheet. Select the range **A13:H13**. On the **Home tab**, in the **Format group**, click the **Styles** button. In the **Cell Styles** gallery, under **Titles and Headings**, click **Heading 4**. In the **Alignment group**, click the **Center Text** button 🖿.

2 On the **View** menu, click **Header and Footer**. In the **Page Setup** dialog box, click **Customize Footer**. With the insertion point positioned in the **Left section** box, click the **Insert File Name** button 🖺, and then click **OK**. In the **Page Setup** dialog box, click **OK**.

3 On the **Home tab**, in the **Themes group**, click the **Themes** button, and then click **Perspective**.

4 On the **Layout tab**, in the **Page Setup group**, click the **Margins** button, and then click **Custom Margins**. In the **Page Setup** dialog box, under **Center on page**, select the **Horizontally** check box, and then click **OK**.

5 In the **Page Setup group**, click **Orientation**, and then click **Landscape**. In the **Print group**, click the **Preview** button. In the **Preview** window, scroll through the document to view how the document will print. Scroll to display the first page, and then compare your screen with Figure 2.27.

> As currently formatted, the worksheet will print on four pages, and the columns will span multiple pages. Additionally, after Page 1, no column titles are visible to identify the data in the columns. The last two columns—*Category* and *Stock Level*—display on pages 3 and 4.

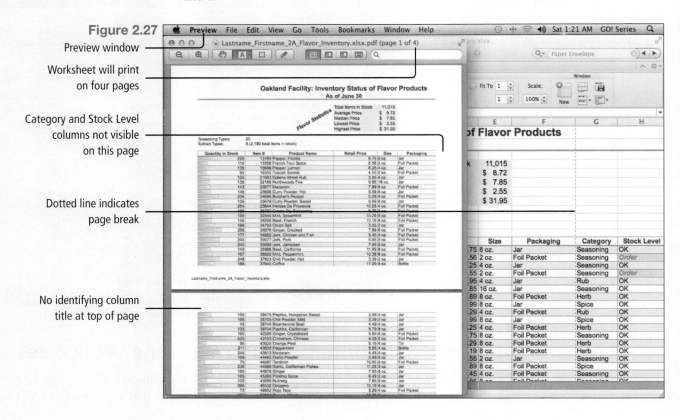

Figure 2.27
Preview window
Worksheet will print on four pages
Category and Stock Level columns not visible on this page
Dotted line indicates page break
No identifying column title at top of page

6 **Close** the **Preview**, and then on the **Preview** menu, click **Quit Preview**. On the **Layout tab**, in the **View** group, click the **Page Layout** button. On the **Layout tab**, in the **Print group**, click the **Repeat Titles** button. In the **Page Setup** dialog box, with the **Sheet tab** active, under **Print titles**, click in the **Rows to repeat at top** box, and then at the right, click the **Collapse Dialog** button.

7 From the **row heading area**, select **row 13**, and then click the **Expand Dialog** button. In the **Page Setup** dialog box, click **OK** to print the column titles in row 13 at the top of every page.

8 Scroll to display the last columns and the rows at the bottom of the worksheet, and notice that the column headings display above the data on every page.

9 On the **Layout tab**, in the **Print group**, click to select the **Fit To** check box, and notice that the worksheet shrinks to fit all on one page. Under **Fit To**, point to the bottom box to display the Screen Tip *Restrict the height to a maximum number of printed pages*. Double-click in this box, type **0**, and then press Return. Scroll to display the bottom of **Page 1** and the top of **Page 2**, and then compare your screen with Figure 2.28.

> All of the columns display on each page, and the rows span two pages. Changing the Fit To Height setting to 0 informs Excel to not shrink the rows to fit on one page.

Figure 2.28

Setting determines number of pages for columns

Worksheet displayed in Page Layout view

Scaling selected by selecting Fit To check box

Setting determines number of pages for rows—blank because you typed 0

Last two columns display on page

Column titles display at top of page 2

Two pages will print

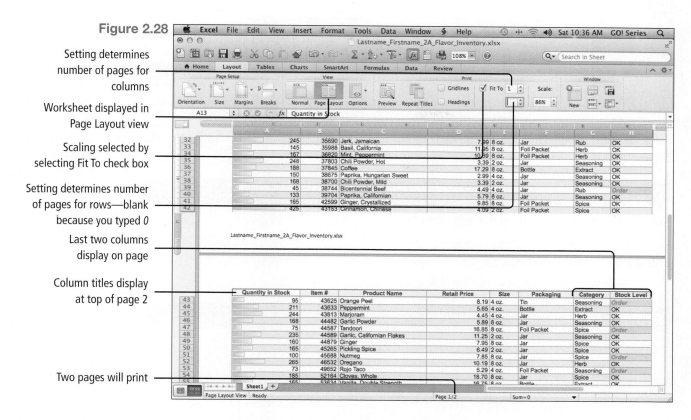

10 On the **Layout tab**, in the **View group**, click the **Normal** button. On the **File** menu, click the **Properties**. In the **Subject** box, type your course name and section number. In the **Author** box, replace the existing text with your firstname and lastname. In the **Keywords** box, type **inventory, Oakland** and then click **OK**.

11 **Save** 💾 your workbook, and then **Print** or submit it electronically as directed.

12 If required by your instructor, print or create an electronic version of your worksheet with formulas displayed by using the instructions in Activity 1.15, and then **Close** your workbook without saving so that you do not save the changes you made to print formulas. On the **Excel** menu, click **Quit Excel**.

More Knowledge | Scaling for Data That Is Slightly Larger Than the Printed Page

If your data is just a little too large to fit on a printed page, you can scale the worksheet to make it fit. Scaling reduces both the width and height of the printed data to a percentage of its original size or by the number of pages that you specify. To adjust the printed output to a percentage of its actual size, for example to 80%, on the Layout tab, in the Print group, click the Scale arrows to select a percentage.

End **You have completed Project 2A** _____

Project 2B Weekly Sales Summary

Project Activities

In Activities 2.16 through 2.26, you will edit an existing workbook for Laura Morales. The workbook summarizes the online and in-store sales of products during a one-week period in July. The worksheets of your completed workbook will look similar to Figure 2.29.

Project Files

For Project 2B, you will need the following file:

e02B_Weekly_Sales

You will save your workbook as:

Lastname_Firstname_2B_Weekly_Sales

Project Results

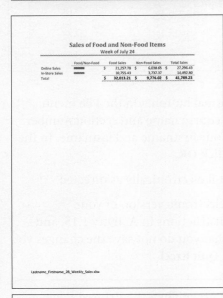

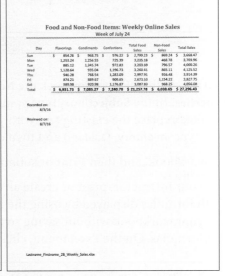

Figure 2.29
Project 2B Weekly Sales

Objective 7 | Navigate a Workbook and Rename Worksheets

Use multiple worksheets in a workbook to organize data in a logical arrangement. When you have more than one worksheet in a workbook, you can **navigate** (move) among worksheets by clicking the **sheet tabs**. Sheet tabs identify each worksheet in a workbook and are located along the lower left edge of the workbook window. When you have more worksheets in the workbook than can be displayed in the sheet tab area, use the four sheet tab scrolling buttons to move sheet tabs into and out of view.

Activity 2.16 | Navigating Among Worksheets, Renaming Worksheets, and Changing the Tab Color of Worksheets

Excel names the first worksheet in a workbook *Sheet1* and each additional worksheet in order—*Sheet2*, *Sheet3*, and so on. Most Excel users rename the worksheets with meaningful names. In this activity, you will navigate among worksheets, rename worksheets, and change the tab color of sheet tabs.

> **Another Way**
>
> Press Command ⌘ + O to display the Open dialog box. Press Shift + Command ⌘ + S to display the Save As dialog box.

1 Open **Excel**. On the **File** menu, click **Open**, and then from your student files, **Open e02B_Weekly_Sales**. If necessary, increase the size of the Excel window to fill the screen by clicking the Zoom button 🔘 or by dragging the lower right corner of the Excel window. If necessary, on the Standard toolbar, click the Zoom arrow 100% ▾, and then click 125%.

2 On the **File** menu, click **Save As**. In the **Save As** dialog box, navigate to your **Excel Chapter 2** folder, and then using your own name, **Save** the workbook as **Lastname_Firstname_2B_Weekly_Sales**

> In the displayed workbook, there are two worksheets into which some data has already been entered. For example, on the first worksheet—Sheet1—the days of the week and sales data for the one-week period display.

3 Along the bottom of the Excel window, point to and then click the **Sheet2 tab**.

> The second worksheet in the workbook displays and becomes the active worksheet.

4 In cell **A1**, notice the text *In-Store*—this worksheet contains data for in-store sales.

5 Click the **Sheet1 tab**. Then, point to the **Sheet1 tab**, and double-click to select the sheet tab name. Type **Online Sales** and press Return.

> The first worksheet becomes the active worksheet, and the sheet tab displays *Online Sales*.

6 Point to the **Sheet2 tab**, press Control and click, and then from the shortcut menu, click **Rename**. Type **In-Store Sales** and press Return. Compare your screen with Figure 2.30.

> You can use either of these methods to rename a sheet tab.

Figure 2.30

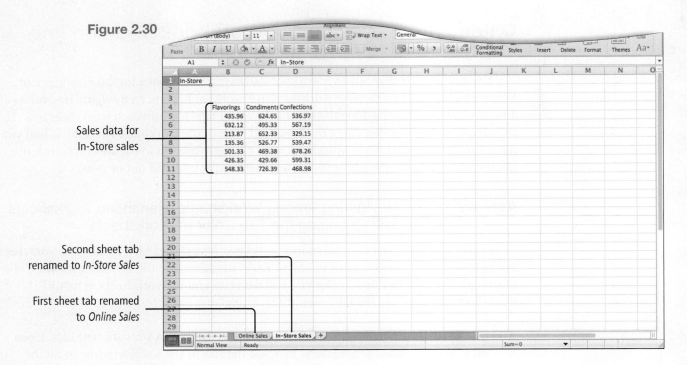

Sales data for In-Store sales

Second sheet tab renamed to *In-Store Sales*

First sheet tab renamed to *Online Sales*

Another Way

On the Format menu, point to Sheet, and then click Tab Color.

7 Point to the **In-Store Sales sheet tab** and press [Control] and click. On the shortcut menu, click **Tab Color**. In the **Tab Color** window, under **Theme Colors**, in the first row, click the last color—**Accent 6**.

8 Click the **Online Sales sheet tab**. In the **Tab Color** window, under **Theme Colors**, in the first row, click the next to the last color—**Accent 5**. **Save** 💾 your workbook, and then compare your screen with Figure 2.31.

Figure 2.31

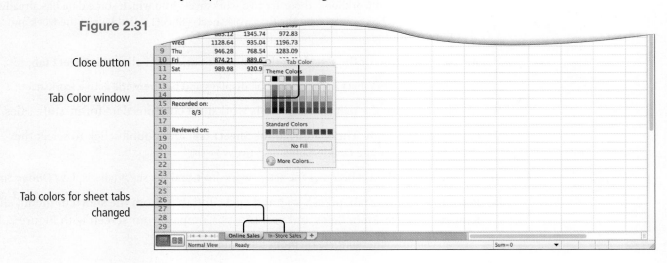

Close button

Tab Color window

Tab colors for sheet tabs changed

9 In the **Tab Color** window, click the **Close** 🔘 button.

Objective 8 | Enter Dates, Clear Contents, and Clear Formats

Dates represent a type of value that you can enter in a cell. When you enter a date, Excel assigns a serial value—a number—to the date. This makes it possible to treat dates like other numbers. For example, if two cells contain dates, you can find the number of days between the two dates by subtracting the older date from the more recent date.

Activity 2.17 | Entering and Formatting Dates

In this activity, you will examine the various ways that Excel can format dates in a cell. Date values entered in any of the following formats will be recognized by Excel as a date:

Format	Example
m/d/yy	7/4/2016
d-mmm	4-Jul
d-mmm-yy	4-Jul-16
mmm-yy	Jul-16

On your keyboard, ⊟ (the hyphen key) and ⊘ (the forward slash key) function identically in any of these formats and can be used interchangeably. You can abbreviate the month name to three characters or spell it out. You can enter the year as two digits, four digits, or even leave it off. When left off, the current year is assumed but does not display in the cell.

A two-digit year value of 30 through 99 is interpreted by the Mac operating system as the four-digit years of 1930 through 1999. All other two-digit year values are assumed to be in the 21st century. If you always type year values as four digits, even though only two digits may display in the cell, you can be sure that Excel interprets the year value as you intended. Examples are shown in Figure 2.32.

How Excel Interprets Dates

Date Typed As:	Completed by Excel As:
7/4/16	7/4/2016
7/4/98	7/4/1998
7/4	4-Jul (current year assumed)
7-4	4-Jul (current year assumed)
July 4	4-Jul (current year assumed)
Jul 4	4-Jul (current year assumed)
Jul/4	4-Jul (current year assumed)
Jul-4	4-Jul (current year assumed)
July 4, 2016	4-Jul-16
July 4, 1998	4-Jul-98
July 2016	Jul-16 (first day of month assumed)
July 1998	Jul-98 (first day of month assumed)

Figure 2.32

1 On the **Online Sales** sheet, click cell **A16** and notice that the cell indicates *8/3* (August 3). In the **Formula Bar**, notice that the full date of August 3, 2016 displays in the format *8/3/2016*.

Another Way

Press Command ⌘ + 1 to display the Format Cells dialog box.

2 With cell **A16** selected, on the **Format** menu, click **Cells** to display the **Format Cells** dialog box with the **Number tab** active.

Under Category, *Date* is selected, and under Type, *3/14* is selected. Cell A16 uses this format type; that is, only the month and day display in the cell.

3 In the **Format Cells** dialog box, under **Type**, click several other date types and watch the **Sample** area to see how applying the selected date format would format your cell. When you are finished, click the **3/14/01** type, and then compare your screen with Figure 2.33.

Figure 2.33

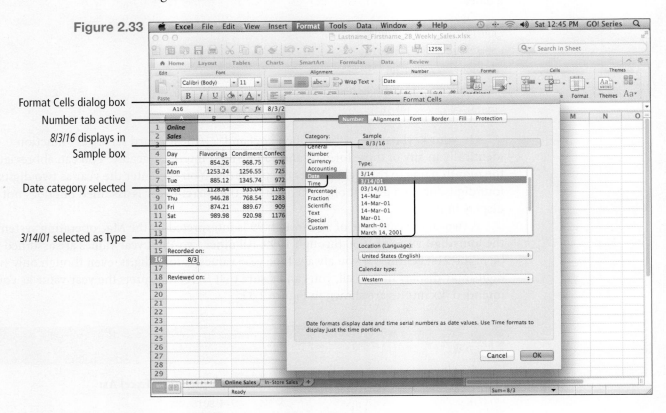

Format Cells dialog box
Number tab active
8/3/16 displays in Sample box
Date category selected
3/14/01 selected as Type

4 At the bottom of the **Format Cells** dialog box, click **OK**. Click cell **A19**, type **8-7-16** and then press Return.

Cell A19 has no special date formatting applied, and thus displays in the default date format *8/7/16*.

> **Alert! | The Date Does Not Display as 8/7/16**
>
> Preference settings in your Mac operating system determine the default format for dates. If your result is different, it is likely that the formatting of the default date was adjusted on the computer at which you are working.

5 Click cell **A19** again. Hold down Control and press ; (semicolon) on your keyboard. Press Return to confirm the entry.

Excel enters the current date, obtained from your computer's internal calendar, in the selected cell using the default date format. Control + ; is a quick method to enter the current date.

6 Click cell **A19** again, type **8/7/16** and then press Return. **Save** 💾 your workbook.

Because the year *16* is less than 30, Excel assumes a 21st century date and changes *16* to *2016* in the formula bar to complete the four-digit year. Typing *98* would result in *1998*. For two-digit years that you type that are between 30 and 99, Excel assumes a 20th century date.

Activity 2.18 | Clearing Cell Contents and Formats

A cell has *contents*—a value or a formula—and a cell may also have one or more *formats* applied, for example, bold and italic font styles, fill color, font color, and so on. You can choose to clear—delete—the contents of a cell, the formatting of a cell, or both.

Clearing the contents of a cell deletes the value or formula typed there, but it does *not* clear formatting applied to a cell. In this activity, you will clear the contents of a cell and then clear the formatting of a cell that contains a date to see its underlying content.

1 In the **Online Sales** worksheet, click cell **A1**. On the **Edit** menu, point to **Clear**, and then click **Contents**. Notice that the text is cleared, but the orange formatting remains.

2 Click cell **A2**, and then press Delete.

> You can use either of these two methods to delete the *contents* of a cell. Deleting the contents does not, however, delete the formatting of the cell; you can see that the orange fill color format applied to the two cells still displays.

3 In cell **A1**, type **Online Sales** and then on the formula bar, click the **Enter** button  so that cell **A1** remains the active cell.

> In addition to the orange fill color, the bold italic text formatting remains with the cell.

4 On the **Edit** menu, point to **Clear**, and then click **Formats**.

> Clearing the formats deletes formatting from the cell—the orange fill color and the bold and italic font styles—but does not delete the cell's contents.

5 Use the same technique to clear the orange fill color from cell **A2**. Click cell **A16**, press Command ⌘ + Y to repeat the last command—Clear Formats. In the **Number group**, in the **Number Format** box, notice that *General* displays.

> Recall that you can quickly repeat the last command by using the keyboard shortcut Command ⌘ + Y. The Number Format box in the Number group indicates the current Number Format of the selected cell. Clearing the date formatting from the cell displays the date's serial number. The date, August 3, 2016, is stored as a serial number that indicates the number of days since January 1, 1900. This date is the 42,585th day since the reference date of January 1, 1900.

Another Way

Press Command ⌘ + Z to Undo the last command.

6 On the Standard toolbar, click the **Undo** button  to restore the date format. **Save** your workbook, and then compare your screen with Figure 2.34.

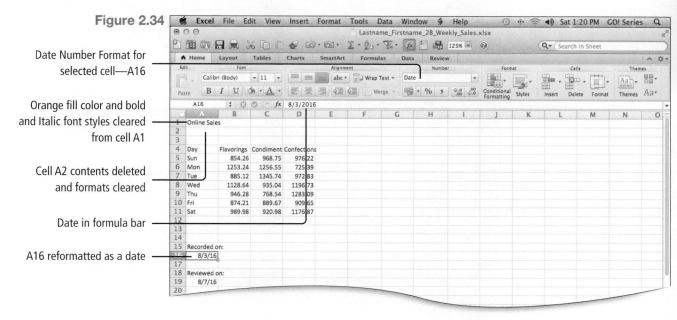

Figure 2.34

Date Number Format for selected cell—A16

Orange fill color and bold and Italic font styles cleared from cell A1

Cell A2 contents deleted and formats cleared

Date in formula bar

A16 reformatted as a date

Excel | Chapter 2

Objective 9 | Copy and Paste Cells

Data in cells can be copied to other cells in the same worksheet, to other sheets in the same workbook, or to sheets in another workbook. The action of placing cell contents that have been copied or moved to the Clipboard into another location is called *paste*.

Activity 2.19 | Copying and Pasting Cells

Recall that the Clipboard is a temporary storage area maintained by your Mac operating system. When you select one or more cells, and then perform the Copy command or the Cut command, the selected data is placed on the Clipboard. From the Clipboard storage area, the data is available for pasting into other cells, other worksheets, other workbooks, and even into other Office programs.

Another Way

To copy, press
⌘Command ⌘ + C; or
press Control and click,
and then from the
shortcut menu, click
Copy.

1 With the **Online Sales** worksheet active, select the range **A4:A19**.

A range of cells identical to this one is required for the *In-Store Sales* worksheet.

2 On the Standard toolbar, click the **Copy** button 🗐 to place a copy of the cells on the Clipboard. Notice that the copied cells display a moving border.

Another Way

To paste, press
⌘Command ⌘ + V; or on
the Home tab, in the
Edit group, click the
Paste button; or press
Control and click, and
then from the shortcut
menu, click Paste.

3 At the bottom of the workbook window, click the **In-Store Sales sheet tab** to make it the active worksheet. Click cell **A4**, and then on the Standard toolbar, click the **Paste** button 🗐. Below the pasted range, click the **Paste Options** button 📋, and then compare your screen with Figure 2.35.

Similar to pasting in Word, the Paste Options button gives you more control over how the data displays once it is copied and pasted. The default paste option is Use Destination Theme—the theme applied to the cells and worksheet in which the cells are pasted. When pasting a range of cells, you need only select the cell in the upper left corner of the *paste area*—the target destination for the data that has been cut or copied using the Clipboard.

Figure 2.35

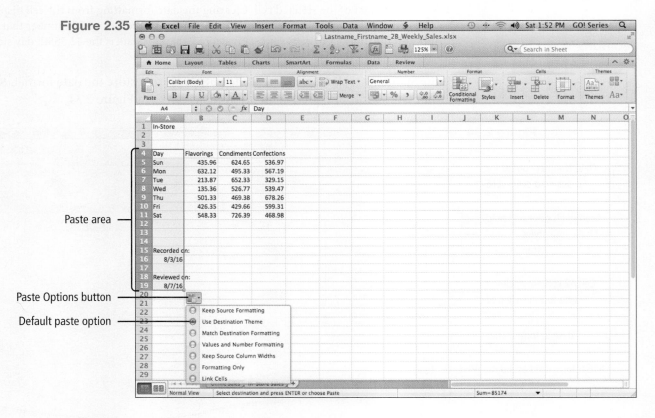

Paste area

Paste Options button

Default paste option

4 Be sure that **Use Destination Theme** is selected, and then click anywhere in the worksheet to close the list. Notice, on the status bar, the message *Select destination and press ENTER or choose Paste*, which indicates that your selected range remains available on the Clipboard.

5 Display the **Online Sales** worksheet. Press Esc to cancel the moving border, and then **Save** 🖫 your workbook.

> The status bar no longer displays the message.

Note | Pressing Enter to Complete a Paste Action

If you want to paste the same text more than one time, click the Paste button so that the copied text remains available on the Clipboard. Otherwise, you can press Return to complete the Paste command.

Objective 10 | Edit and Format Multiple Worksheets at the Same Time

You can enter or edit data on several worksheets at the same time by selecting and grouping multiple worksheets. Data that you enter or edit on the active sheet is reflected in all selected sheets.

Activity 2.20 | Grouping Worksheets for Editing

In this activity, you will group the two worksheets, and then format both worksheets at the same time.

1 With the **Online Sales** sheet active, press Command ⌘ + fn + ← to make cell **A1** the active cell. Point to the **Online Sales sheet tab**, press Control and click, and then from the shortcut menu, click **Select All Sheets**.

2 At the top of your screen, notice that *[Group]* displays in the title bar. Compare your screen with Figure 2.36.

> Both worksheets are selected, as indicated by *[Group]* in the title bar. Data that you enter or edit on the active sheet will also be entered or edited in the same manner on all of the selected sheets in the same cells.

Figure 2.36

[Group] indicates that
sheets have been selected

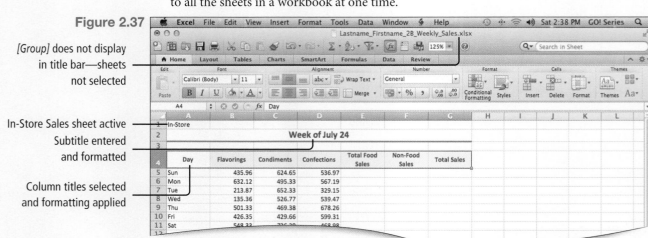

3 Select **columns A:G**, and then by dragging any column border in the selection, change the **Width** to **11.00 (0.99 inches)**.

4 Click cell **A2**, type **Week of July 24** and then on the formula bar, click the **Enter** button to keep cell **A2** as the active cell. Select the range **A2:G2**, and then on **Home tab**, in the **Alignment group**, click the **Merge** button to center the text across the range **A2:G2**. In the **Format group**, click the **Styles** button, and then apply the **Heading 1** cell style.

5 Click cell **E4**, type **Total Food Sales** and then press Tab. In cell **F4**, type **Non-Food Sales** and then press Tab. In cell **G4**, type **Total Sales** and then press Return.

6 Select the range **A4:G4**, and then apply the **Heading 3** cell style. In the **Alignment group**, click the **Center Text** button, and then click the **Align Text Middle** button. Click the **Wrap Text** button, and then click **Wrap Text**. **Save** your workbook.

Another Way

On any sheet tab, press Control and click, and then click Ungroup Sheets.

7 Display the **In-Store Sales** worksheet to cancel the grouping, and then compare your screen with Figure 2.37.

As soon as you select a single sheet, the grouping of the sheets is canceled and *[Group]* no longer displays in the title bar. Because the sheets were grouped, the same new text and formatting were applied to both sheets. In this manner, you can make the same changes to all the sheets in a workbook at one time.

Figure 2.37

[Group] does not display
in title bar—sheets
not selected

In-Store Sales sheet active
Subtitle entered
and formatted

Column titles selected
and formatting applied

Activity 2.21 | Formatting and Constructing Formulas on Grouped Worksheets

Recall that formulas are equations that perform calculations on values in your worksheet and that a formula starts with an equal sign (=). Operators are the symbols with which you specify the type of calculation that you want to perform on the elements of a formula. In this activity, you will enter sales figures for Non-Food items from both Online and In-Store sales, and then calculate the total sales.

1 Display the **Online Sales** worksheet. Verify that the sheets are not grouped—*[Group]* does *not* display in the title bar.

2 Click cell **A1**, type **Food and Non-Food Items: Weekly Online Sales** and then on the formula bar, click the **Enter** button 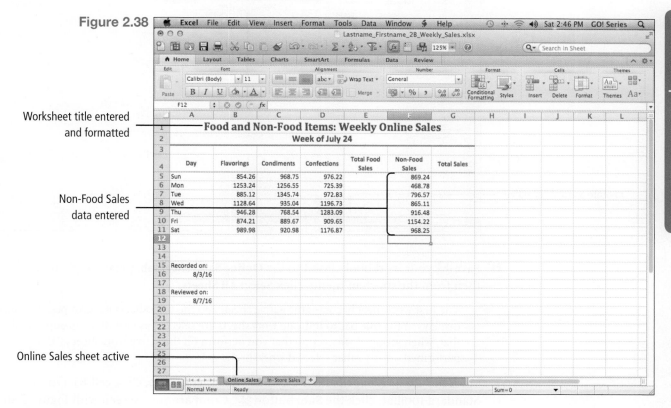 to keep cell **A1** as the active cell. **Merge** the text across the range **A1:G1**, and then apply the **Title** cell style.

3 In the column titled *Non-Food Sales*, click cell **F5**, in the range **F5:F11**, type the following data for Non-Food Sales, and then compare your screen with Figure 2.38.

	Non-Food Sales
Sun	869.24
Mon	468.78
Tue	796.57
Wed	865.11
Thu	916.48
Fri	1154.22
Sat	968.25

Figure 2.38

Worksheet title entered and formatted

Non-Food Sales data entered

Online Sales sheet active

Excel | Chapter 2

4 Display the **In-Store Sales** sheet. In cell **A1**, replace *In-Store* by typing **Food and Non-Food Items: Weekly In-Store Sales** and then on the formula bar, click the **Enter** button to keep cell **A1** as the active cell. **Merge** the text across the range **A1:G1**, and then apply the **Title** cell style.

5 In the column titled *Non-Food Sales*, click cell **F5**. In the range **F5:F11**, type the following data for Non-Food Sales, and then compare your screen with Figure 2.39.

Non-Food Sales	
Sun	569.34
Mon	426.44
Tue	636.57
Wed	721.69
Thu	359.12
Fri	587.99
Sat	436.22

Figure 2.39

Worksheet title entered and formatted

Non-Food Sales data entered

In-Store Sales sheet active

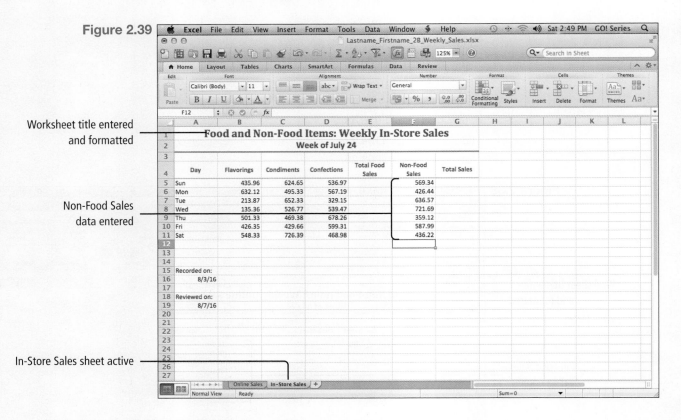

6 **Save** your workbook. Point to the **Online Sales sheet tab**, press Control and click, and then from the shortcut menu, click **Select All Sheets**.

The first worksheet becomes the active sheet, and the worksheets are grouped. *[Group]* displays in the title bar to indicate worksheets are selected as part of the group. Recall that, when grouped, any action that you perform on the active worksheet is *also* performed on any other selected worksheets.

7 With the sheets *grouped* and the **Online Sales** sheet active, click cell **E5**. On the Standard toolbar, click the **Sum** button Σ. Compare your screen with Figure 2.40.

Recall that when you enter the SUM function, Excel looks first above and then left for a proposed range of cells to sum.

Figure 2.40

[Group] indicates worksheets are selected or grouped together

SUM function in formula bar

Proposed range of cells to sum surrounded by moving border

SUM function in cell E5

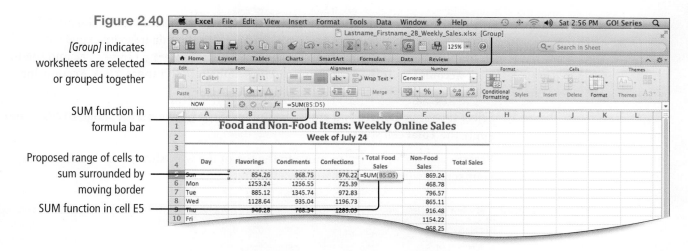

8 Press Return to display *Total Food Sales for Sunday*, which is *2799.23*.

9 Click cell **E5**, and then drag the fill handle down to copy the formula through cell **E11**.

10 Click cell **G5**, type **=** and then click cell **E5**. Type **+** and then click cell **F5**. Compare your screen with Figure 2.41.

> Using the point-and-click technique to construct this formula is only one of several techniques you can use. Alternatively, you can use any other method to enter the SUM function to add the values in these two cells.

Figure 2.41

Formula in cell G5

11 Press Return to display the result *3668.47*, and then copy the formula down through cell **G11**.

12 In cell **A12**, type **Total** and then press Return. Select the range **B5:G12**, which is all of the sales data and the empty cells at the bottom of each column of sales data.

13 With the range **B5:G12** selected, press Command ⌘ + Shift + T to enter the **SUM** function in each empty cell.

> Selecting a range in this manner will place the Sum function in the empty cells at the bottom of each column. Using the keyboard shortcut keys is an alternative way to enter the Sum function in a cell or cells.

14 Select the range **A5:A12**, and then apply the **Heading 4** cell style.

Excel | Chapter 2

15 To apply financial formatting to the worksheets, select the range **B5:G5**, hold down `Command ⌘`, and then select the range **B12:G12**. With the nonadjacent ranges selected, In the **Number group**, click the **Number Format arrow** `General ▾`, and then click **Accounting**. If the formatting did not apply to both ranges, click Accounting one more time.

16 Select the range **B6:G11** and apply the **Comma Style** `,`. Select the range **B12:G12** and apply the **Total** cell style.

17 Press `Command ⌘` + `fn` + `←` to move to the top of the worksheet, and then compare your screen with Figure 2.42.

Figure 2.42

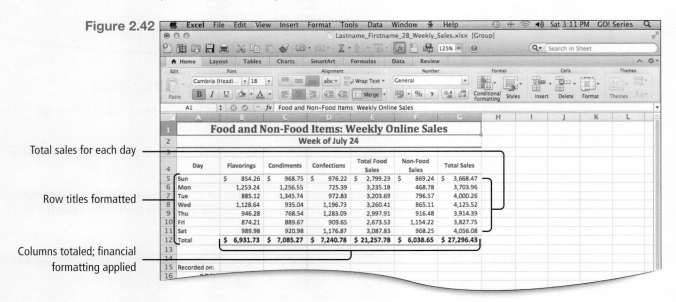

Total sales for each day

Row titles formatted

Columns totaled; financial formatting applied

18 Click the **In-Store Sales sheet tab** to cancel the grouping and display the second worksheet. **Save** 🖫 your workbook, and then compare your screen with Figure 2.43.

With your worksheets grouped, the calculations on the first worksheet were also performed on the second worksheet, and the formatting was applied.

Figure 2.43

Title bar does not display *[Group]*—sheets not selected

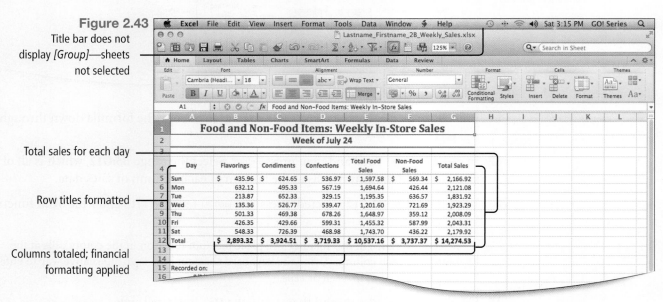

Total sales for each day

Row titles formatted

Columns totaled; financial formatting applied

Objective 11 | Create a Summary Sheet with Column Sparklines

A **summary sheet** is a worksheet where totals from other worksheets are displayed and summarized. Recall that sparklines are tiny charts within a single cell that show a data trend.

Activity 2.22 | Constructing Formulas that Refer to Cells in Another Worksheet

In this activity, you will insert a new worksheet in which you will place the totals from the Online Sales worksheet and the In-Store Sales worksheet. You will construct formulas in the Summary worksheet to display the total sales for both online sales and in-store sales that will update the Summary worksheet whenever changes are made to the other worksheet totals.

1 To the right of the **In-Store Sales sheet tab**, click the **Insert Sheet** button. On the Standard toolbar, click the **Zoom arrow** 100% ▼, and then click **125%**.

2 Point to the **sheet tab** and press Control and click. From the shortcut menu, click **Rename**, type **Summary** and then press Return. Change the **Tab Color** to **Accent 3**—in the first row, the seventh color. **Close** the **Tab Color** window.

3 Widen **columns A:E** to **14.00 (1.23 inches)**. In cell **A1**, type **Sales of Food and Non-Food Items** and then **Merge** the title across the range **A1:E1**. Apply the **Title** cell style.

4 In cell **A2**, type **Week of July 24** and then **Merge** across **A2:E2**. Apply the **Heading 1** cell style.

5 Leave **row 3** blank. To create column titles, in cell **B4**, type **Food/Non-Food** and then press Tab. In cell **C4**, type **Food Sales** and press Tab. In cell **D4**, type **Non-Food Sales** and press Tab. In cell **E5**, type **Total Sales** and then press Return. Select the range **B4:E4**. Apply the **Heading 3** cell style, and then apply **Center Text**.

6 To create row titles, in cell **A5**, type **Online Sales** In cell **A6**, type **In-Store Sales** and then compare your screen with Figure 2.44.

Figure 2.44

Title and subtitle entered —
Row 3 is blank —
Row titles entered —
Column titles entered —
Sheet tab renamed with Accent 3 color —

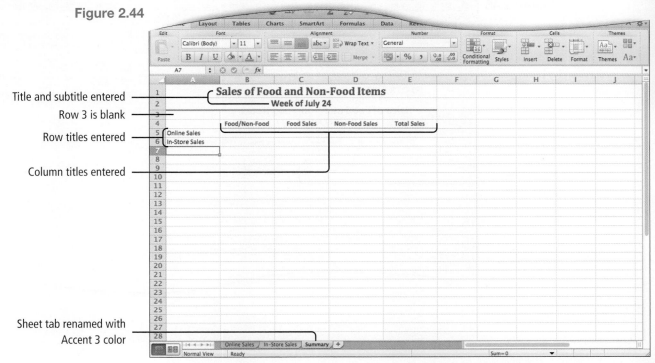

Excel | Chapter 2

7 Click cell **C5**. Type = and then click the **Online Sales sheet tab**. On the **Online Sales** worksheet, click cell **E12**, and then press ⏎Return to redisplay the **Summary** worksheet and insert the total **Food Sales** amount of *$21,257.78*.

8 Click cell **C5** to select it again. Look at the formula bar, and notice that instead of a value, the cell contains a formula that is equal to the value in another cell in another worksheet. Compare your screen with Figure 2.45.

> The value in this cell is equal to the value in cell E12 of the *Online Sales* worksheet. The Accounting Number Format applied to the referenced cell is carried over. By using a formula of this type, changes in cell E12 on the *Online Sales* worksheet will be automatically updated in this *Summary* worksheet.

Figure 2.45

Formula refers to cell in another worksheet

Total Food Sales from the Online Sales worksheet

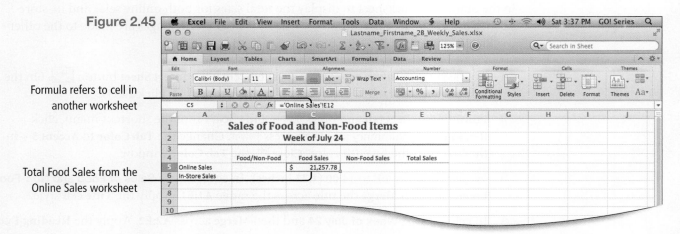

9 Click cell **D5**. Type = and then click the **Online Sales sheet tab**. Click cell **F12**, and then press ⏎Return to redisplay the **Summary** worksheet and insert the total **Non-Food Sales** amount of *$6,038.65*.

10 By using the techniques you just practiced, in cells **C6** and **D6** insert the total **Food Sales** and **Non-Food Sales** data from the **In-Store Sales** worksheet. **Save** 🖫 your workbook, and then compare your screen with Figure 2.46.

Figure 2.46

Totals from two other worksheets

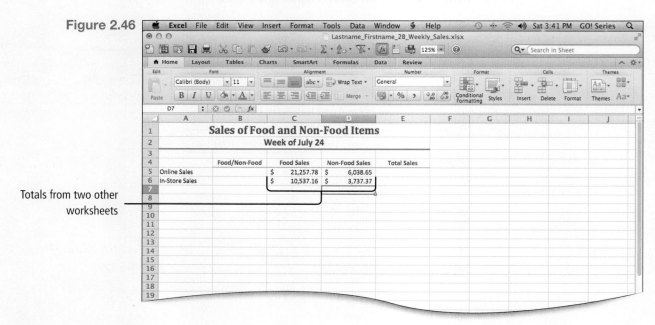

Activity 2.23 | Changing Values in a Detail Worksheet to Update a Summary Worksheet

The formulas in cells C5:D6 display the totals from the other two worksheets. Changes made to any of the other two worksheets—sometimes referred to as *detail sheets* because the details of the information are contained there—that affect their totals will display on this Summary worksheet. In this manner, the Summary worksheet accurately displays the current totals from the other worksheets.

1 In cell **A7**, type **Total** and then select the range **C5:E6**. On the Standard toolbar, click the **Sum** button Σ to total the two rows.

> This technique is similar to selecting the empty cells at the bottom of columns and then inserting the SUM function for each column. Alternatively, you can use any other method to sum the rows. Recall that cell formatting carries over to adjacent cells unless two cells are left blank.

2 Select the range **C5:E7**, and then click the **Sum** button Σ to total the three columns. Compare your screen with Figure 2.47.

Figure 2.47

Rows and columns totaled ────

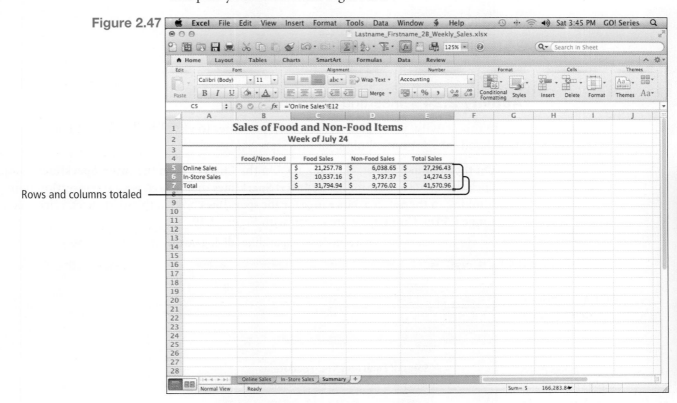

3 In cell **C6**, notice that total **Food Sales** for **In-Store Sales** is *$10,537.16*, and in cell **C7**, notice the total of *$31,794.94*.

4 Display the **In-Store Sales** worksheet, click cell **B8**, type **353.63** and then press Return. Notice that the formulas in the worksheet recalculate.

5 Display the **Summary** worksheet, and notice that in the **Food Sales** column, both the total for the *In-Store Sales* location and the *Total* also recalculated.

> In this manner, a Summary sheet recalculates any changes made in the other worksheets.

6 Select the range **C6:E6** and change the format to the **Comma Style** . Select the range **C7:E7**, and then apply the **Total** cell style. Select the range **A5:A7** and apply the **Heading 4** cell style. **Save** your workbook. Click cell **A1**, and then compare your screen with Figure 2.48.

Excel | Chapter 2

Figure 2.48

Comma Style applied to C6:E6

Food Sales Total recalculates to $32,013.21

Heading 4 style applied to row titles

Total cell style applied to C7:E7

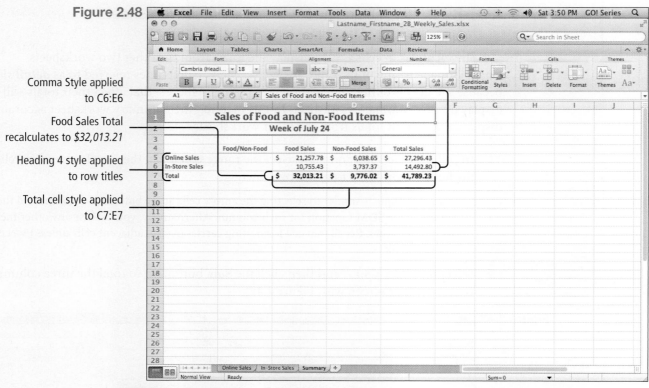

Activity 2.24 | Inserting Sparklines

In this activity, you will insert column sparklines to visualize the ratio of Food to Non-Food sales for both Online and In-Store Sales.

1 On the **Summary** sheet, click cell **B5**. On the **Charts tab**, in the **Insert Sparklines group**, click the **Column** button. In the **Insert Sparklines** dialog box, with the insertion point blinking in the **Select a data range for the sparklines** box, in the worksheet, select the range **C5:D5**. Compare your screen with Figure 2.49.

As you select the range, the Insert Sparklines dialog box temporarily collapses.

Figure 2.49

Column button in Insert Sparklines group

Range C5:D5 selected as indicated by moving border

Insert Sparklines dialog box

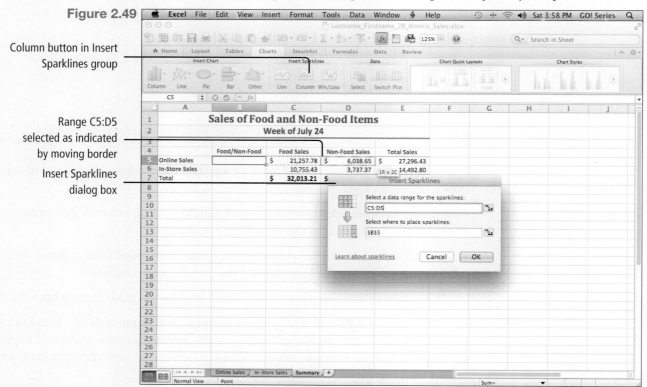

2 In the **Insert Sparklines** dialog box, click **OK**. Click cell **B6**, and then **Insert** a **Column Sparkline** for the range **C6:D6**. In the **Format group**, point to the styles, and then click the **More** button ⊡. Apply **Sparkline Style Accent 2, Darker 25%**. Click in cell **A1**, **Save** ⊟ your workbook, and then compare your screen with Figure 2.50.

You can see, at a glance, that for both Online and In-Store sales, Food Sales are much greater than Non-Food Sales.

Figure 2.50

Column sparklines compare sales of Food to Non-Food for both Online and In-Store sales

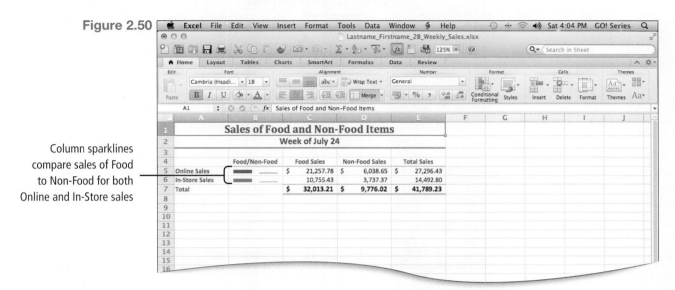

Objective 12 | Format and Print Multiple Worksheets in a Workbook

Each worksheet within a workbook can have different formatting, for example, different headers or footers. If all of the worksheets in the workbook will have the same header or footer, you can select all the worksheets and apply formatting common to all of the worksheets; for example, you can set the same footer in all of the worksheets.

Activity 2.25 | Moving and Formatting Worksheets in a Workbook

In this activity, you will move the Summary sheet so that it becomes the first worksheet in the workbook. Then you will format and prepare your workbook for printing. The three worksheets containing data can be formatted simultaneously.

1 Point to the **Summary sheet tab**, press and hold down the mouse, and drag slightly to the left to display a small black triangle—a caret.

2 Drag to the left until the caret and ⊞ pointer are to the left of the **Online Sales sheet tab**, as shown in Figure 2.51, and then release the mouse.

Use this technique to rearrange the order of worksheets within a workbook.

Excel | Chapter 2

Figure 2.51

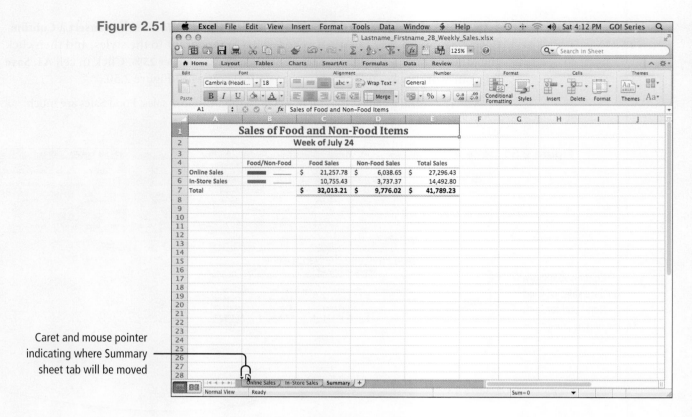

Caret and mouse pointer indicating where Summary sheet tab will be moved

---

3 Be sure the **Summary** worksheet is the active sheet, point to its **sheet tab**, press Control and click, and then click **Select All Sheets** to display *[Group]* in the title bar. On the **View** menu, click **Header and Footer**. In the **Page Setup** dialog box, click **Customize Footer**. With the insertion point positioned in the **Left section** box, click the **Insert File Name** button 📄, and then click **OK**. In the **Page Setup** dialog box, click **OK**.

4 On the **Layout tab**, in the **Page Setup group**, click the **Margins** button, and then click **Custom Margins**. In the **Page Setup** dialog box, under **Center on page**, select the **Horizontally** check box, and then click **OK**. Verify that *[Group]* still displays in the title bar.

By selecting all sheets, you can apply the same formatting to all of the worksheets at the same time. Dotted lines indicate the page breaks in Normal view.

5 On the **File** menu, click **Properties**. In the **Subject** box, type your course name and section number. In the **Author** box, type your firstname and lastname. In the **Keywords** box type **weekly sales, online, in-store** and then click **OK**. **Save** 💾 your workbook.

> **Another Way**
> On the File menu, click Print.

6 Press Command ⌘ + P to display the **Print** dialog box, and then compare your screen with Figure 2.52.

By grouping, you can view all sheets in the Preview in the Print dialog box. If you do not see *1 of 3* at the bottom of the Preview, click Cancel, select all the sheets again, and then redisplay the Print dialog box.

Figure 2.52

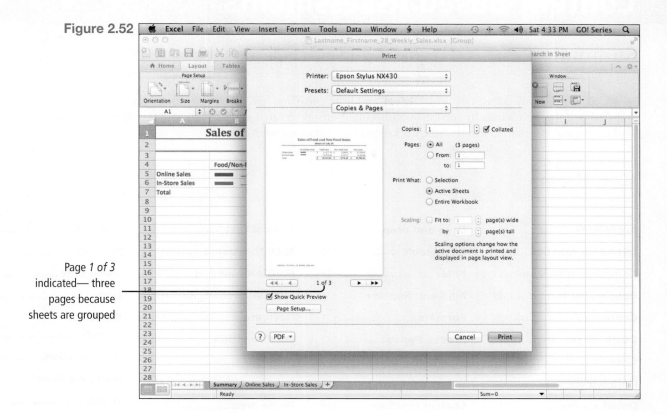

Page *1 of 3*
indicated— three
pages because
sheets are grouped

7 At the bottom of the **Print Preview**, click the **Next Page** ▶ button as many times as necessary to view each page of your workbook.

Activity 2.26 | Printing All the Worksheets in a Workbook

1 If you are required to print your worksheets, in the **Print** dialog box, click **Print**; or submit them electronically as directed.

By grouping, you can print all of the worksheets at one time.

2 If required, print or create an electronic version of your worksheets with formulas displayed by using the instructions in Activity 1.15. **Close** 🔘 your workbook, without saving so that you do not save the changes you made to print formulas. On the **Excel** menu, click **Quit Excel**.

End **You have completed Project 2B**

Content-Based Assessments

Summary

In this chapter, you used the Statistical, Logical, and Date and Time functions. You created a table and analyzed the table's data by sorting and filtering. You also created a workbook with multiple worksheets, and then summarized all the worksheets on a summary worksheet.

Key Terms

Matching

Match each term in the second column with its correct definition in the first column by writing the letter of the term on the blank line in front of the correct definition.

_____ 1. A predefined formula that performs calculations by using specific values in a particular order or structure.

_____ 2. Excel functions such as AVERAGE that are useful to analyze a group of measurements.

_____ 3. A predefined formula that adds all the numbers in a selected range.

_____ 4. A function that adds a group of values, and then divides the result by the number of values in the group.

_____ 5. A function that finds the middle value that has as many values above it in the group as are below it.

_____ 6. A function that determines the smallest value in a range.

_____ 7. A function that determines the largest value in a range.

_____ 8. The action of moving a selection by dragging it to a new location.

_____ 9. A group of functions that tests for specific conditions, and which typically use conditional tests to determine whether specified conditions are true or false.

_____ 10. Conditions that you specify in a logical function.

_____ 11. A statistical function that counts the number of cells within a range that meet the given condition and which has two arguments—the range of cells to check and the criteria.

_____ 12. Any value or expression that can be evaluated as being true or false.

_____ 13. A function that uses a logical test to check whether a condition is met, and then returns one value if true, and another value if false.

A AVERAGE function

B Comparison operators

C Conditional format

D COUNTIF function

E Criteria

F Drag and drop

G Function

H IF function

I Logical functions

J Logical test

K MAX function

L MEDIAN function

M MIN function

N Statistical functions

O SUM function

_____ 14. Symbols that evaluate each value to determine if it is the same (=), greater than (>), less than (<), or in between a range of values as specified by the criteria.

_____ 15. A format that changes the appearance of a cell based on a condition.

Multiple Choice

Circle the correct answer.

1. A shaded bar that provides a visual cue about the value of a cell relative to other cells is a:
   A. data bar   B. detail bar   C. filter

2. The function that retrieves and then displays the date and time from your computer is the:
   A. DATE function   B. NOW function   C. CALENDAR function

3. The command that enables you to select one or more rows or columns and lock them into place is:
   A. drag and drop   B. scale to fit   C. freeze panes

4. A series of rows and columns with related data that is managed independently from other data is a:
   A. table   B. pane   C. detail sheet

5. The process of arranging data in a specific order based on the value in each field is called:
   A. filtering   B. sorting   C. scaling

6. The process of displaying only a portion of the data based on matching a specific value to show only the data that meets the criteria that you specify is called:
   A. filtering   B. sorting   C. scaling

7. The Excel command that enables you to specify rows and columns to repeat on each printed page is:
   A. navigate   B. print titles   C. conditional format

8. The labels along the lower border of the workbook window that identify each worksheet are the:
   A. data bars   B. sheet tabs   C. detail sheets

9. A worksheet where totals from other worksheets are displayed and summarized is a:
   A. summary sheet   B. detail sheet   C. table

10. The worksheets that contain the specifics of the information summarized on a summary sheet are called:
    A. summary sheets   B. detail sheets   C. tables

Content-Based Assessments

Apply 2A skills from these Objectives:

1 Use the SUM, AVERAGE, MEDIAN, MIN, and MAX Functions

2 Move Data, Resolve Error Messages, and Rotate Text

3 Use COUNTIF and IF Functions and Apply Conditional Formatting

4 Use Date and Time Functions and Freeze Panes

5 Create, Sort, and Filter an Excel Table

6 Format and Print a Large Worksheet

Skills Review | Project 2C Gift Inventory

In the following Skills Review, you will edit a worksheet for Laura Morales, President, detailing the current inventory of Gift Assortments at the Portland facility. Your completed workbook will look similar to Figure 2.53.

Project Files

For Project 2C, you will need the following file:

e02C_Gift_Inventory

You will save your workbook as:

Lastname_Firstname_2C_Gift_Inventory

Project Results

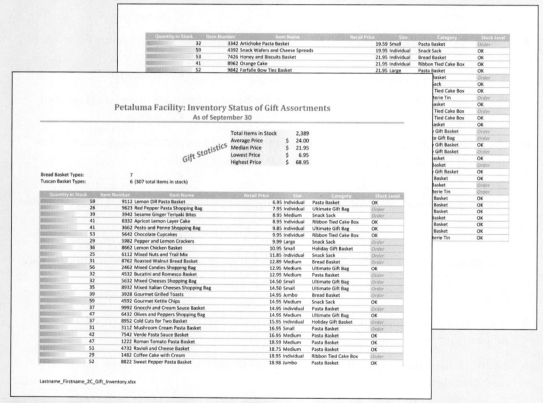

Figure 2.53

(Project 2C Gift Inventory continues on the next page)

Content-Based Assessments

1 Open **Excel**. On the **File** menu, click **Open**, and from your student files, **Open e02C_Gift_Inventory**. If necessary, increase the size of the Excel window to fill the screen by clicking the Zoom button ⬚ or by dragging the lower right corner of the Excel window. If necessary, on the Standard toolbar, click the Zoom arrow 100%▾, and then click 125%. On the **File** menu, click **Save As**, navigate to your **Excel Chapter 2** folder, and then **Save** the workbook as **Lastname_Firstname_2C_Gift_Inventory**

a. Click cell **B4**. On the **Formulas tab**, in the **Function group**, click the **AutoSum** button. Select the range **A14:A68**, and then press Return.

b. With cell **B5** active, in the **Function group**, click the **AutoSum arrow**, and then click **Average**. Type **d14:d68** and then press Return.

c. With cell **B6** active, on the Standard toolbar, click the **Sum arrow**, and then click **More Functions**. In the **Formula Builder** window, in the **Search for a function box**, type **me** and then under **Statistical**, double-click **MEDIAN**. At the bottom of the **Formula Builder** window, in the **Arguments** box, with the range *B4:B5* selected in the **number1** box, in the worksheet, select the range **D14:D68**, and then press Return. **Close** the **Formula Builder** window.

d. Click cell **B7**. On the Standard toolbar, click the **Sum arrow**, and then click **Min**. In the worksheet, select the range **D14:D68** and then press Return to determine the lowest **Retail Price**. In cell **B8**, insert the **Max** function to determine the highest **Retail Price**. **Save** your workbook.

2 Click cell **B4**. On the **Home tab**, in the **Number group**, click the **Comma Style** button, and then click the **Decrease Decimal** button two times. Select the range **B5:B8**, and apply the **Number Format** of **Accounting**.

a. Select the range **A4:B8**. Point to the right edge of the selected range to display the ✋ pointer. Drag the selected range to the right until the **ScreenTip** displays *D4:E8*, and then release the mouse.

b. With the range **D4:E8** selected, on the **Home tab**, in the **Format group**, click the **Styles** button to display the **Cell Styles** gallery. Under **Themed Cell Styles**, click **20% - Accent1**.

c. In cell **C6**, type **Gift Statistics** and then press Return. Select the range **C4:C8**, and then on the **Home tab**, in the **Alignment group**, click the **Merge** button. On the

Format menu, click **Cells**. In the **Format Cells** dialog box, click the **Alignment tab**. Under **Orientation**, point to the **red diamond**, and then drag the diamond upward until the **Degrees** box indicates **20**. In the **Format Cells** dialog box, click **OK**.

d. With the merged cell still selected, on the **Home tab**, in the **Font group**, change the **Font Size** to **18**, and then apply **Bold** and **Italic**. Click the **Font Color arrow**, and then in the first row, click the fourth color—**Text 2**. In the **Alignment group**, click the **Align Text Right** button, and then **Save** your workbook.

3 Click cell **B10**. On the **Formulas tab**, in the **Function group**, click the **Formula Builder** button. In the **Formula Builder** window, in the **Search for a function** box, type **countif** and then under **Statistical**, double-click **COUNTIF**.

a. Without clicking in the worksheet, scroll to display **column F**. In the worksheet, select the range **F14:F68** to display *F14:F68* in the **range** box. In the **Formula Builder** window, click in the **criteria** box, type **bread basket** and then press Return to calculate the number of Bread Basket types in cell **B10**.

b. Click cell **G14**. In the **Formula Builder** window, in the **Search** box, if necessary, type **if** and then under **Logical**, double-click **IF**. Without clicking in the worksheet, scroll to display cell *A14*.

c. In the **Formula Builder** window, in the **Arguments** box, click in the **value1** box. In the worksheet, click cell **A14**. In the **Formula Builder** window, to the right of **is True**, click the **arrows**, and then click **<** (**Less Than**). In the **value2** box, type **40** In the **then** box, type **Order** In the **else** box, type **OK** and then press Return. **Close** the **Formula Builder** window, and then scroll to display **column G**. Using the fill handle, copy the function in cell **G14** down through cell **G68**. **Save** your workbook.

4 With the range **G14:G68** selected, on the **Home tab**, in the **Format group**, click the **Conditional Formatting** button. In the list, point to **Highlight Cells Rules**, and then click **Text that Contains**.

a. In the **New Formatting Rule** dialog box, with the insertion point blinking in the empty box, type **Order** and then in the **Format with** box, click the **arrows**, and then click **custom format**.

b. In the **Format Cells** dialog box, on the **Font tab**, under **Font style**, click **Bold Italic**. Click the **Color**

(Project 2C Gift Inventory continues on the next page)

Excel | Chapter 2

arrow, and then under **Theme Colors**, in the first row, click the eighth color—**Accent 4**. Click **OK**, and then in the **New Formatting Rule** dialog box, click **OK** to apply the font color, bold, and italic to the cells that contain the word *Order*.

c. Select the range **A14:A68**. In the **Format group**, click the **Conditional Formatting** button. Point to **Data Bars**, and then under **Gradient Fill**, click **Green Data Bar**. Click anywhere to cancel the selection.

d. Select the range **F14:F68**. On the **Edit** menu, click **Replace**. In the **Replace** dialog box, in the **Find what** box, type **Board** and then in the **Replace with** box type **Sack** Click the **Replace All** button, and then in the message box, click **OK**. In the **Replace** dialog box, click **Close**.

e. Scroll as necessary, and then click cell **A70**. Type **Edited by Hilary Albright** and then press Return. With cell **A71** as the active cell, on the **Formulas tab**, in the **Function group**, click the **Insert** button, point to **Date and Time**, and then click **NOW**. Press Return to enter the current date and time, and then **Save** your workbook.

5 Press Command ⌘ + fn + ← to make cell **A1** active. Click in any cell in the data below row 13. On the **Tables tab**, in the **Table Options group**, click the **New arrow**, and then click **Insert Table with Headers**. On the **Tables tab**, in the **Table Styles group**, click the **More** button, and then under **Light**, locate and click **Table Style Light 9**.

a. In the header row of the table, click the **Retail Price arrow**, and in the **Sort and Filter** task pane, click **Ascending**. If necessary, point to the title bar of the task pane, and drag the task pane up slightly so that the top of the table header row displays. In the header row, click the **Category arrow**. In the **Sort and Filter** task pane, click the **(Select All)** check box to clear all of the check boxes. Scroll as necessary, and then click to select only the **Tuscan Basket** check box. Click any cell in the table so that the task pane closes and the table is selected.

b. On the **Tables tab**, in the **Table Options group**, select the **Total Row** check box. Click cell **A69**, click the **arrows** that display to the right of cell **A69**, and then click **Sum**. In cell **B11**, type the result **6** and then press Tab. In cell **C11**, type **(307 total items in stock)** and then press Return.

c. In the header row of the table, click the **Category arrow**, and then in the **Sort and Filter** task pane, click the **Clear Filter** button to redisplay all of the data. Click anywhere in the table. On the **Tables tab**, in the **Table Options group**, clear the **Total Row** check box, and then in the **Tools group**, click the **Convert to Range** button. In the message box, click **Yes**, and then **Save** your workbook.

6 On the **Layout tab**, click the **Margins** button, and then click **Custom Margins**. On the **Margins tab**, under **Center on page**, select the **Horizontally** check box. In the **Page Setup** dialog box, click the **Page tab**. Under **Scaling**, click **Fit to**. Be sure that *1* displays in the **pages(s) wide box**. In the **tall** box, type **0** and then click **OK**. Alternatively, you can set scaling on the Layout tab, in the Print group.

a. On the **Layout tab**, in the **Print group**, click the **Repeat Titles** button. In the **Page Setup** dialog box, with the **Sheet tab** active, under **Print titles**, click in the **Rows to repeat at top** box, and then at the right, click the **Collapse Dialog** button. From the row heading area, select **row 13**, and then click the **Expand Dialog** button.

b. In the **Page Setup** dialog box, click the **Header/Footer tab**. Alternatively, if the Page Setup dialog box is not displayed, from the Edit menu, click Header and Footer to create a footer. Click the **Customize Footer** button, and in the **Left section**, **Insert** the **File Name**, and then click **OK**. In the **Page Setup** dialog box, click **OK**. Make cell **A1** the active cell.

c. Display the **File Properties**, and then add your course name and section, your name, and the keywords **inventory, Petaluma, gifts** and then click **OK**. **Save** your workbook, and then on the **File** menu, click **Print** to view your worksheet in the **Preview** section of the **Print** dialog box—the worksheet will print on two pages.

d. **Print** or submit electronically as directed by your instructor. If required by your instructor, print or create an electronic version of your worksheet with formulas displayed by using the instructions in Activity 1.15, and then **Close** the workbook without saving so that you do not save the changes you made to print formulas. On the **Excel** menu, click **Quit Excel**.

End **You have completed Project 2C**

Content-Based Assessments

Apply **2B** skills from these Objectives:

7 Navigate a Workbook and Rename Worksheets

8 Enter Dates, Clear Contents, and Clear Formats

9 Copy and Paste Cells

10 Edit and Format Multiple Worksheets at the Same Time

11 Create a Summary Sheet with Column Sparklines

12 Format and Print Multiple Worksheets in a Workbook

Skills Review | Project **2D** Texas Sales

In the following Skills Review, you will edit a workbook that summarizes dessert and spice sales in the Texas retail locations. Your completed workbook will look similar to Figure 2.54.

Project Files

For Project 2D, you will need the following file:

e02D_Texas_Sales

You will save your workbook as:

Lastname_Firstname_2D_Texas_Sales

Project Results

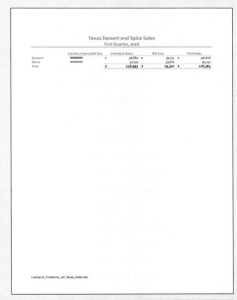

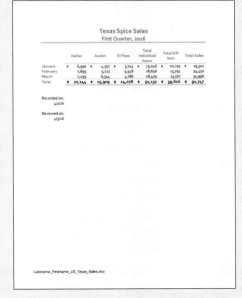

Figure 2.54

(Project 2D Texas Sales continues on the next page)

Excel | Chapter 2

1 Open **Excel**. On the **File** menu, click **Open**, and then from your student files, **Open e02D_Texas_Sales**. If necessary, increase the size of the Excel window to fill the screen by clicking the Zoom button or by dragging the lower right corner of the Excel window. If necessary, on the Standard toolbar, click the Zoom arrow, and then click 125%. On the **File** menu, click **Save As**, navigate to your **Excel Chapter 2** folder, and then using your own name, save the file as **Lastname_Firstname_2D_Texas_Sales**

a. Point to the **Sheet1 tab**, and then double-click to select the sheet tab name. Type **Dessert Sales** and then press Return.

b. Point to the **Sheet2 tab**, press Control and click, and then from the shortcut menu, click **Rename**. Type **Spice Sales** and press Return.

c. Point to the **Dessert Sales sheet tab**, press Control and click. On the shortcut menu, click **Tab Color**. In the **Tab Color** window, under **Theme Colors**, in the first row, click the last color—**Accent 6**. Click the **Spice Sales tab**, and then change the **Tab Color** to **Accent 2**—in the first row, the sixth color. **Close** the **Tab Color** window.

d. Click the **Dessert Sales sheet tab**, and then click cell **A12**. On the **Format** menu, click **Cells**. In the **Format Cells** dialog box, with the **Number tab** active, under **Type**, click **3/14/01**, and then at the bottom of the dialog box, click **OK**. Click cell **A15**, type **4/5/16** and then press Return.

e. Click cell **A1**. On the **Edit** menu, point to **Clear**, and then click **Formats**.

f. Select the range **A5:A15**. On the Standard toolbar, click the **Copy** button. At the bottom of the workbook window, click the **Spice Sales sheet tab** to make it the active worksheet. Click cell **A5**, and then on the Standard toolbar, click the **Paste** button. Display the **Dessert Sales** sheet. Press Esc to cancel the moving border, and then **Save** your workbook.

2 With the **Dessert Sales** sheet active, make cell **A1** the active cell. Point to the **sheet tab**, press Control and click, and then on the shortcut menu, click **Select All Sheets**. Verify that *[Group]* displays in the title bar.

a. **Merge** the text in cell **A1** across the range **A1:G1**, and then apply the **Title** cell style. Select **columns A:G**, and then by dragging any column border in the selection, change the **Width** to **10.00 (0.90 inches)**.

b. Click cell **A2**, type **First Quarter, 2016** and then on the formula bar, click the **Enter** button to keep cell **A2** as the active cell. **Merge** the text across the range **A2:G2**, and then apply the **Heading 1** cell style.

c. Select the range **B4:G4**, and then apply the **Heading 3** cell style. In the **Alignment group**, click the **Center Text** button, and then click the **Align Text Middle** button. Click the **Wrap Text** button, and then click **Wrap Text**.

d. With the sheets still grouped and the **Dessert Sales** sheet active, click cell **E5**. On the Standard toolbar, click the **Sum** button, and then on the formula bar, click the **Enter** button to keep cell **E5** active. Drag the fill handle down to copy the formula through cell **E7**.

e. Click cell **G5**, type **=** and then click cell **E5**. Type **+** and then click cell **F5**. On the formula bar, click the **Enter** button. Copy the formula down through cell **G7**. In cell **A8**, type **Total** and then press Return. Select the range **B5:G8**, and then press Command ⌘ +Shift + T to enter the SUM function for all the columns. Select the range **A5:A8**, and then apply the **Heading 4** cell style.

f. Select the range **B5:G5**, hold down Command ⌘, and then select the range **B8:G8**. Apply the **Number Format** of **Accounting** and decrease the decimal places to zero. If the Accounting format does not display for the second range, click Accounting again. Select the range **B6:G7**, and then apply the **Comma Style** with zero decimal places. Select the range **B8:G8**, apply the **Total** cell style, and then **Save** your workbook.

3 Click the **Spice Sales sheet tab** to cancel the grouping and display the second worksheet.

a. To the right of the **Spice Sales sheet tab**, click the **Insert Sheet** button. On the Standard toolbar, click the **Zoom arrow**, and then click **125%**. **Rename** the new **sheet tab Summary** and then change the **Tab Color** to **Accent 4**—in the first row, the eighth color. **Close** the **Tab Color** window.

b. Widen **columns A:E** to **20.00 (1.73 inches)**. In cell **A1**, type **Texas Dessert and Spice Sales** and then **Merge** the title across the range **A1:E1**. Apply the **Title** cell style. In cell **A2**, type **First Quarter, 2016** and then **Merge** the text across the range **A2:E2**. Apply the **Heading 1** cell style. In cell **A5**, type **Desserts** and in cell **A6**, type **Spices**

c. In cell **B4**, type **Individual Items/Gift Sets** and in cell **C4**, type **Individual Items** In cell **D4**, type **Gift**

(Project 2D Texas Sales continues on the next page)

Skills Review | Project **2D** Texas Sales (continued)

Sets and in cell **E4**, type **Total Sales** Select the range **B4:E4**, apply the **Heading 3** cell style, and then apply **Center Text** to these column titles.

d. Click cell **C5**. Type = and then click the **Dessert Sales sheet tab**. In the **Dessert Sales** worksheet, click cell **E8**, and then press Return. Click cell **D5**. Type = and then click the **Dessert Sales sheet tab**. Click cell **F8**, and then press Return.

e. By using the technique you just practiced, in cells **C6** and **D6**, insert the total **Individual Items** and **Gift Sets** data from the **Spice Sales** worksheet.

f. In the **Summary** worksheet, select the range **C5:E6**, and then on the Standard toolbar, click the **Sum** button to total the two rows. In cell **A7**, type **Total** and then select the range **C5:E7**. Click the **Sum** button to total the three columns. Select the nonadjacent ranges **C5:E5** and **C7:E7**, and then apply the **Number Format** of **Accounting** with zero decimal places. Be sure the Accounting format is applied to both ranges. Select the range **C6:E6**, and then apply the **Comma Style** with zero decimal places. Select the range **C7:E7**, and then apply the **Total** cell style. Select the range **A5:A7** and apply the **Heading 4** cell style.

g. Click cell **B5**. On the **Charts tab**, in the **Insert Sparklines group**, click the **Column** button. In the **Create Sparklines** dialog box, with the insertion point blinking in the **Select a data range for the sparklines** box, in the worksheet, select the range **C5:D5**, and then in the **Insert Sparklines** dialog box, click **OK**.

h. Click cell **B6**, and then **Insert** a **Column Sparkline** for the range **C6:D6**. In the **Format group**, point to the styles, click the **More** button, and then apply the **Sparkline Style Accent 2, Darker 25%** style to this sparkline. **Save** your workbook.

4 Point to the **Summary sheet tab**, press down the mouse, and drag to the left until the caret and pointer are to the left of the **Dessert Sales sheet tab**, and then release the mouse to move the Summary sheet to the first position.

a. Be sure that the **Summary** worksheet is the active sheet, point to its **sheet tab**, press Control and click, and then click **Select All Sheets** to display [Group] in the title bar. On the **View** menu, click **Header and Footer**. In the **Page Setup** dialog box, click **Customize Footer**. With the insertion point blinking in the **Left section** box, click the **Insert File Name** button, and then click **OK**.

b. In the **Page Setup** dialog box, click the **Margins tab**, and then under **Center on page**, select the **Horizontally** check box. In the **Page Setup** dialog box, click the **Page tab**, and then under **Scaling**, click **Fit to**, and change the **tall** box setting to **0** to be sure that all of the columns will print on one page. In the **Page Setup** dialog box, click **OK**, and then make cell **A1** active.

c. On the **File** menu, click **Properties**. Add your course name and section, your name, and the keywords **desserts, spices, sales** and then click **OK**.

d. **Save** your workbook. Verify that the worksheets in your workbook are still grouped—[Group] displays in the title bar—and then on the **File** menu, click **Print** to display your worksheets in the **Preview** in the **Print** dialog box—3 pages will print. **Print** or submit electronically as directed.

e. If required by your instructor, print or create an electronic version of your worksheets with formulas displayed by using the instructions in Activity 1.15, and then **Close** the workbook without saving so that you do not save the changes you made to print formulas. On the **Excel** menu, click **Quit Excel**.

End **You have completed Project 2D**

Excel | Chapter 2

Content-Based Assessments

Apply 2A skills from these Objectives:

1 Use the SUM, AVERAGE, MEDIAN, MIN, and MAX Functions

2 Move Data, Resolve Error Messages, and Rotate Text

3 Use COUNTIF and IF Functions and Apply Conditional Formatting

4 Use Date and Time Functions and Freeze Panes

5 Create, Sort, and Filter an Excel Table

6 Format and Print a Large Worksheet

Mastering Excel | Project 2E Dressings

In the following Mastery project, you will edit a worksheet for Laura Morales, President, detailing the current inventory of dressings and oils produced at the San Diego facility. Your completed worksheet will look similar to Figure 2.55.

Project Files

For Project 2E, you will need the following files:

e02E_Dressings

You will save your workbook as:

Lastname_Firstname_2E_Dressings

Project Results

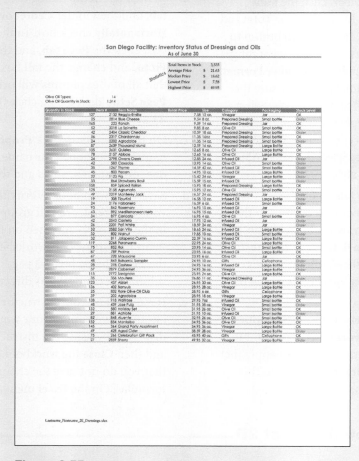

Figure 2.55

(Project 2E Dressings continues on the next page)

Content-Based Assessments

Mastering Excel | Project 2E Dressings (continued)

1 Open **Excel**. On the **File** menu, click **Open**, and then from your student files, **Open e02E_Dressings**. If necessary, increase the size of the Excel window to fill the screen and change the Zoom setting to 125%. On the **File** menu, click **Save As**, and then **Save** the file in your **Excel Chapter 2** folder as **Lastname_Firstname_2E_Dressings**

2 In cell **B4**, calculate the **Total Items in Stock** by summing the **Quantity in Stock** data, and then apply the **Comma Style** with zero decimal places to the result. In each cell in the range **B5:B8**, insert formulas to calculate the Average, Median, Lowest, and Highest **Retail Price**, and then apply the **Number Format** of **Accounting** to each result.

3 Move the range **A4:B8** to the range **D4:E8**, and then apply the **20% - Accent1** cell style. Widen **column D** to **17.00 (1.49 inches)**. In cell **C6**, type **Statistics** and then select the range **C4:C8**. **Merge** the selected cells, and then in the **Format Cells** dialog box, change the text **Orientation** to **25 Degrees**, and then apply **Bold** and **Italic**. Change the **Font Size** to **14** and the **Font Color** to **Text 2**. Apply **Align Text Middle** and **Align Text Right**.

4 In cell **B10**, use the **COUNTIF** function to count the number of **Olive Oil** items in the **Category** column. In the **Category** column, **Replace All** occurrences of **Viniger** with **Vinegar**.

5 In cell **H14**, enter an **IF** function to determine the items that must be ordered. If the **Quantity in Stock** is less than **50 then** display **Order else** display **OK** Fill the formula down through cell **H65**. Apply **Conditional Formatting** to the **Stock Level** column so that cells that

contain the text *Order* are formatted with **Bold Italic** and with a **Color** of **Accent 1**. Apply **Conditional Formatting** to the **Quantity in Stock** column by applying a **Gradient Fill Green Data Bar**.

6 Format the range **A13:H65** as a **Table** with headers, and apply the **Table Style Light 9** style. **Sort** the table in **Ascending Order** by **Retail Price**, and then filter the records based on the **Category** column to display the **Olive Oil** types. Display a **Total Row** in the table and then in cell **A66**, **Sum** the **Quantity in Stock** for the **Olive Oil** items. Type the result in cell **B11**. Click in the table, and then on the **Tables tab**, remove the **Total Row** from the table. Clear the **Category** filter, and then convert the table to a range.

7 Change the theme to **Executive**. **Insert** the **File Name** in the **Left section** of the footer. Center the worksheet **Horizontally**, and then adjust scaling to be sure the columns print on one page. Make cell **A1** the active cell, and then display the **Print** dialog box to be sure the worksheet prints on one page. If necessary, make corrections to the worksheet.

8 In the **File Properties**, add your course name and section, your name, and the keywords **dressings, inventory, San Diego Save**, and then **Print** or submit electronically as directed. If required by your instructor, print or create an electronic version of your worksheet with formulas displayed by using the instructions in Activity 1.15, and then **Close** the workbook without saving so that you do not save the changes you made to print formulas. **Quit Excel**.

End **You have completed Project 2E**

Content-Based Assessments

Apply **2B** skills from these Objectives:

7 Navigate a Workbook and Rename Worksheets

8 Enter Dates, Clear Contents, and Clear Formats

9 Copy and Paste Cells

10 Edit and Format Multiple Worksheets at the Same Time

11 Create a Summary Sheet with Column Sparklines

12 Format and Print Multiple Worksheets in a Workbook

Mastering Excel | Project **2F** Expenses

In the following Mastery project, you will edit a workbook that summarizes the Laurales Herb and Spices Advertising and Marketing expenses for the month of June in two states. Your completed worksheets will look similar to Figure 2.56.

Project Files

For Project 2F, you will need the following file:

e02F_Expenses

You will save your workbook as:

Lastname_Firstname_2F_Expenses

Project Results

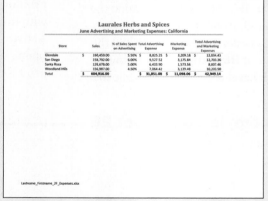

Figure 2.56

(Project 2F Expenses continues on the next page)

Mastering Excel | Project 2F Expenses (continued)

1 Open **Excel**. On the **File** menu, click **Open**, and then from your student files, **Open e02F_Expenses**. If necessary, increase the size of the Excel window to fill the screen and change the Zoom setting to 125%. On the **File** menu, click **Save As**, and then **Save** the file in your **Excel Chapter 2** folder as **Lastname_Firstname_ 2F_Expenses**

2 Rename **Sheet1** as **California** and change the **Tab Color** to **Accent 1**. Rename **Sheet2** as **Washington** and change the **Tab Color** to **Accent 3**.

3 Click the **California sheet tab** to make it the active sheet, and then group the worksheets. In cell **A1**, type **Laurales Herbs and Spices** and then **Merge** the text across the range **A1:F1**. Apply the **Title** cell style. **Merge** the text in cell **A2** across the range **A2:F2**, and then apply the **Heading 1** cell style.

4 With the sheets still grouped, in cell **D5**, calculate **Total Advertising Expense** for *Glendale* by multiplying the **Sales** by the **% of Sales Spent on Advertising**. Use the fill handle to copy the formula down through cell **D8**. In cell **F5**, calculate **Total Advertising and Marketing Expenses** by adding the **Total Advertising Expense** and **Marketing Expense** for *Glendale*. Use the fill handle to copy the formula down through the cell **F8**.

5 In **row 9**, sum the **Sales**, **Total Advertising Expense**, **Marketing Expense**, and **Total Advertising and Marketing Expenses** columns. Apply the **Number Format** of **Accounting** with two decimal places to the appropriate cells in **row 5** and **row 9** (do not include the percentages). Apply the **Comma Style** with two decimal places to the appropriate cells in **rows 6:8** (do not include the percentages). Apply the **Total** cell style to the appropriate cells in the **Total** row. **Ungroup** the sheets.

6 **Insert** a new **Sheet**, and change the **Zoom** setting to **125%**. Change the sheet name to **Summary** and then change the **Tab Color** to **Accent 5**. Widen **column A** to **25.00 (2.16 inches)**, and then widen **columns B:E** to **18.00 (1.57 inches).** Move the **Summary** sheet so that it is the first sheet in the workbook. In cell **A1**, type **Laurales Herbs and Spices** and then **Merge** the title across the range **A1:E1**. Apply the **Title** cell style. In cell **A2**, type **June Advertising and Marketing Expenses: California and Washington** and then **Merge** the text across the range **A2:E2**. Apply the **Heading 1** cell style.

7 In the range **A5:A8**, type the following row titles and then apply the **Heading 4** cell style:

Sales
Advertising Expense
Marketing Expense
Total Marketing and Advertising

8 In the range **B4:E4**, type the following column titles, and then apply **Center Text** and the **Heading 3** cell style.

California/Washington
California
Washington
Total

9 In cell **C5**, enter a formula that references cell **B9** in the **California** worksheet so that the total sales value for California displays in **C5**. Create similar formulas to enter the total **Advertising Expense**, **Marketing Expense** and **Total Marketing and Advertising** values for California in the range **C6:C8**. Using the same technique, enter formulas in the range **D5:D8** so that the **Washington** totals display.

10 In **column E**, **Sum** the **Sales**, **Advertising Expense**, **Marketing Expense**, and **Total Marketing and Advertising** rows.

11 In cell **B5**, insert a **Column Sparkline** for the range **C5:D5**. In cells **B6**, **B7**, and **B8**, insert column sparklines for the appropriate ranges to compare California totals with Washington totals. To the sparkline in **B6**, apply **Sparkline Style Accent 2**, (**no dark or light**). In cell **B7** apply **Sparkline Style Accent 3**, (**no dark or light**). In cell **B8** apply **Sparkline Style Accent 4**, (**no dark or light**).

12 **Group** the three worksheets, and then in the **Left section** of the footer, **Insert** the **File Name**. Center the worksheets **Horizontally** on the page, and then change the **Orientation** to **Landscape**. Adjust scaling so that all of the columns print on one page. Three pages will print.

13 In **File Properties**, add your course name and section, your name, and the keywords **June, advertising expenses, marketing expenses Save** your workbook, and then **Print** or submit electronically as directed. If required by your instructor, print or create an electronic version of your worksheets with formulas displayed by using the instructions in Activity 1.15, and then **Close** the workbook without saving so that you do not save the changes you made to print formulas. **Quit Excel**.

End **You have completed Project 2F**

Content-Based Assessments

1 Use the SUM, AVERAGE, MEDIAN, MIN, and MAX Functions

2 Move Data, Resolve Error Messages, and Rotate Text

3 Use COUNTIF and IF Functions and Apply Conditional Formatting

4 Use Date and Time Functions and Freeze Panes

5 Create, Sort, and Filter an Excel Table

6 Format and Print a Large Worksheet

7 Navigate a Workbook and Rename Worksheets

8 Enter Dates, Clear Contents, and Clear Formats

9 Copy and Paste Cells

10 Edit and Format Multiple Worksheets at the Same Time

11 Create a Summary Sheet with Column Sparklines

12 Format and Print Multiple Worksheets in a Workbook

Mastering Excel | Project **2G** Inventory Summary

In the following Mastery project, you will edit a worksheet that summarizes the inventory status at the Petaluma production facility. Your completed workbook will look similar to Figure 2.57.

Project Files

For Project 2G, you will need the following file:

e02G_Inventory_Summary

You will save your workbook as

Lastname_Firstname_2G_Inventory_Summary

Project Results

Figure 2.57

(Project 2G Inventory Summary continues on the next page)

Content-Based Assessments

Mastering Excel | Project 2G Inventory Summary (continued)

1 Open **Excel**. From your student files, **Open e02G_ Inventory_Summary. Save** the file in your **Excel Chapter 2** folder as **Lastname_Firstname_2G_Inventory_Summary**

2 **Rename Sheet1** as **Condiments** and **Sheet2** as **Toppings** Make the following calculations in each of the two worksheets *without* grouping the sheets:

- In cell **B4**, enter a formula to **Sum** the **Quantity in Stock** data, and then apply the **Comma Style** with zero decimal places to the result.

- In cells **B5:B8**, enter formulas to calculate the Average, Median, Lowest, and Highest **Retail Price**, and then apply the **Number Format** of **Accounting**.

3 In each of the two worksheets, make the following calculations *without* grouping the sheets:

- In cell **B10**, enter a **COUNTIF** function to determine how many different types of **Relish** products are in stock on the **Condiments** sheet and how many different types of **Salsa** products are in stock on the **Toppings** worksheet.

- In cell **G15**, enter an **IF** function to determine the items that must be ordered. If the **Quantity in Stock** is less than **50 then** display **Order else** display **OK** Fill the formula down through all the rows.

- Apply **Conditional Formatting** to the **Stock Level** column so that cells that contain the text *Order* are formatted with **Bold Italic** with a **Font Color** of **Accent 1, Darker 25%**. Apply **Gradient Fill Green Data Bars** to the **Quantity in Stock** column.

4 In the **Condiments** sheet, format the range **A14:G64** as a table with headers and apply the **Table Style Medium 2** style. Insert a **Total Row**, filter by **Category** for **Relish**, **Sum** the **Quantity in Stock** column, and then record the result in cell **B11**.

5 Click in the table, clear the filter, **Sort** the table on the **Item #** column in **Ascending** order, remove the **Total Row**, and then convert the table to a range. On the **Layout tab**, click **Repeat Titles**, and then set **Print titles** so that **row 14** repeats at the top of each page.

6 In the **Toppings** sheet, format the range **A14:G61** as a table with headers and apply the **Table Style Light 16** style. Insert a **Total Row**, filter by **Category** for **Salsa**, **Sum** the **Quantity in Stock** column, and then record the result in cell **B11**.

7 Click in the table, clear the filter, **Sort** the table on the **Item #** column in **Ascending** order, remove the **Total Row**, and then convert the table to a range. Be sure that the values in cell **D52** and cell **D60** display two decimal places.

8 On the **Layout tab**, click **Repeat Titles**, and then set **Print titles** so that **row 14** repeats at the top of each page, and then **Save** your workbook. **Group** the two worksheets. Center the worksheets **Horizontally**, and set scaling so that the columns print on one page. **Ungroup** the sheets.

9 **Insert** a new **Sheet**. In the Standard toolbar, change the **Zoom** setting to **125%**. **Rename** the new sheet name to **Summary** and then widen **columns A:D** to **18.00 (1.82 inches)**. Move the **Summary** sheet so that it is the first sheet in the workbook. In cell **A1**, type **Petaluma Inventory Summary Merge** the title across the range **A1:D1**, and then apply the **Title** cell style. In cell **A2**, type **As of June 30, 2016** and then **Merge** the text across the range **A2:D2**. Apply the **Heading 1** cell style.

10 On the **Condiments sheet**, **Copy** the range **A4:A8**. Display the **Summary sheet**, and then **Paste** the selection to cell **A5**. Apply the **Heading 4** cell style to the selection. In the **Summary sheet**, in cell **B4**, type **Condiments** In cell **C4**, type **Toppings** and in cell **D4**, type **Condiments/ Toppings**Apply **Center Text** and the **Heading 3** cell style to the column titles.

11 In cell **B5**, enter a formula that references cell **B4** in the **Condiments sheet** so that the **Condiments Total Items in Stock** displays in **B5**. Create similar formulas to enter the **Average Price**, **Median Price**, **Lowest Price**, and **Highest Price** from the **Condiments sheet** into the **Summary** sheet in the range **B6:B9**.

12 Enter formulas in the range **C5:C9** that reference the appropriate cells in the **Toppings** worksheet. To the range **B5:C5**, apply the **Comma Style** with zero decimal places. In cells **D5**, **D6**, **D7**, **D8**, and **D9**, insert column sparklines using the values in the *Condiments* and *Toppings* columns. Format each sparkline using the first five Sparkline styles in the first row.

13 Center the **Summary** worksheet **Horizontally** and change the **Orientation** to **Landscape**. **Group** the worksheets and in the **Left section** of the footer, **Insert** the **File Name**. Make cell **A1** the active cell. Display **File Properties**. Add your course name and section, your name, and the keywords **Petaluma inventory**

(Project 2G Inventory Summary continues on the next page)

Excel | Chapter 2

Mastering Excel | Project **2G** Inventory Summary (continued)

14 **Save** your workbook, and then **Print** or submit electronically as directed—five pages result. If required by your instructor, print or create an electronic version of your worksheets with formulas displayed by using the instructions in Activity 1.15, and then **Close** the workbook without saving so that you do not save the changes you made to print formulas. **Quit Excel**.

 You have completed Project 2G ————————————————————————

Content-Based Assessments

GO! Fix It | Project 2H Confections

Project Files

For Project 2H, you will need the following file:

    e02H_Confections

You will save your workbook as:

    Lastname_Firstname_2H_Confections

In this project, you will correct a worksheet that contains the confection inventory for the month of June at the Laurales Herb and Spices Petaluma production facility. From the student files that accompany this textbook, open the file e02H_Confections, and then save the file in your Excel Chapter 2 folder as **Lastname_Firstname_2H_Confections**

To complete the project, you must find and correct errors in formulas and formatting. View each formula in cells B4:B8 and edit as necessary. In addition to errors that you find, you should know:

- The table should be sorted in Ascending order by Item #.
- New stock should be ordered when the Quantity in Stock is less than 50, and the word *Order* should be formatted with bold italic in color Accent 3.
- The table should be converted to a range.
- Gradient fill red data bars should be applied to the Quantity in Stock column.

Insert the file name in the left section of the footer, center the worksheet horizontally, and repeat the table column titles on each page. Edit the file properties to include your course and section, your name, and the keywords **Petaluma, confections** Save your file, and then print or submit your worksheet electronically as directed by your instructor—two pages result. If required by your instructor, print or create an electronic version of your worksheet with formulas displayed by using the instructions in Activity 1.15, and then close the workbook without saving so that you do not save the changes you made to print formulas. Then Quit Excel.

End You have completed Project 2H ———————————

Apply a combination of the 2A and 2B skills.

GO! Make It | Project 2I Salary Summary

Project Files

For Project 2I, you will need the following file:

e02I_Salary_Summary

You will save your workbook as:

Lastname_Firstname_2I_Salary_Summary

Open e02I_Salary_Summary and save the file in your Excel Chapter 2 folder as **Lastname_Firstname_2I_Salary_Summary** Edit the worksheet as shown in Figure 2.58. To calculate Commission for each salesperson, multiply the Sales by the Commission Rate, using absolute cell references as necessary. To determine the Bonus, construct an IF function where the Logical Test determines if Sales are greater than **21500**, then display **500**, else display **0** Calculate Total Compensation by adding the Commission and the Bonus for each salesperson. Determine the Sales and Compensation totals, averages, medians, and highest and lowest amounts. Insert a table, apply Table Medium Style 16, sort the table as shown in Figure 2.58, apply cell styles and number formatting as indicated, and convert the table to a range. Insert a footer with the file name in the left section, center the worksheet horizontally, and add your course name and section, your name, and the keywords **commission, sales** to the file properties. Print or submit electronically as directed by your instructor—one page results.

Project Results

Laurales Herbs and Spices

January Sales and Compensation

	Sales	Compensation
Total	$ 394,393.00	$ 64,658.95
Average	$ 23,199.59	$ 3,803.47
Median	$ 22,924.00	$ 3,938.60
Highest	$ 33,909.00	$ 5,586.35
Lowest	$ 12,320.00	$ 1,848.00

Commission Rate 15%

Name	Sales	Commission	Bonus	Total Compensation
Anderson	12,320.00	1,848.00	-	1,848.00
Antonetti	22,299.00	3,344.85	500.00	3,844.85
Belitti	12,523.00	1,878.45	-	1,878.45
Caprio	12,932.00	1,939.80	-	1,939.80
Chiu	33,909.00	5,086.35	500.00	5,586.35
Cloutier	30,550.00	4,582.50	500.00	5,082.50
Fernandez	21,345.00	3,201.75	-	3,201.75
Hernandez	22,045.00	3,306.75	500.00	3,806.75
Hutchins	31,309.00	4,696.35	500.00	5,196.35
Jackson	29,505.00	4,425.75	500.00	4,925.75
Johnson	25,340.00	3,801.00	500.00	4,301.00
Lee	13,500.00	2,025.00	-	2,025.00
Lin	32,950.00	4,942.50	500.00	5,442.50
Maya	23,950.00	3,592.50	500.00	4,092.50
Nguyen	22,924.00	3,438.60	500.00	3,938.60
Ochoa	25,900.00	3,885.00	500.00	4,385.00
Patel	21,092.00	3,163.80	-	3,163.80

Lastname_Firstname_2I_Salary Summary.xlsx

Figure 2.58

End **You have completed Project 2I**

Content-Based Assessments

GO! Solve It | Project **2J** Toppings

Project Files

For Project 2J, you will need the following file:

e02J_Toppings

You will save your workbook as:

Lastname_Firstname_2J_Toppings

Open the file e02J_Toppings and save it as **Lastname_Firstname_2J_Toppings** in your Excel Chapter 2 folder. Complete the worksheet by entering appropriate formulas in cells B5 and B6. In the Stock Level column, enter an IF function that determines whether the quantity in stock is greater than 65. If the Quantity in Stock is greater than 65, then the Stock Level should display the text **OK** Otherwise the Stock Level should display the text **Order** Insert a Table with a total row and apply an attractive table style. Sort the table by Item #, calculate the values for B7 and B8, and then clear all filters and remove the total row from the table. Convert the table to a range. Format the worksheet attractively, and apply appropriate Data Bars to the Quantity in Stock column and conditional formatting to the Stock Level column so that items that need to be ordered are easily identified. Include the file name in the footer, add appropriate file properties, center horizontally, be sure the columns all print on one page, and submit as directed.

	Performance Level		
	Exemplary: You consistently applied the relevant skills	**Proficient:** You sometimes, but not always, applied the relevant skills	**Developing:** You rarely or never applied the relevant skills
Create formulas	All formulas are correct and are efficiently constructed.	Formulas are correct but not always constructed in the most efficient manner.	One or more formulas are missing or incorrect; or only numbers were entered.
Insert and format a table	Table was created and formatted properly.	Table was created but incorrect data was selected or the table was not formatted.	No table was created.
Format worksheet data attractively and appropriately	Formatting is attractive and appropriate.	Adequately formatted but difficult to read or unattractive.	Inadequate or no formatting.

(Performance Criteria)

End **You have completed Project 2J** ——————————

Content-Based Assessments

GO! Solve It | Project **2K** First Quarter Summary

Project Files

For Project 2K, you will need the following file:

e02K_First_Quarter

You will save your workbook as:

Lastname_Firstname_2K_First_Quarter

Open the file e02K_First_Quarter and save it as **Lastname_Firstname_2K_First_Quarter** in your Excel Chapter 2 folder. This workbook contains two worksheets; one that includes California sales data by product and one that includes Oregon sales data by product. Complete the two worksheets by calculating totals by product and by month. Then calculate the Percent of Total by dividing the Product Total by the Monthly Total, using absolute cell references as necessary. Format the worksheets attractively with a title and subtitle, and apply appropriate financial formatting. Insert a new worksheet that summarizes the monthly totals by state. Enter the months as the column titles and the states as the row titles. Include a Product Total column and a column for sparklines titled **Jan./Feb./March** Format the Summary worksheet attractively with a title and subtitle, insert column sparklines that compare the months, and apply appropriate financial formatting. Include the file name in the footer, add appropriate file properties, center horizontally, be sure the columns all print on one page, and submit as directed.

		Performance Level		
		Exemplary: You consistently applied the relevant skills	**Proficient:** You sometimes, but not always, applied the relevant skills	**Developing:** You rarely or never applied the relevant skills
Performance Criteria	**Create formulas**	All formulas are correct and are efficiently constructed.	Formulas are correct but not always constructed in the most efficient manner.	One or more formulas are missing or incorrect; or only numbers were entered.
	Create Summary worksheet	Summary worksheet created properly.	Summary worksheet was created but the data, sparklines, or formulas were incorrect.	No Summary worksheet was created.
	Format attractively and appropriately	Formatting is attractive and appropriate.	Adequately formatted but difficult to read or unattractive.	Inadequate or no formatting.

End You have completed Project 2K ————————

Outcomes-Based Assessments

Rubric

The following outcomes-based assessments are open-ended assessments. That is, there is no specific correct result; your result will depend on your approach to the information provided. Make Professional Quality your goal. Use the following scoring rubric to guide you in how to approach the problem and then to evaluate how well your approach solves the problem.

The *criteria*—Software Mastery, Content, Format and Layout, and Process—represent the knowledge and skills you have gained that you can apply to solving the problem. The *levels of performance*—Professional Quality, Approaching Professional Quality, or Needs Quality Improvements—help you and your instructor evaluate your result.

	Your completed project is of Professional Quality if you:	Your completed project is Approaching Professional Quality if you:	Your completed project Needs Quality Improvements if you:
1-Software Mastery	Choose and apply the most appropriate skills, tools, and features and identify efficient methods to solve the problem.	Choose and apply some appropriate skills, tools, and features, but not in the most efficient manner.	Choose inappropriate skills, tools, or features, or are inefficient in solving the problem.
2-Content	Construct a solution that is clear and well organized, contains content that is accurate, appropriate to the audience and purpose, and is complete. Provide a solution that contains no errors in spelling, grammar, or style.	Construct a solution in which some components are unclear, poorly organized, inconsistent, or incomplete. Misjudge the needs of the audience. Have some errors in spelling, grammar, or style, but the errors do not detract from comprehension.	Construct a solution that is unclear, incomplete, or poorly organized; contains some inaccurate or inappropriate content; and contains many errors in spelling, grammar, or style. Do not solve the problem.
3-Format and Layout	Format and arrange all elements to communicate information and ideas, clarify function, illustrate relationships, and indicate relative importance.	Apply appropriate format and layout features to some elements, but not others. Overuse features, causing minor distraction.	Apply format and layout that does not communicate information or ideas clearly. Do not use format and layout features to clarify function, illustrate relationships, or indicate relative importance. Use available features excessively, causing distraction.
4-Process	Use an organized approach that integrates planning, development, self-assessment, revision, and reflection.	Demonstrate an organized approach in some areas, but not others; or, use an insufficient process of organization throughout.	Do not use an organized approach to solve the problem.

Outcomes-Based Assessments

GO! Think | Project 2L Seasonings

Project Files

For Project 2L, you will need the following file:

e02L_Seasonings

You will save your workbook as:

Lastname_Firstname_2L_Seasonings

Laura Morales, President of Laurales Herbs and Spices, has requested a worksheet that summarizes the seasonings inventory data for the month of March. Laura would like the worksheet to include the total Quantity in Stock and Number of Items for each category of items, and she would like the items to be sorted from lowest to highest retail price.

Edit the workbook to provide Laura with the information requested. Format the worksheet titles and data and include an appropriately formatted table so that the worksheet is professional and easy to read and understand. Insert a footer with the file name, add appropriate file properties, center horizontally, and be sure that the columns print on one page and column titles print on all pages. Save the file in your Excel Chapter 2 folder as **Lastname_Firstname_2L_Seasonings** and print or submit as directed by your instructor.

End **You have completed Project 2L** ————————————

GO! Think | Project 2M Expense Summary

Project Files

For Project 2M, you will need the following file:

e02M_Expense_Summary

You will save your workbook as:

Lastname_Firstname_2M_Expense_Summary

Sara Lopez, Director of the San Diego production facility, has requested a summary analysis of the administrative expenses the facility incurred in the last fiscal year. Open e02M_Expense_Summary and then complete the calculation in the four worksheets containing the quarterly data. Summarize the information in a new worksheet that includes formulas referencing the totals for each expense category for each quarter. Sum the expenses to display the yearly expense by quarter and expense category. Format the worksheets in a manner that is professional and easy to read and understand. Insert a footer with the file name, add appropriate file properties, center horizontally, and be sure that the columns print on one page. Save the file in your Excel Chapter 2 folder as **Lastname_Firstname_2M_Expense_Summary** and print or submit as directed by your instructor.

End **You have completed Project 2M** ————————————

Outcomes-Based Assessments

Apply a combination of the **2A** and **2B** skills.

You and GO! | Project **2N** Annual Expenses

Project Files

For Project 2N, you will need the following file:

New Excel workbook

You will save your workbook as:

Lastname_Firstname_2N_Annual_Expenses

Develop a workbook that details the expenses you expect to incur during the current year. Create four worksheets, one for each quarter of the year and enter your expenses by month. For example, the Quarter 1 sheet will contain expense information for January, February, and March. Some of these expenses might include, but are not limited to, Mortgage, Rent, Utilities, Phone, Food, Entertainment, Tuition, Child Care, Clothing, and Insurance. Include monthly and quarterly totals for each category of expense. Insert a worksheet that summarizes the total expenses for each quarter. Format the worksheet by adjusting column width and wrapping text, and by applying appropriate financial number formatting and cell styles. Insert a footer with the file name, add appropriate file properties, center horizontally, and be sure that the columns print on one page. Save your file in your Excel Chapter 2 folder as **Lastname_Firstname_2N_Annual_Expenses** and submit as directed by your instructor.

End **You have completed Project 2N** ———————————

Apply a combination of the **2A** and **2B** skills.

GO! Group Business Running Case | Project **2O**
Bell Orchid Hotels Group Running Case

This project relates to the **Bell Orchid Hotels**. Your instructor may assign this group case project to your class. If your instructor assigns this project, he or she will provide you with information and instructions to work as part of a group. The group will apply the skills gained thus far to help the Bell Orchid Hotels achieve their business goals.

End **You have completed Project 2O** ———————————

Excel | Chapter 2

Analyzing Data with Pie Charts, Line Charts, and What-If Analysis Tools

OUTCOMES

At the end of this chapter you will be able to:

PROJECT 3A
Present budget data in a pie chart.

PROJECT 3B
Make projections using what-if analysis and present projections in a line chart.

OBJECTIVES

Mastering these objectives will enable you to:

1. Chart Data with a Pie Chart (p. 375)
2. Format a Pie Chart (p. 378)
3. Edit a Workbook and Update a Chart (p. 385)
4. Use Goal Seek to Perform What-If Analysis (p. 387)

5. Design a Worksheet for What-If Analysis (p. 392)
6. Answer What-If Questions by Changing Values in a Worksheet (p. 398)
7. Chart Data with a Line Chart (p. 401)

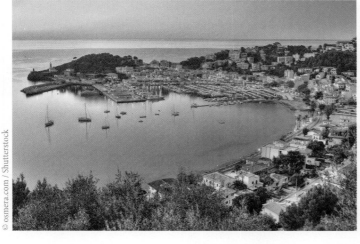

© osmera.com / Shutterstock

In This Chapter

In this chapter, you will work with two different types of commonly used charts that make it easy to visualize data. You will create a pie chart in a separate chart sheet to show how the parts of a budget contribute to a total budget. You will also practice using parentheses in a formula, calculate the percentage rate of an increase, answer what-if questions, and then chart data in a line chart to show the flow of data over time. In this chapter, you will also practice formatting the axes in a line chart.

The projects in this chapter relate to **The City of Orange Blossom Beach**, a coastal city located between Fort Lauderdale and Miami. The city's access to major transportation provides both residents and businesses an opportunity to compete in the global marketplace. Each year, the city welcomes a large number of tourists who enjoy the warm climate and beautiful beaches and who embark on cruises from this major cruise port. The city encourages best environmental practices and partners with cities in other countries to promote sound government at the local level.

Project 3A Budget Pie Chart

Project Activities

In Activities 3.01 through 3.11, you will edit a worksheet for Lila Darius, City Manager, that projects expenses from the city's general fund for the next fiscal year, and then present the data in a pie chart. Your completed worksheet will look similar to Figure 3.1.

Project Files

For Project 3A, you will need the following file:

> e03A_Fund_Expenses

You will save your workbook as:

> Lastname_Firstname_3A_Fund_Expenses

Project Results

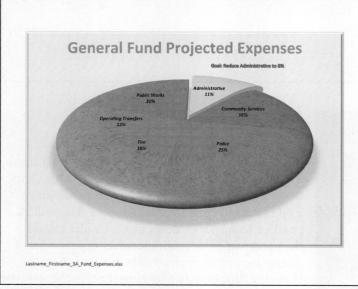

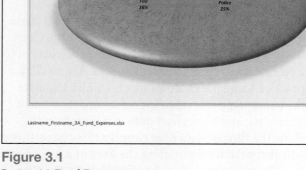

Figure 3.1
Project 3A Fund Expenses

Objective 1 | Chart Data with a Pie Chart

A **pie chart** shows the relationship of each part to a whole. The size of each pie slice is equal to its value compared to the total value of all the slices. The pie chart style displays data that is arranged in a single column or single row, and shows the size of items in a single data series proportional to the sum of the items. Whereas a column or bar chart can have two or more data series in the chart, a pie chart can have only one data series.

Consider using a pie chart when you have only one data series to plot, when you do not have more than seven categories, and when the categories represent parts of a total value.

Activity 3.01 | Creating a Pie Chart and a Chart Sheet

A **fund** is a sum of money set aside for a specific purpose. In a municipal government like the city of Orange Blossom Beach, the **general fund** is money set aside for the normal operating activities of the city, such as operating the police department and fire department and administering the everyday functions of the city.

1 Open **Excel**. From the student files that accompany this textbook, **Open e03A_Fund_ Expenses**. If necessary, increase the size of the Excel window to fill the screen. If necessary, on the Standard toolbar, click the Zoom arrow 100% ▾, and then click 125%.

2 On the **File** menu, click **Save As**. In the **Save As** dialog box, navigate to the location where you are storing your projects for this chapter. **Create** a new folder named **Excel Chapter 3** and then in the **Save As** box, type **Lastname_Firstname_3A_Fund_Expenses** Click **Save** or press Return.

> The worksheet indicates the expenses for the current year and the projected expenses for the next fiscal year.

3 Click cell **D5**, and then type **=** to begin a formula.

4 Click cell **C5**, which is the first value that is part of the total Projected Expenses, to insert it into the formula. Type **/** to indicate division, and then click cell **C11**, which is the total Projected Expenses.

> Recall that to determine the percentage by which a value makes up a total, you must divide the value by the total. The result will be a percentage expressed as a decimal.

5 Press Command ⌘ + T to make the reference to the value in cell **C11** absolute, which will enable you to copy the formula. Compare your screen with Figure 3.2.

> Recall that an **absolute cell reference** refers to a cell by its fixed position in the worksheet. The reference to cell C5 is a **relative cell reference**, because when you copy the formula, you want the reference to change *relative* to its row.

> Recall also that dollar signs display to indicate that a cell reference is absolute.

Figure 3.2

Formula bar displays formula

Cell C5 bordered and shaded in blue, indicating it is part of an active formula

Reference to cell C11 with $ signs to indicate an absolute cell reference

Cell C11 selected as part of active formula

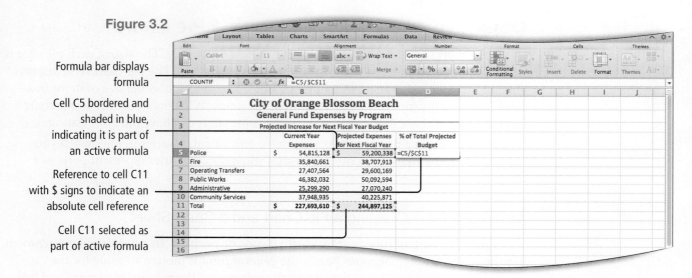

6 On the formula bar, click the **Enter** button 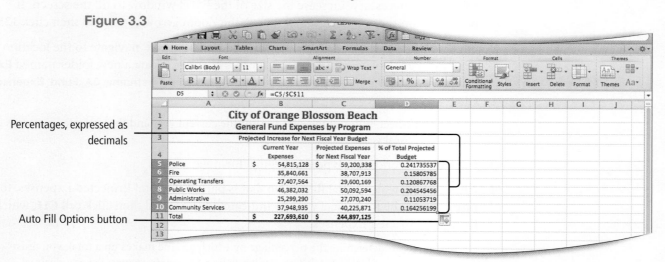 to confirm the entry and to keep cell **D5** the active cell. Using the fill handle, copy the formula down through cell **D10**, and then compare your screen with Figure 3.3.

Figure 3.3

Percentages, expressed as decimals

Auto Fill Options button

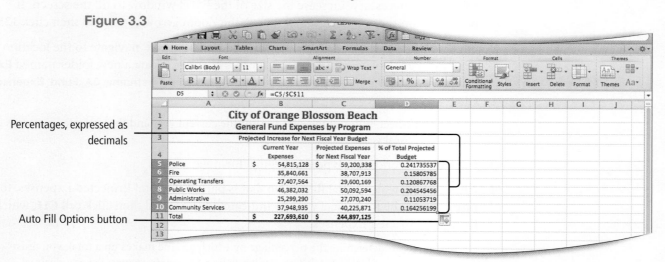

7 With the range **D5:D10** still selected, on the **Home tab**, in the **Number group**, click the **Percent Style** button 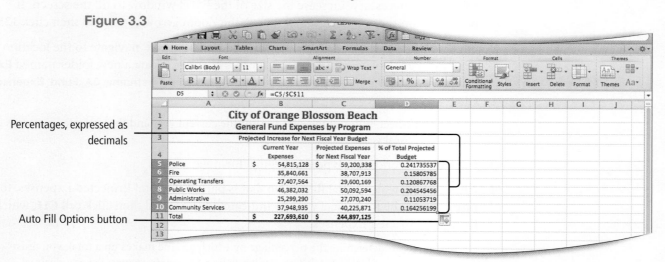, and then in the **Alignment group**, click the **Center Text** button . Click cell **A1** to cancel the selection, and then **Save** your workbook. Compare your screen with Figure 3.4.

Figure 3.4

Percent of Total for each program calculated, expressed as percentage

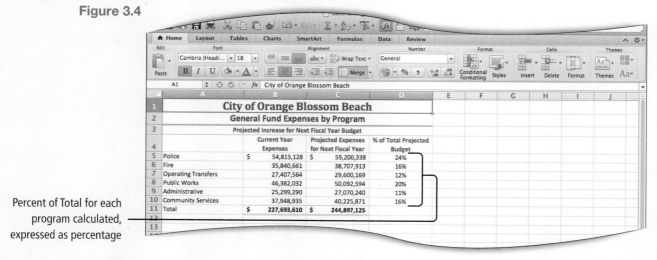

8 Select the range **A5:A10**, hold down Command ⌘, and then select the range **C5:C10** to select the nonadjacent ranges with the program names and the projected expense for each program, respectively.

> To create a pie chart, you must select two ranges. One range contains the labels for each slice of the pie chart, and the other range contains the values that add up to a total. The two ranges must have the same number of cells and the range with the values should *not* include the cell with the total.

> The program names (Police, Fire, and so on) are the category names and will identify the slices of the pie chart. Each projected expense is a *data point*—a value that originates in a worksheet cell and that is represented in a chart by a *data marker*. In a pie chart, each pie slice is a data marker. Together, the data points form the *data series*—related data points represented by data markers—and determine the size of each pie slice.

9 With the nonadjacent ranges selected, click the **Charts tab**, and then in the **Insert Chart group**, click the **Pie** button. Under **3-D Pie**, click the first chart—**3-D Pie**—to create the chart on your worksheet.

Another Way

On the Chart menu, click Move Chart.

10 Point to the white area of the chart, press Control and click, and then from the shortcut menu, click **Move Chart**. In the **Move Chart** dialog box, click the **New sheet** option button.

11 In the **New sheet** box, replace the highlighted text *Chart1* by typing **Projected Expenses Chart** and then click **OK** to display the chart on a separate worksheet in your workbook. Compare your screen with Figure 3.5.

> The pie chart displays on a new sheet in your workbook, and a *legend* identifies the pie slices. Recall that a legend is a chart element that identifies the patterns or colors assigned to the categories in the chart.

> A *chart sheet* is a workbook sheet that contains only a chart; it is useful when you want to view a chart separately from the worksheet data. The sheet tab displays *Projected Expenses Chart*.

Figure 3.5

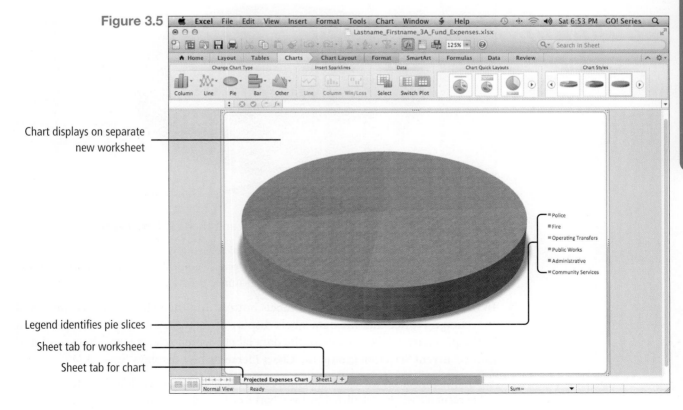

Chart displays on separate new worksheet

Legend identifies pie slices

Sheet tab for worksheet

Sheet tab for chart

Objective 2 | Format a Pie Chart

Activity 3.02 | Applying Percentages to Labels in a Pie Chart

In your worksheet, for each expense, you calculated the percent of the total in column D. These percentages can also be calculated by the Chart feature and added to the pie slices as labels.

1 On the **Chart Layout tab**, in the **Labels group**, click the **Chart Title** button, and then click **Title Above Chart**.

2 With the **Chart Title** box selected, type **General Fund Projected Expenses** and then click the border of the **Chart Title** box to remove the insertion point from the box. On the **Chart Layout tab**, in the **Current Selection group**, notice that the **Chart Elements** box displays *Chart Title*.

From the *Chart Elements box*, you can select a chart element so that you can format it.

<table>
<tr><td>

Another Way

To format the title, click the Home tab, and in the Font group, change the settings.

</td><td>

3 In the **Current Selection group**, click the **Format Selection** button. In the **Format Title** dialog box, change the **Font size** to **36** and change the **Font color** to **Accent 1, Darker 25%**—in the fifth row, the fifth color. In the **Format Title** dialog box, click **OK**, and then compare your screen with Figure 3.6.

</td></tr>
</table>

Figure 3.6

Chart Elements box

Format Selection button

New chart title text entered, selected, and formatted

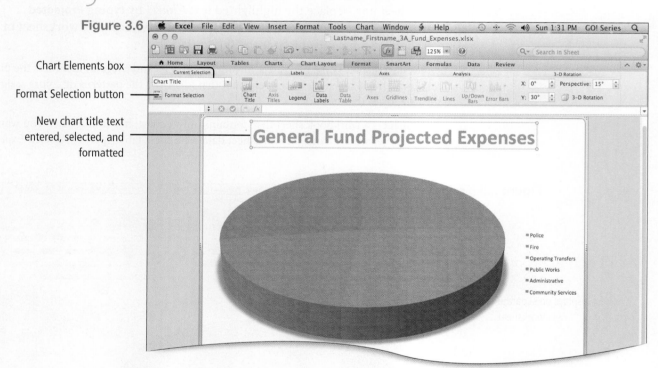

4 In the **Labels group**, click the **Legend** button, and then click **No Legend**.

The chart expands to fill the new space. In a pie chart, it is usually more effective to place the labels within, or close to, each pie slice. Because you will place the program names (the categories) on the pie slices, a legend is unnecessary.

5 In the **Labels group**, click the **Data Labels** button, and then click **Category Name and Percentage**. Notice that the data labels display the category name and the percentage in the pie chart. Click any one of the data labels, which selects all of them, and notice in the **Current Selection group**, the **Chart Elements** box displays *Series 1 Data Labels*.

In the worksheet, you calculated the percentage of the total in column D. Here, the percentage will be calculated by the Chart feature and added to the chart as a label.

6 With the data labels selected, in the **Current Selection group**, click the **Format Selection** button. In the **Format Data Labels** dialog box, on the **Font tab**, change the **Font style** to **Bold Italic** and the **Font size** to **11**. On the left side of the **Format Data Labels** dialog box, click **Labels**. Under **Label options**, click in the **Label position** box, and then click **Center**. In the **Format Data Labels** dialog box, click **OK**.

7 **Save** 🖫 your workbook. Press Esc to deselect the labels, and then compare your screen with Figure 3.7.

Figure 3.7

Data labels on pie slices replace legend, include category name and percentage, centered in slice, and formatted

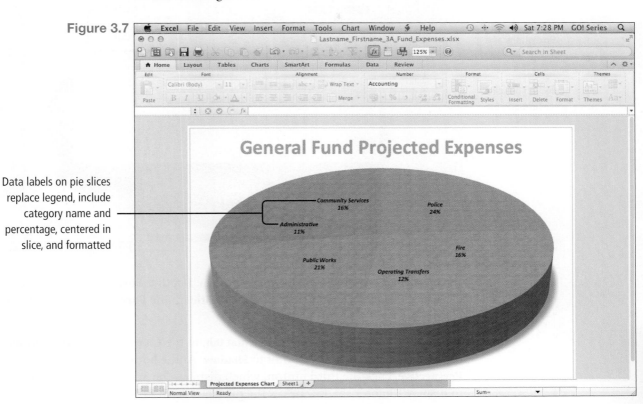

Activity 3.03 │ Formatting a Pie Chart with 3-D

The abbreviation for *three-dimensional* is *3-D*, which refers to an image that appears to have all three spatial dimensions—length, width, and depth.

1 Click in any pie slice—do not click the label in the slide—to select the entire pie; notice that selection handles display on the outside corners of each slice.

2 Click the **Format tab**. In the **Chart Element Styles group**, click the **Effects** button, point to **Bevel**, and then click **Bevel Options**.

3 In the **Format Data Series** dialog box, with the **Bevel tab** active, under **Bevel**, click in the **Top** box, and then click **Circle**. Click in the **Bottom** box, and then click **Circle**.

Bevel is a shape effect that uses shading and shadows to make the edges of a shape appear to be curved or angled.

4 In the four **Width** and **Height** boxes, select the existing text, type **512** and then compare your screen with Figure 3.8.

After typing *512* and moving to another box, *pt* is automatically added to the number.

Excel │ Chapter 3

Figure 3.8

Depth & Surface tab

Format Data Series
dialog box

Bevel tab

Box widths and
heights set to 512 pt

Selection handles
surround pie

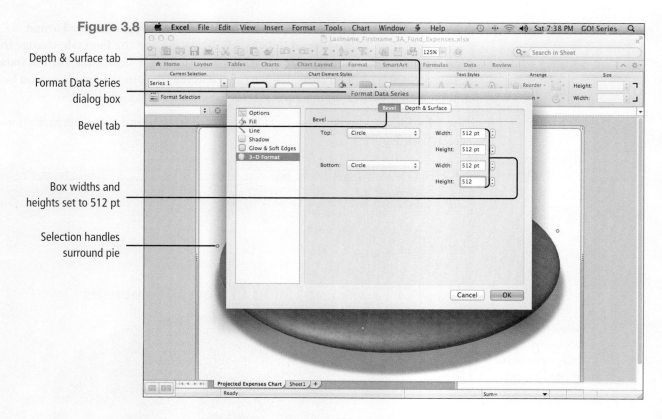

5 In the **Format Data Series** dialog box, click the **Depth & Surface tab**. Under **Surface**, click in the **Material** box, and then click **Plastic**. In the **Format Data Series** dialog box, click **OK**.

6 With the pie still selected, on the **Format tab**, in the **Chart Element Styles group**, click the **Effects** button, and then point to **Shadow**. At the bottom of the gallery, under **Perspective**, click the third button, which displays the ScreenTip *Perspective Bottom* to display a lighter shadow below the pie chart. **Save** 🖫 your workbook.

Activity 3.04 | Rotating a Pie Chart

The order in which the data series in pie charts are plotted in Excel is determined by the order of the data on the worksheet. To gain a different view of the chart, you can rotate the chart within the 360 degrees of the circle of the pie shape to present a different visual perspective of the chart.

1 Notice the position of the **Fire** and **Police** slices in the chart. Then, with the pie chart still selected—sizing handles surround the pie—on the **Format tab**, in the **Current Selection group**, click the **Format Selection** button.

2 In the **Format Data Series** dialog box, on the left, click **Options**. On the right, change the **Angle of first slice** to **100** to rotate the chart 100 degrees to the right. In the **Format Data Series** dialog box, click **OK**. **Save** 🖫 your workbook, and then compare your screen with Figure 3.9.

Rotating the chart can provide a better perspective of the chart. Here, rotating the chart in this manner emphasizes that the Fire and Police programs represent a significant portion of the total expenses.

Figure 3.9

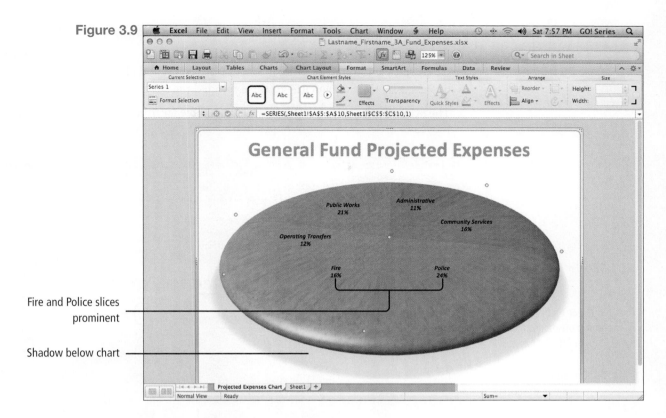

Fire and Police slices prominent

Shadow below chart

Activity 3.05 | Exploding and Coloring a Pie Slice

You can pull out—**explode**—one or more slices of a pie chart to emphasize a specific slice or slices. Additionally, there is a different chart type you can select if you want *all* the slices to explode and emphasize all the individual slices of a pie chart—the exploded pie or exploded pie in 3-D chart type. The exploded pie chart type displays the contribution of *each* value to the total, while at the same time emphasizing individual values.

1 Press Esc to deselect all chart elements. Click in any colored section of a slice to select the entire pie—do not click on the data labels within a slice—and then click the **Administrative** slice to select only that slice. Compare your screen with Figure 3.10.

Figure 3.10

Only *Administrative* slice selected as indicated by selection handles

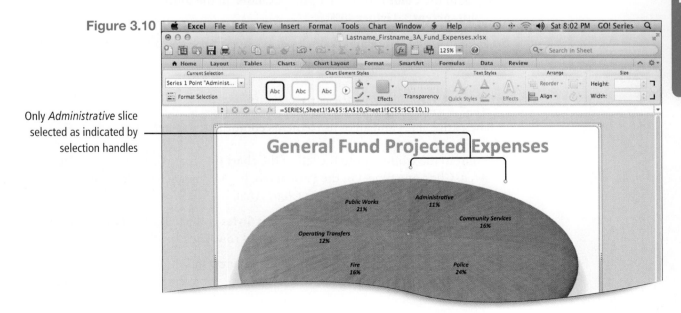

2 Point to the **Administrative** slice to display the 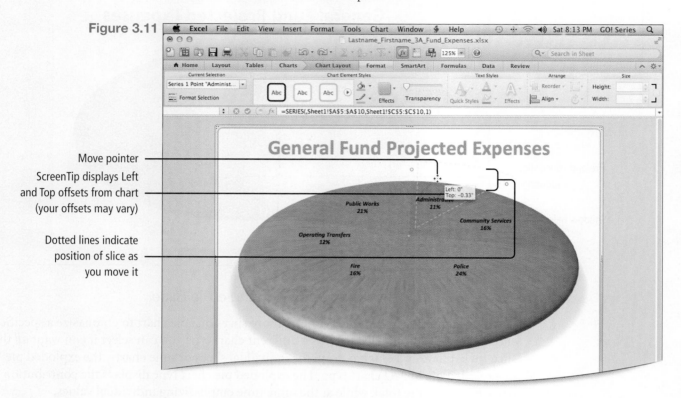pointer and a ScreenTip. Drag the slice slightly upward and away from the center of the pie, as shown in Figure 3.11, and then release the mouse button. Do not be concerned about the exact location—as displayed by the ScreenTip—of the exploded pie slice.

The ScreenTip displays how far to the left and how far from the top the slice will be moved or offset from its current position.

Figure 3.11

Move pointer

ScreenTip displays Left and Top offsets from chart (your offsets may vary)

Dotted lines indicate position of slice as you move it

3 With the **Administrative** slice still selected, on the **Format tab**, in the **Current Selection group**, click the **Format Selection** button.

4 In the **Format Data Point** dialog box, on the left, click **Fill**. With the **Solid tab** active, click in the **Color** box. Under **Theme Colors**, in the fourth row, click the seventh color, **Accent 3, Lighter 40%**.

5 In the **Format Data Point** dialog box, click **OK**. **Save** your workbook, and notice that the exploded pie slice has a gold fill color.

Activity 3.06 | Formatting the Chart Area

The entire chart and all of its elements comprise the *chart area*.

1 Point to the white area to the left of the chart title to display the ScreenTip *Chart Area*. Click one time. On the **Format tab**, in the **Current Selection group**, notice that the **Chart Elements** box displays *Chart Area*.

2 On the **Format tab**, in the **Chart Element Styles group**, click the **Effects** button, point to **Bevel**, and then under **Bevel**, in the second row, click the third bevel—**Convex**.

3 Press Esc to deselect the chart element and view this effect—a convex beveled frame around your entire chart—and then compare your screen with Figure 3.12.

Figure 3.12

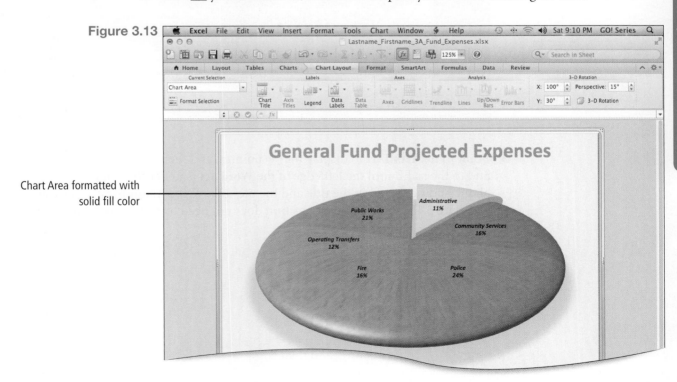

Convex beveled frame surrounds chart sheet

4 Point slightly inside the border of the chart to display the ScreenTip *Chart Area*, click, and then on the **Format tab**, in the **Current Selection group**, click **Format Selection**.

5 In the **Format Chart Area** dialog box, on the left, be sure that **Fill** is selected. With the **Solid tab** active, click in the **Color** box, and then under **Theme Colors**, in the third row, click the fifth color, **Accent 1, Lighter 60%**. In the **Format Chart Area** dialog box, click **OK**.

6 **Save** 🖫 your workbook, and then compare your screen with Figure 3.13.

Figure 3.13

Chart Area formatted with solid fill color

Excel | Chapter 3

Activity 3.07 | Inserting WordArt in a Chart

WordArt is a gallery of text styles with which you can create decorative effects, such as shadowed or mirrored text. In an Excel chart, WordArt can be effective if you plan to highlight a specific area of the chart.

1 With the **Chart Area** selected, on the **Insert** menu, point to **Picture**, and then click **WordArt**.

The WordArt indicating *Your Text Here* displays on top of the pie chart.

2 With the **WordArt** selected, on the **Home tab**, in the **Font group**, change the **Font Size** to **11**. Click the **Font Color arrow** $\boxed{\text{A}}$ ⋅, and then under **Theme Colors**, in the first row, click the second color—**Text 1**. Type **Goal: Reduce Administrative to 8%** and then compare your screen with Figure 3.14.

Figure 3.14

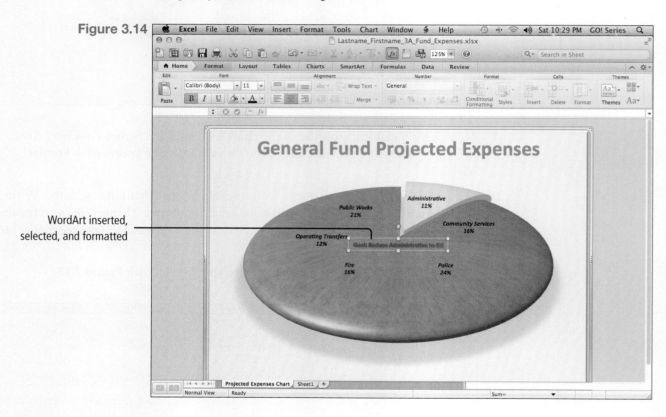

WordArt inserted, selected, and formatted

3 Point to the **WordArt** to display the ⊕ pointer, and then drag the **WordArt** upward and to the right until the left edge of the **Word Art** is under the *c* in *Projected* and about midway between the title and the pie—above the **Administrative** slice as shown in Figure 3.15; your WordArt position does not need to match precisely.

Figure 3.15

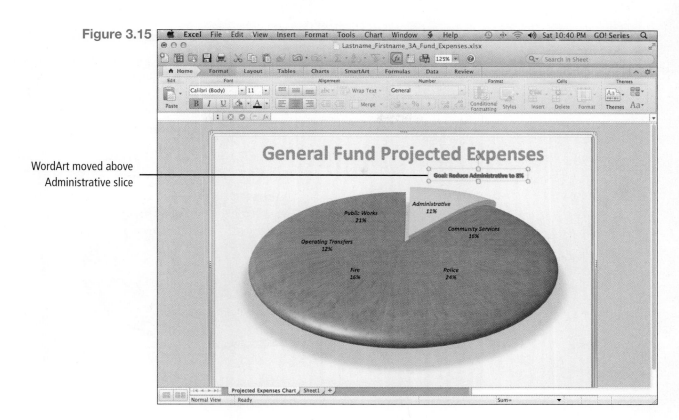

WordArt moved above
Administrative slice

4 On the **Home tab**, in the **Font group**, click the **Bold** button **B** to remove the bold formatting. Press Esc to cancel the selection of the **WordArt**, and then **Save** 🖫 your workbook.

Objective 3 | Edit a Workbook and Update a Chart

Activity 3.08 | Editing a Workbook and Updating a Chart

If you edit the data in your worksheet, the chart data markers—in this instance the pie slices—will adjust automatically to accurately represent the new values.

1 On the pie chart, notice that *Police* represents 24% of the total projected expenses.

2 In the sheet tab area at the bottom of the workbook, click the **Sheet1 tab** to redisplay the worksheet.

> **Another Way**
> Double-click the cell to position the insertion point in the cell, and then edit.

3 Click cell **C5**, and then in formula bar, change *59200338* to **62200388**

4 Press Return, and notice that the total in cell **C11** recalculates to *$247,897,175*, and the percentages in **column D** also recalculate.

5 Display the **Projected Expenses Chart** sheet. Notice that the pie slices adjust to show the recalculation—*Police* is now *25%* of the projected expenses. **Save** 🖫 your workbook, and then compare your screen with Figure 3.16.

Excel | Chapter 3

Figure 3.16

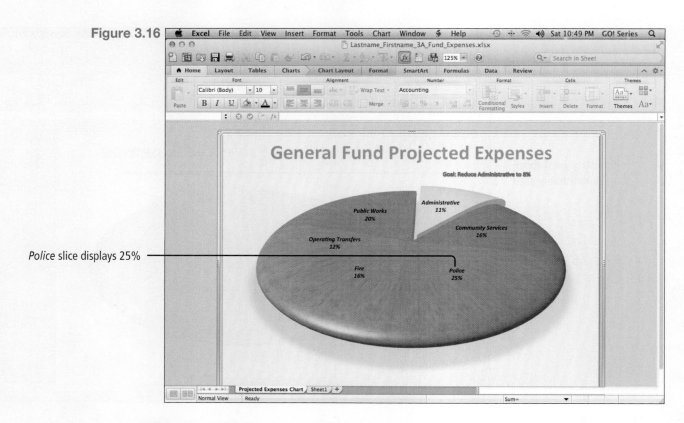

Police slice displays 25%

Activity 3.09 | Inserting WordArt in a Worksheet

In an Excel worksheet, WordArt can be effective if you plan to display your worksheet in a PowerPoint presentation, or if readers will be viewing the worksheet data online.

1 In the sheet tab area at the bottom of the workbook, click the **Sheet1 tab** to redisplay the worksheet. On the **Insert** menu, click **WordArt**.

>The WordArt indicating *Your Text Here* displays in the worksheet.

2 On the **Format tab**, in the **Text Styles group**, click the **Quick Styles** button. **Under Applies to All Text in the Shape**, on the second row, click the last button—the letter *A* displays in solid olive green with a reflection under the letter.

3 With the **WordArt** selected, type **general fund expenses** and then point anywhere on the border surrounding the WordArt object. Click the border one time to select the entire **WordArt** and to remove the insertion point from the text in the WordArt.

4 On the **Home tab**, in the **Font group**, change the **Font Size** to **28**.

5 Point to the **WordArt** border to display the ⊕ pointer, and then drag to position the upper left corner of the WordArt approximately as shown in Figure 3.17. If necessary, press any of the arrow keys on your keyboard to nudge the WordArt object into position in small increments. Click any cell to deselect the WordArt, and then **Save** 🖫 your workbook.

Figure 3.17

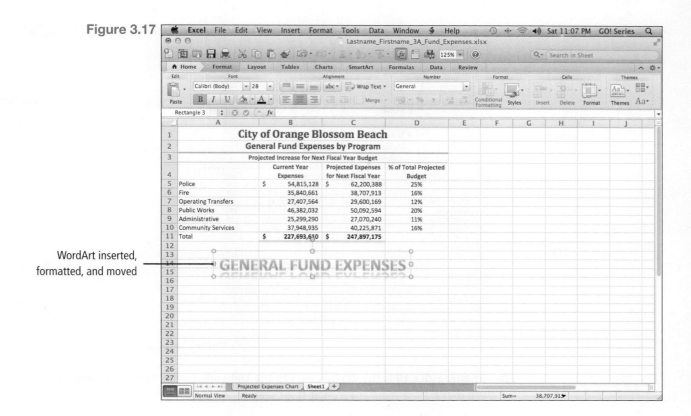

WordArt inserted,
formatted, and moved

Objective 4 | Use Goal Seek to Perform What-If Analysis

Activity 3.10 | Using Goal Seek to Perform What-If Analysis

The process of changing the values in cells to see how those changes affect the outcome of formulas in your worksheet is referred to as *what-if analysis*. A what-if analysis tool that is included with Excel is *Goal Seek*, which finds the input needed in one cell to arrive at the desired result in another cell.

1 In cell **A17**, type **Goal: To Reduce Administrative Expenses from 11% to 8% of Total Expenses** and then press Return. **Merge** the text across the range **A17:D17**. On the **Home tab**, in the **Format group**, click the **Styles** button. In the **Cell Styles** gallery, under **Titles and Headings**, click **Heading 3**.

2 In cell **A18**, type **Goal Amount:** and then press Return.

3 Select the range **C9:D9**, and then on the Standard toolbar, click the **Copy** button. Click cell **B18**, and then on the Standard toolbar, click the **Paste** button.

4 Press Esc to cancel the moving border, click cell **C18**, and then compare your screen with Figure 3.18.

Excel | Chapter 3

Figure 3.18

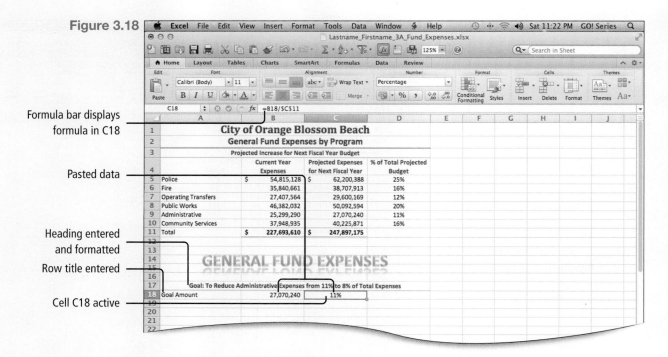

Formula bar displays formula in C18

Pasted data

Heading entered and formatted

Row title entered

Cell C18 active

5 Be sure cell **C18** is the active cell. On the **Data tab**, in the **Analysis group**, click the **What-If** button, and then click **Goal Seek**.

6 In the **Goal Seek** dialog box, notice that the active cell, **C18**, is indicated in the **Set cell** box. Press Tab to move to the **To value** box, and then type **8%**

> C18 is the cell in which you want to set a specific value; 8% is the percentage of the total expenses that you want to budget for Administrative expenses. The Set cell box contains the formula that calculates the information you seek.

7 Press Tab to move the insertion point to the **By changing cell** box, and then click cell **B18**. Compare your screen with Figure 3.19.

> Cell B18 contains the value that Excel changes to reach the goal. Excel formats this cell as an absolute cell reference.

Figure 3.19

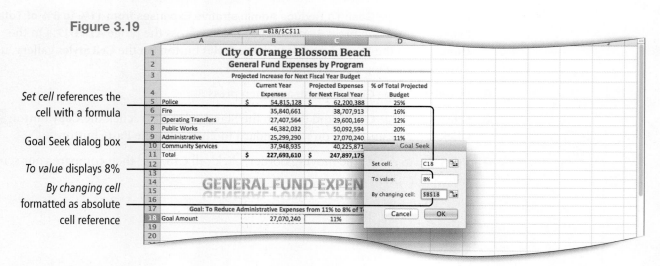

Set cell references the cell with a formula

Goal Seek dialog box

To value displays 8%

By changing cell formatted as absolute cell reference

8 In the **Goal Seek** dialog box, click **OK**. In the **Goal Seek Status** dialog box, click **OK**.

> Excel calculates that the city must budget for $19,831,774 in Administrative expenses in order for this item to become 8% of the total projected budget.

9 Select the range **A18:C18**. On the **Home tab**, in the **Format group**, click the **Styles** button to display the **Cell Styles** gallery. Under **Themed Cell Styles**, click **20% - Accent3**. Click cell **B18**, and then from the **Cell Styles** gallery, scroll to display the bottom of the gallery, and under **Number Format**, click **Currency [0]**.

10 Click cell **A1**, **Save** 🖫 your workbook, and then compare your screen with Figure 3.20.

Figure 3.20

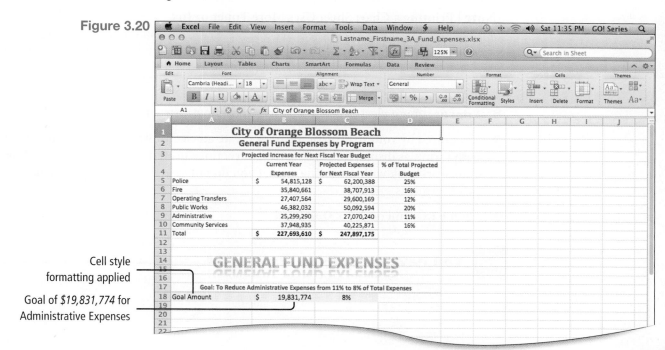

Cell style formatting applied ———
Goal of *$19,831,774* for Administrative Expenses ———

Activity 3.11 | Preparing and Printing a Workbook with a Chart Sheet

Another Way

Point to the sheet tab, press Control and click, and from the shortcut menu, click Rename.

1 With your worksheet displayed, in the sheet tab area, double-click *Sheet1* to select the text, type **Projected Expenses Data** and then press Return.

2 On the **View** menu, click **Header and Footer**. In the **Page Setup** dialog box, click **Customize Footer**. With the insertion point in the **Left section**, click the **Insert File Name** button 🖹, and then click **OK**.

3 In the **Page Setup** dialog box, click the **Margins tab**. Under **Center on page**, select the **Horizontally** check box, and then click **OK**. **Save** 🖫 your workbook.

Recall that dotted lines display to indicate the page breaks.

4 Click the **Projected Expenses Chart** sheet tab to display the chart sheet. On the **View** menu, click **Header and Footer**, and then using the steps you just practiced, insert the file name in the **Left section** of the footer.

5 On the **File** menu, click **Properties**. In the **Subject** box, type your course name and section number. In the **Author** box, replace the existing text with your firstname and lastname. In the **Keywords** box type **general fund, expenses, pie chart** and then click **OK**.

6 Point to either of the sheet tabs, press Control and click, and then from the shortcut menu, click **Select All Sheets**. Verify that *[Group]* displays in the title bar. **Save** 🖫 your workbook.

Recall that by selecting all sheets, you can print all sheets at one time.

7 On the **File** menu, click **Print**. In the **Print** dialog box, examine the first page of the previewed document, and then under the preview of the document, click the **Next Page** button to view the second page of your workbook.

The preview of the worksheet is too small to see, but the worksheet will print at its full size.

> **Note** | Printing a Chart Sheet Uses More Toner or Ink
>
> Printing a chart that displays on a chart sheet will use more toner or ink than a small chart that is part of a worksheet. If you are printing your work, check with your instructor to verify whether or not you should print the chart sheet.

8 **Print** or submit electronically as directed by your instructor.

9 If required by your instructor, print or create an electronic version of your worksheet with formulas displayed by using the instructions in Activity 1.15, and then **Close** your workbook without saving so that you do not save the changes you made to print formulas.

10 On the **Excel** menu, click **Quit Excel**.

End **You have completed Project 3A** ————————————

Project 3B Growth Projection with Line Chart

Project Activities

In Activities 3.12 through 3.19, you will assist Lila Darius, City Manager, in creating a worksheet to estimate future population growth based on three possible growth rates. You will also create a line chart to display past population growth. Your resulting worksheet and chart will look similar to Figure 3.21.

Project Files

For Project 3B, you will need the following files:

e03B_Population_Growth
e03B_Beach.JPG

You will save your workbook as:

Lastname_Firstname_3B_Population_Growth

Project Results

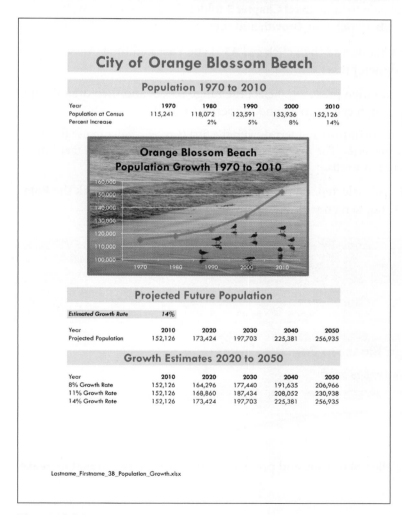

Figure 3.21
Project 3B Population Growth

Objective 5 | Design a Worksheet for What-If Analysis

Excel recalculates; if you change the value in a cell referenced in a formula, Excel automatically recalculates the result of the formula. Thus, you can change cell values to see *what* would happen *if* you tried different values. Recall that this process of changing the values in cells to see how those changes affect the outcome of formulas in your worksheet is referred to as what-if analysis.

Activity 3.12 | Using Parentheses in a Formula to Calculate a Percentage Rate of Increase

Ms. Darius has the city's population figures for the past five 10-year census periods. In each 10-year census period, the population has increased. In this activity, you will construct a formula to calculate the *percentage rate of increase*—the percent by which one number increases over another number—for each 10-year census period since 1970. From this information, future population growth can be estimated.

1 Open **Excel**. From your student files, **Open e03B_Population_Growth**. If necessary, increase the size of the Excel window to fill the screen. If necessary, on the Standard toolbar, click the Zoom arrow ⌈100%▾⌉, and then click 125%. On the **File** menu, click **Save As**, and then navigate to your **Excel Chapter 3** folder. In the **Save As** box, type **Lastname_Firstname_3B_Population_Growth** and then click **Save** or press ⌈Return⌉.

2 Be sure to leave **row 4** blank, and then click cell **A5**. Type **Year** and then press ⌈Tab⌉. In cell **B5**, type **1970** and then press ⌈Tab⌉.

3 In cell **C5**, type **1980** and then press ⌈Tab⌉. Select the range **B5:C5**, and then drag the fill handle to the right through cell **F5** to extend the series to 2010.

> By establishing a pattern of 10-year intervals with the first two cells, you can use the fill handle to continue the series. The AutoFill feature will do this for any pattern that you establish with two or more cells.

4 With the range **B5:F5** still selected, on the **Home tab**, in the **Font group**, click the **Bold** button ⌈B⌉. Compare your screen with Figure 3.22.

Figure 3.22

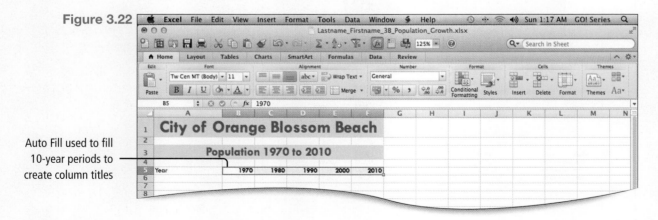

Auto Fill used to fill 10-year periods to create column titles

5 In cell **A6**, type **Population at Census** and press ⌈Return⌉. In cell **A7**, type **Percent Increase** and press ⌈Return⌉.

6 Click cell **B6**, and then beginning in cell **B6**, and by pressing ⌨Tab to move across the row, enter the following values for the population in the years listed:

1970	1980	1990	2000	2010
115241	**118072**	**123591**	**133936**	**152126**

7 Select the range **B6:F6**, and then on the **Home tab**, in the **Number group**, click the **Comma Style** button ⟨,⟩. In the **Number group**, click the **Decrease Decimal** button ⟨.00→.0⟩ two times.

8 Click cell **C7**. Being sure to include the parentheses, type **=(c6-b6)/b6** and then on the formula bar, click the **Enter** button ⟨✓⟩ to keep cell **C7** active—your result is *0.0245659* (or *0.02*). Compare your screen with Figure 3.23.

Figure 3.23

Formula bar displays formula in cell C7—the active cell

Values entered for population, formatted as Comma Style with no decimal places

Formula result displays in cell C7 (yours may display 0.02)

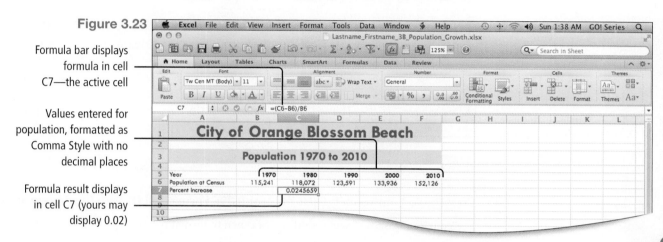

9 With cell **C7** active, on the **Home tab**, in the **Number group**, click the **Percent Style** button ⟨%⟩, and then examine the formula in the formula bar.

The mathematical formula *rate = amount of increase/base* is used to calculated the percentage rate of population increase from 1970 to 1980. The formula is applied as follows:

First, determine the *amount of increase* by subtracting the *base*—the starting point represented by the 1970 population—from the 1980 population. Thus, the *amount of increase* = 118,072 – 115,241 or 2,831. Between 1970 and 1980, the population increased by 2,831 people. In the formula, this calculation is represented by *C6-B6*.

Second, calculate the *rate*—what the amount of increase (2,831) represents as a percentage of the base (1970's population of 115,241). Determine this by dividing the amount of increase (2,831) by the base (115,241). Thus, 2,831 divided by 115,241 is equal to 0.0245659 or, when formatted as a percent, 2%.

10 In the formula bar, locate the parentheses enclosing *C6-B6*.

Excel follows a set of mathematical rules called the *order of operations*, which has four basic parts:

- Expressions within parentheses are processed first.

- Exponentiation, if present, is performed before multiplication and division.

- Multiplication and division are performed before addition and subtraction.

- Consecutive operators with the same level of precedence are calculated from left to right.

11 Click cell **D7**, type **=** and then by typing, or by using a combination of typing and clicking cells to reference them, construct a formula similar to the one in cell **C7** to calculate the rate of increase in population from 1980 to 1990. Compare your screen with Figure 3.24.

> Recall that the first step is to determine the *amount of increase*—1990 population minus 1980 population—and then to write the calculation so that Excel performs this operation first; that is, place it in parentheses.
>
> The second step is to divide the result of the calculation in parentheses by the *base*—the population for 1980.

Figure 3.24

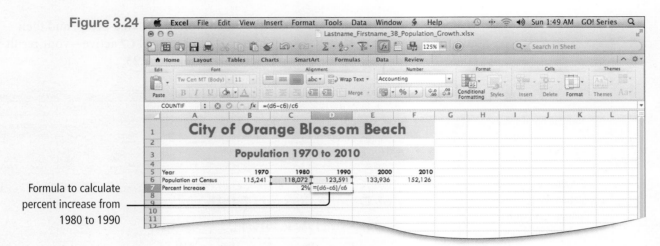

Formula to calculate percent increase from 1980 to 1990

12 Press Return. Your result is *0.0467427* (or *0.05*). Format cell **D7** with the **Percent Style** %.

> Your result is *5%*; Excel rounds up or down to format percentages.

13 With cell **D7** selected, drag the fill handle to the right through cell **F7**. Click any empty cell to cancel the selection, **Save** 💾 your workbook, and then compare your screen with Figure 3.25.

> Because this formula uses relative cell references—that is, for each year, the formula is the same but the values used are relative to the formula's location—you can copy the formula in this manner. For example, the result for 1990 uses the 1980 population as the base, the result for 2000 uses the 1990 population as the base, and the result for 2010 uses the 2000 population as the base.
>
> The formula results show the percent of increase for each 10-year period between 1970 and 2010. You can see that in each 10-year period, the population has grown as much as 14%—from 2000 to 2010—and as little as 2%—from 1970 to 1980.

Figure 3.25

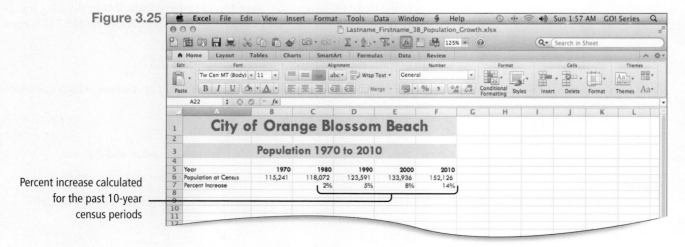

Percent increase calculated for the past 10-year census periods

> **More Knowledge | Use of Parentheses in a Formula**
>
> When writing a formula in Excel, use parentheses to communicate the order in which the operations should occur. For example, to average three test scores of 100, 50, and 90 that you scored on three different tests, you would add the test scores and then divide by the number of test scores in the list. If you write this formula as =100+50+90/3, the result would be 180, because Excel would first divide 90 by 3 and then add 100+50+30. Excel would do so because the order of operations states that multiplication and division are calculated *before* addition and subtraction.
>
> The correct way to write this formula is =(100+50+90)/3. Excel will add the three values, and then divide the result by 3, or 240/3, resulting in a correct average of 80. Parentheses play an important role in ensuring that you get the correct result in your formulas.

Activity 3.13 | Using Format Painter and Formatting as You Type

You can format numbers as you type them. When you type numbers in a format that Excel recognizes, Excel automatically applies that format to the cell. Recall that once applied, cell formats remain with the cell, even if the cell contents are deleted. In this activity, you will format cells by typing the numbers with percent signs and use Format Painter to copy formats.

1 Be sure to leave **row 8** blank, and then click cell **A9**. Type **Projected Future Population** and then press Return.

2 Click cell **A3**. On the Standard toolbar, click the **Format Painter** button, and then click cell **A9**.

> The format of cell A3 is *painted*—applied to—cell A9, including the merging and centering of the text across the range A9:F9.

3 Be sure to leave **row 10** blank, and then click cell **A11**, type **Estimated Growth Rate** and then press Return.

4 Be sure to leave **row 12** blank, and then click cell **A13**. Type **Year** and then in cell **A14**, type **Projected Population**

5 In cell **B13**, type **2010** and then press Tab. In cell **C13**, type **2020** and then press Tab.

6 Select the range **B13:C13**, and then drag the fill handle through cell **F13** to extend the pattern of years to *2050*. Apply **Bold** B to the selected range, and then compare your screen with Figure 3.26.

Figure 3.26

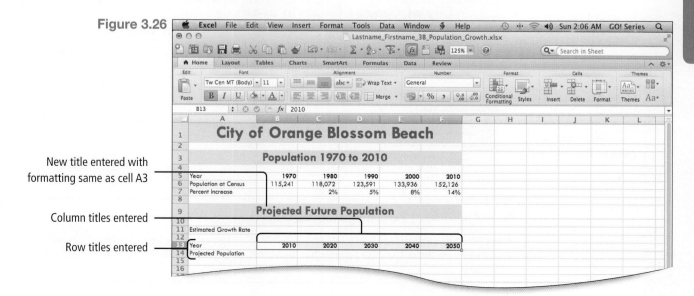

New title entered with formatting same as cell A3

Column titles entered

Row titles entered

7 Click cell **B14**, and then on the **Home tab**, in the **Number group**, notice that the **Number Format** box indicates *General*. Then, being sure to type the comma, type **152,126**

8 On the formula bar, click the **Enter** button 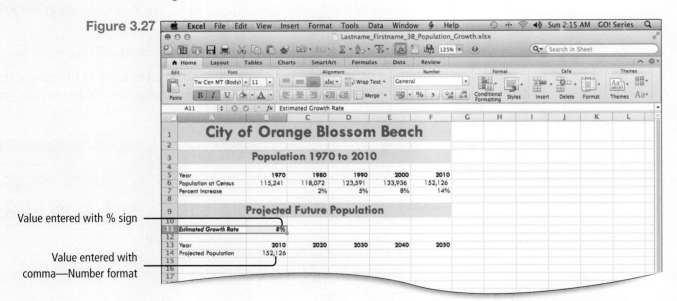 to keep the cell active, and then in the **Number group**, notice that the format changed to *Number*.

9 Press Delete, and then in the **Number group**, notice that the *Number* format is still indicated.

> Recall that deleting the contents of a cell does not delete the cell's formatting.

10 *Without* typing a comma, in cell **B14**, type **152126** and then press Return.

> The comma displays even though you did not type it. When you type a number and include a formatting symbol such as a comma or dollar sign, Excel applies the format to the cell. Thus, if you delete the contents of the cell and type in the cell again, the format you established remains applied to the cell. This is referred to as *format as you type*.

11 Examine the format of the value in cell **B14**, and then compare it to the format in cell **B6** where you used the **Comma Style** button to format the cell. Notice that the number in cell **B14** is flush with the right edge of the cell, but the number in cell **B6** leaves a small amount of space on the right edge.

> When you type commas as you enter numbers, Excel applies the *Number* format, which does *not* leave a space at the right of the number for a closing parenthesis in the event of a negative number. This is different from the format that is applied when you use the *Comma Style* button on the Ribbon, as you did for the numbers entered in row 6. Recall that the Comma Style format leaves space on the right for a closing parenthesis in the event of a negative number.

12 In cell **B11**, type **8%** and then press Return. Select the range **A11:B11**, and then apply **Bold** B and **Italic** I. **Save** 💾 your workbook, and then compare your screen with Figure 3.27.

Figure 3.27

Value entered with % sign

Value entered with comma—Number format

More Knowledge | Percentage Calculations

When you type a percentage into a cell—for example *8%*—the percentage format, without decimal points, displays in both the cell and the formula bar. Excel will, however, use the decimal value of *0.08* for actual calculations.

Activity 3.14 | Calculating a Value After an Increase

A growing population results in increased use of city services. Thus, city planners in Orange Blossom Beach must estimate how much the population will increase in the future. The calculations you made in the previous activity show that the population has increased at varying rates during each 10-year period from 1970 to 2010, ranging from a low of 2% to a high of 14% per 10-year census period.

Population data from the state and surrounding areas suggests that future growth will trend close to that of the recent past. To plan for the future, Ms. Darius wants to prepare three forecasts of the city's population based on the percentage increases in 2000, in 2010, and for a percentage increase halfway between the two; that is, for 8%, 11%, and 14%. In this activity, you will calculate the population that would result from an 8% increase.

1 Click cell **C14**. Type **=b14*(100%+b11)** and then on the formula bar, click the **Enter** button to display a result of *164296.08*. Compare your screen with Figure 3.28.

> Recall that as you type, a list of Excel functions that begin with the letter *B* may briefly display. This is **Formula AutoComplete**, an Excel feature that, after typing an = (equal sign) and the beginning letter or letters of a function name, displays a list of function names that match the typed letter(s). In this instance, the letters represent cell references, *not* the beginning of a function name.
>
> This formula calculates what the population will be in the year 2020, assuming an increase of 8% over 2010's population. Use the mathematical formula *value after increase = base × percent for new value* to calculate a value after an increase as follows:
>
> First, establish the *percent for new value*. The **percent for new value = base percent + percent of increase**. The *base percent* of 100% represents the base population and the *percent of increase* in this instance is 8%. Thus, the population will equal 100% of the base year plus 8% of the base year. This can be expressed as 108% or 1.08. In this formula, you will use 100% + the rate in cell B11, which is 8%, to equal 108%.
>
> Second, enter a reference to the cell that contains the *base*—the population in 2010. The base value resides in cell B14—*152,126*.
>
> Third, calculate the *value after increase*. Because in each future 10-year period the increase will be based on 8%—an absolute value located in cell B11—this cell reference can be formatted as absolute by typing dollar signs.

Figure 3.28

Formula includes absolute cell reference to B11

Result of formula

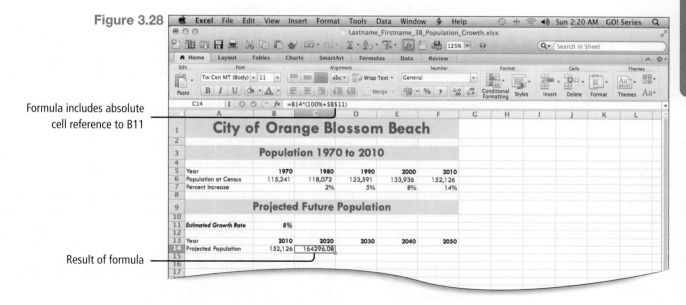

2 With cell **C14** as the active cell, drag the fill handle to copy the formula to the range **D14:F14**.

3 Click cell **B14**, and then on the Standard toolbar, click the **Format Painter** button [icon]. Select the range **C14:F14** to apply the Number format to the cells in the range. Click an empty cell to cancel the selection, **Save** [icon] your workbook, and then compare your screen with Figure 3.29.

> This formula uses a relative cell address—B14—for the *base*; the population in the previous 10-year period is used in each of the formulas in cells D14:F14 as the *base* value. Because the reference to the *percent of increase* in cell B11 is an absolute reference, each *value after increase* is calculated with the value from cell B11.
>
> The population projected for 2020—*164,296*—is an increase of 8% over the population in 2010. The projected population in 2030—*177,440*—is an increase of 8% over the population in 2020, and so on.

Figure 3.29

Projection calculated using an 8% growth rate

Each value represents an 8% increase over the previous base year

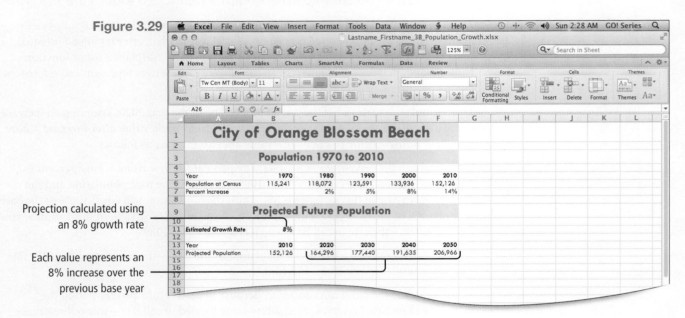

More Knowledge | Percent Increase or Decrease

The basic formula for calculating an increase or decrease can be done in two parts. First determine the percent by which the base value will be increased or decreased, and then add or subtract the results to the base. The formula can be simplified by using (1+amount of increase) or (1–amount of decrease), where 1, rather than 100%, represents the whole. Thus, the formula used in Step 1 of Activity 3.14 could also be written =b14*(1+b11), or =(b14*b11)+b14.

Objective 6 | Answer What-If Questions by Changing Values in a Worksheet

If a formula depends on the value in a cell, you can see what effect it will have if you change the value in that cell. Then, you can copy the value computed by the formula and paste it into another part of the worksheet where you can compare it to other values.

Activity 3.15 | Answering What-If Questions and Using Paste Special

A growth rate of 8% in each 10-year period will result in a population of almost 207,000 people by 2050. The city planners will likely ask: *What if* the population grows at the highest rate (14%)? *What if* the population grows at a rate that is halfway between the 2000 and 2010 rates (11%)?

Because the formulas are constructed to use the growth rate displayed in cell B11, Ms. Darius can answer these questions quickly by entering different percentages into that cell. To keep the results of each set of calculations so they can be compared, you will paste the results of each what-if question into another area of the worksheet.

1 Be sure to leave **row 15** blank, and then click cell **A16**. Type **Growth Estimates 2020 to 2050** and then press Return. Use **Format Painter** 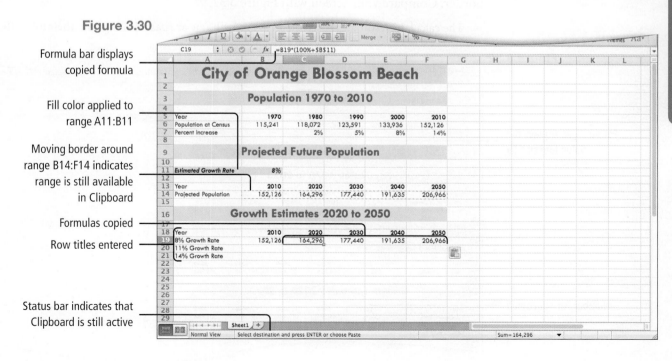 to copy the format from cell **A9** to cell **A16**.

2 Select the range **A11:B11**. On the **Home tab**, in the **Font group**, click the **Fill Color arrow** , and then under **Theme Colors**, in the third row, click the first color—**Background 1, Darker 15%**.

3 Be sure to leave **row 17** blank, and then, in the range **A18:A21**, type the following row titles:

> **Year**
>
> **8% Growth Rate**
>
> **11% Growth Rate**
>
> **14% Growth Rate**

4 Select the range **B13:F13**, and then press Command ⌘ + C to copy the range to the Clipboard.

5 Click cell **B18,** and then press Command ⌘ + V to paste the range to the range B18:F18.

> Recall that when pasting a group of copied cells to a target range, you need only click the first cell of the range.

6 Select and **Copy** the range **B14:F14**, and then in cell **B19**, **Paste** the range.

7 Click cell **C19**. On the formula bar, notice that the *formula* was pasted into the cell, as shown in Figure 3.30.

> This is *not* the desired result. The actual *calculated values*—not the formulas—are needed in the range.

Figure 3.30

Formula bar displays copied formula

Fill color applied to range A11:B11

Moving border around range B14:F14 indicates range is still available in Clipboard

Formulas copied

Row titles entered

Status bar indicates that Clipboard is still active

Excel | Chapter 3

8 On the Standard toolbar, click the **Undo** button. With the range **B14:F14** still copied to the Clipboard—as indicated by the message in the status bar and the moving border—click cell **B19**. On the **Home tab**, in the **Edit group**, click the **Paste arrow**, and then click **Paste Special**.

9 In the **Paste Special** dialog box, under **Paste**, click the **Values and number formats** option button, and then compare your screen with Figure 3.31.

> The *Values and number formats* Paste Special setting enables you to paste the calculated values that result from the calculation of formulas along with the formatting of the cells that are copied.

Figure 3.31

Paste Special dialog box

Values and number formats selected

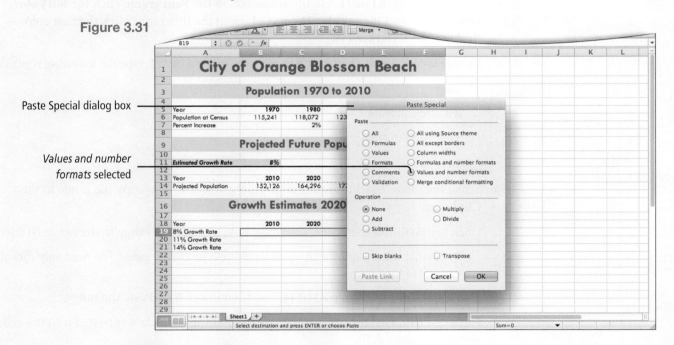

10 In the **Paste Special** dialog box, click **OK**. Click cell **C19**, and notice on the formula bar that the cell contains a *value*, not a formula. Press Esc to cancel the moving border. Compare your screen with Figure 3.32.

> The calculated estimates based on an 8% growth rate are pasted along with their formatting.

Figure 3.32

Formula bar displays the value for cell C19

Number Format copied

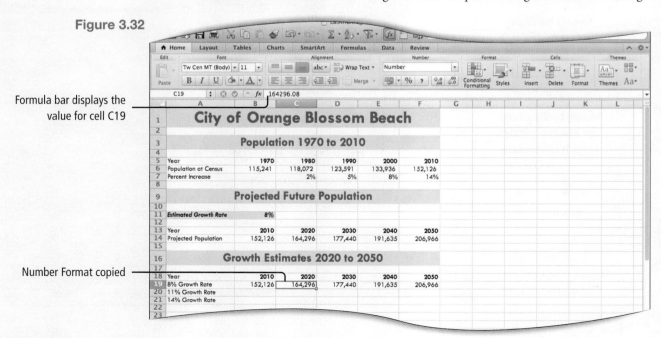

11 Click cell **B11**. Type **11** and then watch the values in **C14:F14** *recalculate* as, on the formula bar, you click the **Enter** button ⊘.

> The value *11%* is halfway between 8% and 14%—the growth rates from the two most recent 10-year periods.

12 Select and **Copy** the new values in the range **B14:F14**. Click cell **B20**, and then on the **Home tab**, in the **Edit group**, click the **Paste arrow**. Click **Paste Special**, and in the **Paste Special** dialog box, click the **Values and number formats** option button. In the **Paste Special** dialog box, click **OK**.

13 In cell **B11**, change the percentage by typing **14** and then press Return. Notice that the projected values in **C14:F14** recalculate.

14 Using the skills you just practiced, select and **Copy** the recalculated values in the range **B14:F14**, and then **Paste** the **Values and number formats** to the range **B21:F21**.

15 Press Esc to cancel the moving border, click cell **A1**, **Save** 🖫 your workbook, and then compare your screen with Figure 3.33.

> With this information, Ms. Darius can answer several what-if questions about the future population of the city and provide a range of population estimates based on the rates of growth over the past 10-year periods.

Figure 3.33

Values and number formats copied for each what-if question

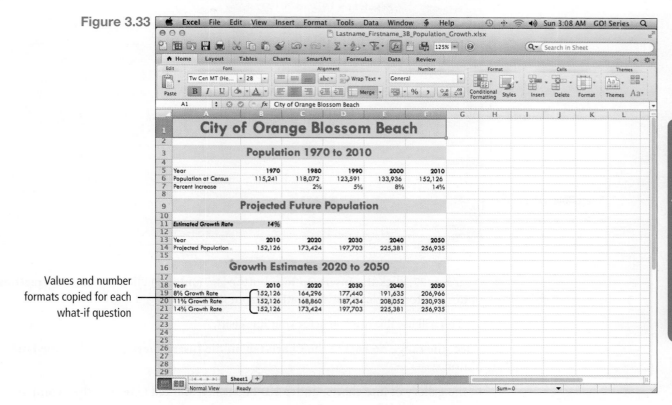

Objective 7 | Chart Data with a Line Chart

A *line chart* displays trends over time. Time is displayed along the bottom axis, and the data point values connect with a line. The curve and direction of the line make trends obvious to the reader.

Whereas the columns in a column chart and the pie slices in a pie chart emphasize the distinct values of each data point, the line in a line chart emphasizes the flow from one data point value to the next.

Activity 3.16 | Inserting Multiple Rows and Creating a Line Chart

In this activity, you will chart the actual population figures from 1970 to 2010 in a line chart so that city council members can see how the population has increased over the past five census periods.

1 In the **row header area**, point to **row 8** to display the ➡ pointer, and then drag down to select **rows 8:26**. On the **Home tab**, in the **Cells group**, click the **Insert** button to insert the same number of blank rows as you selected. Compare your screen with Figure 3.34.

Use this technique to insert multiple rows quickly.

Figure 3.34

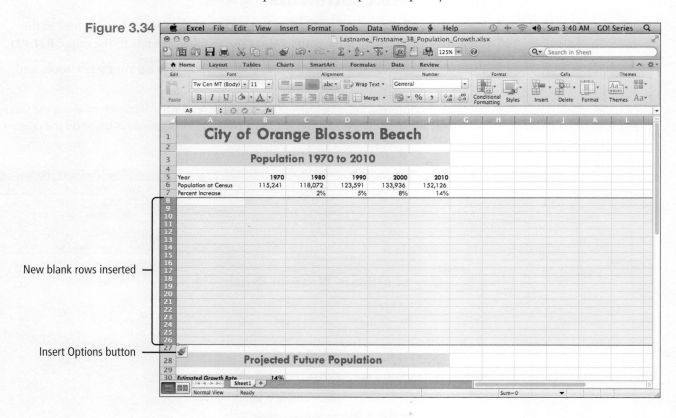

New blank rows inserted

Insert Options button

2 Near **row 27**, click the **Insert Options** button 🖌, and then click the **Clear Formatting** option button to clear any formatting from these rows.

You will use this blank area for your line chart.

3 Select the range **A6:F6**. On the **Charts tab**, in the **Insert Chart group**, click the **Line** button.

4 In the gallery of line charts, under **2-D Line**, click **Marked Line**, and then compare your screen with Figure 3.35.

The line chart displays as an embedded chart in the worksheet.

Figure 3.35

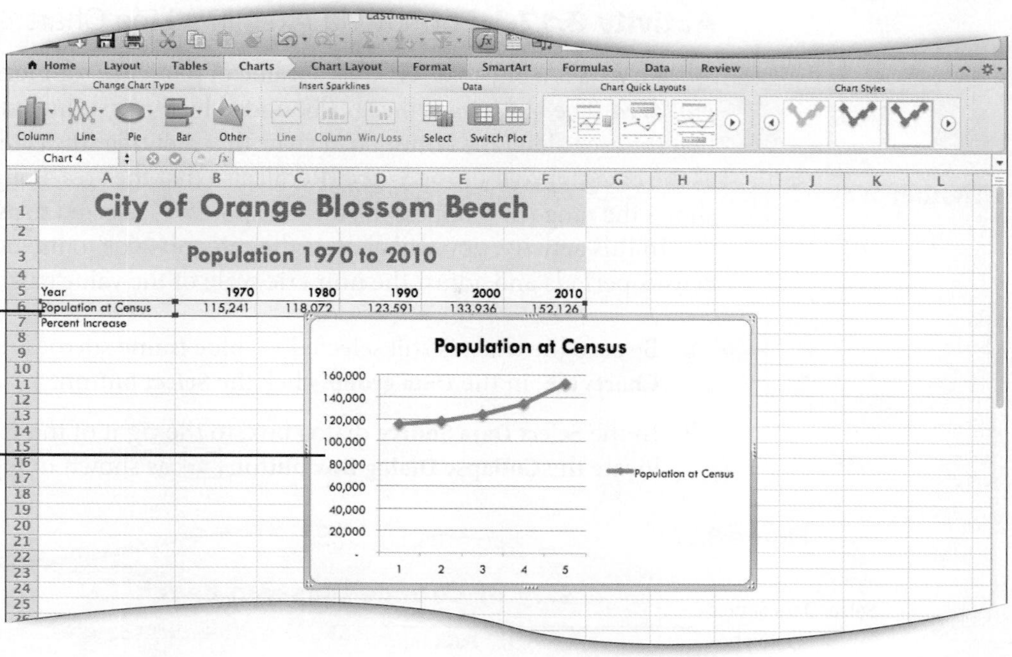

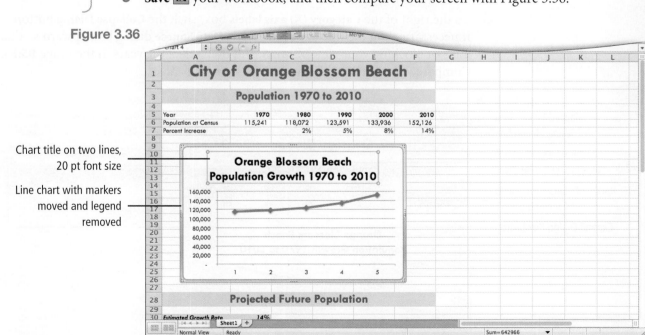

Data selected for charting

Line chart with markers inserted

5 Point to the left border of the chart to display the ⊹ pointer, and then drag the chart so that its upper left corner is positioned in cell **A9**, aligned approximately under the *t* in the word *Percent* above.

6 On the **Chart Layout tab**, in the **Labels group**, click the **Legend** button, and then click **No Legend**.

7 Click the chart title one time to select it and display a border around the title. Type **Orange Blossom Beach** and then press Return to begin a new line.

8 Type **Population Growth 1970 to 2010** Click the border around the chart title to remove the insertion point from the title. On the **Home tab**, in the **Font group**, change the **Font Size** to **20**.

9 **Save** 💾 your workbook, and then compare your screen with Figure 3.36.

Another Way

With the border of the title box selected, on the Chart Layout tab or on the Format tab, in the Current Selection group, click the Format Selection button, and then change the Font size.

Figure 3.36

Chart title on two lines, 20 pt font size

Line chart with markers moved and legend removed

Excel | Chapter 3

Activity 3.17 | Formatting Axes in a Line Chart

An *axis* is a line that serves as a frame of reference for measurement; it borders the chart *plot area*. The plot area is the area bounded by the axes, including all the data series. Recall that the area along the bottom of a chart that identifies the categories of data is referred to as the *category axis* or the *x-axis*. Recall also that the area along the left side of a chart that shows the range of numbers for the data points is referred to as the *value axis* or the *y-axis*.

In this activity, you will change the category axis to include the names of the 10-year census periods and adjust the numeric scale of the value axis.

Another Way

At the bottom of the chart, point to any of the numbers 1 through 5 to display the ScreenTip *Horizontal (Category) Axis*. Press Control and click, and then from the shortcut menu, click Select Data.

1. Be sure the chart is still selected—a blue frame surrounds the chart area. On the **Charts tab**, in the **Data group**, click the **Select** button.

2. In the **Select Data Source** dialog box, to the right of the **Category (X) axis labels** box, locate the **Collapse Dialog Box** button, as shown in Figure 3.37.

Figure 3.37

Select Data Source dialog box

Category (X) axis requires labels to identify each 10-year period

Collapse Dialog Box button

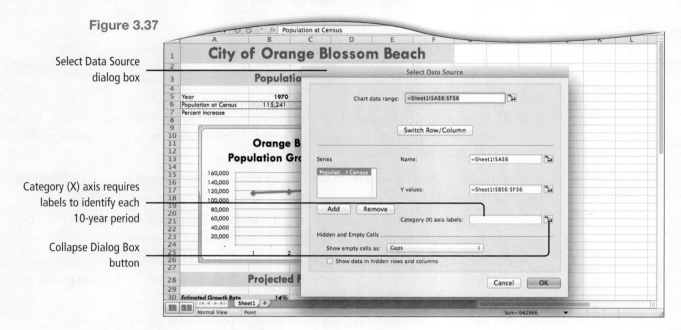

3. To the right of the **Category (X) axis labels** box, click the **Collapse Dialog** button. If necessary, drag the title bar of the **Select Data Source** dialog box upward so that it is not blocking your view of **row 5**, and then select the years in the range **B5:F5**. Compare your screen with Figure 3.38.

Figure 3.38

Collapsed Select Data Source dialog box

Range indicated with absolute cell references

Range of years surrounded by moving border

Expand Dialog Box button

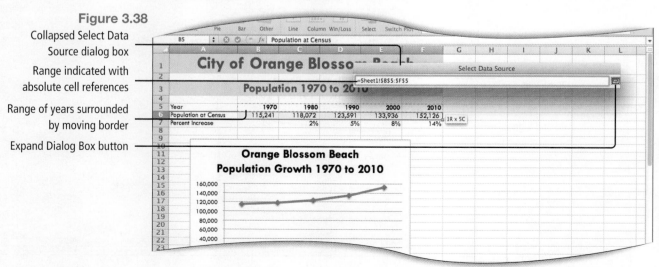

4 In the collapsed **Select Data Source** dialog box, click the **Expand Dialog Box** button 🔲. In the **Select Data Source** dialog box, click **OK**, and then compare your screen with Figure 3.39.

The years display as the category labels on the category (X) axis.

Figure 3.39

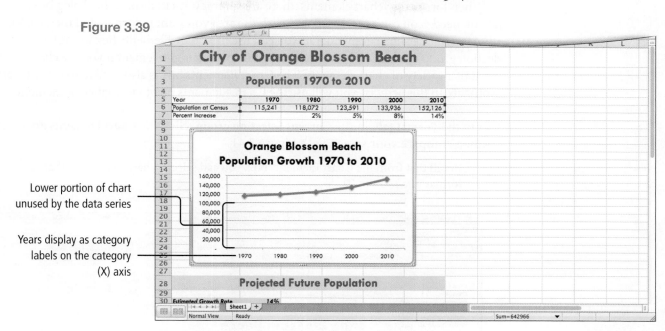

Lower portion of chart unused by the data series

Years display as category labels on the category (X) axis

Another Way

On the left side of the chart, point to any of the numbers to display the ScreenTip *Vertical (Value) Axis*, and then press [Control] and click. From the shortcut menu, click Format Axis.

5 On the chart, notice that the blue line—the data series—does not display in the lower portion of the chart. On the **Chart Layout tab**, in the **Axes group**, click the **Axes** button. Point to **Vertical Axis**, and then click **Axis Options**.

6 In the **Format Axis** dialog box, on the left, click **Scale**. On the right, under **Vertical axis scale**, double-click in the **Minimum** box to select the existing value, and then type **100000**

Because none of the population figures are under 100,000, changing the Minimum number to 100,000 will enable the data series to occupy more of the plot area.

7 Notice that the **Major unit** box displays a value of *10000.0*. In the **Format Axis** dialog box, click **OK**. **Save** 💾 your workbook, and then compare your screen with Figure 3.40.

The *Major unit* value determines the spacing between *tick marks* and thus between the gridlines in the plot area. Tick marks are the short lines that display on an axis at regular intervals. By default, Excel started the values at zero and increased in increments of 20,000. By setting the Minimum value on the value axis to 100,000, the Major unit changed from 20,000 to 10,000. The line chart shows a clearer trend in the population growth.

Figure 3.40

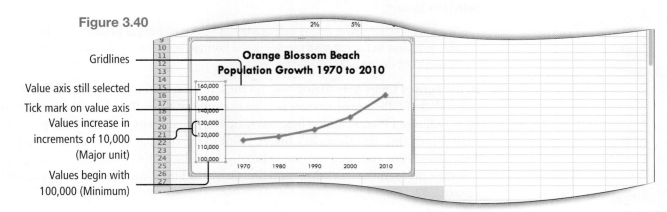

Gridlines

Value axis still selected

Tick mark on value axis

Values increase in increments of 10,000 (Major unit)

Values begin with 100,000 (Minimum)

Excel | Chapter 3

Activity 3.18 | Formatting the Chart and Plot Areas

An Excel chart has two background elements—the plot area and the chart area—which, by default display a single fill color. To add visual appeal to a chart, you can insert a graphic image as the background.

When formatting chart elements, there are several ways to display the dialog boxes that you need. You can press Control and click the area you want to format and then click a command on the shortcut menu. Or, you can use the Chart Elements box in the Current Selection group on the Format tab of the Ribbon, which is convenient if you are changing the format of a variety of chart elements. The Chart Elements box is also available on the Chart Layout tab. In this activity, you will use the Chart Elements box to format chart elements.

1 On the **Format tab**, in the **Current Selection group**, click the **Chart Elements arrow**, and then compare your screen with Figure 3.41.

> Recall that from the Chart Elements box, you can select a chart element so that you can format it.

Figure 3.41

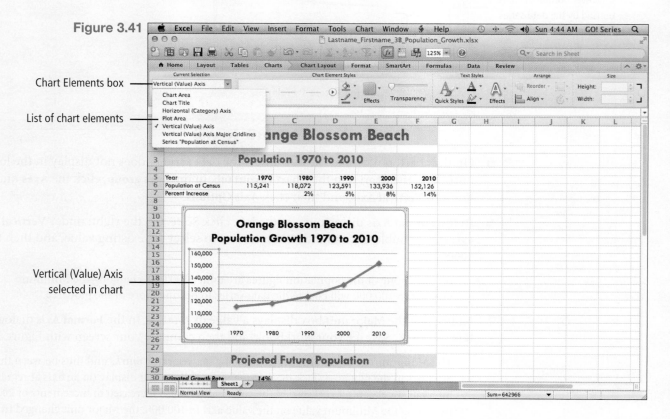

Chart Elements box

List of chart elements

Vertical (Value) Axis selected in chart

2 In the list, click **Chart Area**. Directly below the **Chart Elements** box, click the **Format Selection** button.

> The Format Chart Area dialog box displays. Use this technique to select the chart element that you want to format, and then click the Format Selection button to display the appropriate dialog box.

3 In the **Format Chart Area** dialog box, on the left, be sure that **Fill** is selected. On the right, click the **Picture or Texture tab**. To the right of **From file**, click **Choose Picture**. In the **Choose a Picture** dialog box, navigate to your student files, click the picture **e03B_Beach.JPG**, and then click **Insert**. Point to the title bar of the **Format Chart Area** dialog box, and drag the dialog box to the right of the worksheet so that you can view more of the worksheet and line chart, and then compare your screen with Figure 3.42.

Figure 3.42

Chart Area selected in the Chart Elements box

Format Selection button selected

Format Chart Area dialog box

Picture or Texture tab

Preview of Beach picture

Beach picture displays in the chart

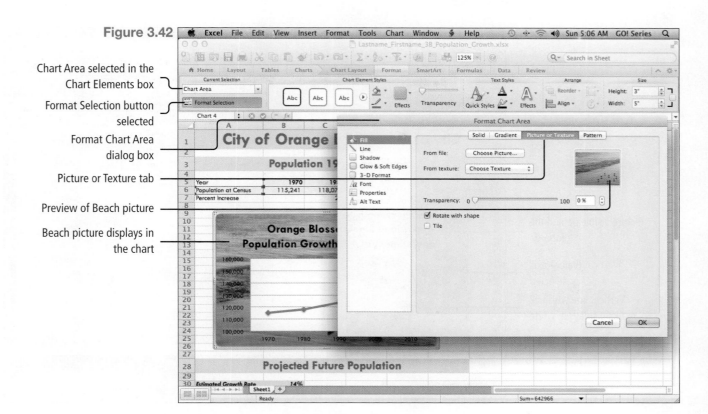

4 In the **Format Chart Area** dialog box, on the left, click **Line**. In the **Format Chart Area** dialog box, with the **Solid tab** active, click in the **Color** box, and then under **Theme Colors**, in the first row, click the fourth color—**Text 2**.

5 In the **Format Chart Area** dialog box, click the **Weights & Arrows tab**. On the right, with the text in the **Weight** box selected, type **4** and then click **OK** to close the dialog box and apply the formatting changes.

> A 4 pt teal border frames the chart.

6 In the **Current Selection group**, click the **Chart Elements arrow**, click **Plot Area**, and then click the **Format Selection** button.

7 In the **Format Plot Area** dialog box, on the left, click **Fill**. On the right, click in the **Color** box, and then click **No Fill**. In the **Format Plot Area** dialog box, click **OK**.

> The fill is removed from the plot area, and the picture is visible as the background.

8 Click the **Chart Elements arrow**, click **Vertical (Value) Axis**, and then click the **Format Selection** button.

9 In the **Format Axis** dialog box, on the left, verify that **Line** is selected. In the **Format Axis** dialog box with the **Solid tab** active, click in the **Color** box, and then click the first color—**Background 1**. Compare your screen with Figure 3.43.

> The vertical line with tick marks displays in white.

Excel | Chapter 3

Figure 3.43

Format Axis dialog box —

Picture visible behind the plot area

Vertical (Value) axis selected

Vertical line with tick marks displays in white

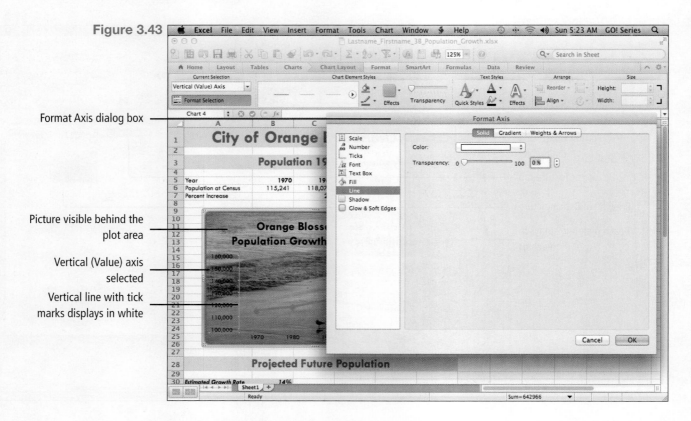

10 In the **Format Axis** dialog box, click **OK**. Click the **Chart Elements arrow**, click **Vertical (Value) Axis Major Gridlines**, and then click the **Format Selection** button. Change the **Line Color** to the **Background 1** color (White). In the **Format Gridlines** dialog box, click **OK**.

11 Click the **Chart Elements arrow**, click **Horizontal (Category) Axis**, and then click the **Format Selection** button. In the **Format Axis** dialog box, change the **Line Color** to the **Background 1** color (White). In the **Format Axis** dialog box, click **OK**.

12 Point to any of the numbers on the vertical value axis to display the **ScreenTip** of *Vertical (Value) Axis*, and then click. Notice that the **Chart Elements** box displays *Vertical (Value) Axis*. On the **Home tab**, in the **Font group**, change the **Font Color** to **Background 1** (White). Click any of the years on the horizontal category axis, and then click the **Font Color** button to change the color to **Background 1** (White).

13 Click any cell to deselect the chart, press Command ⌘ + fn + ← to move to cell **A1**. **Save** your workbook, and then compare your screen with Figure 3.44.

Figure 3.44

4 pt teal border surrounds chart

Gridlines display in white

Values display in white

Years display in white

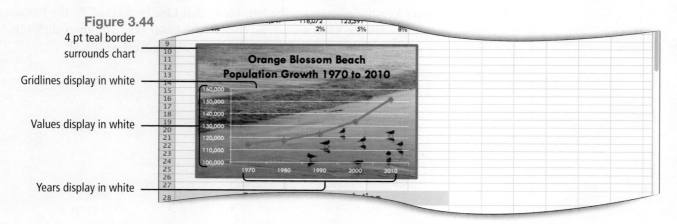

Activity 3.19 | Preparing and Printing Your Worksheet

1 On the **File** menu, click **Properties**. In the **Subject** box, type your course name and section number. In the **Author** box, replace the existing text with your firstname and lastname. In the **Keywords** box, type **population** and then click **OK**.

2 On the **View** menu, click **Header and Footer**. In the **Page Setup** dialog box, click **Customize Footer**. With the insertion point in the **Left section**, click the **Insert File Name** button , and then click **OK**.

3 In the **Page Setup** dialog box, click the **Margins tab**, and then under **Center on page**, select the **Horizontally** check box. Click **OK** to close the dialog box.

4 **Save** 🖫 your workbook. On the **File** menu, click **Print** to display the preview of your worksheet. Compare your screen with Figure 3.45.

Figure 3.45

Print dialog box

Preview of worksheet

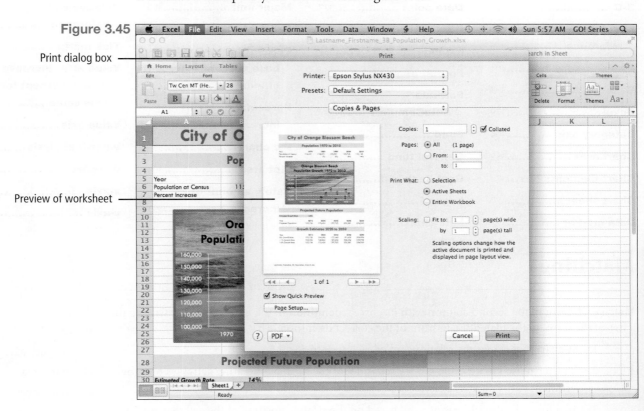

5 If necessary, return to the worksheet to make any necessary adjustments or corrections, and then **Save** 🖫 your workbook.

6 **Print** or submit electronically as directed by your instructor.

7 If required by your instructor, print or create an electronic version of your worksheet with formulas displayed by using the instructions in Activity 1.15, and the **Close** your workbook without saving so that you do not save the changes you made to print formulas.

8 On the **Excel** menu, click **Quit Excel**.

End **You have completed Project 3B**

Content-Based Assessments

Summary

In this chapter, you created a pie chart to show how the parts of a budget contribute to a total budget. Then you formatted the pie chart attractively and used Goal Seek. You also practiced using parentheses in a formula, calculating the percentage rate of an increase, answering what-if questions, and charting data in a line chart to show trends over time.

Key Terms

Matching

Match each term in the second column with its correct definition in the first column by writing the letter of the term on the blank line in front of the correct definition.

_____ 1. A chart that shows the relationship of each part to a whole.

_____ 2. The term used to describe money set aside for the normal operating activities of a government entity such as a city.

_____ 3. In a formula, the address of a cell based on the relative position of the cell that contains the formula and the cell referred to.

_____ 4. A column, bar, area, dot, pie slice, or other symbol in a chart that represents a single data point.

_____ 5. A workbook sheet that contains only a chart.

_____ 6. A shape effect that uses shading and shadows to make the edges of a shape appear to be curved or angled.

_____ 7. The entire chart and all of its elements.

_____ 8. The process of changing the values in cells to see how those changes affect the outcome of formulas in a worksheet.

_____ 9. The mathematical formula to calculate a rate of increase.

_____ 10. The mathematical rules for performing multiple calculations within a formula.

_____ 11. The Excel feature by which a cell takes on the formatting of the number typed into the cell.

A Axis

B Bevel

C Category axis

D Chart area

E Chart sheet

F Data marker

G Format as you type

H General fund

I Order of operations

J Pie chart

K Rate = amount of increase/base

L Relative cell reference

M Tick marks

N Value axis

O What-if analysis

_____ 12. A line that serves as a frame of reference for measurement and that borders the chart plot area.

_____ 13. The area along the bottom of a chart that identifies the categories of data; also referred to as the *x*-axis.

_____ 14. A numerical scale on the left side of a chart that shows the range of numbers for the data points; also referred to as the *y*-axis.

_____ 15. The short lines that display on an axis at regular intervals.

Multiple Choice

Circle the correct answer.

1. A sum of money set aside for a specific purpose is a:
    A. value axis   **B.** fund   **C.** rate

2. A cell reference that refers to a cell by its fixed position in a worksheet is referred to as being:
    A. absolute   **B.** relative   **C.** mixed

3. A value that originates in a worksheet cell and that is represented in a chart by a data marker is a data:
    A. point   **B.** cell   **C.** axis

4. Related data points represented by data markers are referred to as the data:
    A. slices   **B.** set   **C.** series

5. The action of pulling out a pie slice from a pie chart is called:
    A. extract   **B.** explode   **C.** plot

6. A gallery of text styles with which you can create decorative effects, such as shadowed or mirrored text is:
    A. WordArt   **B.** shape effects   **C.** text fill

7. The percent by which one number increases over another number is the percentage rate of:
    A. decrease   **B.** change   **C.** increase

8. A chart type that displays trends over time is a:
    A. pie chart   **B.** line chart   **C.** column chart

9. The area bounded by the axes of a chart, including all the data series, is the:
    A. chart area   **B.** plot area   **C.** axis area

10. The x-axis is also known as the:
    A. category axis   **B.** value axis   **C.** data axis

Excel | Chapter 3

Content-Based Assessments

Apply **3A** skills from
these Objectives:

1 Chart Data with a Pie
Chart

2 Format a Pie Chart

3 Edit a Workbook and
Update a Chart

4 Use Goal Seek to
Perform What-If
Analysis

Skills Review | Project **3C** Improvement Expenditures

In the following Skills Review, you will edit a worksheet for Jennifer Carson, City Finance Manager, that details the city general fund facilities improvement expenditures. Your completed worksheets will look similar to Figure 3.46.

Project Files

For Project 3C, you will need the following file:

e03C_Improvement_Expenditures

You will save your workbook as:

Lastname_Firstname_3C_Improvement_Expenditures

Project Results

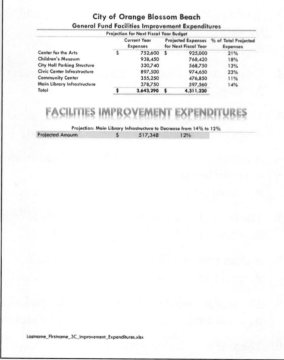

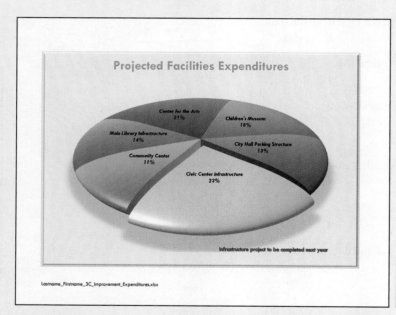

Figure 3.46

(Project 3C Improvement Expenditures continues on the next page)

Content-Based Assessments

Skills Review | Project **3C** Improvement Expenditures (continued)

1 Open **Excel**. From your student files, **Open e03C_Improvement_Expenditures**. If necessary, increase the size of the Excel window to fill the screen. If necessary, on the Standard toolbar, click the Zoom arrow, and then click 125%. On the **File** menu, click **Save As**, navigate to your **Excel Chapter 3** folder, and **Save** the file as **Lastname_Firstname_3C_Improvement_Expenditures**

a. Click cell **D5**, and then type = to begin a formula. Click cell **C5**, type **/** and then click cell **C11**. Press Command ⌘ + T to make the reference to the value in cell **C11** absolute. On the formula bar, click the **Enter** button, and then fill the formula down through cell **D10**.

b. With the range **D5:D10** selected, on the **Home tab**, in the **Number group**, click the **Percent Style** button. In the **Alignment group**, click the **Center Text** button.

2 Select the nonadjacent ranges **A5:A10** and **C5:C10** to select the expense names and the projected expenses. On the **Charts tab**, in the **Insert Chart group**, click the **Pie** button, and then under **3-D Pie**, click **3-D Pie**.

a. Point to the chart, press Control and click, and from the shortcut menu, click **Move Chart**. In the **Move Chart** dialog box, click the **New sheet** option button. In the **New sheet** box, replace the highlighted text *Chart1* by typing **Projected Expenditures Chart** and then click **OK**.

b. On the **Chart Layout tab**, in the **Labels group**, click the **Chart Title** button, and then click **Title Above Chart**. With the **Chart Title** box selected, type **Projected Facilities Expenditures** and then click the **Chart Title border** to remove the insertion point from the box.

c. In the **Current Selection group**, click the **Format Selection** button. In the **Format Title** dialog box, with the **Font tab** active, change the **Font size** to **28** and change the **Font color** to **Accent 1**—in the first row, the fifth color. In the **Format Title** dialog box, click **OK**.

d. On the **Chart Layout tab**, in the **Labels group**, click the **Legend** button, and then click **No Legend**. In the **Labels group**, click the **Data Labels** button, and then click **Category Name and Percentage**.

e. Click any one of the data labels to select them all. In the **Current Selection group**, click the **Format Selection** button. In the **Format Data Labels** dialog

box, with the **Font tab** active, change the **Font style** to **Bold Italic** and change the **Font size** to **12**. On the left side of the **Format Data Labels** dialog box, click **Labels**. Under **Label options**, click in the **Label position** box, and then click **Center**. In the **Format Data Labels** dialog box, click **OK**, and the **Save** your workbook.

3 Click in any pie slice outside of the label to select the entire pie. On the **Format tab**, in the **Chart Element Styles group**, click the **Effects** button, point to **Bevel**, and then click **Bevel Options**.

a. In the **Format Data Series** dialog box, with the **Bevel tab** active, under **Bevel**, click in the **Top** box, and then click **Circle**. Click in the **Bottom** box, and then click **Circle**. In the four **Width** and **Height** boxes, type **512**

b. In the **Format Data Series** dialog box, click the **Depth & Surface tab**. Under **Surface**, click the **Material** box, click **Plastic**, and then click **OK**.

c. On the **Format tab**, in the **Chart Element Styles group**, click the **Effects** button, and then point to **Shadow**. Under **Perspective**, click the third button—**Perspective Bottom**.

d. With the pie chart still selected, on the **Format tab**, in the **Current Selection group**, click the **Format Selection** button. In the **Format Data Series** dialog box, on the left, click **Options**. On the right, change the **Angle of first slice** to **300** to move the largest slice—*Civic Center Infrastructure*—to the center front of the pie. In the **Format Data Series** dialog box, click **OK**.

e. Press Esc to deselect all chart elements. Click any slice to select the entire pie, and then click the **Civic Center Infrastructure** slice to select only that slice.

f. Point to the **Civic Center Infrastructure** slice, and then explode the slice by dragging it down slightly away from the center of the pie.

g. With the **Civic Center Infrastructure** slice still selected, on the **Format tab**, in the **Current Selection group**, click the **Format Selection** button. In the **Format Data Point** dialog box, on the left, click **Fill**. With the **Solid tab** active, click in the **Color** box. Under **Theme Colors**, in the fourth row, click the fifth color—**Accent 1, Lighter 40%**, and then click **OK**. **Save** your workbook.

(Project 3C Improvement Expenditures continues on the next page)

Excel | Chapter 3

4 Point to the white area just inside the border of the chart to display the ScreenTip *Chart Area*, and then click one time.

   a. On the **Format tab**, in the **Chart Element Styles** group, click the **Effects** button, point to **Bevel**, and then under **Bevel**, in the second row, click the third bevel—**Convex**.

   b. With the chart area still selected, on the **Format tab**, in the **Current Selection group**, click the **Format Selection** button. In the **Format Chart Area** dialog box, on the left, be sure that **Fill** is selected. With the **Solid tab** active, click in the **Color** box, and then under **Theme Colors**, in the third row, click the last color, **Accent 6, Lighter 60%.** In the **Format Chart Area** dialog box, click **OK**, and then **Save** your workbook.

   c. With the **Chart Area** still selected, on the **Insert** menu, point to **Picture**, and then click **WordArt**. With the **WordArt** selected, on the **Home tab**, in the **Font group**, change the **Font Size** to **12**. Click the **Font Color arrow**, and then under **Theme Colors**, in the first row, click the second color—**Text 1**. Click the **Bold** button to remove the bold formatting, and then type **Infrastructure project to be completed next year** Point to the **WordArt** to display the 🔀 pointer, and then drag the WordArt down and to the right until the left edge of the WordArt displays in the approximate middle of the *Civic Center Infrastructure* slice and about midway between the pie and the bottom border of the chart as shows in Figure 3.46—your WordArt position does not need to match precisely. Press Esc to cancel the selection of the WordArt, and then **Save** your workbook.

5 In the sheet tab area at the bottom of the workbook, click the **Sheet1 tab** to redisplay the worksheet.

   a. On the **Insert** menu, click **WordArt**. On the **Format tab**, in the **Text Styles group**, click the **Quick Styles** button. Under **Applies to All Text in the Shape**, on the second row, click the last button—a solid letter with a reflection under the letter.

   b. With the **WordArt** selected, type **facilities improvement expenditures** and then click anywhere on the border surrounding the WordArt object. On the **Home tab**, in the **Font group**, change the **Font Size** to **24**.

   c. Drag to position the upper left corner of the **WordArt** in cell **A13**—use the arrow keys as necessary to nudge the WordArt to approximately center the WordArt under the columns in the worksheet.

6 In cell **A17**, type **Projection: Main Library Infrastructure to Decrease from 14% to 12%** and then press Return. **Merge** the text across the range **A17:D17**. On the **Home tab**, in the **Format group**, click the **Styles** button. In the **Cell Styles** gallery, click **Heading 3**.

   a. In cell **A18**, type **Projected Amount:** and press Return. Select the range **C10:D10**, and then on the Standard toolbar, click the **Copy** button. Click cell **B18**, and then on the Standard toolbar, click the **Paste** button. Press Esc to cancel the moving border.

   b. Click cell **C18**. On the **Data tab**, in the **Analysis group**, click the **What-If** button, and then click **Goal Seek**. In the **Goal Seek** dialog box, press Tab to move to the **To value** box, and then type **12%**

   c. Press Tab to move the insertion point to the **By changing cell** box, and then click cell **B18**. In the **Goal Seek** dialog box, click **OK**. In the **Goal Seek Status** dialog box, click **OK**.

   d. Select the range **A18:C18**. On the **Home tab**, in the **Format group**, click the **Styles** button to display the **Cell Styles** gallery. Under **Themed Cell Styles**, apply **40% - Accent3**. Click cell **B18**, and then from the **Cell Styles** gallery, apply the **Currency [0]** cell style. Click cell **A1**, and then **Save** your workbook.

7 With your worksheet displayed, in the sheet tab area, double-click *Sheet1* to select the text, type **Projected Expenditure Data** and then press Return.

   a. On the **View** menu, click **Header and Footer**. In the **Page Setup** dialog box, click **Customizer Footer**. With the insertion point in the **Left section**, click the **Insert File Name** button, and then click **OK**.

   b. In the **Page Setup** dialog box, click the **Margins tab**. Under **Center on page**, select the **Horizontally** check box, and then click **OK**. **Save** your workbook.

   c. Click the **Projected Expenditures Chart sheet tab** to display the chart sheet. On the **View** menu, click **Header and Footer**. In the **Page Setup** dialog box, click **Customize Footer**. With the insertion point in the **Left section**, click the **Insert File Name** button,

(Project 3C Improvement Expenditures continues on the next page)

Skills Review | Project **3C** Improvement Expenditures (continued)

and then click **OK**. In the **Page Setup** dialog box, click **OK**.

d. On the **File** menu, click **Properties**. In the **Subject** box, type your course name and section number. In the **Author** box, replace the existing text with your firstname and lastname. In the **Keywords** box, type **facilities expenditures** and then click **OK**. **Save** your workbook.

e. Point to either of the sheet tabs, press Control and click, and then from the shortcut menu, click **Select All Sheets**. Verify that *[Group]* displays in the title bar, and then **Save** your workbook. On the **File**

menu, click **Print**, and then in the **Print** dialog box, in the preview area, view the two pages of your workbook—the worksheet displays too small to view, but will print in full size.

f. **Print** or submit electronically as directed by your instructor. If required by your instructor, print or create an electronic version of your worksheet with formulas displayed by using the instructions in Activity 1.15, and then **Close** the workbook without saving so that you do not save the changes you made to print formulas. On the **Excel** menu, click **Quit Excel**.

End **You have completed Project 3C** ————————————————————————

Excel | Chapter 3

Apply **3B** skills from
these Objectives:

5 Design a Worksheet
for What-If Analysis

6 Answer What-If
Questions by Changing
Values in a Worksheet

7 Chart Data with a Line
Chart

Skills Review | Project **3D** License Projection

In the following Skills Review, you will edit a worksheet for Jennifer Carson, City Finance Manager, that forecasts the revenue from business licenses that the City of Orange Blossom Beach expects to collect in the five-year period 2012–2016. Your completed worksheet will look similar to Figure 3.47.

Project Files

For Project 3D, you will need the following files:

> e03D_License_Projection
> e03D_Water_Scene.JPG

You will save your workbook as:

> Lastname_Firstname_3D_License_Projection

Project Results

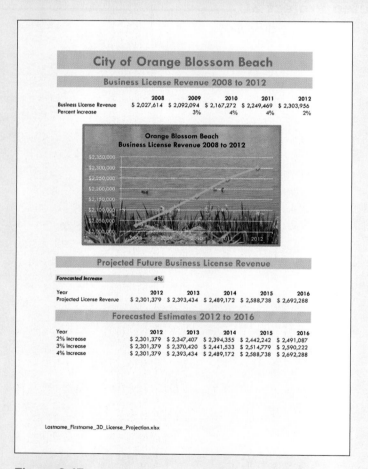

Figure 3.47

(Project 3D License Projection continues on the next page)

Skills Review | Project **3D** License Projection (continued)

1 Open **Excel**. From your student files, **Open e03D_ License_Projection**. If necessary, increase the size of the Excel window to fill the screen. If necessary, on the Standard toolbar, click the Zoom arrow, and then click 125%. **Save** the file in your **Excel Chapter 3** folder as **Lastname_Firstname_3D_License_Projection**

a. Click cell **C7**. Being sure to include the parentheses, type **=(c6-b6)/b6** and then on the formula bar, click the **Enter** button. On the **Home tab**, in the **Number group**, click the **Percent Style** button.

b. Click cell **D7**, type **=** and then by typing, or by using a combination of typing and clicking cells to reference them, construct a formula similar to the one in cell **C7** to calculate the rate of increase in business license revenue from 2009 to 2010. Format cell **D7** with the **Percent Style**. With cell **D7** selected, drag the fill handle to the right through cell **F7**.

c. In cell **A9**, type **Projected Future Business License Revenue** and then press Return. Click cell **A3**, and then on the Standard toolbar, click the **Format Painter** button, and then click cell **A9**. In cell **A11**, type **Forecasted Increase** and then in cell **A13**, type **Year**

d. In cell **A14**, type **Projected License Revenue** and then in cell **B13**, type **2012** and press Tab. In cell **C13**, type **2013** and then press Tab. Select the range **B13:C13**, and then drag the fill handle through cell **F13** to extend the pattern of years to *2016*. Apply **Bold** to the selection.

e. Click cell **B14**, type **2301379** and then on the formula bar, click the **Enter** button. On the **Home tab**, in the **Format group**, click the **Styles** button. From the **Cell Styles** gallery, apply the **Currency [0]** style.

f. In cell **B11**, type **2%** which is the percent of increase from 2011 to 2012, and then on the formula bar, click the **Enter** button. Select the range **A11:B11**, and then apply **Bold** and **Italic**.

g. Click cell **C14**. Type **=b14*(100%+b11)** and then on the formula bar, click the **Enter** button. With cell **C14** as the active cell, drag the fill handle to copy the formula to the range **D14:F14**. Click cell **B14**. On the Standard toolbar, click the **Format Painter** button, and then select the range **C14:F14**.

2 In cell **A16**, type **Forecasted Estimates 2012 to 2016** and then press Return. Use **Format Painter** to copy the format from cell **A9** to cell **A16**.

a. Select the range **A11:B11**. On the **Home tab**, in the **Font group**, click the **Fill Color arrow**, and then under **Theme Colors**, in the third row, click the first color—**Background 1, Darker 15%**.

b. In the range **A18:A21**, type the following row titles:

Year

2% Increase

3% Increase

4% Increase

c. Select the range **B13:F13**, and then press Command ⌘ + C to copy the range to the Clipboard. Click cell **B18**, and then press Command ⌘ + V to paste the selection to the range **B18:F18**.

d. Select and **Copy** the range **B14:F14**. Click cell **B19**, and then on the **Home tab**, in the **Edit group** click the **Paste arrow**, and then click **Paste Special**. In the **Paste Special** dialog box, under **Paste**, click the **Values and number formats** option button, and then click **OK**. Press Esc to cancel the moving border.

e. Click cell **B11**. Type **3** and then press Return. Select and **Copy** the new values in the range **B14:F14**. Click cell **B20**, and then by using the **Paste Special** dialog box, paste as **Values and number formats**. Press Esc to cancel the moving border.

f. In cell **B11**, type **4** and then press Return. Select and **Copy** the range **B14:F14**. Click cell **B21**, and then by using the **Paste Special** dialog box, paste as **Values and number formats**. Press Esc to cancel the moving border, click cell **A1**, and then **Save** your workbook.

3 In the **row header area**, point to **row 8** to display the ➡ pointer, and then drag down to select **rows 8:26**. On the **Home tab**, in the **Cells group**, click the **Insert** button to insert the same number of blank rows as you selected. Under the selection area, near cell **A27**, click the **Insert Options** button, and then click the **Clear Formatting** option button to clear formatting from these rows.

a. Select the range **A6:F6**. On the **Charts tab**, in the **Insert Chart group**, click the **Line** button. In the gallery of line charts, under **2-D Line**, click **Marked Line** to create the chart as an embedded chart in the worksheet.

(Project 3D License Projection continues on the next page)

Excel | Chapter 3

b. Point to the border of the chart to display the ✶ pointer, and then drag the chart so that its upper left corner is positioned in cell **A9**, aligned approximately under the *r* in the word *Increase* above.

c. On the **Chart Layout tab**, in the **Labels group**, click the **Legend** button, and then click **No Legend**. Click the chart title one time to select it. Type **Orange Blossom Beach** and then press ⟨Return⟩.

d. Type **Business License Revenue 2008 to 2012** and then click the border around the chart title remove the insertion point from the title. On the **Home tab**, in the **Font group**, change the **Font Size** to **14**. **Save** your workbook.

e. Be sure the chart is still selected—a blue frame surrounds it. On the **Charts tab**, in the **Data group**, click the **Select** button. In the **Select Data Source** dialog box, to the right of the **Category (X) axis labels** box, click the **Collapse Dialog Box** button. If necessary, drag the title bar of the Axis Labels dialog box upward so that it is not blocking your view of **row 5**, and then select the years in the range **B5:F5**. In the collapsed **Select Data Source** dialog box, click the **Expand Dialog Box** button. In the **Select Data Source** dialog box, click **OK** to display the years as category labels in the chart.

4 On the **Chart Layout tab**, in the **Axes group**, click the **Axes** button. Point to **Vertical Axis**, and then click **Axis Options**. In the **Format Axis** dialog box, on the left, be sure **Scale** is selected. On the right, double-click in the **Minimum** box, and then type **2000000**

a. Notice that the **Major unit** box displays a value of *50000.0*. In the **Format Axis** dialog box, click **OK**.

b. On the **Chart Layout tab**, in the **Current Selection group**, click the **Chart Elements arrow**, and then click **Chart Area**. Directly below the **Chart Elements** box, click the **Format Selection** button.

c. In the **Format Chart Area** dialog box, on the left, be sure that **Fill** is selected. On the right, click the **Picture or Texture tab**. To the right of **From file**, click **Choose Picture**. In the **Choose a Picture** dialog box, navigate to your student files, click the picture **e03D_Water_Scene.JPG**, and then click **Insert**.

d. In the **Format Chart Area** dialog box, on the left, click **Line**. In the **Format Chart Area** dialog box,

with the **Solid tab** active, click in the **Color** box. Under **Theme Colors**, in the first row, click the fourth color—**Text 2**.

e. In the **Format Chart Area** dialog box, click the **Weights & Arrows tab**. On the right, with the text in the **Width** box selected, type **4** and then click **OK**.

5 In the **Current Selection group**, click the **Chart Elements arrow**, click **Plot Area**, and then click the **Format Selection** button. In the **Format Plot Area** dialog box, on the left, click **Fill**. On the right, click in the **Color** box, and then click **No Fill**. In the **Format Plot Area** dialog box, click **OK**.

a. Click the **Chart Elements arrow**, click **Vertical (Value) Axis**, and then click the **Format Selection** button. In the **Format Axis** dialog box, on the left, click **Line**. On the right, with the **Solid tab** active, click in the **Color** box, and then click the first color—**Background 1**. In the **Format Axis** dialog box, click **OK**.

b. From the **Chart Elements** box, click **Vertical (Value) Axis Major Gridlines**, and then click the **Format Selection** button. Change the **Line Color** to **Background 1** (White), and then click **OK** to close the dialog box.

c. From the **Chart Elements** box, click **Horizontal (Category) Axis**, and then click the **Format Selection** button. Change the **Line Color** to **Background 1** (White), and then click **OK** to close the dialog box.

d. Click any of the numbers on the vertical value axis, and then on the **Home tab**, in the **Font group**, change the **Font Color** to **Background 1** (White). Click any of the years on the horizontal category axis, and then change the **Font Color** to **Background 1** (White). Click any cell to deselect the chart, and then press ⟨Command ⌘⟩ + ⟨fn⟩ + ⟨←⟩ to move to cell **A1**.

6 On the **View** menu, click **Header and Footer**. In the **Page Setup** dialog box, click **Customize Footer**. With the insertion point in the **Left section**, click the **Insert File Name** button, and then click **OK**. In the **Page Setup** dialog box, click the **Margins tab**. Under **Center on page**, select the **Horizontally** check box, and then click **OK** to close the dialog box. **Save** your workbook.

a. On the **File** menu, click **Properties**. In the **Subject** box, type your course name and section number.

(Project 3D License Projection continues on the next page)

Content-Based Assessments

Skills Review | Project **3D** License Projection (continued)

In the **Author** box, replace the existing text with your firstname and lastname. In the **Keywords** box type **business license revenue, forecast** and then click **OK**. **Save** your workbook.

b. **Print** or submit electronically as directed by your instructor. If required by your instructor, print

or create an electronic version of your worksheet with formulas displayed by using the instructions in Activity 1.15, and then **Close** your workbook without saving so that you do not save the changes you made to print formulas. On the **Excel** menu, click **Quit Excel**.

 You have completed Project 3D

Apply **3A** skills from these Objectives:

1 Chart Data with a Pie Chart

2 Format a Pie Chart

3 Edit a Workbook and Update a Chart

4 Use Goal Seek to Perform What-If Analysis

Mastering Excel | Project **3E** Capital Projects

In the following project, you will edit a worksheet for Jennifer Carson, City Finance Manager, that summarizes the budget for capital projects in the City of Orange Blossom Beach. Your completed worksheets will look similar to Figure 3.48.

Project Files

For Project 3E, you will need the following files:

e03E_Capital_Projects

You will save your workbook as:

Lastname_Firstname_3E_Capital_Projects

Project Results

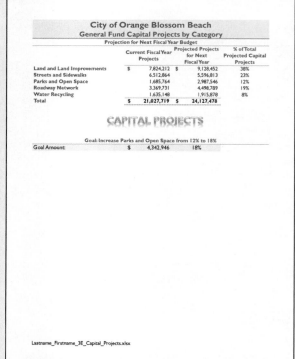

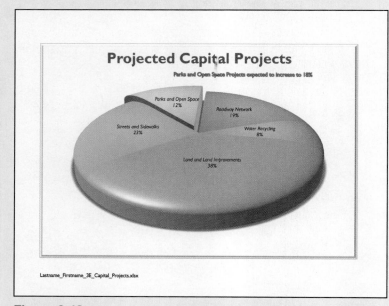

Figure 3.48

(Project 3E Capital Projects continues on the next page)

Content-Based Assessments

1 Open **Excel**. From your student files, **Open e03E_ Capital_Projects**. If necessary, increase the size of the Excel window to fill the screen. If necessary, on the Standard toolbar, click the Zoom arrow, and then click 125%. **Save** the file in your **Excel Chapter 3** folder as **Lastname_Firstname_3E_Capital_Projects**

2 In cells **B10** and **C10**, enter formulas to calculate totals for each column. Then, in cell **D5**, enter a formula to calculate the % of Total Projected Capital Projects for Land and Land Improvements by dividing the **Projected Projects for Next Fiscal Year** for **Land and Land Improvements** by the **Total Projected Projects for Next Fiscal Year**. Use absolute cell references as necessary, format the result as **Percent Style**, and apply **Center Text** to the percentage. Fill the formula down through cell **D9**.

3 Select the nonadjacent ranges **A5:A9** and **C5:C9**, and then insert a **3-D Pie** chart. Move the chart to a **New sheet** named **Projected Capital Projects** Insert a **Chart Title** above the chart with the text **Projected Capital Projects** Change the chart title **Font Size** to **32** and change the **Font Color** to **Text 2**—in the first row, the fourth color.

4 Remove the **Legend** from the chart, and then add **Data Labels** formatted so that only the **Category Name and Percentage** display positioned in the **Center** of each slice. For the data labels, change the **Font Size** to **11**, and then apply **Italic**.

5 Select the entire pie, display the **Effects** gallery, point to **Bevel**, and then click **Bevel Options**. Change the **Top** and **Bottom** options to the last **Bevel** type—**Art Deco**. Set the **Top Width** and **Height** boxes to **256** and then set the **Bottom Width** and **Height** boxes to **0** In the **Format Data Series** dialog box, on the **Depth & Surface tab**, change the **Material** to **Plastic**.

6 With the pie chart selected, click the **Format Selection** button, and in the **Format Data Series** dialog box, click **Options**. Change the **Angle of first slice** to **100** to move the *Parks and Open Space* slice to the top of the pie. Select the **Parks and Open Space** slice, and then explode the slice slightly.

7 Change the **Fill Color** of the **Land and Land Improvements** slice to **Text 1, Lighter 50%**—in the fourth row, the second color. Format the **Chart Area** by applying a **Convex Bevel** effect. To the **Chart Area**, apply a **Fill Color** of **Accent 3, Lighter 80%**—in the second row, the seventh color.

8 Insert a **WordArt** box, and change the **Font Size** to **12** and the **Font Color** to **Text 1**—in the first row, the second color. Remove the **Bold** formatting, and then type **Parks and Open Space Projects expected to increase to 18%** Drag the **WordArt** upward until the left edge of the Word Art is positioned approximately halfway between the *Parks and Open Space* pie slice and the *d* in the word *Projected* in the title as shown in Figure 3.48—your WordArt position does not need to match precisely. Press Esc to deselect the WordArt.

9 Display **Sheet1** and rename the sheet as **Capital Projects Data** Click in any blank cell to cancel any selections. **Insert** a **WordArt**, and then by using **Quick Styles**, under **Applies to All Text in the Shape**, click the last style. Type **capital projects** and then change the **Font Size** to **20**. Drag to position the upper left corner of the **WordArt** into cell **A12** to visually center the WordArt between the columns of the worksheet. Nudge as necessary.

10 In cell **A16**, type **Goal: Increase Parks and Open Space from 12% to 18%** and then **Merge** the text across the range **A16:D16**. Apply the **Heading 3** cell style. In cell **A17**, type **Goal Amount:**

11 **Copy** the range **C7:D7** to cell **B17**. Click cell **C17**, and then use **Goal Seek** to determine the projected amount of Parks and Open Space projects in cell **B17** if the value in **C17** is **18%**

12 Select the range **A17:C17**, and then apply the **20% - Accent2** cell style. In cell **B17**, from the **Cell Styles** gallery, apply the **Currency [0]** cell style.

13 Insert the file name in the **Left section** of the footer, and then center the worksheet **Horizontally** on the page. If necessary, click cell **A1**. Display the **Projected Capital Projects** sheet and insert the file name in the **Left section** of the footer.

14 In **File Properties**, add your course name and section, your name, and the keywords **Parks and Open Space, capital projects**

15 Group the sheets, and then **Save** your workbook. **Print** or submit electronically as directed by your instructor. If required by your instructor, print or create an electronic version of your worksheet with formulas displayed by using the instructions in Activity 1.15, and then **Close** the workbook without saving so that you do not save the changes you made to print formulas. On the **Excel** menu, click **Quit Excel**.

 End You have completed Project 3E

Excel | Chapter 3

Apply **3B** skills from these Objectives:

5 Design a Worksheet for What-If Analysis

6 Answer What-If Questions by Changing Values in a Worksheet

7 Chart Data with a Line Chart

Mastering Excel | Project **3F** Fee Projection

In the following project, you will edit a worksheet that Jeffrey Lovins, Human Resources Director, will use to prepare a five-year forecast of the revenue generated by community development fees. Your completed worksheet will look similar to Figure 3.49.

Project Files

For Project 3F, you will need the following file:

e03F_Fee_Projection

You will save your workbook as:

Lastname_Firstname_3F_Fee_Projection

Project Results

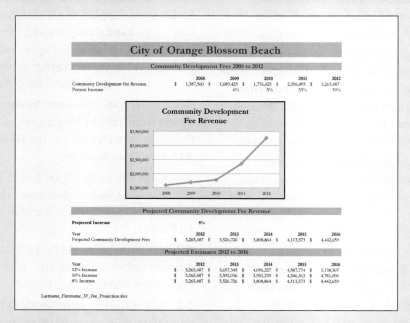

Figure 3.49

(Project 3F Fee Projection continues on the next page)

Mastering Excel | Project **3F** Fee Projection (continued)

1 Open **Excel**. From your student files, **Open e03F_ Fee_Projection**. If necessary, increase the size of the Excel window to fill the screen. If necessary, on the Standard toolbar, click the Zoom arrow, and then click 125%. **Save** the file in your **Excel Chapter 3** folder as **Lastname_ Firstname_3F_Fee_Projection**

2 In cell **C7**, construct a formula to calculate the percent of increase in employee annual benefit costs from 2008 to 2009. Format the result with the **Percent Style** and then fill the formula through cell **F7**.

3 In cell **A9**, type **Projected Community Development Fee Revenue** and then use **Format Painter** to copy the formatting from cell **A3** to cell **A9**. In cell **A11**, type **Projected Increase** and then in cell **A13**, type **Year** In cell **A14**, type **Projected Community Development Fees** and then in the range **B13:F13**, use the fill handle to enter the years **2012** through **2016**. Apply **Bold** to the years. In cell **B14**, type **3265487** and then from the **Cell Styles** gallery, apply the **Currency [0]** format. In cell **B11**, type **12%** which is the projected increase estimated by the city financial analysts. To the range **A11:B11**, apply **Bold**.

4 In cell **C14**, construct a formula to calculate the annual projected community development fees for the year 2013 after the projected increase of 12% is applied. Fill the formula through cell **F14**, and then use **Format Painter** to copy the formatting from cell **B14** to the range **C14:F14**.

5 In cell **A16**, type **Projected Estimates 2012 to 2016** and then use **Format Painter** to copy the format from cell **A9** to cell **A16**. In cells **A18:A21**, type the following row titles:

Year

12% Increase

10% Increase

8% Increase

6 **Copy** the range **B13:F13**, and then **Paste** the selection to **B18:F18**. **Copy** the range **B14:F14**, and then by using the **Paste Special** dialog box, paste the **Values and number formats** to the range **B19:F19**. Complete the Projected Estimates section of the worksheet by changing the *Projected Increase* in **B11** to **10%** and then to **8%** copying and pasting the **Values and number formats** to the appropriate ranges in the worksheet.

7 Select **rows 8:26**, **Insert** rows, and then **Clear Formatting** from the inserted rows. By using the data in **A5:F6**, insert a **Marked Line** chart in the worksheet. Move the chart so that its upper left corner is positioned in cell **A9** and centered under the data above. Remove the **Legend**, and then modify the chart title so the text *Fee Revenue* displays on the second line. Be sure to delete the space between *Development* and *Fee*.

8 Format the **Vertical (Value) Axis** so that the **Minimum** is **1500000** and be sure the **Major unit** displays *500000.0*. Format the **Chart Area** with a **Fill Color** of **Background 2, Lighter 40%**—in the fourth row, the third color. Change the **Line Color** to **Text 1**—in the first word, the second color. Change the **Width** of the line to **2**

9 Deselect the chart, and then insert the file name in the **Left section** of the footer. Center the worksheet **Horizontally** on the page. In the **Page Setup** dialog box, on the **Page tab**, change the **Orientation** to **Landscape**, and then under **Scaling**, click the **Fit to** option button. In **File Properties**, add your course name and section, your name, and the keywords **fee projection**

10 Click cell **A1**, and then **Save** your workbook. **Print** or submit electronically as directed by your instructor. If required by your instructor, print or create an electronic version of your worksheet with formulas displayed by using the instructions in Activity 1.15, and then **Close** the workbook without saving so that you do not save the changes you made to print formulas. On the **Excel** menu, click **Quit Excel**.

End **You have completed Project 3F** ———————————————————

1 Chart Data with a Pie Chart

2 Format a Pie Chart

3 Edit a Workbook and Update a Chart

4 Use Goal Seek to Perform What-If Analysis

5 Design a Worksheet for What-If Analysis

6 Answer What-If Questions by Changing Values in a Worksheet

7 Chart Data with a Line Chart

Mastering Excel | Project **3G** Operations Analysis

In the following project, you will you will edit a workbook for Jennifer Carson, City Finance Manager, that summarizes the operations costs for the Public Works Department. Your completed worksheets will look similar to Figure 3.50.

Project Files

For Project 3G, you will need the following file:

e03G_Operations_Analysis

You will save your workbook as

Lastname_Firstname_3G_Operations_Analysis

Project Results

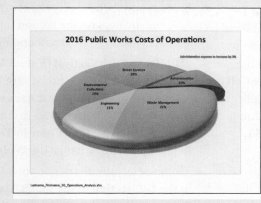

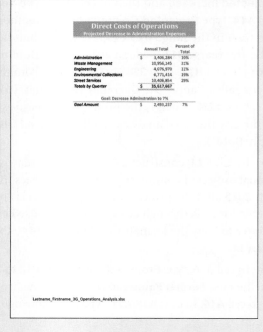

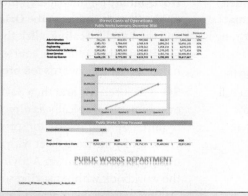

Figure 3.50

(Project 3G Operations Analysis continues on the next page)

Content-Based Assessments

Mastering Excel | Project 3G Operations Analysis (continued)

1 Open **Excel**. From your student files, **Open e03G_Operations_Analysis**. If necessary, increase the size of the Excel window to fill the screen. If necessary, on the Standard toolbar, click the Zoom arrow, and then click 125%. **Save** the file in your **Excel Chapter 3** folder as Lastname_Firstname_3G_Operations_Analysis

2 In the **Public Works** sheet, calculate totals in the ranges **F5:F9** and **B10:F10**. In cell **G5**, construct a formula to calculate the Percent of Total by dividing the **Annual Total** for **Administration** in cell **F5** by the **Annual Total** for all quarters in cell **F10**. Use absolute cell references as necessary, format the result in **Percent Style**, and then apply **Center Text** alignment. Fill the formula down through cell **G9**.

3 Select the nonadjacent ranges **A5:A9** and **F5:F9**, and then insert a **3-D Pie** chart. Move the chart to a **New sheet** with the name **Public Works Summary Chart** Insert a **Chart Title** above the chart with the text **2016 Public Works Costs of Operations** and then change the **Font Size** to **28**.

4 Remove the **Legend** from the chart and then add **Data Labels** formatted so that only the **Category Name and Percentage** display positioned in the **Center** of each slice. For the data labels, change the **Font Size** to **12**, and then apply **Bold** and **Italic**.

5 Select the pie chart, and then modify **Effects** by changing the **Bevel Options**. Change the **Top** and **Bottom** options to the **Circle**. Set the **Top Width** and **Height** boxes to **256** and then set the **Bottom Width** and **Height** boxes to **50** For **Depth & Surface**, change the **Material** to **Metal**.

6 With the pie chart selected, in the **Format Data Series** dialog box, on the left, click **Options**, and then change the **Angle of first slice** to **50** Explode the **Administration** slice slightly away from the pie. Format the **Chart Area** with a **Fill Color** of **Accent 2, Lighter 80%**—in the second row, the sixth color.

7 Insert a **WordArt** box with a **Font Size** of **10.5** and a **Font Color** of **Text 2**—in the first row, the fourth color. Remove the **Bold** formatting, and then type **Administration expense to increase by 3%** Move the **WordArt** so that it is positioned in close proximity to the *Administration* pie slice as displayed in Figure 3.50—the position of your WordArt need not be precise. On this chart sheet, insert the file name in the **Left section** of the footer.

8 In the **Public Works** sheet, using the data in the nonadjacent ranges **B4:E4** and **B10:E10**, insert a **Marked Line** chart in the worksheet. Move the chart so that its

upper left corner is positioned in cell **A12**, visually centered between the columns in the worksheet. Remove the **Legend** and then add a **Chart Title** above the chart with the text **2016 Public Works Cost Summary** Edit the **Vertical (Value) Axis** so that the **Minimum** is set to **8600000** and the **Major unit** is **200000** Format the **Chart Area** with a **Fill Color** of **Accent 2, Lighter 40%**—in the fourth row, the sixth color.

9 In cell **B35**, type **35617667** and then apply the **Currency [0]** cell style. In cell **C35**, construct a formula to calculate the **Projected Operations Costs** after the forecasted increase is applied. Fill the formula through cell **F35**, and then use **Format Painter** to copy the formatting from cell **B35** to the range **C35:F35**.

10 **Insert** a **WordArt** and format using the last **Quick Style** under **Applies to All Text in the Shape**. Type **public works department** and then change the **Font Size** to **32**. Drag to position the **WordArt** in cell **A38**, centered between the columns of the worksheet.

11 Change the **Orientation** to **Landscape**, and then adjust the **Scaling** so that the worksheet prints on one page. Insert the file name in the **Left section** of the footer. Center the worksheet **Horizontally** on the page.

12 Display the **Projected Decrease sheet**. In cell **C5**, calculate the Percent of Total by dividing the **Administration Annual Total** by the **Totals by Quarter**, using absolute cell references as necessary. Apply **Percent Style** and then fill the formula from **C5:C9**.

13 **Copy** cell **B5**, and then use **Paste Special** to paste the **Values and number formats** to cell **B13**. **Copy** and **Paste** cell **C5** to **C13**. With cell **C13** selected, use **Goal Seek** to determine the goal amount of administration expenses in cell **B13** if the value in **C13** is set to **7%**

14 On the **Projected Decrease** sheet, insert the file name in the **Left section** of the footer, and then center the worksheet **Horizontally** on the page. In **File Properties**, add your course name and section, your name, and the keywords **public works**

15 Group the sheets, and then **Save** your workbook. **Print** or submit electronically as directed by your instructor. If required by your instructor, print or create an electronic version of your worksheets with formulas displayed by using the instructions in Activity 1.15, and then **Close** the workbook without saving so that you do not save the changes you made to print formulas. On the **Excel** menu, click **Quit Excel**.

End **You have completed Project 3G**

y

Excel | Chapter 3

GO! Fix It | Project **3H** Recreation

Project Files

For Project 3H, you will need the following file:

> e03H_Recreation

You will save your workbook as:

> Lastname_Firstname_3H_Recreation

In this project, you will correct a worksheet that contains the annual enrollment of residents in city-sponsored recreation programs. From the student files that accompany this textbook, open e03H_Recreation, and then save the file in your Excel Chapter 3 folder as **Lastname_Firstname_3H_Recreation**

To complete the project, you must find and correct errors in formulas and formatting. View each formula in the worksheet and edit as necessary. Review the format and title of the pie chart and make corrections and formatting changes as necessary. In addition to errors that you find, you should know:

- The pie chart data should include the Age Group and the Total columns.

- The Chart Area should include a blue fill color, and the title font color should be white.

- The pie chart should be in a separate worksheet named **Enrollment Analysis Chart**

Insert the file name in the footer of both sheets, and add your course name and section, your name, and the keywords **Parks and Recreation, enrollment** to the file properties. Group your sheets, save your file, and then print or submit your worksheet electronically as directed by your instructor. If required by your instructor, print or create an electronic version of your worksheet with formulas displayed by using the instructions in Activity 1.15, and then close the workbook without saving so that you do not save the changes you made to print formulas. Then Quit Excel.

End **You have completed Project 3H** ———————————————

Content-Based Assessments

GO! Make It | Project **3I** Tax Projection

Project Files

For Project 3I, you will need the following file:

 New Excel workbook

You will save your workbook as:

 Lastname_Firstname_3I_Tax_Projection

Start a new blank Excel workbook and create the worksheet shown in Figure 3.51. Save the workbook in your Excel Chapter 3 folder as **Lastname_Firstname_3I_Tax_Projection** In the range C7:F7, calculate the rate of increase from the previous year. In the range C31:F31, calculate the projected property tax for each year based on the forecasted increase. Complete the worksheet by entering in the range B36:F38, the projected property tax revenue for each year based on 2%, 3%, and 4% increases. Insert the chart as shown, using the 2010 through 2014 Property Tax Revenue data. For the chart area use a fill color of Accent 1, Lighter 60%, and change the chart title font size to 14. Change the orientation to landscape, scale the height to fit to one page, and center horizontally on the page. Insert the file name in the footer, and then add your course name and section, your name, and the keywords **property tax** to the file properties. Save the workbook, and then print or submit electronically as directed by your instructor. If required by your instructor, print or create an electronic version of your worksheet with formulas displayed by using the instructions in Activity 1.15, and then close the workbook without saving changes. Then Quit Excel.

Project Results

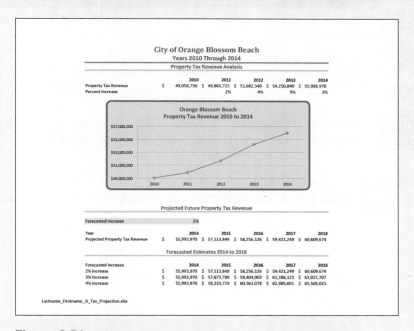

Figure 3.51

End   **You have completed Project 3I** ————————————

Content-Based Assessments

GO! Solve It | Project **3J** Staffing

Project Files

For Project 3J, you will need the following file:

e03J_Staffing

You will save your workbook as:

Lastname_Firstname_3J_Staffing

Open the file e03J_Staffing and save it in your Excel Chapter 3 folder as **Lastname_Firstname_3J_Staffing** Complete the worksheet by calculating totals and the % of Total Employees. Format the worksheet attractively, including appropriate number formatting. Insert a pie chart in a separate sheet that illustrates the Two-Year Projection staffing levels by department, and use the techniques that you practiced in this chapter to format the chart so that it is attractive and easy to understand. Change the angle of the first slice so that the Public Safety slice displays below the title and explode the slice slightly. Then, insert WordArt that indicates that the increase in Public Safety staffing is contingent upon City Council approval. Include the file name in the footer, center the worksheet horizontally on the page, add appropriate file properties, and then save and submit as directed.

		Performance Level		
		Exemplary: You consistently applied the relevant skills	**Proficient:** You sometimes, but not always, applied the relevant skills	**Developing:** You rarely or never applied the relevant skills
Performance Criteria	**Create formulas**	All formulas are correct and are efficiently constructed.	Formulas are correct but not always constructed in the most efficient manner.	One or more formulas are missing or incorrect; or only numbers were entered.
	Chart inserted and formatted	Chart was inserted and formatted properly.	Chart was inserted but incorrect data was selected or the chart was not formatted.	No chart was inserted.
	Format attractively and appropriately	Formatting is attractive and appropriate.	Adequately formatted but difficult to read or unattractive.	Inadequate or no formatting.

End You have completed Project 3J

Content-Based Assessments

GO! Solve It | Project **3K** Water Usage

Project Files

For Project 3K, you will need the following files:

> New Excel workbook
> e03K_Beach.JPG

You will save your workbook as:

> Lastname_Firstname_3K_Water_Usage

The City of Orange Blossom Beach is a growing community and the City Council has requested an analysis of future resource needs. In this project, you will create a worksheet for the Department of Water and Power that lists residential water usage over the past ten years and that forecasts the amount of water that city residents will use in the next ten years. Save the workbook in your Excel Chapter 3 folder as **Lastname_Firstname_3K_Water_Usage** Create a worksheet with the following data:

	2008	2010	2012	2014	2016
Water Use in Orange Blossom Beach	62500	68903	73905	76044	80342

Calculate the percent increase for the years 2010 to 2016. Below the Percent Increase, insert a line chart that illustrates the city's water usage from 2008 to 2016. Below the chart, add a section to the worksheet to calculate the projected water usage for the years 2016 to 2024 in two-year increments based on a 4% annual increase. The 2016 amount is 80,342. Format the chart and worksheet attractively with a title and subtitle, and apply appropriate formatting. If you choose to format the chart area with a picture, you can use e03K_Beach.JPG located with your student files. Include the file name in the footer and enter appropriate file properties. Save, and then print or submit as directed.

	Performance Level		
Performance Criteria	**Exemplary:** You consistently applied the relevant skills	**Proficient:** You sometimes, but not always, applied the relevant skills	**Developing:** You rarely or never applied the relevant skills
Create formulas	All formulas are correct and are efficiently constructed.	Formulas are correct but not always constructed in the most efficient manner.	One or more formulas are missing or incorrect or only numbers were entered.
Insert and format line chart	Line chart created correctly and is attractively formatted.	Line chart was created but the data was incorrect or the chart was not appropriately formatted.	No line chart was created.
Format attractively and appropriately	Formatting is attractive and appropriate.	Adequately formatted but difficult to read or unattractive.	Inadequate or no formatting.

End **You have completed Project 3K** ————————————

Outcomes-Based Assessments

Rubric

The following outcomes-based assessments are open-ended assessments. That is, there is no specific correct result; your result will depend on your approach to the information provided. Make Professional Quality your goal. Use the following scoring rubric to guide you in how to approach the problem and then to evaluate how well your approach solves the problem.

The *criteria*—Software Mastery, Content, Format and Layout, and Process—represent the knowledge and skills you have gained that you can apply to solving the problem. The *levels of performance*—Professional Quality, Approaching Professional Quality, or Needs Quality Improvements—help you and your instructor evaluate your result.

	Your completed project is of Professional Quality if you:	Your completed project is Approaching Professional Quality if you:	Your completed project Needs Quality Improvements if you:
1-Software Mastery	Choose and apply the most appropriate skills, tools, and features and identify efficient methods to solve the problem.	Choose and apply some appropriate skills, tools, and features, but not in the most efficient manner.	Choose inappropriate skills, tools, or features, or are inefficient in solving the problem.
2-Content	Construct a solution that is clear and well organized, contains content that is accurate, appropriate to the audience and purpose, and is complete. Provide a solution that contains no errors in spelling, grammar, or style.	Construct a solution in which some components are unclear, poorly organized, inconsistent, or incomplete. Misjudge the needs of the audience. Have some errors in spelling, grammar, or style, but the errors do not detract from comprehension.	Construct a solution that is unclear, incomplete, or poorly organized; contains some inaccurate or inappropriate content; and contains many errors in spelling, grammar, or style. Do not solve the problem.
3-Format and Layout	Format and arrange all elements to communicate information and ideas, clarify function, illustrate relationships, and indicate relative importance.	Apply appropriate format and layout features to some elements, but not others. Overuse features, causing minor distraction.	Apply format and layout that does not communicate information or ideas clearly. Do not use format and layout features to clarify function, illustrate relationships, or indicate relative importance. Use available features excessively, causing distraction.
4-Process	Use an organized approach that integrates planning, development, self-assessment, revision, and reflection.	Demonstrate an organized approach in some areas, but not others; or, use an insufficient process of organization throughout.	Do not use an organized approach to solve the problem.

Outcomes-Based Assessments

Apply a combination of the 3A and 3B skills.

GO! Think | Project 3L School Enrollment

Project Files

For Project 3L, you will need the following file:

> New Excel workbook

You will save your workbook as:

> Lastname_Firstname_3L_School_Enrollment

Marcus Chavez, the Superintendent of Schools for the City of Orange Blossom Beach, has requested an enrollment analysis of students in the city public elementary schools in order to plan school boundary modifications resulting in more balanced enrollments. Enrollments in district elementary schools for the past two years are as follows:

School	2015 Enrollment	2016 Enrollment
Orange Blossom	795	824
Kittridge	832	952
Glenmeade	524	480
Hidden Trails	961	953
Beach Side	477	495
Sunnyvale	515	502

Create a workbook to provide Marcus with the enrollment information for each school and the total district enrollment. Save the file in your Excel Chapter 3 folder as **Lastname_Firstname_3L_School_Enrollment** Insert a column to calculate the percent change from 2015 to 2016. Note that some of the results will be negative numbers. Format the percentages with two decimal places. Insert a pie chart in its own sheet that illustrates the 2016 enrollment figures for each school and format the chart attractively. Format the worksheet so that it is professional and easy to read and understand. Insert a footer with the file name and add appropriate file properties. Save, and then print or submit as directed by your instructor.

End You have completed Project 3L ————————

Apply a combination of the **3A** and **3B** skills.

GO! Think | Project **3M** Park Acreage

Project Files

For Project 3M, you will need the following files:

New Excel workbook
e03M_Park.JPG

You will save your workbook as:

Lastname_Firstname_3M_Park_Acreage

The City of Orange Blossom Beach wants to maintain a high ratio of parkland to residents and has established a goal of maintaining a minimum of 50 parkland acres per 1,000 residents. The following table contains the park acreage and the population, in thousands, since 1980. Start a new blank Excel workbook, save the workbook in your Excel Chapter 3 folder as **Lastname_Firstname_3M_Park_Acreage** and then enter appropriate titles. Then, enter the following data in the worksheet and calculate the *Acres per 1,000 residents* by dividing the Park acreage by the Population in thousands.

	1980	1990	2000	2010
Population in thousands	118.4	123.9	133.5	152.6
Park acreage	5,800	6,340	8,490	9,200
Acres per 1,000 residents				

Create a line chart that displays the Park Acres Per 1,000 Residents for each year. Format the chart professionally and insert the picture e03M_Park.JPG from your student files in the chart fill area. Below the chart, create a new section titled **Park Acreage Analysis** and then copy and paste the Years and the Park acreage values to the new section. Calculate the *Percent increase* from the previous ten years for the 1990, 2000, and 2010 years. Below the Park Acreage Analysis section, create a new worksheet section titled **Park Acreage Forecast** and then enter the following values.

	2010	2020	2030	2040
Population in thousands	152.6	173.2	197.7	225.3
Park acreage necessary				
Percent increase				

Calculate the *Park acreage necessary* to reach the city's goal by multiplying the Population in thousands by 50. Then calculate the *Percent increase* from the previous ten years for the 2020, 2030, and 2040 years. Use techniques that you practiced in this chapter to format the worksheet professionally. Insert a footer with the file name and add appropriate file properties. Save, and then print or submit as directed by your instructor.

 You have completed Project 3M ───────────────

Apply a combination of the 3A and 3B skills.

You and GO! | Project **3N** Expense Analysis

Project Files

For Project 3N, you will need the following file:

New Excel workbook

You will save your workbook as:

Lastname_Firstname_3N_Expense_Analysis

Develop a worksheet that details the expenses you have incurred during the past two months and list the expenses for each month in separate columns. Save your file in your Excel Chapter 3 folder as **Lastname_Firstname_3N_Expense_Analysis** Calculate totals for each column and then add a column in which you can calculate the percent of change from one month to the next. Insert and format a pie chart that illustrates the expenses that you incurred in the most recent month. After reviewing the pie chart, determine a category of expense in which you might be overspending, and then pull that slice out of the pie and insert a WordArt box indicating how you might save money on that expense. Insert a footer with the file name, center the worksheet horizontally on the page, and add appropriate file properties. Save, and then print or submit as directed.

 You have completed Project 3N ——————————————————

Apply a combination of the 3A and 3B skills.

GO! Group Business Running Case | Project **3O**
Bell Orchid Hotels Group Running Case

This project relates to the **Bell Orchid Hotels**. Your instructor may assign this group case project to your class. If your instructor assigns this project, he or she will provide you with information and instructions to work as part of a group. The group will apply the skills gained thus far to help the Bell Orchid Hotels achieve their business goals.

 You have completed Project 3O ——————————————————

Getting Started with Microsoft Office PowerPoint

OUTCOMES

At the end of this chapter you will be able to:

PROJECT 1A
Create a new PowerPoint presentation.

PROJECT 1B
Edit and format a PowerPoint presentation.

OBJECTIVES

Mastering these objectives will enable you to:

1. Create a New Presentation (p. 437)
2. Edit a Presentation in Normal View (p. 441)
3. Add Pictures to a Presentation (p. 448)
4. View and Print a Presentation (p. 452)

5. Edit an Existing Presentation (p. 457)
6. Format a Presentation (p. 462)
7. Use Slide Sorter View (p. 465)
8. Apply Slide Transitions (p. 467)

© Bridget Zawitoski / Shutterstock

In This Chapter

In this chapter, you will study presentation skills, which are among the most important skills you will learn. Good presentation skills enhance your communications—written, electronic, and interpersonal. In this technology-enhanced world, communicating ideas clearly and concisely is a critical personal skill. Microsoft PowerPoint for Mac 2011 is presentation software with which you create electronic slide presentations. Use PowerPoint to present information to your audience effectively. You can start with a new, blank presentation and add content, pictures, and themes, or you can collaborate with colleagues by inserting slides that have been saved in other presentations.

The projects in this chapter relate to **Lehua Hawaiian Adventures**. Named for the small, crescent-shaped island that is noted for its snorkeling and scuba diving, Lehua Hawaiian Adventures offers exciting but affordable adventure tours. Hiking tours go off the beaten path to amazing remote places on the islands. If you prefer to ride into the heart of Hawaii, try the cycling tours. Lehua Hawaiian Adventures also offers Jeep tours. Whatever you prefer—mountain, sea, volcano—our tour guides are experts in the history, geography, culture, and flora and fauna of Hawaii.

Project 1A Company Overview

Project Activities

In Activities 1.01 through 1.13, you will create the first four slides of a new presentation that Lehua Hawaiian Adventures Tour Manager Carl Kawaoka is developing to introduce the tour services that the company offers. Your completed presentation will look similar to Figure 1.1.

Project Files

For Project 1A, you will need the following files:

New Presentation
p01A_Helicopter
p01A_Beach

You will save your presentation as:

Lastname_Firstname_1A_LHA_Overview

Project Results

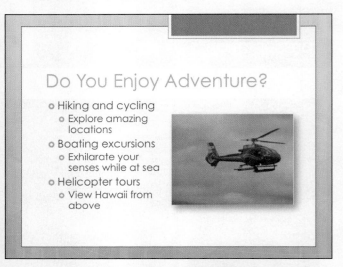

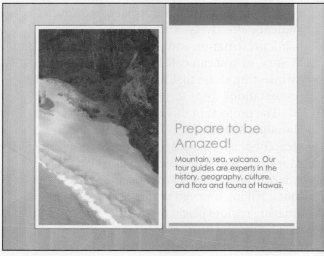

Figure 1.1
Project 1A LHA Overview

Objective 1 | Create a New Presentation

Microsoft PowerPoint for Mac 2011 is software with which you can present information to your audience effectively. You can edit and format a blank presentation by adding text, a presentation theme, and pictures.

Activity 1.01 | Identifying Parts of the PowerPoint Window

In this activity, you will open PowerPoint and identify the parts of the PowerPoint window.

> **Another Way**
> Press Command ⌘ + N; or from the PowerPoint Presentation Gallery, select White, and then click Choose.

1 Open **PowerPoint**. On the **File** menu, click **New Presentation** to display a new presentation in Normal view. If necessary, increase the width of the window to fill the entire screen. Compare your screen with Figure 1.2.

Normal view is the primary editing view in PowerPoint where you write and design your presentations. Normal view includes the Notes pane, the Slide pane, and the Slides/Outline pane.

Figure 1.2

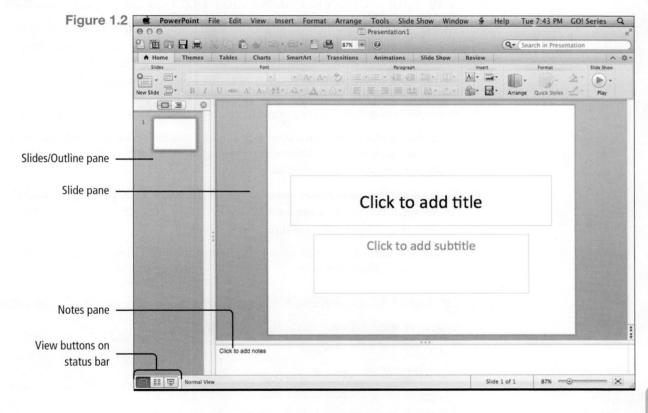

2 Take a moment to study the parts of the PowerPoint window described in the table in Figure 1.3.

Microsoft PowerPoint Screen Elements

Screen Element	Description
Notes pane	Displays below the Slide pane and provides space for you to type notes regarding the active slide.
Slide pane	Displays a large image of the active slide.
Slides/Outline pane	Displays either the presentation in the form of miniature images called **thumbnails** (Slides tab) or the presentation outline (Outline tab).
Status bar	Displays, in a horizontal bar at the bottom of the presentation window, the current slide number, number of slides in a presentation, theme, View buttons, Zoom slider, and Fit slide to current window button; you can customize this area to include additional helpful information.
View buttons	Control the look of the presentation window with a set of commands.

Figure 1.3

Activity 1.02 | Entering Presentation Text and Saving a Presentation

PowerPoint displays a new presentation with a single *slide*—a *title slide* in Normal view. A presentation slide—similar to a page in a document—can contain text, pictures, tables, charts, and other multimedia or graphic objects. The title slide is the first slide in a presentation and provides an introduction to the presentation topic.

1 In the **Slide pane**, click in the text *Click to add title*, which is the title *placeholder*.

> A placeholder is a box on a slide with a border that holds title and body text or other content such as charts, tables, and pictures. This slide contains two placeholders, one for the title and one for the subtitle.

2 Type **Lehua Hawaiian Adventures** point to *Lehua*, and then press Control and click. On the shortcut menu, click **Ignore All** so *Lehua* is not flagged as a spelling error in this presentation. Compare your screen with Figure 1.4.

> Recall that a red wavy underline indicates that the underlined word is not in the Microsoft Office dictionary.

Figure 1.4

Red wavy line no longer displays under *Lehua*

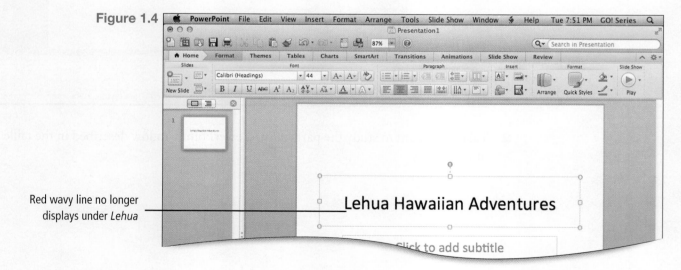

3 Click in the subtitle placeholder—*Click to add subtitle*—and then type **Carl Kawaoka**

4 Press Return to create a new line in the subtitle placeholder. Type **Tour Manager**

5 Point to **Kawaoka**, press Control and click, and then on the shortcut menu, click **Ignore All**. Compare your screen with Figure 1.5.

Figure 1.5

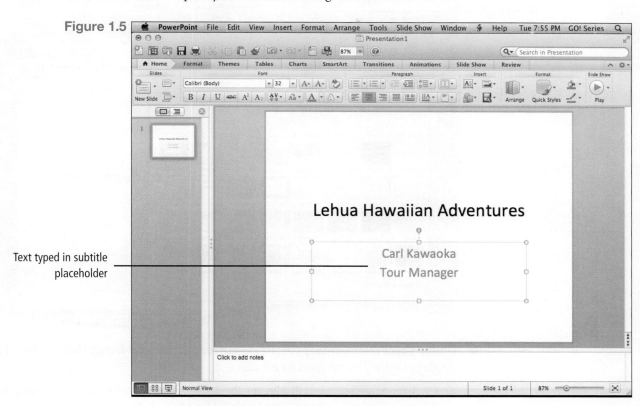

Text typed in subtitle placeholder

6 On the **File** menu, click **Save As**, and then navigate to the location where you will store your files for this chapter. Create a new folder named **PowerPoint Chapter 1** In the **Save As** box, replace the existing text with **Lastname_Firstname_1A_LHA_Overview** and then click **Save**.

Activity 1.03 | Applying a Presentation Theme

A *theme* is a set of unified design elements that provides a look for your presentation by applying colors, fonts, and effects.

1 On the Ribbon, click the **Themes tab**. In the **Themes group**, point to the bottom of the gallery of themes, and then click the **More** ▼ button to display the **Themes** gallery. Compare your screen with Figure 1.6.

Figure 1.6

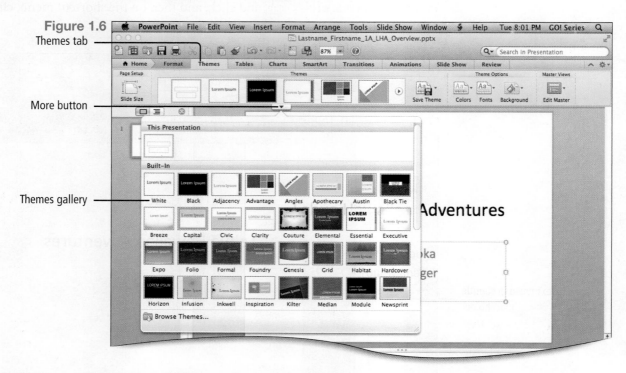

Themes tab

More button

Themes gallery

2 Under **This Presentation**, point to the current theme and notice that a ScreenTip displays *Office Theme: used by all slides.*

Click the More button to display the theme gallery, or on the Ribbon, point to a theme to display a ScreenTip that will display the name of the theme.

3 Under **Built-In**, click the **Austin** theme to change the presentation theme. **Save** 🖫 your presentation, and then compare your screen with Figure 1.7.

Figure 1.7

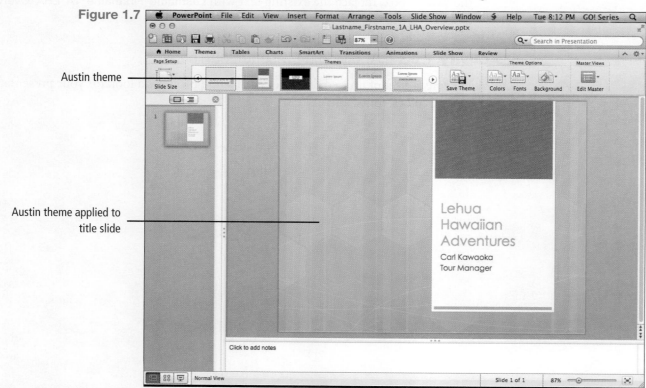

Austin theme

Austin theme applied to title slide

Objective 2 | Edit a Presentation in Normal View

Editing is the process of modifying a presentation by adding and deleting slides or by changing the contents of individual slides.

Activity 1.04 | Inserting a New Slide

To insert a new slide in a presentation, display the slide that will precede the slide that you want to insert.

1 On the **Home tab**, in the **Slides group**, point to the **New Slide** button. Compare your screen with Figure 1.8.

> The New Slide button is a split button. Recall that clicking the main part of a split button performs a command and clicking the arrow opens a menu, list, or gallery. The left, main part of the New Slide button, when clicked, inserts a slide without displaying any options. The right part—the New Slide arrow—when clicked, displays a gallery of slide *layouts*. A layout is the arrangement of elements, such as title and subtitle text, lists, pictures, tables, charts, shapes, and movies, on a slide.

Figure 1.8

New Slide arrow

New Slide button

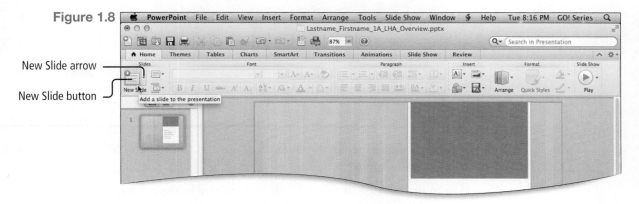

2 In the **Slides group**, click the **New Slide arrow** to display the gallery, and then compare your screen with Figure 1.9.

Figure 1.9

Layout gallery for Austin theme

New Slide arrow

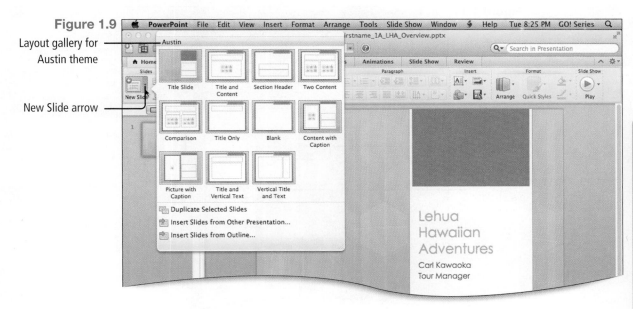

3 In the gallery, click the **Two Content** layout to insert a new slide. Notice that the new blank slide displays in the **Slide pane** and in the **Slides/Outline pane**. Compare your screen with Figure 1.10.

Figure 1.10

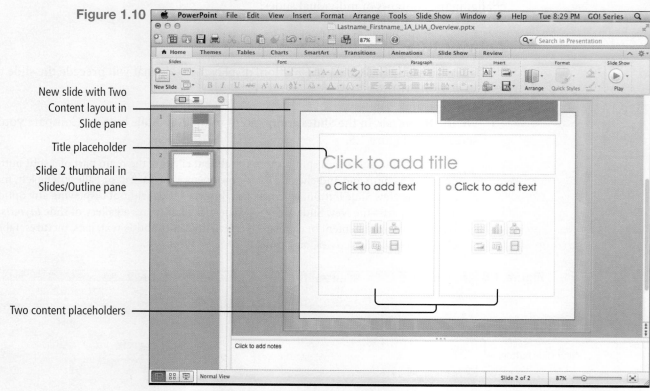

New slide with Two Content layout in Slide pane

Title placeholder

Slide 2 thumbnail in Slides/Outline pane

Two content placeholders

4 In the **Slide pane**, on the slide, click the text *Click to add title*, and then type **Do You Enjoy Adventure?**

5 On the left side of the slide, click anywhere in the content placeholder. Type **Hiking and cycling** and then press Return.

6 Type **Explore locations** and then compare your screen with Figure 1.11.

Figure 1.11

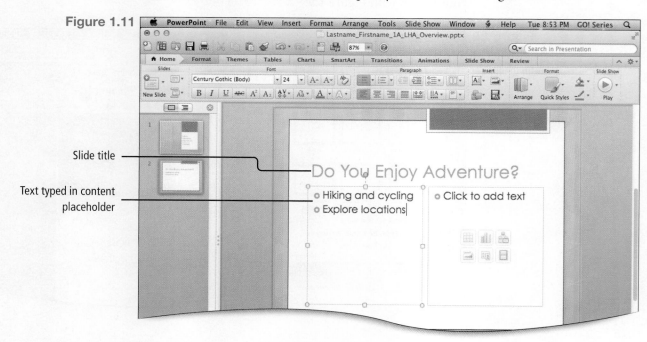

Slide title

Text typed in content placeholder

7 Save 💾 your presentation.

Activity 1.05 | Increasing and Decreasing List Levels

Text in a PowerPoint presentation is organized according to *list levels*. List levels, each represented by a bullet symbol, are similar to outline levels. On a slide, list levels are identified by the bullet style, indentation, and the size of the text.

The first level on an individual slide is the title. Increasing the list level of a bullet point increases its indent and results in a smaller text size. Decreasing the list level of a bullet point decreases its indent and results in a larger text size.

1 On **Slide 2**, if necessary, click at the end of the last bullet point after the word *locations*, and then press Return to insert a new bullet point.

2 Type **Boating excursions** and then press Return.

3 Press Tab, and then notice that the green bullet is indented. Type **Exhilarate your senses while at sea**

> By pressing Tab at the beginning of a bullet point, you can increase the list level and indent the bullet point.

Another Way
Press Shift + Tab to decrease the indent.

4 Press Return. Notice that a new bullet point displays at the same level as the previous bullet point. Then, on the **Home tab**, in the **Paragraph group**, click the **Decrease Indent** button. Type **Helicopter tours** and then compare your screen with Figure 1.12.

Figure 1.12

Increase Indent button

Decrease Indent button— unavailable because you cannot decrease this bullet level any further

List level of bullet point increased by pressing Tab before typing

List level of bullet point decreased by clicking Decrease Indent button

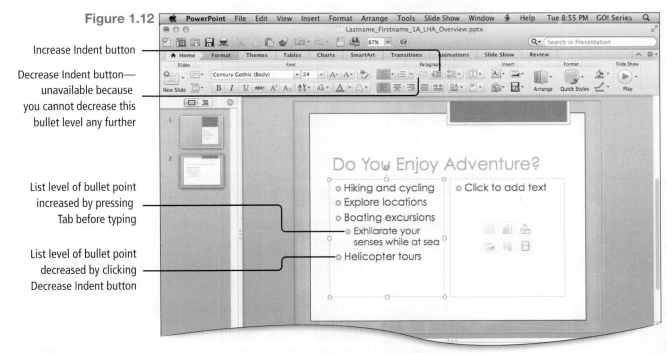

5 Press Return, and then press Tab to increase the list level. Type **View Hawaii from above**

6 Click anywhere in the second bullet point—*Explore locations*. On the **Home tab**, in the **Paragraph group**, click the **Increase Indent** button. Compare your screen with Figure 1.13.

> The bullet point is indented, and the size of the text decreases.

Figure 1.13

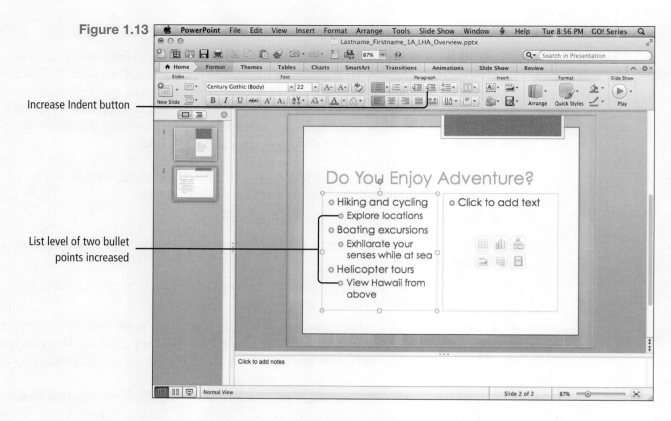

Increase Indent button

List level of two bullet
points increased

7 **Save** 🖫 your presentation.

Activity 1.06 | Adding Speaker's Notes to a Presentation

Recall that when a presentation is displayed in Normal view, the Notes pane displays below the Slide pane. Use the Notes pane to type speaker's notes that you can print below a picture of each slide. Then, while making your presentation, you can refer to these printouts while making a presentation, thus reminding you of the important points that you want to discuss during the presentation.

1 With **Slide 2** displayed, on the **Home tab**, in the **Slides group**, click the **New Slide arrow** to display the **Slide Layout** gallery, and then click **Section Header**.

The section header layout changes the look and flow of a presentation by providing text placeholders that do not contain bullet points.

2 Click in the title placeholder, and then type **About Our Company**

3 Click in the content placeholder below the title, and then type **Named for the crescent-shaped island noted for scuba diving, Lehua Hawaiian Adventures offers exciting and affordable tours throughout Hawaii.** Compare your screen with Figure 1.14.

Figure 1.14

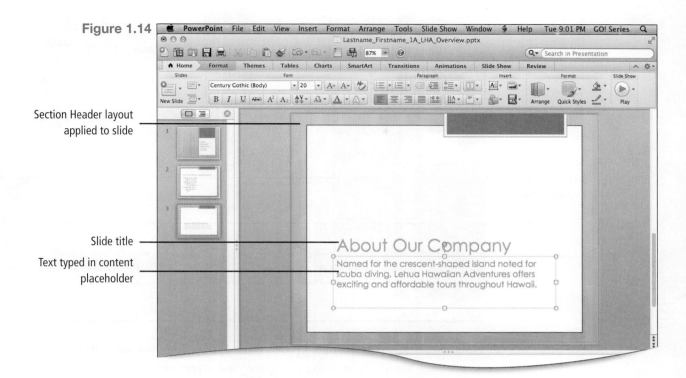

Section Header layout
applied to slide

Slide title

Text typed in content
placeholder

4 Below the slide, click in the **Notes pane**. Type **Lehua Hawaiian Adventures is based in Honolulu but has offices on each of the main Hawaiian islands.** Compare your screen with Figure 1.15, and then **Save** 🖫 your presentation.

Figure 1.15

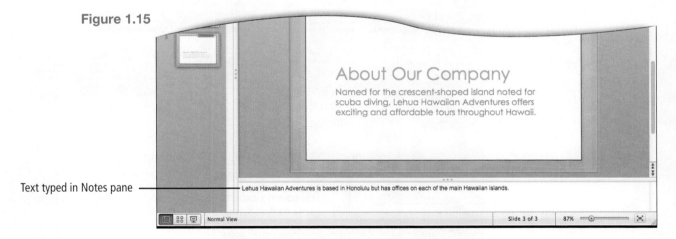

Text typed in Notes pane

Activity 1.07 | Displaying and Editing Slides in the Slide Pane

To edit a presentation slide, display the slide in the Slide pane.

1 Look at the **Slides/Outline pane**, and then notice that the presentation contains three slides. At the right side of the PowerPoint window, in the vertical scroll bar, point to the scroll slider, and then press the mouse to display a ScreenTip indicating the slide number and title.

Another Way

Point anywhere in the Slide pane, and then swipe down on your mouse to move between slides.

2 Drag the scroll slider up until the ScreenTip displays *Slide 2: Do You Enjoy Adventure?* Compare your screen with Figure 1.16, and then release the mouse to display **Slide 2**.

PowerPoint | Chapter 1

Figure 1.16

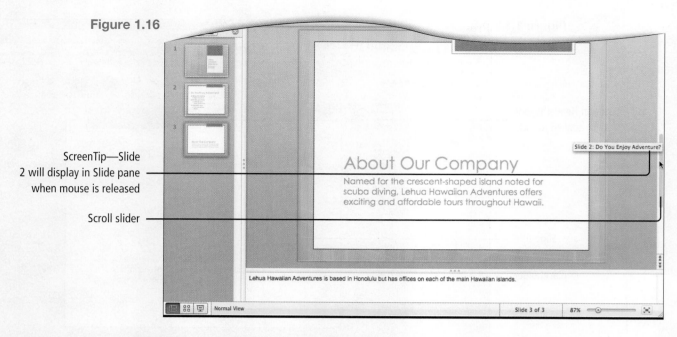

ScreenTip—Slide 2 will display in Slide pane when mouse is released

Scroll slider

3 On **Slide 2**, in the second bullet point, click at the end of the word *Explore*. Press Spacebar, and then type **amazing** Compare your screen with Figure 1.17.

> The placeholder text is resized to fit within the placeholder. The AutoFit Options button displays.

Figure 1.17

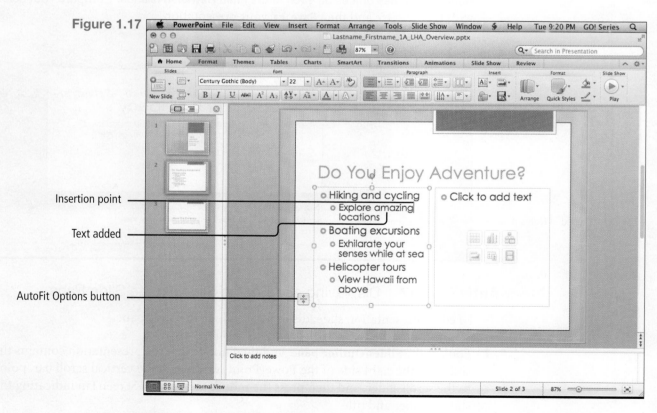

Insertion point

Text added

AutoFit Options button

4 Click the **AutoFit Options** button, and then notice that **AutoFit Text to Placeholder** is selected.

> The default *AutoFit Text to Placeholder* option keeps the text contained within the placeholder by reducing the size of the text. The *Stop Fitting Text to This Placeholder* option turns off the AutoFit option so that the text can flow beyond the placeholder border; the text size remains unchanged.

5 Press [Esc] to close the options list. Below the vertical scroll bar, locate the **Previous Slide** [▲] and **Next Slide** [▼] buttons as shown in Figure 1.18.

Figure 1.18

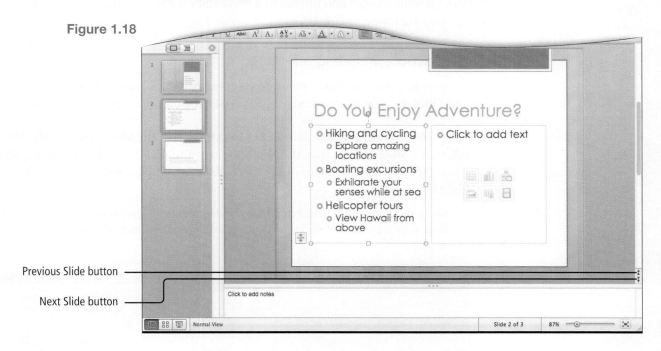

Previous Slide button

Next Slide button

6 In the vertical scroll bar, click the **Previous Slide** button [▲] so that **Slide 1** displays. Then click the **Next Slide** button [▼] two times until **Slide 3** displays.

By clicking the Next Slide or the Previous Slide buttons, you can scroll through your presentation one slide at a time.

7 On the left side of the PowerPoint window, in the **Slides/Outline pane**, point to **Slide 1**, and then notice that a ScreenTip displays the slide title. Compare your screen with Figure 1.19.

In the Slides/Outline pane, the slide numbers display to the left of the slide thumbnails.

Figure 1.19

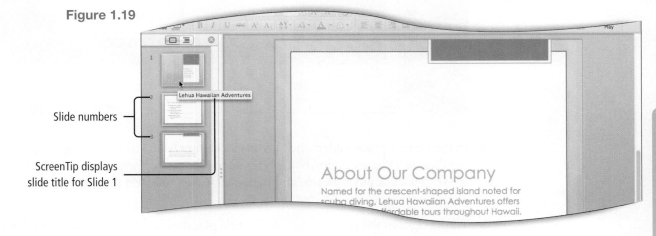

Slide numbers

ScreenTip displays
slide title for Slide 1

8 In the **Slides/Outline pane**, click **Slide 1** to display it in the **Slide pane**, and then in the slide subtitle, click at the end of the word *Tour*. Press [Spacebar], and then type **Operations**

Clicking a slide thumbnail is the most common method used to display a slide in the Slide pane.

9 **Save** [💾] your presentation.

Objective 3 | Add Pictures to a Presentation

Photographic images add impact to a presentation and help the audience visualize the message you are trying to convey.

Activity 1.08 | Inserting a Picture from a File

Many slide layouts in PowerPoint accommodate digital picture files so that you can easily add pictures you have stored on your system or on a portable storage device.

1 In the **Slides/Outline pane**, click **Slide 2** to display it in the **Slide pane**. On the **Home tab**, in the **Slides group**, click the **New Slide arrow** to display the **Slide Layout** gallery. Click **Picture with Caption** to insert a new **Slide 3**. Compare your screen with Figure 1.20.

Recall that a new slide is inserted after the selected slide. The previous Slide 3 is now Slide 4. In the center of the large picture placeholder, the *Insert Picture from File* button displays.

Figure 1.20

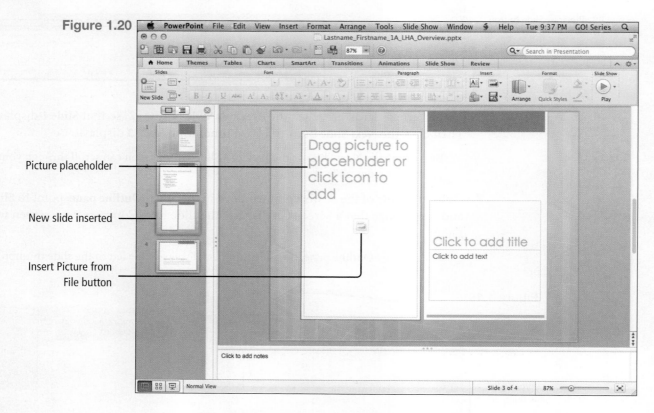

Picture placeholder

New slide inserted

Insert Picture from File button

2 In the picture placeholder, click the **Insert Picture from File** button ☐ to open the **Choose a Picture** dialog box. Navigate to the location where your student files are stored, click **p01A_Beach**, and then click **Insert** to insert the picture in the placeholder.

3 To the right of the picture, click in the title placeholder. Type **Prepare to be Amazed!**

4 Below the title, click in the caption placeholder, and then type **Mountain, sea, volcano. Our tour guides are experts in the history, geography, culture, and flora and fauna of Hawaii.** Compare your screen with Figure 1.21.

Figure 1.21

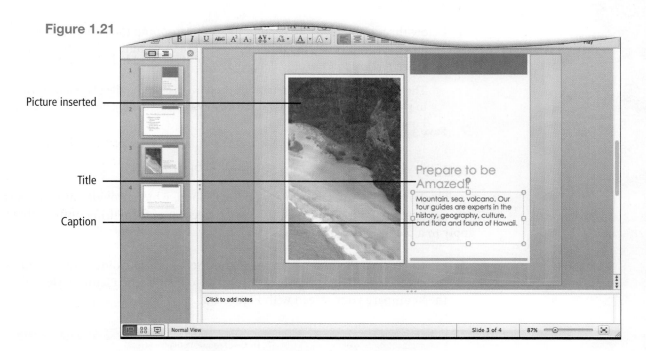

Picture inserted

Title

Caption

5 Display **Slide 2**. In the placeholder on the right side of the slide, click the **Insert Picture from File** button ⬚. Navigate to your student files, and then click **p01A_Helicopter**. Click **Insert**, and then compare your screen with Figure 1.22.

Small circles and squares—*sizing handles*—surround the inserted picture and indicate that the picture is selected and can be modified or formatted. The *rotation handle*—a green circle above the picture—provides a way to rotate a selected image. Cropping tools display below the picture to enable you to change the display of the picture in the content placeholder. *Crop* is a command that reduces the size of a picture by removing vertical or horizontal edges.

Figure 1.22

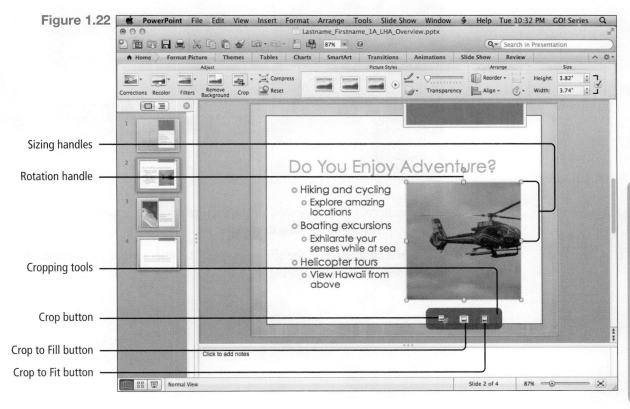

Sizing handles

Rotation handle

Cropping tools

Crop button

Crop to Fill button

Crop to Fit button

PowerPoint | Chapter 1

6 Below the picture, point to each of the three cropping tools to display the ScreenTip, and then click the **Crop to Fit** button 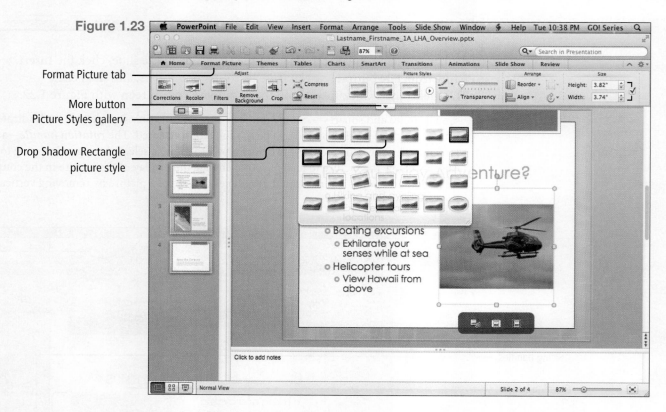—the third button that displays a ScreenTip of *Resize picture to fit inside placeholder.*

> The picture is resized and retains its proportions to fit in the placeholder. As you progress in your study of Office, you will learn more about cropping pictures.

7 **Save** 💾 your presentation.

Activity 1.09 | Applying a Style to a Picture

The Format Picture tab displays on the Ribbon, which provides numerous *styles* that you can apply to your pictures. A style is a collection of formatting options that you can apply to a picture, text, or an object.

1 On the **Format Pictures tab**, in the **Picture Styles group**, point to the bottom of the gallery of styles. Click the **More** button ▼ to display the **Picture Styles** gallery, and then compare your screen with Figure 1.23.

Figure 1.23

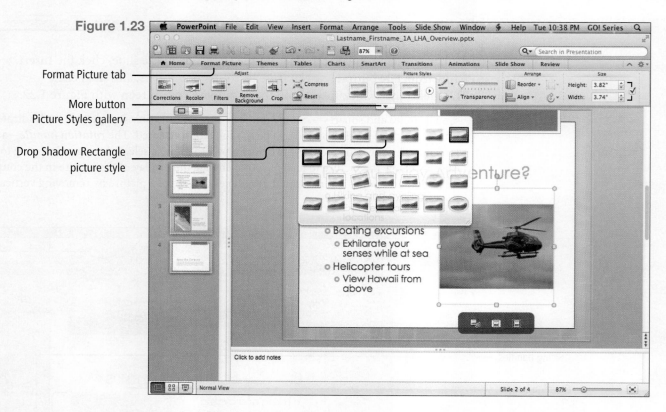

2 In the gallery, point to several of the picture styles to display the ScreenTips. In the first row, click **Drop Shadow Rectangle**.

3 Click in a blank area of the slide to cancel the selection of the picture, and then compare your screen with Figure 1.24.

Figure 1.24

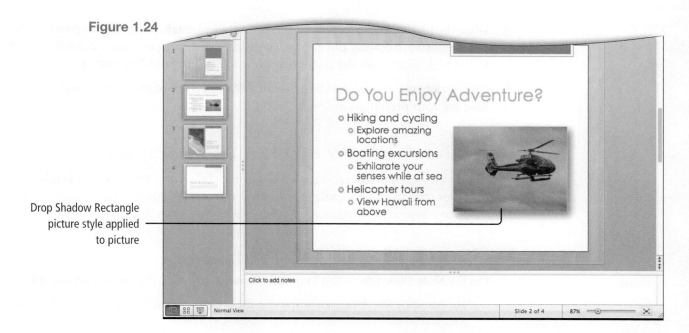

Drop Shadow Rectangle picture style applied to picture

4 **Save** 💾 your presentation.

Activity 1.10 │ Applying and Removing Picture Artistic Filters

Artistic filters are formats applied to images that make pictures resemble sketches or paintings.

1 With **Slide 2** displayed, select the picture of the helicopter.

2 On the **Format Picture tab**, in the **Adjust group**, click the **Filters** button to display the **Artistic Filters** gallery. Compare your screen with Figure 1.25.

Figure 1.25

Filters button

Artistic Filters gallery

None filter

Paint Strokes filter

3 In the gallery, point to several of the artistic filters to display the ScreenTips. Then, in the second row, click the **Paint Strokes** filter.

4 With the picture still selected, on the **Format Picture tab**, in the **Adjust group**, click the **Filters** button to display the gallery. In the first row, click the first filter—**None**—to remove the filter from the picture and restore the previous formatting.

5 Click in a blank area of the slide to cancel the selection of the picture, and then **Save** 🖫 your presentation.

Objective 4 | View and Print a Presentation

When you view a presentation as an electronic slide show, the entire slide fills the computer screen, and an audience can view your presentation if your computer is connected to a projection system.

Activity 1.11 | Viewing a Slide Show

Another Way

Press Command ⌘ + Shift + Return to start the slide show from the beginning. Or, display the first slide you want to show and click the Slide Show button on the lower right side of the status bar.

1 On the **Slide Show tab**, in the **Play Slide Show group**, click the **From Start** button.

The first slide fills the screen, displaying the presentation as the audience would see it if your computer were connected to a projection system.

2 Click the mouse, or press Spacebar, or press → to advance to the second slide.

3 Using any of the methods, advance the slides until the last slide displays, and then advance the slide one more time.

After the last slide in a presentation, the default PowerPoint setting is to end the presentation by returning to the PowerPoint window. It is a good idea to end a presentation with a final closing slide.

4 On the **PowerPoint** menu, click **Preferences**. In the **PowerPoint Preferences** dialog box, click the **View** button. Under **Slide show**, select the **End with black slide** check box, and then click **OK**.

Recall that Preference settings are applied every time you open the application, so you do not need to change it every time you open PowerPoint.

5 Press Command ⌘ + Shift + Return to start the presentation from Slide 1. Advance through the slides by clicking the mouse, or pressing Spacebar or →.

After the last slide in a presentation, a **black slide** displays, indicating that the presentation is over. In this manner, the audience does not see the PowerPoint window. An alternative is to create a final slide; but when you display your presentation, you must remember that it is the final slide.

6 With the black slide displayed, click the mouse or press Spacebar or → to exit the slide show and return to the presentation.

More Knowledge | Starting a Slide Show from the Current Slide and Exiting a Slide Show Before the End

To start a slide show from the current or active slide, press Command ⌘ + Return; or on the Slide Show tab, in the Play Slide Show group, click the From Current Slide button; or on the status bar, click the Slide Show button. To exit a slide show at any time and return to the PowerPoint window, press Esc.

Activity 1.12 | Inserting Headers and Footers

A **header** is text that prints at the top of each sheet of **slide handouts** or **notes pages**. Slide handouts are printed images of slides on a sheet of paper. Notes pages are printouts that contain the slide image on the top half of the page and notes that you have created on the Notes pane in the lower half of the page.

In addition to headers, you can insert *footers*—text that displays at the bottom of every slide or that prints at the bottom of a sheet of slide handouts or notes pages.

Another Way
On the View menu, click Header and Footer.

1 On the **Home tab**, in the **Insert group**, click the **Text** button [A], and then click **Header and Footer**.

2 In the **Header and Footer** dialog box, click the **Notes and Handouts tab**. Under **Include on page**, select the **Date and time** check box, and as you do so, watch the **Preview** box in the lower right corner of the **Header and Footer** dialog box.

> The Preview box indicates the placeholders on the printed Notes and Handouts pages. The two narrow rectangular boxes at the top of the Preview box indicate placeholders for the header text and date. When you select the Date and time check box, the placeholder in the upper right corner is outlined, indicating the location in which the date will display. By default, the Page number is selected; the placeholder is the lower right corner.

3 If necessary, click the Update automatically option button so that the current date prints on the notes and handouts each time the presentation is printed.

4 If necessary, *clear* the Header check box to omit this element. Notice that in the **Preview** box, the corresponding placeholder is not selected.

5 If necessary, select the Page number check box. Select the **Footer** check box, and then notice that the insertion point displays in the **Footer** box. Using your own name, type **Lastname_Firstname_1A_LHA_Overview** so that the file name displays as a footer, and then compare your screen with Figure 1.26.

Figure 1.26

Text button in Insert group
Header and Footer dialog box
Notes and Handouts tab
Update automatically selected
File name typed in Footer box

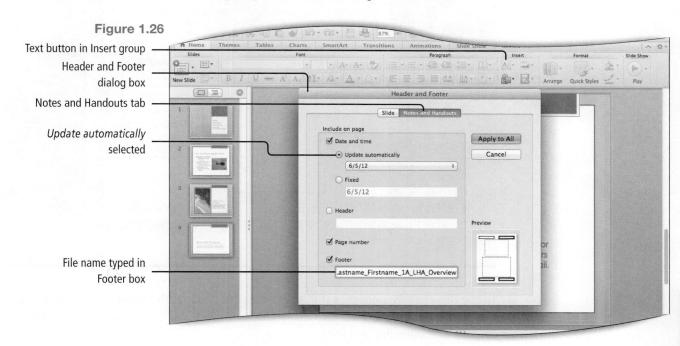

6 In the **Header and Footer** dialog box, click **Apply to All** to display the footer on the bottom of every printed page for Notes and Handouts. **Save** [💾] your presentation.

More Knowledge | Adding Footers to Slides

You can also add footers to the actual slides, which will display during your presentation, by using the Slide tab in the Header and Footer dialog box. Headers cannot be added to individual slides.

Activity 1.13 | Printing a Presentation

Use the Print dialog box to preview the arrangement of slides on the notes and handouts pages.

1 Display **Slide 1**. On the **File** menu, click **Print**.

The Print dialog box displays the tools you need to select your print settings and also to view a preview of your presentation. On the left, Print Preview displays your presentation exactly as it will print on a color printer.

2 To the right of the **Print Preview**, click in the **Print What** box, and then compare your screen with Figure 1.27.

The list displays either the default print setting—Slides—or the most recently selected print setting. Thus, on your system, this button might indicate the presentation Notes, Outline, or one of several arrangements of Handouts—depending on the most recently used setting.

Figure 1.27

Print dialog box

Print Preview

Print What options

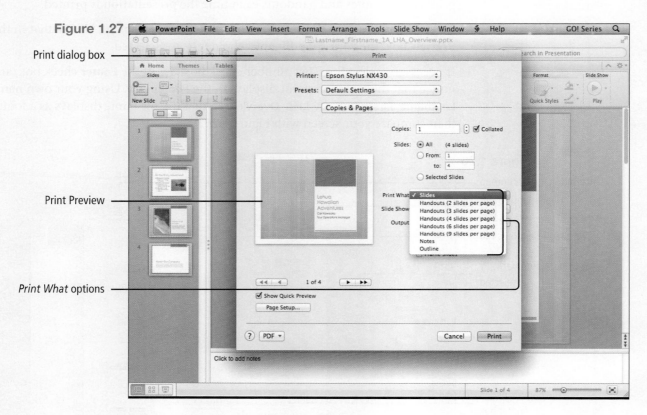

3 In the list, click **Handouts (4 slides per page)**. Notice that the **Print Preview** on the left displays the slide handout, and that the current date, file name, and page number display in the header and footer.

By default, Notes, Handouts, and Outlines print in Portrait Orientation; and Slides print in Landscape Orientation. To change the Orientation, in the Print dialog box, click the Page Setup button.

4 To print your handout, be sure your system is connected to a printer, and then in the **Print** dialog box, click the **Print** button.

The handout will print on your default printer—on a black and white printer, the colors will print in shades of gray. The Print dialog box closes, and your slides redisplay in the PowerPoint window.

Another Way

Press Command ⌘ + P.

5 On the **File** menu, click **Print**. Click in the **Print What** box, and then click **Notes**. The Notes page for **Slide 1** displays; recall, however, that you created notes for **Slide 4**.

Indicated below the Print Preview of the Notes page are the current slide number and the number of pages that will print when Notes is selected. You can use the Next Page and Previous Page arrows to display each Notes page in the presentation.

6 Below the **Print Preview**, click the **Next Page** button ▶ three times so that **Page 4** displays. Compare your screen with Figure 1.28.

The notes that you created for Slide 4 display below the image of the slide.

Figure 1.28

Page 4 displays

Notes you typed for Slide 4

Notes selected

Page 4 indicated

Next page button

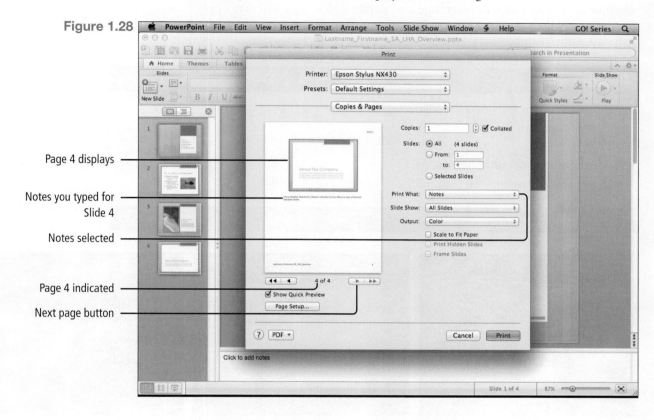

7 Under **Slides**, double-click in the **From** box, and then type **4** so that only the Notes page for **Slide 4** will print. Click the **Print** button to print the Notes page for Slide 4.

8 On the **File** menu, click **Properties**. In the **Subject** box, type your course name and section number. In the **Author** box, delete any text and type your firstname and lastname. In the **Keywords** box, type **company overview** and then click **OK**.

9 Save 💾 and then Close ⊗ your presentation. On the **PowerPoint** menu, click **Quit PowerPoint**.

End **You have completed Project 1A**

PowerPoint | Chapter 1

Project 1B New Product Announcement

Project Activities

In Activities 1.14 through 1.22, you will combine two presentations that the marketing team at Lehua Adventure Travels developed describing their new Ecotours. You will combine the presentations by inserting slides from one presentation into another, and then you will rearrange and delete slides. You will also apply font formatting and slide transitions to the presentation. Your completed presentation will look similar to Figure 1.29.

Project Files

For Project 1B, you will need the following files:

p01B_Ecotours
p01B_Slides

You will save your presentation as:

Lastname_Firstname_1B_Ecotours

Project Results

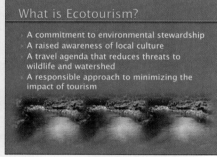

Figure 1.29
Project 1B Ecotours

Objective 5 | Edit an Existing Presentation

Recall that editing refers to the process of adding, deleting, and modifying presentation content. You can edit presentation content in either the Slide pane or the Slides/Outline pane.

Activity 1.14 | Displaying and Editing the Presentation Outline

You can display the presentation outline in the Slides/Outline pane and edit the presentation text. Changes that you make in the outline are immediately displayed in the Slide pane.

1 Open **PowerPoint**. On the **File** menu, click **Open**. From your student files, **Open** the **p01B_Ecotours** presentation file. If necessary, increase the width of the window to fill the entire screen. On the **File** menu, click **Save As**, navigate to your **PowerPoint Chapter 1** folder, and then using your own name, **Save** the file as **Lastname_Firstname_1B_Ecotours**

2 In the **Slides/Outline pane**, click the **Outline** button ▤ to display the presentation outline—if you have a wide screen or the width of the Slides/Outline pane is increased, you will see an Outline tab instead of the button. Compare your screen with Figure 1.30.

> The outline tab is wider than the Slides tab so that you have additional space to type your text. Each slide in the outline displays the slide number, slide icon, and the slide title in bold. The active slide—Slide 1—is selected in the Slides/Outline pane.

Figure 1.30

Outline tab —

Slide numbers and titles —

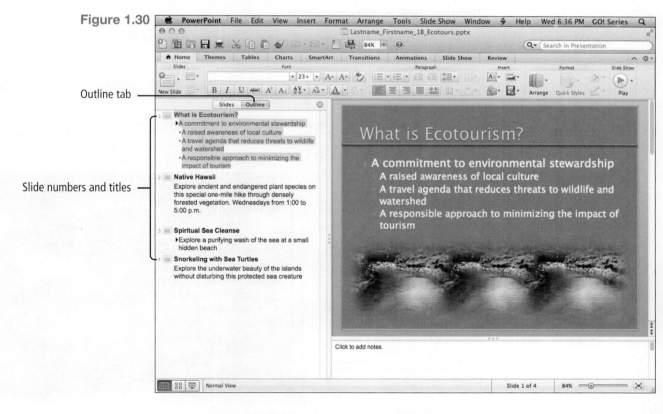

3 In the **Outline tab**, in **Slide 1**, click to the right of the title to cancel the selection of the entire slide. Then select the three bullet points, and compare your screen with Figure 1.31.

Figure 1.31

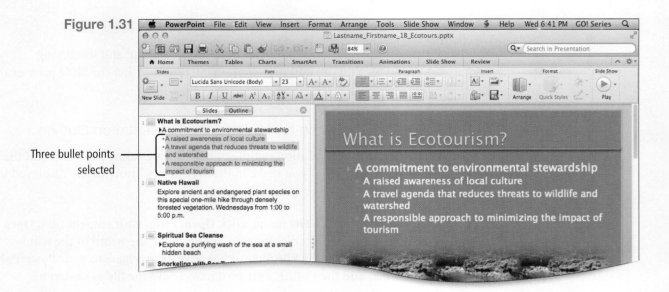

Three bullet points selected

4 On the **Home tab**, in the **Paragraph group**, click the **Decrease Indent** button one time to decrease the list level of the selected bullet points.

> When you type in the outline or change the list level, the changes also display in the Slide pane.

5 In the **Outline tab**, click anywhere in **Slide 3**, and then click at the end of the bullet point after the word *beach*. Press Return to create a new bullet point at the same list level as the previous bullet point. Type **Offered Tuesdays and Thursdays one hour before sunset, weather permitting**

6 Press Return to create a new bullet point. Type **Fee: $30** and then compare your screen with Figure 1.32.

Figure 1.32

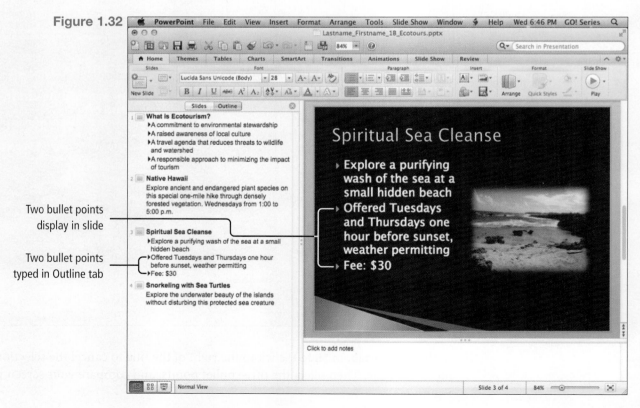

Two bullet points display in slide

Two bullet points typed in Outline tab

7 In the **Slides/Outline pane**, click the **Slides tab** to display the slide thumbnails, and then **Save** 🖫 your presentation.

> You can type text in the Slide pane or in the Outline tab. Displaying the Outline tab enables you to view the entire flow of the presentation.

Activity 1.15 | Inserting Slides from an Existing Presentation

Presentation content is commonly shared among group members in an organization. Rather than re-creating slides, you can insert slides from an existing presentation into the current presentation. In this activity, you will insert slides from an existing presentation into your 1B_Ecotours presentation.

1 Display **Slide 1**. On the **Home tab**, in the **Slides group**, click the **New Slide arrow** to display the **Slide Layout** gallery and additional commands for inserting slides. Compare your screen with Figure 1.33.

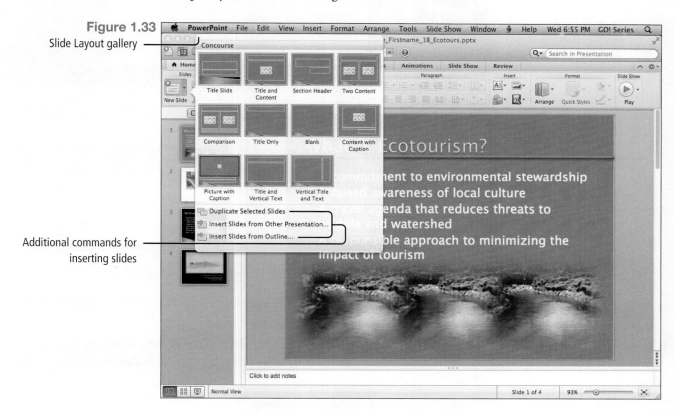

Figure 1.33
Slide Layout gallery

Additional commands for inserting slides

2 Below the gallery, click **Insert Slides from Other Presentation**. In the **Choose a File** dialog box, navigate to the location where your student files are stored, and then double-click **p01B_Slides** to display the slides in the **Slide Finder** dialog box.

3 At the lower left corner of the **Slide Finder** dialog box, select the **Keep design of original slides** check box, and then compare your screen with Figure 1.34.

> By selecting the *Keep design of original slides* check box, you retain the formatting applied to the slides when inserted into the existing presentation. When the *Keep design of original slides* check box is cleared, the theme formatting of the presentation in which the slides are inserted is applied.

Figure 1.34

Slide Finder dialog box

Slides from *p01B_Slides* presentation display in Slide Finder dialog box with Slide number and title

Keep design of original slides check box selected

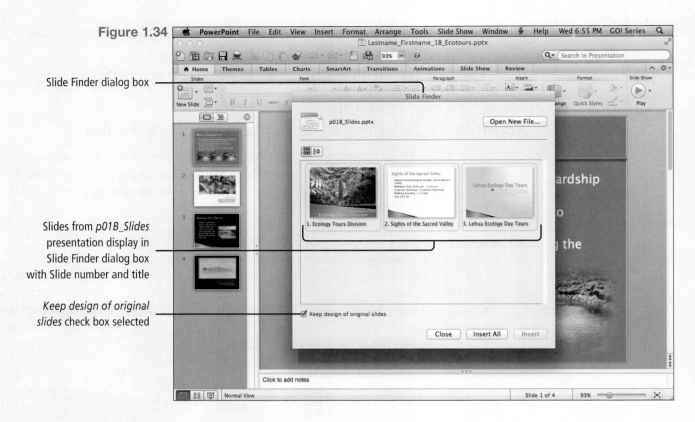

4 In the **Slide Finder** dialog box, double-click the first slide—**Ecology Tours Division**—to insert the slide into the current presentation after Slide 1, and then notice that the original slide background formatting is retained.

> **Note** | Inserting Slides
>
> You can insert slides into your presentation in any order; remember to display the slide that will precede the slide that you want to insert.

5 In your **1B_Ecotours** presentation, in the **Slides/Outline pane**, click **Slide 5** to display it in the **Slide pane**.

6 In the **Slide Finder** dialog box, double-click the second slide and then double-click the third slide to insert both slides after **Slide 5**. In the **Slide Finder** dialog box, click **Close**.

Your presentation contains seven slides.

7 On **Slide 7**, click in the word *Lehua*, and then press Control and click to display the shortcut menu. Click **Ignore All**. Use the same technique to ignore the spelling of the word *Ecotour*. Compare your screen with Figure 1.35, and then **Save** your presentation.

Figure 1.35

Inserted slides

> **More Knowledge | Inserting All Slides**
>
> You can insert all of the slides from an existing presentation into the current presentation at one time. In the Slide Finder dialog box, click Insert All.

Activity 1.16 | Finding and Replacing Text

The Replace command enables you to locate all occurrences of specified text and replace it with alternative text.

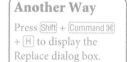

Another Way

Press Shift + Command ⌘ + H to display the Replace dialog box.

1 Display **Slide 1**. On the **Edit** menu, point to **Find**, and then click **Replace**. In the **Replace** dialog box, in the **Find what** box, type **Ecology** and then in the **Replace with** box, type **Eco** Compare your screen with Figure 1.36.

Figure 1.36

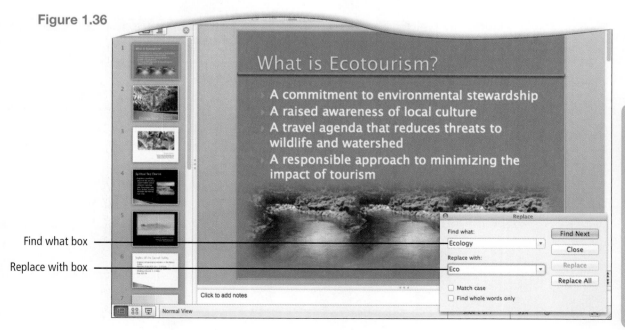

Find what box

Replace with box

PowerPoint | Chapter 1

2 In the **Replace** dialog box, click the **Replace All** button.

A message box displays indicating the number of replacements that were made.

3 In the message box, click **OK**, **Close**  the **Replace** dialog box, and then **Save** 🖫 your presentation.

Objective 6 | Format a Presentation

Formatting refers to changing the appearance of the text, layout, and design of a slide. You will find it easiest to do most of your formatting changes in PowerPoint in the Slide pane.

Activity 1.17 | Changing Fonts, Font Sizes, Font Styles, and Font Colors

Recall that a font is a set of characters with the same design and shape and that fonts are measured in points. Font styles include bold, italic, and underline, and you can apply any combination of these styles to presentation text. Font styles and font color are useful to provide emphasis and are a visual cue to draw the reader's eye to important text.

1 On the right side of the **Slides/Outline pane**, drag the scroll slider down—or point to the gray area in the Slides/Outline pane and slide your finger on the mouse—until **Slide 7** displays, and then click **Slide 7** to display it in the **Slides** pane.

When a presentation contains a large number of slides, a scroll slider displays to the right of the slide thumbnails so that you can scroll and then select the thumbnails.

2 In the **Slide pane**, select the title text—*Lehua Eco Day Tours*. On the **Home tab**, in the **Font group**, click the **Font arrow**, and then click **Arial Black**.

3 Select the light green text in the placeholder below the title, and then in the **Font group**, change the **Font** to **Arial Black** and the **Font Size** to **28**. Then, click the **Font Color arrow** 🅰, and compare your screen with Figure 1.37.

The colors in the top row of the color gallery are the colors associated with the presentation theme—*Concourse*. The colors in the rows below the first row are light and dark variations of the theme colors.

Figure 1.37
Font Color arrow
Font Size changed to 28
Font changed to Arial Black
Theme colors
Theme color variations

4 Point to several of the colors and notice that a ScreenTip displays the color name.

5 In the first row of colors, click the second color—**Text 1**—to change the font color. Notice that on the **Home tab**, in the **Font group**, the **Font Color** button displays the most recently applied font color—Black or *Text 1*.

> When you click the Font Color button instead of the Font Color arrow, the color displayed in the Font Color button is applied to selected text without displaying the color gallery.

6 Display **Slide 2**, and then select the title *Eco Tours Division*. In the **Font group**, click the **Font Color** button [A] to apply the font color **Text 1** (Black) to the selection. Press [Esc] two times to cancel the selection of text and to hide the placeholder border. Select the subtitle—*Lehua Adventure Tours*—and then change the **Font Color** to **Text 1**. Compare your screen with Figure 1.38.

Figure 1.38

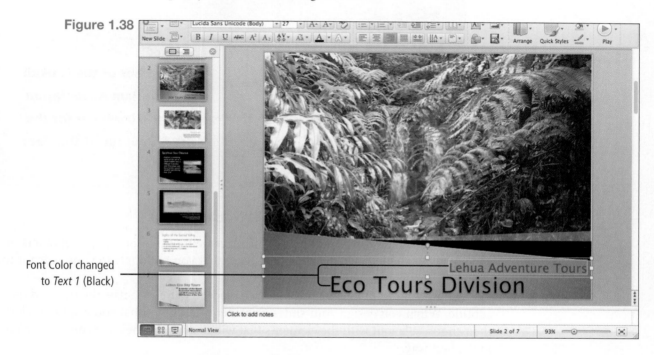

Font Color changed to *Text 1* (Black)

7 Display **Slide 3**, and then select the title—*Native Hawaii*. On the **Home tab**, in the **Font group**, apply **Bold** [B] and **Italic** [I], and then **Save** [💾] your presentation.

Activity 1.18 | Aligning Text and Changing Line Spacing

In PowerPoint, ***text alignment*** refers to the horizontal placement of text within a placeholder. You can align left, centered, right, or justified.

1 Display **Slide 2**. Click anywhere in the title—*Eco Tours Division*.

2 On the **Home tab**, in the **Paragraph group**, click the **Align Text Right** button [≡] to right align the text within the placeholder.

3 Display **Slide 7**. Click anywhere in the text below the title. In the **Paragraph group**, click the **Line Spacing** button. In the list, click **1.5** to change from single-spacing between lines to one-and-a-half spacing between lines. **Save** your presentation, and then compare your screen with Figure 1.39.

Figure 1.39

Line Spacing button

Line Spacing changed to 1.5

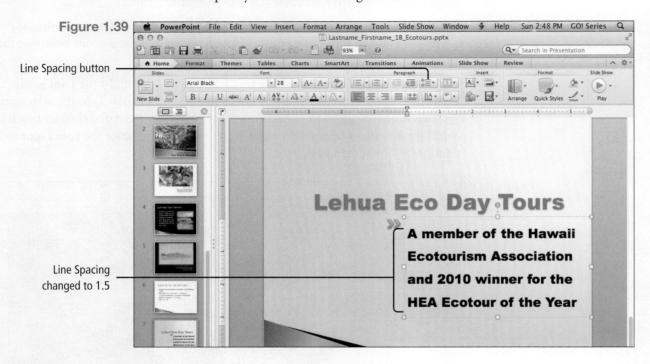

Activity 1.19 | Modifying Slide Layout

Recall that the slide layout defines the placement of the content placeholders on a slide. PowerPoint includes predefined layouts that you can apply to your slide for the purpose of arranging slide elements.

For example, a Title Slide contains two placeholder elements—the title and the subtitle. When you design your slides, consider the content that you want to include, and then choose a layout with the elements that will display the message you want to convey in the best way.

1 Display **Slide 3**. On the **Home tab**, in the **Slides group**, click the **Layout** button to display the **Slide Layout** gallery. Notice that *Content with Caption* is selected. Also, notice that the theme—*Concourse*—for the slide displays.

The selection indicates the layout of the current slide. In the Slide Layout gallery, there is a section entitled Concourse, the theme that was applied to the p01B_Ecotours student data file. The second section is entitled 1_Concourse—this second layout section displays because you kept the design of the original slides when you inserted the slides from the p01B_Slides presentation.

The order that these sections display when clicking the Layout button depends on the active slide—if you click on a slide that was in the p01B_Ecotours file, *Concourse* will display as the first section. If the active slide is one that was in the second file, p01B_ Slides, *1_Concourse* will display as the first section.

2 Under **Concourse**, click **Picture with Caption** to change the slide layout, **Save**  your presentation, and then compare your screen with Figure 1.40.

The Picture with Caption layout emphasizes the picture more effectively than the Content with Caption layout.

Figure 1.40

Slide layout changed to
Picture with Caption

Native Hawaii »

Explore ancient and endangered plant species on this special one-mile hike
through densely forested vegetation. Wednesdays from 1:00 to 5:00 p.m.

Objective 7 | Use Slide Sorter View

Slide Sorter view displays thumbnails of all of the slides in a presentation. Use Slide Sorter view to rearrange and delete slides and to apply formatting to multiple slides.

Another Way

From the View menu, click Slide Sorter; or press Command ⌘ + 2.

Activity 1.20 | Deleting Slides in Slide Sorter View

1 In the lower left corner of the PowerPoint window, click the **Slide Sorter View** button ⊞ to display all of the slide thumbnails, and then compare your screen with Figure 1.41.

Your slides may display larger or smaller than those shown in Figure 1.41.

Figure 1.41

Slides display in
Slide Sorter view

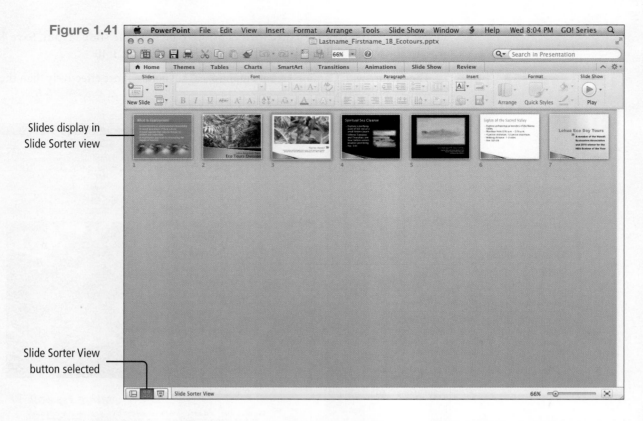

Slide Sorter View
button selected

2 Click **Slide 6**, and notice that an orange outline surrounds the slide, indicating that it is selected. On your keyboard, press ⌫elete to delete the slide. **Save** 💾 your presentation.

Activity 1.21 | Moving Slides in Slide Sorter View

1 With the presentation displayed in Slide Sorter view, point to **Slide 2**. Drag the slide to the left until **Slide 2** displays to the left of **Slide 1** and a dimmed **Slide 2** displays in its original location, as shown in Figure 1.42.

Figure 1.42

Position slide will be
moved to when
mouse is released

Original position of Slide 2

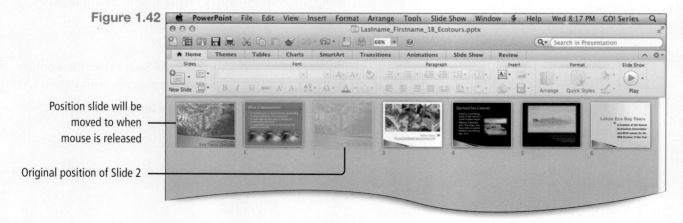

2 Release the mouse to move the slide to the first position in the presentation.

3 Click **Slide 4**, hold down Command ⌘, and then click **Slide 5**. Compare your screen with Figure 1.43.

> Both slides are outlined, indicating that both are selected. By holding down Command ⌘, you can create a group of selected slides.

Figure 1.43

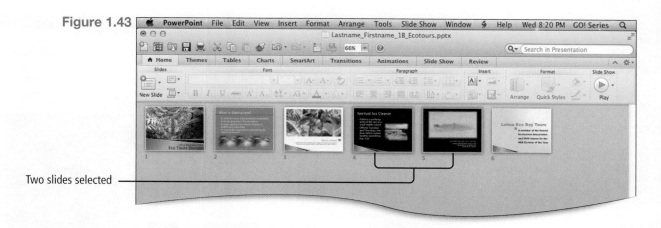

Two slides selected

4 Point to either of the selected slides, and then drag to position the slides to the left of **Slide 3**, and compare your screen with Figure 1.44.

As you drag the selected slides to their new position, a red circle with the number of selected slides—in this case, 2—displays in the lower right corner of the slide. In their original positions, the selected slides are dimmed.

Figure 1.44

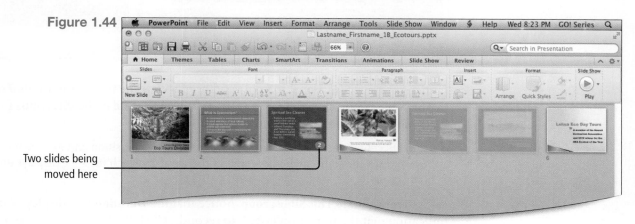

Two slides being moved here

5 Release the mouse to move the slides. In the status bar, click the **Normal View** button to return to Normal view. **Save** your presentation.

Objective 8 | Apply Slide Transitions

Slide transitions are the motion effects that occur in Slide Show view when you move from one slide to the next during a presentation. You can choose from a variety of transitions, and you can control the speed and method with which the slides advance.

Activity 1.22 | Applying Slide Transitions to a Presentation

1 Display **Slide 1**. On the **Transitions tab**, in the **Transition to This Slide group**, point to the bottom of the gallery, and then click the **More** button ▾ to display the **Transitions** gallery. Compare your screen with Figure 1.45.

Figure 1.45

More button

Transitions gallery

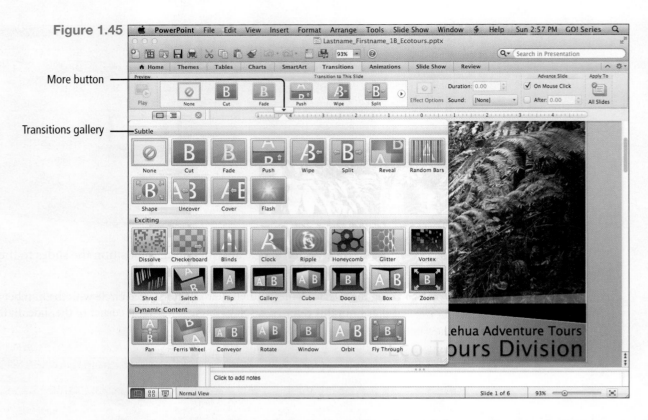

2 Under **Exciting**, click **Doors** to apply and briefly view the transition. In the **Transition to This Slide group**, click the **Effect Options** button to display the directions from which the slide enters the screen. Click **Horizontal**.

> The Effect Options vary depending upon the selected transition and include the direction from which the slide enters the screen or the shape in which the slide displays during the transition.

3 In the **Transition to This Slide group**, notice that the **Duration** box displays *1.40*, indicating that the transition lasts 1.40 seconds. Click the **Duration** box **up spin arrow** three times so that *1.70* displays. In the **Advance Slide group**, verify that the **On Mouse Click** check box is selected—select it if necessary. Compare your screen with Figure 1.46.

> When the On Mouse Click option is selected, the presenter controls when the current slide advances to the next slide by clicking the mouse or by pressing Spacebar or →. In the Slides/Outline pane the icon with a right-pointing arrow displays under the slide number for Slide 1, indicating that a transition has been applied to this slide.

Figure 1.46

Duration changed to *1.70*

Doors transition selected

Indicates transition applied to this slide

On Mouse Click check box selected

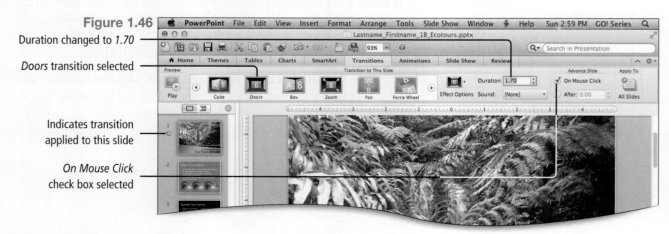

4 In the **Apply To group**, click the **All Slides** button so that the Doors, Horizontal with a Duration of 1.70 seconds transition is applied to all of the slides in the presentation. Notice that in the **Slides/Outline pane**, under each slide number, the small icon with a right-pointing arrow displays, providing a visual cue that a transition has been applied to each slide.

5 With **Slide 1** selected, on the status bar, click the **Slide Show** button . View your presentation, clicking the mouse to advance through the slides. When the black slide displays, click the mouse one more time to display the presentation in Normal view. **Save** 🖫 your presentation.

> **Note | Applying Multiple Slide Transitions**
>
> You can apply more than one type of transition in your presentation by displaying the slides one at a time, and then clicking the transition that you want to apply instead of clicking the All Slides button.

6 On the **View** menu, click **Header and Footer**. In the **Header and Footer** dialog box, click the **Notes and Handouts tab**. Under **Include on page**, select the **Date and time** check box, and be sure that **Update automatically** is selected. Be sure that **Page number** is selected. Select the **Footer** check box. In the **Footer** box, using your own name, type **Lastname_Firstname_1B_Ecotours** and then click **Apply to All**.

7 On the **File** menu, click **Properties**. In the **Subject** box, type your course name and section number, and then in the **Author** box, delete any text and type your firstname and lastname. In the **Keywords** box, type **ecotours, ecotourism** and then click **OK**.

8 **Save** 🖫 your presentation. **Print Handouts (6 slides per page)** or submit electronically as directed by your instructor.

9 **Close** 🗙 the presentation, and then **Quit PowerPoint**.

> **More Knowledge | Broadcasting a Slide Show**
>
> You can broadcast a slide show to remote viewers by using the PowerPoint Broadcast Service or another broadcast service. To broadcast a slide show, on the Slide Show tab, in the Play Slide Show group, click the Broadcast Show button, and then follow the instructions in the Broadcast Slide Show dialog box to start the broadcast.

End **You have completed Project 1B** ————————————————

Content-Based Assessments

Summary

In this chapter, you created a new PowerPoint presentation and edited an existing presentation by reusing slides from another presentation. You entered, edited, and formatted text in Normal view; worked with slides in Slide Sorter view; and viewed the presentation as a slide show. You also added emphasis to your presentations by inserting pictures, applying font formatting, and modifying layout, alignment, and line spacing.

Key Terms

Matching

Match each term in the second column with its correct definition in the first column. Write the letter of the term on the blank line in front of the correct definition.

_____ 1. The PowerPoint view in which the window is divided into three panes—the Slide pane, the Slides/Outline pane, and the Notes pane.

_____ 2. A presentation page that can contain text, pictures, tables, charts, and other multimedia or graphic objects.

_____ 3. The first slide in a presentation, the purpose of which is to provide an introduction to the presentation topic.

_____ 4. On a slide, a box with a border that holds title and body text or other content such as charts, tables, and pictures.

_____ 5. A set of unified design elements that provides a look for your presentation by applying colors, fonts, and effects.

_____ 6. An outline level in a presentation represented by a bullet symbol and identified in a slide by the indentation and the size of the text.

_____ 7. Small circles and squares that indicate that a picture is selected.

_____ 8. A green circle located above a selected picture with which you can rotate the selected image.

_____ 9. A collection of formatting options that can be applied to a picture, text, or object.

_____ 10. A slide that displays at the end of every slide show to indicate that the presentation is over.

A Black slide

B Formatting

C List level

D Normal view

E Notes page

F Placeholder

G Rotation handle

H Sizing handles

I Slide

J Slide handouts

K Slide transitions

L Style

M Text alignment

N Theme

O Title slide

_____ 11. Printed images of slides on a sheet of paper.

_____ 12. A printout that contains the slide image on the top half of the page and notes that you have created in the Notes pane on the lower half of the page.

_____ 13. The process of changing the appearance of the text, layout, and design of a slide.

_____ 14. The term that refers to the horizontal placement of text within a placeholder.

_____ 15. Motion effects that occur in Slide Show view when you move from one slide to the next during a presentation.

Multiple Choice

Circle the correct response.

1. In Normal view, the pane that displays a large image of the active slide is the:
   A. Slide pane   B. Slides/Outline pane   C. Notes pane

2. In Normal view, the pane that displays below the Slide pane is the:
   A. Slide Sorter pane   B. Slides/Outline pane   C. Notes pane

3. The buttons in the lower right corner that control the look of the presentation window are the:
   A. Normal buttons   B. View buttons   C. Thumbnails buttons

4. The process of modifying a presentation by adding and deleting slides or by changing the contents of individual slides is referred to as:
   A. Editing   B. Formatting   C. Aligning

5. The arrangement of elements, such as title and subtitle text, lists, pictures, tables, charts, shapes, and movies, on a PowerPoint slide is referred to as:
   A. Theme modification   B. Editing   C. Layout

6. Text that prints at the top of a sheet of slide handouts or notes pages is a:
   A. Header   B. Footer   C. Page number

7. Text that displays at the bottom of every slide or that prints at the bottom of a sheet of slide handouts or notes:
   A. Header   B. Footer   C. Page number

8. The command that locates all occurrences of specific text and replace it with alternative text is:
   A. Replace   B. Find   C. Edit

9. The view in which all of the slides in your presentation display in miniature is:
   A. Slide Sorter view   B. Normal view   C. Slide Show view

10. Formats applied to images that make pictures resemble sketches or paintings are:
    A. Styles   B. Slide transitions   C. Artistic filters

Content-Based Assessments

Apply **1A** skills from these Objectives:

1 Create a New Presentation

2 Edit a Presentation in Normal View

3 Add Pictures to a Presentation

4 View and Print a Presentation

Skills Review | Project **1C** Nature Preserve

In the following Skills Review, you will create a new presentation by inserting content and pictures, adding notes and footers, and applying a presentation theme. Your completed presentation will look similar to Figure 1.47.

Project Files

For Project 1C, you will need the following files:

New Presentation
p01C_Bay
p01C_Snorkel

You will save your presentation as:

Lastname_Firstname_1C_Nature_Preserve

Project Results

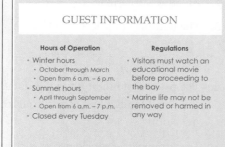

Figure 1.47

(Project 1C Nature Preserve continues on the next page)

Content-Based Assessments

Skills Review | Project **1C** Nature Preserve (continued)

1 Open **PowerPoint**. On the **File** menu, click **New Presentation** to display a new presentation in Normal view.

   a. In the **Slide pane**, click in the title placeholder, which contains the text *Click to add title*. Type **Hanauma Bay**

   b. Click in the subtitle placeholder, and then type **Oahu's Nature Preserve**

   c. In the title, point to *Hanauma*, press Control and click, and then on the shortcut menu, click **Ignore All**.

   d. On the **Themes tab**, in the **Themes group**, point to the bottom of the gallery, and then click the **More** button. In the **Themes gallery**, click **Apothecary** to apply the Apothecary theme to the presentation.

   e. On the **File** menu, click **Save As**, and then navigate to your **PowerPoint Chapter 1** folder. In the **Save As** box, replace the existing text with **Lastname_Firstname_1C_Nature_Preserve** and then click **Save**.

2 On the **Home tab**, in the **Slides group**, click the **New Slide arrow**. In the gallery, click the **Picture with Caption** layout to insert a new slide.

   a. In the **Slide pane**, click the text *CLICK TO ADD TITLE*, and then type **marine life conservation district** You do not have to capitalize any of the letters in the title because the Apothecary theme placeholder indicates that every letter will be capitalized.

   b. Click in the text placeholder below the title, and then type **founded in 1990**

   c. In the picture placeholder, click the **Insert Picture from File** button, and then navigate to your student data files. Click **p01C_Bay**, and then click **Insert** to insert the picture in the placeholder. Do not be concerned about the Crop tools—the picture displays correctly.

   d. With the picture selected, on the **Format Picture tab**, in the **Picture Styles group**, point to the bottom of the gallery, and then click the **More** button. In the **Picture Styles** gallery, use the ScreenTips to locate and then click the **Drop Shadow Rectangle** style.

   e. In the **Adjust group**, click the **Filters** button, and then in the fourth row, click the second effect—**Texturizer**. **Save** your presentation.

3 On the **Home tab**, in the **Slides group**, click the **New Slide arrow**. In the gallery, click the **Comparison** layout

to insert a new slide. In the title placeholder, type **guest information**

   a. Below the title, on the left side of the slide, click in the small placeholder containing the bolded words *Click to add text*. Type **Hours of Operation**

   b. On the right side of the slide, click in the small placeholder containing the bolded words *Click to add text*. Type **Regulations**

   c. On the left side of the slide, click in the content placeholder. Type **Winter hours** and then press Return. Press Tab to increase the list level, and then type **October through March** and then press Return. Type **Open from 6 a.m. – 6 p.m.** and then press Return.

   d. On the **Home tab**, in the **Paragraph group**, click the **Decrease Indent** button. Type **Summer hours** and then press Return. On the **Home tab**, in the **Paragraph group**, click the **Increase Indent** button. Type **April through September** and then press Return. Type **Open from 6 a.m. – 7 p.m.** and then press Return.

   e. On the **Home tab**, in the **Paragraph group**, click the **Decrease Indent** button. Type **Closed every Tuesday**

   f. On the right side of the slide, click in the content placeholder. Type **Visitors must watch an educational movie before proceeding to the bay** and then press Return. Type **Marine life may not be removed or harmed in any way**

   g. **Save** your presentation.

4 On the **Home tab**, in the **Slides group**, click the **New Slide arrow**. In the gallery, click **Title and Content** to insert a new slide. In the title placeholder, type **explore the reef!**

   a. In the content placeholder, click the **Insert Picture from File** button, and then navigate to your student data files. Double-click **p01C_Snorkel**, to insert the picture in the placeholder. Below the selected picture, in the **Crop** tools, click the **Crop to Fit** button—the third Crop button under the picture.

   b. With the picture selected, on the **Format Picture tab**, in the **Picture Styles group**, click the **More** button to display the **Picture Styles** gallery. Using the ScreenTips, locate and click the **Soft Edge Rectangle** style.

   c. Below the slide, click in the **Notes pane**, and then type **Visitors should not step on the reef as it can damage the coral.**

(Project 1C Nature Preserve continues on the next page)

PowerPoint | Chapter 1

Skills Review | Project 1C Nature Preserve (continued)

5 Insert a **New Slide** using the **Section Header** layout.

a. In the title placeholder, type **contact lehua hawaiian adventures** In the text placeholder, type **for additional information**

b. If necessary, point to **Lehua**, press Control and click, and then on the shortcut menu, click **Ignore All** to ignore the spelling of *Lehua*.

6 On the **Slide Show tab**, in the **Play Slide Show group**, click the **From Start** button.

a. Click the mouse, or press Spacebar or →, to advance to the second slide. Advance through the slides until the black slide displays.

b. With the black slide displayed, click the mouse to exit the slide show and return to the presentation.

7 On the **Home tab**, in the **Insert group**, click the **Text** button, and then click **Header and Footer**.

a. In the **Header and Footer** dialog box, click the **Notes and Handouts tab**. Under **Include on page**, select the **Date and time** check box. If necessary, click the Update automatically option button so that the current date prints on the notes and handouts.

b. Be sure that the *Header* check box is not selected. Be sure that the **Page number** check box is selected. Select the **Footer** check box. In the **Footer** box, type **Lastname_Firstname_1C_Nature_Preserve** and then click **Apply to All**.

c. On the **File tab**, click **Properties**. In the **Subject** box, type your course name and section number. In the **Author** box, delete any text and type your firstname and lastname. In the **Keywords** box, type **snorkel, nature** and then click **OK**.

d. **Save** your presentation. **Print Handouts (6 slides per page)** or submit electronically as directed by your instructor. **Close** the presentation, and then **Quit PowerPoint**.

End **You have completed Project 1C**

Content-Based Assessments

Skills Review | Project **1D** Kauai Beaches

In the following Skills Review, you will edit an existing presentation by inserting slides from another presentation, applying font and slide formatting, and applying slide transitions. Your completed presentation will look similar to Figure 1.48.

Project Files

For Project 1D, you will need the following files:

p01D_Kauai_Beaches
p01D_Hawaii_Slides

You will save your presentation as:

Lastname_Firstname_1D_Kauai_Beaches

Project Results

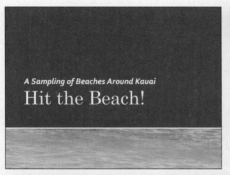

Figure 1.48

(Project 1D Kauai Beaches continues on the next page)

Skills Review | Project **1D** Kauai Beaches (continued)

1 Open **PowerPoint**. On the **File** menu, click **Open**. Navigate to your student files, and then **Open** the **p01D_Kauai_Beaches** presentation. If necessary, increase the size of the window to fill the screen. On the **File** menu, click **Save As**, navigate to your **PowerPoint Chapter 1** folder, and then using your own name, **Save** the file as **Lastname_Firstname_1D_Kauai_Beaches** Take a moment to examine the content of the presentation.

a. In the **Slides/Outline pane**, click the **Outline** button to display the presentation outline.

b. In the **Outline tab**, in **Slide 2**, click anywhere in the second bullet point, which begins with the text *Accessible via.*

c. On the **Home tab**, in the **Paragraph group**, click the **Increase Indent** button one time.

d. In the **Outline tab**, click at the end of the third bullet point after the word *summer.* Press ⌐Return⌐ to create a new bullet point at the same list level as the previous bullet point. On the **Home tab**, in the **Paragraph group**, click the **Increase Indent** button one time. Type **Pounding surf makes the pool dangerous in winter**

e. In the **Slides/Outline pane**, click the **Slides tab** to display the slide thumbnails.

2 Display **Slide 1**. On the **Home tab**, in the **Slides group**, click the **New Slide arrow** to display the **Slide Layout** gallery and additional commands for inserting slides.

a. Below the gallery, click **Insert Slides from Other Presentation**. In the **Choose a File** dialog box, navigate to your student files, and then double-click **p01D_Hawaii_Slides**.

b. At the bottom of the **Slide Finder** dialog box, select the **Keep design of original slides** check box.

c. In the **Slide Finder** dialog box, double-click the first slide—**Hawaii Slides**—to insert the slide into the current presentation after **Slide 1**. In the **Slide Finder** dialog box, double-click the second slide—**Anini Beach**—to insert it as the third slide in your presentation.

d. In your **1D_Kauai_Beaches** presentation, in the **Slides/Outline pane**, click **Slide 4** to display it in the **Slide pane**.

e. In the **Slide Finder** dialog box, double-click the fourth slide—**Mahaulepu Trail**—and then double-click the fifth slide—**Tunnels Beach Outstanding**—to insert both slides after **Slide 4**. In the **Slide Finder** dialog box, click **Close**.

3 Display **Slide 1**, and then select the title—*Hit the Beach!*

a. On the **Home tab**, in the **Font group**, click the **Font arrow** to display the available fonts. Scroll to locate and then click **Century**. Click the **Font Size arrow**, and then click **60** to change the font size.

b. Select the subtitle—*A Sampling of Beaches Around Maui.* Change the **Font Size** to **28**, and then apply **Bold** and **Italic.**

c. On the **Edit** menu, point to **Find**, and then click **Replace**. In the **Replace** dialog box, in the **Find what** box, type **Maui** and then in the **Replace with** box, type **Kauai**

d. In the **Replace** dialog box, click the **Replace All** button to replace two occurrences of *Maui* with *Kauai*. Click **OK** to close the message box, and then in the **Replace** dialog box, click the **Close** button.

e. Display **Slide 3**, and then select the title—*Anini Beach.* On the **Home tab**, in the **Font group**, click the **Font Color arrow**. Under **Theme Colors**, in the fourth row, click the ninth color—**Accent 5, Lighter 40%.**

f. Display **Slide 4**, and then select the title—*Queen's Bath.* Click the **Font Color** button to apply **Accent 5, Lighter 40%** to the selection.

4 Display **Slide 7**, and then click anywhere in the text *Lehua Hawaiian Adventures.*

a. On the **Home tab**, in the **Paragraph group**, click the **Center Text** button to center the text within the placeholder.

b. In the **Paragraph group**, click the **Line Spacing** button. In the list, click **1.5** to change from single-spacing between lines to one-and-a-half spacing between lines.

c. Display **Slide 1**. On the **Home tab**, in the **Slides group**, click the **Layout** button to display the **Slide Layout** gallery. At the top of the gallery, under **Module**, click **Title Slide** to change the slide layout.

(Project 1D Kauai Beaches continues on the next page)

Content-Based Assessments

5 In the lower left corner of the status bar, click the **Slide Sorter View** button to display the slide thumbnails in Slide Sorter view.

a. Click **Slide 2**, and then notice that a thick outline surrounds the slide, indicating that it is selected. Press Delete to delete the slide.

b. Point to **Slide 3**, and then drag to position the slide to the left of **Slide 2**. Release the mouse to move the slide.

c. Point to **Slide 4**, and then drag to position the slide to the left of **Slide 2**. Release the mouse to move the slide.

d. On the status bar, click the **Normal** button to return the presentation to Normal view.

6 Display **Slide 1**. On the **Transitions tab**, in the **Transition to This Slide group**, click the **Wipe** button to apply the Wipe transition to the slide.

a. In the **Transition to This Slide group**, click the **Effect Options** button, and then click **From Top**.

b. In the **Transition to This Slide group**, click the **Duration** box **up spin arrow** five times to change the **Duration** to **1.50**.

c. In the **Advance Slide group**, be sure that the **On Mouse Click** check box is selected.

d. In the **Apply To group**, click the **All Slides** button so that the transition settings are applied to all of the slides in the presentation.

e. With **Slide 1** selected, on the status bar, click the **Slide Show** button, and then view your presentation, clicking the mouse to advance through the slides. When the black slide displays, click the mouse one more time to display the presentation in Normal view.

f. Check the spelling in the presentation. If necessary, select the Ignore All option if proper names are indicated as misspelled.

g. On the **View** menu, click **Header and Footer**. In the **Header and Footer** dialog box, click the **Notes and Handouts tab**. Under **Include on page**, select the **Date and time** check box, and then if necessary, select Update automatically.

h. Select the **Footer** check box. In the **Footer** box, using your own name, type **Lastname_Firstname_1D_Kauai_Beaches** and then click **Apply to All**.

i. On the **File** menu, click **Properties**. In the **Subject** box, type your course name and section number. In the **Author** box, delete any text and type your firstname and lastname. In the **Keywords** box, type **Kauai, beaches** and then click **OK**.

j. **Save** your presentation. **Print Handouts (6 slides per page)** or submit electronically as directed by your instructor. **Close** the presentation, and then **Quit PowerPoint**.

End **You have completed Project 1D**

Content-Based Assessments

Apply **1A** skills from these Objectives:

1 Create a New Presentation

2 Edit a Presentation in Normal View

3 Add Pictures to a Presentation

4 View and Print a Presentation

Mastering PowerPoint | Project **1E** Big Island

In the following Mastering PowerPoint project, you will create a new presentation that Lehua Hawaiian Adventures will use in their promotional materials to describe features of the Big Island of Hawaii. Your completed presentation will look similar to Figure 1.49.

Project Files

For Project 1E, you will need the following files:

New Presentation
p01E_Waves
p01E_Lava_Arch
p01E_Bridge

You will save your presentation as:

Lastname_Firstname_1E_Big_Island

Project Results

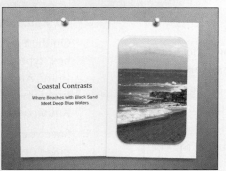
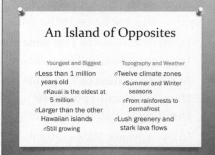

Figure 1.49

(Project 1E Big Island continues on the next page)

Content-Based Assessments

Mastering PowerPoint | Project **1E** Big Island (continued)

1 Open **PowerPoint**. On the **File** menu, click **New Presentation**. If necessary, increase the size of the window to fill the screen. Apply the **Pushpin** theme. For the title of this presentation, type **The Big Island of Hawaii** and for the subtitle, type **Lehua Hawaiian Adventures** Correct possible spelling errors on this slide by choosing the **Ignore All** option for the word *Lehua*. **Save** your presentation in your **PowerPoint Chapter 1** folder as **Lastname_Firstname_1E_Big_Island**

2 Insert a **New Slide** using the **Picture with Caption** layout. In the title placeholder, type **Coastal Contrasts** On the right side of the slide, in the content placeholder, from your student files, insert the picture **p01E_Waves**. Ignore the cropping tools. Format the picture with the **Bevel Rectangle** picture style and the **Paint Brush** artistic filter.

3 On the left side of the slide, in the text placeholder, type **Where Beaches with Black Sand Meet Deep Blue Waters** and then in the **Notes pane**, type **Black sand beaches are formed from ground lava and are primarily located on the southeast side of the island.**

4 Insert a **New Slide** using the **Comparison** layout. In the title placeholder, type **An Island of Opposites** On the left side of the slide, in the placeholder with blue text, type **Youngest and Biggest** and then on the right side of the slide, in the placeholder with blue text, type **Topography and Weather**

5 On the left side of the slide, in the large content placeholder, type the following four bullet points, increasing and decreasing the list level as shown below:

    Less than 1 million years old
        Kauai is the oldest at 5 million
    Larger than the other Hawaiian islands
        Still growing

6 In the large content placeholder on the right side of the slide, type the following four bullet points, increasing and decreasing the list level as shown.

    Twelve climate zones
        Summer and Winter seasons
        From rainforests to permafrost
    Lush greenery and stark lava flows

7 Insert a **New Slide** with the **Title and Content** layout. In the title placeholder, type **Where Lava Meets the Sea** and then in the content placeholder, from your student files, insert the picture **p01E_Lava_Arch**. Ignore the cropping tools. Apply the **Double Frame, Black** picture style.

8 Insert a **New Slide** using the **Picture with Caption** layout. In the title placeholder, type **Explore the Coastline** In the text placeholder, type **Take your time as you meander the over 200 miles of coastline that rings the Big Island. Hike the lava flows, explore the tide pools, and marvel at the deep blue waters that make Hawaii a stunning escape to paradise.**

9 In the placeholder on the right, from your student files, insert the picture **p01E_Bridge**. Ignore the cropping tools. Apply the **Bevel Rectangle** picture style.

10 Insert a **Header and Footer** for the **Notes and Handouts** pages. Include the **Date and time** updated automatically, the **Page number**, and a **Footer**—using your own name—with the text **Lastname_Firstname_1E_Big_Island** and **Apply to All** the slides.

11 Display the **File Properties**. In the **Subject** box, type your course name and section number, and replace the text in the **Author** box with your own firstname and lastname. In the **Keywords** box, type **Big Island** and then click **OK**.

12 **Save** your presentation, and then view the **Slide Show** from the start. **Print Handouts (6 slides per page)** or submit electronically as directed by your instructor. **Close** the presentation, and then **Quit PowerPoint**.

 You have completed Project 1E

Apply **1B** skills from these Objectives:

5 Edit an Existing Presentation

6 Format a Presentation

7 Use Slide Sorter View

8 Apply Slide Transitions

Mastering PowerPoint | Project **1F** Tour

In the following Mastering PowerPoint project, you will edit a presentation describing the land and sea tours offered by Lehua Hawaiian Adventures. Your completed presentation will look similar to Figure 1.50.

Project Files

For Project 1F, you will need the following files:

p01F_Tour
p01F_Sample_Slides

You will save your presentation as:

Lastname_Firstname_1F_Tour

Project Results

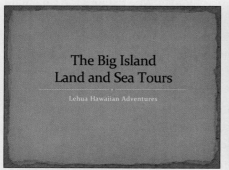

Figure 1.50

(Project 1F Tour continues on the next page)

Content-Based Assessments

Mastering PowerPoint | Project 1F Tour (continued)

1 Open **PowerPoint**, and then from your student data files, **Open** the file **p01F_Tour**. If necessary, increase the size of your window to fill the screen. **Save** the file in your **PowerPoint Chapter 1** folder as **Lastname_Firstname_1F_Tour**

2 Display the presentation **Outline**. In the **Outline tab**, in **Slide 2**, click at the end of the first bullet point after the words *1 p.m.* Press Return, and then increase the list level of the new bullet point. Type **Meet at our LHA office in Kona**

3 In the **Slides/Outline pane**, click the **Slides tab** to display the slide thumbnails, and then display **Slide 1**. **Insert Slides from Other Presentation**, and in the **Choose a File** dialog box, navigate to your student files, and **Insert p01F_Sample_Slides**. In the **Slide Finder** dialog box, select the **Keep design of original slides** check box, and then from this group of slides, insert the second and third slides—*Hamakua Coast and Hilo* and *Akaka Falls*.

4 In the **Slides/Outline pane**, click **Slide 4** to display it in the **Slide pane**, and then from the **Slide Finder** dialog box, insert the fifth, sixth, and eighth slides—*Captain Cook's Monument*, *Explore the Reef!*, and *Start Your Adventure!* **Close** the **Slide Finder** dialog box.

5 Display **Slide 1**, and then change the **Layout** to **Title Slide**. Select the title—*The Big Island Land and Sea Tours*. Change the **Font** to **Constantia**, and the **Font Size** to **48**. Change the **Font Color** to **Background 1**—in the first row, the first color.

6 Display **Slide 3**, and then select the paragraph in the content placeholder. Apply **Bold** and **Italic**, and then apply **Center Text** alignment. Change the **Line Spacing** to **1.5**.

7 In **Slide Sorter** view, delete **Slide 6**. Then select **Slides 4** and **5** and move both slides so that they are positioned after **Slide 1**. In **Normal** view, display **Slide 1**. Apply the **Split** transition and change the **Effect Options** to **Horizontal Out**. Apply the transition to **All Slides** in the presentation. View the **Slide Show** from the start.

8 Check the spelling in the presentation. If necessary, select the Ignore All option if proper names are indicated as misspelled.

9 Insert a **Header and Footer** for the **Notes and Handouts** pages. Include the **Date and time** updated automatically, the **Page number**, and a **Footer**—using your own name—with the text **Lastname_Firstname_1F_Tour** and **Apply to All** the slides.

10 Display the **File Properties**. In the **Subject** box, type your course name and section number, and replace the text in the **Author** box with your own firstname and lastname. In the **Keywords** box, type, type **tours, Big Island** and then click **OK**.

11 **Save** your presentation, and then **Print Handouts (6 slides per page)** or submit electronically as directed by your instructor. **Close** the presentation, and then **Quit PowerPoint**.

End You have completed Project 1F

Mastering PowerPoint | Project **1G** Volcano Tour

In the following Mastering PowerPoint project, you will edit an existing presentation that describes the tour of Volcanoes National Park offered by Lehua Hawaiian Adventures. Your completed presentation will look similar to Figure 1.51.

Project Files

For Project 1G, you will need the following files:

p01G_Crater_Information
p01G_Lava
p01G_Volcano_Tour

You will save your presentation as:

Lastname_Firstname_1G_Volcano_Tour

Project Results

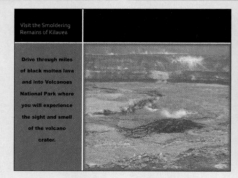

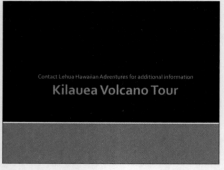

Figure 1.51

(Project 1G Volcano Tour continues on the next page)

Content-Based Assessments

Mastering PowerPoint | Project 1G Volcano Tour (continued)

1 Open **PowerPoint**, and then from your student files, **Open** the file **p01G_Volcano_Tour**. If necessary, increase the size of your window to fill the screen. **Save** the file in your **PowerPoint Chapter 1** folder as **Lastname_Firstname_1G_Volcano_Tour**

2 **Replace** all occurrences of the text **Diamond Head** with **Kilauea** Display **Slide 3**, **Insert Slides from Other Presentation**, navigate to your student files, and then **Insert** the **p01G_Crater_Information** presentation. Be sure that the **Keep design of original slides** check box is clear—not selected—and then insert both slides. The inserted slides use the format in the 1G_Volcano_Tour presentation. **Close** the **Slide Finder** dialog box.

3 Display the presentation **Outline**, and then in **Slide 3**, increase the list level of the bullet point beginning *You will hike*. In either the **Slide pane** or the **Outline**, click at the end of the last bullet point after the word *flow*, and then insert a new bullet point. Decrease its list level. Type **Tour precautions** and then press ⏎Return. Increase the list level, and then type the following two bullet points.

> **Wear sturdy, covered shoes**
> **Expect uneven terrain**

4 Display the **Slides** as thumbnails. In **Slide 1**, select the subtitle—*The Big Island's Most Majestic Sight*—and then change the **Font Color** to **Text 1**—in the first row, the second color—and the **Font Size** to **28**. On **Slide 2**, apply **Center Text** alignment to the caption text that begins with *Witness the forces*, and then apply **Bold** and **Italic** formatting. Change the **Line Spacing** to **2.0**. Click in the content placeholder on the right, and then from your

student files, **Insert** the picture **p01G_Lava**. Ignore the cropping tools. Format the picture with the **Beveled Oval, Black** picture style and the **Paint Brush** artistic filter.

5 In **Slide Sorter** view, move **Slide 5** between **Slides 3** and **4**. In **Normal** view, on **Slide 5**, change the slide **Layout** to **Title Slide**, and then type the following notes in the **Notes pane**: **Recent volcanic activity at the national park site may result in changes to the tour itinerary**. Apply the **Uncover** transition and change the **Effect Options** to **From Top**. Change the timing by increasing the **Duration** to **1.50**. Apply the transition effect to **All Slides**. View the **Slide Show** from the start.

6 Check the spelling in the presentation. If necessary, select the Ignore All option if proper names are indicated as misspelled.

7 Insert a **Header and Footer** for the **Notes and Handouts** pages. Include the **Date and time** updated automatically, the **Page number**, and a **Footer**—using your own name—with the text **Lastname_Firstname_1G_Volcano_Tour** and **Apply to All** the slides.

8 Display the **File Properties**. In the **Subject** box, type your course name and section number, and replace the text in the **Author** box with your own firstname and lastname. In the **Keywords** box, type **Kilauea, volcano** and then click **OK**.

9 **Save** your presentation, and then **Print Handouts (6 slides per page)** or submit electronically as directed by your instructor. **Close** the presentation, and then **Quit PowerPoint**.

End **You have completed Project 1G**

Content-Based Assessments

Apply a combination of the **1A** and **1B** skills.

GO! Fix It | Project **1H** Hawaii Guide

Project Files

For Project 1H, you will need the following files:

> p01H_Hawaii_Guide
> p01H_Islands

You will save your presentation as:

> Lastname_Firstname_1H_Hawaii_Guide

In this project, you will edit a presentation prepared by Lehua Hawaiian Adventures that describes some of the activities on each of the Hawaiian Islands. From the student files that accompany this textbook, open the file p01H_Hawaii_Guide, and then save the file in your PowerPoint Chapter 1 folder as **Lastname_Firstname_1H_Hawaii_Guide**

To complete the project, you should know:

- All of the slides in the p01H_Islands presentation should be inserted in this presentation after Slide 2. Correct two spelling errors and ignore all instances of proper names that are indicated as misspelled.

- The Waveform theme should be applied.

- Slides 3 through 8 should be arranged alphabetically according to the name of the island.

- On the Maui and Molokai slides, the list level of the second bullet points should be decreased.

- The Layout for Slide 2 should be Section Header, the slide should be moved to the end of the presentation, and the Flip transition using the Left Effect Option with a Duration of 1.20 should be applied to all of the slides in the presentation.

- File Properties should include your course name and section, your name, and the keywords **guide, islands** A Header and Footer should be inserted for the Notes and Handouts pages that include the Date and time updated automatically, the Page number, and a Footer with the text **Lastname_Firstname_1H_Hawaii_Guide**

Save your presentation, and then print Handouts (4 slides per page) or submit electronically as directed by your instructor. Close the presentation, and then Quit PowerPoint.

End **You have completed Project 1H** ———————————————

Content-Based Assessments

GO! Make It | Project 1I Dolphin Encounter

Project Files

For Project 1I, you will need the following files:

> p01I_Dolphin_Encounters
> p01I_Dolphin

You will save your presentation as:

> Lastname_Firstname_1I_Dolphin_Encounters

From your student files, open p01I_Dolphin_Encounters, and then save it in your PowerPoint Chapter 1 folder as **Lastname_Firstname_1I_Dolphin_Encounters**

By using the skills you practiced in this chapter, create the slide shown in Figure 1.52 by inserting a new Slide 2 with the layout and text shown in the figure. The title font size is 36, and the font color is Background 1 (Black). The caption text font is Arial, and the font size is 16 with bold and italic applied. To complete the slide, from your student files, insert the picture p01I_Dolphin. Add the date and time updated automatically, the file name, and a page number in the Notes and Handouts header and footer. In the File Properties, add course information, your name, and the keyword **dolphin** Save your presentation, and then print Handouts (2 slides per page) or submit electronically as directed by your instructor. Close the presentation, and then Quit PowerPoint.

Project Results

Figure 1.52

End You have completed Project 1I

Content-Based Assessments

GO! Solve It | Project **1J** Planning Tips

Project Files

For Project 1J, you will need the following file:

> p01J_Planning_Tips

You will save your presentation as:

> Lastname_Firstname_1J_Planning_Tips

Open the file p01J_Planning_Tips and save it in your PowerPoint Chapter 1 folder as **Lastname_Firstname_1J_Planning_Tips** Complete the presentation by applying a theme and by correcting spelling errors. Format the presentation attractively by applying appropriate font formatting and by changing text alignment and line spacing. Change the layout of at least one slide to a layout that will accommodate a picture. Insert a picture that you have taken yourself, or use one of the pictures in your student data files that you inserted in other projects in this chapter. On the last slide, insert an appropriate picture, and then apply picture styles to both pictures. Apply slide transitions to all of the slides in the presentation. Check spelling in the presentation, selecting Ignore All if proper names are indicated as misspelled. Add the date and time updated automatically, the file name, and a page number in the Notes and Handouts header and footer. Add your course name and section number, your name, and the keywords **planning, weather** to the File Properties. Save your presentation, and then print Handouts (6 slides per page) or submit electronically as directed by your instructor. Close the presentation, and then Quit PowerPoint.

		Performance Level	
		Exemplary: You consistently applied the relevant skills	**Proficient:** You sometimes, but not always, applied the relevant skills	**Developing:** You rarely or never applied the relevant skills
Performance Criteria	Apply a theme	An appropriate theme was applied to the presentation.	A theme was applied but was not appropriate for the presentation.	A theme was not applied.
	Apply font and slide formatting	Font and slide formatting is attractive and appropriate.	Adequately formatted but difficult to read or unattractive.	Inadequate or no formatting.
	Use appropriate pictures and apply styles attractively	Two appropriate pictures are inserted and styles are applied attractively.	Pictures are inserted but styles are not applied or are inappropriately applied.	Pictures are not inserted.

End **You have completed Project 1J**

Content-Based Assessments

Apply a combination of the 1A and 1B skills.

GO! Solve It | Project **1K** Hikes

Project Files

For Project 1K, you will need the following file:

p01K_Hikes

You will save your presentation as:

Lastname_Firstname_1K_Hikes

Open the file p01K_Hikes and save it in your PowerPoint Chapter 1 folder as **Lastname_Firstname_1K_Hikes** Complete the presentation by applying an appropriate theme. Move Slide 2 to the end of the presentation, and then change the layout to one appropriate for the end of the presentation. Format the presentation attractively by applying font formatting and by changing text alignment and line spacing. Review the information on Slide 3, and then increase list levels appropriately on this slide. Apply picture styles to the two pictures in the presentation and an artistic filter to at least one picture. Apply slide transitions to all of the slides. Check spelling in the presentation, selecting Ignore All if proper names are indicated as misspelled. Add the date and time updated automatically, the file name, and a page number in the Notes and Handouts header and footer. Add your course name and section number, your name, and the keywords **hiking Akaka Falls, Waimea Canyon** to the File Properties. Save your presentation, and then print Handouts (6 slides per page) or submit electronically as directed by your instructor. Close the presentation, and then Quit PowerPoint.

Performance Criteria		Performance Level		
		Exemplary: You consistently applied the relevant skills	**Proficient:** You sometimes, but not always, applied the relevant skills	**Developing:** You rarely or never applied the relevant skills
	Apply a theme	An appropriate theme was applied to the presentation.	A theme was applied but was not appropriate for the presentation.	A theme was not applied.
	Apply appropriate formatting	Formatting is attractive and appropriate.	Adequately formatted but difficult to read or unattractive.	Inadequate or no formatting.
	Apply appropriate list levels	List levels are applied appropriately.	Some, but not all, list levels are appropriately applied.	Changes to list levels were not made.

End **You have completed Project 1K**

Rubric

The following outcomes-based assessments are open-ended assessments. That is, there is no specific correct result; your result will depend on your approach to the information provided. Make Professional Quality your goal. Use the following scoring rubric to guide you in how to approach the problem and then to evaluate how well your approach solves the problem.

The *criteria*—Software Mastery, Content, Format and Layout, and Process—represent the knowledge and skills you have gained that you can apply to solving the problem. The *levels of performance*—Professional Quality, Approaching Professional Quality, or Needs Quality Improvements—help you and your instructor evaluate your result.

	Your completed project is of Professional Quality if you:	Your completed project is Approaching Professional Quality if you:	Your completed project Needs Quality Improvements if you:
1-Software Mastery	Choose and apply the most appropriate skills, tools, and features and identify efficient methods to solve the problem.	Choose and apply some appropriate skills, tools, and features, but not in the most efficient manner.	Choose inappropriate skills, tools, or features, or are inefficient in solving the problem.
2-Content	Construct a solution that is clear and well organized, contains content that is accurate, appropriate to the audience and purpose, and is complete. Provide a solution that contains no errors in spelling, grammar, or style.	Construct a solution in which some components are unclear, poorly organized, inconsistent, or incomplete. Misjudge the needs of the audience. Have some errors in spelling, grammar, or style, but the errors do not detract from comprehension.	Construct a solution that is unclear, incomplete, or poorly organized; contains some inaccurate or inappropriate content; and contains many errors in spelling, grammar, or style. Do not solve the problem.
3-Format and Layout	Format and arrange all elements to communicate information and ideas, clarify function, illustrate relationships, and indicate relative importance.	Apply appropriate format and layout features to some elements, but not others. Overuse features, causing minor distraction.	Apply format and layout that does not communicate information or ideas clearly. Do not use format and layout features to clarify function, illustrate relationships, or indicate relative importance. Use available features excessively, causing distraction.
4-Process	Use an organized approach that integrates planning, development, self-assessment, revision, and reflection.	Demonstrate an organized approach in some areas, but not others; or, use an insufficient process of organization throughout.	Do not use an organized approach to solve the problem.

Outcomes-Based Assessments

GO! Think | Project **1L** Big Island

Project Files

For Project 1L, you will need the following files:

New Presentation
p01L_Fishing
p01L_Monument

You will save your presentation as:

Lastname_Firstname_1L_Big_Island

Carl Kawaoka, Tour Operations Manager for Lehua Hawaiian Adventures, is developing a presentation describing sea tours on the Big Island of Hawaii to be shown at a travel fair on the mainland. In the presentation, Carl will be showcasing the company's two most popular sea excursions: The Captain Cook Monument Snorkeling Tour and the Kona Deep Sea Fishing Tour.

On the Captain Cook Monument Snorkeling Tour, guests meet at 8:00 a.m. at the Lehua Hawaiian Adventures Kona location and then board a 12-passenger rigid hull inflatable raft. Captained by a U.S. Coast Guard licensed crew, the raft is navigated along the Hawaii coastline, exploring sea caves, lava tubes, and waterfalls. Upon arrival at the Monument, guests snorkel in Hawaii's incredible undersea world of colorful fish, sea turtles, and stingrays. Lehua Hawaiian Adventures provides the lunch, snacks, drinks, and snorkeling equipment and asks that guests bring their own towels, sunscreen, swimsuits, and sense of adventure. This tour lasts 5 hours, and the fee is $85.

On the Kona Deep Sea Fishing Tour, guests meet at 7:00 a.m. at the Lehua Hawaiian Adventures Kona location and then board a 32-foot Blackfin fishing boat. The boat is manned by a U.S. Coast Guard licensed crew of three. A maximum of six guests are allowed on each trip, which sails, weather permitting, every Wednesday, Friday, and Saturday. For deep sea fishing, there is no better place than the Kona Coast. On full-day adventures, it is common for guests to catch marlin, sailfish, ahi, ono, and mahi-mahi. This tour lasts 8 hours, and the fee is $385.

Using the preceding information, create a presentation that Carl can show at the travel fair. The presentation should include four to six slides describing the two tours. Apply an appropriate theme and use slide layouts that will effectively present the content. From your student files, insert the pictures p01L_Fishing and p01L_Monument on appropriate slides and apply picture styles or artistic filters to enhance the pictures. Apply font formatting and slide transitions, and modify text alignment and line spacing as necessary. Check spelling in the presentation, selecting Ignore All if proper names are indicated as misspelled. Save the file as **Lastname_Firstname_1L_Big_Island** and then add the date and time updated automatically, the file name, and a page number in the Notes and Handouts header and footer. Add your course name and section number, your name, and the keywords **sea tours, deep sea fishing, snorkeling tours** to the File Properties. Save your presentation in your PowerPoint Chapter 1 folder, and then print Handouts or submit electronically as directed by your instructor. Close the presentation, and then Quit PowerPoint.

End **You have completed Project 1L** —————————————————

Outcomes-Based Assessments

GO! Think | Project **1M** Beaches

Project Files

For Project 1M, you will need the following files:

New Presentation
p01M_Black_Sand
p01M_Kite_Surf
p01M_Lithified_Cliffs
p01M_Reef
p01M_Tide_Pools

You will save your presentation as:

Lastname_Firstname_1M_Beaches

Katherine Okubo, President of Lehua Hawaiian Adventures, is making a presentation to groups of tourists at a number of hotels on the Hawaiian Islands. She would like to begin the presentation with an introduction to the beaches of Hawaii before discussing the many ways in which her company can assist tourists with selecting the places they would like to visit. The following paragraphs contain some of the information about the shorelines and beaches that Katherine would like to include in the presentation.

The shorelines of Hawaii vary tremendously, from black sand beaches with pounding surf to beaches of pink and white sand with calm waters perfect for snorkeling. Many of the shorelines provide picturesque hiking, shallow tide pools for exploring, a beautiful reef where fish and turtles delight snorkelers, and waves that the most adventurous kite and board surfers enjoy. The terrain and the water make it easy for visitors to find a favorite beach in Hawaii.

The northern shore of Oahu is famous for its surfing beaches, while the southern shores of Kauai provide hikers with amazing views of the lithified cliffs formed by the power of the ocean. Black sand beaches are common on Hawaii, formed by the lava flows that created the islands. The reef that buffers many beaches from the open ocean is home to a wide variety of sea life that can be enjoyed while scuba diving and snorkeling.

Using the preceding information, create the first four to six slides of a presentation that Katherine can show during her discussion. Apply an appropriate theme and use slide layouts that will effectively present the content. Several picture files listed at the beginning of this project have been provided that you can insert in your presentation. Apply font formatting, picture styles, and slide transitions, and modify text alignment and line spacing as necessary. Check spelling in the presentation, selecting Ignore All if proper names are indicated as misspelled. Save the file as **Lastname_Firstname_1M_Beaches** and then add the date and time updated automatically, the file name, and a page number in the Notes and Handouts header and footer. Add your course name and section number, your name, and the keywords **beaches, Black Sands beach, tide pools, lithified cliffs, scuba, snorkeling** to the File Properties. Save your presentation in your PowerPoint Chapter 1 folder, and then print Handouts or submit electronically as directed by your instructor. Close the presentation, and then Quit PowerPoint.

End **You have completed Project 1M** ———————————————

Outcomes-Based Assessments

Apply a combination of the 1A and 1B skills.

You and GO! | Project 1N Travel

Project Files

For Project 1N, you will need the following file:

> New Presentation

You will save your presentation as:

> Lastname_Firstname_1N_Travel

Choose a place to which you have traveled or would like to travel. Create a presentation with at least six slides that describes the location, the method of travel, the qualities of the location that make it interesting or fun, the places you can visit, and any cultural activities in which you might like to participate. Choose an appropriate theme, slide layouts, and pictures, and then format the presentation attractively. Add a header and footer, and include appropriate information in the File Properties. Save your presentation in your PowerPoint Chapter 1 folder as **Lastname_Firstname_1N_Travel** and print handouts or submit electronically as directed. Close the presentation, and then Quit PowerPoint.

End You have completed Project 1N ———————————————

Apply a combination of the 1A and 1B skills.

GO! Group Business Running Case | Project 1O
Bell Orchid Hotels Group Running Case

This project relates to the **Bell Orchid Hotels**. Your instructor may assign this group case project to your class. If your instructor assigns this project, he or she will provide you with information and instructions to work as part of a group. The group will apply the skills gained thus far to help the Bell Orchid Hotels achieve its business goals.

End You have completed Project 1O ———————————————

Formatting PowerPoint Presentations

OUTCOMES

At the end of this chapter you will be able to:

PROJECT 2A
Format a presentation to add visual interest and clarity.

OBJECTIVES

Mastering these objectives will enable you to:

1. Format Numbered and Bulleted Lists (p. 495)
2. Insert Clip Art (p. 499)
3. Insert Text Boxes and Shapes (p. 506)
4. Format Objects (p. 510)

PROJECT 2B
Enhance a presentation with WordArt and diagrams.

5. Remove Picture Backgrounds and Insert WordArt (p. 519)
6. Create and Format a SmartArt Graphic (p. 526)

© karnizz/Shutterstock

In This Chapter

A PowerPoint presentation is a visual aid in which well-designed slides help the audience understand complex information while keeping them focused on the message. Color is an important element that enhances your slides and draws the audience's interest by creating focus. When designing the background and element colors for your presentation, be sure that the colors you use provide contrast so that the text is visible on the background.

Fascination Entertainment Group operates 15 regional theme parks across the United States, Mexico, and Canada. Park types include traditional theme parks, water parks, and animal parks. This year the company will launch three of its new "Fascination Parks," where attractions combine fun and the discovery of math and science information, and where teens and adults enjoy the free Friday night concerts.

Project 2A Employee Training Presentation

Project Activities

In Activities 2.01 through 2.14, you will format a presentation for Yuki Hiroko, Director of Operations for Fascination Entertainment Group, that describes important safety guidelines for employees. Your completed presentation will look similar to Figure 2.1.

Project Files

For Project 2A, you will need the following file:

p02A_Safety

You will save your presentation as:

Lastname_Firstname_2A_Safety

Project Results

Fascination Entertainment Group

Employee Safety Training

Our Top Priority

At Fascination Entertainment Group, guest and employee safety is our top priority. Staff must report all accidents, no matter how minor, so that trained safety and security personnel can properly document and officially report any and all incidents.

Spring Season
- Implementation of new safety guidelines
- Installation of new signage throughout the parks
  - ❖ Ride entrances
  - ❖ Visitor center
  - ❖ Rest areas
- Completion of staff training in new safety guidelines and basic first aid training

Injury Prevention—Protect Yourself
1. Stay well hydrated
2. Choose water over soft drinks or juices
3. Drink whenever you are thirsty
4. Apply sunscreen throughout the day
5. Wear your uniform hat or visor
6. Wear comfortable, supportive shoes

Injury Prevention—Protect Guests
- Complete scheduled equipment checks
- Enforce boarding restrictions for all rides
- Verify height requirements for young children
- Check every seatbelt and harness
- Assist guests to understand regulations
- Refer questions to your supervisor

If Safety is Questionable → STOP

At Fascination Entertainment Group

Safety is Our Top Priority

Figure 2.1
Project 2A Safety

Objective 1 | Format Numbered and Bulleted Lists

Recall that formatting is the process of changing the appearance of the text, layout, or design of a slide. You can format slide content by changing the bulleted and numbered list styles and colors.

Activity 2.01 | Selecting Placeholder Text

Recall that a placeholder is a box on a slide with a border that holds title and body text or other content such as charts, tables, and pictures. You can format placeholder contents by selecting text or by selecting the entire placeholder.

1 Open **PowerPoint**. From the student files that accompany this textbook, locate and **Open p02A_Safety**. If necessary, increase the size of your window to fill the entire screen. On the **File** menu, click **Save As**, and then navigate to the location where you are storing your projects for this chapter. Create a **New Folder** named **PowerPoint Chapter 2** and then in the **Save As** box and using your own name, type **Lastname_ Firstname_2A_Safety** Click **Save** or press Return. Take a moment to view each slide and become familiar with the contents of this presentation.

2 Display **Slide 2**. Click anywhere in the content placeholder with the single bullet point, and then compare your screen with Figure 2.2.

A border displays, indicating that you can make editing changes to the placeholder text. The sizing handles display in white. There is a small dashed line between the top center sizing handle and the rotation handle. The red dashed lines at the top and bottom are part of the decorative elements of the applied theme.

Figure 2.2

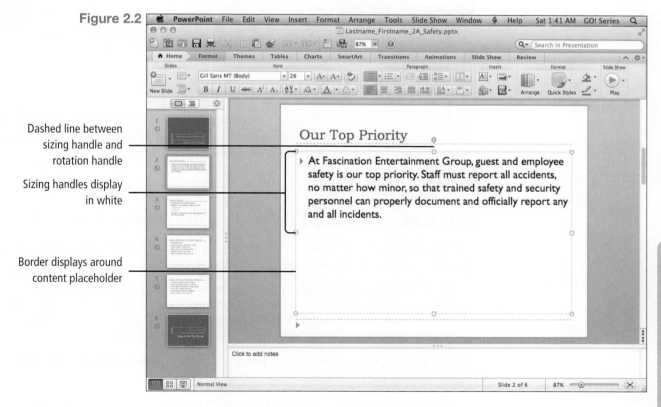

Dashed line between sizing handle and rotation handle

Sizing handles display in white

Border displays around content placeholder

Another Way

Point to a sizing handle and then click to select the entire placeholder.

→ **3** Point anywhere on the border of the placeholder to display the ✛ pointer, and then click one time to remove the insertion point from the placeholder, and notice that the color of the sizing handles changes to a light shade of gray, and there is a solid, light blue line between the top center sizing handle and the rotation handle. Compare your screen with Figure 2.3.

> Using this method, all of the text in the placeholder is selected, and any formatting changes that you make will be applied to *all* of the text in the placeholder.

Figure 2.3

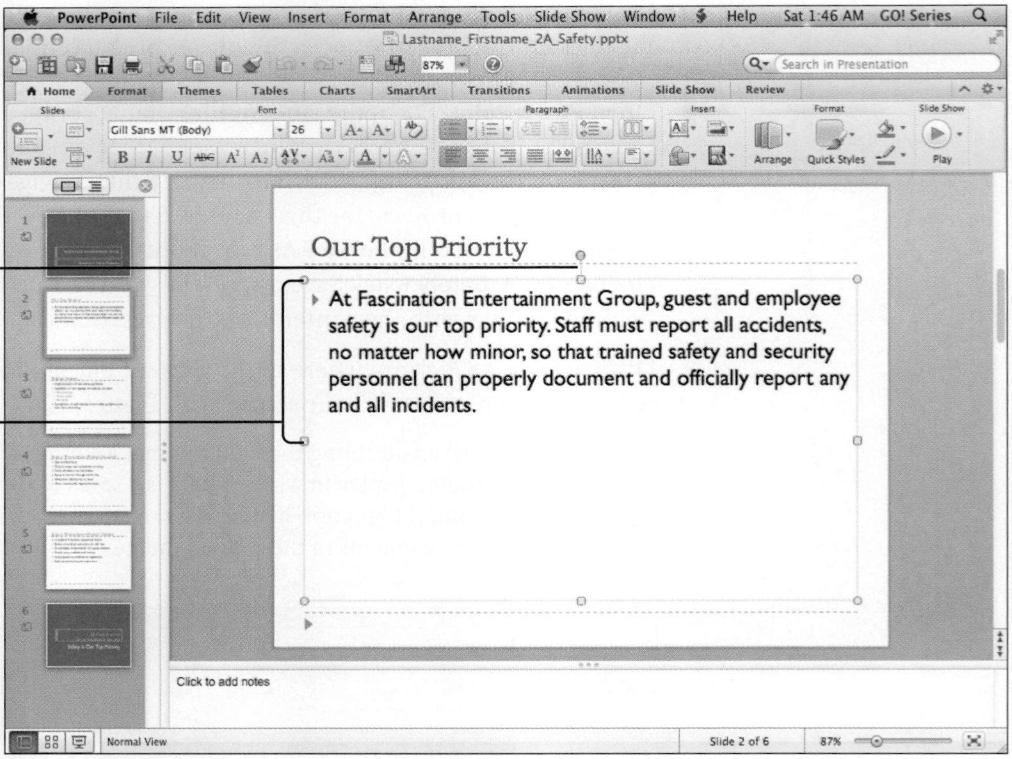

Solid, light blue line between top center sizing handle and rotation handle

Color of sizing handles changes to light gray

4 With the placeholder selected, on the **Home tab**, in the **Font group**, click in the **Font Size** box to select the existing number of *26*, type **30** and then press ⏎Return. Notice that the font size of *all* of the placeholder text increases.

5 **Save** 🖫 your presentation.

Activity 2.02 | Changing a Bulleted List to a Numbered List

1 Display **Slide 4**, and then click anywhere in the bulleted list. Point to any of the sizing handles, and then click one time to select the placeholder.

> Recall that the color of the sizing handles changes to light gray, and the line between the top center sizing handle and the rotation handle changes to a solid, light blue line—indications that the entire placeholder is selected. You can either click the border of the placeholder or click one of the sizing handles to select the placeholder.

2 On the **Home tab**, in the **Paragraph group**, click the **Numbered List** button 📋▾, and then compare your screen with Figure 2.4.

> All of the bullet symbols are converted to numbers. The color of the numbers is determined by the applied theme—*Origin*.

Figure 2.4

Numbered List button

Solid, light blue line, indicating placeholder selected

Bullet symbols converted to numbers

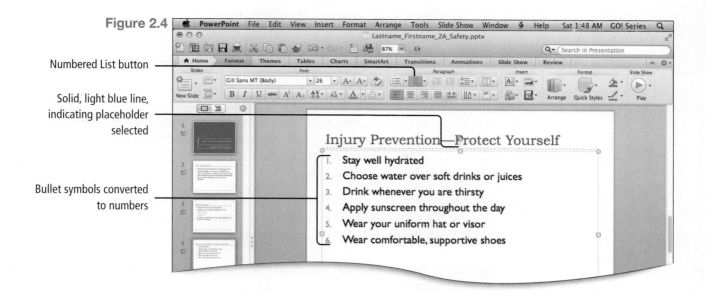

Alert! | Did You Display the Numbering Gallery?

If you clicked the Numbered List arrow instead of the Numbered List button, the Numbering gallery displays. Click the Numbered List arrow again or press [Esc] to close the gallery, and then click the Numbered List button to convert the bullets to numbers.

3 Save [icon] your presentation.

Activity 2.03 | Modifying a Bulleted List Style

The presentation theme includes default styles for the bullet points in content placeholders. You can customize a bullet by changing its style, color, and size.

1 Display **Slide 3**, and then select the three second-level bullet points—*Ride entrances*, *Visitor center*, and *Rest areas*.

2 On the **Home tab**, in the **Paragraph group**, click the **Bulleted List arrow** [icon] to display the **Bullets** gallery, and then compare your screen with Figure 2.5.

The Bullets gallery displays several bullet characters that you can apply to the selection.

Figure 2.5

Bulleted List arrow

Bullets gallery

Current bullet style

Selected bullet points

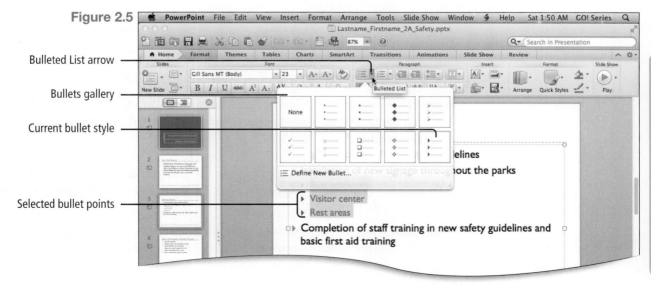

PowerPoint | Chapter 2

3 At the bottom of the **Bullets** gallery, click **Define New Bullet**. In the **Format Text** dialog box, with the **Bullets tab** active, in the second row, click the click the fourth bullet style–❖ (Star Bullets). If the Star Bullets style is not available, in the second row of bullets, click the second bullet style.

4 Below the gallery, click in the **Color** box. Under **Theme Colors**, in the fifth row, click the sixth color—**Accent 2, Darker 25%**. Triple-click in the **Size** box to select the existing number, type **100** and then compare your screen with Figure 2.6.

Figure 2.6

Format Text dialog box

Bullets and Numbering selected

Bullets tab active

Star Bullets selected

Bullet Color changed

Bullet Size changed to 100%—same size as text

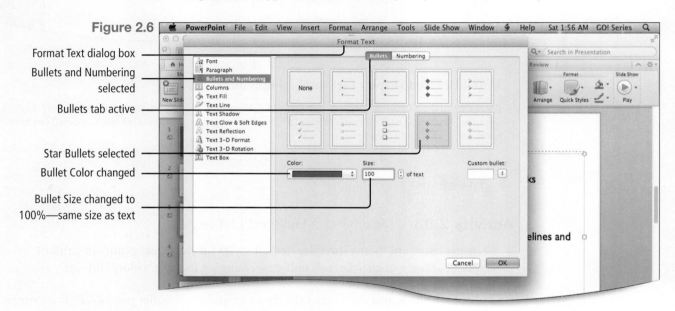

5 In the **Format Text** dialog box, click **OK** to apply the bullet style, and then **Save** 🖫 your presentation.

Activity 2.04 | Removing a Bullet Symbol from a Bullet Point

The Bullet button is a toggle button, enabling you to turn the bullet symbol on and off. A slide that contains a single bullet point can be formatted as a single paragraph *without* a bullet symbol.

1 Display **Slide 2**, and then click anywhere in the paragraph with the bullet symbol. On the **Home tab**, in the **Paragraph group**, click the **Bulleted List** button ⌸▾. Compare your screen with Figure 2.7.

> The bullet symbol no longer displays, and the Bulleted List button is no longer selected. Additionally, the indentation associated with the list level is removed.

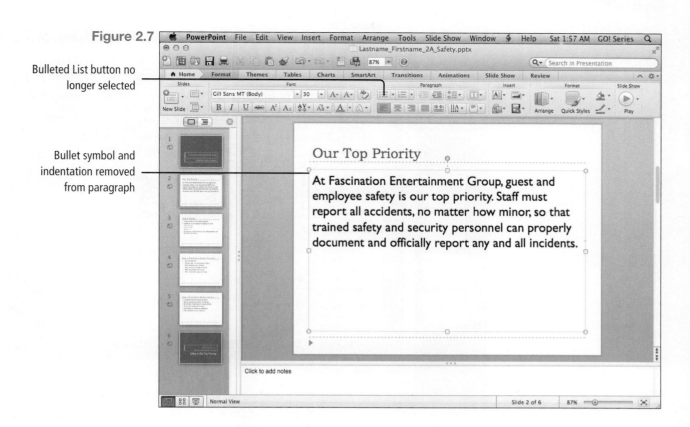

Figure 2.7

Bulleted List button no longer selected

Bullet symbol and indentation removed from paragraph

2 Apply **Center Text** ☰ to the paragraph. On the **Home tab**, in the **Paragraph group**, click the **Line Spacing** button ☵▾, and then click **1.5**.

3 Click any one of the sizing handles or the border to select all of the text in the placeholder, and then apply **Bold** **B** and **Italic** *I*. Click in the slide title, and then click the **Center Text** button ☰. **Save** 🖫 your presentation.

Objective 2 | Insert Clip Art

There are many sources from which you can insert images into a presentation. One type of image that you can insert is a *clip*—a single media file such as art, sound, animation, or a movie.

Activity 2.05 | Inserting Clip Art

1 Display **Slide 4**, and then on the **Home tab**, in the **Slides group**, click the **Layout** button ▦▾. Click **Two Content** to change the slide layout.

2 On the **Home tab**, in the **Insert group**, click the **Picture** button 🖼, and then click **Clip Art Gallery** to display the **Clip Gallery**. Compare your screen with Figure 2.8.

Figure 2.8

Picture button

Clip Gallery

3 At the bottom of the **Clip Gallery**, click the **Online** button. If a message box displays about launching your default Internet browser, click Yes. On the Microsoft Office Images Web page, in the **Search all images** box, type **bottled water, pouring** to search for images that contain the keywords *bottled water* and *pouring*. Compare your screen with Figure 2.9.

Web pages are updated frequently. If the page does not display as shown in Figure 2.9, you should be able to find a search box on the current Web page.

Figure 2.9

Microsoft Office
Images Web page

Search terms entered

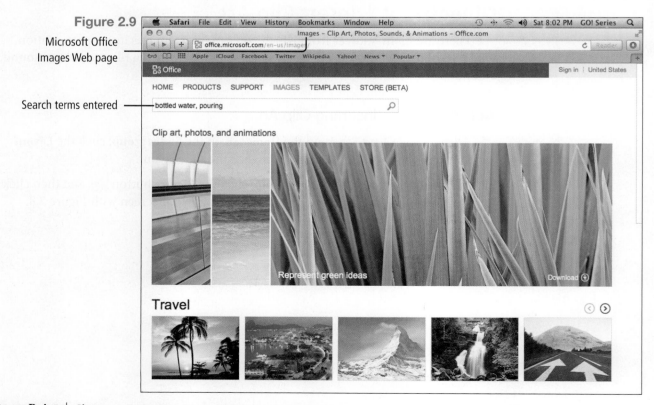

4 Click the **Search** button. On the **Search results** page, locate and point to the image of the water pouring from a glass water bottle on a blue background, and then compare your screen with Figure 2.10.

> When you point to an image on the Search results page, two links display—view details and Download.

Figure 2.10

Search results page

Selected image

Alert! | Is the Water Bottle Image Unavailable?

If you are unable to locate the suggested picture, choose another similar image.

---

5 In the selected image, click **Download**. The downloaded image—MP900401208. JPG—displays in the **Preview** application. **Close** ⊖ the image preview, and then on the **Preview** menu, click **Quit Preview**. **Close** ⊖ the Web page, and then **Quit** your browser to return to the **Clip Gallery**.

6 In the **Clip Gallery**, click the **Import** button. In **Import** dialog box, notice that your **Downloads** folder is selected. Click the file you downloaded—**MP900401208.JPG**—to select it. At the bottom of the **Import** dialog box, click the **Move into Clip Gallery** option button, and then click the **Import** button.

7 In the **Properties** dialog box, in the **Description of this clip** box, type **Water Bottle** and then click **OK**. If you do not see the image of the water bottle in the Clip Gallery, in the **Clip Gallery Search** box, type **water bottle** and then click the **Search** button. If necessary, click the water bottle picture that you downloaded, and then click the **Insert** button to insert it in the content placeholder on the right side of the slide and to close the Clip Gallery. Compare your screen with Figure 2.11.

Figure 2.11

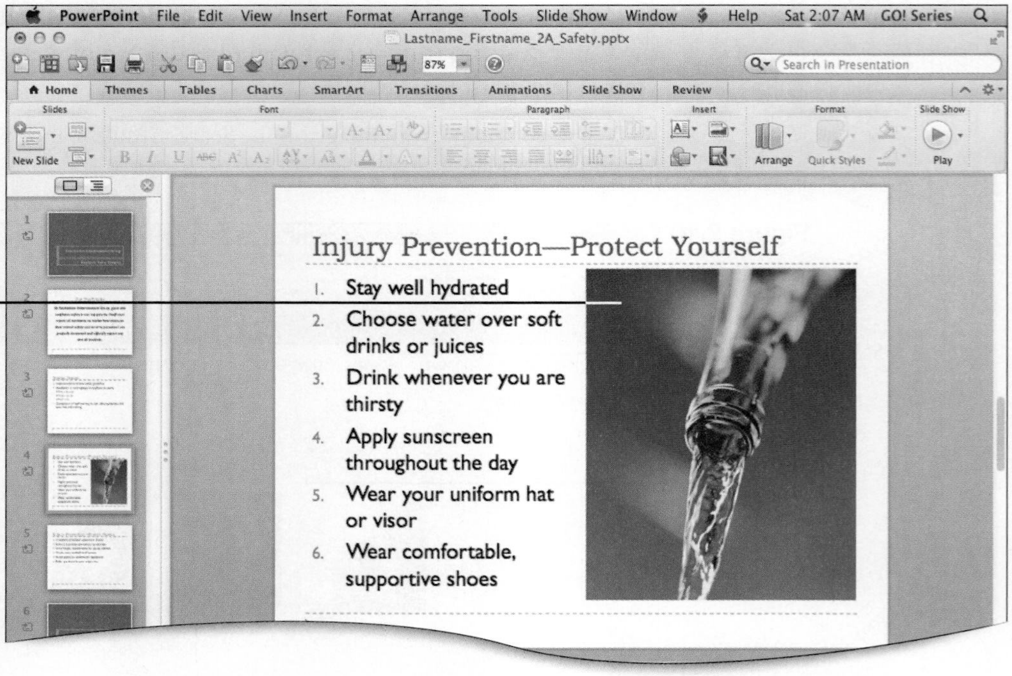

Downloaded image inserted in placeholder

8 Display **Slide 1**. On the **Home tab**, in the **Insert group**, click the **Picture** button, and then click **Clip Art Gallery** to display the **Clip Gallery**. Click the **Online** button. In the message box, click **Yes** to launch your browser. On the Microsoft Office Images Web page, **Search** for images with the key words of **red lights, safety**

9 Point to the picture as shown in Figure 2.12, and then click **Download**.

If you cannot locate the picture, select another appropriate image.

Figure 2.12

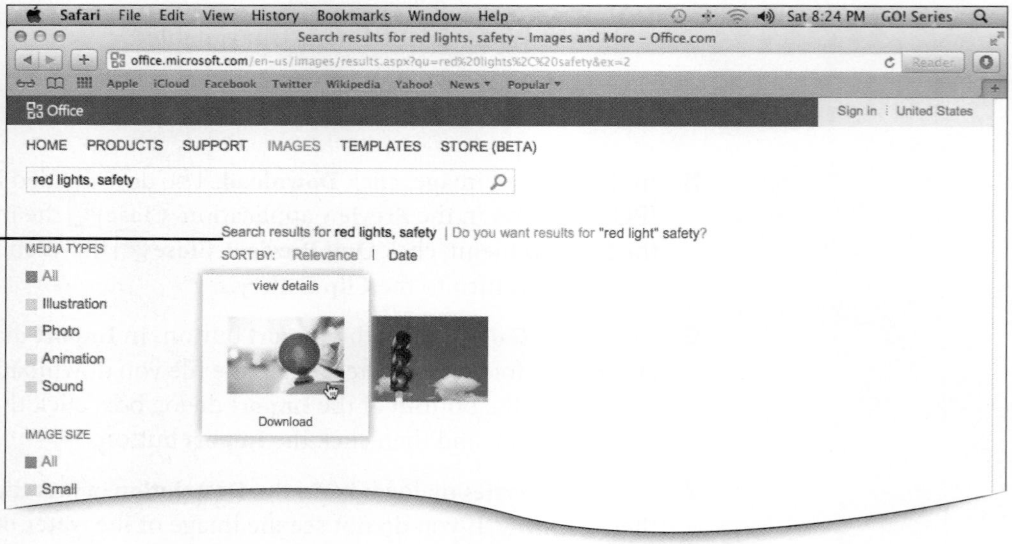

Results for search terms of *red lights, safety*

10 **Close** the preview of the image, and then on the **Preview** menu, click **Quit Preview**. **Close** the Web page, and then **Quit** your browser. In the **Clip Gallery**, click the **Import** button. In the **Import** dialog box, click the **MP900427757.JPG** file, click **Move into Clip Gallery**, and then click **Import**. In the **Properties** dialog box, in the **Description of this clip** box, type **Red Light** and then click **OK**.

11 In the **Clip Gallery**, if the Red Light image does not display, in the Search box, type **red light** and then click Search. If necessary, click the **Red Light** image, and then click **Insert** to insert the image on the slide and to close the Clip Gallery. **Save** 🖫 your presentation.

When a slide layout does not have a placeholder for a picture, the image is inserted and centered in the middle of the slide and may cover existing content.

Activity 2.06 | Sizing and Aligning Images

Recall that when an image is selected, it is surrounded by sizing handles that you can drag to resize the image. You can also resize an image using the Height and Width boxes on the Format Picture tab. You can move pictures by using the Align command or by dragging to the desired location. When you point to the image, rather than pointing to a sizing handle, the move pointer—a four-headed arrow—displays, indicating that you can move the image.

Another Way

Drag a corner sizing handle to resize an image proportionately.

1 On **Slide 1**, select the picture of the red light to surround it with sizing handles. On the **Format Picture tab**, in the **Size group**, triple-click in the **Height** box to select the existing number, and then type **3.5**

2 Press Return to resize the image. Notice that the picture is resized proportionately, and the **Width** box displays *5.26"*. Compare your screen with Figure 2.13.

When a picture is resized in this manner, the width adjusts in proportion to the picture height.

Figure 2.13

Height changed to 3.5"

Picture resized

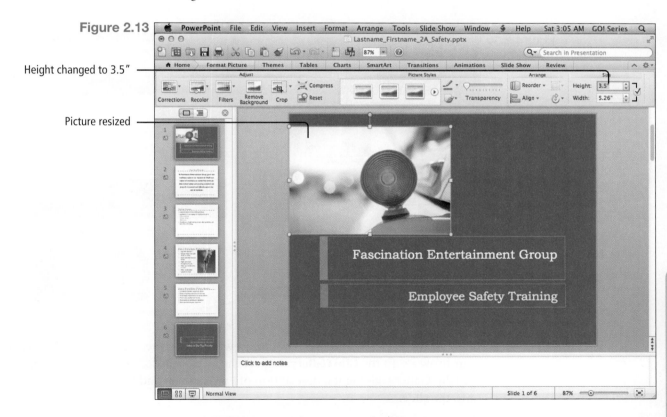

Another Way

Drag the picture to the desired location.

3 On the **Format Picture tab**, in the **Arrange group**, click the **Align** button, and then click **Align Center** to center the picture between the left and right margins of the slide. **Save** 🖫 your presentation, and then compare your screen with Figure 2.14.

Figure 2.14

Align button ——

Picture centered horizontally ——

4 Display **Slide 6**. Using the techniques you have practiced, display the **Clip Gallery**, search **Online** for an image of the Ferris wheel shown in Figure 2.15, and then **Download** that image. If you cannot locate the image, select another appropriate image.

Figure 2.15

Image of Ferris wheel from Microsoft Office Images Web page ——

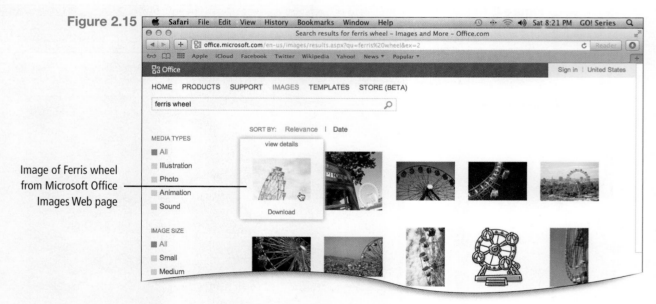

5 **Close** ⊗ the preview, and then **Quit Preview**. **Close** ⊗ the Web page, and the **Quit** your browser. In the **Clip Gallery**, **Import** the **MP900430862.JPG** file by moving it into the Clip Gallery, giving it a description of **Ferris Wheel** and then **Insert** the image onto the slide.

6 On **Slide 6**, select the picture of the Ferris wheel. On the **Format Picture tab**, in the **Size group**, change the **Height** to **2.5** and then press Return to resize the picture. Compare your screen with Figure 2.16.

Figure 2.16

Height changed to 2.5″ ———

Ferris wheel picture inserted and resized ———

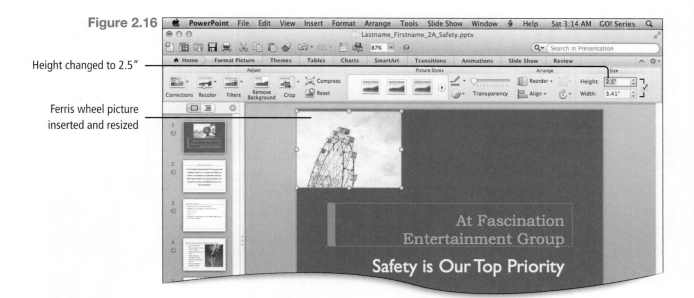

7 **Save** 💾 your presentation.

> **More Knowledge | Moving an Object by Using the Arrow Keys**
>
> You can use the directional arrow keys on your keyboard to move or nudge a picture, shape, or other object in small increments. Select the object so that its outside border displays as a solid line. Then, on your keyboard, hold down the ⌘Command ⌘ key and press the directional arrow keys to move the selected object in precise increments.

Activity 2.07 | Changing the Shape of a Picture

An inserted picture is rectangular in shape; however, you can modify a picture by changing its shape.

1 Display **Slide 1**, and then select the picture.

2 On the **Format Picture tab**, in the **Adjust group**, *point* to the **Crop arrow**, and then compare your screen with Figure 2.17.

> The Crop button is a split button. The left section—the Crop button—enables the *crop* feature, which reduces the size of a picture by removing vertical or horizontal edges. The right section—the Crop arrow—displays cropping options, such as the option to crop a picture to fill or fit the placeholder.

Figure 2.17

Crop arrow ———

3 Click the **Crop arrow**, and then point to **Mask to Shape** to display categories of shapes. Point to **Basic Shapes**, and then compare your screen with Figure 2.18. If you click the Crop button instead of the Crop arrow, press ⎋, and then click the Crop arrow.

Figure 2.18

Selected picture

Oval shape

Crop Mask to Shape option

Categories of shapes

Shapes gallery for Basic Shapes category

4 Under **Basic Shapes**, in the first row, click the first shape—**Oval**—to change the picture's shape to an oval. **Save** 🖫 your presentation.

Objective 3 | Insert Text Boxes and Shapes

You can use objects, including text boxes and shapes, to draw attention to important information or to serve as containers for slide text. Many shapes, including lines, arrows, ovals, and rectangles, are available to insert and position anywhere on your slides.

Activity 2.08 | Inserting a Text Box

A **text box** is an object with which you can position text anywhere on a slide.

1 On the **View** menu, click **Ruler**. On the horizontal and vertical rulers, notice that *0* displays in the center of the slide.

Horizontally, the PowerPoint ruler indicates measurement from the center *out* to the left and to the right. Vertically, the PowerPoint ruler indicates measurements from the center up and down.

2 Display **Slide 5**. On the **Home tab**, in the **Insert group**, click the **Text** button 🔲▾, and then click **Text Box**.

3 Move the 🔲 pointer to several different places on the slide, and as you do so, in the horizontal and vertical rulers, notice that *ruler guides*—vertical and horizontal lines that display in the rulers indicating the pointer's position—move also.

Use the ruler guides to help you position objects on a slide.

4 Position the pointer so that the ruler guides are positioned on the **left half of the horizontal ruler at 4.5 inches** and on the **lower half of the vertical ruler at 1.5 inches**, and then compare your screen with Figure 2.19.

Figure 2.19

Text button —

Ruler guide positioned on left half of horizontal ruler at 4.5 inches —

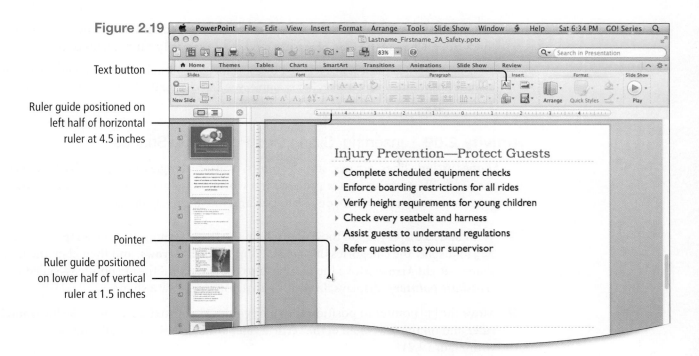

Pointer —

Ruler guide positioned on lower half of vertical ruler at 1.5 inches —

5 Click one time to create a narrow rectangular text box. With the insertion point blinking inside the text box, type **If Safety is Questionable** Notice that as you type, the width of the text box expands to accommodate the text. Compare your screen with Figure 2.20.

Do not be concerned if your text box is not positioned exactly as shown in Figure 2.20.

Figure 2.20

Width of text box indicated on horizontal ruler —

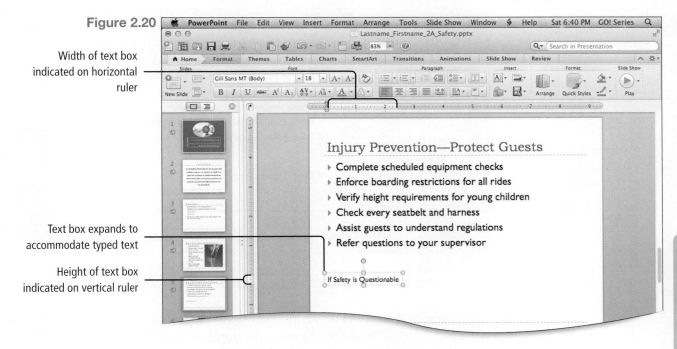

Text box expands to accommodate typed text —

Height of text box indicated on vertical ruler —

> **Alert!** | **Does the Text in the Text Box Display Vertically, One Character at a Time?**
>
> If you move the pointer when you click to create the text box, PowerPoint sets the width of the text box and does not widen to accommodate the text. If this happened to you, your text may display vertically instead of horizontally or it may display on two lines or it may display outside of the text box. Click Undo, and then repeat the steps again, being sure that you do not move the mouse when you click to insert the text box.

6 Click one of the sizing handles of the text box to select the entire text box—or click the border. Change the **Font Size** to **24**, and then **Save** 🖫 your presentation.

> You can format the text in a text box by using the same techniques that you use to format text in any other placeholder. For example, you can change the font, font style, font size, and font color.

Activity 2.09 | Inserting, Sizing, and Positioning Shapes

Shapes include lines, arrows, stars, banners, ovals, rectangles, and other basic shapes you can use to illustrate an idea, a process, or a workflow. Shapes can be sized and moved using the same techniques that you use to size and move clip art images.

1 With **Slide 5** displayed, on the **Home tab**, in the **Insert group**, click the **Shape** button 🔲 to display the categories of shapes. Point to **Block Arrows**, and then click the first shape—**Right Arrow**. Move the pointer into the slide until the ⊞ pointer—called the *crosshair pointer*—displays, indicating that you can draw a shape.

2 Move the ⊞ pointer to position the ruler guides at approximately **0 on the horizontal ruler** and on the **lower half of the vertical ruler at 1.5 inches**. Compare your screen with Figure 2.21.

Figure 2.21

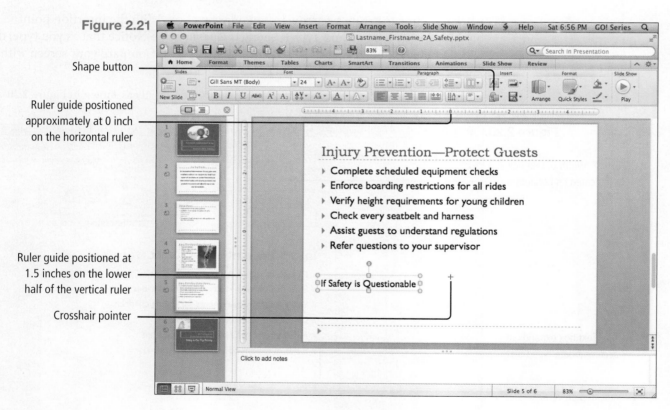

Shape button

Ruler guide positioned approximately at 0 inch on the horizontal ruler

Ruler guide positioned at 1.5 inches on the lower half of the vertical ruler

Crosshair pointer

3 Click the mouse to insert the arrow. On the **Format tab**, in the **Size group**, triple-click the number in the **Height** box to select the number. Type **0.5** and then press ⊞Tab to move to the **Width** box and to select the number in the box. Type **2** and then press Return to resize the arrow. Compare your screen with Figure 2.22.

Figure 2.22

Shape Height changed to 0.5"

Shape Width changed to 2"

Right Arrow shape resized

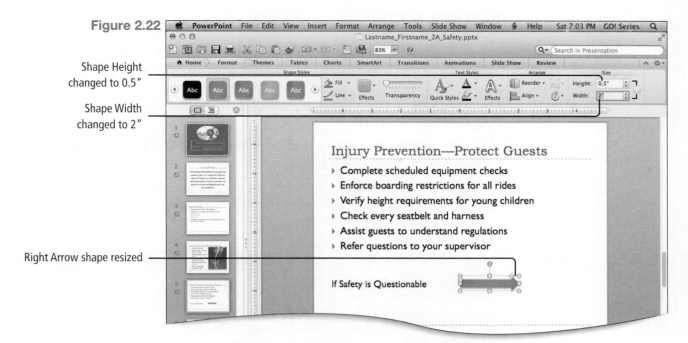

4 On the **Home tab**, in the **Insert group**, click the **Shape** button. Point to **Basic Shapes**, and then in the gallery, in the third row, click the second shape—**Octagon**.

5 Move the pointer to position the ruler guides on the **right half of the horizontal ruler at 2.5 inches** and on the **lower half of the vertical ruler at 1 inch**, and then click one time to insert an octagon.

6 On the **Format tab**, in the **Size group**, triple-click the number in the **Height** box to select the number. Type **2** and then press Tab to select the number in the **Width** box. Type **2** and then press Return to resize the octagon. Compare your screen with Figure 2.23. Do not be concerned if your shapes are not positioned exactly as shown in the figure.

Figure 2.23

Shape Height and Width both changed to 2"

Octagon inserted and resized

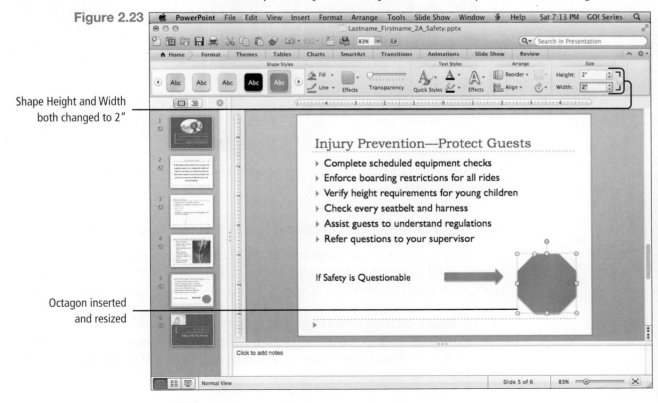

7 **Save** your presentation.

Activity 2.10 | Adding Text to Shapes

Shapes can serve as a container for text. After you add text to a shape, you can change the font and font size, apply font styles, and change text alignment.

1 On **Slide 5**, be sure the octagon is selected. Type **STOP** and notice that the text is centered within the octagon.

2 Select the text *STOP*, and then change the **Font Size** to **32**. Compare your screen with Figure 2.24, and then **Save** 🖫 your presentation.

> To format the text in the octagon, you can select the text as you did here, or you can click the border or one of the sizing handles, which selects all of the text in the octagon, and then apply formatting to the text.

Figure 2.24

Text typed, selected, and Font Size changed to 32

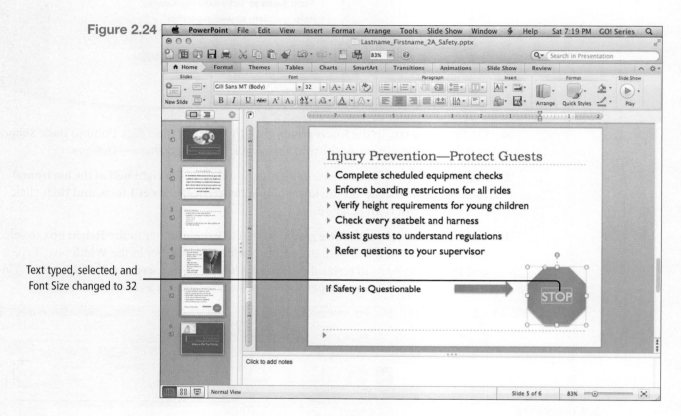

Objective 4 | Format Objects

Apply styles and effects to clip art, shapes, and text boxes to complement slide backgrounds and colors.

Activity 2.11 | Applying Shape Fills, Outlines, and Styles

Changing the inside *fill color* and the outside line color are distinctive ways to format a shape. A fill color is the inside color of text or of an object. Use the Shape Styles gallery to apply predefined combinations of these fill and line colors and also to apply other effects.

1 On **Slide 5**, click anywhere in the text *If Safety is Questionable* to select the text box. On the **Format tab**, in the **Shape Styles group**, point to the bottom of the **Shape Styles** gallery, and then click the **More** button 🔽 to display more styles in the **Shape Styles** gallery.

2 In the last row, click the third style (the last style in the red styles column). Select the **Octagon** shape, and then apply the same style you applied to the text box—in the last row, the third style.

3 Select the **arrow**, and then display **More** of the **Shape Styles** gallery. In the last row, click the second style (the last style in the blue styles column).

4 Click in a blank part of the slide so that no objects are selected, and then compare your screen with Figure 2.25.

Figure 2.25

Shape styles applied to text box, right arrow, and octagon ————

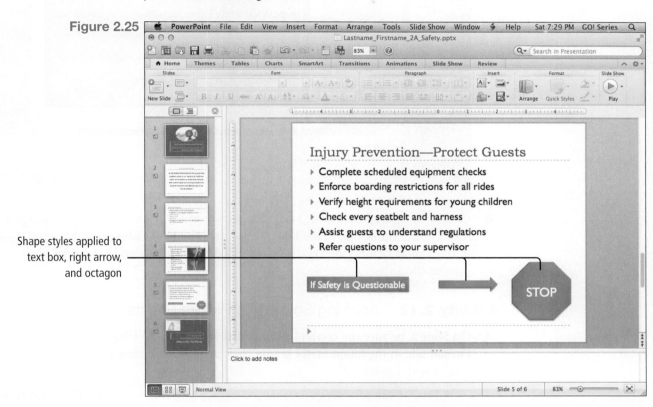

5 Display **Slide 2**, and then click anywhere in the paragraph of text to select the content placeholder.

6 On the **Format tab**, in the **Shape Styles group**, click the **Fill arrow**, and then in the first row, click the fifth color—**Accent 1**.

7 In the **Shape Styles group**, click the **Line arrow**. Point to **Weights**, click **3 pt**, and notice that a thick outline surrounds the text placeholder. Click in a blank area of the slide so that nothing is selected, and then compare your slide with Figure 2.26.

You can use combinations of fill colors, line colors, and line weights to format an object.

Figure 2.26

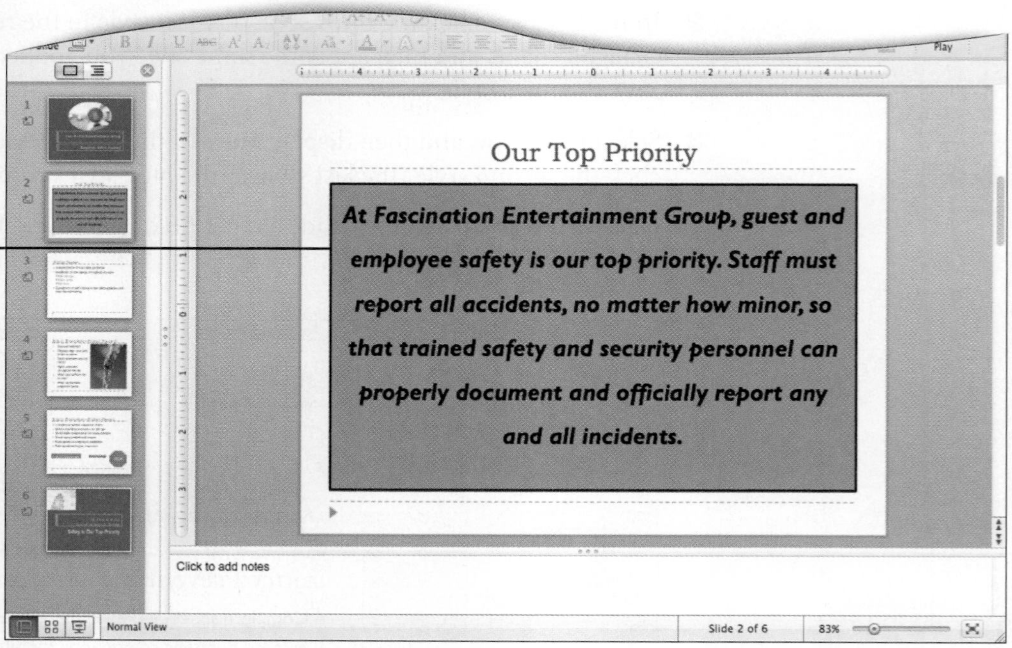

Shape fill and 3 pt line applied to text placeholder

8 Click in the paragraph, and then press Command ⌘ + A to select all of the paragraph text. On the **Home tab**, in the **Font group**, click the **Font Color arrow** A, and then in the **Theme Colors** gallery, click the first color—**Background 1**. **Save** your presentation.

Activity 2.12 | Applying Shape and Picture Effects

1 On **Slide 2**, be sure the content placeholder still displays sizing handles. On the **Format tab**, in the **Shape Styles group**, click the **Effects** button, and then compare your screen with Figure 2.27.

A list with categories of effects that you can apply to shapes displays. These effects can also be applied to pictures and text boxes.

Figure 2.27

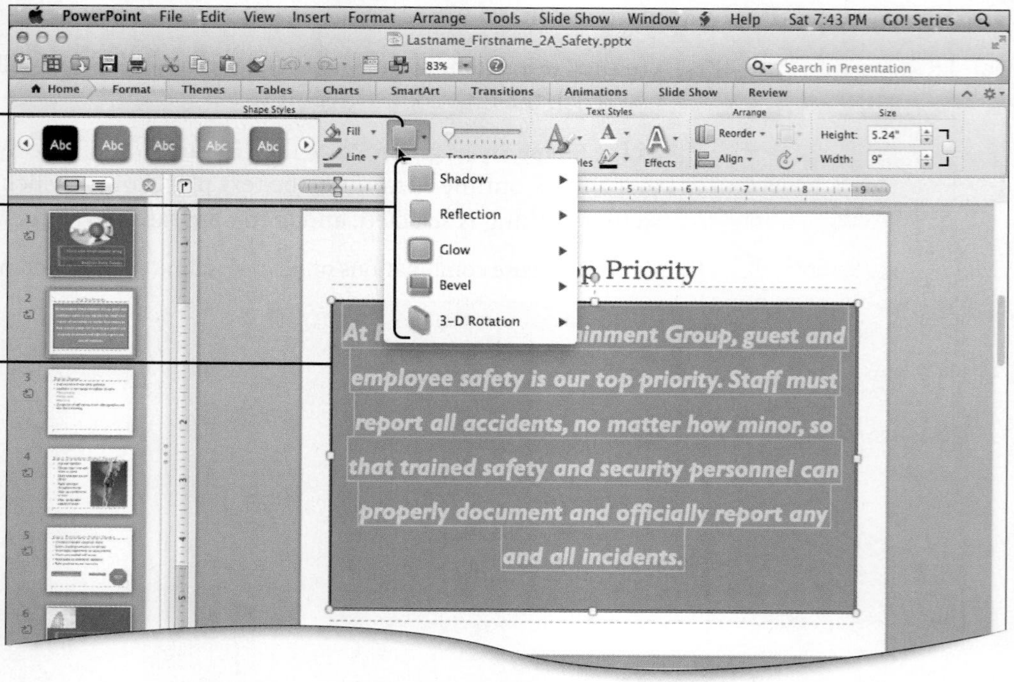

Effects button

Categories of shape effects

Placeholder selected

2 Point to **Bevel** to display the **Bevel** gallery. In the last row, click the last bevel—**Art Deco**.

3 Display **Slide 1**, and then click the picture to select it. On the **Format Picture tab**, in the **Picture Styles group**, click the **Effects** button.

Another Way

On the Format menu, click Picture. On the left side of the Format Picture dialog box, click Glow & Soft Edges.

4 Point to **Glow**, and then at the bottom of the **Glow** gallery, click **Glow Options**. In the **Format Picture** dialog box, under **Soft Edges**, triple-click the number in the **Size** box to select it, type **50** and then click **OK**. Compare your screen with Figure 2.28.

The soft edges effect softens and blurs the outer edge of the picture so that it blends into the slide background. Instead of typing 50 in the Size box, you can drag the slider until 50 pt displays in the Size box.

Figure 2.28

Effects button

50 pt Soft Edges effect applied to selected picture

5 Display **Slide 4**, and then select the picture. On the **Format Picture tab**, in the **Picture Styles group**, click the **Effects** button, and then point to **Glow**. In the **Glow** gallery, in the first row, click the second glow effect—**Accent 1, 8 pt glow**.

6 Click in a blank area of the slide to cancel the selection of the picture. Compare your screen with Figure 2.29, and then **Save** your presentation.

The glow effect applies a colored, softly blurred outline to the selected object.

Figure 2.29

Glow effect applied to picture

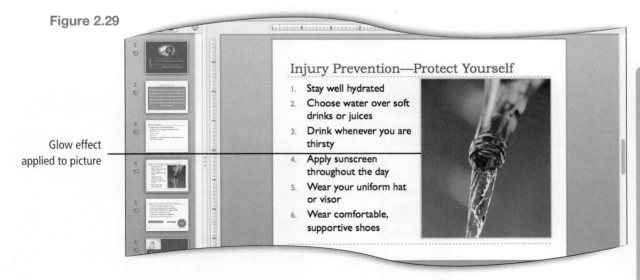

Activity 2.13 | Duplicating Objects

1 Display **Slide 6**, and click the picture to select it. On the **Format Picture tab**, in the **Arrange group**, click the **Align** button, and then click **Align Top**.

> The picture aligns itself with the top left corner of the slide.

2 Press Command ⌘ + D.

> A duplicate of the picture overlaps the original picture and the duplicated image is selected.

3 Point to the duplicated picture to display the ⊕ pointer, and then drag down and to the right approximately 1 inch in both directions so that both pictures are visible. Compare your screen with Figure 2.30. Do not be concerned if your pictures are not positioned exactly as shown in the figure.

Figure 2.30

Original picture aligned at top left corner of slide

Duplicated picture moved so that both pictures are visible

4 With the duplicated image selected, press Command ⌘ + D to insert a third copy of the image.

5 Click anywhere on the slide so that no picture is selected. **Save** 🖫 your presentation, and then compare your screen with Figure 2.31. Do not be concerned if your pictures are not positioned exactly as shown.

Figure 2.31

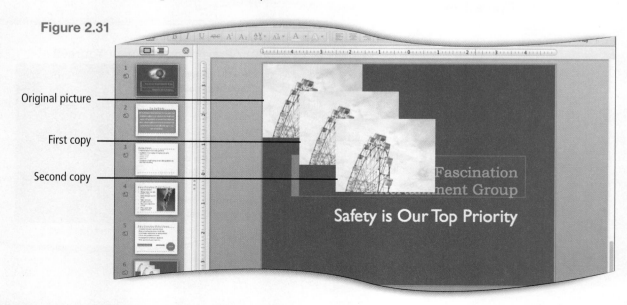

Original picture

First copy

Second copy

Activity 2.14 | Aligning and Distributing Objects

When you insert multiple objects on a slide, you can use commands on the Ribbon to align and distribute the objects precisely.

Another Way

Hold down Shift and click each object that you want to select.

1 With **Slide 6** displayed, position the pointer in the gray area of the **Slide pane** just outside the upper left corner of the slide to display the ▶ pointer. Drag down and to the right to draw a transparent rectangle that encloses the three pictures. Compare your screen with Figure 2.32.

Figure 2.32

Pointer initially positioned outside of slide to begin selection rectangle —

Transparent blue selection rectangle encloses the three pictures—the color of your selection rectangle may differ —

2 Release the mouse to select the three objects, and then compare your screen with Figure 2.33.

Objects completely enclosed by a selection rectangle are selected when the mouse is released.

Figure 2.33

Three pictures selected —

3 On the **Format Picture tab**, in the **Arrange group**, click the **Align** button, and then at the bottom of the list, click **Align to Slide**.

This setting will cause the objects to align with the edges of the slide and not necessarily with each other.

4 In the **Arrange group**, click the **Align** button again, and then click **Align Top**.

The top of each of the three pictures aligns with the top edge of the slide.

5 Click in a blank area of the slide so that nothing is selected. Then, click the third picture. On the **Format Picture tab**, in the **Arrange** group, click the **Align** button, and then click **Align Right**.

The top right corner of the picture aligns with the top right corner of the slide.

6 Hold down Shift and click the remaining two pictures so that all three pictures are selected. In the **Arrange group**, click the **Align** button, and then click **Align Selected Objects**.

This setting will cause the objects that you select to align relative to each other.

7 With the three pictures still selected, click the **Align** button again, and then click **Distribute Horizontally**. Compare your screen with Figure 2.34.

The three pictures are spaced and distributed evenly across the top of the slide and aligned with the top edge of the slide.

Figure 2.34

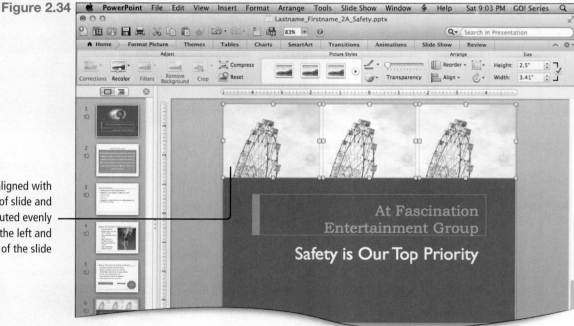

Pictures aligned with top edge of slide and distributed evenly between the left and right margins of the slide

8 With the three pictures selected, on the **Format Picture tab**, in the **Picture Styles group**, click the **Effects** button. Point to **Glow**, and then click **Glow Options**. In the **Format Object** dialog box, under **Soft Edges**, change the **Size** to **50** and then click **OK** to apply the Soft Edges 50 pt effect to all three pictures.

9 Display **Slide 5**, hold down Shift, and then at the bottom of the slide, click the **text box**, the **arrow**, and the **octagon** to select all three objects.

10 With the three objects selected, on the **Format tab**, in the **Arrange group**, click the **Align** button. Be sure that **Align Selected Objects** is still active—a check mark displays to its left. Then, click **Align Middle**. Click the **Align** button again, and then click **Distribute Horizontally**.

The midpoint of each object aligns and the three objects are distributed evenly.

11 Click anywhere on the slide so that no objects are selected, and then compare your screen with Figure 2.35.

Figure 2.35

Text box, arrow, and octagon aligned and distributed evenly between right and left margins

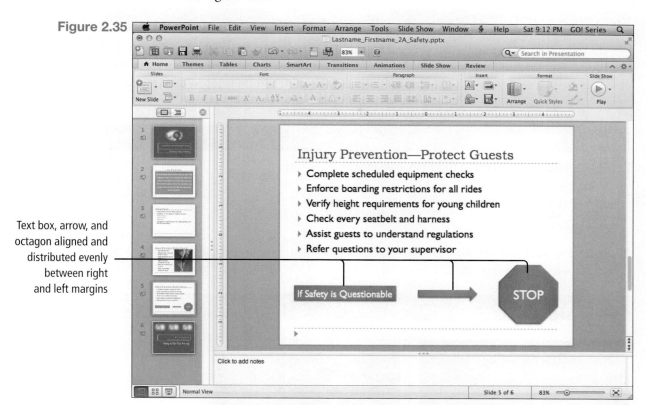

12 Save ⊟ your presentation. On the **Slide Show tab**, in the **Play Slide Show group**, click the **From Start** button, and then view the slide show. Press Esc or click when the black slide displays to exit the slide show.

13 On the **View** menu, click **Header and Footer**. In the **Header and Footer** dialog box, click the **Notes and Handouts tab**. Under **Include on page**, select the **Date and time** check box, and then be sure *Update automatically* is selected. Be sure that the *Page number* check box is selected, and then select the **Footer** check box. In the **Footer** box, using your own name, type **Lastname_Firstname_2A_Safety** and then click **Apply to All**.

14 Display **File Properties**. In the **Subject** box, type your course name and section number. In the **Author** box, replace the text with your own firstname and lastname. In the **Keywords** box, type **safety, injury prevention** and then click **OK**.

15 Save ⊟ your presentation. **Print Handouts (6 slides per page)**, or submit your presentation electronically as directed by your instructor.

16 Close ◎ the presentation, and then **Quit PowerPoint**.

End **You have completed Project 2A**

PowerPoint | Chapter 2

Project 2B Event Announcement

Project Activities

In Activities 2.15 through 2.24, you will format slides in a presentation for the Marketing Director of Fascination Entertainment Group that informs employees about upcoming events at the company's amusement parks. You will enhance the presentation using WordArt and SmartArt graphics. Your completed presentation will look similar to Figure 2.36.

Project Files

For Project 2B, you will need the following files:

> p02B_Celebrations
> p02B_Canada_Contact
> p02B_Mexico_Contact
> p02B_US_Contact

You will save your presentation as:

> Lastname_Firstname_2B_Celebrations

Project Results

Figure 2.36
Project 2B Celebrations

Objective 5 | Remove Picture Backgrounds and Insert WordArt

To avoid the boxy look that results when you insert an image into a presentation, use **Background Removal** to flow a picture into the content of the presentation. Background Removal removes unwanted portions of a picture so that the picture does not appear as a self-contained rectangle.

WordArt is a gallery of text styles with which you can create decorative effects, such as shadowed or mirrored text. You can choose from the gallery of WordArt styles to insert a new WordArt object or you can customize existing text by applying WordArt formatting.

Activity 2.15 | Removing the Background from a Picture and Applying Soft Edge Options

1 Open **PowerPoint**. From your student files, **Open** the **p02B_Celebrations** presentation. If necessary, increase the size of your window to fill the entire screen. If the rulers do not display, on the View menu, click Ruler. **Save** the file as **Lastname_Firstname_2B_ Celebrations** in your **PowerPoint Chapter 2** folder.

2 Display **Slide 6**. Notice how the picture is a self-contained rectangle and that it has a much darker black background than the presentation. Click the picture to select it, and then on the **Format Picture tab**, in the **Adjust group**, click the **Remove Background** button. Compare your screen with Figure 2.37.

> PowerPoint determines what portion of the picture is the foreground—the portion to keep—and what portion is the background—the portion to remove. The background is overlaid in magenta, leaving the remaining portion of the picture as it will look when the background removal is complete. A rectangular selection area displays that can be moved and sized to select additional areas of the picture. In the lower left corner of the Slide pane, the Background Removal box gives instructions for further editing.

Figure 2.37

Remove Background button

Picture background overlaid with magenta color

Selection rectangle

Area of picture in foreground as determined by PowerPoint

Background Removal instructions

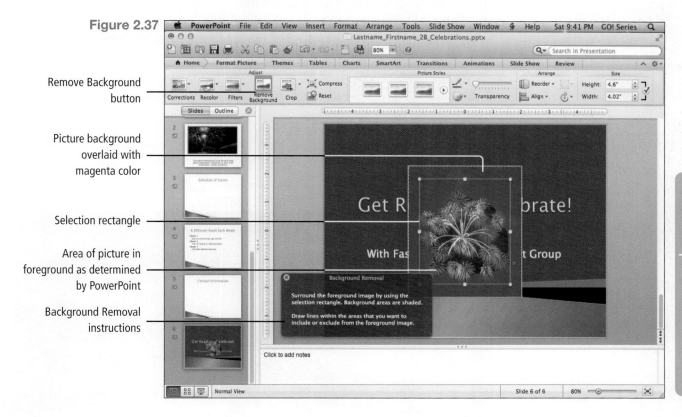

PowerPoint | Chapter 2

3 **Close** ⊗ the **Background Removal** box. On the **selection rectangle**, point to the left center sizing handle to display the ⬚ pointer, and then drag to the left so that the left edge of the selection area aligns with the dashed border surrounding the picture. Compare your screen with Figure 2.38.

> When you move or size the selection area, the areas outside the selection are treated as background and are removed. Thus, you have control over which portions of the picture that you keep. Here, by resizing the selection area on the left, a larger area of each *flower* in the fireworks is included in the foreground of the picture. On the right side of the fireworks picture, some dark red shadowing is visible as part of the picture.

Figure 2.38

Selection rectangle aligns with dashed border

Additional portion of fireworks display as foreground

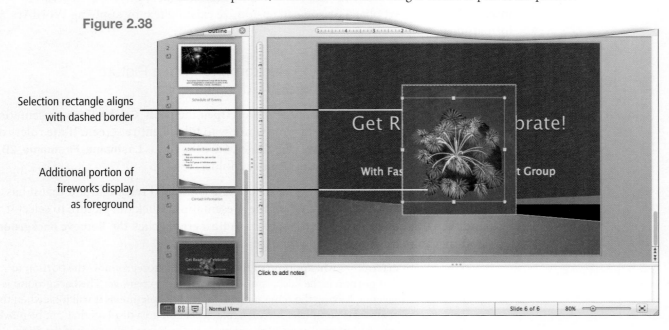

Another Way

In the status bar, drag the Zoom Slider to increase the Zoom to 100%.

4 On the Standard toolbar, click the **Zoom arrow** `100%▾`, and then click **100%** to increase the size of the slide in the Slide pane. Notice on the right side of the fireworks picture the dark red shadowing in a triangular shape that is visible between some of the outer flowers of the fireworks display. Point to the triangular shape, and then compare your screen with Figure 2.39.

> When you move the mouse over an area of the picture that has been identified as part of the foreground, the pointer includes a red circle with a minus sign (−) in it.

Figure 2.39

Zoom increased to 100%

Dark red triangle-shaped shadowing between outer flower of fireworks

Pointer that indicates area will be marked for removal when clicked

5 Position the ⬤ pointer so that the ruler guides align on the **right half of the horizontal ruler slightly to the left of 1 inch** and on the **lower half of the vertical ruler slightly above 0.5 inch**—between the two flowers in the fireworks. Click one time to insert a deletion mark, and then compare your screen with Figure 2.40. If your mark is not positioned as shown in the figure, click Undo and begin again.

> You can surround irregular-shaped areas that you want to remove with deletion marks. Here, you can begin to surround the dark red shadow by placing a deletion mark in one corner of the red triangular area.

Figure 2.40

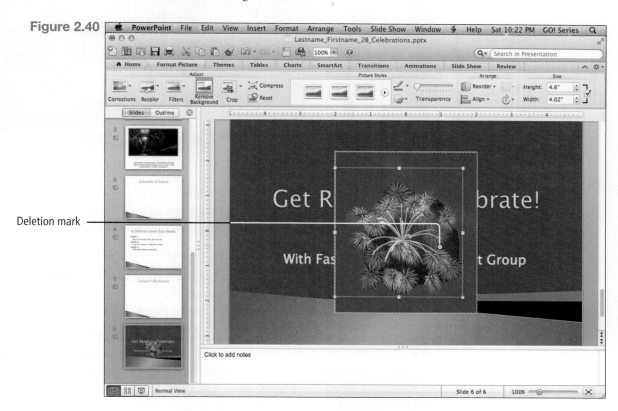

Deletion mark

6 Position the ⬤ pointer so that the ruler guides align on the **right half of the horizontal ruler at approximately 1.5 inches** and on the **lower half of the vertical ruler at approximately 0.75 inch** so that the pointer is aligned on the right edge of the dark red triangle. Click one time to insert another mark, and notice that the two inserted marks provided PowerPoint with sufficient information to remove some of the triangular-shaped red shadowing. Click to insert additional deletion marks until most of the triangular-shaped red shadowing is removed in this area, and then compare your screen with Figure 2.41.

> Do not be concerned if the number of deletion marks varies from those in Figure 2.41— the purpose is to remove the triangular-shaped red shadowing in this area of the picture, so you may use more or fewer deletion marks.

Figure 2.41

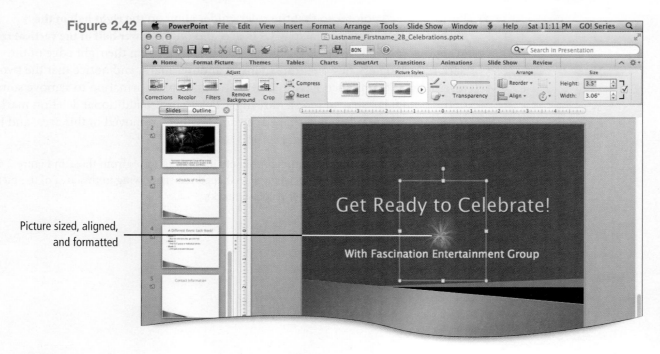

Additional deletion marks
inserted, resulting in
triangle-shaped red
shadowing being
removed (the number of
deletion marks you
insert may vary)

7 **Save** 💾 your presentation. Click in a blank area of the slide to cancel the selection of the picture and to remove the background from the picture. On the far right edge of the status bar, click the **Fit Slide to Current Window** button 🔲.

The Zoom setting changes back to the original setting before you increased it to 100%.

8 Click the picture to select it. On the **Format Picture tab**, in the **Picture Styles group**, click the **Effects** button 🔘, point to **Glow**, and then click **Glow Options**. In the **Format Picture** dialog box, under **Soft Edges**, change the **size** to **50** and then click **OK**.

9 On the **Format Picture tab**, in the **Adjust group**, click the **Filters** button, and then in the fourth row, click the third artistic filter—**Crisscross Etching**. In the **Size group**, change the **Height** to **3.5** and then press Return. In the **Arrange group**, click the **Align** button, and then click **Align Center**. Click the **Align** button again, and then click **Align Middle**. **Save** 💾 your presentation, and then compare your screen with Figure 2.42.

Figure 2.42

Picture sized, aligned,
and formatted

Activity 2.16 | Applying WordArt Styles to Existing Text

1 On **Slide 6**, click anywhere in the word *Get*, and then select the title—*Get Ready to Celebrate!* On the **Format tab**, in the **Text Styles group**, click the **Quick Styles** button.

The WordArt Styles gallery displays in two sections. If you choose a WordArt style in the Applies to Selected Text section, you must first select all of the text to which you want to apply the WordArt. If you choose a WordArt style in the Applies to All Text in the Shape section, the WordArt style is applied to all of the text in the placeholder or shape.

2 Under **Applies to Selected Text**, in the first row, click the fourth style, and then compare your screen with Figure 2.43.

Figure 2.43

Quick Styles button—location of WordArt gallery

WordArt style applied to selected text

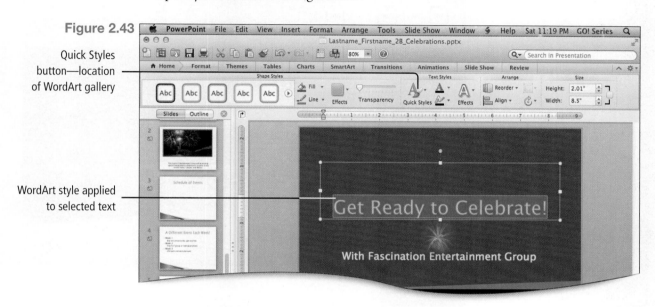

3 With the text still selected, in the **Text Styles group**, click the **Fill arrow** ◭. Under **Theme Colors**, in the fourth row, click the sixth color—**Accent 2, Lighter 40%**, and then compare your screen with Figure 2.44.

Figure 2.44

Fill button displays applied color

Fill color applied to WordArt

4 **Save** 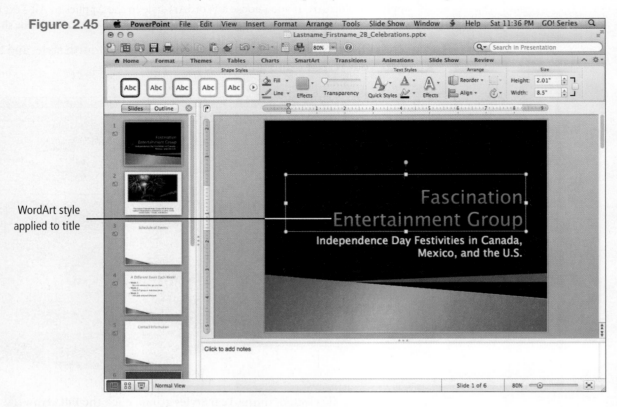 your presentation. Display **Slide 1**, and then click anywhere in the title—
Fascination Entertainment Group.

5 On the **Format tab**, in the **Text Styles group**, click the **Quick Styles** button to display
the **WordArt Styles** gallery. Under **Applies to All Text in the Shape**, in the first row,
click the third style, and then compare your screen with Figure 2.45.

Figure 2.45

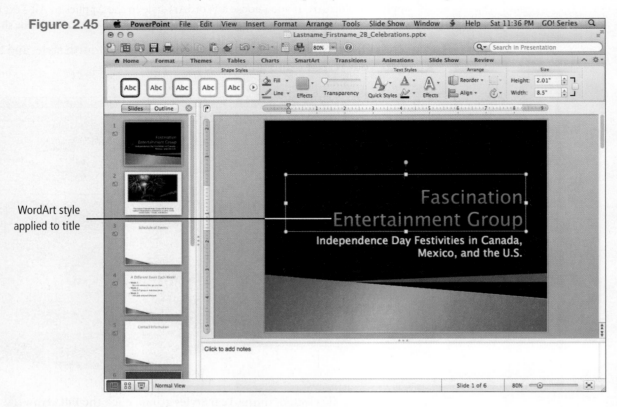

WordArt style
applied to title

6 **Save** 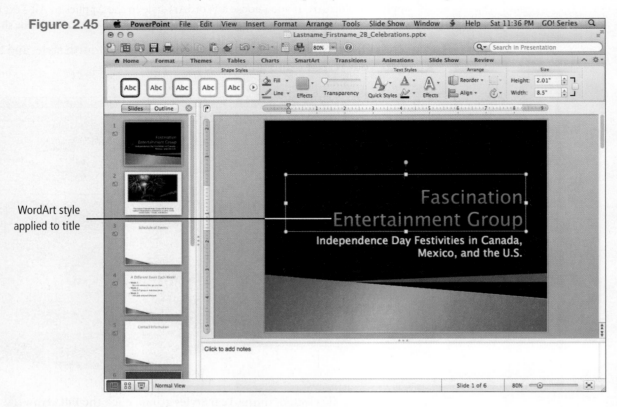 your presentation.

Activity 2.17 | Inserting a WordArt Object

In addition to formatting existing text using WordArt, you can insert a new WordArt
object anywhere on a slide.

1 Display **Slide 2**. On the **Home tab**, in the **Insert group**, click the **Text** button, and
then click **WordArt**.

In the center of your slide, WordArt is inserted that displays *Your Text Here*, but the
placeholder is not selected.

2 Click anywhere between the words in the WordArt placeholder text—*Your Text
Here.* If necessary, click in the same position one more time to display the sizing
handles around the WordArt placeholder. On the **Format tab**, in the **Text Styles
group**, click the **Quick Styles** button to display the **WordArt Styles** gallery. Under
Applies to All Text in the Shape, in the first row, click the third style.

3 Press Command ⌘ + A to select the WordArt placeholder text. Type **Get Ready for 2016!**
to replace the WordArt placeholder text. Compare your screen with Figure 2.46.

Figure 2.46

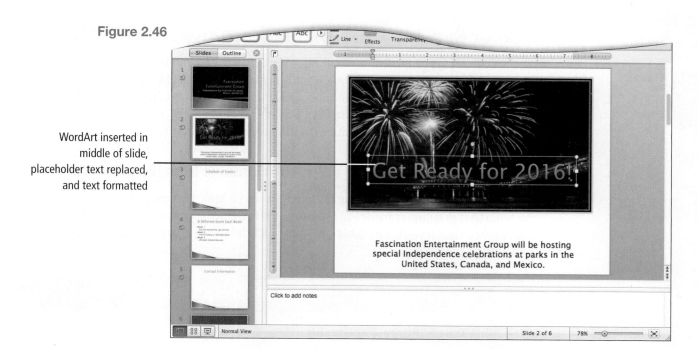

WordArt inserted in
middle of slide,
placeholder text replaced,
and text formatted

4 Point to the **WordArt** border to display the pointer, and then drag down to position the WordArt between the picture and the text at the bottom of the slide. Use the arrow keys on your keyboard to nudge the WordArt in small increments in the direction of the arrow key. On the **Format tab**, in the **Arrange group**, click the **Align** button, and then click **Align Center**. Compare your screen with Figure 2.47, make adjustments, if necessary, and then **Save** your presentation.

Figure 2.47

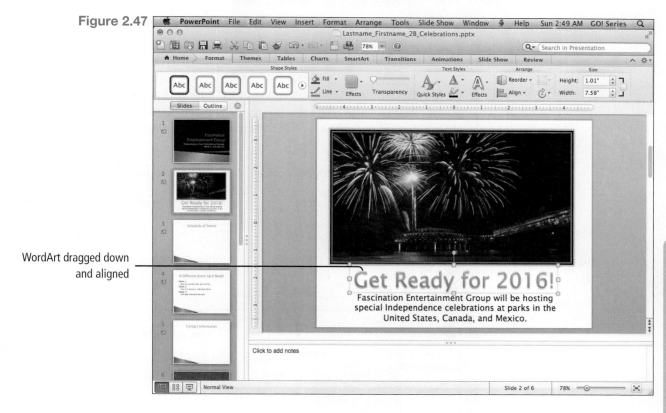

WordArt dragged down
and aligned

PowerPoint | Chapter 2

Objective 6 | Create and Format a SmartArt Graphic

A **SmartArt graphic** is a visual representation of information that you create by choosing from various layouts to communicate your message or ideas effectively. SmartArt graphics can illustrate processes, hierarchies, cycles, lists, and relationships. You can include text and pictures in a SmartArt graphic, and you can apply colors, effects, and styles that coordinate with the presentation theme.

Activity 2.18 | Creating a SmartArt Graphic from Bulleted Points

You can convert an existing bulleted list into a SmartArt graphic. When you create a SmartArt graphic, consider the message that you are trying to convey, and then choose an appropriate layout. The table in Figure 2.48 describes types of SmartArt layouts and suggested purposes.

Microsoft PowerPoint SmartArt Graphic Types	
Graphic Type	**Purpose of Graphic**
List	Shows grouped blocks of information
Process	Shows steps in a process or timeline
Cycle	Shows a continual process
Hierarchy	Shows a decision tree or displays an organization chart or information that is ranked
Relationship	Illustrates connections or associations
Picture	Includes pictures in the layout to communicate messages and ideas
Matrix	Shows how parts relate to a whole
Pyramid	Shows proportional relationships with the largest component on the top or bottom

Figure 2.48

1 Display **Slide 4**, and then click anywhere in the bulleted list placeholder. On the **SmartArt tab**, in the **Insert SmartArt Graphic group**, click the **List** button. Use the ScreenTips to locate the **Vertical Bullet List**, and then compare your screen with Figure 2.49.

Figure 2.49

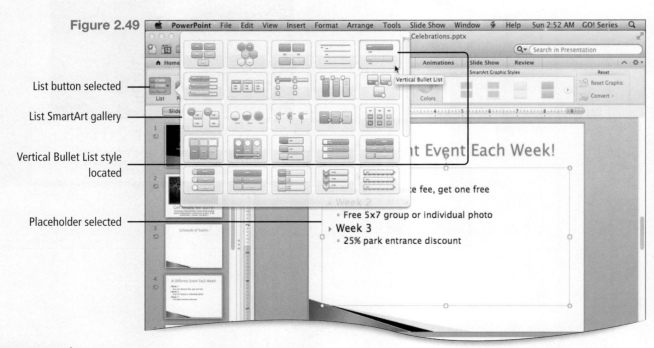

List button selected

List SmartArt gallery

Vertical Bullet List style located

Placeholder selected

2 In the **List** gallery, click **Vertical Bullet List**. If the Text Pane displays, click its Close button ⊗. Compare your screen with Figure 2.50, and then **Save** 🖫 your presentation.

> It is not necessary to select all of the text in the placeholder. By clicking in the list, PowerPoint converts all of the bullet points to the selected SmartArt graphic. On the Ribbon, the SmartArt contextual tools display on the Format tab. The thick border surrounding the SmartArt graphic indicates that it is selected and displays the area that the object will cover on the slide.

Figure 2.50

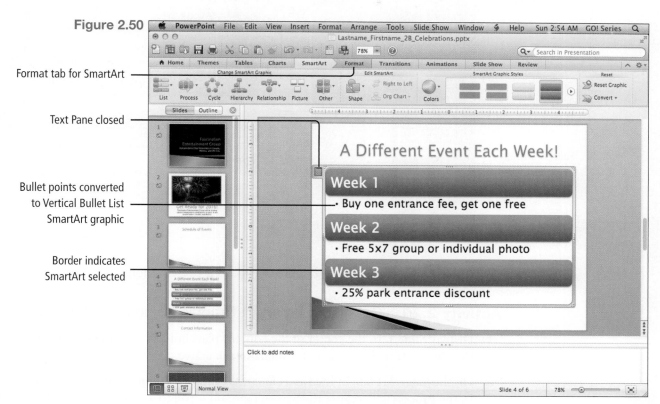

Format tab for SmartArt

Text Pane closed

Bullet points converted to Vertical Bullet List SmartArt graphic

Border indicates SmartArt selected

Activity 2.19 │ Adding Shapes in a SmartArt Graphic

If a SmartArt graphic does not have enough shapes to illustrate a concept or display the relationships, you can add more shapes.

Another Way

Point to the shape, press Control and click, and on the shortcut menu, point to Add Shape, and then click Add Shape After.

1 In the SmartArt graphic, click in the shape that contains the text *Week 3*. On the left side of the SmartArt graphic, click the **Text Pane** button 📋. Point to the title bar of the **Text Pane**, and then drag it to the left so that you can see more of the Slide pane, if necessary. In the **Text Pane**, click the **Add** button 🔳 to add a new shape, and then type **Week 4**

> The text in each of the SmartArt shapes resizes to accommodate the added shape. As you type in the Text Pane, the text displays in the inserted shape.

2 Press Return, and notice that a new shape is added below the *Week 4* shape. In the **Text Pane**, click the **Increase Indent** button 🔳, type **25% discount on food and beverages** and then compare your screen with Figure 2.51.

> The shape is converted to a bullet point under Week 4.

PowerPoint │ Chapter 2

Figure 2.51

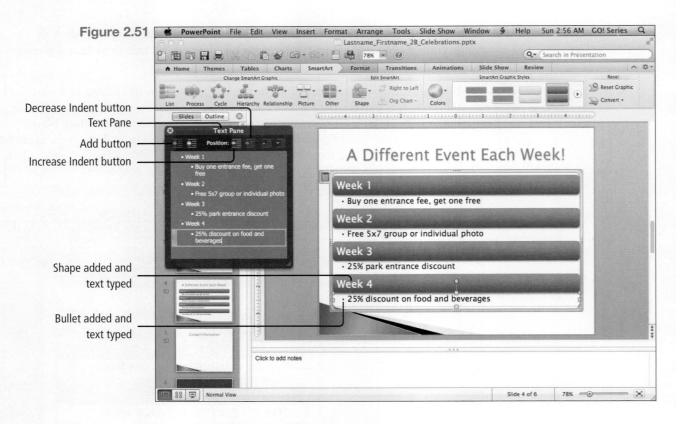

Decrease Indent button

Text Pane

Add button

Increase Indent button

Shape added and
text typed

Bullet added and
text typed

3 **Close** ✕ the **Text Pane**, and then **Save** 🖫 your presentation.

Activity 2.20 | Creating a SmartArt Graphic Using a Content Layout

1 Display **Slide 3**. In the center of the content placeholder, click the **Insert SmartArt Graphic** button 🖼 to make the **SmartArt tab** active.

2 On the **SmartArt tab**, in the **Insert SmartArt Graphic group**, click the **Process** button. In the **Process** gallery, use the ScreenTips and scroll to locate and point to **Vertical Arrow List**. Compare your screen with Figure 2.52.

Figure 2.52

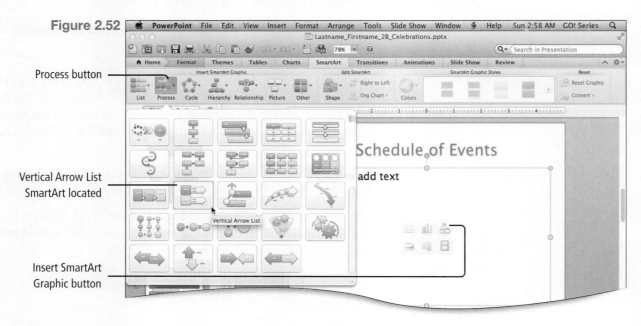

Process button

Vertical Arrow List
SmartArt located

Insert SmartArt
Graphic button

3 In the **Process** gallery, click **Vertical Arrow List** to insert the SmartArt graphic in the slide.

> The SmartArt graphic displays with two rounded rectangle shapes and two arrow shapes. You can type text directly into the shapes or you can type text in the Text Pane, which may display to the left of your SmartArt graphic.

4 In the SmartArt graphic, click in the first orange rectangle, and then type **Canada** In the arrow shape to the immediate right, click in the first bullet point. Type **July 2016** and then click in the second bullet point. Press Delete to remove the second bullet point from the arrow shape.

5 Click in the second orange rectangle, and then type **U.S.** In the arrow shape to the immediate right, click in the first bullet point. Type **July 2016** and then click in the second bullet point. Press Delete, and then compare your screen with Figure 2.53.

Figure 2.53

Text typed in
Vertical Arrow List
SmartArt graphic

6 Click in the *U.S.* rectangle. Press Control and click, and from the shortcut menu, point to **Add Shape**, and then click **Add Shape After** to insert a new rectangle and arrow. Type **Mexico** and then in the arrow shape to the right, type **September 2016**

7 Display **Slide 5**. On the **SmartArt tab**, in the **Insert SmartArt Graphic group**, click the **Picture** button. Scroll as necessary to locate and click **Vertical Picture Accent List** to insert the SmartArt graphic in the slide.

8 In the SmartArt graphic, in the top rectangle shape, type **Rachel Lewis** and then press Return. Type **United States** and then click in the middle rectangle shape. Type **Javier Perez** and then press Return. Type **Mexico** and then click in the last rectangle shape, type **Annette Johnson** and then press Return. Type **Canada**

9 In the top circle shape, click the **Insert Picture from File** button ☐. In the **Choose a Picture** dialog box, navigate to your student files, click **p02B_US_Contact**, and then click **Insert** to insert the picture. Using the technique you just practiced, in the middle circle shape, **Insert** the **p02B_Mexico_Contact** picture. In the last circle shape, **Insert** the **p02B_Canada_Contact** picture. Compare your screen with Figure 2.54, and then **Save** ☐ your presentation.

Figure 2.54

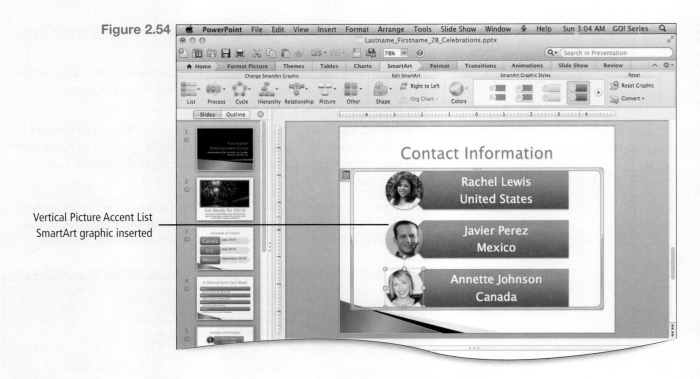

Vertical Picture Accent List SmartArt graphic inserted

Activity 2.21 | Changing the SmartArt Layout

1 Display **Slide 3**, and then click anywhere in the SmartArt graphic. On the **SmartArt tab**, in the **Change SmartArt Graphic group**, click the **Hierarchy** button. Locate and click **Hierarchy List**.

2 Compare your screen with Figure 2.55, and then **Save** 🖫 your presentation.

Figure 2.55

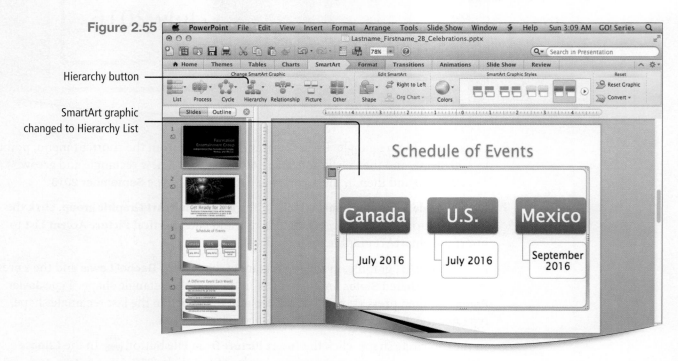

Hierarchy button

SmartArt graphic changed to Hierarchy List

Activity 2.22 | Changing the Color and Style of a SmartArt Graphic

SmartArt Styles are combinations of formatting effects that you can apply to SmartArt graphics.

1 With **Slide 3** displayed and the SmartArt graphic selected, on the **SmartArt tab**, in the **SmartArt Graphic Styles group**, click the **Colors** button. In the **Colors** gallery, under **Colorful**, click the first style—**Colorful - Accent Colors**—to change the colors of the SmartArt graphics.

2 On the **SmartArt tab**, in the **SmartArt Graphic Styles group**, point to the bottom of the **SmartArt Styles** gallery, and then click the **More** button ⏷ to display the **SmartArt Styles** gallery. Using the ScreenTips, locate and click **Inset**. Compare your slide with Figure 2.56.

Figure 2.56

Colors button

Inset style selected in gallery

Color changed and Inset style applied to SmartArt

3 Display **Slide 5**, and select the SmartArt. On the **SmartArt tab**, in the **SmartArt Graphic Styles group**, click the **Colors** button. Under **Accent 2**, click the first style—**Colored Fill - Accent 2**. On the **SmartArt tab**, in the **SmartArt Graphic Styles group**, point to the bottom of the **SmartArt Styles** gallery, and then click the **More** button ⏷ to display the **SmartArt Styles** gallery. Using the ScreenTips, locate and click **Intense Effect**, and then **Save** 🖫 your presentation.

Activity 2.23 | Changing the Shape of a SmartArt Graphic

You can select individual or groups of shapes in a SmartArt graphic and change the selected shapes to another type of shape.

1 With **Slide 5** displayed, click the first circle picture, and then hold down Shift and click the remaining two circles so that all three circles are selected.

2 On the **SmartArt tab**, in the **Edit SmartArt group**, click the **Shape** button. Point to **Rectangles**, and then click the first shape—**Rectangle**—to change the circles to rectangles. Compare your screen with Figure 2.57, and then **Save** 🖫 your presentation.

Figure 2.57

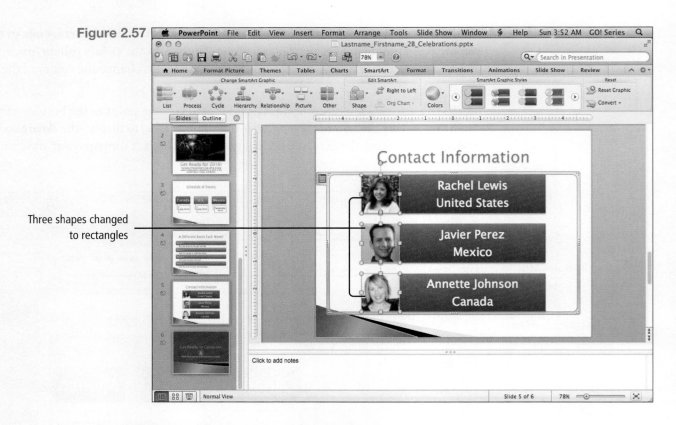

Three shapes changed
to rectangles

Activity 2.24 | Converting a SmartArt to Text

1   Display **Slide 4**, and then click anywhere in the SmartArt graphic. On the **SmartArt tab**, in the **Reset group**, click the **Convert** button, and then click **Convert to Text** to convert the SmartArt graphic to a bulleted list. Compare your screen with Figure 2.58.

Figure 2.58

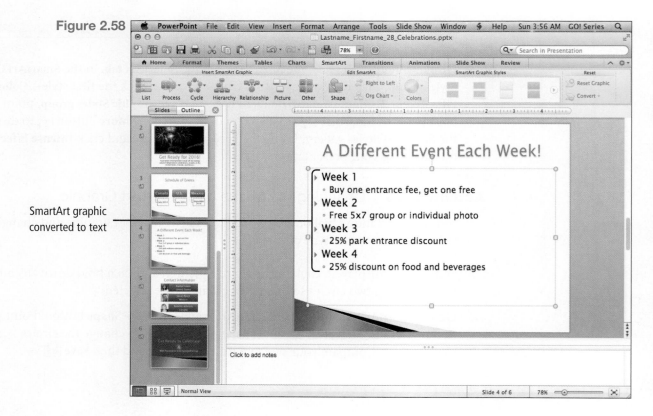

SmartArt graphic
converted to text

2 Add a **Header and Footer** on the **Notes and Handouts** pages. Include the **Date and time updated automatically**, the **Page number**, and a **Footer** with the text **Lastname_Firstname_2B_Celebrations** and apply to all the slides.

3 Display the **File Properties**. In the **Subject** box, type your course name and section number. In the **Author** box, replace the text with your own firstname and lastname. In the **Keywords** box, type **Independence day, celebrations** and then click **OK**. View the **Slide Show** from the start, make any necessary adjustments, and then **Save** 🖫 your presentation.

4 **Print Handouts (6 slides per page)**, or submit your presentation electronically as directed by your instructor. **Close** 🖾 your presentation, and then **Quit PowerPoint**.

End **You have completed Project 2B** ————————————————

Content-Based Assessments

Summary

In this chapter, you formatted a presentation by changing the bullet style and by applying WordArt styles to text. You enhanced your presentations by inserting, sizing, and formatting shapes, pictures, and SmartArt graphics, resulting in a professional-looking presentation.

Key Terms

Background removal 519

Clip 499

Crop 505

Crosshair pointer 508

Fill color 510

Ruler guides 506

Shapes 508

SmartArt graphic 526

SmartArt styles 530

Text box 506

WordArt.....................519

Matching

Match each term in the second column with its correct definition in the first column. Write the letter of the term on the blank line in front of the correct definition.

_____ 1. A transparent rectangle that you create by starting to drag in the gray area of the Slide pane and that is used to select multiple objects on the slide.

_____ 2. A common format for a slide that contains a single point without a bullet symbol.

_____ 3. A single media file, for example art, sound, animation, or a movie.

_____ 4. A four-headed arrow-shaped pointer that indicates that you can reposition an object or image.

_____ 5. An object within which you can position text anywhere on the slide.

_____ 6. Vertical and horizontal lines that display in the rulers to provide a visual indication of the pointer position so that you can draw a shape.

_____ 7. Lines, arrows, stars, banners, ovals, or rectangles used to illustrate an idea, a process, or a workflow.

_____ 8. The pointer that indicates that you can draw a shape.

_____ 9. The inside color of text or an object.

_____ 10. A style gallery displaying predefined combinations of shape fill and line colors.

_____ 11. A setting used to align selected objects.

_____ 12. The command that reduces the size of a picture by removing vertical or horizontal edges.

_____ 13. A gallery of text styles from which you can create shadowed or mirrored text.

_____ 14. A visual representation of information that you create by choosing from many layouts to communicate your message or ideas effectively.

_____ 15. Combinations of formatting effects that are applied to SmartArt graphics.

A Align to Slide

B Clip

C Crop

D Crosshair pointer

E Fill color

F Move pointer

G Paragraph

H Ruler guides

I Selection rectangle

J Shapes

K Shape Styles

L SmartArt graphic

M SmartArt Styles

N Text box

O WordArt

Content-Based Assessments

Multiple Choice

Circle the correct response.

1. The color of the numbers or bullet symbols in a list is determined by the:
   A. Slide layout   B. Theme   C. Gallery

2. When you point to an image in one of the Shape galleries, the screen element that displays the keywords and information about the size of the image is the:
   A. ScreenTip   B. Navigation bar   C. Menu

3. To horizontally or vertically position selected objects on a slide relative to each other, use the:
   A. Align tools   B. Distribute tools   C. Crop tools

4. The command that removes unwanted portions of a picture so that the picture does not appear as a self-contained rectangle is:
   A. Shape height   B. Picture adjust   C. Background removal

5. The SmartArt type that shows sequential steps in a timeline is:
   A. Radial   B. Process   C. List

6. The SmartArt type that shows a continual process is:
   A. Hierarchy   B. Radial   C. Cycle

7. The SmartArt type with which you can show a decision tree or create an organization chart or information that is ranked is:
   A. Matrix   B. Pyramid   C. Hierarchy

8. The SmartArt type that illustrates connections or associations is:
   A. Picture   B. Radial   C. Relationship

9. The SmartArt type that shows how parts relate to a whole is:
   A. Matrix   B. Pyramid   C. Radial

10. The SmartArt type that shows proportional relationships with the largest component on the top or bottom is:
    A. Matrix   B. Pyramid   C. Relationship

Content-Based Assessments

Apply **2A** skills from these Objectives:

1 Format Numbered and Bulleted Lists
2 Insert Clip Art
3 Insert Text Boxes and Shapes
4 Format Objects

Skills Review | Project **2C** 10K Run

In the following Skills Review, you will create a presentation that describes the annual 10K Run sponsored by Fascination Entertainment Group at the Santa Clara Park location. Your completed presentation will look similar to Figure 2.59.

Project Files

For Project 2C, you will need the following file:

p02C_10K_Run

You will save your presentation as:

Lastname_Firstname_2C_10K_Run

Project Results

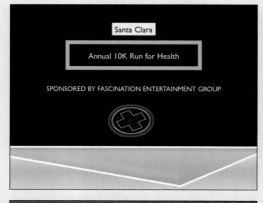

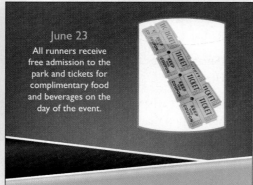

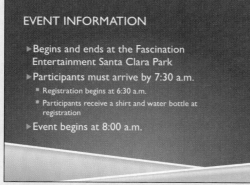

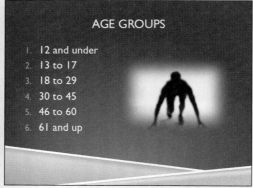

Figure 2.59

(Project 2C 10K Run continues on the next page)

Skills Review | Project **2C** 10K Run (continued)

1 Open **PowerPoint**. From the student files that accompany this textbook, **Open p02C_10K_Run**. If necessary, increase the size of your window to fill the entire screen. If necessary, display the Rulers. **Save** the presentation in your **PowerPoint Chapter 2** folder as **Lastname_Firstname_2C_10K_Run**

a. With **Slide 1** displayed, on the **Home tab**, in the **Insert group**, click the **Shape** button, point to **Basic Shapes**, and in the fourth row, click the fourth shape—**Frame**.

b. Move the pointer to align the ruler guides with the **left half of the horizontal ruler at approximately 3 inches** and with the **upper half of the vertical ruler at approximately 2.5 inches**, and then click to insert the **Frame**.

c. On the **Format tab**, in the **Size group**, triple-click the number in the **Height** box to select the number, type **1.2** and then press Tab. In the **Width** box, replace the selected number with **5.5** and then press Return to resize the shape.

d. In the slide, click the frame border to remove the selection in the **Width** box. With the frame selected, type **Annual 10K Run for Health** and then click the sizing handle or border to select the entire shape. On the **Home tab**, in the **Font group**, change the **Font Size** to **24**. On the **Format tab**, in the **Shape Styles group**, click the **Fill arrow**, and then under **Theme Colors**, in the first row, click the seventh color—**Accent 3**. On the **Format tab**, in the **Arrange group**, click the **Align** button, and then click **Align Center**. **Save** your presentation.

2 In **Slide 1**, select the picture of the cross inside the circle. On the **Format Picture tab**, in the **Picture Styles group**, click the **Effects** button. Point to **Glow**, and then in the second row, click the first effect—**Accent 2, 11 pt glow**.

a. On the **Home tab**, in the **Insert group**, click the **Text** button, and then click **Text Box**. Move the Ａ⌋ pointer to position the ruler guides on the **horizontal ruler at approximately 0 inches** and on the **upper half of the vertical ruler at approximately 3 inches**, and then click to insert the text box.

b. Type **Santa Clara** and then click the border or sizing handle to select the entire text box. Change the **Font Size** to **24**. On the **Format tab**, in the **Shape Styles**

group, point to the bottom of the **Shape Styles** gallery, and then click the **More** button. In the first row, click the fourth style.

c. With the text box selected, hold down Shift, and then click the frame shape, the title placeholder, and the picture so that all four objects are selected. On the **Format tab**, in the **Arrange group**, click the **Align** button, and then click **Align to Slide**. Click the **Align** button again, and then click **Align Center**.

d. With the four objects still selected, click the **Align** button, and then click **Align Selected Objects**. Click the **Align** button again, and then click **Distribute Vertically**. **Save** your presentation.

3 Display **Slide 2**, and then click in the title placeholder containing the text *June 23*.

a. On the **Home tab**, in the **Paragraph group**, click the **Bulleted List** button to remove the bullet symbol from the title, and then apply **Center Text**. Select the placeholder, and then change the **Font Size** to **36**.

b. On the right side of the slide, click in the content placeholder. On the **Home tab**, in the **Insert group**, click the **Picture** button, and then click **Clip Art Gallery**. In the **Clip Gallery**, click the **Online** button. If a message box displays, click Yes.

c. On the Microsoft Offices Images Web page, in the **Search all images** box, type **keep this coupon** and click the **Search** button. On the Search results Web page, point to the first picture of the light yellow tickets, and then click **Download**. The downloaded image—*MP900305705.JPG* (or a different file name)—displays in Preview. **Close** the preview, and then **Quit Preview**. **Close** the Web page, and then **Quit** your browser to return to the **Clip Gallery**.

d. In the **Clip Gallery**, click the **Import** button. In the **Import** dialog box, click the file you downloaded to select it. At the bottom of the **Import** dialog box, click the **Move into Clip Gallery** option button, and then click the **Import** button. In the **Properties** dialog box, change the **Description of this clip** to **Tickets** and then click **OK**. If the Tickets picture does not display in the Clip Gallery, in the Search box, type **tickets** and then click the Search button. Click the **Tickets** picture, and then click **Insert**.

e. In **Slide 2**, click the picture of the tickets to select it. With the picture selected, on the **Format Picture**

(Project 2C 10K Run continues on the next page)

Skills Review | Project **2C** 10K Run (continued)

tab, in the **Adjust group**, click the **Crop arrow**, point to **Mask to Shape**. Point to **Basic Shapes**, and in the sixth row, click the second shape—**Can**—to change the shape of the white area surrounding the tickets. Under the picture, in the **Crop tools**, click the third button—**Crop to Fit**—which displays a ScreenTip of *Resize picture to fit inside placeholder*.

f. On the **Format Picture tab**, in the **Picture Styles group**, click the **Effects** button, point to **Glow**, and then in the second row, click the first effect—**Accent 2, 11 pt glow**. **Save** your presentation.

4 Display **Slide 3**, and then select the two, second-level bullet points, beginning with *Registration begins*.

a. On the **Home tab**, in the **Paragraph group**, click the **Bulleted List arrow**, and then click **Define New Bullet**. In the first row of bullets, click the third style, which displays as filled square bullets. Replace the number in the **Size** box with **125** and then click in the **Color** box. In the first row, click the seventh color—**Accent 3**—and then click **OK** to change the bullet style.

b. Display **Slide 4**, and then click the bulleted list placeholder. Click the border or one of the sizing handles to select the entire placeholder, and then on the **Home tab**, in the **Paragraph group**, click the **Numbered List** button to change the bullets to numbers. **Save** your presentation.

5 Display **Slide 5**, and then select the picture of the shoe. On the **Format Picture tab**, in the **Size group**, change the **Height** to **2.5**

a. With the picture selected, on the **Format Picture tab**, in the **Picture Styles group**, click the **Effects** button,

point to **Glow**, and then click **Glow Options**. In the **Format Picture** dialog box, under **Soft Edges**, change the **Size** to **10** pt and then click **OK**.

b. With the picture still selected, press Command ⌘ + D to create a duplicate of the picture. Drag the duplicated picture to the right about **1 inch**, and then press Command ⌘ + D to create another duplicate.

c. Hold down Shift, and then click the first two shoe pictures so that all three pictures are selected. On the **Format Picture tab**, in the **Arrange group**, click the **Align** button, and then click **Align to Slide**. Click the **Align** button again, and then click **Align Bottom**. Click the **Align** button again, and then click **Distribute Horizontally**. **Save** your presentation.

d. Add a **Header and Footer** for the **Notes and Handouts** pages. Include the **Date and time updated automatically**, the **Page number**, and a **Footer** with the text **Lastname_Firstname_2C_10K_Run** Click **Apply to All**.

e. Display the **File Properties**. In the **Subject** box, type your course name and section number. In the **Author** box, replace the text with your own firstname and lastname. In the **Keywords** box, type **10K, health** and then click **OK**. **Save** your presentation.

f. View the **Slide Show** from the start, make any necessary adjustments, and then **Save** your presentation. **Print Handouts** (**6 slides per page**), or submit your presentation electronically as directed by your instructor. **Close** your presentation, and then **Quit PowerPoint**.

End **You have completed Project 2C** ⎯⎯⎯⎯⎯⎯⎯⎯⎯⎯⎯⎯⎯⎯⎯

Content-Based Assessments

Apply **2B** skills from
these Objectives:

5 Remove Picture
Backgrounds and
Insert WordArt

6 Create and Format a
SmartArt Graphic

Skills Review | Project **2D** Wave Rider

In the following Skills Review, you will format a presentation by inserting and formatting WordArt and SmartArt graphics. Your completed presentation will look similar to Figure 2.60.

Project Files

For Project 2D, you will need the following file:

p02D_Wave_Rider

You will save your presentation as:

Lastname_Firstname_2D_Wave_Rider

Project Results

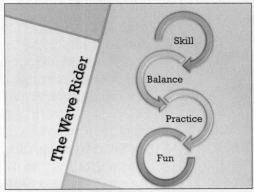
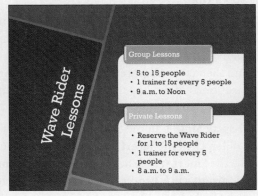

Figure 2.60

(Project 2D Wave Rider continues on the next page)

Skills Review | Project **2D** Wave Rider (continued)

1 Open **PowerPoint**. From the student files that accompany this textbook, **Open p02D_Wave_Rider**. If necessary, increase the size of your window to fill the entire screen. **Save** the presentation in your **PowerPoint Chapter 2** folder as **Lastname_Firstname_2D_Wave_Rider**

a. With **Slide 1** displayed, select the title—*Catch a Wave*. On the **Format tab**, in the **Text Styles group**, click the **Quick Styles** button. Under **Applies to All Text in the Shape**, click the last style. The text displays with a blue fill color and has a reflection below it

b. Display **Slide 2**. On the **Home tab**, in the **Insert group**, click the **Text** button, and then click **WordArt**. In the slide, click anywhere between the words in the WordArt placeholder text, and then click in the same position to display the sizing handles around the WordArt placeholder. Press [Command ⌘] + [A] to select the text in the WordArt placeholder. On the **Format tab**, in the **Text Styles group**, click the **Quick Styles** button. Under **Applies to Selected Text**, in the second row, click the fourth style. With the text *Your text here* still selected, type **Surf's Up!**

c. With the WordArt selected, on the **Format tab**, in the **Arrange group**, click the **Align** button, and then click **Align Top**. Click the **Align** button again, and then click **Align Left** so that the WordArt is positioned in the upper left corner of the slide. **Save** your presentation.

2 Display **Slide 3**. In the center of the content placeholder, click the **Insert SmartArt Graphic** button to make the **SmartArt tab** active. In the **Insert SmartArt Graphic group**, click **Process**, scroll as necessary to locate and click **Circle Arrow Process**. If necessary, Close the Text Pane.

a. In the SmartArt graphic, the first instance of *Text* is selected. Type **Skill** and then in the middle circle arrow, replace *Text* with **Balance** In the last circle arrow, replace *Text* with **Practice**

b. In the SmartArt graphic, click the circle arrow that surrounds *Practice* to place sizing handles around the third circle arrow. Press [Control] and click, and on the shortcut menu, point to **Add Shape**, and then click **Add Shape After** to add a fourth circle arrow. In the selected text box, type **Fun**

c. On the **SmartArt tab**, in the **SmartArt Graphic Styles group**, click the **Colors** button, and then under **Colorful**, click **Colorful Range - Accent Colors 3 to 4**. Point to the bottom of the **SmartArt Graphic Styles** gallery, and then click the **More** button. Using the ScreenTips, locate and click **Intense Effect**. **Save** your presentation.

3 Display **Slide 4**. In the content placeholder, click anywhere in the bulleted list. On the **SmartArt tab**, in the **Insert SmartArt Graphic group**, click the **List** button. Locate and click **Lined List** to change the bulleted list to a SmartArt graphic.

a. On the **SmartArt tab**, in the **SmartArt Graphics Styles group**, click the **Change Colors** button. Under **Colorful**, click the last style—**Colorful Range - Accent Colors 4 to 5**.

b. On the **SmartArt tab**, point to the bottom of the **SmartArt Graphic Styles** gallery, and then click the **More** button. In the **SmartArt Graphic Styles** gallery, in the second row, click the fourth style—**Cartoon**.

c. With the SmartArt selected, on the **SmartArt tab**, in the **Change SmartArt Graphic group**, click the **List** button, and then locate and click **Vertical Box List**.

d. In the SmartArt, under *Group Lessons*, click in the white rectangle that contains the bulleted list to display sizing handles around the white rectangle. Hold down [Shift], and then click in white area of the rectangle under *Private Lessons* that contains the second bulleted list so that both bulleted list rectangles are selected. On the **SmartArt tab**, in the **Edit SmartArt group**, click the **Shape** button. Point to **Rectangles**, and then click the last shape—**Round Diagonal Corner Rectangle**. **Save** your presentation.

4 Display **Slide 5**. On the **Home tab**, in the **Insert group**, click the **Text** button, and then click **WordArt**. Click anywhere between the words in the WordArt placeholder text, and then click one more time to display the sizing handles around the WordArt placeholder. Press [Command ⌘] + [A] to select the placeholder text.

a. On the **Format tab**, in the **Text Styles group**, click the **Quick Styles** button. Under **Applies to Selected Text**, in the second row, click the third style. With the text *Your text here* still selected, type **At Fascination Water Parks!**

(Project 2D Wave Rider continues on the next page)

Content-Based Assessments

Skills Review | Project **2D** Wave Rider (continued)

b. Click the border or one of the sizing handles of the Word Art to select the entire WordArt placeholder. On the **Home tab**, in the **Font group**, change the **Font Size** to **24**. With the WordArt selected, on the **Format tab**, in the **Arrange group**, click the **Align** button, and then click **Align Bottom**. Click the **Align** button again, and then click **Align Left** so that the WordArt is positioned in the lower left corner of the slide. **Save** your presentation.

c. Add a **Header and Footer** for the **Notes and Handouts** pages. Include the **Date and time updated automatically**, the **Page number**, and a **Footer** with the text **Lastname_Firstname_2D_Wave_Rider** and **Apply to All**.

d. Display the **File Properties**. In the **Subject** box, type your course name and section number. In the **Author** box, replace the text with your own firstname and lastname. In the **Keywords** box, type **water parks, wave rider** and then click **OK**. **Save** your presentation.

e. View the **Slide Show** from the start, make any necessary adjustments, and then **Save** your presentation. **Print Handouts (6 slides per page)**, or submit your presentation electronically as directed by your instructor. **Close** your presentation, and then **Quit PowerPoint**.

End **You have completed Project 2D** ————————————————————

Content-Based Assessments

Apply **2A** skills from these Objectives:

1 Format Numbered and Bulleted Lists

2 Insert Clip Art

3 Insert Text Boxes and Shapes

4 Format Objects

Mastering PowerPoint | Project **2E** Job Fair

In the following Mastering PowerPoint project, you will format a presentation describing employment opportunities at the Fascination Entertainment Group theme parks. Your completed presentation will look similar to Figure 2.61.

Project Files

For Project 2E, you will need the following file:

p02E_Job_Fair

You will save your presentation as:

Lastname_Firstname_2E_Job_Fair

Project Results

Figure 2.61

(Project 2E Job Fair continues on the next page)

Content-Based Assessments

Mastering PowerPoint | Project 2E Job Fair (continued)

1 Open **PowerPoint**. From the student files that accompany this textbook, **Open p02E_Job_Fair**. If necessary, increase the size of your window to fill the entire screen. If necessary, display the Rulers. **Save** the file in your **PowerPoint Chapter 2** folder as **Lastname_Firstname_2E_Job_Fair**

2 On **Slide 2**, remove the bullet symbol from the paragraph. Apply **Center Text** to the paragraph, set the **Line Spacing** to **1.5**, and then apply **Bold** and **Italic** to the text. With the content placeholder selected, display the **Shape Styles** gallery, and then in the second row, apply the last style.

3 On **Slide 3**, change the first-level bullet points—*Competitive pay and benefits, Flexible schedules,* and *Perks*—to a **Numbered List**. Under each of the numbered items, change all of the circle bullet symbols to **Checkmark Bullets**, and then change the bullet **Color** to **Accent 6, Darker 50%**—under Theme colors, the last row, the last color.

4 Click in the content placeholder on the right side of the slide. Use the **Clip Art Gallery** to search **Online** for images of **ferris wheel lights** and then **Download** a picture similar to the one displayed in Figure 2.61 at the beginning of this project. **Import** the picture and move it to your **Clip Gallery**, and then **Insert** the picture in your slide. Change the picture **Height** to **3.5** and then **Crop** to **Mask** to a **Shape** of a **Rounded Rectangle**. Modify the **Picture Effect** by applying the a **Glow** style of **Accent 2, 11 pt glow**—second row, first style.

5 Display **Slide 4**. **Insert** a **Shape**—under **Basic Shapes**, click **Bevel**—aligned with the **left half of the horizontal ruler at approximately 1 inch** and the **upper half of the**

vertical ruler at approximately 0.5 inches. Change the shape **Height** to **1** and the **Width** to **4** In the bevel, type **1-800-555-7854** and then change the **Font Size** to **28**.

6 On **Slide 4**, **Insert** a **Text Box** aligned with the **left half of the horizontal ruler at approximately 2 inches** and with the **upper half of the vertical ruler at approximately 2 inches**. In the text box, type **Be a part of our team!** On the **Format tab**, in the **Shape Styles** gallery, in the second row, click the first style. Change the **Font Size** to **28**.

7 Select the text box and the bevel shape, and then, using the **Align Selected Objects** option, apply **Align Center** alignment. Select the text box, the bevel shape, and the *Contact Human Resources Today!* placeholder, and then, using the **Align Selected Objects** option, **Distribute Vertically**. Apply the **Box** transition to all of the slides in the presentation. **Save** your presentation.

8 Add a **Header and Footer** for the **Notes and Handouts** pages. Include the **Date and time updated automatically**, the **Page number**, and a **Footer** with the text **Lastname_Firstname_2E_Job_Fair** and **Apply to All**.

9 Display the **File Properties**. In the **Subject** box, type your course name and section number. In the **Author** box, replace the text with your own firstname and lastname. In the **Keywords** box, type **employment** and then click **OK**. **Save** your presentation.

10 View the **Slide Show** from the start, make any necessary adjustments, and then **Save** your presentation. **Print Handouts (4 slides per page)**, or submit your presentation electronically as directed by your instructor. **Close** your presentation, and then **Quit PowerPoint**.

End You have completed Project 2E

Content-Based Assessments

Apply **2B** skills from
these Objectives:

5 Remove Picture
Backgrounds and
Insert WordArt

6 Create and Format a
SmartArt Graphic

Mastering PowerPoint | Project **2F** Attractions

In the following Mastering PowerPoint project, you will format a presentation describing new attractions at several of the Fascination Entertainment Group parks. Your completed presentation will look similar to Figure 2.62.

Project Files

For Project 2F, you will need the following file:

p02F_Attractions

You will save your presentation as:

Lastname_Firstname_2F_Attractions

Project Results

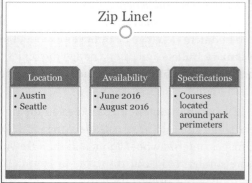

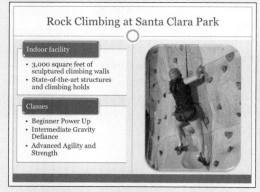

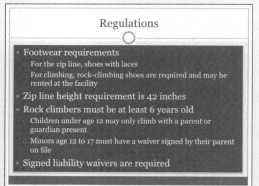

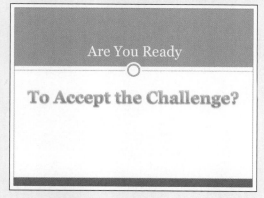

Figure 2.62

(Project 2F Attractions continues on the next page)

Content-Based Assessments

Mastering PowerPoint | Project **2F** Attractions (continued)

1 Open **PowerPoint**. From the student files that accompany this textbook, **Open p02F_Attractions**. If necessary, increase the size of your window to fill the entire screen. **Save** the presentation in your **PowerPoint Chapter 2** folder as **Lastname_Firstname_2F_Attractions**

2 On **Slide 1**, select the title—*Coming Attractions*. On the **Format tab**, in the **Text Styles group**, click the **Quick Styles** button. Under **Applies to Selected Text**, in the last row, apply the second WordArt style.

3 On **Slide 2**, in the content placeholder, insert a **List** type **SmartArt** graphic—**Horizontal Bullet List**. In the top-left rectangle, type **Location** and then in the two bullet points below *Location*, type **Austin** and **Seattle** In the top center rectangle, type **Availability** and then in the rectangle below *Availability*, type **June 2016** and **August 2016** In the top-right rectangle, type **Specifications** and then in the rectangle below *Specifications*, type **Courses located around park perimeters** Delete the extra bullet point.

4 Change the SmartArt color to **Colorful Range - Accent Colors 3 to 4**, and then in the **SmartArt Graphic Styles** gallery, apply the **Inset** style. Select the three upper rectangle shapes—*Location*, *Availability*, and *Specifications*—and then change the shapes to the **Snip Same Side Corner Rectangle** shape.

5 On **Slide 3**, change the bulleted list to a **SmartArt** graphic by applying the **Vertical Box List** graphic. Change

the SmartArt color to **Colorful Range - Accent Colors 3 to 4**, and then apply the **Polished SmartArt Graphic** style.

6 On **Slide 4**, select the content placeholder, and then from the **Shape Styles** gallery, in the third row, apply the last style.

7 On **Slide 5**, **Insert** a **WordArt**. Replace the WordArt placeholder text with **To Accept the Challenge?** Change the **Font Size** to **48**. Using **Quick Styles**, in the **Word Art** gallery, under **Applies to All Text in the Shape**, in the first row, click the third style.

8 Add a **Header and Footer** for the **Notes and Handouts** pages. Include the **Date and time updated automatically**, the **Page number**, and a **Footer** with the text **Lastname_Firstname_2F_Attractions** and **Apply to All**.

9 Display the **File Properties**. In the **Subject** box, type your course name and section number. In the **Author** box, replace the text with your own firstname and lastname. In the **Keywords** box, type **zip line, rock wall** and then click **OK**. **Save** your presentation.

10 View the **Slide Show** from the start, make any necessary adjustments, and then **Save** your presentation. **Print Handouts (6 slides per page)**, or submit your presentation electronically as directed by your instructor. **Close** your presentation, and then **Quit PowerPoint**.

End **You have completed Project 2F**

Apply **2A** and **2B** skills
from these Objectives:

1 Format Numbered
and Bulleted Lists

2 Insert Clip Art

3 Insert Text Boxes and
Shapes

4 Format Objects

5 Remove Picture
Backgrounds and
Insert WordArt

6 Create and Format a
SmartArt Graphic

Mastering PowerPoint | Project **2G** Orientation

In the following Mastering PowerPoint project, you will edit an existing presentation that is shown to Fascination Entertainment Group employees on their first day of a three-day orientation. Your completed presentation will look similar to Figure 2.63.

Project Files

For Project 2G, you will need the following files:

p02G_Orientation
p02G_Maya_Ruiz
p02G_David_Jensen
p02G_Ken_Lee

You will save your presentation as:

Lastname_Firstname_2G_Orientation

Project Results

Figure 2.63

(Project 2G Orientation continues on the next page)

Content-Based Assessments

Mastering PowerPoint | Project **2G** Orientation (continued)

1 Open **PowerPoint**, and then from your student data files, **Open p02G_Orientation**. If necessary, increase the size of your window to fill the entire screen. If necessary, display the Rulers. **Save** the presentation in your **PowerPoint Chapter 2** folder as Lastname_ Firstname_2G_Orientation

2 On **Slide 1**, format the title as **WordArt—Quick Styles**, **Applies to Selected Text**, in the first row, the fourth style. On the right side of the slide, select the five pictures, and then using the **Align to Slide** option, align the pictures by applying **Distribute Vertically** and **Align Right**. On **Slide 2**, change the **Shape Style** of the content placeholder to the second style in the last row.

3 On **Slide 3**, convert the bulleted list to the **Picture** type **SmartArt** graphic—**Title Picture Lineup**. Change the color to **Colorful - Accent Colors**, and then apply the **SmartArt Graphic Style** of **Inset**. In the three picture placeholders, from your student files insert the following pictures: **p02G_Maya_Ruiz**, **p02G_David_Jensen**, and **p02G_Ken_Lee**.

4 On **Slide 4**, change the two bulleted lists to a **Numbered List**. Then, **Insert** a **WordArt** with the text **8 a.m. to 4 p.m.** Drag the WordArt below the two content placeholders, and then **Align Center**. Change the WordArt style—**Quick Styles**, **Applies to Selected Text**, second row, third style. Apply a **Shape Style** to the WordArt—**Shape Styles** gallery, last row, second style.

5 On **Slide 5**, change the bullet symbols to **Checkmark Bullets**, and then in the placeholder on the right, **Insert** a **Clip Art** by using the **Clip Art Gallery** to search **Online** for **first aid kit Photos**. **Download**, **Import**, and **Insert** the picture of an open first aid box. Select the picture, and then below the picture in the **Cropping tools**, click the **Crop to Fit** button—the third button—to resize the picture fit in the placeholder. Use the **Remove Background** command to remove the background from the picture so that only the items in the kit display.

Mark areas to keep and remove as necessary. Change the **Height** to **4.5** and then apply the **Effect** using the **Glow** effect of **Accent 4, 18 pt glow**.

6 On **Slide 5**, **Insert** a **Text Box** aligned with the **left half of the horizontal ruler at approximately 4 inches** and with the **lower half of the vertical ruler at approximately 2.5 inches**. In the text box, type **All employees will be tested on park safety procedures!** Apply **Italic**, and then using the **Align to Slide** option, apply **Align Center**.

7 With **Slide 5** selected, insert a **New Slide** with the **Blank** layout. **Insert** a **Shape**—under **Basic Shapes**, click **Diamond**—of any size anywhere on the slide. Then, resize the diamond so that the **Height** is **6** and the **Width** is **8** Using the **Align to Slide** option, apply **Align Center** and **Align Middle**. In the **Shape Styles** gallery, on the second row, click the second style. In the diamond, type **Fascination Entertainment Group Welcomes You!** Change the **Font Size** to **40**, and then apply the **Effect** of **Bevel Art Deco** to the diamond shape. **Save** your presentation.

8 Add a **Header and Footer** for the **Notes and Handouts** pages. Include the **Date and time updated automatically**, the **Page number**, and a **Footer** with the text **Lastname_Firstname_2G_Orientation** and **Apply to All**.

9 Display the **File Properties**. In the **Subject** box, type your course name and section number. In the **Author** box, replace the text with your own firstname and lastname. In the **Keywords** box, type **orientation, employee training** and then click **OK**. **Save** your presentation.

10 View the **Slide Show** from the start, make any necessary adjustments, and then **Save** your presentation. **Print Handouts** (**6 slides per page**), or submit your presentation electronically as directed by your instructor. **Close** your presentation, and then **Quit PowerPoint**.

End **You have completed Project 2G**

Content-Based Assessments

GO! Fix It | Project **2H** Summer Jobs

Project Files

For Project 2H, you will need the following file:

p02H_Summer_Jobs

You will save your presentation as:

Lastname_Firstname_2H_Summer_Jobs

In this project, you will edit several slides from a presentation prepared by the Human Resources Department at Fascination Entertainment Group regarding summer employment opportunities. From the student files that accompany this textbook, open the file p02H_Summer_Jobs, and then save the file in your PowerPoint Chapter 2 folder as **Lastname_Firstname_2H_Summer_Jobs**

To complete the project, you should know:

- The Theme should be changed to Module, and two spelling errors should be corrected.
- On Slide 1, the pictures should be aligned with the top of the slide and distributed horizontally.
- On Slide 2, the bulleted list should be converted to a Vertical Box List SmartArt, and the Polished SmartArt Graphic style should be applied. The colors should be changed to Colorful Range - Accent Colors 4 to 5.
- On Slide 3, the bulleted list should be formatted as a numbered list.
- On Slide 4, insert a WordArt with the text **Apply Today!** In Quick Styles, under Applies to Selected Text, on the second row, click the third style. Position the WordArt centered approximately 1 inch below the title.
- Add a Header and Footer for the Notes and Handouts pages that includes the Date and time updated automatically, the Page number, and a Footer with the text **Lastname_Firstname_2H_Summer_Jobs** and apply to all.
- File Properties should include your course name and section number, your name, and the keywords **summer jobs, recruitment**

Save your presentation. View the slide show from the start, make any necessary adjustments, and then save the presentation. Print Handouts (4 slides per page), or submit your presentation electronically as directed by your instructor. Close your presentation, and then Quit PowerPoint.

End **You have completed Project 2H** ———————————————————

Content-Based Assessments

GO! Make It | Project 2I Renovation Plans

Project Files

For Project 2I, you will need the following file:

New Presentation

You will save your presentation as:

Lastname_Firstname_2I_Renovation_Plans

By using the skills you practiced in this chapter, create the first two slides of the presentation shown in Figure 2.64. Open PowerPoint to begin a new presentation, and apply the Urban Pop theme and the Breeze color theme. Type the title and subtitle shown in Figure 2.64, and then change the background style to Style 2 and the title font size to 36 and the subtitle font size to 28. Select the text in the title, and then in the WordArt gallery under Quick Styles, on the third row, apply the fourth style. Click the title placeholder, change the Width to **8** and then Align Center. Save the file in your PowerPoint Chapter 2 folder as **Lastname_Firstname_2I_Renovation_Plans**

To locate the picture on Slide 1, using the Clip Gallery, search online for images with the keyword **carnival rides** Resize the picture Height to 2 and then apply soft edges, duplicate, align, and distribute the images as shown in the figure.

Insert a new Slide 2 using the Content with Caption layout. Insert the Basic Matrix SmartArt graphic—located under Other—shown in Figure 2.64 and change the color and style as shown. Type the title and caption text, changing the title Font Size to 36 and the caption text Font Size to 20. Modify line spacing and apply formatting to the caption text as shown in Figure 2.64. Insert the date, file name, and page number in the Notes and Handouts footer. In the File Properties, add your course information, your name, and the keywords **renovation, goals** Save your presentation. View the slide show, make any necessary adjustments, and then Save your presentation. Print Handouts (2 slides per page), or submit your presentation electronically as directed by your instructor. Close your presentation, and then Quit PowerPoint.

Project Results

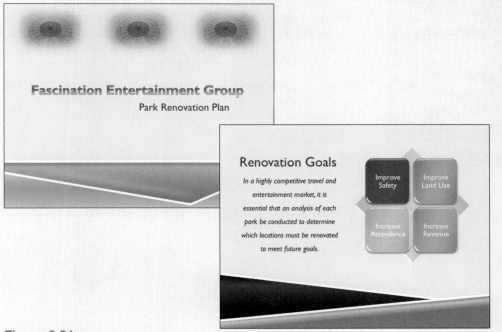

Figure 2.64

 You have completed Project 2I

Content-Based Assessments

GO! Solve It | Project **2J** Business Summary

Project Files

For Project 2J, you will need the following file:

p02J_Business_Summary

You will save your presentation as:

Lastname_Firstname_2J_Business_Summary

Open the file p02J_Business_Summary, and save it in your PowerPoint Chapter 2 folder as **Lastname_Firstname_2J_Business_Summary** Format the presentation attractively by applying appropriate font formatting and by changing text alignment and line spacing. Insert at least one clip art image and change the picture shape and effect. On Slide 2, align and format the text box and shape attractively, and insert a clip art image that can be duplicated, aligned, and distributed across the bottom edge of the slide. On Slide 3, insert an appropriate photo on the right. On Slide 4, convert the bulleted list to an appropriate SmartArt graphic and format the graphic appropriately. Apply slide transitions to all of the slides in the presentation and add a header and footer for the Notes and Handouts pages that includes the date and time updated automatically, the page number, and the file name in the footer. Add your course name and section number, your name, and the keywords **business summary, revenue** to the File Properties. View the slide show, save, and then print handouts or submit electronically as directed by your instructor. Close your presentation, and then Quit PowerPoint.

	Performance Level		
	Exemplary You consistently applied the relevant skills	**Proficient** You sometimes, but not always, applied the relevant skills	**Developing** You rarely or never applied the relevant skills
Insert and format appropriate clip art	Appropriate clip art was inserted and formatted in the presentation.	Clip art was inserted but was not appropriate for the presentation or was not formatted.	Clip art was not inserted.
Insert and format appropriate SmartArt graphic	Appropriate SmartArt graphic was inserted and formatted in the presentation.	SmartArt graphic was inserted but was not appropriate for the presentation or was not formatted.	SmartArt graphic was not inserted.
Format text boxes and shapes attractively	Text boxes and shapes were formatted attractively.	Text boxes and shapes were formatted but the formatting was inappropriately applied.	Inadequate or no formatting.
Insert transitions	Appropriate transitions were applied to all slides.	Transitions were applied to some, but not all slides.	Transitions were not applied.

Performance Criteria (vertical label at left of table)

End You have completed Project 2J ——————————

Content-Based Assessments

GO! Solve It | Project **2K** Hotel

Project Files

For Project 2K, you will need the following file:

p02K_Hotel

You will save your presentation as:

Lastname_Firstname_2K_Hotel

Open the file p02K_Hotel, and save it in your PowerPoint Chapter 2 folder as **Lastname_ Firstname_2K_Hotel** Complete the presentation by inserting a clip art image on the first slide and applying appropriate picture effects. On Slide 2, format the bullet point as a single paragraph. On Slide 3, convert the bulleted list to an appropriate SmartArt graphic, change the SmartArt color, and apply a style. On Slide 4, insert and attractively position a WordArt with the text **Save the Date!** Apply slide transitions to all of the slides. Add a header and footer that includes the date and time updated automatically, the page number, and the file name in the footer. Add your course name and section number, your name, and the keywords **hotel, accommodations** to the File Properties. View the slide show, save, and then print handouts or submit electronically as directed by your instructor. Close your presentation, and then Quit PowerPoint.

<table>
<tr><td rowspan="2"></td><td colspan="3">Performance Level</td></tr>
<tr><td>Exemplary
You consistently applied the relevant skills</td><td>Proficient
You sometimes, but not always, applied the relevant skills</td><td>Developing
You rarely or never applied the relevant skills</td></tr>
<tr><td>Insert and format appropriate clip art</td><td>Appropriate clip art was inserted and formatted in the presentation.</td><td>Clip art was inserted but was not appropriate for the presentation or was not formatted.</td><td>Clip art was not inserted.</td></tr>
<tr><td>Insert and format appropriate SmartArt graphic</td><td>Appropriate SmartArt graphic was inserted and formatted in the presentation.</td><td>SmartArt graphic was inserted but was not appropriate for the presentation or was not formatted.</td><td>SmartArt graphic was not inserted.</td></tr>
<tr><td>Insert and format appropriate WordArt</td><td>Appropriate WordArt was inserted and formatted in the presentation.</td><td>WordArt was inserted but was not appropriate for the presentation or was not formatted.</td><td>WordArt was not inserted.</td></tr>
<tr><td>Insert transitions</td><td>Appropriate transitions were applied to all slides.</td><td>Transitions were applied to some, but not all slides.</td><td>Transitions were not applied.</td></tr>
</table>

Performance Criteria

End You have completed Project 2K ——————————————

Outcomes-Based Assessments

Rubric

The following outcomes-based assessments are open-ended assessments. That is, there is no specific correct result; your result will depend on your approach to the information provided. Make Professional Quality your goal. Use the following scoring rubric to guide you in how to approach the problem and then to evaluate how well your approach solves the problem.

The *criteria*—Software Mastery, Content, Format and Layout, and Process—represent the knowledge and skills you have gained that you can apply to solving the problem. The *levels of performance*—Professional Quality, Approaching Professional Quality, or Needs Quality Improvements—help you and your instructor evaluate your result.

	Your completed project is of Professional Quality if you:	Your completed project is Approaching Professional Quality if you:	Your completed project Needs Quality Improvements if you:
1-Software Mastery	Choose and apply the most appropriate skills, tools, and features and identify efficient methods to solve the problem.	Choose and apply some appropriate skills, tools, and features, but not in the most efficient manner.	Choose inappropriate skills, tools, or features, or are inefficient in solving the problem.
2-Content	Construct a solution that is clear and well organized, contains content that is accurate, appropriate to the audience and purpose, and is complete. Provide a solution that contains no errors in spelling, grammar, or style.	Construct a solution in which some components are unclear, poorly organized, inconsistent, or incomplete. Misjudge the needs of the audience. Have some errors in spelling, grammar, or style, but the errors do not detract from comprehension.	Construct a solution that is unclear, incomplete, or poorly organized; contains some inaccurate or inappropriate content; and contains many errors in spelling, grammar, or style. Do not solve the problem.
3-Format and Layout	Format and arrange all elements to communicate information and ideas, clarify function, illustrate relationships, and indicate relative importance.	Apply appropriate format and layout features to some elements, but not others. Overuse features, causing minor distraction.	Apply format and layout that does not communicate information or ideas clearly. Do not use format and layout features to clarify function, illustrate relationships, or indicate relative importance. Use available features excessively, causing distraction.
4-Process	Use an organized approach that integrates planning, development, self-assessment, revision, and reflection.	Demonstrate an organized approach in some areas, but not others; or, use an insufficient process of organization throughout.	Do not use an organized approach to solve the problem.

Apply a combination of the **2A** and **2B** skills.

GO! Think | Project **2L** Interactive Ride

Project Files

For Project 2L, you will need the following files:

New Presentation

You will save your presentation as:

Lastname_Firstname_2L_Interactive_Ride

As part of its mission to combine fun with the discovery of math and science, Fascination Entertainment Group (FEG) is opening a new interactive roller coaster at its South Lake Tahoe location. FEG's newest roller coaster is designed for maximum thrill and minimum risk. In a special interactive exhibit located next to the coaster, riders can learn about the physics behind this powerful roller coaster and even try their hand at building a roller coaster.

Guests will begin by setting the height of the first hill, which determines the roller coaster's maximum potential energy to complete its journey. Next they will set the exit path and build additional hills, loops, and corkscrews. When completed, riders can submit their roller coaster for a safety inspection to find out whether the ride passes or fails.

In either case, riders can also take a virtual tour of the ride they created to see the maximum speed achieved, the amount of negative G-forces applied, the length of the track, and the overall thrill factor. They can also see how their roller coaster compares with other roller coasters in the FEG family, and they can email the roller coaster simulation to their friends.

Using the preceding information, create a presentation that Marketing Director, Annette Chosek, can use at a travel fair describing the new attraction. The presentation should include four to six slides with at least one SmartArt graphic and one clip art image. Apply an appropriate theme, use slide layouts that will effectively present the content, and use text boxes, shapes, and WordArt if appropriate. Apply font formatting and slide transitions, and modify text alignment and line spacing as necessary. Save the file in your PowerPoint Chapter 2 folder as **Lastname_Firstname_2L_Interactive_Ride** Add a header and footer that includes the date and time updated automatically, the page number, and the file name in the footer. Add your course name and section number, your name, and the keywords **roller coaster, new rides** to the File Properties. View the slide show, save, and then print handouts or submit electronically as directed by your instructor. Close your presentation, and then Quit PowerPoint.

End **You have completed Project 2L** ————————————————

Outcomes-Based Assessments

GO! Think | Project 2M Research

Project Files

For Project 2M, you will need the following file:

New Presentation

You will save your presentation as:

Lastname_Firstname_2M_Research

As the number of theme park vacations continues to rise, Fascination Entertainment Group (FEG) is developing plans to ensure that its top theme parks are a true vacation destination. FEG research has verified that visitors use several factors in determining their theme park destinations: top attractions, overall value, and nearby accommodations.

Visitors, regardless of age, look for thrills and entertainment at a good value. FEG owns four of North America's top 15 roller coasters and two of its top 10 water parks, thus making the parks prime attraction destinations. Typical costs for visitors include park entrance fees, food and beverages, souvenirs, transportation, and lodging. Beginning this year, FEG will offer vacation packages. Package pricing will vary depending on number of adults, number of children, length of stay, and number of parks attended (i.e., theme park, water park, and zoo). Each park will continue to offer annual passes at a discount.

Research shows that visitors who travel more than 100 miles one way will consider the need for nearby accommodations. For its top 10 theme parks, FEG will open hotels at parks that do not currently have them within the next two years. Until then, the company will partner with area hotels to provide discounts to theme park visitors.

Using the preceding information, create the first four slides of a presentation that the Fascination Entertainment Group marketing director can show at an upcoming board of directors meeting. Apply an appropriate theme and use slide layouts that will effectively present the content. Include clip art and at least one SmartArt graphic. Apply font and WordArt formatting, picture styles, and slide transitions, and modify text alignment and line spacing as necessary. If appropriate, insert and format a text box or a shape. Save your presentation in your PowerPoint Chapter 2 folder as **Lastname_Firstname_2M_Research** Add a header and footer that includes the date and time updated automatically, the page number, and the file name in the footer. Add your course name and section number, your name, and the keywords **visitor preferences, research findings** to the File Properties. View the slide show, save, and then print handouts or submit electronically as directed by your instructor. Close your presentation, and then Quit PowerPoint.

End **You have completed Project 2M** ————————————————

Outcomes-Based Assessments

You and GO! | Project **2N** Theme Park

Project Files

For Project 2N, you will need the following file:

New Presentation

You will save your presentation as:

Lastname_Firstname_2N_Theme_Park

Research your favorite theme park and create a presentation with at least six slides that describes the park, its top attractions, nearby accommodations, and the reasons why you enjoy the park. Choose an appropriate theme, slide layouts, and pictures, and format the presentation attractively, including at least one SmartArt graphic and one WordArt object or shape. Save your presentation as Lastname_Firstname_2N_Theme_Park and submit as directed.

 You have completed Project 2N ——————————————

GO! Group Business Running Case | Project **2O**
Bell Orchid Hotels Group Running Case

This project relates to the **Bell Orchid Hotels**. Your instructor may assign this group case project to your class. If your instructor assigns this project, he or she will provide you with information and instructions to work as part of a group. The group will apply the skills gained thus far to help the Bell Orchid Hotels achieve their business goals.

 You have completed Project 2O ——————————————

Enhancing a Presentation with Animation, Movies, Tables, and Charts

OUTCOMES
At the end of this chapter you will be able to:

OBJECTIVES
Mastering these objectives will enable you to:

PROJECT 3A
Customize a presentation with animation and movies.

1. Customize Slide Backgrounds and Themes (p. 559)
2. Animate a Slide Show (p. 566)
3. Insert a Movie (p. 572)

PROJECT 3B
Create a presentation that includes data in tables and charts.

4. Create and Modify Tables (p. 578)
5. Create and Modify Charts (p. 584)

© megumi ito/Shutterstock

In This Chapter

Recall that a presentation theme applies a consistent look to a presentation. You can customize a presentation by modifying the theme and by applying animation to slide elements, and you can enhance your presentations by creating tables and charts that help your audience understand numeric data and trends just as pictures and diagrams help illustrate a concept. The data that you present should determine whether a table or a chart would most appropriately display your information. Styles applied to your tables and charts unify these slide elements by complementing your presentation theme.

The projects in this chapter relate to **Golden Grove**, a growing city located between Los Angeles and San Diego. Just 10 years ago, the population was under 100,000; today, it has grown to almost 300,000. Community leaders have always focused on quality and economic development in decisions on housing, open space, education, and infrastructure, making the city a model for other communities its size around the United States. The city provides many recreational and cultural opportunities with a large park system, thriving arts, and a friendly business atmosphere.

Project 3A Informational Presentation

Project Activities

In Activities 3.01 through 3.10, you will edit and format a presentation that Mindy Walker, Director of Golden Grove Parks and Recreation, has created to inform residents about the benefits of using the city's parks and trails. Your completed presentation will look similar to Figure 3.1.

Project Files

For Project 3A, you will need the following files:

p03A_Park
p03A_Pets
p03A_Trails
p03A_Walking_Trails
p03A_Trails_Video.mov

You will save your presentation as:

Lastname_Firstname_3A_Walking_Trails

Project Results

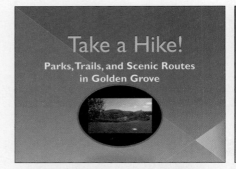
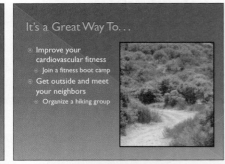

Figure 3.1
Project 3A Walking Trails

Objective 1 | Customize Slide Backgrounds and Themes

You have practiced customizing presentations by applying themes with unified design elements, backgrounds, and colors that provide a consistent look in your presentation. Additional ways to customize a slide include changing theme fonts and colors, applying a background style, modifying the background color, or inserting a picture on the slide background.

Activity 3.01 | Changing the Theme Colors and Theme Fonts

Recall that the presentation theme is a coordinated, predefined set of colors, fonts, lines, and fill effects. In this activity, you will open a presentation in which the Verve theme is applied, and then you will change the *theme colors*—a set of coordinating colors that are applied to the backgrounds, objects, and text in a presentation.

In addition to theme colors, every presentation theme includes *theme fonts* that determine the font to apply to two types of slide text—headings and body. The *Headings font* is applied to slide titles and the *Body font* is applied to all other text. When you apply a new theme font to the presentation, the text on every slide is updated with the new heading and body fonts.

1 Open **PowerPoint**. From the student files that accompany this textbook, locate and **Open p03A_Walking_Trails**. If necessary, increase the size of your window to fill the entire screen. On the **File** menu, click **Save As**, and then navigate to the location where you are storing your projects for this chapter. Create a **New Folder** named **PowerPoint Chapter 3** and then in the **Save As** box and using your own name, type **Lastname_Firstname_3A_Walking Trails** Click **Save** or press Return.

2 Click the **Themes tab**, and then in the **Theme Options group**, click the **Colors** button to display a list of theme colors. If necessary, scroll the list, and then click **Genesis** to change the theme colors.

> Changing the theme colors does not change the overall design of the presentation. In this presentation, the *Verve* presentation theme is still applied to the presentation. By modifying the theme colors, you retain the design of the *Verve* theme. The colors of the *Genesis* theme, which coordinate with the pictures in the presentation, are available as text, accent, and background colors.

3 With **Slide 1** displayed, click anywhere in the title placeholder. Click the **Home tab**, and then in the **Font group**, click the **Font button arrow**. Notice that at the top of the list, Century Gothic (Theme Headings) and Century Gothic (Theme Body) display. Compare your screen with Figure 3.2.

Figure 3.2

Theme fonts

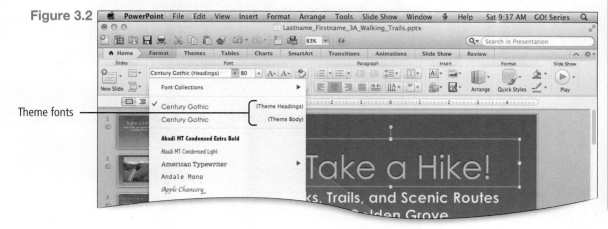

4 Click anywhere on the slide to close the Font list. Click the **Themes tab**, and then in the **Theme Options group**, click the **Fonts** button.

This list displays the name of each theme and the pair of fonts in the theme. The first and larger font in each pair is the Headings font and the second and smaller font in each pair is the Body font.

5 Scroll to the bottom of the list and click **Urban Pop**. Compare your screen with Figure 3.3, and then **Save** 🖫 your presentation.

Figure 3.3

Theme Colors applied to presentation

Theme Fonts applied to presentation

Activity 3.02 | Applying a Background Style

1 With **Slide 1** displayed, on the **Themes tab**, in the **Theme Options group**, click the **Background** button to display the **Background styles** gallery. Compare your screen with Figure 3.4.

A *background style* is a slide background fill variation that combines theme colors in different intensities or patterns.

Figure 3.4

Background button

Background styles gallery—click a style to apply to all slides

Click to open Format Background dialog box to apply background to one or more slides

Click to hide the background graphics on the selected slide

2 Under the gallery of background styles, click **Format Background**. In the **Format Background** dialog box, with the **Solid tab** active, click in the **Color** box. Under **Theme Colors**, on the first row, click the fourth color—**Text 2**—and then click **Apply**. Compare your screen with Figure 3.5.

> The background style is applied only to Slide 1.

Figure 3.5

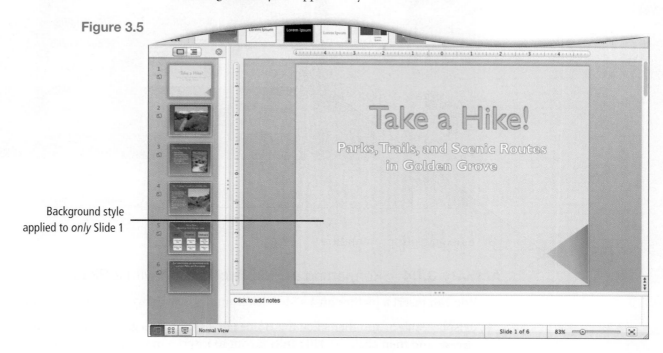

Background style applied to *only* Slide 1

3 Save your presentation.

More Knowledge | Applying Background Styles to All Slides in a Presentation

To change the background style for all of the slides in the presentation, click the background style that you want to apply and the style will be applied to every slide. Or, in the Format Background dialog box, click Apply to All.

Activity 3.03 | Hiding Background Graphics

Many of the PowerPoint 2011 themes contain graphic elements that display on the slide background. In the Verve theme that is applied to this presentation, the background includes a triangle and lines that intersect near the lower right corner of the slide. Sometimes the background graphics interfere with the slide content. When this happens, you can hide the background graphics.

1 Display **Slide 6**, and notice that on this slide, you can clearly see the triangles and lines on the slide background.

> You cannot delete these objects because they are a part of the slide background; however, you can hide them.

2 Display **Slide 5**, and notice that the background graphics distract from the connecting lines on the diagram. On the **Themes tab**, in the **Theme Options group**, click the **Background** button. Under the gallery of background styles, click **Hide Background Graphics**, and then compare your slide with Figure 3.6.

> The background objects no longer display behind the SmartArt diagram on Slide 5.

Figure 3.6

Background graphics do
not display on Slide 5

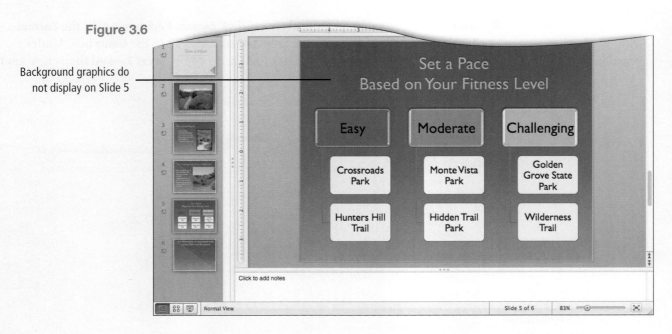

3 **Save** 💾 your presentation.

Activity 3.04 | Formatting a Slide Background with a Picture

You can insert a picture on a slide background so the image fills the entire slide.

1 Display **Slide 3**, and then click the **Home tab**. In the **Slides group**, click the **New Slide arrow**, and then click the **Title Only** layout to insert a new slide after Slide 3.

2 With the new **Slide 4** displayed, click the **Themes tab**. In the **Theme Options group**, click the **Background** button, and then click **Hide Background Graphics**. Click the **Background** button again, and then click **Format Background**.

> In the Format Background dialog box, you can customize a slide background by changing the formatting options.

3 In the **Format Background** dialog box, if necessary, on the left side of the dialog box, click **Fill**. In the **Format Background** dialog box, click the **Picture or Texture tab**. Compare your screen with Figure 3.7.

Figure 3.7

Format Background
dialog box

Picture or Texture
tab active

Hide Background Graphics
selected for Slide 4

New Slide 4 selected

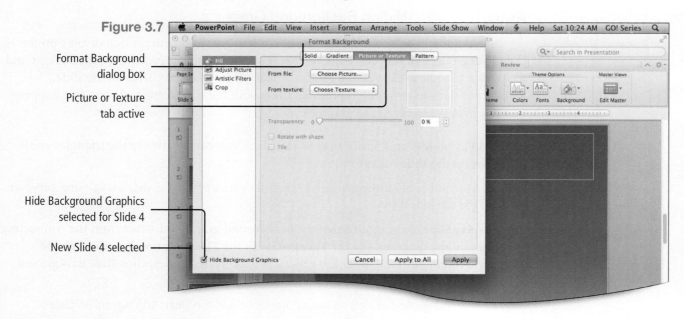

4 To the right of **From file**, click in the **Choose Picture** box. Navigate to your student files, and then click **p03A_Pets**. Click **Insert**, and then at the bottom of the **Format Background** dialog box, click **Apply**. Compare your screen with Figure 3.8, and notice that the picture displays as the background of **Slide 4**.

> When a picture is applied to a slide background using the Format Background option, the picture is not treated as an object. The picture fills the background and you cannot move it or size it.

Figure 3.8

Picture inserted on slide background

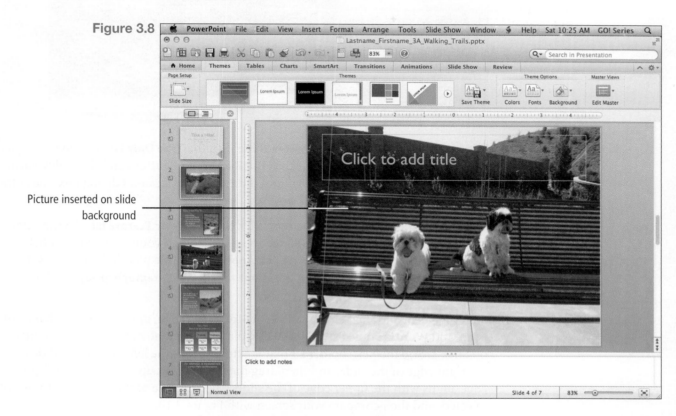

5 Click in the title placeholder, type **Find a Pet Friendly Trail** and then notice that the background picture does not provide sufficient contrast with the text to display the title effectively.

6 With your insertion point still in the title placeholder, click the **Format tab**. In the **Shape Styles group**, click the **Fill arrow**. Under **Theme Colors**, on the last row, click the fifth color—**Accent 1, Darker 50%**. Select the title text, and then on the **Format tab**, in the **Text Styles group**, click the **Quick Styles** button. In the first row, click the third style. On the **Home tab**, in the **Paragraph group**, click the **Center Text** button.

> The green fill color and the white WordArt quick style provide good contrast against the slide background so that the text is readable.

7 Point to the outer edge of the title placeholder to display the pointer, and then drag the placeholder upward and to the left so that its upper left corner aligns with the upper left corner of the slide. Point to the center right sizing handle and drag to the right so that the placeholder extends to the right edge of the slide. Click outside of the placeholder, and then compare your screen with Figure 3.9.

PowerPoint | Chapter 3

Figure 3.9

Title placeholder moved
and resized; fill color
applied

Text centered and
WordArt quick
style applied

8 Display **Slide 5**, and then insert a **New Slide** with the **Title Only** layout. On the **Themes tab**, in the **Theme Options group**, click the **Background** button, and then click **Format Background**. In the lower left corner of the **Format Background** dialog box, select the **Hide Background Graphics** check box.

9 In the **Format Background** dialog box, click the **Picture or Texture tab**. To the right of **From file**, click in the **Choose Picture** box, navigate to your student files, click **p03A_Trails**, click **Insert**, and then click **Apply**. In the title placeholder, type **Get Outside! Get Fit! Get Walking!** On the **Home tab**, in the **Paragraph group**, click the **Center Text** button ☰.

10 Select the text, and then change the **Font Size** to **36**. Then, apply the same **Shape Fill** color and **WordArt** quick style to the title placeholder that you applied to the title on **Slide 4**. Size the placeholder so that it extends from the left edge of the slide to the right edge of the slide, and then drag the placeholder upward so that its upper edge aligns with the upper edge of the slide. Click outside of the title so that it is not selected, and then compare your screen with Figure 3.10.

The green fill color and white text provide good contrast with the slide background and complement the green color of the grass on the slide.

Figure 3.10

Title placeholder sized,
moved, and fill
color applied

Font size changed, text
centered, and WordArt
quick style applied

Picture inserted as
slide background

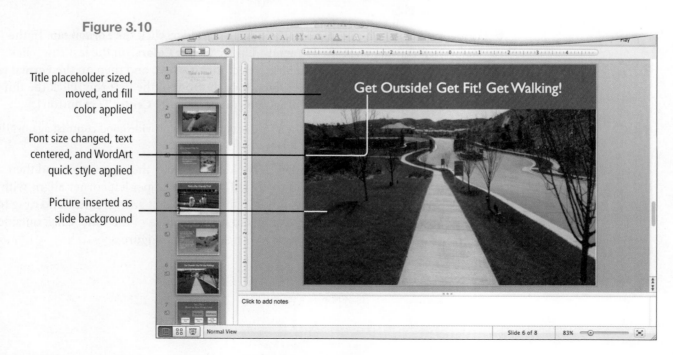

11 Display **Slide 8**, and then format the slide **Background** with a picture from your student files—**p03A_Park**. By using the **Background** button or the **Format Background** dialog box, **Hide Background Graphics**.

12 Select the title placeholder. On the **Format tab**, in the **Shape Styles group**, point to the bottom of the **Shape Styles** gallery, and then click the **More** button ▾. In the **Shape Styles** gallery, in the second row, click the sixth style.

13 Select the text, and then in the **Text Styles group**, click the **Quick Styles** button. In the **WordArt** gallery, on the first row, click the third style. Click outside of the placeholder, and then compare your screen with Figure 3.11. **Save** 🖫 the presentation.

Figure 3.11

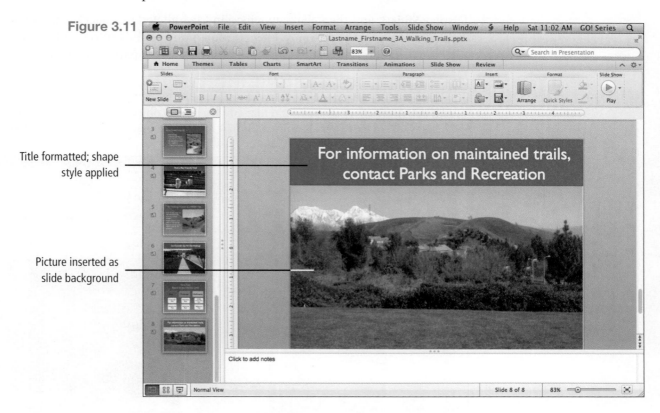

Title formatted; shape style applied

Picture inserted as slide background

Activity 3.05 | Applying a Background Fill Color and Resetting a Slide Background

1 Display **Slide 1**, and then click the **Themes tab**. In the **Theme Options group**, click the **Background** button, and then click **Format Background**.

2 In the **Format Background** dialog box, with **Fill** selected at the left and the **Solid tab** active, click in the **Color** box. Under **Theme Colors**, in the second row, click the first color—**Background 1, Lighter 50%**. Click **Apply**.

The solid fill color is applied to the slide background.

3 On the **Themes tab**, in the **Theme Options group**, click the **Background** button, and then click **Format Background**. In the **Format Background** dialog box, with the **Solid tab** active, click in the **Color** box, click **Automatic**, and then click **Apply**. **Save** 🖫 your presentation.

After making many changes to a slide background, you may decide that the original theme formatting is the best choice for displaying the text and graphics on a slide. The Automatic color feature restores the original color theme formatting to a slide.

Objective 2 | Animate a Slide Show

Animation is a visual or sound effect added to an object or text on a slide. Animation can focus the audience's attention, providing the speaker with an opportunity to emphasize important points using the slide element as an effective visual aid.

Activity 3.06 | Applying Animation Entrance Effects and Effect Options

Entrance effects are animations that bring a slide element onto the screen. You can modify an entrance effect by using the animation Effect Options command.

1 Display **Slide 3**, and then click anywhere in the bulleted list placeholder. On the **Animations tab**, in the **Entrance Effects group**, point to the bottom of the **Entrance Effects** gallery, and then click the **More** button ▾. Compare your screen with Figure 3.12.

> Recall that an entrance effect is animation that brings an object or text onto the screen. An *emphasis effect* is animation that emphasizes an object or text that is already displayed. An *exit effect* is animation that moves an object or text off the screen.

Figure 3.12

Emphasis Effects

Exit Effects

Entrance Effects gallery

More button

2 Under **Basic**, click **Split**, and then notice the animation is applied to the list. Compare your screen with Figure 3.13.

> The numbers *1* and *2* display to the left of the bulleted list placeholder, indicating the order in which the bullet points will be animated during the slide show. For example, the first bullet point and its subordinate bullet are both numbered *1*. Thus, both will display at the same time.

Figure 3.13

Split entrance effect selected

Highlighted numbers indicate animation order

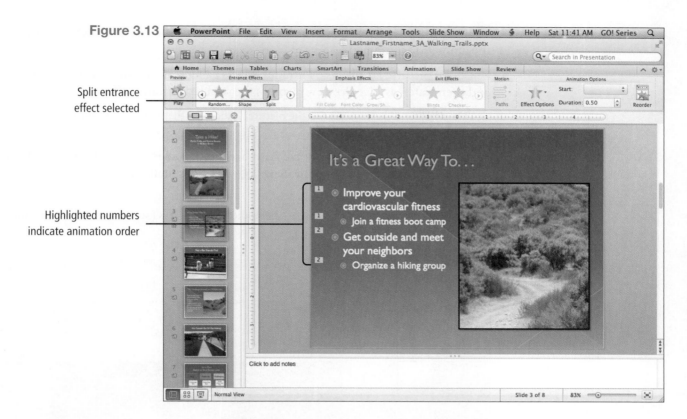

3 In the **Animation Options group**, click the **Effect Options** button, and then compare your screen with Figure 3.14.

Effect Options control the direction and sequence in which the animation displays. Additional options may be available with other entrance effects.

Figure 3.14

Effect Options button

Effect Options list

Animation order numbers are selected

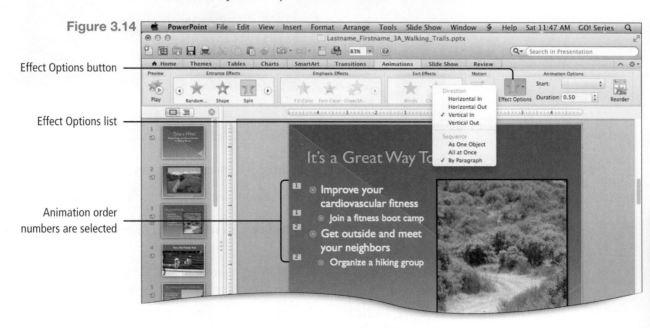

Alert! | Is the Effect Options Button Unavailable?

If the Effect Options button is dimmed or unavailable, you may have clicked in the slide and deselected the numbers that indicate the animation order. Hold down Shift and click each of numbers to select them all, and then the Effect Options button will be available.

PowerPoint | Chapter 3

4 On the list, under **Direction**, click **Vertical Out**, and notice the direction from which the animation is applied.

5 Select the picture. Display the **Entrance Effects** gallery. Under **Basic**, click **Dissolve In**, and then watch as Live Preview displays the selected entrance effect.

> The number *3* displays next to the picture, indicating that it is third in the slide animation sequence.

6 Select the title, and then display the **Entrance Effects** gallery. Under **Basic**, click **Split** to apply the animation to the title. **Save** your presentation, and then compare your screen with Figure 3.15.

> The number *4* displays next to the title, indicating that it is fourth in the slide animation sequence.

Figure 3.15

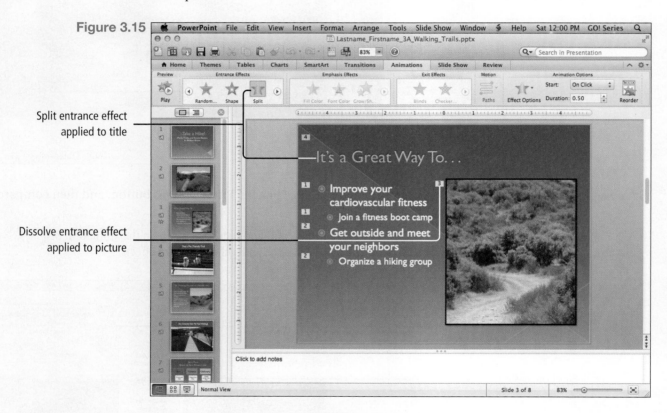

Split entrance effect applied to title

Dissolve entrance effect applied to picture

Activity 3.07 | Setting Animation Timing Options

Timing options control when animated items display in the animation sequence.

1 With **Slide 3** displayed, on the **Animations tab**, in the **Preview group**, click the **Play** button.

> The list displays first, followed by the picture, and then the title. The order in which animation is applied is the order in which objects display during the slide show.

2 If necessary, to the left of the title, click the number **4** to select the animation order for the title. On the **Animations tab**, in the **Animation Options group**, click the **Reorder** button. In the **Custom Animation** tool, click the **up arrow** button two times, and then compare your screen with Figure 3.16.

> To the left of the title placeholder, the number *1* displays. You can use the Reorder button to change the order in which text and objects are animated during the slide show.

Figure 3.16

Custom Animation tool

Animation reordered so that the title displays first

Moves selected element up in animation order

Moves selected element down in animation order

Removes the animation effect from the selected element

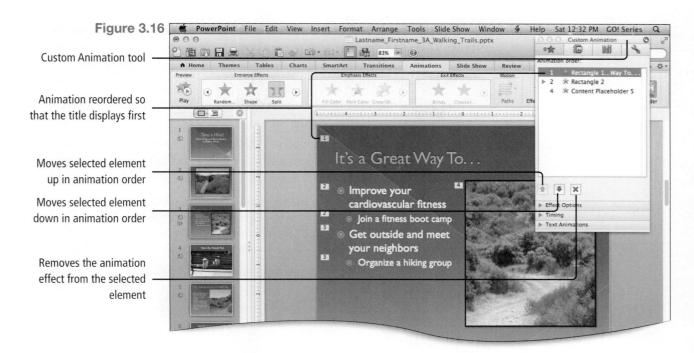

3 **Close**  the **Custom Animation** tool. With the title's animation order—**1**—selected, on the **Animations tab**, in the **Animation Options group**, click in the **Start** box to display three options—*On Click*, *With Previous*, and *After Previous*. Compare your screen with Figure 3.17.

> The ***On Click*** option begins the animation sequence for the selected slide element when the mouse is clicked, or Spacebar or → is pressed. The ***With Previous*** option begins the animation sequence at the same time as the previous animation or slide transition. The ***After Previous*** option begins the animation sequence for the selected slide element immediately after the completion of the previous animation or slide transition.

Figure 3.17

Start options

Selected animation—title

4 Click **After Previous**, and then notice that the number *1* is changed to *0*, indicating that the animation will begin immediately after the slide transition; the presenter does not need to click the mouse or press a key to display the title.

5 Select the picture's animation order—**3**—and then in the **Animation Options group**, click in the **Start** box. Click **With Previous** and notice that the number changes to *2*, indicating that the animation will begin at the same time as the second set of bullet points in the bulleted list.

6 On the **Animations tab**, in the **Preview group**, click the **Play** button, and notice that the title displays first and that the picture displays at the same time as the second set of bullet points.

7 Display **Slide 1**, and then click in the title placeholder. On the **Animations tab**, in the **Entrance Effects group**, in the **Entrance Effects** gallery, click **Fly In**. In the **Animation Options group**, click the **Effect Options button**, and then click **From Top**. In the **Animations Options group**, click in the **Start** box, and then click **After Previous**.

The number *0* displays to the left of the title indicating that the animation will begin immediately after the slide transition.

8 With the title's animation order still selected, in the **Animation Options group**, double-click in the **Duration** box to select the text, and then type **0.25** Compare your screen with Figure 3.18.

Duration controls the speed of the animation. You can set the duration of an animation by typing a value in the Duration box, or you can use the spin box arrows to increase and decrease the duration in 0.10-second increments. When you decrease the duration, the animation speed increases. When you increase the duration, the animation is slowed.

Figure 3.18

Fly In animation applied to title

Duration set to *0.25*

0 displays to the left of title placeholder

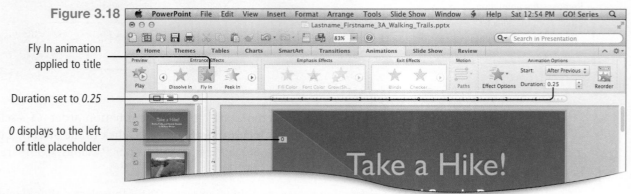

9 Select the subtitle, and then in the **Entrance Effects group**, apply the **Fly In** entrance effect. In the **Animation Options group**, click in the **Start** box, and then click **After Previous**. In the **Animation Options group**, click the **Reorder** button. In the **Custom Animation** tool, click **Timing**. Double-click in the **Delay** box to select the text, type **0.50** and then compare your screen with Figure 3.19.

You can use Delay to begin a selected animation after a specified amount of time has elapsed. Here, the animation is delayed by one-half of a second after the completion of the previous animation—the title animation. You can type a value in the Delay box, or you can use the spin arrows to change the timing.

Figure 3.19

Fly In entrance effect applied to subtitle

Animation starts After Previous animation

Delay set to 0.50 seconds

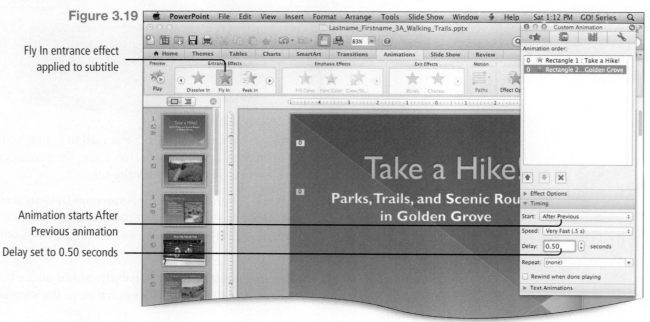

10 **Close** the **Custom Animation** tool. On the **Slide Show tab**, in the **Play Slide Show group**, click the **From Start** button to view the slide show from the beginning and notice the animation on **Slides 1** and **3**. When the black slide displays, press Esc to return to Normal view, and then **Save** your presentation.

Activity 3.08 | Applying More Animation and Removing Animation

1 Display **Slide 5**, and then click anywhere in the bulleted list placeholder. On the **Animations tab**, in the **Entrance Effects group**, apply the **Split** effect. In the **Animation Options group**, click the **Effect Options** button, and then click **Vertical Out**.

2 On **Slide 5**, click the picture. In the **Entrance Effects group**, apply the **Dissolve In** effect. In the **Animation Options group**, click in the **Start** box, and then click **With Previous**. Compare your screen with Figure 3.20.

The numbers displayed to the left of the bulleted list and the picture indicate that animation is applied to the objects.

Figure 3.20

Dissolve In entrance effect starting With Previous animation applied to picture

Animation applied to bulleted list

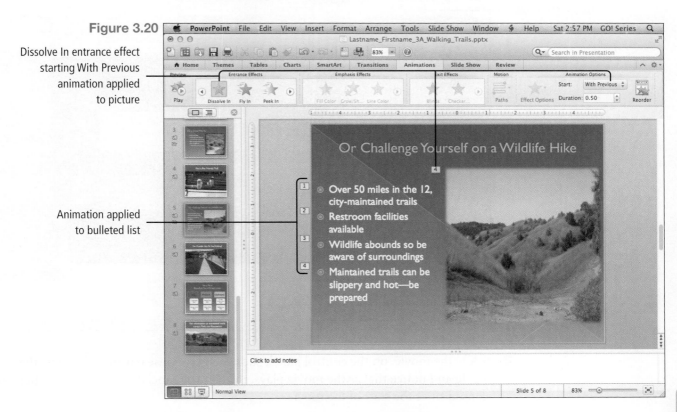

Another Way

With the animation order number selected, in the Animation Options group, click the Reorder button. In the Custom Animation tool, click the X button to remove the animation.

3 Display **Slide 3**, and then click in the title's animation order number—**0**. Press Delete to remove the animation from the title, and then **Save** your presentation.

Objective 3 | Insert a Movie

You can insert, size, and move movies in a PowerPoint presentation, and you can format movies by applying styles and effects.

Activity 3.09 | Inserting a Movie

1 Display **Slide 1**. On the **Home tab**, in the **Insert group**, click the **Media** button ▣▾, and then click **Movie from File**. In the **Choose a Movie** dialog box, navigate to your student files, and then click **p03A_Trails_Video.mov**. Click **Insert**, and then compare your screen with Figure 3.21.

The movie fills most of the slide, and playback and volume controls display in the control panel below the movie. The Format Movie tab displays on the Ribbon.

Figure 3.21

Format Movie tab

Movie inserted

Control panel for playback and volume

2 Below the movie, on the control panel, click the **Play/Pause** button ▶ to view the movie and notice that as the movie plays, the control panel displays the time that has elapsed since the start of the movie.

3 On the **Format Movie tab**, in the **Size group**, triple-click in the **Height** box to select the existing value, type **3** and then press ⏎. Notice that the movie width adjusts proportionately.

4 Point to the movie to display the ✥ pointer, and then drag the movie downward so that the top of the movie is aligned at approximately **0.25 inches on the lower part of the vertical ruler**. Use the arrow keys on your keyboard to nudge the movie as necessary. On the **Format Movie tab**, in the **Arrange group**, click the **Align** button ▤, and then click **Align Center** to center the movie horizontally on the slide. Compare your screen with Figure 3.22.

Figure 3.22

Movie Height changed

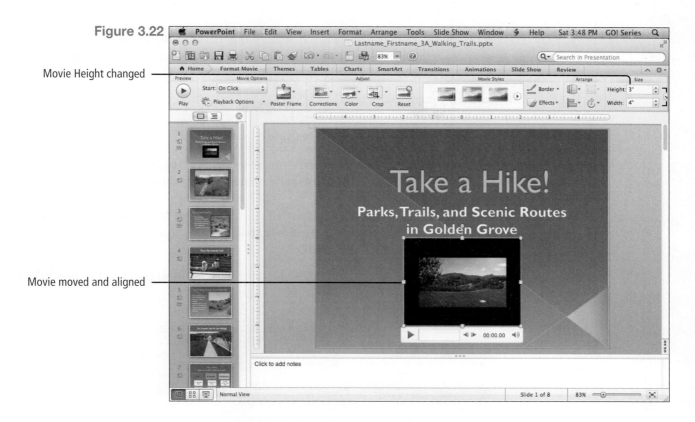

Movie moved and aligned

5 In the lower left corner of the status bar, click the **Slide Show** button to display **Slide 1** in the slide show.

6 Point to the movie to display the pointer, and then compare your screen with Figure 3.23.

When you point to the movie during the slide show, the control panel displays.

Figure 3.23

Slide 1 in Slide Show view

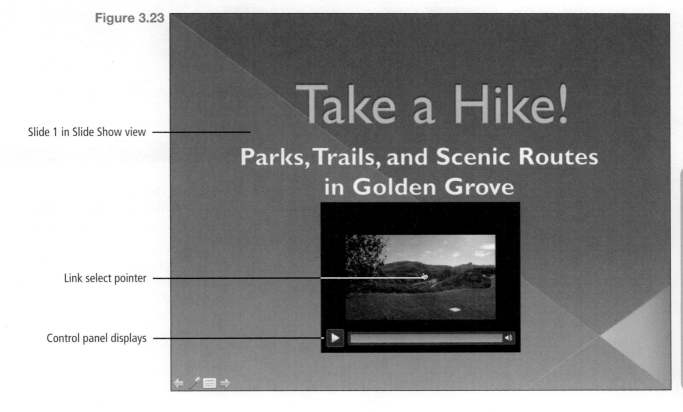

Link select pointer

Control panel displays

7 With the ⌨ pointer displayed, click the mouse to view the movie. Move the pointer away from the movie and notice that the control panel no longer displays. When the movie is finished, press `Esc` to exit the slide show.

8 **Save** 🖫 your presentation.

Activity 3.10 │ Formatting a Movie

You can apply styles and effects to a movie and change the movie shape and border. You can also recolor a movie so that it coordinates with the presentation theme.

1 With **Slide 1** displayed, select the movie. On the **Format Movie tab**, in the **Movie Styles group**, point to the bottom of the **Movie Styles** gallery, and then click the **More** button ▾ to display the **Movie Styles** gallery.

2 Using the ScreenTips to view the style name, under **Moderate**, click the **Beveled Oval, Black** style. Compare your screen with Figure 3.24.

Figure 3.24

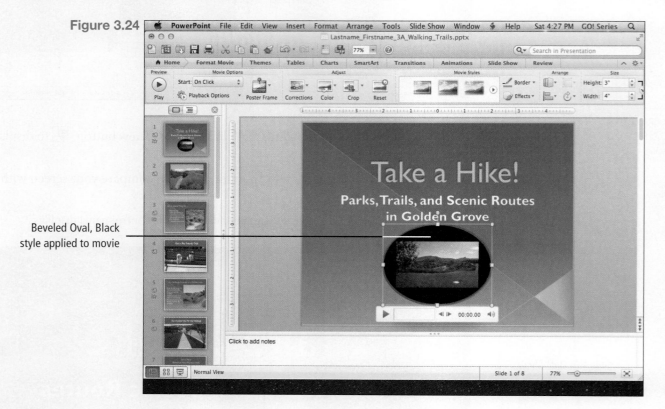

Beveled Oval, Black style applied to movie

3 In the **Movie Styles group**, click the **Border arrow**. Under **Theme Colors**, on the fifth row, click the third color—**Background 2, Darker 25%**. In the **Movie Styles group**, click the **Effects** button, point to **Bevel**, and then click the last bevel—**Art Deco**. Compare your screen with Figure 3.25.

You can format a movie with any combination of styles and effects.

Figure 3.25

Border and bevel
applied to movie

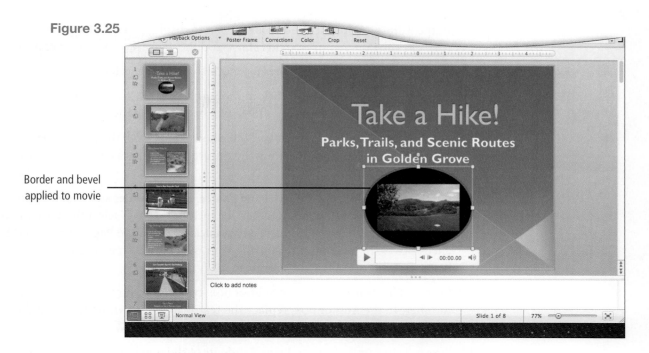

4 On the **Format Movie tab**, in the **Adjust group**, click the **Color** button to display the **Recolor** gallery.

The first row of the Recolor gallery displays options to recolor the movie in grayscale, sepia, washout, or black and white variations. The remaining rows in the gallery display options to recolor the movie in the theme colors.

5 In the **Recolor** gallery, in the second row, point to the first style—**Text Color 2 Dark**, and then compare your screen with Figure 3.26.

Figure 3.26

Color button

Recolor applied to movie

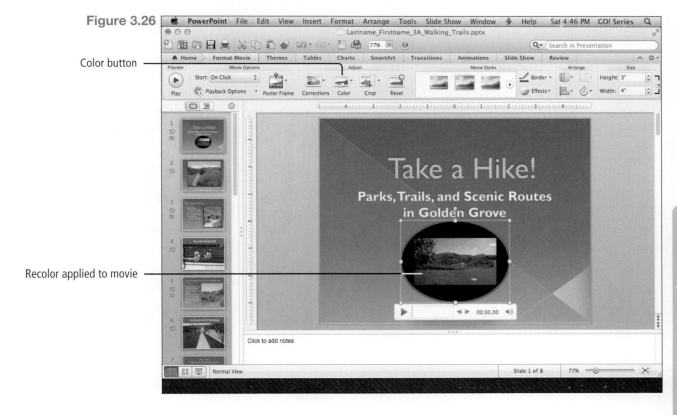

PowerPoint | Chapter 3

6 In the **Adjust group**, click the **Color** button to display the **Recolor** gallery. In the first row, click the first color—**No Recolor**—and then **Save** 🖫 your presentation.

> The No Recolor option restores the movie to its original color.

7 In the **Movie Options group**, click in the **Start** box, and then click **Automatically** so that during the slide show, the movie will begin automatically.

8 On the **Slide Show tab**, in the **Play Slide Show group**, click the **From Start** button, and then view the slide show, clicking the mouse to advance as necessary. Press Esc when the black slide displays.

9 On the **View** menu, click **Header and Footer**. In the **Header and Footer** dialog box, click the **Notes and Handouts tab**. Under **Include on page**, select the **Date and time** check box, and then click **Update automatically**. Select the **Page number** and **Footer** check boxes. In the **Footer** box, using your own name, type **Lastname_Firstname_3A_ Walking_Trails** and then click **Apply to All**.

10 Display **File Properties**. In the **Subject** box, type your course name and section number. In the **Author** box, replace the text with your own firstname and lastname. In the **Keywords** box, type **trails, hiking** and then click **OK**.

11 **Save** 🖫 your presentation. **Print Handouts (4 slides per page)**, or submit your presentation electronically as directed by your instructor.

12 **Close** 🖂 your presentation, and then **Quit PowerPoint**.

End **You have completed Project 3A** ————————————————

Project 3B Summary and Analysis Presentation

Project Activities

In Activities 3.11 through 3.16, you will add a table and two charts to a presentation that Mindy Walker, Director of Parks and Recreation, is creating to inform the City Council about enrollment trends in Golden Grove recreation programs. Your completed presentation will look similar to Figure 3.27.

Project Files

For Project 3B, you will need the following file:

p03B_Recreation_Enrollment

You will save your presentation as:

Lastname_Firstname_3B_Recreation_Enrollment

Project Results

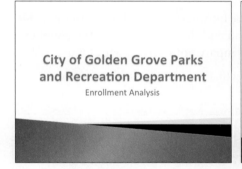

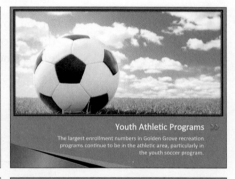

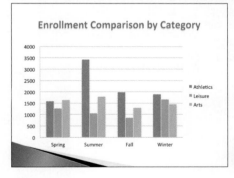

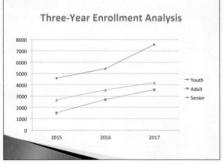

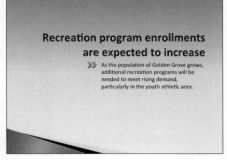

Figure 3.27

Project 3B Recreation Enrollment

Objective 4 | Create and Modify Tables

A *table* is a format for information that organizes and presents text and data in columns and rows. The intersection of a column and row is referred to as a *cell* and is the location in which you type text in a table.

Activity 3.11 | Creating a Table

There are several ways to insert a table in a PowerPoint slide. For example, you can use the Draw Table pointer, which is useful when the rows and columns contain cells of different sizes. Another way is to insert a slide with a Content Layout and then click the Insert Table button. Or, click the Tables tab, and in the Table Options group, click New, and then click a cell to specify the size of the table. In this activity, you will use a Content Layout to create a table.

1 Open **PowerPoint**. From your student files, **Open p03B_Recreation_Enrollment**, and then **Save** the presentation in your **PowerPoint Chapter 3** folder as **Lastname_ Firstname_3B_Recreation_Enrollment**

2 With **Slide 1** displayed, on the **Home tab**, in the **Slides group**, click the **New Slide** button to insert a slide with the **Title and Content** layout. In the title placeholder, type **Recreation Program Summary** and then apply **Center Text** ▤ to the title.

3 In the content placeholder, click the **Insert Table** button ▦ to display the **Insert Table** dialog box. In the **Number of columns** box, type **3** and then press Tab. In the **Number of rows** box, be sure that **2** displays, and then compare your screen with Figure 3.28.

Here you enter the number of columns and rows that you want the table to contain.

Figure 3.28

Insert Table dialog box

Number of columns

Number of rows

Insert Table button

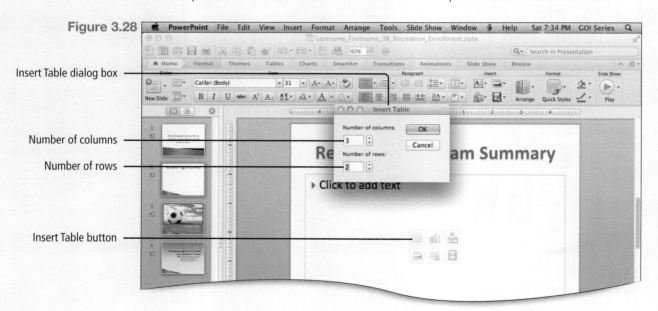

4 Click **OK** to create a table with three columns and two rows. Notice that the insertion point is blinking in the upper left cell of the table.

The table extends from the left side of the content placeholder to the right side, and the three columns are equal in width. By default, a style is applied to the table.

5 With the insertion point positioned in the first cell of the table, type **Athletics** and then press Tab.

Pressing Tab moves the insertion point to the next cell in the same row. If the insertion point is positioned in the last cell of a row, pressing Tab moves the insertion point to the first cell of the next row.

> **Alert! | Did You Press** Return **Instead of** Tab**?**
>
> In a table, pressing Return creates another line in the same cell. If you press Return by mistake, you can remove the extra line by pressing Delete.

6 With the insertion point positioned in the second cell of the first row, type **Leisure** and then press Tab. Type **Arts** and then press Tab to move the insertion point to the first cell in the second row. Compare your screen with Figure 3.29.

Figure 3.29

Text typed in first row

Insertion point positioned in first cell on second row

7 With the insertion point positioned in the first cell of the second row, type **Team sports** and then press Tab. Type **Personal development classes** and then press Tab. Type **Music and dance classes**

8 Press Tab to insert a new blank row.

When the insertion point is positioned in the last cell of a table, pressing Tab inserts a new blank row at the bottom of the table.

9 In the first cell of the third row, type **Youth** and then press Tab. Type **Older adults** and then press Tab. Type **Young adults** and then compare your screen with Figure 3.30. **Save** 💾 your presentation.

Figure 3.30

Text typed in third row

PowerPoint | Chapter 3

Activity 3.12 | Modifying the Layout of a Table

You can modify the layout of a table by inserting or deleting rows and columns, changing the alignment of the text in a cell, adjusting the height and width of the entire table or selected rows and columns, and by merging multiple cells into one cell.

1 Click in any cell in the first column, and then click the **Table Layout tab**. In the **Rows & Columns group**, click the **Left** button.

A new first column is inserted to the left of the column where the insertion point was located, and the widths of the columns are adjusted so that all four columns are the same width.

2 In the *second* row, click in the first cell, and then type **Largest Enrollments**

3 In the third row, click in the first cell, and then type **Primary Market** and then compare your screen with Figure 3.31.

Figure 3.31

Column inserted and text typed

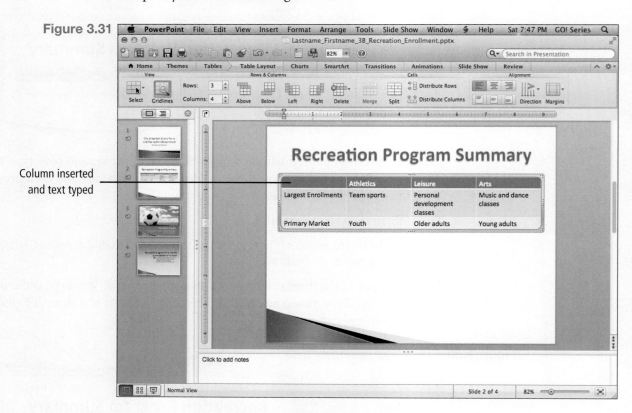

4 With the insertion point positioned in the third row, on the **Table Layout tab**, in the **Rows & Columns group**, click the **Above** button to insert a new third row. In the first cell of the new row, type **Enrollment Capacity** and then press Tab. Type the remaining three entries, pressing Tab to move from cell to cell: **Enrolled at 85% capacity** and **Enrolled at 70% capacity** and **Enrolled at 77% capacity**

5 At the center of the lower border surrounding the table, point to the cluster of four dots—the sizing handle—to display the ⬍ pointer. Compare your screen with Figure 3.32.

Figure 3.32

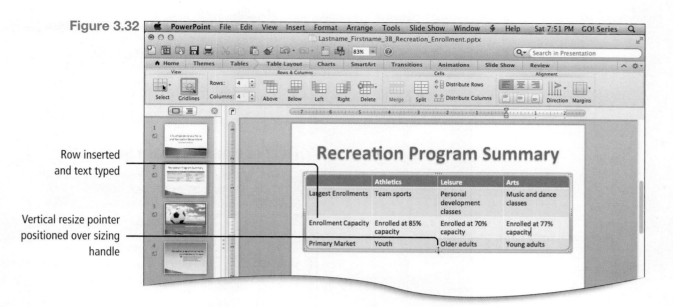

Row inserted
and text typed

Vertical resize pointer
positioned over sizing
handle

6 Drag downward to resize the table until the lower left corner of the table outline is just above the graphic in the lower left corner of the slide. Compare your screen with Figure 3.33.

Figure 3.33

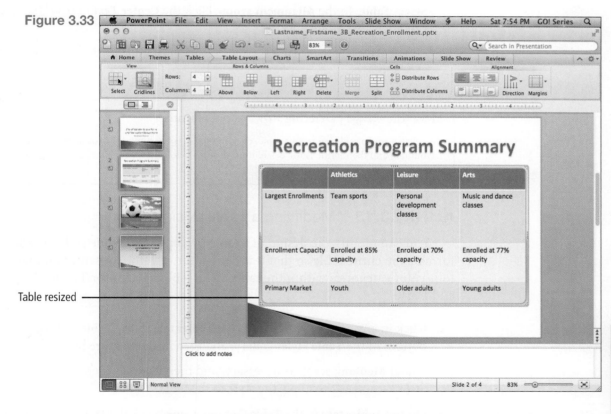

Table resized

7 Click in the first cell of the table. On the **Table Layout tab**, in the **Cells group**, click the **Distribute Rows** button. Compare your screen with Figure 3.34.

The Distribute Rows command adjusts the height of the rows in the table so that they are equal.

Figure 3.34

Distribute Rows button

Table rows equal in height

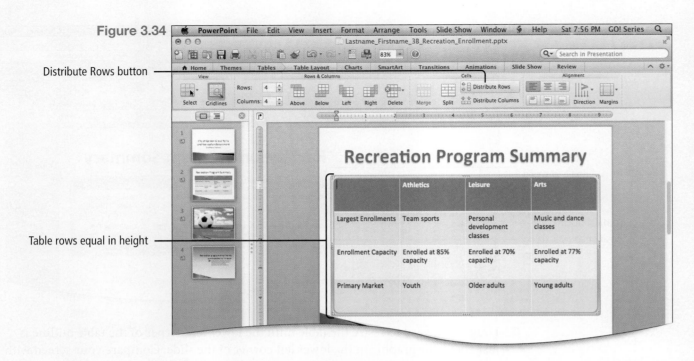

8 On the **Table Layout tab**, in the **View group**, click the **Select** button, and then click **Select Table**. In the **Alignment group**, click the **Center Text** button ▤, and then click the **Align Text Middle** button ▤.

All of the text in the table is centered horizontally and vertically within the cells.

9 **Save** 🖫 your presentation.

> **More Knowledge | Deleting Rows and Columns**
>
> To delete a row or column from a table, click in the row or column that you want to delete. Click the Table Layout tab, and then in the Rows & Columns group, click Delete. In the list, click Delete Columns or Delete Rows.

Activity 3.13 | Modifying a Table Design

You can modify the design of a table by applying a *table style*. A table style formats the entire table so that it is consistent with the presentation theme. There are four color categories within the table styles—Best Match for Theme, Light, Medium, and Dark.

1 Click in any cell in the table. On the **Tables tab**, in the **Table Styles group**, point to the bottom of the **Table Styles** gallery, and then click the **More** button ⯆.

2 Under **Medium**, scroll as necessary, and then using the Screen Tips, click **Medium Style 3 – Accent 2** to apply the style to the table.

3 On the **Tables tab**, in the **Table Options group**, click the **Options** button, and then click **Banded Rows** to clear this option. Notice that each row, except the header row, displays in the same color.

4 Click the **Options** button again, and then click **Banded Rows** to display the rows in alternating colors.

5 Move the pointer outside of the table so that it is positioned to the left of the first row in the table to display the ➡ pointer, as shown in Figure 3.35.

Figure 3.35

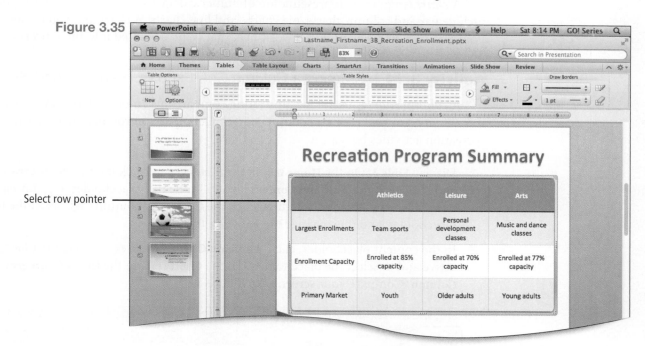

Select row pointer

6 With the ➡ pointer pointing to the first row in the table, click to select the entire row so that you can apply formatting to the selection. On the **Home tab**, in the **Font group**, change the **Font Size** to **28**.

7 With the first row still selected, on the **Tables tab**, in the **Table Styles group**, click the **Effects** button. Point to **Cell Bevel**, and then under **Bevel**, click the first bevel—**Circle**.

8 Position the pointer above the first column to display the ⬇ pointer, and then click to select the first column. On the **Home tab**, in the **Font group**, click the **Bold** button **B**, and then click the **Italic** button **I**.

9 Click in a blank area of the slide, **Save** 💾 your presentation, and then compare your screen with Figure 3.36.

Figure 3.36

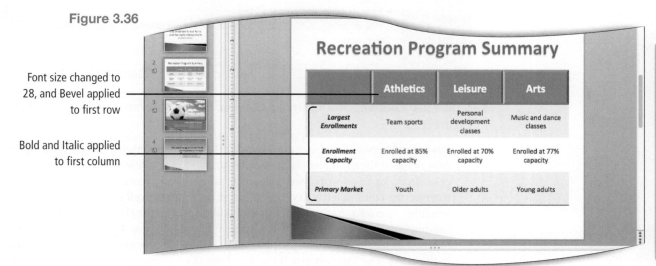

Font size changed to 28, and Bevel applied to first row

Bold and Italic applied to first column

Objective 5 | Create and Modify Charts

A *chart* is a graphic representation of numeric data. Commonly used chart types include bar and column charts, pie charts, and line charts. A chart that you create in PowerPoint is stored in an Excel worksheet that is incorporated into the PowerPoint file.

Activity 3.14 | Creating a Column Chart and Applying a Chart Style

A *column chart* is useful for illustrating comparisons among related numbers. In this activity, you will create a column chart that compares enrollment in each category of recreation activities by season.

1 Display **Slide 3**. On the **Home tab**, in the **Slides group**, click the **New Slide arrow**, and then click the **Title and Content** layout. In the title placeholder, type **Enrollment Comparison by Category** and then click the **Center Text** button ☰. Select the title placeholder, and then change the **Font Size** to **36**.

2 In the content placeholder, click the **Insert Chart** button 📊 to make the **Charts tab** active and to select the placeholder. On the **Charts tab**, in the **Insert Chart group**, click **Column**. Compare your screen with Figure 3.37.

Figure 3.37

Column charts

Insert Chart button

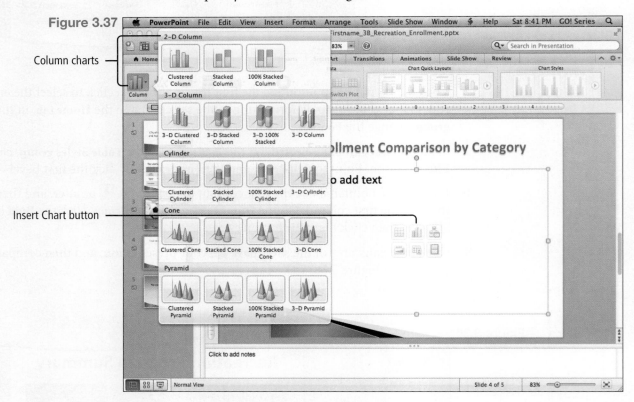

3 Under **2-D Column**, click **Clustered Column**, and then compare your screen with Figure 3.38.

PowerPoint opens Excel and displays a worksheet that contains sample data in a data range outlined in blue, from which the chart in the PowerPoint window will be generated. An Excel worksheet consists of columns and rows. A cell is identified by the intersecting column letter and row number, forming the *cell reference*. The column headings—*Series 1*, *Series 2*, and *Series 3* will display in the chart *legend* and the row headings—*Category 1*, *Category 2*, *Category 3*, and *Category 4*—will display as *category labels*. The legend identifies the patterns or colors that are assigned to the data series in the chart. The category labels display along the bottom of the chart to identify the categories of data.

Figure 3.38

Excel worksheet with sample data

Column headings will display as legend in chart

Row headings will display as category labels in chart

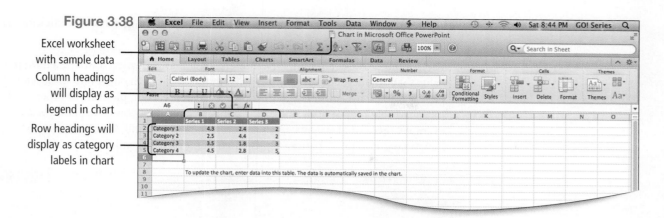

4 Click in cell **B1**, which contains the text *Series 1*. Type **Athletics** and then press Tab to move to cell **C1**.

5 In cell **C1**, which contains the text *Series 2*, type **Leisure** and then press Tab to move to cell **D1**. Type **Arts** and then press Tab. Notice that cell **A2**, which contains the text *Category 1*, is selected. Compare your screen with Figure 3.39.

> The blue box outlining the range of cells defines the area in which you are entering data. When you press Tab in the rightmost cell, the first cell in the next row becomes active.

Figure 3.39

Column headings entered

Cell A2 selected

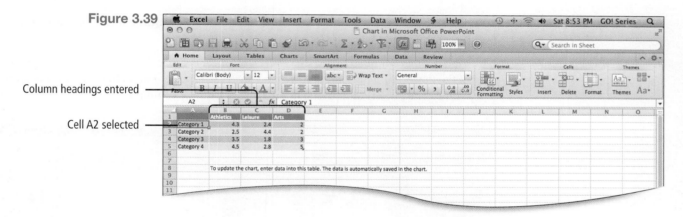

6 Beginning in cell **A2**, type the following data, pressing Tab to move from cell to cell.

	Athletics	Leisure	Arts
Spring	1588	1263	1639
Summer	3422	1058	1782
Fall	1987	852	1293
Winter	1889	1674	

7 In cell **D5**, which contains the value *5*, type **1453** and then press Return.

> Pressing Return in the last cell of the blue outlined area maintains the existing data range.

Alert! | Did You Press Tab After the Last Entry?

If you pressed Tab after entering the data in cell D5, you expanded the chart range. On the Standard toolbar, click the Undo button.

---

8 Compare your screen with Figure 3.40. Correct any typing errors by clicking in the cell that you want to change, and then retype the data.

Each of the 12 cells containing the numeric data that you entered will be a *data point*—a value that originates in a worksheet cell—in the chart. Each data point in the chart will be represented by a *data marker*—a column, bar, area, dot, pie slice, or other symbol in a chart that represents a single data point. Related data points form a *data series*; for example, there will be a data series for *Athletics*, *Leisure*, and *Arts*. Each data series will have a unique color or pattern represented in the chart legend.

Figure 3.40

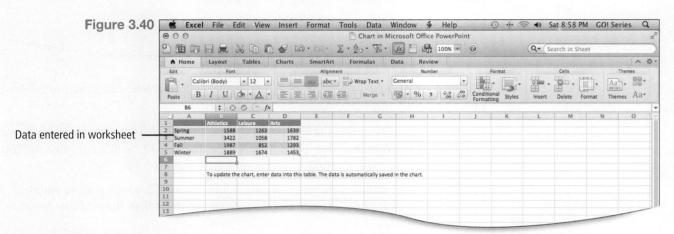

Data entered in worksheet

9 On the **File** menu, click **Close**. On the **Excel** menu, click **Quit Excel**. Compare your screen with Figure 3.41.

You are not prompted to save the Excel worksheet because the worksheet data is a part of the PowerPoint presentation. When you save the presentation, the Excel data is saved with it. The PowerPoint presentation displays with the column chart.

Figure 3.41

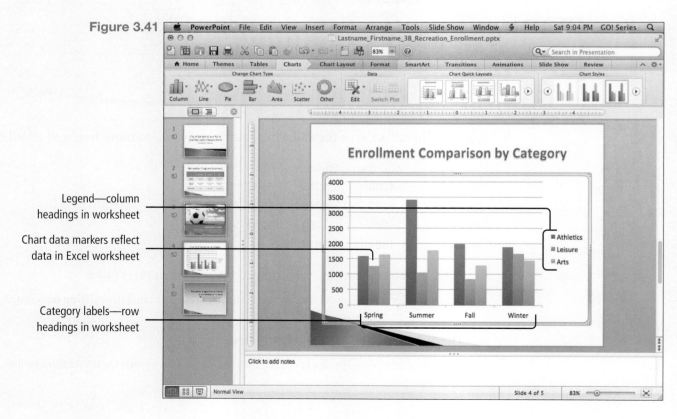

Legend—column headings in worksheet

Chart data markers reflect data in Excel worksheet

Category labels—row headings in worksheet

10 Be sure the chart is selected; click the outer edge of the chart if necessary to select it. On the **Charts tab**, in the **Chart Styles group**, point to the bottom of the gallery, and then click the **More** button ▾ button.

11 In the **Chart Styles** gallery, on the second row, click the second style.

12 Save 🖫 your presentation.

More Knowledge | Editing the Chart Data After Closing Excel

You can redisplay the Excel worksheet and make changes to the data after you have closed Excel. To do so, in PowerPoint, click the chart to select it, and then on the Charts tab in the Data group, click the Edit button.

Activity 3.15 | Creating a Line Chart and Deleting Chart Data

To analyze and compare annual data over a three-year period, the presentation requires an additional chart. Recall that there are a number of different types of charts that you can insert in a PowerPoint presentation. In this activity, you will create a *line chart*, which is commonly used to illustrate trends over time.

1 With **Slide 4** displayed, on the **Home tab**, in the **Slides group**, click the **New Slide arrow**, and then click the **Title and Content** layout. In the title placeholder, type **Three-Year Enrollment Analysis** and then click the **Center Text** button ▤. Select the title placeholder, and then change the **Font Size** to **36**.

2 In the content placeholder, click the **Insert Chart** button 📊. On the **Charts tab**, in the **Insert Chart group**, click the **Line** button. Under **2-D Line**, click **Marked Line**.

3 In the Excel worksheet, click in cell **B1**, which contains the text *Series 1*. Type **Youth** and then press Tab. Type **Adult** and then press Tab. Type **Senior** and then press Tab.

4 Beginning in cell **A2**, type the following data, pressing Tab to move from cell to cell. If you make any typing errors, click in the cell that you want to change, and then retype the data.

	Youth	Adult	Senior
2015	4586	1534	2661
2016	5422	2699	3542
2017	7565	3572	4183

5 In the Excel window, position the pointer over row heading **5** so that the ➡ pointer displays. Compare your screen with Figure 3.42.

Figure 3.42

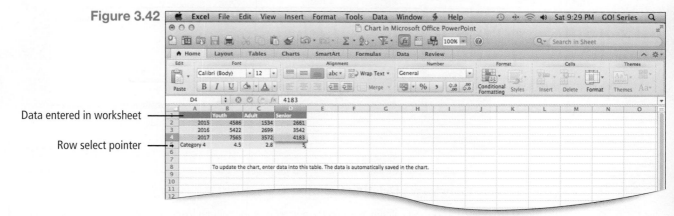

Data entered in worksheet

Row select pointer

6 With the ➡ pointer displayed, click to select the row. On the **Home tab**, in the **Cells group**, click the **Delete** button to delete the extra row from the worksheet, and then compare your screen with Figure 3.43.

> The data in the worksheet contains four columns and four rows, and the blue outline defining the chart data range is resized. You must delete columns and rows that you do not want to include in the chart. You can add additional rows and columns by typing column and row headings and then entering additional data. When data is typed in cells adjacent to the chart range, the range is resized to include the new data.

Figure 3.43

Extra row with sample data deleted

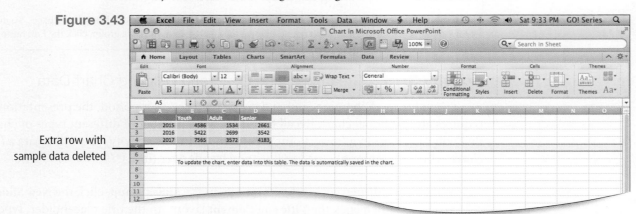

7 On the **File** menu, click **Close**. On the **Excel** menu, click **Quit Excel** to return to the PowerPoint window and to display the chart. On the **Charts tab**, in the **Chart Styles group**, point to the bottom of the **Chart Styles** gallery, and then click the **More** button ▾. In the **Chart Styles** gallery, on the fourth row, click the second style. **Save** 💾 your presentation, and then compare your screen with Figure 3.44.

Figure 3.44

Chart style selected

Line chart with markers

Legend—column headings in worksheet

Category labels—row headings in worksheet

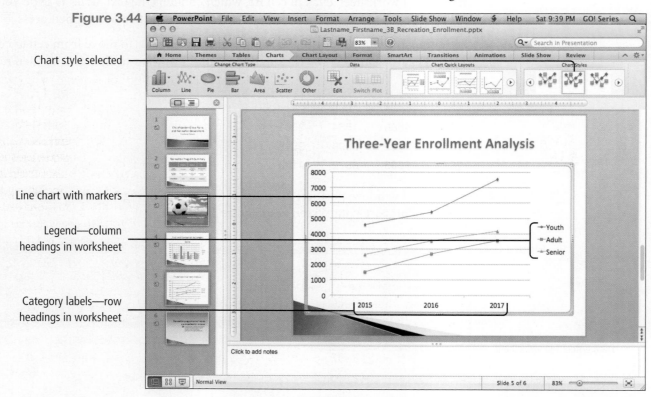

More Knowledge | Deleting Columns

To delete a worksheet column, position the pointer over the column letter that you want to select so that the ⬇ pointer displays. On the Home tab, in the Cells group, click the Delete button.

Activity 3.16 | Animating a Chart

1 Display **Slide 4**, and then click the column chart to select it. On the **Animations tab**, in the **Entrance Effects group**, point to the bottom of the gallery, and then click the **More** button ▾. Under **Basic**, click **Split**.

2 In the **Animation Options group**, click the **Effect Options** button, and then under **Sequence**, click **By Series**. Compare your screen with Figure 3.45.

> The By Series option displays the chart one data series at a time, and the numbers 1, 2, 3, and 4 to the left of the chart indicate the four parts of the chart animation sequence. The chart animation sequence includes the background, followed by the Athletics data series for each season, and then the Leisure series, and then the Arts series.

Figure 3.45

Split animation applied to chart

Numbers indicate animation order

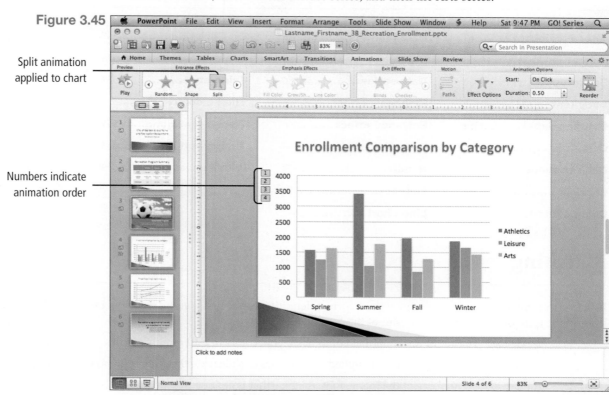

3 On the **Slide Show tab**, in the **Play Slide Show group**, click the **From Current Slide** button to view the animation on **Slide 4**. Click to display the legend and labels. Click again to display the *Athletics* data.

4 Continue to click to advance through the remaining animation effects. After the animations for **Slide 4** are complete, press Esc to end the slide show and return to the presentation.

5 Add a **Header and Footer** for the **Notes and Handouts** pages. Include the **Date and time** that **Update automatically**, the **Page number**, and a **Footer** with the file name **Lastname_ Firstname_3B_Recreation_Enrollment**

6 Display **File Properties**. In the **Subject** box, type your course name and section number. In the **Author** box, replace the text with your own firstname and lastname. In the **Keywords** box, type **enrollment, recreation** and then click **OK**.

7 **Save** 💾 your presentation. **Print Handouts (6 slides per page)**, or submit your presentation electronically as directed by your instructor.

8 **Close** ⊗ the presentation, and then **Quit PowerPoint**.

End **You have completed Project 3B** —————————————

PowerPoint | Chapter 3

Content-Based Assessments

Summary

In this chapter, you formatted a presentation by applying background styles, inserting pictures on slide backgrounds, and changing theme fonts. You enhanced your presentation by inserting a movie, by applying animation effects, and by changing effect and timing options. You practiced creating tables to present information in an organized manner, and you used charts to visually represent data.

Key Terms

Matching

Match each term in the second column with its correct definition in the first column by writing the letter of the term on the blank line in front of the correct definition.

_____ 1. A slide background fill variation that combines theme colors in different intensities.

_____ 2. A theme that determines the font applied to two types of slide text—headings and body.

_____ 3. Of the two types of fonts in the theme font, the type that is applied to slide titles.

_____ 4. Of the two types of fonts in the theme font, the type that is applied to all slide text except titles.

_____ 5. A visual or sound effect added to an object or text on a slide.

_____ 6. Animations that bring a slide element onto the screen.

_____ 7. Animation that emphasizes an object or text that is already displayed.

_____ 8. Animation that moves an object or text off the screen.

_____ 9. A format for information that organizes and presents text and data in columns and rows.

_____ 10. The intersection of a column and row.

_____ 11. Formatting applied to an entire table so that it is consistent with the presentation theme.

_____ 12. A graphic representation of numeric data.

_____ 13. A type of chart used to compare data.

_____ 14. A combination of the column letter and row number identifying a cell.

_____ 15. A chart element that identifies the patterns or colors that are assigned to the each data series in the chart.

A Animation

B Background style

C Body font

D Cell

E Cell reference

F Chart

G Column chart

H Emphasis effect

I Entrance effect

J Exit effect

K Headings font

L Legend

M Table

N Table style

O Theme font

Content-Based Assessments

Multiple Choice

Circle the correct answer.

1. The set of coordinating colors applied to the backgrounds, objects, and text in a presentation is called:
    A. theme colors   B. colors set   C. coordinating colors

2. The command that is used to prevent background graphics from displaying on a slide is:
    A. Hide Background Styles   B. Cover Background Graphics   C. Hide Background Graphics

3. Animation options that control when animated items display in the animation sequence are called:
    A. timing options   B. effect options   C. sequence options

4. An animation that brings a slide element onto the screen is an:
    A. emphasis effect   B. exit effect   C. entrance effect

5. The font that is applied to slide titles is the:
    A. body font   B. headings font   C. titles font

6. A chart element that identifies categories of data is a:
    A. data marker   B. category label   C. category marker

7. A column, bar, area, dot, pie slice, or other symbol in a chart that represents a single data point is a:
    A. data marker   B. data point   C. data series

8. A chart value that originates in a worksheet cell is a:
    A. data marker   B. data point   C. data series

9. A group of related data points is called a:
    A. data marker   B. data point   C. data series

10. A type of chart that shows trends over time is a:
    A. pie chart   B. column chart   C. line chart

Content-Based Assessments

Apply **3A** skills from these Objectives:

1 Customize Slide Backgrounds and Themes

2 Animate a Slide Show

3 Insert a Movie

Skills Review | Project **3C** Park

In the following Skills Review, you will format a presentation by applying slide background styles, colors, pictures, and animation. Your completed presentation will look similar to Figure 3.46.

Project Files

For Project 3C, you will need the following files:

> p03C_Park
> p03C_Park_Scenery
> p03C_Park_Video.mov

You will save your presentation as:

> Lastname_Firstname_3C_Park

Project Results

Figure 3.46

(Project 3C Park continues on the next page)

Content-Based Assessments

Skills Review | Project 3C Park (continued)

1 Open **PowerPoint**. From your student files, **Open p03C_Park**, and then **Save** the presentation in your **PowerPoint Chapter 3** folder as **Lastname_Firstname_3C_Park**

a. On the **Themes tab**, in the **Theme Options group**, click the **Colors** button, and then click **Apothecary** to change the theme colors. In the **Theme Options group**, click the **Fonts** button, and then click **Module** to change the theme fonts.

b. Display **Slide 2**, and then on the **Home tab**, in the **Slides group**, click the **New Slide arrow**. Click **Title Only** to insert a new slide with the Title Only layout. Click in the title placeholder. On the **Format tab**, in the **Shape Styles group**, point to the bottom of the **Shape Styles** gallery, and then click the **More** button. In the last row, click the first style. In the title placeholder, type **Relax in the Shade!**

c. On the **Themes tab**, in the **Theme Options group**, click the **Background** button, and then click **Hide Background Graphics**.

d. Click the **Background** button again. Below the gallery, click **Format Background**, and then in the **Format Background** dialog box, verify that on the left side, **Fill** is selected. In the **Format Background** dialog box, click the **Picture or Texture tab**. To the right of **From file**, click in the **Choose Picture** box. In the **Choose a Picture** dialog box, navigate to your student data files. Click **p03C_Park_Scenery**, and then click **Insert**. In the **Format Background** dialog box, click **Apply** to format the slide background with the picture.

e. Point to the outer edge of the title placeholder to display the ✛ pointer, and then drag the placeholder upward and to the left so that its top left corner aligns with the top left corner of the slide. Point to the center right sizing handle and drag to the right so that the placeholder extends to the right edge of the slide.

2 Display **Slide 4**. On the **Themes tab**, in the **Theme Options group**, click the **Background** button, and then click **Format Background**.

a. In the **Format Background** dialog box, verify that on the left side, **Fill** is selected. Click in the **Color** box. Under **Theme Colors**, in the first row, click the first color—**Background 1**—and then click **Apply** to apply the background fill color to the slide.

b. Display **Slide 2**. On the **Themes tab**, in the **Theme Options group**, click the **Background** button, and then click **Format Background**.

c. In the **Format Background** dialog box, verify that on the left side, **Fill** is selected. Click in the **Color** box. Under **Theme Colors**, in the last row, click the eighth color—**Accent 4, Darker 50%** and then click **Apply** to apply the background fill color to the slide.

3 Display **Slide 5**. On the **Home tab**, in the **Insert group**, click the **Media** button, and then click **Movie from File**. In the **Choose a Movie** dialog box, navigate to your student files, click **p03_Park_Video.mov**, and then click **Insert** to insert the movie.

a. With the movie selected, on the **Format Movie tab**, in the **Size group**, replace the value in the **Height** box with **5.5** and then press ⏎Return⏎.

b. Point to the movie, and then drag upward and to the left so that its upper left corner aligns with the upper left corner of the dark brown rectangle.

c. With the movie selected, on the **Format Movie tab**, in the **Movie Styles** group, click the **Effects** button, point to **Bevel**, and then click the last style—**Art Deco**.

d. With the movie selected, in the **Movie Options group**, click in the **Start** box, and then click **Automatically**.

4 Display **Slide 2**, and then click anywhere in the bulleted list placeholder. On the **Animations tab**, in the **Entrance Effects group**, point to the bottom of the gallery, click the **More** button, and then under **Basic**, click **Split**.

a. In the **Animation Options group**, click the **Effect Options** button, and then click **Vertical Out**.

b. In the **Animation Options group**, click in the **Start** box, and then click **After Previous** so that the list displays after the slide transition.

c. In the **Animation Options group**, click the **Duration up arrow** five times so that **1.00** displays in the **Duration** box.

d. In the **Animation Options group**, click the **Reorder** button. In the **Custom Animation** tool, if necessary, click **Timing** to expand the section. Double-click in the **Delay** box, type **0.25** and then **Close** the **Custom Animation** tool.

5 Display **Slide 3**, and then click in the title placeholder. On the **Animations tab**, in the **Entrance**

(Project 3C Park continues on the next page)

Effects group, point to the bottom of the gallery, and then click the **More** button. Under **Basic**, click **Wipe**. In the **Animation Options group**, click in the **Start** box, and then click **After Previous**.

a. Display **Slide 1**, and then click the subtitle—*A Look at What's New!* Apply an **Entrance Effect** of **Wipe** and **Start** the animation **After Previous**.

b. On **Slide 1**, select the title's animation order number—**1**—and then press Delete to remove the animation from the title.

c. On the **Slide Show tab**, in the **Play Slide Show group**, click the **From Start** button, and then view your presentation, clicking the mouse to advance through the slides. When the black slide displays, press Esc.

d. Add a **Header and Footer** for the **Notes and Handouts** pages. Include the **Date and time** that **Update automatically**, the **Page number**, and a **Footer** with the file name **Lastname_Firstname_3C_ Park** Click **Apply to All**.

e. Display the **File Properties**. In the **Subject** box, type your course name and section number. In the **Author** box, replace the text with your own first and last name. In the **Keywords** box, type **park, summer** and then click **OK**.

f. **Save** your presentation. **Print Handouts (6 slides per page)**, or submit your presentation electronically as directed by your instructor. **Close** the presentation, and then **Quit PowerPoint**.

End **You have completed Project 3C** ——————————————

Content-Based Assessments

Apply **3B** skills from these Objectives:

4 Create and Modify Tables

5 Create and Modify Charts

Skills Review | Project **3D** Technology Budget

In the following Skills Review, you will format a presentation by inserting and formatting a table, column chart, and line chart. Your completed presentation will look similar to Figure 3.47.

Project Files

For Project 3D, you will need the following file:

p03D_Technology_Budget

You will save your presentation as:

Lastname_Firstname_3D_Technology_Budget

Project Results

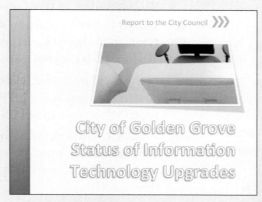
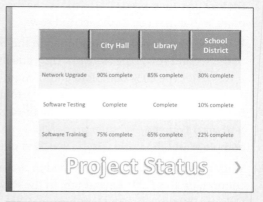
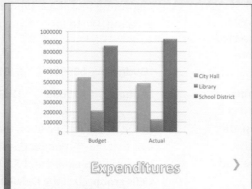
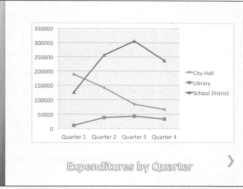

Figure 3.47

(Project 3D Technology Budget continues on the next page)

1 Open **PowerPoint**. From your student files **Open p03D_Technology_Budget**, and then **Save** the presentation in your **PowerPoint Chapter 3** folder as **Lastname_Firstname_3D_Technology_Budget**

a. Display **Slide 2**. In the content placeholder, click the **Insert Table** button to display the **Insert Table** dialog box. In the **Number of columns box**, type **3** and then press Tab. In the **Number of rows** box, verify that *2* displays and then click **OK** to create the table.

b. In the first row of the table, click in the second cell. Type **City Hall** and then press Tab. Type **School District** and then press Tab to move the insertion point to the first cell in the second row.

c. With the insertion point positioned in the first cell of the second row, type **Network Upgrade** and then press Tab. Type **90% complete** and then press Tab. Type **30% complete** and then press Tab to insert a new blank row. In the first cell of the third row, type **Software Training** and then press Tab. Type **75% complete** and then press Tab. Type **22% complete**

d. With the insertion point positioned in the last column, on the **Table Layout tab**, in the **Rows & Columns group**, click the **Left** button. Click in the top cell of the inserted column, and then type **Library** In the second and third rows of the inserted column, type **85% complete** and **65% complete**

e. With the insertion point positioned in the third row, on the **Table Layout tab**, in the **Rows & Columns group**, click the **Above** button. Click in the first cell of the row you inserted, type **Software Testing** and then press Tab. Type the remaining three entries in the row as follows: **Complete** and **Complete** and **10% complete**

2 At the center of the lower border surrounding the table, point to the cluster of four dots—the sizing handle—and make the table larger by dragging downward until the lower edge of the table aligns at **approximately 2 inches on the lower half of the vertical ruler**.

a. Click in the first cell of the table. On the **Table Layout tab**, in the **Cells group**, click the **Distribute Rows** button.

b. On the **Table Layout tab**, in the **View group**, click the **Select** button, and then click **Select Table**. In the **Alignment group**, click the **Center Text** button, and then click the **Align Text Middle** button.

c. Click in any cell in the table. On the **Tables tab**, in the **Table Styles group**, point to the bottom of the gallery, and then click the **More** button. Under **Medium**, using the ScreenTips, click **Medium Style 3 – Accent 1** to apply the style to the table.

d. Move the pointer outside of the table so that is positioned to the left of the first row in the table to display the ➡ pointer, and then click one time to select the entire row. On the **Tables tab**, in the **Table Styles group**, click the **Effects** button. Point to **Cell Bevel**, and then under **Bevel**, click the first bevel—**Circle**. Change the **Font Size** of the text in the first row to **24**.

3 Display **Slide 3**. In the content placeholder, click the **Insert Chart** button to make the **Charts tab** active. On the **Charts tab**, in the **Insert Chart group**, click the **Column** button. Under **2-D Column**, click **Clustered Column**.

a. In the Excel worksheet, click in cell **B1**, which contains the text *Series 1*. Type **City Hall** and then press Tab to move to cell **C1**.

b. In cell **C1**, which contains the text *Series 2*, type **Library** and then press Tab to move to cell **D1**, which contains the text *Series 3*. Type **School District** and then press Tab.

c. Beginning in cell **A2**, type the following data, pressing Tab to move from cell to cell.

	City Hall	Library	School District
Budget	535650	210000	856350
Actual	475895	125760	925785

d. In the worksheet, position the pointer over row heading **4** so that the ➡ pointer displays. Then, drag downward to select both **rows 4** and **5**. On the **Home tab**, in the **Cells group**, click the **Delete** button. On the **File** menu, click **Close**. On the **Excel** menu, click **Quit Excel**.

e. If necessary, click the edge of the chart so that it is selected. On the **Charts tab**, in the **Chart Styles group**, point to the bottom of the gallery, and then click the **More** button. In the **Chart Styles** gallery, on the fourth row, click the second style.

f. With the chart selected, click the **Animations tab**. In the **Entrance Effects group**, point to the bottom of the gallery, and then click the **More** button. Under **Basic**, click **Split**. In the **Animation Options group**, click the **Effect Options** button, and then under **Sequence**, click **By Series**.

(Project 3D Technology Budget continues on the next page)

Content-Based Assessments

Skills Review | Project **3D** Technology Budget (continued)

4 Display **Slide 4**. In the content placeholder, click the **Insert Chart** button. On the **Charts tab**, in the **Insert Chart group**, click the **Line** button, and then under **2-D Line**, click **Marked Line**.

a. In the Excel worksheet, click in cell **B1**, which contains the text *Series 1*. Type **City Hall** and then press Tab. Type **Library** and then press Tab. Type **School District** and then press Tab.

b. Beginning in cell **A2**, type the following data, pressing Tab to move from cell to cell.

	City Hall	Library	School District
Quarter 1	186575	10265	125685
Quarter 2	139670	38675	256830
Quarter 3	83620	42730	305760
Quarter 4	66030	34090	237510

c. On the **File** menu, click **Close**. On the **Excel** menu, click **Quit Excel**.

d. On the **Charts tab**, in the **Chart Styles group**, point to the bottom of the gallery, and then click the **More** button. In the **Chart Styles** gallery, on the fifth row, click the second style.

e. Add a **Header and Footer** for the **Notes and Handouts** pages. Include the **Date and time** that **Update automatically**, the **Page number**, and a **Footer** with the file name **Lastname_Firstname_3D_ Technology_Budget** Click **Apply to All**.

f. Display the **File Properties**. In the **Subject** box, type your course name and section number. In the **Author** box, replace the text with your own first and last name. In the **Keywords** box, type **technology, budget** and then click **OK**.

g. View the **Slide Show** from the start, and then **Save** your presentation. **Print Handouts (4 slides per page)**, or submit your presentation electronically as directed by your instructor. **Close** the presentation, and then **Quit PowerPoint**.

End **You have completed Project 3D** ————————————————

Apply **3A** skills from
these Objectives:

1 Customize Slide
   Backgrounds and
   Themes

2 Animate a Slide Show

3 Insert a Movie

Mastering PowerPoint | Project **3E** Arboretum

In the following Mastering PowerPoint project, you will format a presentation created by the Golden Grove Public Relations Department that describes the City of Golden Grove Arboretum. Your completed presentation will look similar to Figure 3.48.

Project Files

For Project 3E, you will need the following files:

> p03E_Arboretum
> p03E_Arboretum_Flower
> p03E_Arboretum_Video.mov

You will save your presentation as:

> Lastname_Firstname_3E_Arboretum

Project Results

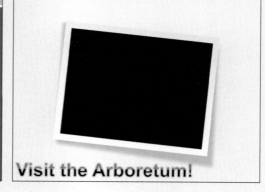

Figure 3.48

(Project 3E Arboretum continues on the next page)

Content-Based Assessments

Mastering PowerPoint | Project **3E** Arboretum (continued)

1 Open **PowerPoint**. From the student files that accompany this textbook, **Open p03E_Arboretum**. **Save** the presentation in your **PowerPoint Chapter 3** folder as **Lastname_Firstname_3E_ Arboretum** Change the **Theme Colors** for the presentation to **Pushpin**, and the **Theme Fonts** to **Clarity**.

2 On **Slide 1**, format the background with a picture from your student files—**p03E_Arboretum_Flower**. In the **Format Background** dialog box, on the **Picture or Texture tab**, clear the **Tile** check box.

3 On **Slide 2**, display the **Format Background** dialog box, and change the **Fill Color**. Under **Theme Colors**, in the second row, click the fifth color—**Accent 1, Lighter 80%**—and then **Apply** the style to this slide only. Select the paragraph on the left side of the slide, and then apply the **Split** entrance effect. Change the **Effect Options** to **Horizontal Out**. Change the **Start** setting to **After Previous**, and then change the **Duration** to **1.00**.

4 On **Slide 3**, format the background with a **Fill Color** of **Dark Purple**—under **Standard Colors**, the last color. **Center** the title, and then remove the entrance effect from the title.

5 On **Slide 4**, **Hide Background Graphics**, and then in the **Format Background** dialog box, apply a **Fill Color** of **Accent 1, Lighter 80%**—under **Theme Colors**, in the second row, the fifth color. From your student files, insert the movie **p03E_Arboretum_Video.mov**. Change the

Height to **4.5** and then using the **Align** button, apply the **Align Center** and **Align Middle** options. Format the movie by applying, from the **Movie Styles** gallery, a **Moderate** style—**Rotated, Gradient**. Change the **Start** setting to **Automatically**.

6 On the **Home tab**, in the **Insert group**, click the **Text** button, and then click **WordArt**. On the **Format tab**, in the **Text Styles group**, click the **Quick Styles** button. On the fourth row, click the third style. Type **Visit the Arboretum!** Drag the **WordArt** so that its lower left corner aligns with the lower left corner of the slide.

7 Display **Slide 3**. For the bulleted list, apply a **Split** entrance effect with an effect option of **Horizontal Out**.

8 Add a **Header and Footer** for the **Notes and Handouts** pages. Include the **Date and time** that **Update automatically**, the **Page number**, and a **Footer** with the text **Lastname_Firstname_3E_Arboretum**

9 Display the **File Properties**. In the **Subject** box, type your course name and section number. In the **Author** box, replace the existing text with your name. In the **Keywords** box, type **arboretum information** and then click **OK**.

10 **Save** your presentation, and then view the **Slide Show** from the start. **Print Handouts (4 slides per page)**, or submit your presentation electronically as directed by your instructor. **Close** the presentation, and then **Quit PowerPoint**.

End **You have completed Project 3E** ————————————————

Apply **3B** skills from these Objectives:

4 Create and Modify Tables

5 Create and Modify Charts

Mastering PowerPoint | Project **3F** Budget

In the following Mastering PowerPoint project, you will format several of the slides in a presentation that the City Manager is developing for an upcoming City Council meeting. Your completed presentation will look similar to Figure 3.49.

Project Files

For Project 3F, you will need the following file:

p03F_Budget

You will save your presentation as:

Lastname_Firstname_3F_Budget

Project Results

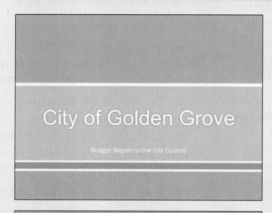

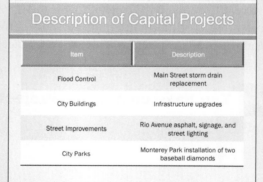

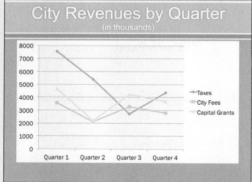

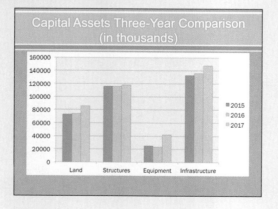

Figure 3.49

(Project 3F Budget continues on the next page)

Content-Based Assessments

Mastering PowerPoint | Project 3F Budget (continued)

1 Open **PowerPoint**. From your student files **Open p03F_Budget**, and then **Save** the presentation in your **PowerPoint Chapter 3** folder as **Lastname_Firstname_3F_Budget**

2 On **Slide 3**, in the content placeholder, insert a **Marked Line** chart. In the Excel worksheet, in cell **B1**, type **Taxes** and then enter the following data:

	Taxes	City Fees	Capital Grants
Quarter 1	7550	3550	4650
Quarter 2	5380	2095	2185
Quarter 3	2695	3260	4220
Quarter 4	4360	2790	3670

3 **Close** the Excel worksheet, and then **Quit Excel**. In the **Chart Styles** gallery, on the fifth row, click the fifth style. Apply the **Wipe** entrance effect to the chart.

4 On **Slide 4**, in the content placeholder, insert a **Table** with **2 columns** and **5 rows**, and then type the text shown in **Table 1** at the bottom of the page.

5 Resize the table so that its lower edge extends to **3 inches on the lower half of the vertical ruler**, and then **Distribute Rows**. Align the table text so that it is centered horizontally and vertically within the cells. Apply table style **Medium Style 3 - Accent 4**, and then apply a **Circle Bevel** to the first row. Change the table text **Font Size** to **20**.

6 On **Slide 5**, in the content placeholder, insert a **Clustered Column** chart. In the Excel worksheet, in cell **B1**, type **2015** and then enter the following data:

	2015	2016	2017
Land	72627	73823	85685
Structures	115746	115920	117812
Equipment	25002	23485	41762
Infrastructure	132586	135860	147873

7 **Close** the Excel worksheet, and then **Quit Excel**. In the **Chart Styles** gallery, on the fifth row, click the second style. Apply the **Wipe** entrance effect to the chart. Change the **Effect Options** so that the animation is applied **By Series**. Change the **Start** setting so that the animation starts **After Previous**.

8 On **Slide 1**, change the title's **Font Size** to **60**. On **Slide 4**, change the title's **Font Size** to **44**. On **Slide 5**, change the title's **Font Size** to **36**.

9 Add a **Header and Footer** for the **Notes and Handouts** pages. Include the **Date and time** that **Update automatically**, the **Page number**, and a **Footer** with the file name **Lastname_Firstname_3F_Budget** Display the **File Properties**, and in the **Subject** box, type your course name and section number. In the **Author** box, replace the existing text with your name. In the **Keywords** box, type **budget, revenue, capital** and then click **OK**.

10 View the **Slide Show** from the start, and then **Save** your presentation. **Print Handouts (6 slides per page)**, or submit your presentation electronically as directed by your instructor. **Close** the presentation, and then **Quit PowerPoint**.

Table 1

Item	Description
Flood Control	Main Street storm drain replacement
City Buildings	Infrastructure upgrades
Street Improvements	Rio Avenue asphalt, signage, and street lighting
City Parks	Monterey Park installation of two baseball diamonds

- - ▶ (Return to Step 5)

 End **You have completed Project 3F** ——————————————

PowerPoint | Chapter 3

Apply **3A** and **3B** skills
from these Objectives:

1 Customize Slide
Backgrounds and
Themes

2 Animate a Slide Show

3 Insert a Movie

4 Create and Modify
Tables

5 Create and Modify
Charts

Mastering PowerPoint | Project **3G** Restaurants

In the following Mastering PowerPoint project, you will format a presentation that the Golden Grove Public Relations Director will show at a meeting of the National Restaurant Owners Association to encourage new restaurant and catering business in the city. Your completed presentation will look similar to Figure 3.50.

Project Files

For Project 3G, you will need the following files:

p03G_Restaurants
p03G_Town_Center.mov
p03G_Catering

You will save your presentation as:

Lastname_Firstname_3G_Restaurants

Project Results

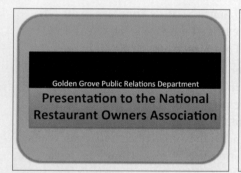

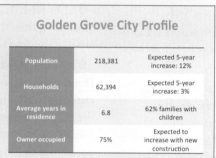

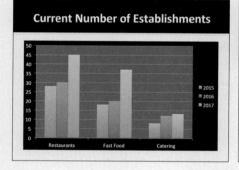

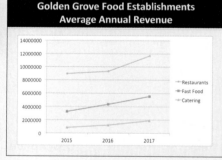

Figure 3.50

(Project 3G Restaurants continues on the next page)

Mastering PowerPoint | Project 3G Restaurants (continued)

1 Open **PowerPoint**. From the student files that accompany this textbook, **Open p03G_Restaurants**. **Save** the presentation in your **PowerPoint Chapter 3** folder as **Lastname_Firstname_3G_Restaurants** Change the **Theme Colors** for the presentation to **Apothecary**, and the **Theme Fonts** to **Expo**.

2 On **Slide 2**, insert a **Table** with **3 columns** and **4 rows**. Apply table style **Medium Style 3 - Accent 2**, and then type the information in **Table 1**, shown at the bottom of this page, into the inserted table.

3 On the **Tables tab**, in the **Table Options group**, click the **Options** button, and then click as needed to select *only* **First Column** and **Banded Rows**. Resize the table so that its lower edge extends to **3 inches on the lower half of the vertical ruler**, and then **Distribute Rows**. Align the table text so that it is centered horizontally and vertically within the cells, and then change the **Font Size** of all of the table text to **24**.

4 On **Slide 3**, display the **Format Background** dialog box, and then apply the **Canvas Texture** to this slide only. Animate the **SmartArt** graphic using the **Wipe** entrance effect starting **After Previous**. Apply the **Split** entrance effect to the bulleted list placeholder, and then change the **Effect Options** to **Vertical Out**.

5 On **Slide 4**, insert a **Clustered Column** chart. In the Excel worksheet, in cell **B1** type **2015** and then enter the following data:

	2015	2016	2017
Restaurants	28	30	45
Fast Food	18	20	37
Catering	8	12	13

6 In the Excel worksheet, **Delete row 5**, and then **Close** the Excel worksheet and **Quit Excel**. In the **Chart Style** gallery, on the sixth row, click the second style. Apply the **Wipe** entrance effect to the chart.

7 On **Slide 5**, from your student files, insert the movie **p03G_Town_Center.mov**. Change the **Height** to **3** and then drag the movie downward so that its top edge aligns **at 0 on the vertical ruler**. Apply the **Align Center** alignment

option, display the **Movie Styles** gallery, and then apply the first **Moderate** style—**Compound Frame, Black.** Change the **Border** to **Accent 1, Darker 50%**—under **Theme Colors**, in the last row, the fifth color. Change the **Movie Options** to **Start** the movie **Automatically**.

8 On **Slide 6**, in the content placeholder, insert a **Marked Line** chart. In the Excel worksheet, in cell **B1**, type **Restaurants** and then enter the following data:

	Restaurants	Fast Food	Catering
2015	8956231	3284680	856700
2016	9326852	4369571	1235640
2017	11689730	5526895	1894325

9 In the Excel worksheet, **Delete row 5**, and then **Close** the Excel worksheet and **Quit Excel**. In the **Chart Styles** gallery, on the fifth row, click the second style. Apply the **Wipe** entrance effect to the chart.

10 On **Slide 7**, **Hide Background Graphics**. Format the slide background by inserting a picture from your student files—**p03G_Catering**. Change the title placeholder **Shape Styles Fill** color to **Text 1**—under **Theme Colors**, in the first row, the second color. Change the **Font Color** to **Accent 2**—under **Theme Colors**, in the first row, the sixth color. Size the placeholder so that it extends from the left edge of the slide to the right edge of the slide, and then move it so that its lower edge aligns with the lower edge of the slide. Apply **Center Text** to the title.

11 Add a **Header and Footer** for the **Notes and Handouts** pages. Include the **Date and time** that **Update automatically**, the **Page number**, and a **Footer** with the file name **Lastname_Firstname_3G_Restaurants** Display the **File Properties**. In the **Subject** box, type your course name and section number. In the **Author** box, replace the existing text with your name. In the **Keywords** box, type **catering, restaurants** and then click **OK**.

12 View the **Slide Show** from the start, and then **Save** your presentation. **Print Handouts (4 slides per page)**, or submit your presentation electronically as directed by your instructor. **Close** the presentation, and then **Quit PowerPoint**.

Table 1

Population	218,381	Expected 5-year increase: 12%
Households	62,394	Expected 5-year increase: 3%
Average years in residence	6.8	62% families with children
Owner occupied	75%	Expected to increase with new construction

- - → (Return to Step 3)

End **You have completed Project 3G**

Content-Based Assessments

GO! Fix It | Project 3H Housing Developments

Project Files

For Project 3H, you will need the following file:

   p03H_Housing_Developments

You will save your presentation as:

   Lastname_Firstname_3H_Housing_Developments

In this project, you will edit several slides from a presentation prepared by the Golden Grove Planning Department regarding real estate developments in the city. From the student files that accompany this textbook, open the file p03H_Housing_Developments, and then save the file in your PowerPoint Chapter 3 folder as **Lastname_Firstname_3H_Housing_Developments**

To complete the project, you should know:

- The Theme Colors should be changed to Module, and the Theme Fonts should be changed to Adjacency.

- The titles on Slides 2 and 3 should be centered.

- On Slide 2, the table style of Light Style 2 - Accent 2 should be applied, and a column should be added to right of the last column in the table. In the inserted column, the following text should be entered in the three cells: **Bering** and **37%** and **August 2016**

- On Slides 3 and 4, the charts should be animated with the Wipe entrance effect.

- A Header and Footer should be added for the Notes and Handouts pages that includes the Date and Time that Update Automatically, the Page number and a Footer with the text **Lastname_Firstname_3H_Housing_Developments** File Properties should include your course name and section, your name, and the Keywords **property tax, housing**

Save and Print Handouts (4 slides per page), or submit your presentation electronically as directed by your instructor. Close the presentation, and then Quit PowerPoint.

End **You have completed Project 3H** ─────────────────────────

Content-Based Assessments

GO! Make It | Project 3I Arboretum

Project Files

For Project 3I, you will need the following files:

> New Presentation
> p03I_Flowers

You will save your presentation as:

> Lastname_Firstname_3I_Arboretum

Open PowerPoint to begin a new presentation, and apply the Advantage theme. Save the presentation in your PowerPoint Chapter 3 folder as **Lastname_Firstname_3I_Arboretum**

By using the skills you practiced in this chapter, create the first two slides of the presentation as shown in Figure 3.51. The layout for Slide 1 is Title Only, and the background is formatted with the picture from your student data files—p03I_Flowers. The title Font Color is Accent 5, Lighter 40%—under Theme Colors, in the fourth row, the ninth color. The title Shape Fill color is, Accent 2, Lighter 10%—under Theme colors, in the last row, the sixth color. The Title Font Size is 54. On Slide 2, insert and format the table as shown. Change the Font Size of the text in the first row to 28. Add a Header and Footer for the Notes and Handouts that includes the Date and Time that Update Automatically, the Page number and a Footer with the text **Lastname_Firstname_3I_Arboretum** In File Properties, add your course information, your name, and the keywords **arboretum, events** Save, and then Print Handouts (2 slides per page), or submit your presentation electronically as directed by your instructor. Close the presentation, and then Quit PowerPoint.

Project Results

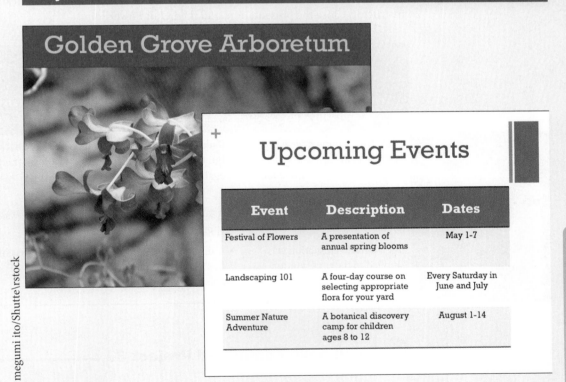

megumi ito/Shutte\rstock

Figure 3.51

End You have completed Project 3I

Content-Based Assessments

GO! Solve It | Project **3J** Aquatic Center

Project Files

For Project 3J, you will need the following file:

    p03J_Aquatic_Center

You will save your presentation as:

    Lastname_Firstname_3J_Aquatic_Center

Open the file p03J_Aquatic_Center, and save it in your PowerPoint Chapter 3 folder as **Lastname_Firstname_3J_Aquatic_Center** Complete the presentation by changing the Theme Fonts and then formatting the slide background of at least one of the slides using a Background Style or Fill Color. On Slide 4, insert and format a table with the following information regarding the fee schedule for swim passes.

Membership	Monthly	Seasonal
Youth	$10	$25
Adult	$25	$50
Senior	$15	$30

Apply appropriate animation and slide transitions to the slides. Insert a Header and Footer for the Notes and Handouts pages that includes the Date and Time that Update Automatically, the Page number, and the file name in the Footer. In File Properties, add your course name and section number, your name, and the Keywords **aquatic center, swim program** Save and then Print Handouts (3 slides per page), or submit your presentation electronically as directed by your instructor. Close the presentation, and then Quit PowerPoint.

		Performance Level		
		Exemplary: You consistently applied the relevant skills	**Proficient:** You sometimes, but not always, applied the relevant skills	**Developing:** You rarely or never applied the relevant skills
Performance Elements	**Format slide with a background style**	Slide background style was applied to at least one slide and text displayed with good contrast against the background.	Slide background was formatted but text did not display well against the chosen background.	Slide background was not formatted with a background style.
	Insert and format appropriate table	Appropriate table was inserted and formatted.	A table was inserted but was not appropriately formatted.	Table was not inserted.
	Apply appropriate animation	Appropriate animation was applied to the presentation.	Animation was applied but was not appropriate for the presentation.	Animation was not applied.

End **You have completed Project 3J**

Content-Based Assessments

GO! Solve It | Project **3K** Power

Project Files

For Project 3K, you will need the following files:

    p03K_Power
    p03K_Tower

You will save your presentation as:

    Lastname_Firstname_3K_Power

Open the file p03K_Power, and save it in your PowerPoint Chapter 3 folder as **Lastname_Firstname_3K_Power** Complete the presentation by applying a theme and then formatting the slide background of one of the slides with the picture found in your student files—p03K_Tower. Adjust the size, position, fill color, and font color of the slide titles as necessary so that the title text displays attractively against the background picture. Format the background of at least one other slide using a Background Style or Fill Color. Insert a new Slide 3 that includes an appropriate title and a table with the following information regarding the power sources that the city uses.

Power Sources	Percent Used by City
Natural Gas	32%
Hydroelectric	17%
Renewables	18%
Coal	23%
Nuclear	10%

On Slide 4, insert and format an appropriate chart to demonstrate the revenue collected from residential power sales over the past three years. Revenue in 2015 was 35.5 million dollars, in 2016 revenue was 42.6 million dollars, and in 2017 revenue was 48.2 million dollars. Apply appropriate animation and slide transitions to the slides. Add a Header and Footer for the Notes and Handouts pages that includes the Date and Time that Update Automatically, the Page number, and the file name in the Footer. In File Properties, add your course name and section number, your name, and the Keywords **power sources, revenue**. Save and then Print Handouts (4 slides per page) or submit the presentation electronically as directed by your instructor. Close the presentation, and then Quit PowerPoint.

	Performance Level		
	Exemplary: You consistently applied the relevant skills	**Proficient:** You sometimes, but not always, applied the relevant skills	**Developing:** You rarely or never applied the relevant skills
Format two slide backgrounds with pictures and styles	Two slide backgrounds were formatted attractively and text displayed with good contrast against backgrounds.	Slide backgrounds were formatted but text did not display well against the chosen background, or only one slide background was formatted.	Slide backgrounds were not formatted with pictures or styles.
Insert and format appropriate table and chart	Appropriate table and chart were inserted and formatted and the entered data was accurate.	A table and a chart were inserted but were not appropriate for the presentation or either a table or a chart was omitted.	Table and chart were not inserted.
Apply appropriate animation	Appropriate animation was applied to the presentation.	Animation was applied but was not appropriate for the presentation.	Animation was not applied.

Performance Elementst

End You have completed Project 3K

Outcomes-Based Assessments

Rubric

The following outcomes-based assessments are *open-ended assessments*. That is, there is no specific correct result; your result will depend on your approach to the information provided. Make *Professional Quality* your goal. Use the following scoring rubric to guide you in *how* to approach the problem, and then to evaluate *how well* your approach solves the problem.

    The *criteria*—Software Mastery, Content, Format and Layout, and Process—represent the knowledge and skills you have gained that you can apply to solving the problem. The *levels of performance*—Professional Quality, Approaching Professional Quality, or Needs Quality Improvements—help you and your instructor evaluate your result.

	Your completed project is of Professional Quality if you:	Your completed project is Approaching Professional Quality if you:	Your completed project Needs Quality Improvements if you:
1-Software Mastery	Choose and apply the most appropriate skills, tools, and features and identify efficient methods to solve the problem.	Choose and apply some appropriate skills, tools, and features, but not in the most efficient manner.	Choose inappropriate skills, tools, or features, or are inefficient in solving the problem.
2-Content	Construct a solution that is clear and well organized, contains content that is accurate, appropriate to the audience and purpose, and is complete. Provide a solution that contains no errors in spelling, grammar, or style.	Construct a solution in which some components are unclear, poorly organized, inconsistent, or incomplete. Misjudge the needs of the audience. Have some errors in spelling, grammar, or style, but the errors do not detract from comprehension.	Construct a solution that is unclear, incomplete, or poorly organized; contains some inaccurate or inappropriate content; and contains many errors in spelling, grammar, or style. Do not solve the problem.
3-Format and Layout	Format and arrange all elements to communicate information and ideas, clarify function, illustrate relationships, and indicate relative importance.	Apply appropriate format and layout features to some elements, but not others. Overuse features, causing minor distraction.	Apply format and layout that does not communicate information or ideas clearly. Do not use format and layout features to clarify function, illustrate relationships, or indicate relative importance. Use available features excessively, causing distraction.
4-Process	Use an organized approach that integrates planning, development, self-assessment, revision, and reflection.	Demonstrate an organized approach in some areas, but not others; or, use an insufficient process of organization throughout.	Do not use an organized approach to solve the problem.

Apply a combination of the 3A and 3B skills.

GO! Think | Project **3L** Animal Sanctuary

Project Files

For Project 3L, you will need the following file:

New Presentation

You will save your presentation as:

Lastname_Firstname_3L_Animal_Sanctuary

The Golden Grove Animal Sanctuary, a nonprofit organization, provides shelter and care for animals in need, including dogs, cats, hamsters, and guinea pigs. The sanctuary, which celebrates its tenth anniversary in July, has cared for more than 12,000 animals since it opened and is a state-of-the-art facility. Funding for the sanctuary comes in the form of business sponsorships, individual donations, and pet adoption fees. The following table indicates revenue generated by the sanctuary during the past three years.

	Fees	Donations	Sponsorships
2015	125,085	215,380	175,684
2016	110,680	256,785	156,842
2017	132,455	314,682	212,648

In addition to shelter services, the sanctuary offers community service and training programs, veterinarian services, and vaccine clinics. Examples of these services include Canine Obedience classes, microchipping ($25 fee), and the Healthy Pet Hotline (free). Canine Obedience classes are for puppies and adult dogs to improve obedience, socialization, and behavior. Classes last two, three, or four months and cost $150 to $250.

Using the preceding information, create the first five slides of a presentation that the director of the Golden Grove Animal Sanctuary will show at an upcoming pet fair. Apply an appropriate theme and use slide layouts that will effectively present the content. Include a line chart with the revenue data, a table with the community service programs information, and at least one slide formatted with a dog or cat on the slide background. Apply styles to the table and chart, and apply animation and slide transitions to the slides. Use the techniques that you practiced in this chapter so that your presentation is professional and attractive. Save the file in your PowerPoint Chapter 3 folder as **Lastname_Firstname_3L_Animal_Sanctuary** and then add a Header and Footer for the Notes and Handouts pages that includes the Date and Time that Update Automatically, the Page number, and the file name in the Footer. In File Properties, add your course name and section number, your name, and the Keywords **animals, pets** Save and then Print Handouts (6 slides per page), or submit the presentation electronically as directed by your instructor. Close the presentation, and then Quit PowerPoint.

End **You have completed Project 3L** ——————————————

Outcomes-Based Assessments

GO! Think | Project **3M** Water Sources

Project Files

For Project 3M, you will need the following file:

New Presentation

You will save your presentation as:

Lastname_Firstname_3M_Water_Sources

The Golden Grove Department of Water and Power operations are financed solely through sales of water and electric services. A portion of capital expenditures are funded through the sale of municipal bonds. The city's water supply is generated from a number of sources, with 35% from the Sierra Nevada aqueduct system, 42% from water districts, 18% from groundwater, and 5% from recycled sources. This supply provides water for the city's residents and commercial and industrial customers.

In the past three years, the department has renovated several reservoirs and pump stations, resulting in better reserves and emergency preparedness capacity. The following table details the in-city reservoir capacities over the past three years. Water capacity is measured in acre feet, in which one acre foot is equal to approximately 325,000 gallons. Years in which zero or low capacity is specified indicate years in which the reservoir was undergoing renovation.

	2015	2016	2017
Elkhart Reservoir	350	1250	2243
Gold Lake Reservoir	3685	865	2865
Diamond Canyon Reservoir	2650	3850	4635

Using the preceding information, create a title slide and four additional slides of a presentation that the Golden Grove chief water engineer can show at an upcoming City Council meeting. Apply an appropriate theme and use slide layouts that will effectively present the content. Include a table that details the water supply sources and a column chart with the reservoir information. Apply animation and slide transitions and use the techniques that you practiced in this chapter so that your presentation is professional and attractive. Save the file in your PowerPoint Chapter 3 folder as **Lastname_Firstname_3M_ Water_Sources** and then add a Header and Footer for the Notes and Handouts pages that includes the Date and Time that Update Automatically, the Page number, and the file name in the Footer. In File Properties, add your course name and section number, your name, and the Keywords **reservoirs, water capacity**. Save, and then Print Handouts (6 slides per page), or submit the presentation electronically as directed by your instructor. Close the presentation, and then Quit PowerPoint.

End **You have completed Project 3M** ————————————

Outcomes-Based Assessments

Apply a combination of the 3A and 3B skills.

You and GO! | Project **3N** Recreation Programs

Project Files

For Project 3N, you will need the following file:

New Presentation

You will save your presentation as:

Lastname_Firstname_3N_Recreation_Programs

Research the recreation programs available in the city in which you live, and then create a presentation about the program. Include a table that describes some of the activities, the location in which they are held, and the fees. Choose an appropriate theme, slide layouts, and pictures, and format the presentation attractively, including at least one slide with a picture on the slide background. Save your presentation in your PowerPoint Chapter 3 folder as **Lastname_Firstname_3N_Recreation_Programs** and submit as directed.

 You have completed Project 3N _____

Apply a combination of the 3A and 3B skills.

GO! Collaborate | Project **3O** Bell Orchid Hotels Group Running Case

This project relates to the **Bell Orchid Hotels**. Your instructor may assign this group case project to your class. If your instructor assigns this project, he or she will provide you with information and instructions to work as part of a group. The group will apply the skills gained thus far to help the Bell Orchid Hotels achieve their business goals.

 You have completed Project 3O _____

Glossary

3-D The shortened term for *three-dimensional*, which refers to an image that appears to have all three spatial dimensions—length, width, and depth.

Absolute cell reference A cell reference that refers to cells by their fixed position in a worksheet; an absolute cell reference remains the same when the formula is copied.

Accounting Number Format The Excel number format that applies a thousand comma separator where appropriate, inserts a fixed U.S. Dollar sign aligned at the left edge of the cell, applies two decimal places, and leaves a small amount of space at the right edge of the cell to accommodate a parenthesis for negative numbers.

Active cell The cell, surrounded by a border, ready to receive data or be affected by the next Excel command.

After Previous An animation command that begins the animation sequence for the selected PowerPoint slide element immediately after the completion of the previous animation or slide transition.

Alignment The placement of paragraph text relative to the left and right margins.

American Psychological Association (APA) One of two commonly used style guides for formatting research papers.

Anchor The symbol that indicates to which paragraph an object is attached.

Animation A visual or sound effect added to an object or text on a slide.

Apple menu A menu that enables you to configure your computer, shut down your computer, and log out.

Application A set of instructions used by a computer to perform a task, such as word processing or accounting; also called a *program*.

Archived file A file that has been reduced in size and thus takes up less storage space and can be transferred to other computers quickly; also called a *zipped file* or *compressed file*.

Arguments The values that an Excel function uses to perform calculations or operations.

Arithmetic operators The symbols +, −, *, /, %, and ^ used to denote addition, subtraction (or negation), multiplication, division, percentage, and exponentiation in an Excel formula.

Artistic effects Formats applied to images that make pictures resemble sketches or paintings.

Artistic filters Formats applied to images that make pictures resemble sketches or paintings.

Auto Fill An Excel feature that generates and extends values into adjacent cells based on the values of selected cells.

AutoComplete (Excel) A feature that speeds your typing and lessens the likelihood of errors; if the first few characters you type in a cell match an existing entry in the column, Excel fills in the remaining characters for you.

AutoCorrect A feature that corrects common spelling errors as you type, for example, changing *teh* to *the*.

AutoFit An Excel feature that adjusts the width of a column to fit the cell content of the widest cell in the column.

AutoSum Another name for the *SUM* function.

AutoText A feature that enables you to quickly insert stored information into a document; for example, a file name, a page number, or the author of the document.

AVERAGE function An Excel function that adds a group of values, and then divides the result by the number of values in the group.

Axis A line that serves as a frame of reference for measurement and that borders the chart plot area.

Background Removal A command that removes unwanted portions of a picture so that the picture does not appear as a self-contained rectangle.

Background style A slide background fill variation that combines theme colors in different intensities or patterns.

Base The starting point; used in calculating the rate of increase, which is the amount of increase divided by the base.

Bevel A shape effect that uses shading and shadows to make the edges of a shape appear to be curved or angled.

Bibliography A list of cited works in a report or research paper, also referred to as *Works Cited*, *Sources*, or *References*, depending upon the report style.

Black slide A slide that displays at the end of an electronic slide show, indicating that the presentation is over.

Body The text of a letter.

Body font A font that is applied to all slide text except titles.

Bulleted list A list of items with each item introduced by a symbol such as a small circle or check mark, and which is useful when the items in the list can be displayed in any order.

Bullets Text symbols such as small circles or check marks that precede each item in a bulleted list.

Category axis The area along the bottom of a chart that identifies the categories of data; also referred to as the *x-axis*.

Category labels The labels that display along the bottom of a chart to identify the categories of data; Excel uses the row titles as the category names.

Cell The intersection of a column and a row.

Cell address Another name for a *cell reference*.

Cell content Anything typed into a cell.

Cell reference The identification of a specific cell by its intersecting column letter and row number.

Cell style A defined set of formatting characteristics, such as font, font size, font color, cell borders, and cell shading.

Center alignment The alignment of text or objects that is centered horizontally between the left and right margins.

Chart A graphic representation of numeric data.

Chart area The entire chart and all of its elements.

Chart Elements box The box in Current Selection group on the Chart Layout or Format tabs from which you can select a chart element so that you can format it.

Chart layout The combination of chart elements that can be displayed in a chart such as a title, legend, labels for the columns, and the table of charted cells.

Chart Quick Layouts gallery A group of predesigned chart layouts that you can apply to an Excel chart.

Chart sheet A workbook sheet that contains only a chart.

Chart styles The overall visual look of a chart in terms of its graphic effects, colors, and backgrounds; for example, you can have flat or beveled columns, colors that are solid or transparent, and backgrounds that are dark or light.

Chart Styles gallery A group of predesigned chart styles that you can apply to an Excel chart.

Chart types Various chart formats used in a way that is meaningful to the reader; common examples are column charts, pie charts, and line charts.

Citation A note inserted into the text of a research paper that refers the reader to a source in the bibliography.

Click The action of tapping or pressing the mouse or pointing device one time.

Clip A single media file, for example, art, sound, animation, or a movie.

Clip art Predefined graphics included with Microsoft Office or downloaded from the Web.

Clip Gallery An Office feature that organizes collections of clip art, photographs, animations, sounds, and movies.

Clipboard A temporary storage area on your computer that holds text or graphics that you select and then copy or cut.

Close button A button on the left side of the title bar that closes the document but does not exit the application.

Cloud service Online storage of data hosted by third parties such as Microsoft's SkyDrive.

Column A vertical group of cells in a worksheet.

Column break indicator A single dotted line with the text *Column Break* that indicates where a manual column break was inserted.

Column chart A chart in which the data is arranged in columns and that is useful for showing data changes over a period of time or for illustrating comparisons among items.

Column heading The letter that displays at the top of a vertical group of cells in a worksheet; beginning with the first letter of the alphabet, a unique letter or combination of letters identifies each column.

Columns view In Finder, a view that displays folders and files in columns.

Comma Style The Excel number format that inserts thousand comma separators where appropriate and applies two decimal places; Comma Style also leaves space at the right to accommodate a parenthesis when negative numbers are present.

Command An instruction to a computer program that causes an action to be carried out.

Common dialog boxes The set of dialog boxes that includes Open, Save, and Save As, which are provided by the Mac programming interface, and which display and operate in all of the Office programs in the same manner.

Comparison operator Symbols that evaluate each value to determine if it is the same (=), greater than (>), less than (<), or in between a range of values as specified by the criteria.

Compatibility The ability of a file to work with other applications.

Complimentary closing A parting farewell in a business letter.

Compressed file A file that has been reduced in size and thus takes up less storage space and can be transferred to other computers quickly; also called a *zipped file* or *archived file*.

Conditional format A format that changes the appearance of a cell—for example, by adding cell shading or font color—based on a condition; if the condition is true, the cell is formatted based on that condition, and if the condition is false, the cell is *not* formatted.

Constant value Numbers, text, dates, or times of day that you type into a cell.

Content control In a template, an area indicated by placeholder text that can be used to add text, pictures, dates, or lists.

Context sensitive command A command associated with activities in which you are engaged; often activated by pressing Control and clicking a screen item.

Contextual tabs Tabs that are added to the Ribbon automatically when a specific object, such as a picture, is selected, and that contain commands relevant to the selected object.

Copy A command that duplicates a selection and places it on the Clipboard.

COUNTIF function A statistical function that counts the number of cells within a range that meet the given condition and that has two arguments—the range of cells to check and the criteria.

Cover Flow view In Finder, a view that is similar to List view, except that it adds a set of previews in the top part of the window that you can flip through.

Criteria Conditions that you specify in a logical function.

Crop A command that reduces the size of a picture by removing vertical or horizontal edges.

Crosshair pointer A pointer that indicates that you can draw a shape.

Cut A command that removes a selection and places it on the Clipboard.

Data Text or numbers in a cell.

Data bar A cell format consisting of a shaded bar that provides a visual cue to the reader about the value of a cell relative to other cells; the length of the bar represents the value in the cell—a longer bar represents a higher value and a shorter bar represents a lower value.

Data marker A column, bar, area, dot, pie slice, or other symbol in a chart that represents a single data point; related data points form a data series.

Data point A value that originates in a worksheet cell and that is represented in a chart by a data marker.

Data series Related data points represented by data markers; each data series has a unique color or pattern represented in the chart legend.

Data source A list of variable information, such as names and addresses, that is merged with a main document to create customized form letters or labels.

Date line The first line in a business letter that contains the current date and that is positioned just below the letterhead if a letterhead is used.

Default The term that refers to the current selection or setting that is automatically used by a computer program unless you specify otherwise.

Deselect The action of canceling the selection of an object or block of text by clicking outside of the selection.

Desktop On a Mac, the opening screen that simulates your work area.

Desktop folder A folder that includes files that you save on your desktop.

Detail sheets The worksheets that contain the details of the information summarized on a summary sheet.

Dialog box A small window that contains options for completing a task.

Disclosure triangle A triangle that displays to the left of a folder name, which, when clicked, expands the folder to display the contents of that folder.

Displayed value The data that displays in a cell.

Dock Area at the bottom of the Mac desktop that displays icons for applications.

Document properties Details about a file that describe or identify it, including the title, author name, subject, and keywords that identify the document's topic or contents; also known as *metadata*.

Documents folder A folder that is a convenient place to store most of the files you create.

Dot leader A series of dots preceding a tab that guides the eye across the line.

Double-click The action of tapping or pressing the mouse or pointing device two times in rapid succession.

Drag The action of pressing down on the mouse while moving your mouse.

Drag and drop The action of moving a selection by dragging it to a new location.

Drawing objects Graphic objects, such as shapes, diagrams, lines, or circles.

Edit The action of making changes to text or graphics in an Office file.

Editing (PowerPoint) The process of modifying a presentation by adding and deleting slides or by changing the contents of individual slides.

Ellipsis A set of three dots indicating incompleteness; when following a command name, indicates that a dialog box will display.

Emphasis effect Animation that emphasizes an object or text that is already displayed.

Enclosures Additional documents included with a business letter.

Endnote In a research paper, a note placed at the end of a document or chapter.

Entrance effect Animation that brings a slide element onto the screen.

Excel table A series of rows and columns that contains related data that is managed independently from the data in other rows and columns in the worksheet.

Exit effect Animation that moves an object or text off the screen.

Expand formula bar button An Excel window element with which you can increase the height of the Formula Bar to display lengthy cell content.

Expand horizontal scroll bar button An Excel window element with which you can increase the width of the horizontal scroll bar.

Explode The action of pulling out one or more pie slices from a pie chart for emphasis.

Extract To decompress, or pull out, files from a compressed form.

Fields In a mail merge, the column headings in the data source.

File A collection of information stored on a computer under a single name, for example a Word document or a PowerPoint presentation.

Fill Color The inside color of text or of an object.

Fill handle The small square in the lower right corner of a selected cell.

Filter The process of displaying only a portion of the data based on matching a specific value to show only the data that meets the criteria that you specify.

Find and Replace (Excel) A command that searches the cells in a worksheet—or in a selected range—for matches and then replaces each match with a replacement value of your choice.

Finder The Mac program that displays the files and folders on your computer, and which is at work anytime you are viewing the contents of files and folders in a window.

Floating object A graphic that can be moved independently of the surrounding text characters.

Folder A container in which you store files.

Font A set of characters with the same design and shape.

Font styles Formatting emphasis such as bold, italic, and underline.

Footer A reserved area for text or graphics that displays at the bottom of each page in a document, worksheet, slide, or slide handout or notes page.

Footnote In a research paper, a note placed at the bottom of the page.

Format Changing the appearance of cells and worksheet elements to make a worksheet attractive and easy to read.

Format as you type The Excel feature by which a cell takes on the formatting of the number typed into the cell.

Format Painter An Office feature that copies formatting from one selection of text to another.

Formatting The process of establishing the overall appearance of text, graphics, and pages in an Office file.

Formatting marks Characters that display on the screen, but do not print, indicating where the Return key, the Spacebar, and the Tab key were pressed; also called *nonprinting characters*.

Formula An equation that performs mathematical calculations on values in a worksheet.

Formula AutoComplete An Excel feature, which, after typing an = (equal sign) and the beginning of letter or letters of a function name, displays a list of function names that match the typed (letters(s).

Formula bar An element in the Excel window that displays the value or formula contained in the active cell; here you can also enter or edit values or formulas.

Freeze Panes A command that enables you to select one or more rows or columns and freeze (lock) them into place; the locked rows and columns become separate panes.

Function A predefined formula—a formula that Excel has already built for you—that performs calculations by using specific values in a particular order or structure.

Fund A sum of money set aside for a specific purpose.

Gallery An Office feature that displays a list of potential results instead of just the command name.

General format The default format that Excel applies to numbers; this format has no specific characteristics—whatever you type in the cell will display, with the exception that trailing zeros to the right of a decimal point will not display.

General fund The term used to describe money set aside for the normal operating activities of a government entity such as a city.

Goal Seek A what-if analysis tool that finds the input needed in one cell to arrive at the desired result in another cell.

Gradient fill A fill option where one color fades into another.

Graphics Pictures, clip art images, charts, or drawing objects.

Groups On the Office Ribbon, the sets of related commands that you might need for a specific type of task.

Hanging indent An indent style in which the first line of a paragraph extends to the left of the remaining lines, and that is commonly used for bibliographic entries.

Header A reserved area for text or graphics that displays at the top of each page in a document, worksheet, slide, or slide handout or notes page.

Headings font The font that is applied to slide titles.

Home folder A folder with the same name as the user account that contains your personal folders and files and that cannot be renamed.

Horizontal window split bar An Excel window element with which you can split the worksheet into two horizontal views of the same worksheet.

Hypertext Markup Language (HTML) The language used to format documents that can be opened using any Web browser.

Icons Pictures that represent a program, a file, a folder, or some other object.

Icons view In Finder, a view that displays folders and files as icons or small pictures.

IF function A function that uses a logical test to check whether a condition is met, and then returns one value if true and another value if false.

Inline object An object or graphic inserted in a document that acts like a character in a sentence.

Insert Worksheet button Located on the row of sheet tabs, a sheet tab that, when clicked, inserts an additional worksheet into the workbook.

Insertion point A blinking vertical line that indicates where text or graphics will be inserted.

Inside address The name and address of the person receiving the letter; positioned below the date line.

Justified alignment An arrangement of text in which the text aligns evenly on both the left and right margins.

Keyboard shortcut A combination of two or more keyboard keys, used to perform a task that would otherwise require a mouse.

Keyword A word that is searchable and helps to describe the content of a document, part of the *metadata*.

Label Another name for a text value, and which usually provides information about number values.

Landscape orientation A page orientation in which the paper is wider than it is tall.

Layout The arrangement of elements, such as title and subtitle text, lists, pictures, tables, charts, shapes, and movies, on a PowerPoint slide.

Leader character Characters that form a solid, dotted, or dashed line that fill the space preceding a tab stop.

Left alignment (Excel) The cell format in which characters align at the left edge of the cell; this is the default for text entries and is an example of formatting information stored in a cell.

Left alignment (Word) An arrangement of text in which the text aligns at the left margin, leaving the right margin uneven.

Legend A chart element that identifies the patterns or colors that are assigned to the categories in the chart.

Lettered column headings The area along the top edge of a worksheet that identifies each column with a unique letter or combination of letters.

Letterhead The personal or company information that displays at the top of a letter.

Line break indicator A small, nonprinting bent arrow that displays where a manual line break was inserted.

Line chart A chart type that is useful to display trends over time; time displays along the bottom axis and the data point values are connected with a line.

Line spacing The distance between lines of text in a paragraph.

List level An outline level in a presentation represented by a bullet symbol and identified in a slide by the indentation and the size of the text.

List view In Finder, a view that displays details about the folders and files, including the date modified, the size of a file, and the type of a file such as Word.

Location Any disk drive, folder, or other place in which you can store files and folders.

Logical functions A group of functions that test for specific conditions and that typically use conditional tests to determine whether specified conditions are true or false.

Logical test Any value or expression that can be evaluated as being true or false.

Mail merge A Microsoft Word feature that joins a main document and a data source to create customized letters or labels.

Main document In a mail merge, the document that contains the text or formatting that remains constant.

Major unit The value in a chart's value axis that determines the spacing between tick marks and between the gridlines in the plot area.

Manual column break An artificial end to a column to balance columns or to provide space for the insertion of other objects.

Manual line break The action of ending a line, before the normal end of the line, without creating a new paragraph.

Manual page break The action of forcing a page to end and placing subsequent text at the top of the next page.

Margins The space between the text and the top, bottom, left, and right edges of the paper.

MAX function An Excel function that determines the largest value in a selected range of values.

MEDIAN function An Excel function that finds the middle value that has as many values above it in the group as are below it; it differs from AVERAGE in that the result is not affected as much by a single value that is greatly different from the others.

Menu bar A horizontal bar at the top of a window that contains the menus of commands.

Merge A command that joins selected cells in an Excel worksheet into one larger cell and centers the contents in the new cell.

Metadata Details about a file that describe or identify it, including the title, author name, subject, and keywords that identify the document's topic or contents; also known as *document properties*.

Microsoft Document Connection An Office application used for sharing and managing files on a Microsoft SharePoint site or on Microsoft's SkyDrive cloud service.

Microsoft Excel A spreadsheet application, which enables you to calculate and analyze numbers and create charts.

Microsoft Office for Mac 2011 A Microsoft suite of products that includes applications for individuals, small organizations, and large enterprises to perform specific tasks.

Microsoft Outlook An Office application, which enables you to manage email and organizational activities.

Microsoft PowerPoint A presentation application, which enables you to communicate information with high-impact graphics and movies.

Microsoft Word A word processing application, which enables you to create and share documents by using its writing tools.

MIN function An Excel function that determines the smallest value in a selected range of values.

Minimize button A button on the left side of the title bar that hides the window by placing it on the Dock.

Modern Language Association (MLA) One of two commonly used style guides for formatting research papers.

More arrow An arrow that when clicked expands the selection to enable you to select more options.

Name box An element of the Excel window that displays the name of the selected cell, table, chart, or object.

Nameplate The banner on the front page of a newsletter that identifies the publication; also referred to as a *banner*, *flag*, or *masthead*.

Navigate The process of exploring within the organizing structure of the Mac operating system or moving among pages for documents or worksheets in Excel.

Nonprinting characters Characters that display on the screen, but do not print, indicating where the Return key, the Spacebar, and the Tab key were pressed; also called *formatting marks*.

Normal template The template that serves as a basis for all new Word documents.

Normal View (Excel) A screen view that maximizes the number of cells visible on your screen and keeps the column letters and row numbers close to the columns and rows.

Normal View (PowerPoint) The primary editing view in PowerPoint in which you write and design your presentations; consists of the Notes pane, the Slide pane, and the Slides/Outline pane.

Note In a research paper, information that expands on the topic, but that does not fit well in the document text.

Notes page A printout that contains the slide image on the top half of the page and notes that you have created on the Notes pane in the lower half of the page.

Notes pane The PowerPoint screen element that displays below the Slide pane with space to type notes regarding the active slide.

NOW function An Excel function that retrieves the date and time from your computer's calendar and clock and inserts the information into the selected cell.

Nudge The action of moving an object on the page in small, precise increments.

Number format A specific way in which Excel displays numbers in a cell.

Number values Constant values consisting of only numbers.

Numbered list A list of items in which each item is introduced by a consecutive number to indicate definite steps, a sequence of actions, or chronological order.

Numbered row headings The area along the left edge of a worksheet that identifies each row with a unique number.

On Click An animation command that begins the animation sequence for the selected PowerPoint slide element when the mouse button is clicked or the spacebar is pressed.

Open dialog box A dialog box from which you can navigate to, and then open on your screen, an existing file that was created in that same program.

Operators The symbols with which you can specify the type of calculation you want to perform in an Excel formula.

Order of operations The mathematical rules for performing multiple calculations within a formula.

Page break indicator A dotted line with the text *Page Break* that indicates where a manual page break was inserted.

Page Layout View A screen view in which you can use the rulers to measure the width and height of data, set margins for printing, hide or

display the numbered row headings and the lettered column headings, and change the page orientation; this view is useful for preparing your worksheet for printing.

Pane A portion of a worksheet window bounded by and separated from other portions by vertical and horizontal bars.

Paragraph symbol The symbol ¶ that represents a paragraph and displays when the Show/Hide command is active.

Parenthetical reference In MLA style, a citation that refers to items on the *Works Cited* page, and which is placed in parentheses; the citation includes the last name of the author or authors, and the page number in the referenced source.

Paste The action of placing text or objects that have been copied or moved from one location to another location.

Paste area The target destination for data that has been cut or copied using the Office clipboard.

Paste Options A list of various options for changing the format of a pasted item.

PDF (Portable Document Format) file A file format that creates an image that preserves the look of your file, but that cannot be easily changed; a popular format for sending documents electronically, because the document will display on most computers.

Percent for new value = base percent + percent of increase The formula for calculating a percentage by which a value increases by adding the base percentage—usually 100%—to the percent increase.

Percent Style The Excel number format that multiples the value in the cell by 100, rounds to the nearest hundredth and displays a percent symbol (%) on the right side of the displayed value.

Percentage rate of increase The percent by which one number increases over another number.

Picture styles Frames, shapes, shadows, borders, and other special effects that can be added to an image to create an overall visual style for the image.

Pie chart A chart that shows the relationship of each part to a whole.

Placeholder On a slide, a box with a border that holds title and body text or other content such as charts, tables, and pictures.

Placeholder text Text in a content control that indicates the type of information to be entered in a specific location.

Platform Underlying hardware or software for a system.

Plot area The area bounded by the axes of a chart, including all the data series.

Point The action of moving your mouse pointer over something on your screen.

Point and click method The technique of constructing a formula by pointing to and then clicking cells; this method is convenient when the referenced cells are not adjacent to one another.

Pointer Any symbol that displays on your screen in response to moving your mouse.

Points A measurement of the size of a font; there are 72 points in an inch, with 10 to12 points being the most commonly used font size.

Pop-up menu A menu that displays—pops up—when you select an option and that contains a menu of commands that stay on the screen only until a command is selected.

Portrait orientation A page orientation in which the paper is taller than it is wide.

Preferences dialog box A dialog box in each Microsoft Office for Mac 2011 application with which you can select application settings and other options and preferences such as how you view and edit files.

Print Preview A view of a document as it will appear when you print it.

Print Titles An Excel command that enables you to specify rows and columns to repeat on each printed page.

Program A set of instructions used by a computer to perform a task, such as word processing or accounting; also called an *application*.

Pt The abbreviation for *point*; for example, when referring to a font size.

Public folder A folder that is used to store files that you want to share with others.

Range Two or more selected cells on a worksheet that are adjacent or nonadjacent; because the range is treated as a single unit, you can make the same changes or combination of changes to more than one cell at a time.

Range finder An Excel feature that outlines cells in color to indicate which cells are used in a formula; useful for verifying which cells are referenced in a formula.

Rate = amount of increase/base The mathematical formula to calculate a rate of increase.

Read-Only A property assigned to a file that prevents the file from being modified or deleted; it indicates that you cannot save any changes to the displayed document unless you first save it with a new name.

Record In a mail merge, a row of information that contains data for one person.

Relative cell reference In a formula, the address of a cell based on the relative position of the cell that contains the formula and the cell referred to.

Ribbon The user interface in Office for Mac 2011 that groups the commands for performing related tasks on tabs below the Standard toolbar in the application window.

Ribbon tabs The tabs on the Office Ribbon that display the names of the task-oriented groups of commands.

Right alignment An arrangement of text in which the text aligns at the right margin, leaving the left margin uneven.

Rotation handle A green circle that provides a way to rotate a selected image.

Row A horizontal group of cells in a worksheet.

Row heading The numbers along the left side of an Excel worksheet that designate the row numbers.

Ruler guides Vertical and horizontal lines that display in the rulers, indicating the pointer's position.

Salutation The greeting line of a business letter.

Sans serif A font design with no lines or extensions on the ends of characters.

Scale to Fit Excel commands that enable you to stretch or shrink the width, height, or both the width and height of printed output to fit a maximum number of pages.

Scaling The process of shrinking the width and/or height of printed output to fit a maximum number of pages.

Screenshot An image of an active window that you can paste into a document.

ScreenTip A small box that that displays useful information when you perform various mouse actions, such as pointing to screen elements or dragging.

Scroll The action of sliding or swiping your finger on the mouse or other pointing device to display a part of the window that is hidden from view.

Search box In a dialog box or window, the box in which you can type a word or a phrase to look for an item.

Section A portion of a document that can be formatted differently from the rest of the document.

Section break A double dotted line that indicates the end of one section and the beginning of another section.

Select To highlight, by clicking or dragging with your mouse, areas of text or data or graphics, so that the selection can be edited, formatted, copied, or moved.

Select All box A box in the upper left corner of the worksheet that, when clicked, selects all the cells in a worksheet.

Series A group of things that come one after another in succession; for example, January, February, March, and so on.

Serif A font design that includes small line extensions on the ends of the letters to guide the eye in reading from left to right.

Shapes Lines, arrows, stars, banners, ovals, rectangles, and other basic shapes with which you can illustrate an idea, a process, or a workflow.

Sheet tab scrolling buttons Buttons to the left of the sheet tabs used to display Excel sheet tabs that are not in view; used when there are more sheet tabs than will display in the space provided.

Sheet tabs The labels along the lower border of the Excel window that identify each worksheet.

Shortcut menu A menu that displays commands and options relevant to the selected text or object.

Sidebar An area on the left side of the Finder window that displays icons that help you locate files, applications, documents, shared computers, and devices such as CDs, DVDs, or removable storage.

Single File Web Page A document saved using HTML and that opens using a Web browser.

Sizing handles Small circles and squares that indicate that a picture is selected.

Slide A presentation page that can contain text, pictures, tables, charts, and other multimedia or graphic objects.

Slide handouts Printed images of slides on a sheet of paper.

Slide pane A PowerPoint screen element that displays a large image of the active slide.

Slide Sorter view A presentation view that displays thumbnails of all of the slides in a presentation.

Slide transitions The motion effects that occur in Slide Show view when you move from one slide to the next during a presentation.

Slides/Outline pane A PowerPoint screen element that displays the presentation either in the form of thumbnails (Slides tab) or in outline format (Outline tab).

Small caps A font effect, usually used in titles, that changes lowercase text into capital (uppercase) letters using a reduced font size.

SmartArt A designer-quality visual representation of your information that you can create by choosing from among many different layouts to effectively communicate your message or ideas.

SmartArt graphic A visual representation of information that you can create by choosing from many different layouts to communicate your message or ideas effectively.

SmartArt Styles Combinations of formatting effects that you can apply to SmartArt graphics.

Sort The process of arranging data in a specific order based on the value in each field.

Sparkline A tiny chart in the background of a cell that gives a visual trend summary alongside your data; makes a pattern more obvious.

Spin box A small box with an upward- and downward-pointing arrow that lets you move rapidly through a set of values by clicking.

Spreadsheet Another name for a *worksheet*.

Standard toolbar The toolbar that displays a row of buttons that provide a one-click method to perform the most common commands in the application such as Save and Print.

Statistical functions Excel functions, including the AVERAGE, MEDIAN, MIN, and MAX functions that are useful to analyze a group of measurements.

Status bar The area along the lower edge of an Office program window that displays file information, the progress of current tasks, and the status of certain commands and keys. On the left side are buttons to change the view of the document. On the right side is a Zoom slider to adjust the size of the displayed document.

Status menus On a Mac, menus displayed as icons on the right side of the menu bar that display the status of your computer or give you quick access to features such as volume control or wireless connections.

Style A group of formatting commands, such as font, font size, font color, paragraph alignment, and line spacing that can be applied to a paragraph with one command.

Style guide A manual that contains standards for the design and writing of documents.

Subfolder A folder within a folder.

Subject line The optional line following the inside address in a business letter that states the purpose of the letter.

Subpoints Secondary-level information in a SmartArt graphic.

SUM function A predefined formula that adds all the numbers in a selected range of cells.

Summary Sheet A worksheet in which totals from other worksheets are displayed and summarized.

Swipe The action of moving your finger across the mouse or pointing device to scroll left, right, up, or down.

Synonyms Words with the same or similar meaning.

Tab stop Specific locations on a line of text, marked on the Word ruler, to which you can move the insertion point by pressing the Tab key, and which is used to align and indent text.

Table A format for information that organizes and presents text and data in columns and rows.

Table style Formatting applied to an entire table so that it is consistent with the presentation theme.

Tabs The name of each activity area in the Office Ribbon.

Template An existing document that you use as a starting point for a new document; it opens a copy of itself, unnamed, and then you use the structure—and possibly some content, such as headings—as the starting point for the new document.

Text alignment The horizontal placement of text within a placeholder.

Text box A movable resizable container for text or graphics.

Text control A content control that accepts only a text entry.

Text effects Decorative formats, such as shadowed or mirrored text, text glow, 3-D effects, and colors that make text stand out.

Text values Constant values consisting of only text, and which usually provides information about number values; also referred to as *labels*.

Text wrapping The manner in which text displays around an object.

Theme A predesigned set of colors, fonts, lines, and fill effects that go well together and that can be applied to your entire document or to specific items.

Theme colors A set of coordinating colors that are applied to the backgrounds, objects, and text in a presentation.

Theme font A theme that determines the font applied to two types of slide text—headings and body.

Thesaurus A research tool that provides a list of synonyms.

Thumbnail A miniature version of the file.

Thumbnails Miniature images of presentation slides.

Tick marks The short lines that display on an axis at regular intervals.

Timing options Animation options that control when animated items display in the animation sequence.

Title bar The bar at the top edge of the program window that indicates the name of the current file and the program name.

Title slide The first slide in a presentation, whose purpose is to provide an introduction to the presentation topic.

Toggle button A button that can be turned on by clicking it once, and then turned off by clicking it again.

Top-level points The main text points in a SmartArt graphic.

Underlying formula The formula entered in a cell and visible only on the Formula Bar.

Underlying value The data that displays in the Formula Bar.

USB flash drive A small data storage device that plugs into a computer USB port.

Value Another name for a *constant value*.

Value after increase = base x percent for new value The formula for calculating the value after an increase by multiplying the original value—the base—by the percent for new value (see the *Percent for new value* formula).

Value axis A numerical scale on the left side of a chart that shows the range of numbers for the data points; also referred to as the *y-axis*.

Vertical window split bar A small box on the vertical scroll bar with which you can split the window into two vertical views of the same worksheet.

Volatile A term used to describe an Excel function that is subject to change each time the workbook is reopened; for example, the NOW function updates itself to the current date and time each time the workbook is opened.

What-if analysis The process of changing the values in cells to see how those changes affect the outcome of formulas in a worksheet.

Window A rectangular area on a computer screen in which programs and content appear, and which can be moved, resized, minimized, or closed.

Windows metafile A graphics file format for Microsoft Windows systems; file has a .wmf extension.

With Previous An animation command that begins the animation sequence on a PowerPoint slide at the same time as the previous animation or slide transition.

WordArt A gallery of text styles with which you can create decorative effects, such as shadowed or mirrored text.

Wordwrap The feature that moves text from the right edge of a paragraph to the beginning of the next line as necessary to fit within the margins.

Workbook An Excel file that contains one or more worksheets.

Workbook-level buttons Buttons at the far right of the Ribbon tabs that minimize or restore a displayed workbook.

Works Cited In MLA style, a list of cited works placed at the end of a research paper or report.

Worksheet The primary document that you use in Excel to work with and store data, and which is formatted as a pattern of uniformly spaced horizontal and vertical lines.

Writer's identification The name and title of the author of a letter, placed near the bottom of the letter under the complimentary closing—also referred to as the *writer's signature block*.

Writer's signature block The name and title of the author of a letter, placed near the bottom of the letter, under the complimentary closing—also referred to as the *writer's identification*.

x-axis The horizontal (*category*) *axis*.

y-axis The vertical (*value*) *axis*.

Zipped file A file that has been reduced in size and thus takes up less storage space and can be transferred to other computers quickly; also called a *compressed file* or *archived file*.

Zoom The action of increasing or decreasing the viewing area on the screen.

Zoom button A button on the left side of the title bar that increases or decreases the size of the window.

Index

column breaks, 198, 200–201
column charts, 258–262, 584–587
column headings, 245
columns
  Excel
    adding, 279–281
    defined, 245
    deleting, 279–281
    freezing, 323
    width of, 249–250, 281–283
  PowerPoint, deleting, 582, 588
  Word
    multiple, 198–200
    in newsletters, 198–201
    selecting, 126
    width of table, 122–123
Columns view, 6
Comma Style, 257, 273
commands
  defined, 3
  from dialog boxes, 14–16
  from the menu/Standard toolbar/Ribbon, 32–40
common dialog boxes, 24
comparison operators, 317–318
compatibility, 27–29
Compatibility Reports, 27–29
complimentary closing, 135
compressed files, 52–53
conditional formatting, 319–320
constant values, 246
content
  cell, 246, 335
  controls, 150
  defined, 335
  layout, 528–530
context sensitive, 248
context-sensitive commands, 13
contextual tabs, 38, 40
copying
  cell data, 336–337
  Clipboard and, 45–49
  defined, 45
  formulas, 254–255, 274–277
corporate authors, 189
COUNTIF function, 316–317
Cover Flow view, 6–7
cover letters
  creating, 133–138
  format of, 135
  letterhead on, 132–133
  proofing, 144–148
creating
  Excel
    chart sheets, 375–377
    line charts, 402–403
    pie charts, 375–377
    Sparklines, 262–263
    tables, 323–324
    workbooks, 243–244
    worksheet footers, 263–265
  Office folders, 16–20
  PowerPoint
    column charts, 584–587
    line charts, 587–588
    presentations, 437–440

SmartArt graphics, 526–530
  tables, 578–580
Word
  cover letters, 133–138
  documents, 59–61, 132–135, 148–155
  letterhead, 132–133
  lists, 82–86, 121
  mailing labels, 208–215
  research papers, 181–184
  resumes, 148–155
  tables, 117–118
  template files, 133
criteria, 316
cropping, 449, 505
crosshair pointers, 508
cutting text, 45–49

D

data. See also text
  Excel
    charting, 258–262
    defined, 246
    entering, 246–251
    moving, 314
    numerical, 250–251, 256–258
    ranges of, 271–272
data bars, 319–320
data markers, 259, 377, 586
data points, 259, 377, 586
data series, 259, 377, 586
data sources, 208
date lines, 135–136
dates, 321–324
decimal tab alignment, 87
defaults, 5
defining arguments, 312
Delay, 570
deleting. See also removing
  chart data, 587–588
  slides, 466
deselecting, 40
Desktop folder, 5
desktops, 3–4
detail sheets, 345–346
dialog boxes, 13–16, 24
dictionaries, 13–14, 270–271
disclosure triangle, 6
displayed values, 250–251
displaying
  Clipboard, 49
  formulas, 266–267
  presentation outlines, 457–459
  Ribbon, 40–41
  slides, 445–447
Distribute Rows command, 581
distributing objects, 515–517
Dock, 3–4, 10
document headings, 182
documents. See also files; Word (Microsoft)
  closing, 50
  opening, 6
  properties, 20–22, 195–196
  settings, 60
  viewing, 60

Documents folder, 5
dollar sign ($), 276
dot leaders, 88–89
double spacing, 78–79
double-clicking, 4
drag-and-drop feature, 141–143, 314
dragging, 13
drawing objects, 61
duplicating objects, 514
duration, animation, 570

E

Edit Data Source button, 211
editing, 441
effects
  animation, 566–568
  artistic, 65–66
  picture, 512–513
  text, 61–62
ellipsis (...), 13
emphasis effects, 566
enclosures, 135
endnotes, 184
entrance effects, 566–568
equal sign (=), 252
errors
  Excel
    formula, 275–276
    moving data, 314
  Word
    grammatical, 13–14, 138, 144–147
    spelling, 13–14, 138, 144–147, 269–271
    word usage, 138
Excel (Microsoft). See also cells; charts; formulas; workbooks; worksheets
  chart sheets
    creating, 375–377
    defined, 377
    preparing/printing workbooks with, 389–390
  closing, 267, 587
  functions
    AVERAGE, 309–311
    COUNTIF, 316–317
    IF, 317–319
    MAX, 313
    MEDIAN, 311–313
    MIN, 313
    NOW, 321–322
    SUM, 251–254, 309–311, 341
  Goal Seek, 387–389
  Help feature, 50–52
  Normal View, 265
  overview, 8
  Page Layout View, 263
  Sparklines, 258, 262–263
  starting, 243–244
  tables
    converting into a range of data, 326–327
    creating, 323–324
    defined, 323
    filtering, 324–326
    freezing columns, 323
    sorting, 324–326